ANTIDEPRESSANTS

Drugs in psychiatry

Volume 1

1983

ELSEVIER

AMSTERDAM · NEW YORK · OXFORD

Antidepressants

Edited by

GRAHAM D. BURROWS
TREVOR R. NORMAN
and
BRIAN DAVIES

Department of Psychiatry,
University of Melbourne,
Australia

1983

ELSEVIER
AMSTERDAM · NEW YORK · OXFORD

ISBN Vol. 1: 0-444-80474-9
ISBN Series: 0-444-80490-0

PUBLISHED BY:

Elsevier Science Publishers
P.O. Box 211
1000 AZ Amsterdam
The Netherlands

SOLE DISTRIBUTORS FOR THE U.S.A. AND CANADA:

Elsevier Science Publishing Company Inc.
52 Vanderbilt Avenue,
New York, N.Y. 10017

Library of Congress Cataloging in Publication Data
Main entry under title:

Antidepressants.

    (Drugs in psychiatry ; v. 1)
    Includes index.
    1. Antidepressants. I. Burrows, Graham D.
II. Norman, Trevor R. III. Davies, Brian, 1928-   .
IV. Series. [DNLM: 1. Antidepressive agents. W1 DR893T
v.1 / QV 77.5]
RM332.A573 1983   616.85'27061   82-24242
ISBN 0-444-80474-9

Printed in the Netherlands

Preface

This volume on antidepressants is the first of a series planned on drugs used in psychiatry. It was decided to attempt to cover the area from basic pharmacology to clinical applications. Frequently, volumes on this subject highlight one aspect only. We hope this volume will be suitable for both the researcher, the specialist and the general practitioner. The second volume to follow will be on *Antianxiety agents*.

GRAHAM D. BURROWS
TREVOR R. NORMAN
BRIAN DAVIES

List of contributors

Contents

SECTION VI. ENDORPHINS

Section I

INTRODUCTION

Burrows/Norman/Davies (eds) Antidepressants
© *1983, Elsevier Science Publishers*

Chapter 1

Recognition of depression – An overview

GRAHAM D. BURROWS

and

BRIAN DAVIES

Department of Psychiatry, University of Melbourne, Australia

This initial introductory chapter is written for the primary doctor, be it family doctor, general physician or specialist and therefore it focusses on the *recognition* of the depressed patient. It is not intended to describe all the classifications of depression. The interested reader could refer to a previous volume (Burrows, 1977). Management of the depressed patient will be considered in Chapter 10.

DEFINITION

Depressive illness is an illness of mood, i.e., an affective disorder. The actual neurophysiological basis of mood control is not clearly defined, yet most people experience a fairly constant mood, with only brief changes, either elevation or lowering of mood. In affective disorders there is a *fixed change of mood* which profoundly influences behaviour and thinking. In depressive illness there is a persistent lowering of mood, while in the uncommon manic illness there is persistent elevation of mood.

RECOGNITION

Nearly half the patients with depressive illness first report to the doctor with complaints that suggest physical illness. If the actual depressive symptoms are not enquired about the diagnosis of depression may be overlooked and many fruitless investigations made. Such complaints are: Fatigue and tiredness; appetite disturbance and consequent changes in weight; decreased energy; constipation; menstrual changes; bodily aches and pains; head-aches; difficulty in breathing; dryness in the mouth. Unusual sensations in the abdomen, chest or head may be *interpreted by the doctor* as dyspepsia, dyspnoea or headaches. If the *actual phenomenology* is enquired into, these errors will not occur.

These 'physical' symptoms are caused by changes in bodily functions associated with the depressive illness, mediated through the autonomic nervous system.

It is important that enquiry should be made into the characteristic depressive symptoms.

DEPRESSIVE SYMPTOMS

Mood change

This is present in all depressed patients, and is the essential abnormality. There is a feeling of sadness that can range from mild despondency to abject despair that overwhelms the patient. Every patient is aware of this change in his or her feeling state, yet few complain spontaneously of it, particularly in the early stages of the illness. There is a great variation in how patients describe this mood change. Patients must be asked, 'Have you been feeling miserable lately? – Have you felt like crying? – How do you feel in yourself?'

Loss of interest

Perhaps the next most important symptom is the loss of interest that accompanies the lowered mood. Patients again will not usually mention this. Loss of interest in the house, work, hobbies, recreation and religion are most important symptoms of depressive illness, as is loss of sexual interest. Loss of interest in personal appearance and hygiene is a most significant sign.

Sleep disturbance

This is often the earliest symptom of a depressive illness. Sometimes it is overlooked as the patient has been given sleeping tablets and forgets to mention that he had never needed hypnotics until a few months previously. Patients may complain that they cannot get to sleep because of their worries and when they sleep they have disturbing dreams. Other patients may say they fall asleep quite easily but wake up early in the morning, cannot sleep again, and feel particularly depressed.

Difficulty in thinking and concentrating

Patients with depressive illness cannot concentrate on simple tasks like reading or house-work. They find it difficult to converse or to make decisions. Elderly patients with de-pression may do badly on tests of memory because of these difficulties and an incorrect diagnosis of dementia may be made.

Painful thoughts

The depressed patient becomes preoccupied with himself; his thoughts are painful and concerned with his liabilities. He cannot 'count his blessings'. He blames himself, magnifies his misdeeds and worries over any minor problems. He ruminates over the past and his peccadilloes. The present and future appear black.

Suicidal thoughts

Depressed patients, because of the mood change and these painful thoughts, often have suicidal thoughts. They should be asked about these. 'Have you thought that life is not worth living?' Most depressed patients will recognize these thoughts and are helped by being asked to talk about them.

Anxiety

Depressed patients are usually anxious. It is important not to miss depressive symptoms in some patients who present with anxiety. Anxious depressed patients are often restless and this motor restlessness is called agitation. It is not uncommon for middle aged and elderly depressed patients to be treated with anti-anxiety drugs for some months, until it is realized that the anxiety symptoms are part of a depression that needs antidepressant treatment. It varies in degree from mild to severe.

Hypochondriasis

Anxious concern over general health or conviction of a particular disease is a most important symptom of depressive illness.

Irritability

Undue or unusual irritability, particularly at home, is an important depressive symptom.

Paranoid ideas

Depressed patients often think that people are against them and know about their defects. These ideas are in keeping with the depressed mood.

Retardation

Depressed patients become slow in their movements and in severe cases the patient can become stuporous. By contrast, their thinking often seems to be speeded up — particularly with circular worrying thoughts about the past or future.

SIGNS

The facial appearance of most depressed patients is characteristic with a furrowed brow,

6

immobile face, down-turned mouth and an expression of troubled perplexity. This appearance should be recognized at a glance. The stooped posture and slowed movements, or the restless agitation, are also important signs.

THE PATIENT'S MENTAL STATE

The doctor should enquire: 'Do you feel it is your fault you are like this?' and 'Have you felt so bad that life doesn't seem worth living?'. 'How have you coped with these feelings?'

These questions asked properly, at the appropriate time, show the patient that the doctor understands how he feels and thinks. Such questions do not put ideas in the patient's head. They are already there.

Severely depressed patients will express guilt, remorse, and persistent suicidal thoughts.

It is the persistence of these depressive symptoms and signs that make up the syndrome of depressive illness. It is important to recognize that clinically:

1) Depressive symptoms occur in many physical and psychiatric illnesses. They form a subsidiary part of the symptomatology and are often a reaction to the main illness. This association, as will be mentioned, is of the greatest importance in general medical practice. Any acute or chronic medical condition may be associated with depressive symptoms. Psychiatric illnesses frequently associated with depression are chronic brain syndromes and schizophrenia. The patient's prognosis in these cases is dependent upon that of the main condition, though the depressive symptoms may be relieved with treatment.
2) *In primary depressive illness,* the predominant feature is the persistent mood change from which the depressive symptoms and signs stem.

ONSET AND COURSE

The onset is usually gradual over the course of a few months, but can be abrupt, and a florid illness may develop in a few days.

The course of the illness is a self-limiting one. Before the days of active treatment it was known that illnesses of mood (depression or mania) remitted completely, leaving the patient as he was before the illness came on. It was also known that some patients tended to get further attacks of depression or mania.

The actual length of the illness is very variable. The mild form (particularly in the elderly) tends to be more chronic than the severe which often develops acutely. In general, without treatment most severe depressive illnesses would have cleared within a year, and it would be unusual for symptoms to persist for more than 2 years.

CULTURAL AND SOCIAL FACTORS, AGE AND SEX

Depressive illness occurs throughout the world but is probably more frequent in people of European origin.

It is evenly distributed throughout the social classes in Europe and the United States.

Depressive illness occurs at all ages from childhood to advanced age, but is more frequent in the 50s, 60s and 70s. This also corresponds to the peak age for suicide. Women are more liable to depressive symptoms than men.

CAUSES OF DEPRESSION

It has been mentioned already that depressive illness is an illness of mood, and that its actual neurophysiological basis is not yet known.

In recent years, much research interest has centred about the chemical basis of mood. Clinical observations on the actions of three drugs, reserpine, iproniazid and imipramine led to suggestions about the biochemical basis of disorders of mood. Studies have suggested changes in brain monoamines (the catecholamines and indoleamines) are related to severe disorders of mood. A monoamine hypothesis could be stated thus 'that depressive illnesses are associated with a relative deficiency of certain monoamines in certain parts of the brain. Antidepressant treatments produce improvement by altering monoamine metabolism in certain parts of the brain. The converse applies to mania and anti-manic treatments'.

It has been shown by studies of twins and families of depressed patients that there is a genetic predisposition to depressive illness, though this may not become manifest till late in life and in the presence of precipitating factors, e.g. bereavement or a cerebrovascular accident.

Psychopathological theories that stem from Freud's study On Mourning and Melancholia have given important insights into psychological mechanisms of depression. In particular, the loss of some source of self-esteem can, in some people with a certain personality structure, cause depression. This loss may be bereavement, or physical health, loss of status on retiring, loss of home, property, etc. These factors may be important in some patients with depressive illness, but are by no means always present.

DIFFERENTIAL DIAGNOSIS

Physical causes

The many symptoms that depressed patients may complain of can suggest the presence of many diseases. In excluding physical causes, a full physical examination and if necessary, ancillary investigations may be needed. Frequent clinical problems are neoplasms, anaemia and myxoedema.

Anxiety

Patients who present with anxiety symptoms often have a depressive illness and enquiry into all depressive symptoms is important. Other anxious patients do not have depressive symptoms. It is important to try and decide about this because treatment with antidepressive or antianxiety drugs may be an essential part of the management of the patient. These will be discussed later.

Hysteria

Hysterical illness *per se* is uncommon, though hysterical symptoms are frequent and can be precipitated by a depressive illness. Here again, enquiry into all depressive symptoms is important. Again, it is important to decide whether to treat the hysterical symptoms with antidepressive treatment or by other means.

Obsessional symptoms

Obsessional symptoms are frequent in depressive illness. These symptoms occurring for the first time in an elderly patient are due to the presence of a depressive illness. In all patients with obsessional symptoms an important practical question is whether to use antidepressive treatment or tranquillizing drugs in the total management of the patient.

Neurotic personality

It is apparent in clinical work that many patients with a history of long standing neurotic personality features may present with an exacerbation of these symptoms, be they anxiety, phobic, obsessional or hysterical ones. This exacerbation often is due to the development of a depressive illness though the depressive symptoms can be overlooked by the inexperienced. These patients are important, as the appropriate treatment may be supportive care and antidepressive treatment and not psychotherapy.

Schizophrenia

In depression (and mania) thought content is appropriate to the mood disorder. This may not be so in schizophrenia. Complex paranoid ideas are more usually due to schizophrenia.

Hypochondriasis

Hypochondriacal symptoms are frequent in depressive illness, but usually the cardinal symptoms and signs of a depressive illness are also present. Some patients are seen who have had marked hypochondriacal symptoms for many years, yet lack the other definite symptoms of depressive illness. It is often best to treat these patients with antidepressive medication, as some of them respond satisfactorily.

HISTORY FROM RELATIVES

A history from the nearest relative is of great importance in diagnosing depressive illness. The doctor should recognize that he cannot compare the patient's present state with his usual self. Only someone who has known the patient for some time can do this. Some patients who do not appear severely depressed have been active energetic people prior to their illness, and the illness may even seem to 'normalize' them. Yet, in fact, this sort of depressive illness can have the same suicidal risk as more obviously depressed patients.

TYPES OF DEPRESSION

In clinical practice there seem to be two contrasting types of depressive illness, and a third which has elements of both types.

Endogenous depression

In the predominantly endogenous type of depression, symptoms are thought to be determined to a large extent by genetic constitutional factors. The symptoms are usually severe, and the onset may have been independent of adverse environmental circumstances (though precipitation by the factors already mentioned is common). Symptoms tend to be worse in the morning and improve later in the day (diurnal variation), while the patient tends to wake early in the morning. Loss of weight and sex drive may be marked. Perhaps most characteristic is the fact that the depressed mood is not altered by pleasing environmental circumstances.

Reactive depression

In the predominantly reactive type of depression, symptoms are understandable as a reaction of a particular sort of personality to a particular situation. Often the situation is one which has produced anger or hostility in the patient and depressive symptoms follow. Symptoms are usually variable and mild and tend to be worse in the evening. Anxiety symptoms are usually prominent. Patients find it difficult to fall off to sleep because of worrying thoughts about the events of the day. The symptoms respond (albeit temporarily) to favourable environmental circumstances. This syndrome with anxiety and depression is the most frequently diagnosed neurotic group of symptoms. Patients with reactive depression are usually younger than those with the endogenous type.

Mixed depression

There is a mixed type in which features of both endogenous and reactive depression are present.

Statistical evaluation of clinical data, using methods of factor analysis, has given support to the clinical distinction between reactive and endogenous depression.

In recent years it has been shown that some 60% of endogenous depressed patients show abnormal plasma cortisol levels after a midnight dose of dexamethasone. This dexamethasone nonsuppression is now a routine test in many hospitals that treat depressed patients.

Psychiatrists in psychiatric hospitals will see mainly endogenous depression, general practitioners mainly reactive depression, while in outpatient and general hospital work mixed pictures are usual.

What matters in each patient is the recognition of the symptoms present and their severity as judged by the way they have interfered with the patient's life and the assessment of possible causative factors. Some illnesses clearly fall into the 'endogenous' group, and some into the 'reactive' group; but many do not and it is not important in these last cases to decide 'endogenous' or 'reactive'.

Modern techniques of cluster analysis of depressive phenomenology have suggested four types of depression:

1) A severe depression in older patients often with delusions and a good premorbid personality. There are usually no precipitating events (i.e. 'endogenous').

2) A moderately severe depression with high levels of anxiety in middle-aged patients, often with an obsessional personality.

3) A middle-aged depressed patient with marked hostility and self-pitying features in the behaviour and mental state.

4) A young, anxious group with evidence of precipitating life events (i.e. 'neurotic or reactive').

RELATIONSHIP OF MANIA TO DEPRESSION

It has been noted in historical medical writings that there is an occasional association of manic and depressive attacks in the same patient (bipolar). This is unusual. Depressive illness alone (unipolar) is commonest. Manic illness alone is an uncommon illness that is essentially the concern of the psychiatrist. The symptoms are the exact converse of depression — elation, grandiose thoughts, overactivity and pressure of talk and activity. Sleep is disturbed and sex drive increased.

THE CAUSES OF DEPRESSION ARE MANY

In young people, problems of family and personal relationships are important as are employment and academic problems. Sexual problems may be of significance.

In the middle-aged, family problems, physical illness, deaths within the family and of friends have great relevance. Women at the menopause are particularly liable to depression.

In the older patient loneliness, and loss of family, friends and health, are important factors.

At all ages, anger, hostility and loss are important precipitants of depression. Operations at any age can be followed by depression. Certain drugs can produce depression (e.g. steroids, the contraceptive pill, reserpine and some other hypotensive drugs).

Depression in children is diagnosed more frequently now and is sometimes treated with antidepressants.

The family doctor should keep the following questions in mind:

1) Is the depression a primary or secondary illness?
2) Are the symptoms mild, moderate or severe?
3) What seem the likely causes?

These questions, if answered, are more important than asking 'Is the depression endogenous or reactive?'

Are the symptoms mild, moderate or severe?

The severity of symptoms is best judged by the way they have interfered with the normal everyday behaviour of the patient. To see the husband or wife of the patient is very helpful.

Usually, despite being tired, irritable and not sleeping well, the patient is coping but under difficulty.

Sometimes the patient is more depressed than appears to be the case. (Often called 'masked depression'.)

Two common reasons for this are:

1) The patient is, normally, a particularly active, 'overenergetic' individual and the depression makes him more 'normal'.
2) The very obsessional patient cannot express his distress easily and keeps at his routine despite his symptoms.

Another use of the term 'masked depression' is any symptoms that appear to respond to antidepressants!

Young patients with personality problems can appear very depressed, yet sudden fluctuations can occur in response to interpersonal and environmental changes. In general, vigorous treatment by drugs or electroconvulsive therapy are not indicated in adolescents and patients under 30. These patients usually have problems which pills cannot solve.

REFERENCES

Burrows, G. D. (Ed.) (1977) Handbook of Studies on Depression. Excerpta Medica, Amsterdam.

Chapter 2

Biochemical and behavioural effects of antidepressant drugs

S.-O.ÖGREN, S. ROSS, H. HALL

and

T. ARCHER

*Astra Läkemedel AB, Research and Development Laboratories,
Pharmacology, S-151 85 Södertälje, Sweden*

INTRODUCTION

The involvement of monoamine neurotransmitters – catecholamines and serotonin (5-HT) – in affective disorders was derived partly from the observation in the late 50s that the monoamine oxidase inhibitors (MAOIs) and tricyclic antidepressant drugs (TCAs), e.g. imipramine, possessed antidepressant properties and the subsequent discovery that these two groups of drugs altered the availability of the monoamines in the brain (Spector et al., 1958; Hertting et al., 1961; Glowinski and Axelrod, 1964). Most TCAs, with some exceptions, have the ability to inhibit the neuronal reuptake of noradrenaline (NA) and 5-HT (Carlsson et al., 1969a,b; Ross and Renyi, 1975a,b). Since reuptake into nerve endings represents the main mechanism by which the action of the monoamines are terminated, the TCAs by increasing the synaptic concentration of monoamine neurotransmitters in certain areas of the brain were suggested to alleviate a hypothesized transmitter deficiency (Schildkraut, 1965; Lapin and Oxenkrug, 1969; Coppen, 1967). The MAO inhibitors were suggested to act by an analogous mechanism, i.e. through inhibition of neuronal MAO which results in an enhanced availability of the transmitters. Thus, the two major classes of drugs effective in depressive disorders would enhance the functional activity of one or more brain monoamine transmitters via actions at the presynaptic level.

However, the relationship between the acute primary effects of the TCAs and MAO inhibitors and their clinical effect is poorly understood. It is not clear whether actions on both NA and 5-HT are involved in their therapeutic effects. Since the prototype TCAs such as imipramine, amitriptyline and more recently clomipramine (Ross and Renyi, 1975b; Träskman et al., 1979) affect both NA and 5-HT reuptake *in vivo* and thus presumably enhance the functional activity of both amines, the relative role of NA and 5-HT is still controversial. Another major problem refers to the relationship between NA and 5-HT uptake inhibition and the receptors possibly involved in the mediation of antidepressant action. Thus, TCAs show direct antagonistic effects on α-adrenergic (U'Prichard et al., 1978; Hall and Ögren, 1981), serotonergic (Bennett and Snyder, 1976; Ögren et al., 1979; Tang and Seeman, 1980) histaminergic (Kanof and Greengard, 1978; Richelson, 1979; Hall and Ögren, 1981) and muscarinic (Rehavi et al., 1977; Snyder and Yamamura, 1977) receptors. In addition, chronic administration of certain TCAs and MAOIs produce alterations in both adrenergic β-receptors (Vetulani et al., 1976; Banerjee et al., 1977) and certain 5-HT receptors (Fuxe et al., 1979; Segawa et al., 1979; Takahashi et al., 1981). Since the receptor alterations observed in monoaminergic neurons develop on a time scale similar to the antidepressant effect they have been suggested to be of clinical importance (Sulser et al., 1978).

The complexity of the biochemical and behavioural effects of the TCAs makes it difficult to analyse their mode of action. The introduction in recent years of antidepressant drugs which differ markedly from the TCAs both in their chemical structure and in their pharmacological profile offers a new approach to examine more critically the relative role of different transmitter mechanisms in depression. In this paper we summarize and compare the acute and long-term biochemical and behavioural properties of TCAs e.g. imipramine and new compounds belonging to 'the second generation' of antidepressant drugs (see Leonard, 1980).

EFFECTS ON MONOAMINERGIC UPTAKE SITE

Various methods have been employed in studies to elucidate the effects of antidepressive drugs on the monoaminergic uptake systems. Rat brain slices (Ross and Renyi, 1975a) or synaptosomes (Snyder and Coyle, 1969) are convenient preparations for examining the *in vitro* potencies. *Ex vivo* experiments in which the uptake is measured *in vitro* in slices or synaptosomes prepared from drug-treated animals have been used as a measure of the *in vivo* activity (Ross and Renyi, 1975b; Wong et al., 1975). Other frequently used *in vivo* methods are the determination of the antagonism of the amine depletion in the rat brain after injections of compounds which are dependent on the neuronal uptake mechanism for releasing the amines. Examples of such compounds are α-4-dimethyl-m-tyramine (H77/77) (Carlsson et al., 1969a) or α-methyl-m-tyrosine forming α-methyl-m-tyramine in the brain (Fuller et al., 1979) for the catecholaminergic neurons and α-ethyl-4-methyl-m-tyramine (H75/12) (Carlsson et al., 1969b) or p-chloroamphetamine (Fuller et al., 1975) for serotonergic neurons. Studies in several laboratories have shown a fairly good correlation between results obtained with the *ex vivo* method measuring amine uptake in brain synaptosomes or slices and those obtained with the H77/77 and H75/12 technique (Maître et al., 1980; cf. Table 2).

TABLE 1

A comparison of the relative inhibitory potency of antidepressant and related drugs on the uptake of NA, 5-HT and DA in the rat brain *in vitro* (synaptosomes), *in vivo* (various techniques) and 5-HT uptake in human platelets under clinical conditions. The data are compiled from numerous reports. Very high potency +++, high potency ++, moderate potency +, low potency −.

| Drug | Rat brain | | | | | | Human platelets |
| | In vitro | | | In vivo | | | |
	NA	5-HT	DA	NA	5-HT	DA	5-HT
Desipramine	+++	(+)	−	+++	(+)	−	+
Imipramine	++	+(+)	−	+++	+	−	++
Clomipramine	++	+++	−	++	+(+)	−	+++
Nortriptyline	++	(+)	−	++	(+)	−	
Amitriptyline	++	++	−	+	(+)	−	+(+)
Maprotiline	++	−	−	++	−	−	−
Doxepin	+	+	−	+	+	−	+
Mianserin	+	−	−	−	−	−	
Iprindole	−	−	−	−	−	−	
Nomifensine	++	−	+	++	−	+	
Viloxazine	+	−	−	(+)	−	−	
Zimelidine	(+)	++	−	(+)	++	−	++
Fluvoxamine	−	++	−	−	+	−	
Femoxetine	+	++	−	+	++	−	++
Fluoxetine	+	++	−	−	++	−	++
Citalopram	−	+++	−	−	+++	−	++
Alaproclate	−	+(+)	−	−	++	−	+

Table 1 summarizes the relative potencies of antidepressant drugs and some experimental drugs on the monoaminergic uptake systems *in vitro* and *in vivo*. The table has been compiled from numerous reports using various methods and experimental conditions and will only give a general picture of the relative potencies.

Some of the tertiary TCAs, e.g. imipramine and amitriptyline, are rather nonselective inhibitors of NA and 5-HT uptake *in vitro*. After systemic administration these compounds become markedly more potent on the NA uptake than on 5-HT uptake inhibition (Table 2), probably because of the formation of the demethylated metabolites, which are selective NA uptake inhibitors *in vitro*. The effect of biotransformation of tertiary to the secondary amines in changing the pharmacological profile of tricyclic antidepressants has also been demonstrated for clomipramine. This drug is a selective 5-HT uptake inhibitor *in vitro* being 10 times more potent to inhibit the uptake mechanism in serotonergic neurons than in noradrenergic neurons. However, after systemic administration clomipramine is a nonselective inhibitor both in rats (Table 2) and also in humans (Träskman et al., 1979) due to the formation of chlordesipramine, which is a selective NA uptake inhibitor (Carlsson et al., 1969a,b).

Selective 5-HT uptake inhibition

The hypothesis that serotonergic neurons may be involved in the aetiology of depres-

TABLE 2

In vivo effects of some antidepressants on the uptake mechanisms in noradrenergic (NA) and serotonergic (5-HT)neurons in the rat brain comparing two different methods: *ex vivo* technique in hypothalamic slices and antagonism of the amine depletion by H77/77 (NA) and H75/12 (5-HT).

| | *Ex vivo* ED_{50} µmol/kg | | | | H77/77 (NA) | H75/12 5-HT |
| | NA | | 5-HT | | ED_{50} µmol/kg | |
	p.o	i.p.	p.o.	i.p.	i.p	
Desipramine	26		>160			
Imipramine	25	19	158	158	47	>157
Clomipramine	58	71	102	28	102	71
Amitriptyline	>160	35	>160	>80	>160	>160
Zimelidine	61	>49	17	14	>98	10

Data from Ross and Renyi (1975b, 1977), Ögren et al. (1981a) and unpublished data.

sive disorders (Coppen, 1967; Lapin and Oxenkrug, 1969) has initiated a search for selective 5-HT uptake inhibitors. During recent years, several such inhibitors have been developed, e.g. fluoxetine (Wong et al., 1974), femoxetine (Buus Lassen et al., 1975), zimelidine (Ross et al., 1976), citalopram (Hyttel, 1977), fluvoxamine (Claassen et al., 1977), indalpine (LeFur and Uzan, 1977), alaproclate (Lindberg et al., 1978), Org-6582 (Mireylees et al., 1978), CGP-6085A (Waldmeier et al., 1979) and Wy-25093 (Diggory et al., 1980). One of these compounds, zimelidine, has been found in several double-blind controlled clinical studies (Coppen et al., 1978; Åberg, 1981; Montgomery et al., 1981) to be an effective antidepressant.

Zimelidine is in itself a moderately potent and selective 5-HT uptake inhibitor. However, its demethylated metabolite norzimelidine is about six times more potent than zimelidine and retains the 5-HT selectivity (Ross and Renyi, 1977). Since the concentration of norzimelidine in plasma markedly exceeds that of the parent compound after administration *in vivo* to rats (Ross et al., 1981) and humans (Åberg-Wistedt et al., 1981) the uptake inhibition *in vivo* is mainly caused by norzimelidine.

Inhibition of the 5-HT uptake in platelets. The 5-HT uptake in platelets has frequently been used as a model system for the uptake in serotonergic neurons (Sneddon, 1973). Because of the easy availability of platelets it is possible to obtain information on the inhibition of the 5-HT uptake under clinical conditions. Treatment with zimelidine (100 mg b.i.d.) reduced the uptake of 5-HT in platelets and decreased 5-HT concentration in whole blood with about 70% at steady state (Åberg-Wistedt et al., 1981). Chronic zimelidine treatment of rats produced similar dose response curves for the inhibition of the uptake of 5-HT in brain slices *ex vivo* and the decrease in whole blood 5-HT (Ross et al., 1981). Extrapolation from rats to man indicates that a clinically effective dose of zimelidine produces about 50% inhibition of the 5-HT uptake in the human brain. This dose corresponds to approximately 10 µmol/kg b.i.d. in the rat. The plasma concentration of norzimelidine was five times higher in the rat compared to that in humans at equipotent doses. This difference is in accordance with the observation that the 5-HT uptake mechanism in human platelets is more sensitive to uptake inhibitors than is that of the rat platelets (Wieloz et al., 1976). This species difference probably explains the observation that also desipramine (75 mg b.i.d.), which does not affect platelet uptake in the rat, caused a marked inhibition (40–50%) of the uptake of 5-HT in human platelets (Åberg-Wistedt et al., 1981).

^{3}H-Imipramine binding. The recent findings that ^{3}H-imipramine binds in platelets (Briley et al., 1979; Talvenheimo et al., 1979; Paul et al., 1980) and in brain (Raisman et al., 1979) to sites which are closely related to the 5-HT uptake sites (for review see Langer and Briley, 1981) open the possibility to evaluate the relative potencies of the 5-HT uptake inhibitors in human brain tissue. The observation that the density of the ^{3}H-imipramine binding site in the rat brain is reduced by chronic treatment with TCAs (Raisman et al., 1980) suggests that the number of binding sites for uptake inhibitors are reduced following chronic treatment.

Selective NA uptake inhibitors

Of the established antidepressants maprotiline is almost a specific NA uptake inhibitor (Baumann and Maître, 1979). Nomifensine is also a selective NA uptake inhibitor with negligible effects on the 5-HT uptake (Koe, 1976). However, this drug also inhibits DA uptake (Hunt et al., 1974) which may contribute to the clinical effect and/or adverse effects. Several experimental drugs are potent and selective NA uptake inhibitors, e.g. nisoxetine (Wong and Bymaster, 1976), mazindol (Koe, 1976) and tandamine (Pugsley and Lippmann, 1979).

Atypical antidepressants

Antidepressants without or with weak effects on the amine uptake and monoamine oxidase are classified as atypical antidepressants. Iprindole, mianserin, viloxazine and trazodone belong to this group. Although mianserin and viloxazine have some inhibitory effect on the NA uptake and trazodone on the 5-HT uptake in vitro, it appears that their in vivo potencies, at least in rats, are too low to be of clinical significance. Iprindole has virtually no uptake inhibitory effects (Gluckman and Baum, 1969; Ross et al., 1971).

Some possible modes of action may be considered: a) that atypical antidepressants interact with the monoaminergic systems by mechanisms unrelated to uptake inhibition, resulting in a similar end response as resulting from the uptake inhibition; or b) that all antidepressant drugs, with the exception of the MAO inhibitors, act by an as yet unknown common mechanism. Several recent observations are in line with the former hypothesis. Thus, chronic treatment of rats with iprindole similar to desipramine causes a down-regulation of the β-adrenoceptor system, which is dependent upon intact noradrenaline neurons (Wolfe et al., 1978). The effect of iprindole can possibly be explained by enhanced release of NA (Hendley, 1978). Similarly, mianserin is a presynaptic α_2-receptor antagonist and can therefore produce an increased release of NA (Baumann and Maître, 1977). Trazodone has been reported to be a 5-HT antagonist, whereas its metabolite m-chlorophenylpiperazine is a 5-HT agonist (Maj et al., 1979). Since trazodone potentiates the 5-HTP induced head twitches in mice (Ögren, unpublished observation) the main effect on serotonergic neurons appears to be a facilitation of 5-HT neurotransmission.

EFFECTS ON REGULATORY MECHANISMS IN MONOAMINERGIC NEURONS

NA and 5-HT neurons

Monoamine transmitter functions in central neurons are influenced by several regulatory mechanisms including synthesis, compartmentation, intraneuronal metabolism, and uptake and neuronal firing. Antidepressant drugs have been shown to affect each of these regulatory mechanisms. Inhibition of monoamine uptake is generally believed to increase the concentration of the transmitter at the synaptic cleft and cause an increased post-synaptic activity. As a consequence, the impulse activity (Aghajanian, 1972) and the monoamine utilization (Corrodi and Fuxe, 1969) and synthesis (Carlsson and Lindqvist, 1978) in the presynaptic neuron is reduced, possibly due to pre- and postsynaptic feedback mechanisms. In view of the number of possible interactions it is not surprising that both acute and chronic administration of antidepressant drugs have yielded quite inconsistent results (for a recent review, see Sugrue, 1981). In spite of this, the ability of antidepressant drugs to modify rat NA and 5-HT brain turnover/synthesis and spontaneous neuronal firing rate in the rat is roughly related to their inhibitory effects on NA and 5-HT uptake, respectively. Thus, demethylated TCAs such as desipramine and protriptyline, which are more potent inhibitors of NA uptake than corresponding tertiary amines, are inhibitors of NA turnover (Sugrue, 1981), synthesis (Carlsson and Lindqvist, 1978) and impulse flow in the locus coeruleus (Nybäck et al., 1975; Scuvée-Moreau and Dresse, 1979). A decline in desipramine-induced decrease in NA turnover has been shown with several techniques including attenuation of the fall in NA content induced by the tyrosinehydroxylase inhibitor α-methyl-p-tyrosine (α-MT) and decreased concentration of the major NA metabolites 3-methoxy-4-hydroxyphenylglycol (MHPG) (Roffman et al., 1977; Sugrue, 1980, 1981).

On the other hand, acute treatment with 5-HT uptake blockers such as zimelidine, Org-6582 and citalopram does not result in any significant changes in noradrenaline turnover and synthesis in the rat brain (Carlsson and Lindqvist, 1978; Sugrue, 1981; Ögren et al., 1981a). Selective 5-HT uptake blockers markedly reduce 5-HT synthesis as determined by a significant reduction in the accumulation of 5-hydroxytryptophan (5-HTP) after decarboxylase inhibition (Carlsson and Lindqvist, 1978; Ögren et al., 1981a) and also antagonize the decline in 5-HT concentration following inhibition of 5-HT synthesis by α-propyldopacetamide (H22/54) (Ögren et al., 1981a).

The decrease in 5-HT synthesis is accompanied by a relatively selective reduction of impulse flow in dorsal raphe neurons (Scuvée-Moreau and Dresse, 1979). Thus, drugs which are selective uptake inhibitors appear to produce more or less selective effects in NA and 5-HT neurons, respectively. In contrast to most antidepressant drugs, acute administration of mianserin appears to increase NA and 5-HT turnover/utilization in the rat brain (Kafoe et al., 1976; Maj et al., 1978a). The increase in NA-turnover may be due to a blocking action on α_2-presynaptic receptors (Baumann and Maître, 1977) located on NA nerve terminals and controlling NA release (Langer, 1977).

Long-term administration of antidepressant drugs has been found to result in several types of adaptive changes in pre- and postsynaptic regulatory mechanisms (see Sugrue, 1981). Whereas acute administration of TCAs generally reduces NA turnover/synthesis, there is evidence in some studies for an increase in NA turnover in the rat brain using several different methods following chronic administration of desipramine, protriptyline (Schildkraut et al., 1971) and imipramine (Schildkraut et al., 1971; Roffman et al., 1977). It is notable that chronic mianserin and trazodone treatment also increases NA turnover in the rat brain (Fludder and Leonard, 1979; Sugrue, 1980; Przegalinski et al., 1981). The increase in NA turnover observed in the rat brain may be linked to the potent α_2-blocking action of these drugs secondary to the development of α_2-adrenoceptor subsensitivity (Crews and Smith, 1978). Another possible explanation is the antiserotonergic action of some of these drugs. There is evidence that reduction of serotonergic transmission results in activation of NA neurons (Przegalinski et al., 1981).

In contrast to NA neurons, no subsensitivity seems to develop in the presynaptic 5-HT mechanisms mediating the reduction of 5-HT turnover and release following treatment with selective 5-HT uptake blockers (Ögren et al., 1981a; Sugrue, 1981). The synthesis of 5-HT, as well as the concentrations of 5-hydroxyindoleacetic acid (5-HIAA), were still decreased in different brain regions of the rat after chronic treatment with zimelidine and Org-6582 (Fuxe et al., 1979; Sugrue, 1980; Ögren et al., 1981a) while no significant changes in NA synthesis or turnover were observed in several brain regions.

Interestingly, chronic but not acute administration of zimelidine, imipramine and Org-6582 produce a consistent reduction of 5-HT concentration (Alpers and Himwich, 1972; Sugrue, 1980; Ross et al., 1981). A similar reduction in NA levels has also been observed following chronic desipramine, imipramine and protriptyline treatment (Schildkraut et al., 1971; Roffler-Tarlov et al., 1973). These findings may indicate that a new steady state equilibrium is obtained in both NA and 5-HT neurons, i.e. less transmitter is released per nerve impulse. This may be an additional feedback-regulating mechanism in order to compensate for the increase in postsynaptic activity resulting from uptake inhibition. Taken together, chronic treatment with antidepressant drugs in the rat produces changes in regulatory mechanisms which are relatively specific for NA and 5-HT neurons. The different effects of antidepressant drugs on NA and 5-HT neurons may therefore be important in categories of patients characterized by disturbances in either NA or 5-HT metabolism.

DA neurons

Antidepressant drugs, with the exception of nomifensine, are weak DA uptake blockers. However, high doses of some TCAs such as chlorimipramine and amitriptyline increase levels of the DA metabolites DOPAC and HVA in rat striatum possibly due to a blockade of DA receptors (Keller et al., 1980). Interestingly, in very low doses (3 mg/kg) amitriptyline, desipramine and also zimelidine have been found to decrease DA turnover particularly in limbic DA systems (Fuxe et al., 1977). The reduction of DA turnover caused by these drugs does not appear to be related to any direct effect on NA, DA or 5-HT receptors (see below).

Chronic administration of TCAs has not revealed any marked changes in rat brain DA turnover in studies of whole brain regions (see Sugrue, 1981). A recent study in the rat also shows, however, that chronic zimelidine treatment produces, in contrast to acute administration, an increased DA turnover in certain areas of the striatum and limbic areas (Fuxe et al., 1982c). The increase in DA turnover was attributed to a down-regulation of the activity in inhibitory 5-HT synapses in the substantia nigra. Thus, the neuronal activity in the ascending meso-striatal neurons can be increased as a result of less 5-HT mediated inhibition (Fuxe et al., 1982c).

Behavioural evidence for such adaptions in nigral neurons have also been found (Sugrue, 1981). Another possibility is that chronic treatment with antidepressant drugs induces subsensitivity at presynaptic DA receptors (Serra et al., 1979). Thus, chronic treatment with imipramine, amitriptyline and mianserin blocked the motor activity inhibitory effect of a small dose of apomorphine. Chronic imipramine treatment also prevented the decrease in DOPAC levels induced by apomorphine (Serra et al., 1979).

EFFECTS ON BRAIN RECEPTORS

Most antidepressant drugs are believed to cause an increased postsynaptic activity of monoaminergic receptors due to an increased availability of the neurotransmitter. A number of functional as well as receptor binding studies have revealed, however, that several of these drugs are inhibitors of postsynaptic receptors. This receptor blocking action could theoretically antagonize the postulated effect of the antidepressant drugs.

Effects on adrenergic receptors

The effects on different receptors are summarized in Table 3. The TCAs, including maprotiline and mianserin inhibit the binding of ^{3}H-WB4101, a radioligand that binds to the α_1-adrenergic receptors in the brain (U'Prichard et al., 1978; Maggi et al., 1980; Hall and Ögren, 1981). The affinities of amitriptyline and imipramine for the α_1-receptor are in the same concentration range in which they affect the neuronal NA uptake. This suggests that several antidepressant drugs may in fact reduce α_1-adrenergic activity in the brain at about the same concentrations at which they enhance NA activity due to NA uptake inhibition. In contrast, zimelidine, norzimelidine, nomifensine and iprindole were all found to be weak α_1-receptor blockers.

Antidepressant drugs may also enhance central NA activity by increasing NA release from the presynaptic neurons. There is pharmacological evidence that mianserin, which is a weak NA uptake inhibitor *in vivo,* could increase NA release due to blockade of presynaptic α_2-adrenergic receptors (Baumann and Maître, 1977). The high potency of mianserin in displacing ^{3}H-clonidine (Hall and Ögren, 1981) which has the pharmacological characteristics of an α_2-adrenergic presynaptic receptor ligand (Titeler et al., 1978; Maggi et al., 1980) is thus in line with pharmacological findings. However, it is not clear at present whether the ^{3}H-clonidine binding site is postsynaptic to NA terminals (U'Prichard et al., 1979). Moreover, since mianserin is an even more potent α_1-receptor blocker in the brain, it is questionable whether an increase in NA release could result in enhanced activity at α_1-receptor sites. Mianserin has been reported not to cause a reduction in the number of β-receptors (Clements-Jewery, 1978) but appears to cause a reduced response to NA sensitive adenylate cyclase in the forebrain (Mobley and Sulser, 1981).

TABLE 3

Effects of some antidepressant drugs on various receptor systems in the rat brain (IC$_{50}$; μM).

	Cholinergic rec. Muscarinic receptors ^{3}H-QNB binding[a]	Adrenergic rec. α$_1$-rec. ^{3}H-WB4101 binding[a]	α$_2$-rec. ^{3}H-clonidine binding[a]	5-HT$_1$-rec. ^{3}H-5-HT binding[a]	Serotonin rec. 5-HT$_1$+5-HT$_2$-rec. ^{3}H-d-LSD binding[a]	5-HT$_2$-rec. ^{3}H-spiroperidol binding[b]	Histamine rec. H$_1$-rec. ^{3}H-mepyramine binding[a]
Amitriptyline	0.062	0.022	0.550	1.52	0.150	0.123	0.006
Clomipramine	0.184	0.035	5.04	21.2	0.917	0.180	0.064
Desipramine	0.848	0.250	10.6	16.1	3.45	–	0.457
Imipramine	0.181	0.097	4.12	24.6	1.35	0.270	0.029
Iprindole	2.37	6.81	6.70	15.2	5.80	–	0.250
Mianserin	0.566	0.067	0.126	1.21	0.097	0.010	0.006
Nomifensine	48.8	1.27	4.56	9.88	3.47	1.77	8.87
Zimelidine	33.7	1.18	3.85	33.2	10.9	>3.0	2.90

a Data from Hall and Ögren, 1981.
b Data from Fuxe et al., 1982a; Ögren et al., 1982.

Contrary to findings by Clements-Jewery (1978), Hall et al. (unpublished observation) have observed that subchronic treatment of rats with mianserin caused a reduction of β-receptors in the central cortex. Since this effect was antagonized by chemical lesion of the cerebral noradrenergic nerve terminals, it appears to have a presynaptic origin, presumably blockade of α_2-receptor. Thus, the acute blockade of α_2-receptors by mianserin appears to result in functional β-adrenergic subsensitivity. With the exception of mianserin, the other antidepressant drugs have low affinity of the ^{3}H-clonidine binding site. It therefore seems unlikely that acute blockade of α_2-receptors modulating NA release could significantly contribute to the action of antidepressant drugs with the exception of mianserin.

The action on α-adrenergic receptors does not appear to be directly linked to the clinical efficacy of antidepressant drugs in view of their marked differences in potency. It has been suggested that the α_1-adrenergic blocking action is partly related to the sedative properties of these drugs (U'Prichard et al., 1978; Cott and Ögren, 1980; Ögren et al., 1981b). However, other pharmacological properties also seem to contribute to the sedative action, for example, the blockade of histamine-H_1-receptors (Quach et al., 1979; Richelson, 1979; Ögren et al., 1981b).

Antidepressant drugs have not been found to have any significant affinity for the β-adrenergic receptor, as measured by displacement of ^{3}H-dihydroalprenolol (Hall and Ögren, 1981). The decrease in β-adrenergic receptor binding following long-term treatment with both TCAs and non-TCAs (Banerjee et al, 1977; Sarai et al., 1978; Sulser et al., 1978; Ross et al., 1981) does not appear, therefore, to be related to a direct action of these drugs on the ^{3}H-dihydroalprenolol binding site.

Effects on 5-HT receptors

Recent evidence indicates the existence of multiple 5-HT receptors in the brain. Two different classes of 5-HT receptors in the brain have been proposed on the basis of ligand-binding assays (Peroutka and Snyder, 1979). Serotonin receptors in the brain can bind tritium-labelled lysergic acid diethylamide (^{3}H-d-LSD), serotonin (^{3}H-5-HT) and spiroperidol (^{3}H-spiroperidol) (Bennett and Snyder, 1976; Leysen et al., 1978). It has been demonstrated that ^{3}H-5-HT and ^{3}H-spiroperidol bind to distinct populations of serotonin receptors in the brain, whereas ^{3}H-LSD binds to both of these sites (Fuxe et al., 1978; Ögren et al., 1979; Peroutka and Snyder, 1979). The receptors that bind ^{3}H-5-HT have been designated 5-HT$_1$-receptors whereas the binding sites in ^{3}H-spiroperidol have been designated 5-HT$_2$-receptors (Peroutka and Snyder, 1979). Most antidepressants have a very low affinity in inhibiting binding to 5-HT$_1$-receptor sites (Ögren et al., 1979; Peroutka and Snyder, 1980; Hall and Ögren, 1981) while several antidepressant drugs very potently inhibit 5-HT$_2$-receptors labelled by ^{3}H-d-LSD (Fuxe et al., 1977, 1978; Ögren et al., 1979; Hall and Ögren, 1981) and ^{3}H-spiroperidol (Peroutka and Snyder, 1979; Fuxe et al., 1982a, c).

Table 3 summarizes data on the 5-HT receptor affinities of different antidepressant drugs. Amitriptyline, nortriptyline and mianserin have high affinities for d-LSD binding sites in the dorsal cerebral cortex with IC_{50} values ranging from 100–200 nM. Several antidepressants, including imipramine, amitriptyline, clomipramine, desipramine and mianserin, also displace ^{3}H-spiroperidol with IC_{50} values from 10–270 nM. The observation that these drugs also block behaviours (head twitches) possibly mediated via activation of 5-HT receptors indicates that they possess a 5-HT receptor blocking action at some 5-HT receptor sites (Fuxe et al., 1977, 1978; Maj et al., 1978b; Ögren et al., 1979) possibly 5-HT$_2$-sites in the brain (Peroutka et al., 1981). When comparing the 5-HT receptor blocking action of antidepressant drugs with their ability to inhibit 5-HT/NA uptake both *in vitro* and *in vivo,* it is found that certain types of antidepressants such as amitriptyline, nortriptyline, mianserin, dibenzepine, nomifensine and doxepin possess 5-HT$_2$-receptor blocking activity in concentrations of doses near to or below those causing 5-HT and NA uptake inhibition (Ögren et al., 1979, 1982; Hall and Ögren, 1981). In contrast, 5-HT uptake blockers such as zimelidine, norzimelidine and fluoxetine have a very low affinity for both ^{3}H-d-LSD and ^{3}H-spiroperidol (Ögren et al., 1979; Fuxe et al., 1981a,b; Hall and Ögren, 1981).

The findings that several antidepressant drugs can act as receptor antagonists at certain 5-HT receptors in the brain are of particular interest in view of recent theories of depression developed independently by Aprison and Hingten (1981) and Takahashi and coworkers (1981). This theory suggests that some types of depression are associated with the development of hypersensitive 5-HT receptors.

Besides a blocking action at 5-HT$_2$-receptors, antidepressant drugs may also exert a direct action on 5-HT$_1$-receptors. Thus, preincubation with antidepressant drugs including iprindole and mianserin induces increases in the affinity and reduces the number of ^{3}H-5-HT binding sites in synaptosomal membranes from the rat brain (Fillion and Fillion, 1981).

EFFECTS ON DOPAMINERGIC RECEPTORS

Most antidepressant drugs with the exception of clomipramine and amitriptyline, have no significant effects on postsynaptic DA receptors (Keller et al., 1980). Clomipramine has also been shown to block DA sensitive adenylate cyclase in the striatum (Karobath, 1975). Clomipramine also appears to be a DA antagonist *in vivo* as it has been shown to reduce the behavioural effects of apomorphine in several studies (Delini-Stula and Vassout, 1979; Hall and Ögren, 1981).

EFFECTS ON MUSCARINIC RECEPTORS

It is well established that TCAs can produce peripheral and central anticholinergic effects (dryness of the mouth, urinary retention, dizziness). Receptor binding studies using the labelled muscarinic antagonist, ^{3}H-QNB, have thus demonstrated that several TCAs are potent muscarinic antagonists *in vitro* (Snyder and Yamamura, 1977; Hall and Ögren, 1981). The affinity of the TCAs for the muscarinic receptor appears to be clearly related to their propensity to produce anticholinergic effects in animals and man. Some newer antidepressants, such as iprindole, nomifensine and zimelidine, are very weak muscarinic antagonists in the brain and periphery compared to the TCAs. Amitriptyline is the most potent muscarinic antagonist of the TCAs followed by imipramine and desipramine (Rehavi et al., 1977; Snyder and Yamamura, 1977; Hall and Ögren, 1981). The relative

24

potency of these drugs in blocking the pharmacological effects induced by the acetyl-choline agonist oxotremorine is in complete agreement with their affinity for muscarinic receptors *in vitro*.

EFFECTS ON HISTAMINERGIC RECEPTORS

Several TCAs and also some non-TCAs have been shown to be highly potent antagonists of histamine-H_1-receptors in the brain and periphery (Figge et al., 1979; Quach et al., 1979; Richelson, 1979). In contrast, zimelidine and norzimelidine failed to affect ^{3}H-mepyramine binding, a ligand for H_1-receptors, and inhibited histamine-induced contraction in the guinea pig ileum only in high concentrations (Hall and Ögren, 1981) The H_1-receptor blocking actions of the antidepressant drugs appear to be partly related to their sedative action (Quach et al., 1979, Cott and Ögren, 1980; Hall and Ögren, 1981; Ögren et al., 1981b). There is a good correlation between the sedative effects of antidepressant drugs and their affinities for central histamine-H_1-receptors both *in vitro* (Fig. 1, modified from Ögren et al., 1981b) and *in vivo* (Quach et al., 1979). Thus, compounds with weak histamine-H_1-receptor blocking properties are largely devoid of sedative effects. The propensity of different drugs to enhance the behavioural action of ethanol has also been found to correlate well with central histamine-H_1-receptor blockade (Cott and Ögren, 1980).

Antidepressants have also been shown to be potent inhibitors of histamine sensitive adenylate cyclase in the brain which is linked to an H_2-receptor (Kanof and Greengard, 1978). However, in contrast to most antidepressant drugs including mianserin, both zimelidine and norzimelidine were recently found to display a negligible blocking action on H_2-receptors. This suggests that histamine H_2-receptor blocking action is not neces-

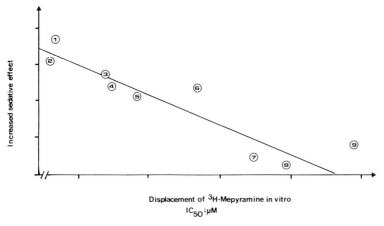

Fig. 1. Relationship between sedative effects of antidepressants and central H_1-receptor blocking properties. The means of ranks in nine different ranking tests for sedative effects in mice has been used as a measure of sedation. The IC_{50}-values for displacement of ^{3}H-mepyramine binding in rat cortex are from Hall and Ögren, 1981. The compounds used are: 1) amitriptyline, 2) mianserin, 3) maprotiline, 4) imipramine, 5) clomipramine, 6) desipramine, 7) zimelidine, 8) norzimelidine, 9) alaproclate.

sary for the therapeutic activity at antidepressant drugs, which earlier was suggested by Kanof and Greengard (1978).

EFFECTS ON OTHER RECEPTORS

Most antidepressant drugs do not show significant affinity (IC_{50}; 10 μM) for the benzo-diazepine (^{3}H-flunitrazepam), the GABA (^{3}H-muscimol) or the opiate (^{3}H-naloxone) receptors (Hall and Ögren, 1981).

ADAPTIVE CHANGES IN MONOAMINERGIC RECEPTOR AND EFFECTOR SYSTEMS FOLLOWING CHRONIC TREATMENT WITH ANTIDEPRESSANT DRUGS

In the previous sections of this paper the acute effects of the different antidepressants have been discussed. However, during the last few years, several studies have focused on the effects of long-term antidepressant treatment on brain receptor mechanisms. The first common feature of long-term treatment with various antidepressant drug was the down-regulation of the noradrenaline stimulated adenylate cyclase (Vetulani and Sulser, 1975). Various types of antidepressant treatment, such as uptake inhibitors, monoamine oxidase inhibitors and electroconvulsive treatment, elicit these changes in β-adrenergic adenylate cyclase, and also in β-adrenergic receptors as measured by receptor binding techniques. More recently, it has been shown that long-term treatment with antidepressant drugs causes down-regulation of both 5-HT receptors (Fuxe et al., 1978, 1979) and of α_2-adrenergic receptors (Crews and Smith, 1978) in the rat brain.

Effects on β-adrenergic receptor and β-adrenergic receptor linked adenylate cyclase

Since Mobley and Sulser (1981) recently reviewed this field only a short account will be given. As mentioned previously, antidepressant drugs have no significant affinity for the β-adrenergic receptor. Thus, the reduction in β-adrenergic receptor binding following long-term treatment with TCAs such as desipramine (Banerjee et al., 1977; Sarai et al., 1978; Sulser et al., 1978) does not appear to be related to a direct action of these drugs on the ^{3}H-dihydroalprenolol binding site. Besides reduction of the density of β-adrenergic receptors, several antidepressant drugs have also been reported to produce a subsensitivity to the NA receptor-linked adenylate cyclase system in the forebrain following chronic treatment (Vetulani and Sulser, 1975; Sulser et al., 1978) and to desensitize cortical neurons to microiontophoretically administered noradrenaline (Olpe and Schellenberg, 1980). These alterations are thought to reflect a 'down-regulation' of NA receptor activity and to be of clinical importance (Sulser et al., 1978). The neurochemical mechanism for this down-regulation has not yet been described. However, noradrenaline uptake inhibitors seem to require the noradrenergic presynaptic nerve terminal for this down-regulation (Wolfe et al., 1978; Schweitzer et al., 1979).

Effects of chronic treatment on 5-HT receptors and receptor activity

Chronic administration of TCAs and other types of antidepressant drugs have also recently been observed to result in 5-HT receptor modifications. Changes seem to occur in both 5-HT_1 and 5-HT_2-receptor sites following chronic antidepressant treatment but the changes are dissimilar. The changes observed in 5-HT_1-receptors labelled by ^{3}H-5-HT in the dorsal cerebral cortex upon chronic treatment with zimelidine, desipramine and imipramine have been found to involve both changes in affinity and changes in receptor numbers (Fuxe et al., 1982a, c). After chronic treatment with these drugs at clinically relevant doses ($2 \times 10\ \mu\text{mol/kg}$ p.o. for 14 days) two binding sites for ^{3}H-5-HT appear (Fuxe et al., 1979; Fuxe et al., 1981, 1982a, c). Following chronic zimelidine, the low affinity site had a more than 100% higher K_D value than the K_D value of control group and the high affinity component had a K_D value around 1 nM compared with 4–6 nM in the control group (Fuxe et al., 1981). In addition, the number of high affinity ^{3}H-5-HT binding sites was markedly reduced. Thus, chronic treatment with active antidepressants seems to increase the affinity for ^{3}H-5-HT to its own receptor while the number of high affinity receptor binding sites is reduced (Fuxe et al., 1982a, c). Also i.p. injections of imipramine, clomipramine and desipramine (Segawa et al., 1979; Maggi et al., 1980, Takahashi et al., 1981) and the MAO inhibitors nialamide and clorgyline (Savage et al., 1980), have been reported to reduce the density of ^{3}H-5-HT binding.

However, not all clinically active antidepressant drugs appear to cause changes in ^{3}H-5-HT binding. For instance, mianserin (Fuxe et al., 1982a, c) iprindole (Peroutka and Snyder, 1980) and the selective 5-HT uptake inhibitor fluoxetine (Maggi et al., 1980; Savage et al., 1980) have been reported not to change ^{3}H-5-HT binding. Recent studies indicate, however, that both fluoxetine and the highly selective 5-HT uptake inhibitor alaproclate produce changes in ^{3}H-5-HT binding similar to imipramine and zimelidine (Fuxe et al., 1981, 1982a, c, unpublished). In general, most of the antidepressants tested, with a high affinity for the 5-HT uptake site (^{3}H-imipramine site) (Langer and Briley, 1981), seem to induce similar changes in ^{3}H-5-HT binding. However, changes in 5-HT_1-receptors *in vivo* appear not to be strictly related to an increased 5-HT availability, since prior degeneration of the 5-HT terminal system in the cerebral cortex failed to counteract the changes in 5-HT_1-receptor binding induced by desipramine and zimelidine (Fuxe et al., 1982c).

Active antidepressants, on the other hand, appear not to produce affinity changes in 5-HT_2-receptors but mainly a reduction in the number of receptors (Peroutka and Snyder, 1980). Subchronic oral treatment with desipramine, imipramine and zimelidine produced a reduction in the number of 5-HT_2-binding sites labelled by ^{3}H-spiroperidol in the frontal cortex (Fuxe et al., 1982a, c). Also i.p. administration of desipramine, imipramine, amitriptyline, mianserin and iprindole (Peroutka and Snyder, 1980) and of clinically effective MAOIs, such as clorgyline, pargyline and nialamide (Savage et al., 1980), have been reported to decrease ^{3}H-spiroperidol binding. Also, selective A-type monoamine oxidase inhibitors such as FLA 336(+) reduce ^{3}H-spiroperidol binding in frontal cortex (Hall et al., unpublished). The mechanism behind the reduction in 5-HT_2-receptors is, however, not known. Changes in 5-HT_2-receptors may be induced, at least in part, by a presynaptic action on the 5-HT terminals, since degeneration of the 5-HT forebrain nerve terminals by a high dose of p-chloro-amphetamine blocked the reduction in ^{3}H-spiroperidol induced by desipramine and zimelidine (Fuxe et al., 1982c).

In view *inter alia* of the fact that many of the antidepressant drugs are 5-HT_2-receptor blocking agents but still reduce the number of 5-HT_2-receptors (desipramine and imipramine), it is postulated that antidepressant drugs may also activate pre- and postsynaptic receptors for comodulators in the 5-HT nerve terminals which subsequently leads to a reduction in the number of 5-HT$_2$-binding sites (see Fuxe et al., 1982a, c).

The analysis of the functional and physiological consequences of the observed changes in 5-HT receptor binding is not clear. Some neurophysiological studies indicate the existence of serotonergic supersensitivity upon subchronic treatment with antidepressant compounds (de Montigny and Aghajanian, 1978). Thus, repeated treatment with TCAs and iprindole was found to increase the sensitivity of hippocampal and geniculate neurons to iontophoretically applied 5-HT (de Montigny and Aghajanian, 1978). On the other hand, neither desipramine, clomipramine nor CGP-6085A administered chronically changed the sensitivity to 5-HT in cortical areas (Olpe and Schellenberg, 1980). Some neurophysiological studies indicate, however, a subsensitivity to 5-HT in the cortex following long-term zimelidine and amitriptyline treatment (Stach et al., 1981). Behavioural and neuroendocrinological findings also suggest that adaptive changes occur in 5-HT synapses which can be interpreted as a subsensitivity development. Thus, chronic zimelidine and desipramine treatment resulted in a reduced number of head-twitches induced by 5-HT agonists (Fuxe et al., 1981). The changes in neuroendocrine functions which are linked to 5-HT neurons in the hypothalamus are in line with a development of subsensitivity. Acute treatment of rats with zimelidine increases prolactin and LH secretion while following subchronic treatment in clinically relevant doses zimelidine reduces prolactin and LH secretion (Fuxe et al., 1982b). These changes can be interpreted as related to the development of a subsensitivity in 5-HT receptors with a facilitory influence on

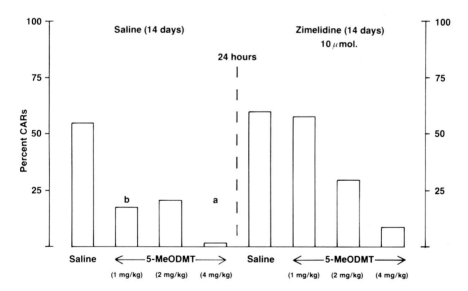

Fig. 2. Subchronic zimelidine treatment causes a consistent trend for an attenuation of the 5-methoxy-N,N-dimethyltryptamine (5-MeO-DMT) induced avoidance impairment. Zimelidine was given once daily (10 μmol/kg, p.o.) for 14 days. 5-MeO-DMT (1–4 mg/μg) was injected s.c. 24 hours following the last administration. * $p<0.05$, a) vs. control, b) versus zimelidine treated rats (Ögren et al., 1982, with permission).

the secretion of prolactin and LH, since zimelidine did not reduce dopamine turnover in the tuberoinfundibular dopamine systems (Fuxe et al., 1982c).

Studies on two-way active avoidance acquisition following long-term treatment with zimelidine and TCAs also indicated a tendency toward some development of subsensitivity at the central 5-HT receptors involved in avoidance learning. Recent studies have indicated that serotonin neurons in the forebrain play an inhibitory role in active avoidance learning possibly by an involvement in storage and/or retrieval processes (Ögren et al., 1982). Serotonin agonists such as 5-methoxy-N,N-dimethyltryptamine (5-MeO-DMT) and high doses of 5-hydroxytryptophan (5-HTP) produce active avoidance impairments which appear to be due to postsynaptic serotonin receptor stimulation. Recent studies indicate an attenuation of the 5-MeO-DMT induced active avoidance deficit in subchronically treated zimelidine rats (Ögren et al., 1982). There is a clear tendency of a reduction in the 5-MeO-DMT induced impairment of avoidance learning in animals treated with zimelidine (10 μmol/kg p.o., once daily) for a period of 14 days (Fig. 2).

Thus, the behavioural findings, utilizing head-twitch responses and conditioned avoidance learning, suggest that some degree of subsensitivity may also develop in the receptors involved in the regulation of avoidance learning, following subchronic zimelidine treatment. Thus, certain types of brain stem mediated behaviours such as head twitches as well as forebrain mediated behaviours such as avoidance learning which are controlled by 5-HT receptors show signs of subsensitivity after chronic or subchronic treatment with zimelidine. It is possible that these changes represent a stabilization of 5-HT neurotransmission which will reduce the synaptic noise and attenuate the possible over- and underactivation of 5-HT synaptic transmission in affective disorders.

SUMMARY

The present review has shown that antidepressant drugs differ considerably in their biochemical and behavioural properties. Most TCAs have potent effects on several neurotransmitter receptor sites at the same concentrations at which they affect NA and 5-HT uptake. Antidepressants of the 'second' generation, such as zimelidine, seems to preferentially block the 5-HT uptake site while mianserin has little affinity for NA and 5-HT uptake sites but potent effects on several receptor sites. The receptor interactions of different antidepressants correlate with the incidence of e.g. anticholinergic side effects and probably are related to sedative properties. Some receptor interactions e.g. the blockade of α_2-receptors and the 5-HT$_2$-receptor blocking action may contribute to the clinical action.

Recent attempts to characterize the mode of action of antidepressant drugs have centered on their effects on monoaminergic mechanisms after chronic treatment. Despite marked pharmacological differences antidepressants produce as a group quite consistent changes in some receptor systems following chronic administration. Most antidepressant drugs produce changes in the sensitivity of the NA coupled adenylate cyclase system generally linked to corresponding changes in the density of β-adrenergic receptors. In addition, some antidepressants cause a reduction of α_2-receptors.

Chronic treatment with antidepressants also decreases the density and changes the affinity of 5-HT$_1$-receptor binding and reduces the number of 5-HT$_2$-receptors. The physiological implications of these receptor alterations are unknown and indicate that antidepressant drugs can alter receptor mediated biological signals in both NA and 5-HT neurons possibly via several different mechanisms.

REFERENCES

Åberg, A. (1981) Controlled cross-over study of a 5-HT uptake inhibiting and a NA uptake inhibiting antidepressant. Acta Psychiatr. Scand. 63 (Suppl. 290), 244−255.

Åberg-Wistedt, A., Jostell, K. G., Ross, S. B. and Westerlund, D. (1981) Effects of zimelidine and desipramine on serotonin and noradrenaline uptake mechanisms in relation to plasma concentrations and to therapeutic effects during treatment of depression. Psychopharmacology 74, 297−305.

Aghajanian, G. K. (1972) Influence of drugs on the firing of serotonin-containing neurons in brain. Fed. Proc. 31, 91−96.

Alpers, H. S. and Himwich, H. E. (1972) The effect of chronic imipramine administration on rat brain levels of serotonin, 5-hydroxyindoleacetic acid, norepinephrine and dopamine. J. Pharmacol. Exp. Ther. 180, 531−538.

Aprison, M. H. and Hingten, J. N. (1981) Hypersensitive serotonergic receptors: a new hypothesis for one subgroup of unipolar depression derived from an animal model. In: B. Haber, S. Gabay, M. R. Issidorides and S. G. A. Alivisatos (Eds), 'Serotonin. Current Aspects of Neurochemistry and Function'. Plenum Press, New York, pp. 627−656.

Banerjee, S. P., Kung, L. S., Riggi, S. J. and Chanda, S. K. (1977) Development of β-adrenergic receptor subsensitivity by antidepressants. Nature 268, 455−456.

Baumann, P. A. and Maitre, L. (1977) Blockade of presynaptic α-receptors and of amine uptake in the rat brain by the antidepressant mianserin. Naunyn-Schmiedeberg's Arch. Pharmacol. 300, 31−37.

Bauman, P. A. and Maitre, L. (1979) Neurobiochemical aspects of maprotiline (Ludiomil[R]) action. J. Int. Med. Res. 7, 391−400.

Bennett, J. P. and Snyder, S. H. (1976) Serotonin and lysergic acid diethylamide binding in rat brain membranes. Relationship to postsynaptic serotonin receptors. Mol. Pharmacol. 12, 373−389.

Briley, M. S., Raisman. R. and Langer, S. Z. (1979) Human platelets possess high-affinity binding sites for ^{3}H-imipramine. Eur. J. Pharmacol. 58, 347−348.

Buus Lassen, J., Squires, R. F., Christensen, J. A. and Molander, L. (1975) Neurochemical and pharmacological studies of a new 5-HT uptake inhibitor, FG 4963, with potential antidepressant properties. Psychopharmacology 42, 21−26.

Carlsson, A. and Lindqvist, M. (1978) Effects of antidepressant agents on the synthesis of brain monoamines. J. Neural Trans. 43, 73−91.

Carlsson, A., Corrodi, H., Fuxe, K. and Hökfelt, T. (1969a) Effect of antidepressant drugs on the depletion of intraneuronal brain 5-hydroxytryptamine stores caused by 4-methyl-α-ethyl-meta-tyramine. Eur. J. Pharmacol. 5, 357−366.

Carlsson, A., Corrodi, H., Fuxe, K. and Hökfelt, T. (1969b) Effect of some antidepressant drugs on the depletion of intraneuronal brain catecholamine stores caused by 4,α-dimethyl-meta-tyramine. Eur. J. Pharmacol 5, 367−373.

Claassen, V., Davies, J. E., Hertting, G. and Placheta, P. (1977) Fluvoxamine, a specific 5-hydroxytryptamine uptake inhibitor. Br. J. Pharmacol. 60, 505−516.

Clements-Jewery, S. (1978) The development of cortical β-adrenoreceptor subsensitivity in the rat by chronic treatment with trazodone, doxepine and mianserin. Neuropharmacology 17, 779−781.

Coppen, A. (1967) The biochemistry of affective disorders. Br. J. Psychiatry 113, 1237−1264.

Coppen, A, Swade, C. and Wood, K. (1978) Platelet 5-hydroxytryptamine accumulation in depressive illness. Clin. Chim. Acta 87, 165−168.

Coppen, A., Rama Rao, V. A., Swade, C. and Wood, K. (1979) Zimelidine: a therapeutic and pharmacokinetic study in depression. Psychopharmacology, 63, 199−202.

Corrodi, H. and Fuxe, K. (1969) Decreased turnover in central 5-HT nerve terminals induced by antidepressant drugs of the imipramine type. Eur. J. Pharmacol. 7, 56−59.

Cott, J. M. and Ögren, S. O. (1980) Antidepressant drugs and ethanol: behavioural and pharmacokinetic interactions in mice. J. Neural Trans. 48, 223–240.

Crews, F. T. and Smith, C. B. (1978) Presynaptic alpha-receptor subsensitivity after long-term antidepressant treatment. Science 202, 322–324.

Delini-Stula, A. and Vassout, A. (1979) Modulation of dopamine-mediated behavioural responses by antidepressants: effects of single and repeated treatment. Eur. J. Pharmacol. 58, 443–451.

De Montigny, C. and Aghajanian, G. K. (1978) Tricyclic antidepressants: long term treatment increases responsitivity of rat brain forebrain neurons to serotonin. Science 202, 1303–1305.

Diggory, G. L., Stephens, R. J., Dickison, S. E., Moser, P. and Wood, M. D. (1980) Behavioural and neurochemical properties of 1-[1-([Indol-3-yl]-methyl)piperid-4-yl]-3-benzoylurea (Wy 25093) in rodents. Arch. Int. Pharmacodyn. 248, 96–104.

Figge, J., Leonard, P. and Richelson, E. (1979) Tricyclic antidepressants: potent blockade of histamine H_1 receptors of guinea pig ileum. Eur. J. Pharmacol. 58, 479–483.

Fillion, G. and Fillion, M. D. (1981) Modulation of affinity of postsynaptic serotonin receptors by antidepressant drugs. Nature 292, 349–351.

Fludder, J. M. and Leonard, B. E. (1979) Chronic effects of mianserin on noradrenaline metabolism in the rat brain: evidence for a presynaptic α-adrenolytic action in vivo. Psychopharmacology 64, 329–332.

Fuller, R. W., Perry, K. W., Snoddy, H. D. and Molloy B. B. (1974) Comparison of the specificity of 3-(p-trifluoromethylphenoxy)-N-methyl-3-phenylpropylamine and chlorimipramine as amine uptake inhibitors in mice. Eur. J. Pharmacol. 28, 233–236.

Fuller, R. W., Perry, K. W. and Molloy, B. B. (1975) Reversible and irreversible phases of serotonin depletion by 4-chloroamphetamine. Eur. J. Pharmacol. 33, 119–124.

Fuller, R. W., Snoddy, H. D. and Perry, K. W. (1979) Nisoxetine antagonism of norepinephrine depletion in brain and heart after α-methyl-m-tyrosine administration. Neuropharmacology 18, 767–770.

Fuxe, K., Ögren, S. O., Agnati, L., Gustavsson, J. Å. and Jonsson, G. (1977) On the mechanism of action of the antidepressant drugs amitriptyline and nortriptyline. Evidence for 5-hydroxytryptamine receptor-blocking activity. Neurosci. Lett. 6, 339–343.

Fuxe, K., Ögren, S. O., Everitt, B. J., Agnati, L. F., Eneroth, P., Gustafsson, J. Å., Jonsson, G., Skett, P. and Holm, A. C. (1978) The effect of antidepressant drugs of the imipramine type on various monoamine systems and their relation to changes in behaviour and neuroendocrine function. In: S. Garattini (Ed.), Symposium Medicum Hoechst on depressive disorders. F. K. Schattauer, Stuttgart, pp. 69–94.

Fuxe, K., Ögren, S. O. and Agnati, L. F. (1979) The effects of chronic treatment with the 5-hydroxytryptamine uptake blocker zimelidine on central 5-hydroxytryptamine mechanisms. Evidence for the induction of a low affinity binding site for 5-hydroxytryptamine. Neurosci. Lett. 13, 307–312.

Fuxe, K., Ögren, S. O., Agnati, L. F., Eneroth, P., Holm, A. C. and Andersson, K. (1981) Long-term treatment with zimelidine leads to a reduction in 5-hydroxytryptamine neurotransmission within the central nervous system of the mouse and rat, Neurosci. Lett. 21, 57–62.

Fuxe, K., Ögren, S. O., Agnati, L. F., Andersson, K. and Eneroth, P. (1982a) Effects of subchronic antidepressant drug treatment on central serotonergic mechanisms in the male rat. In: G. Racagni and E. Costa (Eds), International Symposium 'Typical and atypical antidepressants'. Raven Press, New York, pp. 91–107.

Fuxe, K., Ögren, S. O., Andersson, K., Eneroth, P. and Agnati, L. F. (1982b) The effects of subchronic antidepressant drug treatment on the secretion of adenohypophyseal hormones and of corticosterone in the male rat. In: G. Racagni and E. Costa (Eds), International Symposium 'Typical and Atypical Antidepressants'. Raven Press, New York, pp. 109–120.

Fuxe, K., Ögren, S. O., Agnati, L. F., Andersson, K. and Eneroth, P. (1982c) On the mechanism of action of antidepressant drugs: indications of reductions in 5-HT neurotransmission in some brain regions upon subchronic treatment. In: S. Z. Langer, R. Takahashi, T. Segawa and M. Briley (Eds), 'New Vistas in Depression'. Pergamon Press, New York, pp. 49–63.

Glowinski, J. and Axelrod, J. (1964) Inhibition of uptake of triated-noradrenaline in the intact rat brain by imipramine and structurally related compounds. Nature 204, 1318–1319.

Gluckman, M. I. and Baum, T. (1969) The pharmacology of iprindole, a new antidepressant. Psychopharmacology 15, 169–185.

Hall, H. and Ögren, S. O. (1981) Effects of antidepressant drugs on different receptors in the brain. Eur. J. Pharmacol. 70, 393–407.

Hendley, E. D. (1978) Iprindole is a potent enhancer of spontaneous and KCl-induced efflux of norepinephrine from rat brain slices. Soc. Neurosci. Abstr. 494.

Hertting, G., Axelrod, J. and Whitby, L. G. (1961) Effect of drugs on the uptake and metabolism of ^{3}H-norepinephrine. J. Pharmacol. Exp. Ther. 134, 146–153.

Hunt, P., Kannengiesser, M-H. and Raynaud, J-P. (1974) Nomifensine: a new potent inhibitor of dopamine uptake into synaptosomes from rat brain corpus striatum. J. Pharm. Pharmacol. 26, 370–371.

Hyttel, J. (1977) Neurochemical characterization of a new potent and selective serotonin uptake inhibitor: Lu 10-171. Psychopharmacology 51, 225–233.

Kafoe, W. F., de Ridder, J. J. and Leonard, B. E. (1976) The effects of a tetracyclic antidepressant compound, Org. GB 94, on the turnover of biogenic amines in the rat brain. Biochem. Pharmacol. 25, 2455–2460.

Kanof, P. D. and Greengard, P. (1978) Brain histamine receptors as targets for antidepressant drugs. Nature 272, 329–333.

Karobath, M. E. (1975) Tricyclic antidepressive drugs and dopamine-sensitive adenylate cyclase from rat brain striatum. Eur. J. Pharmacol. 30, 159.

Keller, H. H., Buchaes, W. P. and Da Prada, M. (1980) Dopamine receptor blockade in rat brain after acute and subchronic treatment with tricyclic antidepressants. In: T. Cattabeni, G. Racagni, P. F. Spano and E. Costa (Eds), Long-term Effects of Neuroleptics. Raven Press, New York, pp. 175–179.

Koe, B. K. (1976) Molecular geometry of inhibitors of the uptake of catecholamines and serotonin in synaptosomal preparations of rat brain. J. Pharmacol. Exp. Ther. 199, 649–661.

Langer, S. Z. (1977) Presynaptic receptors and their role in the regulaton of transmitter release. Br. J. Pharmacol. 60, 481–497.

Langer, S. Z. and Briley, M. (1981) High-affinity ^{3}H-imipramine binding: a new biological tool for studies in depression. Trends Neurosci. 4, 28–31.

Lapin, I. P. and Oxenkrug, G. F. (1969) Intensification of the central serotonergic processes as a possible determinant of the thymoleptic effect. Lancet 1, 132–136.

LeFur, G. and Uzan, A. (1977) Effects of 4-(3-indolylalkyl)piperidine derivatives on uptake and release of noradrenaline, dopamine and 5-hydroxytryptamine in rat brain synaptosomes, rat heart and human blood platelets. Biochem. Pharmacol. 26, 497–503.

Leonard, B. E. (1980) Pharmacological properties of some 'second generation' antidepressant drugs. Neuropharmacology 19, 1175–1183.

Leysen, J. E., Niemegeers, C. J. E., Tollenaere, J. P. and Laduron, P. M. (1978) Serotonergic component of neuroleptic receptors. Nature 272, 168–171.

Lindberg, U. H., Thorberg, S. O., Bengtsson, S., Renyi, A. L., Ross, S. B. and Ögren, S. O. (1978) Inhibitors of neuronal monoamine uptake 2. Selective inhibition of 5-hydroxytryptamine uptake by α-aminoacid esters of phenethylalcohols. J. Med. Chem. 21, 448–456.

Maggi, A., U'Prichard, D. C. and Enna, S. J. (1980) Differential effects of antidepressant treatment on brain monoaminergic receptors. Eur. J. Pharmacol. 61, 91–98.

Maitre, L., Moser, P., Baumann, P. A. and Waldmeier, P. C. (1980) Amine uptake inhibitors: criteria of selectivity. Acta Psychiatr. Scand. 61 (Suppl. 280), 97–110.

Maj, J., Mogilnicka, E. and Klimek, V. (1978a) The influence of mianserin and danitracen, 5-hydroxytryptamine receptor blockers, on the 5-hydroxytryptamine disappearance induced by H 22/54 in the rat brain. Pol. Pharmacol. Pharm. 30, 413–420.

Maj, J., Sowinska, H., Baran, L., Gancarczyk, L. and Rawlow, A. (1978b) The central antiserotonergic action of mianserin. Psychopharmacology 59, 79–84.

Maj, J., Palider, W. and Rawlow, A. (1979) Trazodone, a central serotonin antagonist and agonist. J. Neural Trans. 44, 237–248.

Mireylees, S. E., Goolet, I. and Sugrue, M. F. (1978) Effects of Org. 6582 on monoamine uptake in vitro. Biochem. Pharmacol. 27, 1023–1027.

Mobley, P. L. and Sulser, F. (1981) Down-regulation of the central noradrenergic receptor system by antidepressant therapies: biochemical and clinical aspects. In: S. J. Enna, J. B. Matick and E. Richelson (Eds), Antidepressants: Neurochemical Behavioural and Clinical Perspectives. Raven Press, New York, pp. 31–55.

Montgomery, S. A., Rami, S. J., McAuley, R., Roy, D. and Montgomery, D. B. (1981) The antidepressant efficacy of zimelidine and maprotiline. Acta Psychiatr. Scand. 63 (Suppl. 290), 219–224.

Nybäck, H. V., Valters, J. R., Aghajanian, G. K. and Roth, R. H. (1975) Tricyclic antidepressants: effects on the firing rate of brain noradrenergic neurons. Eur. J. Pharmacol. 32, 302–312.

Ögren, S. O., Fuxe, K., Agnati, L. F., Gustavsson, J. Å., Jonsson, G. and Holm, A. C. (1979) Re-evaluation of the indoleamine hypothesis of depression. Evidence for a reduction of functional activity of central 5-HT systems by antidepressant drugs. J. Neural Trans. 46, 85–103.

Ögren, S. O., Ross, S. B., Hall, H., Holm, A. C. and Renyi, A. L. (1981a) The pharmacology of zimelidine: a 5-HT selective reuptake inhibitor. Acta Psychiatr. Scand. 63 (Suppl. 290), 127–151.

Ögren, S. O., Cott, J. and Hall, H. (1981b) Sedative anxiolytic effects of antidepressants in animals. Acta Psychiatr. Scand. 63 (Suppl. 290), 277–288.

Ögren, S. O., Fuxe, K., Archer, T., Johansson, G. and Holm, A. C. (1982) Behavioural and biochemical studies on the effects of acute and chronic administration of antidepressant drugs on central serotonergic receptor mechanisms. In: S. Z. Langer, R. Takahashi, T. Segawa and M. Briley (Eds), New Vistas in Depression. Pergamon Press, New York, pp. 11–19.

Olpe, H. R. and Schellenberg, A. (1980) Reduced sensitivity of neurons to noradrenaline after chronic treatment with antidepressant drugs. Eur. J. Pharmacol. 63, 7–13.

Olpe, H. R. and Schellenberg, A. (1981) The sensitivity of cortical neurons to serotonin: effect of chronic treatment with antidepressants, serotonin uptake inhibitors and monoamine-oxidase blocking drugs. J. Neural Trans. 51, 233–244.

Paul, S. M., Rehavi, M., Skolnick, P. and Goodwin, F. K. (1980) Demonstration of specific 'high affinity' binding sites for [^{3}H] imipramine on human platelets. Life Sci. 26, 953–959.

Peroutka, S. J. and Snyder, S. H. (1979) Multiple serotonin receptors: differential binding of (^{3}H)-5-hydroxytryptamine, (^{3}H)-lysergic acid diethylamide and (^{3}H)-spiroperidol. Mol. Pharmacol. 16, 687–699.

Peroutka, S. J. and Snyder, S. H. (1980) Long-term antidepressant treatment lowers spiroperidol labelled serotonin receptor binding. Science 210, 88–90.

Peroutka, S. J., Lebovitz, R. M. and Snyder, S. H. (1981) Two distinct central serotonin receptors with different physiological functions. Science 212, 827–829.

Przegalinski, E., Kordecka-Magiera, A., Mogilnicka, E. and Maj, J. (1981) Chronic treatment with some atypical antidepressants increases the brain level of 3-methoxy-4-hydroxyphenylglycol (MHPG) in rats. Psychopharmacology 74, 187–190.

Pugsley, T. A. and Lippmann, W. (1979) Effect of acute and chronic treatment of tandamine, a new heterocyclic antidepressant, on biogenic amine metabolism and related activities. Arch. Pharmacol. 308, 239–247.

Quach, T. T., Duchemin, A. M., Rose, C. and Schwartz, J. C. (1979) In vivo occupation of cerebral histamine H_1-receptors evaluated with ^{3}H-mepyramine may predict sedative properties of psychotropic drugs. Eur. J. Pharmacol. 60, 391–392.

Raisman, R., Briley, M. and Langer, S. Z. (1979) High-affinity ^{3}H-imipramine binding in rat cerebral cortex. Eur. J. Pharmacol. 54, 307–308.

Raisman, R., Briley, M. S. and Langer, S. Z. (1980) Specific tricyclic antidepressant binding sites in rat brain characterised by high affinity ^{3}H-imipramine binding. Eur. J. Pharmacol. 61, 373–380.

Rehavi, M., Maayani, S. and Sokolovsky, M. (1977) Tricyclic antidepressant as antimuscarinic drugs: in vivo and in vitro studies. Biochem. Pharmacol. 26, 1559–1567.

Richelson, E. (1979) Tricyclic antidepressants and histamine H_1-receptors. Mayo Clin. Proc. 54, 669–674.

Roffler-Tarlov, S., Schildkraut, J. J. and Draskoczy, P. R.   (1973)   Effects of acute and chronic administration of desipramine on the content of norepinephrine and other monoamines in the rat brain. Biochem. Pharmacol. 22, 2923–2926.

Roffman, M., Kling, M. A., Cassens, G., Orsulak, P. J., Reigle, T. G. and Schildkraut, J. J.   (1977) The effects of acute and chronic administration of tricyclic antidepressants on MHPG-SO$_4$ in rat brain. Psychopharmacol. Commun. 1, 195–206.

Ross, S. B. and Renyi, A. L.   (1975a)   Tricyclic antidepressants agents. I. Comparison of the inhibition of the uptake of ^{3}H-noradrenaline and ^{14}C-5-hydroxytryptamine in slices and crude synaptosome preparations of the midbrain-hypothalamus region of the rat brain. Acta Pharmacol. Toxicol. 36, 382–394.

Ross, S. B. and Renyi, A. L.   (1975b)   Tricyclic antidepressants agents. II. Effects of oral administration on the uptake of ^{3}H-noradrenaline and ^{14}C-5-hydroxytryptamine in slices from the midbrain-hypothalamus region of the rat brain. Acta Pharmacol. Toxicol. 36, 395–408.

Ross, S. B. and Renyi, A. L.   (1977)   Inhibition of the neuronal uptake of 5-hydroxytryptamine and noradrenaline in rat brain by (Z)- and (E)-3-(4-bromophenyl)-N,N-dimethyl-3-(3-pyridyl)allylamines and their secondary analogues. Neuropharmacology 16, 57–63.

Ross, S. B., Renyi, A. L. and Ögren, S. O.   (1971)   A comparison of the inhibitory activities of iprindole and imipramine on the uptake of 5-hydroxytryptamine and noradrenaline in brain slices. Life Sci. 10, 1267–1277.

Ross, S. B., Ögren, S. O. and Renyi, A. L.   (1976)   Z-Dimethylamino-1-(4-bromophenyl)-1-(3-pyridyl)propene (H 102/09), a new selective inhibitor of the neuronal 5-hydroxytryptamine uptake. Acta Pharmacol. Toxicol. 39, 152–166.

Ross, S. B., Hall, H., Renyi, A. L. and Westerlund, D.   (1981)   Effects of zimelidine on serotonergic and noradrenergic neurons after repeated administration in the rat. Psychopharmacology 72, 219–225.

Sarai, K., Frazer, A., Brunswick, D. and Mendels, J.   (1978)   Desmethylimipramine-induced decrease in β-adrenergic receptor binding in rat cerebral cortex. Biochem. Pharmacol. 27, 2179–2181.

Savage, D. D., Mendels, J. and Frazer, A.   (1980)   Monoamine oxidase inhibitors and serotonin uptake inhibitors: differential effects of (^{3}H)-serotonin binding sites in rat brain. J. Pharmacol. Exp. Ther. 212, 259–263.

Schildkraut, J. J.   (1965) The catecholamine hypothesis of affective disorders. A review of supporting evidence. Am. J. Psychiatry 122, 509–522.

Schildkraut, J. J., Winokur, A., Draskoczy, P. R. and Hensle, J. H.   (1971)   Changes in norepinephrine turnover in rat brain during chronic administration of imipramine and protriptyline: a possible explanation for the delay in onset of clinical antidepressant effects. Am. J. Psychiatry 127, 72–79.

Schweitzer, J. W., Schwartz, R. and Friedhoff, A. J.   (1979)   Intact presynaptic terminals required for β-adrenergic receptor regulation by desipramine. J. Neurochem. 33, 377–379.

Scuvée-Moreau, J. J. and Dresse, A. E.   (1979)   Effect of various antidepressant drugs on the spontaneous firing rate of locus coeruleus and dorsal raphe neurons of the rat. Eur. J. Pharmacol. 57, 219–225.

Segawa, T., Mizuta, T. and Nomura, Y.   (1979)   Modification of cental 5-hydroxytryptamine binding sites in synaptic membranes from rat brain after long-term administration of tricyclic antidepressants. Eur. J. Pharmacol. 58, 75–83.

Serra, G., Argiolas, A., Klimek, V., Fadda, F. and Gessa, G. L.   (1979)   Chronic treatment with antidepressants prevents the inhibitory effect of small doses of apomorphine on dopamine synthesis and motor activity. Life Sci. 25, 415–424.

Sneddon, J. M.   (1973)   Blood platelets as a model for monoamine-containing neurones. Prog. Neurobiol. 1, 151–198.

Snyder, S. H. and Coyle, J. T.   (1969)   Regional differences in ^{3}H-norepinephrine and ^{3}H-dopamine uptake into rat brain homogenates. J. Pharmacol. Exp. Ther. 165, 78–88.

Snyder, S. H. and Yamamura, H. I.   (1977) Antidepressants and the muscarinic acetylcholine receptor. Arch. Gen. Psychiatry 34, 236–239.

Spector, S., Prockop, D., Shore, P. A. and Brodie, B. B.   (1958)   Effect of iproniazid on brain levels

34

of norepinephrine and serotonin. Science 127, 704.

Stach, R., Kacz, D. and Pawlowski, L. (1981) Alterations of the central electophysiological effects of serotonin after chronic administration of amitriptyline and zimelidine. Abstract at the III world congress of Biological Psychiatry, Stockholm, June 28—July 3, 1981.

Sugrue, M. F. (1980) Changes in rat brain monoamine turnover following chronic antidepressant administration. Life Sci. 26, 423–429.

Sugrue, M. F. (1981) Chronic antidepressant administration and adaptive changes in central monoaminergic systems. In: S. J. Enna, J. B. Malick and E. Richelson (Eds), Antidepressants: Neurochemical, Behavioural and Clinical Perspectives. Raven Press, New York, pp. 13–30.

Sulser, F., Vetulani, J. and Mobley, P. L. (1978) Mode of action of antidepressant drugs. Biochem. Pharmacol. 27, 257–261.

Takahashi, R., Tateishi, T., Yoshida, H., Nagayama, H. and Tachiki, L. (1981) Serotonin metabolism of animal model of depression. In: B. Harber, S. Gabay, M. R. Issidorides and S. G. A. Alivisator (Eds), Serotonin. Current Aspects of Neurochemistry and Function. Plenum Press, New York, pp. 603–625.

Talvenheimo, J. T., Nelson, P. J. and Rudnick, G. (1979) Mechanism of imipramine inhibition of platelets 5-hydroxytryptamine transport. J. Biol. Chem. 254, 4631–4635.

Tang, S. W. and Seeman, P. (1980) Effect of antidepressant drugs on serotonergic and adrenergic receptors. Naunyn-Schmideberg's Arch. Pharmacol. 311, 4631–4635.

Titeler, M., Tedesco, J. L. and Seeman, P. (1978) Selective labeling of presynaptic receptors by (^{3}H)-dopamine, (^{3}H)-apomorphine and (^{3}H)clonidine; labeling of post-synaptic sites by (^{3}H)neuroleptics. Life Sci. 23, 587–592.

Träskman, L., Åsberg, M., Bertilsson, L., Cronholm, B., Mellström, B., Neckers, L. M., Sjöqvist, F., Thorén, P. and Tybring, G. (1979) Plasma levels of chlorimipramine and its demethyl metabolite during treatment of depression. Clin. Pharmacol. Ther. 26, 600–610.

U'Prichard, D. C., Greenberg, D. A., Sheehan, P. P. and Snyder, S. H. (1978) Tricyclic antidepressants: therapeutic properties and affinity for α-noradrenergic receptor binding sites in the brain. Science 199, 197–198.

U'Prichard, D. C., Bechtel, W. D., Rouot, B. M. and Snyder, S. H. (1979) Multiple apparent α-noradrenergic receptor binding sites in rat brain: effect of 6-hydroxydopamine. Mol. Pharmacol. 16, 47–60.

Vetulani, J. and Sulser, F. (1975) Action of various antidepressant treatments reduces reactivity of noradrenergic cyclic AMP-generating system in limbic forebrain. Nature 257, 495–496.

Vetulani, J., Stawarz, R. J., Pingell, J. V. and Sulser, F. (1976) A possible common mechanism of action of antidepressant treatments. Naunyn-Schmiedeberg's Arch. Pharmacol. 293, 109–114.

Waldmeier, P. C., Baumann, P. A. and Maitre, L. (1979) CGP 6085A, a new, specific inhibitor on serotonin uptake: neurochemical characterization and comparison with other serotonin uptake blockers. J. Pharmacol. Exp. Ther. 211, 42–49.

Wieloz, M., Salmona, M., de Gaetano, G. and Garattini, S. (1976) Uptake of ^{14}C-5-hydroxytryptamine by human and rat platelets and its pharmacological inhibition. A comparative kinetic analysis. Arch. Pharmacol. 296, 59–65.

Wolfe, B. B., Harden, T. K., Sporn, J. R. and Molinoff, P. B. (1978) Presynaptic modulation of beta-adrenergic receptors in rat cerebral cortex after treatment with antidepressants. J. Pharmacol. Exp. Ther. 207, 446–457.

Wong, D. T. and Bymaster, F. P. (1976) Effect of nisoxetine on uptake of catecholamines in synaptosomes isolated from discrete regions of rat brain. Biochem. Pharmacol. 25, 1979–1983.

Wong, D. T., Horng, J. S., Bymaster, F. P., Hauser, K. L. and Molloy, B. B. (1974) A selective inhibitor of serotonin uptake: Lilly 110140, 3-(p-trifluoromethylphenoxy)-N-methyl-3-phenylpropylamine. Life Sci. 15, 471–479.

Wong, D. T., Bymaster, F. P., Horng, J. S. and Molloy, B. B. (1975) A new selective inhibitor for uptake of serotonin into synaptosomes of rat brain: 3-(p-trifluoromethylphenoxy)-N-methyl-3-phenylpropylamine. J. Pharmacol. Exp. Ther. 193, 804–811.

Chapter 3

Urinary MHPG and response to antidepressants

K. P. MAGUIRE

and

T . R. NORMAN

Department of Psychiatry, University of Melbourne, Parkville, Australia

INTRODUCTION

Research in recent years has been directed towards finding a biochemical test for either classification of subgroups of depressive illness or predicting response to the various antidepressant drugs available. Most approaches have their origins in the so-called monoamine theory of depression which postulates that depressive illness is associated with a deficiency of either noradrenaline or serotonin in the central nervous system. Measurement of the noradrenaline metabolite, 3-methoxy-4-hydroxy phenylethyleneglycol (MHPG) has received much attention.

This chapter will attempt to summarise briefly the rationale for the measurement of urinary MHPG, outline the factors which affect this metabolite, and review the studies which have investigated the value of urinary MHPG in predicting response to antidepressants.

BACKGROUND

MHPG is the main metabolite of noradrenaline produced centrally and urinary levels are presumed to reflect this. Earlier studies estimated that up to 60% of urinary MHPG is derived from the central nervous system (Maas et al., 1979). A more recent study has

TABLE 1

Studies investigating urinary MHPG and response to antidepresants.

Study	No. patients	Diagnosis	Drug used	Low VMA diet	No. urine samples	Drug-free period	Analysis of data and conclusions reached
Maas et al., 1972	12	Severe depression	IMI DMI	yes 1 week	1–5	2–3 weeks	Patients divided into responders or non-responders on basis of nurses ratings.
	16	Severe depression	IMI	1 week	1–5	2–3 weeks	Responders (n = 4) and intermediate group (n = 4) had lower predrug MHPG than non-responders. Significant inverse relationship between predrug MHPG and response as measured by nurses rating at week 4
Schildkraut, 1973	6	Manic-depressives (2) Involutional (4)	AT	no	2–7	1 week	Responders (defined as having a 50% decrease in HDRS, sustained for 6 weeks, n = 3) had higher predrug MHPG than nonresponders (n = 3)
Beckman and Goodwin, 1975	39	Primary affective disorder – unipolar	AT IMI	no	3–5	2 weeks	Responders (defined as decreasing ≥ 3 on nurses rating) to AT had significantly higher predrug MHPG than IMI responders. Partial responders (n = 15) excluded from analysis
Sacchetti et al., 1976	5	Primary affective disorder	AT	yes 2 days	2–5	3 weeks	Response determined using a self-rating scale 4/5 improved despite wide range of predrug MHPG
Steinbrook et al., 1979	19	Major depressive disorder	IMI AMOX	yes 3 days	1	4 days	Significant correlation observed between HDRS at week 4 and predrug MHPG for IMI group (n = 9) but not for AMOX (n = 10)
Coppen et al., 1979	12	Primary depressive illness – unipolar	AT	no	1	7–10 days	No significant correlation between HDRS at week 6 and predrug MHPG

Reference	n	Diagnosis	Drug	Placebo	No.	Duration	Comments
Cobbin et al., 1979	35	Unipolar and bipolar depressives	AT IMI DMI NT	no	1	?	Patients with low predrug MHPG (females < 1300 µg/24 h; males < 1600 µg/24 h) treated with IMI, DMI, NT and high predrug MHPG treated with AT. Response assessed on a 5-point scale and compared to a previously treated group (n = 44) who were rated retrospectively. Response significantly better than in control group
Spiker et al., 1980	18	Major depressive disorder, unipolar, endogenous	AT	no	2	5–7 days	No significant correlation between predrug MHPG and HDRS at week 4. No significant difference between unequivocal responders (n = 6) and nonresponders (n = 6)
Rosenbaum et al., 1980	13	Primary affective disorder, unipolar	IMI MAP	yes 24 hrs	1	10 days	Responders defined as HDRS at week 4 ≥ 16 and 60% less than baseline. Low MHPG defined as < 1950 µg/24 h. 5/6 'low' responded to IMI/MAP; 1/7 'high' responded to IMI/MAP
Hollister et al., 1980	17	Unipolar and bipolar	NT	no	1–5	2–3 weeks	No significant association between predrug MHPG and change in HDRS (week 4–week 0). When 6 lowest excretors were compared with the 6 highest; 4/6 highest improved while 1/6 lowest improved, a significant difference

IMI = imipramine; DMI = desipramine; AT = amitriptyline; AMOX = amoxapine; NT = nortriptyline; MAP = maprotiline; HDRS = Hamilton depression rating score; VMA = vanillylmandelic acid.

questioned this and suggested that only 20% of total urinary MHPG is derived from brain (Blombery et al., 1980). The amount of urinary MHPG which is derived from the brain is still open to question.

Despite this uncertainty, studies have been undertaken to compare the 24 hour urinary excretion in depressed patients with normal controls. Maas et al. (1968) found that urinary excretion of MHPG was lower in 16 patients of mixed depressive subgroups compared with 11 normal controls. De Leon-Jones et al. (1975) also found lower excretion in 33 severely depressed women than in 21 controls. More recent studies have tended to look at the different subtypes of depressive illness. Schildkraut et al. (1978) found that bipolar manic-depressives and schizo-affectives excreted less MHPG than unipolar nonendogenous depressives. They also found that the unipolar endogenous group was heterogeneous and included both 'low' and 'high' excretors. Other studies have suggested that the low excretion of MHPG in depressives returns to normal on recovery (Pickar et al., 1978). Overall, the evidence does tend to suggest a lowered excretion of MHPG in some depressives but many have normal or even high levels. Studies in normal volunteers have shown a range of 900–3,500 $\mu g/24$ h (Hollister et al., 1978). This range covers the majority of values reported for depressed patients.

Further studies dealing with urinary MHPG in depressive patients noted a relationship between clinical improvement and pretreatment urinary excretion of MHPG (Maas et al., 1972; Schildkraut, 1973). This led to the suggestion that two distinct subgroups of depressives existed, one which excreted low levels of urinary MHPG ans showed a favourable response to imipramine or desipramine, and one which had normal levels of MHPG in urine and responded to amitriptyline. The first group were thought to have an alteration in noradrenaline in the central nervous system whereas the latter would have an alteration in serotonin. The known activities of the antidepressants involved in preventing reuptake of noradrenaline and serotonin were consistent with these ideas (Maas, 1975).

STUDIES INVESTIGATING URINARY MHPG AND RESPONSE TO ANTIDEPRESSANTS

Including the two studies referred to above, 10 studies have now been published and are presented in detail in Table 1. The many differences in study methodology make comparison difficult. Some studies have differentiated their patients into responders and non-responders and then compared urinary MHPG in each group, while other studies have divided their patients into 'low' or 'high' excretors and looked at response rates in those groups. Still further studies have looked for a correlation between pretreatment urinary MHPG and response as measured by Hamilton rating scores.

Half of the studies have looked at mixed depressive subtypes, the other half have studied only unipolar depressives. Four studies have put their patients on a low monoamine diet whereas six have not. All studies have included a drug-free period prior to measuring pretreatment urinary MHPG but some were not long enough to ensure complete clearance of previous drugs. Completeness of urine collections was generally well controlled but some studies relied on a single 24-hour collection to provide a measure of pretreatment MHPG. Hollister et al. (1978) have suggested that, due to variations between daily samples, at least three separate collections should be made and the average excretion calculated.

All but one study used gas-chromatography to measure levels of MHPG. One cannot strictly compare results from one laboratory to another without quality control samples, however, the similarity in reported results suggests that most assays would be in agreement. Cobbin et al. (1979) used spectrophotometry which in general is a less reliable method.

This latter study is the only one which has actually assigned patients to a particular treatment on the basis of their urinary MHPG levels. The response rate amongst these patients was compared to an earlier group of patients treated by the same psychiatrist. The major criticism is that the control group responses were determined by retrospective analysis of case reports.

Ignoring the differences outlined above and looking only at the results, four studies have found that low predrug MHPG excretion is associated with a favourable response to imipramine, desipramine or maprotiline; three studies have found that normal/high pretreatment excretion of MHPG is associated with favourable response to amitriptyline or nortriptyline, and four studies have found no association between pretreatment urinary MHPG and response to either amitriptyline or nortriptyline. As all studies can be criticised on methodological grounds, the value of urinary MHPG in predicting response to antidepressants must remain inconclusive until further studies are carried out.

FACTORS INFLUENCING URINARY EXCRETION OF MHPG

Many factors have been shown to affect excretion of MHPG and must thus be taken into consideration when evaluating or designing studies. Several studies have shown that age, urine volume, creatinine excretion and severity of depression prior to treatment were not correlated to pretreatment urinary MHPG (De Leon-Jones et al., 1975; Edwards et al., 1980; Hollister et al., 1980a; Spiker et al., 1980).

Some studies find that females excrete less than males (Maas et al., 1968; Edwards et al., 1980) but that this is related to body weight and disappears when excretion rate is expressed as μg MHPG/mg creatinine. Hollister et al. (1978) found no systematic sex differences in MHPG excretion based on five estimations per subject.

The effect of activity on excretion of MHPG remains unclear. Ebert et al. (1972) found that increased physical activity increased MHPG excretion in six patients while Goode et al. (1973) found that exercise did not influence urinary MHPG in five normal controls. Hollister et al. (1978) could find no consistent relationship between activity and excretion in 17 normal volunteers. Similarly, Sweeney et al. (1978) found no significant effect of either enhanced or restricted activity on urinary MHPG in 24 patients. This was despite highly significant changes in activity levels as confirmed by telemetric monitoring.

In the same study (Sweeney et al., 1978) a significant relationship was found between changes in state anxiety and MHPG excretion within an individual. No relationship between baseline anxiety and urinary MHPG was evident in the overall group. This suggests that stress or anxiety does influence MHPG excretion confirming earlier studies (Maas et al., 1971). The effect of diet is also controversial. Studies in normal subjects have indicated negligible dietary influences (Muscettola et al., 1977; Sharpless, 1977) but the latter study found a significant increase in MHPG when depressed patients were taken off their low monoamine diet. The authors could not come up with any satisfactory explanation for the difference between depressives and controls.

Two recent studies report on dietary influences on excretion of MHPG. Hollister et al. (1980b) found urinary excretion was elevated during the first day of alcohol withdrawal, in some cases to levels well above that normally observed (5,000–14,000 μg/24 h). Caffeine withdrawal produced a similar effect (Gibson, 1981). The increases seen are probably due to sympathetic activation and of peripheral rather than central origin. Since both alcohol and caffeine are restricted in some studies this could lead to discrepancies.

The effect of drugs on the excretion of urinary MHPG has not been systematically studied. Most investigations have been largely carried out in drug-free patients or normal controls. The antidepressants have been shown to both increase and decrease excretion of MHPG (Pickar et al., 1978; Cobbin et al., 1979) hence washout periods prior to studying patients are necessary. Hollister et al. (1980b) found increases excretion in eight patients with asthma. This was attributed to the concomitant administration of sympathomimetic agents of the β-adrenergic receptor stimulating type or the phosphodiesterase inhibitor type. Obviously, any drugs which influence catecholamines either centrally or peripherally must be restricted.

CONCLUSIONS

From the above, it is obvious that many issues remain unresolved and further studies are necessary to clarify problems such as sex differences, effects of activity, diet etc. on the urinary excretion of MHPG. Future patient studies need careful planning to take all these factors into account, and should include an experimental group who are assigned to treatment on the basis of their urinary MHPG levels and a control group who are randomly treated.

A further advance in design over previous studies would be to use the pharmacologically 'purer' antidepressants which are now available. The older drugs such as amitriptyline and imipramine do not act only on noradrenaline or serotonin but on both to some extent. Newer drugs such as zimelidine are much more selective, in this case for serotonin, or maprotiline which is active mainly on noradrenergic systems. If the two subgroups postulated previously do exist, then the 'low' MHPG excretors might be expected to respond to maprotiline while the 'normal/high' excretors might respond better to zimelidine.

Until studies of this type are carried out in large patient groups, the routine measurement of urinary MHPG excretion in depressive illness is not warranted. Theoretical problems such as the amount of urinary MHPG which is derived from the brain also need resolution. These considerations are important if urinary MHPG studies are to help in elucidating the biochemical mechanisms underlying depressive disorders.

REFERENCES

Beckman, H. and Goodwin, F. K. (1973) Antidepressant response to tricyclics and urinary MHPG in unipolar patients. Arch. Gen. Psychiatry 32, 17–21.

Blombery, P. A., Kopin, I. J., Gordon, E. K., Markey, S. P. and Ebert, M. H. (1980) Conversion of MHPG to vanillylmandelic acid. Arch. Gen. Psychiatry 37, 1095–1098.

Cobbin, D. M., Requin-Blow, B., Williams, L. R. and Williams, W. O. (1979) Urinary MHPG levels and tricyclic antidepressant drug selection. Arch. Gen. Psychiatry 36, 1111–1115.

Coppen, A., Rama Rao, V. A., Ruthven, C. R. J., Goodwin, B. L. and Sandler, M. (1979) Urinary MHPG is not a predictor for clinical response to amitriptyline in depressive illness. Psychopharmacology 64, 95–97.

DeLeon-Jones, J., Maas, J. W., Dekirmenjian, H. and Sanchez, J. (1975) Diagnostic subgroups of affective disorders and their urinary excretion of catecholamine metabolites. Am. J. Psychiatry 132, 1141–1148.

Ebert, M. H., Post, R. M. and Goodwin, F. K. (1972) Effect of physical activity on urinary MHPG excretion in depressed patients. Lancet ii, 766.

Edwards, D. J., Spiker, D. G., Neil, J. F., Kupfer, D. J. and Rizk, M. (1980) MHPG excretion in depression. Psychiatr. Res. 2, 295–305.

Gibson, C. J. (1981) Caffeine withdrawal elevates urinary MHPG excretion. N. Engl. J. Med. 304, 363.

Goode, D. J., Dekirmenjian, H., Meltzer, H. Y. and Maas, J. W. (1973) Relation of exercise to MHPG excretion in normal subjects. Arch. Gen. Psychiatry 29, 391–396.

Hollister, L. E., Davis, K. L., Overall, J. E. and Anderson, T. (1978) Excretion of MHPG in normal subjects. Arch. Gen. Psychiatry 35, 1410–1415.

Hollister, L. E., Davis, K. L. and Berger, P. A. (1980a) Subtypes of depression based on excretion of MHPG and response to nortriptyline. Arch. Gen. Psychiatry 37, 1107–1110.

Hollister, L. E., Prusmack, J. J., Knopes, K. and Kanaske, K. (1980b) Asthma and alcohol withdrawal as sources of artefact in urinary excretion of MHPG. Commun. Psychopharmacol. 4, 135–140.

Maas, J. W. (1975) Biogenic amines and depression. Arch. Gen. Psychiatry 32, 1357–1361.

Maas, J. W., Fawcett, J. and Dekirmenjian, H. (1968) MHPG excretion in depressive states. Arch. Gen. Psychiatry 19, 129–134.

Maas, J. W., Dekirmenjian, H. and Fawcett, J. (1971) Catecholamine metabolism, depression and stress. Nature 230, 330–331.

Maas, J. W., Fawcett, J. A. and Dekirmenjian, H. (1972) Catecholamine metabolism, depressive illness and drug response. Arch. Gen. Psychiatry 26, 252–262.

Maas, J. W., Hattox, S. E., Greene, N. M. and Landis, D. H. (1979) MHPG production by human brain in vivo. Science 205, 1025–1027.

Muscettola, G., Wehr, T. and Goodwin, F. K. (1977) Effect of diet on urinary MHPG excretion in depressed patients and normal control subjects. Am. J. Psychiatry 134, 914–916.

Pickar, D., Sweeney, D. R., Maas, J. W. and Heninger, G. R. (1978) Primary affective disorder, clinical state change and MHPG excretion. Arch. Gen. Psychiatry 35, 1378–1383.

Rosenbaum, A. H., Schatzberg, A. F., Maruta, T., Orsulak, P. J., Cole, J. O., Grab, E. L. and Schildkraut, J. (1980) MHPG as a predictor of antidepressant response to imipramine and maprotiline. Am. J. Psychiatry 137, 1090–1092.

Sacchetti, E., Smeraldi, E., Cagnasso, M., Biondi, P. A. and Bellodi, L. (1976) MHPG, amitriptyline and affective disorders. Int. Pharmacopsychiatry 11, 157–162.

Schildkraut, J. J. (1973) Norepinephrine metabolites as biochemical criteria for classifying depressive disorders and predicting responses to treatment: preliminary findings. Am. J. Psychiatry 130, 695–698.

Schildkraut, J. J., Orsulak, P. J., Schatzberg, A. F., Gudeman, J. E., Cole, J. O., Rohde, W. A. and LaBrie, R. A. (1978) Toward a biochemical classification of depressive disorders. Arch. Gen. Psychiatry 35, 1427–1433.

Sharpless, N. S. (1977) Determination of MHPG in urine and the effect of diet on its excretion. Res. Comm. Chem. Pathol. Pharmacol. 18, 257–273.

Spiker, D. G., Edwards, D., Hanin, I., Neil. J. F. and Kupfer, D. J. (1980) Urinary MHPG and clinical response to amitriptyline in depressed patients. Am. J. Psychiatry 137, 1183–1187.

Steinbrook, R. M., Jacobsen, A. F., Weiss, B. L. and Goldstein, B. J. (1979) Amoxapine, imipramine and placebo: a double-blind study with pretherapy urinary MHPG levels. Curr. Ther. Res. 26, 490–496.

Sweeney, D. R., Maas, J. W. and Heninger, G. R. (1978) State anxiety, physical activity and MHPG excretion. Arch. Gen. Psychiatry 35, 1418–1423.

Burrows/Norman/Davies (eds) Antidepressants
© *1983, Elsevier Science Publishers*

Chapter 4

The platelet model

ODD LINGJAERDE

Department of Psychiatry, University of Tromsø, Asgard, Norway

'The platelet model', in this context, refers to the study of biochemical and pharmacological phenomena in platelets that are reflecting identical – or at least similar – phenomena in the brain. What makes the platelets suitable as a model system in depression, is especially that they have a similar mechanism for active uptake and storage of serotonin (5-hydroxytryptamine) as have the serotonergic neurons, in view of the presumed role of serotonin in the pathophysiology and treatment of affective disorders (see Chapter 2). This survey will therefore concentrate on different aspects of serotonin function, although other possibilities for utilizing the platelet model in affective disorder will also be mentioned.

In relation to affective disorders, the platelet model can be used for two different purposes: 1) For the study of possible abnormalities connected with the disease process. This may be of interest both with regard to the investigation of this group of disorders in general, and – possibly – as a diagnostic or prognostic tool. 2) For the study of drug effects. Again, this may be part of the study of the mode of action of such drugs in general, or it may be used in the individual patient as a method for drug monitoring.

Before presenting some of the relevant findings within this field, some main features of platelet physiology and biochemistry will be briefly outlined. Since monoamine oxidase (MAO) is discussed in Chapters 15 and 16, it will be left out here.

THE BLOOD PLATELET

The mammalian blood platelets are anucleate cells only about 2 μm in diameter. They are formed from megakaryocytes in the bone marrow. In man, the circulating platelet count is about 2×10^8 per ml blood, and the life span of each platelet is around 10 days.

The platelets have a rather complicated structure, with microtubules, a complex canalicular system, mitochondria, and several kinds of granules. Platelets are important in coagulation, but they also have the capacity to participate in several other physiological and pathological processes (for comprehensive reviews of platelet biology and pathology, see Gordon, 1976 and 1981).

One of the more characteristic features of platelets, and one especially important in this context, is the ability to actively take up and store serotonin. Most platelet serotonin is stored in specialized granules − often referred to as the 'dense granules' − probably in a complex with ATP and Ca^{2+} and Mg^{2+} (for survey, see Da Prada et al., 1981). Uptake into the granules is inhibited by reserpine.

The inward transport of serotonin through the plasma membrane has the following main characteristics (Lingjaerde, 1977a):

1) At low, and physiological substrate concentrations it seems that the only inward passage of serotonin is by way of an active, saturable transport process − the so-called 'serotonin pump'.

2) This active uptake follows simple saturation or Michaelis-Menten kinetics, with an apparent K_m (the concentration giving half maximal uptake rate), of about $5 \times 10^{-7}M$. The maximal uptake rate, V_{max}, is more dependent on the experimental conditions; in human plasma at physiological pH it is about 100 pmole/10^8 platelets/min (Lingjaerde, 1979a).

3) The uptake is highly dependent on temperature (there is no measurable active uptake at $0-4°C$), and decreases markedly with increasing pH, at least within the pH range of 6.0−8.0. The uptake is dependent on the presence of Na^+ and Cl^- (or other small, but unphysiological anions), and is stimulated and stabilized by K^+. It is also energy-dependent, probably because the uptake requires an intact 'sodium pump' and membrane potential.

4) The uptake is inhibited by a great number of different compounds. The most potent inhibitors are some of the tricyclic and related antidepressants, to be discussed below.

There also seems to be a slow efflux of serotonin from the platelets, at least *in vitro* (Lingjaerde, 1981a). The efflux may also be influenced by certain drugs, but this process has so far not been studied systematically in relation to affective disorders or antidepressant treatment, and is not to be discussed further.

The platelet surface has different receptors for serotonin. One of them is the transport receptor, but there is at least one other receptor that mediates the effect of serotonin on platelet shape and aggregation. Serotonin has a higher affinity for this receptor than for the uptake receptor (Drummond, 1976). Although this receptor seems to have certain similarities with one kind of serotonin receptor in brain (Graf and Pletscher, 1979), it is at present uncertain whether it can be used for model purposes in relation to affective disorders. There is also possibly a third, low affinity serotonin receptor on the platelet surface, of uncertain function (Drummond and Gordon, 1975, Drummond, 1976).

Noradrenaline and adrenaline, as well as metaraminol, are also accumulated by platelets *in vitro,* possibly by a low affinity active transport process plus passive diffusion (Drummond, 1976). These transport processes cannot be considered as valid models for the high-affinity uptake of noradrenaline (and adrenaline) in the brain. As for dopamine, there has been some controversy as to the mode of transfer through the platelet membrane. However, according to recent studies, there is no specific active uptake of dopamine in platelets, but only uptake via the serotonin uptake mechanism, plus facilitated diffusion. None of these mechanisms are valid as a model system in relation to dopaminergic neurons in the brain (Lingjaerde and Kildemo, 1981).

Catecholamines have an aggregatory action on platelets, and also (in lower concentrations) enhance platelet aggregation induced by ADP. Both these effects are probably mediated by α-adrenergic receptors, different from the uptake receptors (Bygdeman and Johnsen, 1969). The platelet surface also has β-adrenergic receptors, mediating an increase in platelet cAMP (Drummond, 1976).

There are several other receptors on the platelet surface as well (Mills and MacFarlane, 1976), and several other transport processes have been shown to take place through the platelet plasma membrane (Lingjaerde, 1977a). So far, however, these receptors and transport processes are of limited interest here.

The use of platelets as a model system for neurons in the brain has been discussed in several surveys, e.g. by Sneddon (1973), Stahl (1977), Gaetano (1978) and Pletscher et al. (1979). On the whole, platelets seem to be valid and useful models for the study of serotonin uptake and storage, although some differences have been found between platelets and synaptosomes in this respect (Smith et al., 1978). They may also be used for the study of α-adrenergic and β-adrenergic receptor functions, and − of course − for the study of MAO (see Chapters 15 and 16).

ABNORMALITIES OF PLATELET FUNCTION IN AFFECTIVE DISORDERS

The platelet model has been used for several years in an attempt to reveal abnormalities of serotonin uptake and storage and in MAO activity (see Chapters 15 and 16) related to affective disorder. As usual, in biochemical studies in psychiatry, the results have been somewhat divergent, but some findings now seem to be well established.

Changes in content of serotonin in whole blood or in the platelets (whichever was measured) have been claimed by several investigators. Thus, *increased* serotonin level was found in both psychotic and nonpsychotic depression by Todrick et al. (1960); in several kinds of acute psychoses, also depressives, by Jus et al. (1960), and in bipolar depressives by Wirz-Justice and Pühringer (1978). On the other hand, *decreased* serum or platelet level of serotonin in depressive patients has been reported by Banki (1978) and by Coppen et al. (1976), whereas Gayford et al. (1973) reported endogenously depressed patients to have blood serotonin levels at the lower end of the normal range. Finally, Murphy and Weiss (1972) found normal levels of platelet serotonin, as well as normal platelet number, in both bipolar and non-bipolar depressed patients. How can these discrepant findings be explained? Some of the patients claimed to have *low* serotonin levels may not have been free from antidepressant medication long enough. As will be discussed below, several tricyclic antidepressants reduce platelet serotonin markedly, and this reduction may take at least 2 weeks to be normalized after the drug is withdrawn. According to Jus et al. (1960) the *increased* serotonin level seen in acutely disturbed patients may decline in a few days, and is possibly an unspecific reaction seen in several mental disorders.

Another aspect of platelet serotonin has been brought into the discussion by Wirz-Justice and Pühringer (1978a): a circadian variation in platelet serotonin as well as in serotonin uptake rate, and possible disturbances in these rhythms. According to these authors, the lowest platelet serotonin level occurs normally at about 4 p.m., whereas in some unipolar depressed patients it was found to occur already at about 12 noon or earlier.

Whereas the results have been rather confusing with regard to platelet or blood serotonin levels in affective disorders, there is much more agreement with regard to serotonin *uptake rate.* Although some investigators have not found any changes in serotonin uptake rate in uni- or bipolar depression (Shaw et al., 1971; Murphy and Costa, 1975; Wirz-Justice and Pühringer, 1978a), several investigators have found reduced uptake rate in untreated uni- and/or bipolar depressed patients (Pare et al., 1974; Hallstrom et al., 1976; Tuomisto and Tukiainen, 1976; Coppen et al., 1978; Dreux et al., 1979; Scott et al., 1979; Tuomisto et al., 1979; Meltzer et al., 1980; Rausch et al., 1980; Ross et al., 1980). Most of these investigators have performed kinetic analyses of the uptake, and have found that there is reduced V_{max} without alterations in K_m. Since antidepressants with inhibitory effect on platelet serotonin uptake always increase K_m and usually have no effect on V_{max} (Lingjaerde, 1979b), and since the patients included in the studies above have almost always been without antidepressant drug treatment for at least some weeks, one can probably rule out the possibility that the reduced V_{max} is a drug effect.

There is some controversy as to whether reduced serotonin uptake is also found in recovered depressed patients. Coppen et al. (1978) report this to be the case, whereas Scott et al. (1979) report *increased* uptake in recovered unipolar patients.

There has also been reported a disturbance of circadian variation in uptake rate in depression, with reduced variation during the day (Oxenkrug et al., 1978; Rausch et al., 1980).

How can this reduced uptake of serotonin in depression be interpreted? Reduced V_{max}, without an altered K_m, may be due either to a reduced number of transport carriers per platelet, or to the presence of a compound in plasma with a noncompetitive inhibitory effect on the uptake. So far, it is difficult to say which possibility is the more likely one, and whether the same reduction in uptake capacity also applies to the serotonergic neurones in the brain.

Can the reduced platelet serotonin uptake be used diagnostically or prognostically? Perhaps some time in the future; more has to be known about the diagnostic and prognostic correlates of serotonin uptake before this variable can have any great value in this respect. At least for the time being, therefore, reduced serotonin uptake rate is of more scientific than practical interest.

Except for these studies on serotonin content and uptake rate, platelets have been little utilized for the study of the psychobiology of affective disorders. It may be mentioned that Frazer (1975) found no abnormal effects of noradrenaline or prostaglandin PGE_1 on cAMP synthesis in platelets from depressive patients.

PLATELETS AS A MODEL SYSTEM FOR ANTIDEPRESSANT DRUG EFFECTS

The platelet serotonin uptake and storage mechanisms have been extensively used for the

study of drug effects, especially the effects of tricyclic and related antidepressants
thermore, platelet MAO has been used for assessing the effect of MAO inhibitors; t ͏
discussed in Chapters 15 and 16. Some attempts have also been made to use platelets as a
model system for studying the effects of drugs on other monoaminergic uptake mechanisms, but according to the discussion above, this is of doubtful relevance in relation to
the specific processes going on in the brain. Therefore, this discussion will concentrate on
the effects of tricyclic and related antidepressants on platelet content and uptake of
serotonin.

EFFECT ON SEROTONIN UPTAKE

Many tricyclic and related antidepressants have a strong inhibitory effect on serotonin
uptake in platelets (Marshall et al., 1960; Yates et al., 1964; Todrick and Tait, 1969).
However, antidepressants vary widely in their inhibitory potency. As a general rule, the
tertiary amines, having a dimethylamino group in the end of the side chain (such as imipramine, amitriptyline and chlorimipramine) have a stronger inhibitory effect than their
secondary amine or demethylated analogues (such as desipramine, nortriptyline and
desmethylchlorimipramine). At a serotonin concentration near to the K_m value, and in a
medium without protein, 50% inhibition of serotonin uptake rate in human platelets is
obtained with, e.g. approximately 2×10^{-9}M chlorimipramine, 10^{-8}M imipramine,
3×10^{-8}M amitriptyline, 2×10^{-7}M desipramine but only with about $5-7 \times 10^{-6}$M
maprotiline or mianserin (Lingjaerde, 1977b). The relative potencies of various antidepressants reported here, are in good accordance with the results of several other investigators (Spankova et al., 1972; Todrick, 1973; Tuomisto, 1974). Hydroxylated metabolites of several antidepressants are at least equipotent with their parent compound as uptake inhibitors (Calil et al., 1978).

The relative potency of the drugs in inhibiting serotonin uptake in platelets is practically the same as for the inhibition of high-affinity serotonin uptake in the brain, although
the *absolute* potency seems to be somewhat higher in synaptosomes than in platelets
(Hyttel, 1978). Thus, with a reservation as to the absolute potency, blood platelets are
a useful model for the study of the effect of antidepressants on serotonin uptake also in
the brain.

The inhibition of serotonin uptake in platelets is seen not only *in vitro,* but also *ex
vivo,* i.e. in platelets (or plasma) from patients treated with therapeutic doses of such
drugs. Here also, however, the inhibition varies markedly for different drugs. Thus, ordinary doses of chlorimipramine have about 10 times stronger effect (measured as increase
in K_m) than amitriptyline on serotonin uptake in the patient's own platelets *ex vivo*
(Lingjaerde, 1979a). For both drugs, a very good correlation was found between daily
dose and uptake inhibition (see also below). Some of the weaker uptake inhibitors do
not seem to give measurable inhibition of platelet serotonin uptake *ex vivo;* this has, for
instance, been reported for maprotiline (Waldmeier et al., 1974).

In kinetic terms, the inhibition by antidepressants of serotonin uptake in platelets is
usually of the competitive type, with an increase in K_m without alteration of V_{max}. It is
reasonable to assume that this type of inhibition is caused by the binding of drug to the
serotonin transport receptor. This reduces the binding of serotonin to the same receptor.

48

The binding of imipramine to the platelet's surface was directly demonstrated by Boullin and O'Brien (1968), and it was shown later by Briley et al. (1979) that this was a high-affinity binding, probably to a receptor that is identical with the serotonin transport carrier (Talvenheimo et al., 1979; Langer et al., 1980).

However, not all antidepressants have a pure competitive inhibitory effect on serotonin uptake. The effect of chlorimipramine thus seems to be a combination of a competitive and a noncompetitive inhibitory effect, giving both increased K_m and reduced V_{max} (Lingjaerde, 1979b). The basic mechanism of serotonin uptake inhibition may therefore be more complicated than has been assumed.

Is there a relation between platelet (or brain) serotonin uptake inhibition and therapeutic effect of tricyclic antidepressants? According to 'the serotonin hypothesis' (Lapin and Oxenkrug, 1969), the inhibition of the serotonin reuptake system at serotonergic synapses should have a therapeutic effect by increasing the postsynaptic activity of the transmitter. However, many clinically effective tricyclic antidepressants do not seem to have this effect in therapeutically effective doses. Therefore, this effect does not at least seem to be a *sine qua non* for antidepressant effect. On the other hand, a specific serotonin uptake inhibitor like zimelidine, has been reported to have an antidepressant effect which cannot (at least so far) be attributed to *other* relevant pharmacological effects (Carlsson et al., 1981). There are two possible explanations for these findings: 1) Serotonin uptake inhibition is only one of several possible mechanisms for obtaining a therapeutic 'final common path' in endogenous depression. 2) Serotonin uptake inhibition is therapeutically effective only in a subgroup of endogenous depression. For further discussion, see Chapter 2.

Anyhow, for the tricyclic antidepressants as a group there is obviously no correlation between serotonin uptake inhibition, in platelets or in brain, and antidepressant effect. For the individual drug, on the other hand, uptake inhibition correlates with the dose given (Lingjaerde, 1979a) and with the plasma concentration of the drug and possible active metabolites (Coppen et al., 1979). Therefore, measuring the serotonin uptake inhibition in patients on antidepressant drugs can be used for drug monitoring. This must be based on empirical data about the degree of inhibition to be expected from therapeutically effective doses or plasma concentrations of a given drug. Thus, an average therapeutic dose of chlorimipramine will increase the K_m of platelet serotonin uptake (in plasma from the patient) from the untreated value of about $5 \times 10^{-7}M$ to about $2 \times 10^{-5}M$; for amitriptyline, the expected K_m value will be about $2 \times 10^{-6}M$ (Lingjaerde, 1979a). Values much higher or lower than the expected ones would indicate a too high or a too low dose, respectively.

Theoretically, at least, this method for drug monitoring has the advantage over the measurement of plasma drug level, that the inhibition reflects only the free and active fraction of drug in plasma, avoiding the error due to unknown individual variations in plasma protein binding. The fact that the uptake inhibition is due to both parent compound and active metabolites may also be considered an advantage *if* the measured serotonin uptake inhibition is therapeutically relevant, or if it at least reflects the therapeutic potency (Lingjaerde, 1981b). However, it will often be difficult to say whether these conditions apply.

The main disadvantage of using serotonin uptake inhibition for drug monitoring is that the method is rather time-consuming, especially if one wants to do a complete kinetic analysis with calculation of the kinetic parameters K_m and V_{max}. Furthermore, the method can only be used with antidepressants having a fairly strong inhibitory effect on serotonin uptake.

In light of the above, one would, for a given drug, expect at least as good a correlation between serotonin uptake inhibition and therapeutic effect, as between drug plasma concentration and therapeutic effect. However, so far the very few studies on this inhibition-therapeutic effect relationship have not shown a significant correlation (Coppen et al., 1979; Tuomisto et al., 1979). Further studies are needed to clarify whether there is such a correlation for all, or possibly for only a subgroup of endogenously depressed patients, and whether this correlation is different from the correlation between drug plasma concentration and clinical effect.

Since only the free and not the protein-bound fraction of drug in plasma is active as an inhibitor of serotonin uptake, assessment of serotonin uptake inhibition can also be used for calculation of protein binding of drugs in plasma (Todrick, 1973; Lingjaerde, 1976, 1981c). In principle, one measures the inhibitory effect of various known concentrations of drug in plasma and in platelets resuspended in a protein-free medium, and from this calculates the IC_{50} (the total drug concentration giving 50% uptake inhibition) in the two media. Assuming that the difference in IC_{50} in plasma and in protein-free medium is due to protein binding in the former, one can then calculate the per cent protein binding. As an example: if IC_{50} is 10^{-6}M in plasma and 10^{-7}M in protein-free medium, we have

$$\frac{10^{-6}-10^{-7}}{10^{-6}} \times 100 = 90$$

giving a protein binding of 90%.

It should be noted that this method can only be used *in vitro* (since the drug has to be added in known concentrations to both media), and that certain precautions have to be taken, expecially with regard to pH (Lingjaerde, 1981c).

EFFECT ON PLATELET OR TOTAL BLOOD SEROTONIN

Inhibition of platelet serotonin uptake *in vivo* leads to a gradual reduction in platelet serotonin level. Since practically all blood serotonin is localized in the platelets, and the platelet count does not seem to be altered by antidepressant drugs (Lingjaerde, unpublished observation), this effect can be demonstrated by measuring either platelet serotonin or total blood serotonin. In the following, the term 'platelet serotonin' will be used whether platelet or total blood serotonin has been measured.

Marshall and coworkers as far back as 1960, reported that treatment with imipramine leads to an exponential decline in platelet serotonin (Marshall et al., 1960; Todrick, 1973), with maximal depletion being obtained after approximately 2 weeks. Reduction of platelet serotonin has since been shown for several other antidepressants, usually with maximal depletion after 1 to 3 weeks (Lund et al., 1978; Wirz-Justice and Pühringer, 1978b; Ross et al., 1980). Ross et al. (1980) calculated the 'half-life' of platelet serotonin to be about 5 days during treatment with chlorimipramine or zimelidine, and found that the serotonin level increased to normal values in about 2 weeks or more after termination of medication. Lund et al. (1978), however, found that normal serotonin level may not be obtained until 3 or 4 weeks after termination of treatment with paroxetin. There seems to be no tolerance to this serotonin-depleting effect even after several months treatment (Petersen et al., 1978). This is in accordance with the observation that platelet serotonin uptake inhibition is not altered even after some years of treatment with chlorimipramine or amitriptyline (personal observation).

So far, there has been no convincing documentation of correlation between platelet serotonin depletion and therapeutic effect. No such correlation was, e.g. found by Børup et al. (1979) in 12 patients treated with femoxetine.

Whereas inhibition of serotonin uptake in platelets can be demonstrated only a few hours after an effective dose, and can actually be regarded as an immediate effect of drug in plasma, serotonin depletion is a slower process, taking weeks to reach the maximal effect of a given dose. This restricts the usefulness of this variable in drug monitoring.

LITHIUM AND PLATELET SEROTONIN

There has been considerable confusion with regard to the effect of lithium on platelet serotonin uptake and level. Murphy et al. (1969) reported that lithium treatment leads to increased platelet serotonin uptake *ex vivo,* and Coppen et al. (1980) found that lithium treatment restored the low serotonin uptake in depression to normal levels. On the other hand, Scott et al. (1979) found that lithium treatment does not influence the serotonin uptake parameters, and Meltzer et al. (1980) even found that lithium treatment reduces V_{max} for platelet serotonin uptake. *In vitro* experiments have also given controversial results. Some investigators have found no effect of lithium, added *in vitro,* on platelet serotonin uptake (Murpy et al., 1969; Lingjaerde, unpublished), whereas others have found a moderate inhibitory effect (Genefke, 1972; Coppen et al., 1980). A possible error in such experiments is that pH in the incubation medium may be increased upon adding Li_2CO_3 if this is the lithium salt used.

These controversial results would seem to warrant considerable caution in using the platelet model for the study of lithium effects on serotonin uptake and storage.

REFERENCES

Banki, C. M. (1978) 5-Hydroxytryptamine content of the whole blood in psychiatric illness and alcoholism. Acta Psychiatr. Scand. 57, 232–238.

Børup, C., Petersen, I.-M., Honoré, P. le Fèvre and Wetterberg, L. (1979) Reduction of whole blood serotonin in depressed patients treated with a new, selective serotonin-uptake inhibitor, femoxetine. Psychopharmacology 63, 241–243.

Boullin, D. J. and O'Brien, R. A. (1968) The binding of imipramine to the outer membrane of blood platelets. J. Pharm. Pharmacol. 20, 583–584.

Briley, M. S., Raisman, R. and Langer, S. Z. (1979) Human platelets possess high-affinity binding sites for ^{3}H-imipramine. Eur. J. Pharmacol. 58, 347–348.

Bygdeman, S. and Johnsen, O. (1969) Studies on the effect of adrenergic blocking drugs on catecholamine-induced platelet aggregation and uptake of noradrenaline and 5-hydroxytryptamine. Acta Physiol. Scand. 75, 129–138.

Calil, H. M., Potter, W. Z., Zavadil, A. and Goodwin, F. K. (1978) Hydroxylated metabolites of tricyclic antidepressants inhibit amine uptake. Presented at the 11th C.I.N.P. Congress, Vienna, Austria, July 9–14.

Carlsson, A., Gottfries, C.-G., Holmberg, G., Modigh, K., Svensson, T. and Ögren, S.-O. (Eds) (1981) Recent Advances in the Treatment of Depression. Munksgaard, Copenhagen.

Coppen, A., Turner, P., Rowsell, A. R. and Padgham, C. (1976) 5-Hydroxytryptamine (5-HT) in the whole blood of patients with depressive illness. Postgrad. Med. J. 52, 156–158.

Coppen, A., Swade, C. and Wood, K. (1978) Platelet 5-hydroxytryptamine accumulation in depressive illness. Clin. Chim. Acta 87, 165–168.

Coppen, A., Rama Rao, V. A., Swade, C. and Wood, K. (1979) Inhibition of 5-hydroxytryptamine reuptake by amitriptyline and zimelidine and its relationship to their therapeutic action. Psychopharmacology 63, 125–129.

Coppen, A., Swade, C. and Wood, K. (1980) Lithium restores abnormal platelet 5-HT transport in patients with affective disorders. Br. J. Psychiatry 136, 235–238.

Da Prada, M., Richards, J. G. and Kettler, R. (1981) Amine storage organelles in platelets. In: J. L. Gordon (Ed.), Platelets in Biology and Pathology, Vol. 2. Elsevier/North-Holland, Amsterdam, pp. 107–146.

De Gaetano, G. (1978) Blood platelets as a pharmacological model of serotoninergic synaptosomes. In: G. de Gaetano and S. Garattini (Eds), Platelets: A Multidisciplinary Approach. Raven Press, New York, pp. 373–384.

Dreux, C., Launay, J. M. and Giret, M. (1979) Le modèle plaquettaire appliqué à l'étude de la dépression. Ann. Biol. Clin. 37, 41–47.

Drummond, A. H. (1976) Interactions of blood platelets with biogenic amines: uptake, stimulation and receptor binding. In: J. L. Gordon (Ed.), Platelets in Biology and Pathology. Elsevier/North-Holland, Amsterdam, pp. 203–239.

Drummond, A. H. and Gordon, J. L. (1975) Specific binding sites for 5-hydroxytryptamine on rat bood platelets, Biochem. J. 150, 129–132.

Frazer, A. (1975) Adrenergic responses in depression: Implications for a receptor deficit. In: J. Mendels (Ed.), The Psychobiology of Depression. Spectrum Publications, New York, pp. 7–26.

Gayford, J. J., Parker, A. L., Phillips, E. M. and Rowsell, A. R. (1973) Whole blood 5-hydroxytryptamine during treatment of endogenous depressive illness. Br. J. Psychiatry 122, 597–598.

Genefke, I. K. (1972) The active uptake of 5-hydroxytryptamine in rat and human blood platelets under the influence of lithium in vivo and in vitro. Acta Psychiatr. Scand. 48, 394–399.

Gordon, J. L. (Ed.) (1976) Platelets in Biology and Pathology. Elsevier/North-Holland, Amsterdam.

Gordon, J. L. (Ed.) (1981) Platelets in Biology and Pathology, Vol. 2, Elsevier/North-Holland, Amsterdam.

Graf, M. and Pletscher, A. (1979) Shape change of blood platelets – a model for cerebral 5-hydroxytryptamine receptors? Br. J. Pharmacol. 65, 601–608.

Hallstrom, C. O. S., Linford Rees, W., Pare, C. M. B., Trenchard, A. and Turner, P. (1976) Platelet uptake of 5-hydroxytryptamine and dopamine in depression. Postgrad. Med. J. 52 (Suppl. 3), 40–44.

Hyttel, J. (1978) Effect of a specific 5-HT uptake inhibitor, citalopram (Lu 10-171), on ^{3}H-5-HT uptake by rat brain synaptosomes in vitro. Psychopharmacology 60, 13–18.

Jus, A., Laskowska, D. and Zimny, S. (1960) Studies on the serotonin level in blood serum in acute psychotic states (exogenous psychoses, and certain psychoses of the schizophrenic group) (Orig. in Polish). Neurol. Neurochir. Psychiatr. Polska 11, 353–359.

Langer, S. Z., Moret, C., Raisman, R., Dubocovich, M. L. and Briley, M. (1980) High-affinity (^{3}H)imipramine binding in rat hypothalamus: association with uptake of serotonin but not norepinephrine. Science 210, 1133–1135.

Lapin, I. P. and Oxenkrug, G. F. (1969) Intensification of the central serotoninergic processes as a possible determinant of thymoleptic effect. Lancet I, 132–136.

Lingjaerde, O. (1976) Effect of doxepin on uptake and efflux of serotonin in human blood platelets in vitro. Psychopharmacology 47, 183–186.

Lingjaerde, O. (1977a) Platelet uptake and storage of serotonin. In: W. B. Essman (Ed.), Serotonin in Health and Disease, Vol. 4. Spectrum Publications, New York, pp. 139–199.

Lingjaerde, O. (1977b) Nomifensine symposium: discussion after paper by R. Ehsanullah and P.

Turner. Br. J. Clin. Pharmacol. 4, 165S–166S.

Lingjaerde, O. (1979a) Inhibition of platelet uptake of serotonin in plasma from patients treated with clomipramine and amitriptyline. Eur. J. Clin. Pharmacol. 15, 335–340.

Lingjaerde, O. (1979b) Inhibitory effect of clomipramine and related drugs on serotonin uptake in platelets: more complicated than previously thought. Pscyhopharmacology 61, 245–249.

Lingjaerde, O. (1981a) The kinetics of serotonin efflux from human blood platelets, and how it is influenced by different drugs in vivo and in vitro. In: B. Angrist, G. D. Burrows, M. Lader, O. Lingjaerde, G. Sedvall and D. Wheatley (Eds), Recent Advances in Neuropsychopharmacology, Pergamon Press, Oxford, pp. 161–167.

Lingjaerde, O. (1981b) Biological assay systems for tricyclic antidepressants. In: E. Usdin, S. Dahl, L. Gram and O. Lingjaerde (Eds), Clinical Pharmacology in Psychiatry: Neuroleptic and Antidepressant Research. Macmillan Press, London, pp. 27–32.

Lingjaerde, O. (1981c) Protein binding of an antidepressant drug, trazodone, calculated from inhibition of platelet serotonin uptake in plasma vs. protein-free medium in vitro. Presented at 3rd World Congress of Biological Psychiatry, Stockholm, June 28–July 3.

Lingjaerde, O. and Kildemo, O. (1981) Dopamine uptake in platelets: two different low-affinity, saturable mechanisms. Agents Actions 11, 410–416.

Lund, J., Lomholt, B., Fabricius, J., Christensen, J. A. and Bechgaard, E. (1978) Paroxetine: pharmacokinetics, tolerance and depletion of blood 5-HT in man. Acta Pharmacol. Toxicol. 44, 289–295.

Marshall, E. F., Stirling, G. S., Tait, A. C. and Todrick, A. (1960) The effect of iproniazide and imipramine on the blood platelet 5-hydroxytryptamine level in man. Br. J. Pharmacol. 15, 35–41.

Meltzer, H. Y., Arora, R., Baber, R., Busch, D., Kaskey, G., Nasr, S., Piyakalamala, S. and Tricou, B. J. (1980) Serotonin uptake in blood platelets of depressed patients. Presented at the meeting 'New Directions in Biological Psychiatry', Boston, September 5–7.

Mills, D. C. B. and Macfarlane, D. E. (1976) Platelet receptors. In: J. L. Gordon (Ed.), Platelets in Biology and Pathology. Elsevier/North-Holland, Amsterdam, pp. 159–172.

Murphy, D. L. and Costa, J. L. (1975) Utilization of cellular studies of neurotransmitter-related enzymes and transport processes in man for the investigation of biological factors in behavioral disorders. In: J. Mendels (Ed.), The Psychobiology of Depression. Spectrum Publications, New York, pp. 27–46.

Murphy, D. L. and Weiss, R. (1972) Reduced monoamine oxidase activity in blood platelets from bipolar depressed patients. Am. J. Psychiatry 128, 1351–1357.

Murphy, D. L., Colburn, R. W., Davis, J. M. and Bunney, W. E. (1969) Stimulation by lithium of monoamine uptake in human platelets. Life Sci. 8, 1187–1194.

Murphy, D. L., Colburn, R. W., Davis, J. M. and Bunney, W. E. (1970) Imipramine and lithium effects on biogenic amine transport in depressed and manic-depressed patients. Am. J. Psychiatry 127, 339–345.

Oxenkrug, G. F., Prakhje, I. and Mikhalenko, I. N. (1978) Disturbed circadian rhythm of 5-HT uptake by blood platelets in depressive psychosis. Activ. Nerv. Superior 20, 66–67.

Pare, C. M. B., Trenchard, A. and Turner, P. (1974) 5-Hydroxytryptamine in depression. Adv. Biochem. Psychopharmacol. 11, 275–279.

Petersen, E. N., Bechgaard, E., Sortwell, R. J. and Wetterberg, L. (1978) Potent depletion of 5-HT from monkey whole blood by a new 5-HT uptake inhibitor, paroxetine (FG 7051). Eur. J. Pharmacol. 52, 115–119.

Pletscher, A., Laubscher, A., Graf, M. and Saner, A. (1979) Blood platelets as models for central 5-hydroxytryptaminergic neurons. Ann. Biol. Clin. 37, 35–39.

Rausch, J. L., Shah, N. S., Yates, J. D. and Burch, E. A. (1980) Platelet serotonin uptake in patients with major depression. Presented at the meeting 'New Directions in Biological Psychiatry', Boston, September 5–7.

Ross, S. B., Jansa, S., Wetterberg, L., Fyrö, B. and Hellner, B. (1976) Decreased blood level of 5-hydroxytryptamine by inhibitors of the membranal 5-hydroxytryptamine uptake. Life Sci. 19, 205–210.

Ross, S. B., Aperia, B., Beck-Friis, J., Jansa, S., Wetterberg, L. and Åberg, A. (1980) Inhibition of

5-hydroxytryptamine uptake in human platelets by antidepressant agents in vivo. Psychopharmacology 67, 1–7.

Scott, M., Reading, H. W. and Loudon, J. B. (1979) Studies on human blood platelets in affective disorders. Psychopharmacology 60, 131–135.

Shaw, D. M., MacSweeney, D. A., Woolcock, N. and Bevan-Jones, A. B. (1971) Uptake and release of ^{14}C-5-hydroxytryptamine by platelets in affective illness. J. Neurol. Neurosurg. Psychiatry 34, 224–225.

Smith, L. T., Hanson, D. R. and Omenn, G. S. (1978) Comparisons of serotonin uptake by blood platelets and brain synaptosomes. Brain Res. 146, 400–403.

Sneddon, J. M. (1973) Blood platelets as a model for monoamine-containing neurones. In: G. A. Kerkut and J. W. Phillis (Eds), Progress in Neurobiology, Vol. 1, Part 2. Pergamon Press, New York, pp. 153–198.

Spankova, H, Rysanek, K. and Ruzickova, S. (1972) Inhibition of serotonin uptake by human thrombocytes and inhibition of thrombocyte aggregation. Activ. Nerv. Superior 14, 133–134.

Stahl, S. M. (1977) The human platelet. A diagnostic and research tool for the study of biogenic amines in psychiatric and neurologic disorders. Arch. Gen. Psychiatry 34, 509–516.

Talvenheimo, J., Nelson, P. J. and Rudnick, G. (1979) Mechanism of imipramine inhibition of platelet 5-hydroxytryptamine transport. J. Biol. Chem. 254, 4631–4635.

Todrick, A. (1973) The laboratory assessment of the antidepressive action of clomipramine (anafranil). J. Int. Med. Res. 1, 291–295.

Todrick, A. and Tait, C. (1969) The inhibition of human platelet 5-hydroxytryptamine uptake by tricyclic antidepressive drugs. The relationship between structure and potency. J. Pharm. Pharmacol. 21, 751–762.

Todrick, A., Tait, A. C. and Marshall, E. F. (1960) Blood platelet 5-hydroxytryptamine levels in psychiatric patients. J. Ment. Sci. 106, 884–886.

Tuomisto, J. (1974) A new modification for studying 5-HT uptake by blood platelets: a re-evaluation of tricyclic antidepressants as uptake inhibitors. J. Pharm. Pharmacol 26, 92–100.

Tuomisto, J. and Tukiainen, E. (1976) Decreased uptake of 5-hydroxytryptamine in blood platelets from depressed patients. Nature 262, 596–598.

Tuomisto, J., Tukiainen, E. and Ahlfors, U. G. (1979) Decreased uptake of 5-hydroxytryptamine in blood platelets from patients with endogenous depression. Psychopharmacology 65, 141–147.

Waldmeier, P. C., Greengrass, P. M. and Maitre, L. (1974) Does maprotiline (Ludiomil) influence serotonin uptake and free tryptophan concentration in human plasma? Experientia 30, 697.

Wirz-Justice, A. and Pühringer, W. (1978a) Seasonal incidence of an altered diurnal rhythm of platelet serotonin in unipolar depression. J. Neural Trans. 42, 45–53.

Wirz-Justice, A. and Pühringer, W. (1978b) Chronic treatment with clomipramine and maprotiline depletes platelet serotonin and modifies its diurnal rhythm. Prog. Neuro-Psychopharmacol. 2, 217–224.

Yates, C. M., Todrick, A. and Tait, A. C. (1964) Effect of imipramine and some analogues on the uptake of 5-hydroxytryptamine by human blood platelets in vitro. J. Pharm. Pharmacol. 15, 460–463.

Section II

TRICYCLIC ANTIDEPRESSANTS

Burrows/Norman/Davies (eds) Antidepressants
© *1983, Elsevier Science Publishers*

Chapter 5

Metabolism of tricyclic antidepressant drugs

G. RUBINSTEIN, I. MCINTYRE, G. D. BURROWS, T. R. NORMAN

and

K. P. MAGUIRE

Department of Psychiatry, University of Melbourne, Australia

INTRODUCTION

The tricyclic antidepressant drugs are highly lipid soluble. They are mostly biotransformed into more water-soluble compounds which can be excreted by the kidney; the transformation may involve one or more metabolic steps, and the metabolites may be more or less pharmacologically active than the parent compound and even toxic compounds may be formed. Furthermore, metabolic processes may be altered by concomitant medication, by pre-existing disease, and a number of other factors. Which pathway will predominate depends on the route of administration of the drug.

GENERAL METABOLIC PATHWAYS

With oral administration, and even although complete absorption occurs in the gut, only a small proportion of the administered drug is biologically available. The primary decrease in availability is attributed to the 'first pass' effect, or metabolism of the drug which occurs during its first passage through the gastrointestinal tract and liver. Drugs can be metabolized in various parts of the body, however, the liver seems to be quantitatively the most important organ in this respect.

The tricyclic antidepressant imipramine is metabolized by the action of at least five enzyme systems, including the liver microsomal P-450 system (Bickel, 1970). The major metabolic pathways for elimination of tricyclic antidepressants (TCAs) are by oxidation and conjugation, only 1–3% being eliminated unchanged through the kidneys (Christiansen et al., 1967; Alexanderson and Borga 1973; Gram and Fredericson Over∅, 1975). Extrahepatic metabolism in man is probably negligible (Minder et al., 1971; Dencker et al., 1976). Metabolites formed by the P-450 system are further metabolized to sulphuric esters and glucuronides, but the most important reactions in man are N-demethylation and hydroxylation, followed by glucuronide coupling. (For review and further references see von Bahr, 1972.)

N-oxidation and dealkylation are minor pathways (Christiansen et al., 1967; Alexanderson and Borga, 1973; Gram, 1974). Gram and Christiansen have shown (1975) that all three metabolic steps, demethylation, hydroxylation and glucuronide coupling occur during one passage through the liver — so-called 'first pass' metabolism. This probably reflects the close functional and anatomical link between the microsomal cytochrome P-450 oxidation enzyme system and the system mediating glucuronide coupling of the hydroxy metabolites (von Bahr, 1972; Bickel and Börner, 1974; Gram, 1980). The markedly hydrophilic glucuronides are readily reabsorbed and excreted via the kidney tubule and small bowel.

Imipramine and desmethylimipramine

Following oral administration, imipramine (IMI) is essentially entirely absorbed (Crammer et al., 1968). The product of IMI demethylation, desmethylimipramine (DMI), is itself an antidepressant. Crammer and Scott (1966) after administration of DMI, identified the following metabolites in the urine of patients: unchanged DMI; 2-hydroxy-DMI (the main component); 10-hydroxy-DMI; didesmethyl-DMI (DDMI); 2-hydroxy-DDMI; 10-hydroxy-DDMI; iminodibenzyl which resulted from the destruction of the tricyclic skeleton of the drug; 2-hydroxy-DMI-glucuronide and 10-hydroxy-DDMI-glucuronide. Crammer and Scott (1966) suggested that 2-hydroxylation and 10-hydroxylation may be alternate pathways. Demethylation converting IMI to DMI is controlled by nonspecific hepatic microsomal enzymes and in humans does not appear to be readily reversible (Bickel and Baggiolini, 1966).

In a study by Bickel and Weder (1968) on the total fate of IMI in the rat, the formation of 14 metabolites was detected. Of these, Bickel and Weder (1969) showed that only IMI, DMI and iminodibenzyl crossed easily from plasma to brain. They pointed out that medium polarity metabolites which can appear in liver and other cellular tissues (Bickel and Weder, 1968) do not enter the brain. IMI is hydroxylated more rapidly than DMI (Bickel and Weder, 1968).

In a study of 'first pass' metabolism, Gram and Christiansen (1975) gave test doses of ^{14}C-IMI either p.o. or i.v. to four subjects. The following metabolites were identified in the urine: IMI, DMI, IMI-N-oxide, 2-hydroxy-DMI, IMI-2-O-glucuronide, DMI-2-O-glucuronide, and unknown metabolites. More drug is metabolized after p.o. than after i.v. administration, as it is delivered directly to the liver. Only 10% of the increased metabolism is due to hydroxylation, the major part being an increase in demethylation yielding DMI. Demethylation accounts for 60–85% of the first pass metabolism (Gram and Christiansen, 1975).

Enterohepatic circulation. Dencker et al. (1976) found no evidence that IMI was deme-

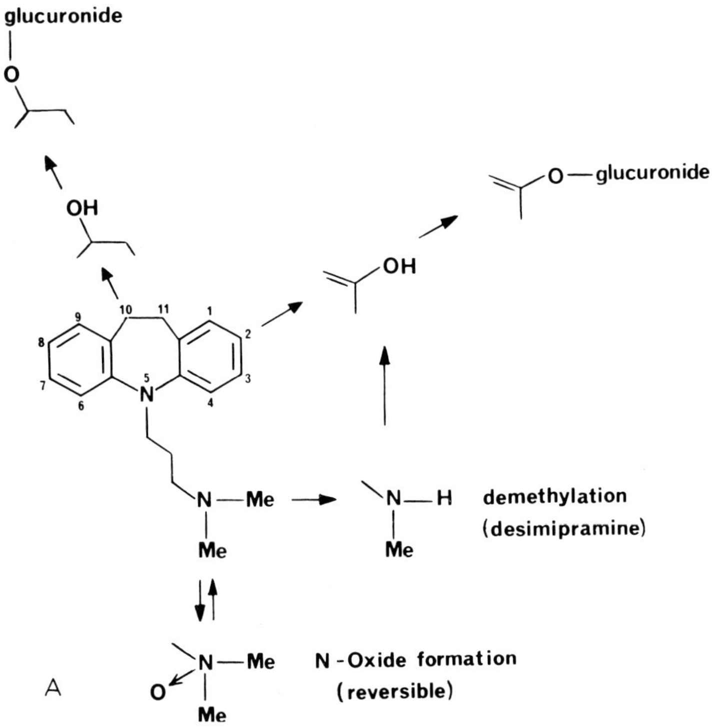

glucuronide

O

OH

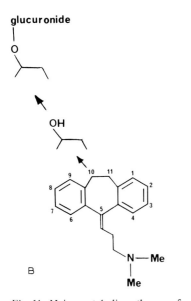

9 10 11 1
8 2
7 3
6 5 4
N

N—Me → N—H   **demethylation**
| | **(desimipramine)**
Me   Me

O—glucuronide

OH

A

N—Me   **N-Oxide formation**
O↙ | **(reversible)**
Me

Fig. 1a. Major metabolic pathways of imipramine.

glucuronide

O

OH

9 10 11 1
8 2
7 3
6 5 4

N—Me
|
Me

B

Fig. 1b. Major metabolic pathways of amitriptyline.

thylated during passage across the intestinal wall. However, the level of IMI in the portal vein remained considerably higher than in the cubital vein, indicating biliary excretion and reabsorption of the drug, i.e. an enterohepatic circulation. These results agree with those of Bickel and Weder (1968) and Crammer et al. (1968).

Self-inhibition by DMI. Several reports in the literature have suggested that DMI could inhibit the metabolism of other drugs (see later). Using isolated perfused rat liver, Moldowan and Bellward (1974) studied three metabolic reactions of IMI: aromatic hydroxylation, N-demethylation (formation of DMI) and N-oxidation (formation of IMI-N-oxide). Exogenous DMI was found to inhibit hydroxylation, but only at higher concentrations was demethylation inhibited. The hydroxylated metabolites quickly conjugated to form glucuronides, suggesting that the conjugation reaction is much more rapid than hydroxylation. The concentration of N-oxide was very low. Crammer et al. (1969) found that the formation of N-oxide, which is reversible and short lived, accounts for only 1–2% of the administered dose.

Imipramine-N-oxide. This is available as an antidepressant drug in some countries, and undergoes a quite different form of metabolism. It is reduced to IMI, mainly intracellularly in erythrocytes, brain tissue, and possibly other cells (Bickel et al., 1968; Nagy and Hansen, 1978) but not to any major extent in the liver. Concentrations of IMI and DMI were found to be very low. Probably the succession of metabolic steps, as with amitriptyline N-oxide, is primarily 10-hydroxylation then N-oxide reduction followed by N-demethylation.

Amitriptyline and nortriptyline

In the rat, Eschenhof and Rieder (1969) found the following metabolites of amitriptyline (AT) in urine and faeces: unchanged AT; 10-hydroxy-AT; monodemethylated AT, i.e. nortriptyline (NT); the didemethylated derivative desmethylnortriptyline DNT; 10-hydroxy-NT; AT-N-oxide; the glucuronide of 10-hydroxy-AT; the glucuronide of 10-hydroxy-NT; the glucuronide of 10-hydroxy-DNT. In the urine of man they identified NT; DNT; NT-glucuronide; 10-hydroxy-NT-glucuronide; 10-hydroxy-DNT and AT-N-oxide. In the faeces of man only AT was present. Compounds of AT are secreted by the gastric mucosa into the stomach lumen, and by the liver via bile into the small intestine. The bile contains two conjugated metabolites exclusively but these are absorbed in the small intestine and not excreted. AT and NT are hydroxylated in the aliphatic ring position 10, compared with the aromatic hydroxylation at position 2 in IMI and DMI. Both possible stereoisomers of hydroxy-NT have been shown to be formed (Bertilsson and Alexanderson, 1972).

In patients treated with AT, the ratios of plasma levels NT/AT vary widely, with an average of about unity. Rollins et al. (1980) found demethylation of AT ranged from 25 to 89% in six subjects. Gram and Fredericson Overø (1975) using p.o. and i.v. administration of NT in six subjects found mean oral availability to be 0.50. In a study of Burch and Hullin (1981a), NT resulting from an AT dose, averaged 48% of the plasma level after an equal dose of NT. Allowing for first pass metabolism, the conversion of AT to systemic NT is 48% × 0.5 or 24%. The remainder was presumably either hydroxylated directly or demethylated to NT and further metabolized before reaching the systemic circulation. Santagostino et al. (1974) in a single dose AT study found NT metabolites (NT, DNT and 10-hydroxy-NT) constituted 59% of excretion, and AT metabolites (AT, AT-N-oxide, 10-hydroxy-AT) only 41%. This suggests that unlike IMI, hydroxylation is more important than demethylation with AT. First pass metabolism studies resulted in the figures 30–69% NT, mean 49% (Burch and Hullin, 1981), compare 60–85% DMI from IMI (see earlier).

Amitriptyline-N-oxide. After a single dose of AMI, the total amount of N-oxide excreted accounted for about 1% of the dose. It appears in the urine soon after administration of the parent compound but disappears within 9 hours (Santagostino et al. 1974). Midgley et al. (1981) and Breyer Pfaff et al. (1981) studied the metabolic fate of AT-N-oxide in man. Only polar metabolites appeared, not AT and NT. Biotransformation of this compound appears to be successively first 10-hydroxylation, then N-oxide reduction followed by N-demethylation.

Slow release amitriptyline. AT is often administered as a single evening dose; this may result in the risk of toxicity from the high peak plasma levels. For this reason slow release products have been developed. Burch and Hullin (1981b) found greater individual variation between subjects, but no reduction in peak levels, with the slow release compound compared with ordinary AT tablets. Jørgensen (1977), however, found later and lower peaks of slow release AT. Jørgensen also obtained similar results with the product used by Burch and Hullin (unpublished results). Further experiments appear to be necessary to determine whether failure of the slow release mechanism is due to the presence of food absorption in the gut.

Chlorimipramine

Demethylation of chlorimipramine (CMI) produces desmethylchlorimipramine (DCMI). CMI is a fairly specific inhibitor of serotonin uptake (Carlsson et al., 1969). DCMI which forms and accumulates to greater than plasma concentration of the parent compound (Mellström and Tybring, 1977) is a potent inhibitor of noradrenaline uptake. Hence, the metabolite DCMI is an important determinant of effects during drug treatment. Perel et al. (1977) identified two series of chlorimipramine metabolites in humans, corresponding to the 8-hydroxy and 2-hydroxy compounds and their corresponding demethylated products.

Doxepin

Metabolic transformations include demethylation, N-oxidation, hydroxylation and glucuronide formation as with other TCAs. Doxepin (DOX) and desmethyldoxepin (DDOX) represent only about 2% of the total drug-related material present in plasma, the remainder must represent polar metabolites. Of the many metabolites only DOX and DDOX were found to be present in rat brain (Hobbs, 1969). An estimated first pass metabolism in a study by Ziegler et al. (1978b) ranged from 55 to 87% in seven volunteers.

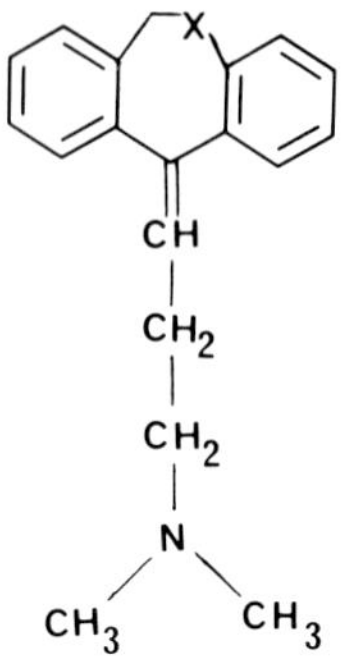

62

X = CH$_2$, AMITRIPTYLINE

X = S, DOTHIEPIN

X = O, DOXEPIN

Fig. 2.

Dothiepin

Crampton et al. (1978) found that the major metabolites recovered from urine were the S-oxides of dothiepin and northiaden (desmethyl dothiepin). Maguire et al. (1981) investigated the metabolism of dothiepin after single dose administration to seven healthy volunteers. S-oxidation was found to be a more important pathway in the biotransformation of dothiepin than demethylation. Peak concentrations of dothiepin S-oxide were higher than peak concentrations of northiaden in all volunteers, and higher than dothiepin in all but one. Dothiepin and its S-oxide are eliminated at a similar rate, northiaden more slowly. Northiaden S-oxide could not be measured by the same procedure due to different extraction characteristics. A major peak observed during analysis for dothiepin and northiaden was subsequently identified as dothiepin S-oxide and quantitated. This metabolite has recently been found to inhibit uptake of 5-HT into platelets (Norman et al., 1981) which is suggestive of antidepressant activity. Concentrations of this metabolite and probably also northiaden S-oxide should thus be included in any clinical studies of this drug (Maguire et al., 1981).

Protriptyline

Protriptyline, a secondary amine, is structurally similar to nortriptyline. As with other secondary amine TCAs, its elimination is largely dependent on liver hydroxylation and conjugation. Biggs et al. (1975) reported that protriptyline levels were higher, based on drug dosage, than plasma levels of other TCAs. Ziegler et al. (1978a) in a study using eight healthy volunteers estimated the first pass metabolism of protriptyline at 10–25% of the oral dose, which is relatively small compared with other TCAs. Ziegler et al.,

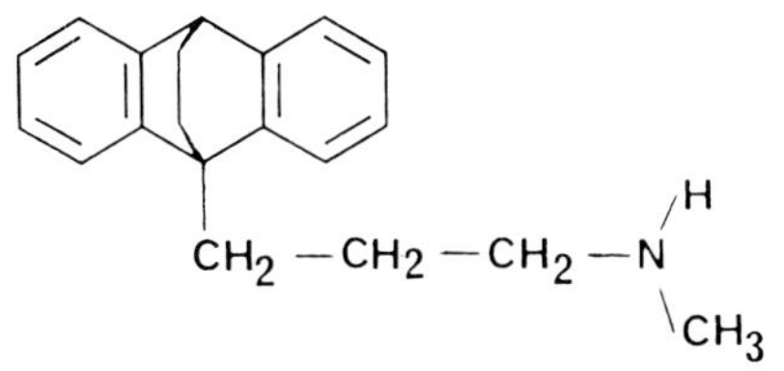

Fig. 3. Maprotiline.

point out that the unusually long half-life of protriptyline is due to its slow rate of metabolism, and the well documented delay between the onset of TCA treatment and recovery, may result in confusion. Therapeutic doses may wrongly be considered ineffective, and a potentially lethal dose may be initiated.

Lofepramine

This drug is an IMI analogue with a chlorophenacyl grouping replacing one N-methyl group. Increasing the lipophilicity in this way, it was hoped, should speed up absorption. It has a high first pass metabolism, apparent bioavailability is only 6.6% (Plym Forshell et al., 1976). DMI is a major metabolite of this drug.

Maprotiline

Maprotiline (MAP) is distinguished from conventional tricyclic antidepressants only by the rigid flexure imposed upon its molecular skeleton by an ethylene bridge (Wilhelm, 1972). Its structure is not sufficiently different to substantiate claims that it represents a new class of psychotropic agent. The principal metabolite is the desmethyl derivative, but both this metabolite and maprotiline itself may be further transformed to numerous minor metabolites by simple and multiple hydroxylation of the aromatic parts of the molecule and oxidative modification of the propylamino side chain. These phenolic derivatives may then be further converted to aromatic methoxy ethers or excreted in the urine as glucuronide conjugates. On chronic dosing, blood concentrations of the desmethyl derivative reach appreciable levels, but those of the principal monohydroxy (phenolic) derivative are negligible (Riess et al., 1975). The other hydroxylated and methoxylated derivatives are clearly only trace metabolites (Pinder et al., 1977). Unchanged maprotiline in the urine accounts for only 2% of the administered dose (Jones and Luscombe, 1976). Desmethyl maprotiline and maprotiline-N-oxide have similar pharmacological properties to the parent drug in animals (Shibuya et al., 1975).

NEWER ANTIDEPRESSANT DRUGS

These have been developed in an attempt to improve on the therapeutic qualities of the tricyclic antidepressant drugs; mainly to increase speed of onset of therapeutic effect, to reduce cardiotoxicity and to reduce anticholinergic side effects. There has been a considerable degree of success in the two latter aims, as a result of which newer antidepressants are suitable for use in the elderly. However, Blackwell (1981) advocates caution in

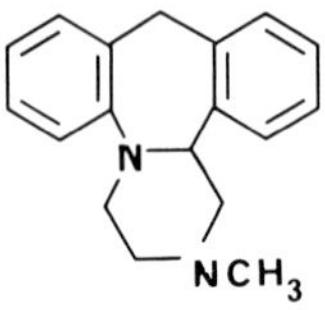

64

Fig. 4.

assessment of these compounds since accurate evaluation of relative efficacy and adverse effects is a slow, cumulative process.

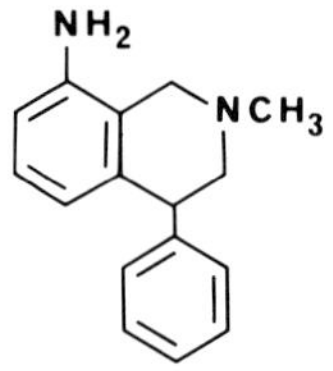

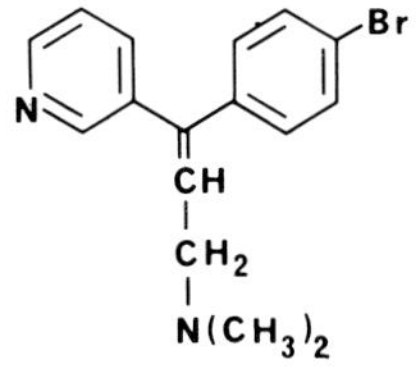

The greatly altered chemical structure has resulted in very different metabolic pathways from those common to the classical TCAs. In particular, there is in some cases conjugation of the parent compound, which with TCAs occurs only after hydroxylation. Knowledge of the kinetics of conjugation is required to evaluate the plasma level of unchanged drug, since only the free fraction exerts the antidepressive effect.

Mianserin

Mianserin is a tetracyclic piperazino-azepine compound with a pharmacological profile of action different from that of the TCAs (Brogden et al., 1978). The predominant route of biotransformation of mianserin in the human is aromatic hydroxylation, N-oxidation, and N-demethylation, the major metabolites being 8-hydroxy mianserin, N-desmethyl mianserin and mianserin-N-oxide (Kopera, 1975). Most of a dose is metabolized, only 4–7% being present in the urine as unchanged drug. There are no published data indicating whether or not the metabolites are pharmacologically active (Brogden et al., 1978), but all may be active on peripheral serotonin uptake mechanisms (Coppen et al., 1978).

Zimelidine

Zimelidine, a 'monocyclic' antidepressant drug, was developed as a specific blocking agent for serotonin at the neuronal membrane. It was shown that zimelidine is rapidly demethylated in animals and man. In a study in five healthy subjects, peak plasma norzimelidine concentrations were attained within 3 to 5 hours after the administration of single oral and intravenous doses of zimelidine, indicating that hepatic 'first pass' metabolism plays a major role in the formation of the active metabolite (Love et al., 1981).

Norzimelidine retains the specificity of action and greater potency with regard to sero-tonin action and is regularly monitored along with zimelidine in patients taking the drug (Ögren et al., 1981).

The major metabolic routes involve oxidation at both nitrogens, N-demethylation and deamination of the aliphatic nitrogen. The major excretion products in urine were zimeli-dine N-oxide and an acrylic acid derivative, these were also identified in human urine (Lundström et al., 1981).

Nomifensine

Nomifensine is a tetrahydroisoquinoline antidepressant which is chemically distinct from the tricyclic or tetracyclic antidepressants, monoamine oxidase inhibitors and other cur-rently available agents.

Three principal metabolites formed by hydroxylation and methoxylation of the phenyl ring are found in equal proportion (about 7%) in human serum and urine (Heptner et al., 1978). Of these, only the 4-hydroxyphenyl derivative is consistently active *in vitro* and *in vivo*. The proportion of nomifensine and of the conjugated drug in urine is dependent on the pH of the extraction process, the glucuronide conjugate being split when the pH is below 7.1. Following single doses, the amount of unchanged drug in serum is 5%, nomifensine being present mainly as the conjugate (Heptner et al., 1978; McIntyre et al., 1982). Four further metabolites have been found; desmethyl-nomifensine; dihydroxy-nomifensine; dimethoxynomifensine; and hydroxy-dimethoxynomifensine; but these account for less than 1% of the administered dose (Heptner et al., 1978).

INTERINDIVIDUAL VARIATION OF METABOLISM

It has been shown by many researchers that patients treated with identical doses of TCAs reveal great interindividual differences in their steady-state plasma concentrations. Ham-mer and Sjöqvist (1967) demonstrated a 36-fold difference between the lowest and highest steady-state level of desimipramine in patients taking equal amounts of the drug. Most of the variability was considered to be genetically determined unless they were simultane-ously exposed to other drugs (Alexanderson et al., 1969). Among determinants of varia-bility are genetic differences in the hepatic microsomal enzyme system and hepatic blood flow. Tissue binding, plasma protein binding and binding to erythrocytes are a much lower source of variability. Alexanderson et al., investigated inter- and intra-pair differen-ces in monozygotic (MZ) and dizygotic (DZ) twins, all given the same dose of nortrip-tyline. MZ twins showed almost identical steady-state plasma levels, with significant be-tween-pair differences. DZ twins showed intra-pair differences of up to 8-fold. Administra-tion of enzyme stimulating drugs reduced plasma concentrations threefold. A major factor in determining steady-state plasma concentrations would thus appear to be the genetic determination of the hepatic oxidizing system.

CLINICAL EFFECTS OF METABOLITES

The most widely discussed difference in action of metabolites is that between tertiary amines and the secondary amines which result from demethylation. This is discussed in Chapter 7. Further demethylation of DMI and NT probably does not occur to any great extent (Christiansen et al., 1967; Eschenhof and Rieder, 1969).

In addition, there is the question as to whether the hydroxy metabolites, possessing *in vitro* effects comparable to the parent compound, exert comparable clinical effects. Although Bickel and Weder (1969) discounted a pharmacological effect of hydroxy derivatives, the point has been raised again by Potter et al. (1979, 1980), and De Vane et al. (1981). Studies using synaptosomal preparations showed that 2-hydroxy DMI is a potent inhibitor of neurotransmitter uptake; quantitative amounts of 2-hydroxy DMI are present in the cerebrospinal fluid (CSF) of patients taking DMI, and it accumulates to a significant proportion of the parent compound.

There is a tendency for older patients to have a higher proportion of metabolites, possibly due to impairment of renal function, which may reduce clearance of polar metabolites in the CSF during NT treatment; this was confirmed by Bertilsson et al. (1979). Perel et al. (1978) reported indications from animal studies of CNS effects of 2-hydroxy desimipramine. Since previous consensus has been that only nonpolar metabolites cross the blood-brain barrier (see above), further investigation is needed.

Cardiac effects

Several studies have indicated that hydroxy metabolites of TCAs may be implicated in the well known cardiac effects of TCAs (see Chapter 13). In dogs, 2-hydroxy imipramine was found to be highly cardiotoxic (Jandhyala et al., 1977). There was a lesser degree of cardiotoxicity with 3-chlorimipramine hydroxy compounds. Wilkerson (1978) found 2-hydroxy imipramine to be more potent than imipramine and desimipramine in counteracting digoxin induced cardiac arrhythmias in dogs.

Further clinical studies are needed to clarify the significance of the various TCA metabolites in relation to therapy and toxicity.

FACTORS INFLUENCING METABOLISM

Effects of age

The results of studies of Gurland et al. (1982) in London and New York confirm that there are between 13 and 16% of the elderly in both cities who suffer from psychiatric illness (Copeland, 1981). Gottfries (1981) has found depression associated with physical illness in the elderly to be difficult to treat, mainly because of side effects which make it difficult to achieve a therapeutic dose.

In particular, reduction of acetylcholine associated enzymes in the elderly requires caution in the use of drugs with anticholinergic properties (Davies et al., 1971) Cardiovascular function is also more vulnerable.

It appears that the elderly may have a decreased rate of elimination of antidepressants compared with younger subjects (Castleden and George, 1979; Luscombe and John, 1980). To date, there is sufficient work on first pass extraction and hepatic blood flow to suggest that any drug with a high extraction ratio will be eliminated more slowly in the elderly, and thus, if they are given the same dose as young subjects, they will develop high steady-state plasma levels (WHO, 1981). A recent pharmacokinetic evaluation of mianserin, for example, showed that elderly depressed patients eliminate the drug more slowly than young healthy volunteers (Maguire et al., 1982). Such results may indicate the use of divided or lower dosages of antidepressants in the elderly to prevent increased concentrations, and consequent side effects. (See also Chapter 13 for cardiotoxic effects of TCAs; Chapter 14 for reduced cardiotoxic effects of newer antidepressants; and Chapter 16, p. 240 for the use of MAOIs in depressed elderly patients.) In contrast to adults, children (age range 2–12) treated with IMI for hyperkinesis or childhood depression demethylate to a much greater extent due to the greater percentage of body occupancy by hepatic tissue (Perel et al., 1978).

Effects of smoking

While the effects of cigarette smoking on the metabolism of a number of drugs and chemicals have been investigated (Hart et al., 1976) effect on tricyclic metabolism is not well known. The constituents of tobacco and tobacco smoke are believed to increase the rate of metabolism by inducing drug-metabolizing enzymes (Hart et al., 1976). Smokers and nonsmokers therefore might show differences in their steady-state tricyclic plasma levels. A significant difference between smokers and nonsmokers has been observed in steady-state levels of imipramine taken with desipramine (Perel et al., 1975). Patients smoking 15 or more cigarettes a day have been found to tolerate daily doses of 75 mg clomipramine far better than nonsmokers, but this was *not* reflected in lower plasma tricyclic levels in smokers (Luscombe and John, 1980). Other studies have found no correlation between the number of cigarettes smoked per day and plasma nortriptyline levels (Alexanderson et al., 1969) and no effect of smoking on the steady-state plasma levels of nortriptyline (Norman et al., 1977).

Other effects

Sex differences in metabolism of TCAs were found in rats by Pscheidt (1962), but no clinical evidence of sex differences in man has been reported.

Ziegler and Biggs (1977) considered the effects of age, sex, race and smoking on plasma levels of amitriptyline and nortriptyline. Only race showed evidence of significant difference in metabolism. This was supported by Lewis et al. (1980) with a study of clomipramine in British and Asian volunteers. They considered there was evidence of both genetic and environmentally controlled ethnic factors for alteration in metabolism.

Circadian rhythm. Nakano and Hollister (1978) found no effects of circadian rhythm on metabolism of nortriptyline.

Effects of disease

There is a high prevalence of chronic renal failure and depressive symptoms are common in this condition. Dawling et al. (1981) studied nortriptyline pharmacokinetics in patients with chronic renal failure. Hepatic oxidation mechanisms are usually unaltered (Reidenberg, 1977) and comparisons between patients and physically healthy subjects revealed no significant difference in NT half-life and clearance. However, the authors point out that; a) a major part of NT is excreted following glucuronide conjugation of 10-hydroxy nortriptyline (Alexanderson and Borga, 1973) and in renal insufficiency these products may accumulate; and b) protein binding of the drug may be diminished (Reidenberg, 1977), which may result in abnormal sensitivity to the drug. The authors recommend single dose prediction tests or plasma level monitoring in these patients. In other illness states, interaction with concomitant medication should be considered, e.g. barbiturates in epilepsy (Braithwaite and Flanagan, 1975).

DRUG INTERACTIONS

It is well documented that concomitant prescribing of other drugs with tricyclics has an effect on plasma tricyclic concentrations and conversely TCAs may influence the concentration of the concomitant medication.

Barbiturates

Chronic administration of barbiturates was shown by Hammer and Sjöqvist (1967) to lower TCA levels, due to enzyme induction of the hepatic microsomal system (Conney, 1967). Burrows and Davies (1971) reported that amylobarbitone taken for a few nights may lower plasma NT levels. Ballinger et al. (1974) studied effects of amylobarbitone and nitrazepam. They found no apparent effects on depression, sleep or side effects. It is recommended that barbiturates should not be prescribed for depressed patients receiving tricyclics, but the clinical implications are insufficiently clarified.

Antipsychotics

Gram and Overø (1972) and Gram (1976) have reported inhibition of the metabolism of tricyclics by chlorpromazine, perphenazine, and haloperidol. Similar effects were found by Moody et al. (1967) with chlorpromazine and Olivier-Martin et al. (1975) with levomepromazine.

Antianxiety drugs

The benzodiazepine compounds nitrazepam, diazepam, oxazepam and chlordiazepoxide have been found to have no effect on plasma NT levels (Silverman and Braithwaite, 1973). Lorazepam at 7.5 mg for 10 days significantly raised plasma concentration of NT in one patient (Burrows, 1976). More investigation is required on the effects of antianxiety compounds.

Steroids

Burrows and his colleagues (1974) found decreased nortriptyline steady-state levels in two of five female patients after 2 months of 'Eugynon' (norgestrel 0.5 mg, ethinyloestradiol 0.05 ng). Norethisterone, a progestogen may also affect the plasma level of nortriptyline. One patient previously unresponsive to NT in doses of up to 250 mg daily, showed greatly diminished depressive symptoms after 5 mg norethisterone for 5 days premenstrually for three consecutive menstrual cycles. In the other two women, similar therapy with norethisterone had no effect on the plasma NT.

Antiobesity agents

Fenfluramine administered for a few weeks to four patients who had complained of weight gain following chronic TCA therapy resulted in significant elevation of plasma NT levels. No change of note occurred in their affective state. (Burrows et al., 1974).

Thyroid hormones

Some authors have suggested that the response of depressed patients to imipramine can be substantially altered by small induced changes in endocrine state, particularly the thyroid axis (Prange et al., 1976; Swartz, 1982). Another investigation of the role of thyroid hormones in depressive illness, where triiodothyronine (T_3) 20 μg was added to the therapy of six depressed women aged 30–60 years who were receiving TCAs, found no significant response. No effect was found on either the clinical state or plasma nortriptyline levels (Burrows et al., 1974).

NEWER ANTIDEPRESSANTS AND DRUG INTERACTION

Some tricyclic antidepressants inhibit microsomal drug metabolizing enzymes and may alter the metabolism of drugs such as propanolol and antipyrine when administered simultaneously (O'Malley et al., 1972). Maprotiline has no such effects in animals (Riess et al., 1975) and there is no evidence of either induction or inhibition of enzymes in man (Briant and George, 1974). Zimelidine has been found to be devoid of any significant interaction with phenobarbital, pentobarbital and diazepam (Cott and Ögren, 1980). A preliminary determination of the effects of subchronic antidepressant medication on liver enzymes was done by measuring cytochrome P-450 concentrations (Cott and Ögren, 1980). Amitriptyline significantly increased cytochrome P-450 concentration but zimelidine did not. Zimelidine and norzimelidine had no effect even at high dosages on the sedation of mice by alcohol. Zimelidine appears to be a particularly safe antidepressant in view of its lack of interaction with sedative/hypnotic drugs (Cott and Ögren, 1980). Few studies have evaluated drug interactions with mianserin. Mattila and coworkers (1978) found that mianserin did not interact with alcohol in learning and memory tasks, however, coordination and reaction skills were impaired, and mianserin was shown to interact additively with alcohol. Coadministration of mianserin and adrenergic blocking drugs such as bethanidine or guanethidine, or beta-adrenergic blocking drugs (e.g. propranolol or propranolol + hydralazine) does not produce any effect on blood pressure (Burgess et al., 1978; Coppen et al., 1978). Kopera (1979) also found no effect of mianserin on the anticoagulant doses of phenprocoumon.

CONCLUSION

This chapter gives a brief account of the metabolism of the classical tricyclic antidepressant drugs. It also draws attention to the renewed realization that a number of metabolites of the tricyclic antidepressants may themselves have significant pharmacological action, both desirable and adverse.

Mention is made of a number of factors which influence metabolism, including interaction with concomitant medication. In this context, the special case of the elderly depressive patient is important, where imperfect metabolic function and elimination is likely to be compounded by a coexisting illness and concomitant medication.

Finally, a short account is given of metabolism of a few of the 'second generation' antidepressants, which have been developed with the aim of overcoming some inadequacies of the classical tricyclic antidepressants.

REFERENCES

Alexanderson, B., and Borga, O. (1973) Urinary excretion of nortriptyline and five of its metabolites in man after single and multiple doses. Eur. J. Clin. Pharmacol. 5, 174–180.

Alexanderson, B. A., Price-Evans, D. A. and Sjöqvist, F. (1969) Steady-state plasma levels of nortriptyline in twins: influence of genetic factors and drug therapy. Br. Med. J. 4, 764–768.

Ballinger, B. R., Presley, A., Reid, A. H. and Stevenson, I. H. (1974) The effect of hypnotics on imipramine treatment. Psychopharmacology 39, 267–274.

Bellward, G. D., Morgan, R. G. and Szombathy, V. H. (1974) The effects of pretreatment of mice with norethindrone on the metabolism of ^{14}C-imipramine by the liver microsomal drug-metabolizing enzymes. Can. J. Physiol. Pharmacol. 52, 28–38.

Bertilsson, L. and Alexanderson, B. (1972) Stereospecific hydroxylation of nortriptyline in man in relation to interindividual differences in its steady-state plasma level. Eur. J. Clin. Pharmacol. 4, 201–205.

Bertilsson, L., Mellström, B. and Sjöqvist, F. (1979) Pronounced inhibition of noradrenaline uptake by 10-hydroxy metabolites of nortriptyline. Life Sci. 25, 1285–1292.

Bickel, M. H. (1969) The pharmacology and biochemistry of N-oxides. Pharmacol. Rev. 21, 325–355.

Bickel, M. H. (1970) Antidepressants and tranquillizers. Biochemical aspects. Humangenetik 9, 202–204.

Bickel, M. H. and Baggiolini, M. (1966) The metabolism of imipramine and its metabolites by rat liver microsomes. Biochem. Pharmacol. 15, 1155–1169.

Bickel, M. H. and Börner, H. (1974) Uptake, subcellular distribution and transfer process of imipramine and its metabolites formed in rat liver perfusion systems. Naunyn-Schmiedeberg's Arch. Pharmacol. 284, 339–352.

Bickel, M. H. and Weder, H. J. (1968) The total fate of a drug: kinetics of distribution, excretion and formation of 14 metabolites in rats treated with imipramine. Arch. Int. Pharmacodyn. 173, 433–463.

Bickel, M. H. and Weder, H. J. (1969) Buccal absorption and other properties of pharmacokinetic importance of imipramine and its metabolites. J. Pharm. Pharmacol. 21, 160–168.

Bickel, M. H. Flückiger, M. and Baggiolini, M. (1967) Vergleichende Demethylierung von tricyclischen Psychopharmaka durch Rattenleber-Mikrosomen. Naunyn-Schiedeberg's Arch. Pharmacol. 256, 360–366.

Bickel, M. H., Weder, H. J. and Aebi, H. (1968) Metabolic interconversions between imipramine, its N-oxide, and its desmethyl derivative in rat tissues in vitro. Biochem. Biophys. Res. Comm. 33, 1012–1018.

Biggs, J. T., Holland, W. H. and Sherman, W. R. (1975) Steady-state protriptyline levels in an outpatient population. Am. J. Psychiatry 132, 960–962.

Blackwell, B. (1981) Adverse effects of antidepressant drugs. Part 2: 'Second generation' antidepressants and rational decision making in antidepressant therapy. Drugs 21, 273–282.

Borga, O. and Garle, M. (1972) A gas chromatographic method for the quantitative determination of nortriptyline and some of its metabolites in human plasma and urine. J. Chromatogr. 68, 77–88.

Braithwaite, R. A. and Flanagan, R. J. (1975) Steady-state plasma nortriptyline concentrations in epileptic patients. Br. J. Clin. Pharmacol. 2, 469–471.

Breyer-Pfaff, U., Ewert, M. and Wiatr. R. (1978) Comparative single-dose kinetics of amitriptyline and its N-oxide in a volunteer. Arzneim.-Forsch. 28, 1916–1920.

Briant, R. H. and George C. F. (1974) The assessment of potential drug interactions with a new tricyclic antidepressant. Br. J. Clin. Pharmacol. 1, 113.

Brogden, R. N., Heel, R. C., Speight, T. M. and Avery, G. S. (1978) Mianserin: a review of its pharmacological properties and therapeutic efficacy in depressive illness. Drugs 16, 273.

Burch, J. F. and Hullin, R. P. (1981a) Amitriptyline pharmacokinetics. A crossover study with single doses of amitriptyline and nortriptyline. Psychopharmacology 74, 35–42.

Burch, J. F. and Hullin, R. P. (1981b) Amitriptyline pharmacokinetics. Single doses of Lentizol compared with ordinary amitriptyline tablets. Psychopharmacology 74, 43–50.

Burgess, C. D., Turner, P. and Wadsworth, J. (1978) Cardiovascular responses to mianserin hydrochloride: a comparison with tricyclic antidepressants. Br. J. Clin. Pharmacol. 5, 215.

Burrows, G. D. (1976) Plasma Nortriptyline and Lorazepam. Presented at C.I.N.P. meeting, Quebec 1976.

Burrows, G. D. and Davies, B. (1971) Barbiturates and tricyclic antidepressants. Br. Med. J. 4,3.

Burrows, G. D., Davies, B. and Scoggins, B. A. (1974) Plasma tricyclic levels and drug interactions. J. Pharmacol. 5 (Suppl. 2).

Carlsson, A., Corrodi, H., Fuxe, K. and Hökfelt, T. (1969) Effect of antidepressant drugs on the depletion of intraneural brain 5-hydroxytryptamine stores caused by 4-methyl-alpha-meta-tyramin. Eur. J. Pharmacol. 5, 357–366.

Castleden, C. M. and George, C. F. (1979) The effect of ageing on the hepatic clearance of propanolol. Br. J. Clin. Pharmacol. 7, 49–54.

Christiansen, J., Gram, L. F., Kofod, B., and Rafaelsen, O. (1967) Imipramine metabolism in man. Psychopharmacology 11, 255–264.

Conney, A. H. (1967) Pharmacological implication of microsomal enzyme induction. Pharmacol. Rev. 19, 317–366.

Copeland, J. S. (1981) Discussion, treatment of depression in the elderly. In: Proceedings of the Corfu symposium. Acta Psychiatr. Scand. 63 (Suppl. 290) 433.

Coppen, A., Ghose, K., Swade, C. and Wood, K. (1978) Effect of mianserin chloride on peripheral uptake mechanisms for noradrenaline and 5-hydroxytryptamine in man. Br. J. Clin. Pharmacol. 5, (Suppl. 1), 13S–17S.

Cott, J. M. and Ögren, S. O. (1980) Antidepressant drugs and ethanol: behavioural and pharmacokinetic interaction in mice. J. Neural Trans. 48, 223–240.

Crammer, J. L. and Scott, B. (1966) New metabolites of imipramine. Psychopharmacology 8, 461.

Crammer, J. L., Scott, B., Woods, H. and Rolfe, B. (1968) Metabolism of ^{14}C-imipramine. 1. Excretion in the rat and in man. Psychopharmacology 12, 263–277.

Crammer, J. L., Scott, B. and Rolfe, B. (1969) Metabolism of ^{14}C-imipramine. 11. Urinary metabolites in man. Psychopharmacology 15, 207–225.

Crampton, E. L., Dickinson, W., Haran, G., Marchant, B. and Risdall, P. C. (1978) The metabolism of dothiepin hydrochloride in vivo and in vitro. Br. J. Pharmacol. 64, 405P.

Davies, R. K., Tucker, E. J., Harrow, M. and Detre, T. P. (1971) Confusional episodes and antidepressant medication. Am. J. Psychiatry 128, 127.

Dawling, S., Lynn, K., Rosser, R. and Braithwaite, R. (1981) The pharmacokinetics of nortriptyline in patients with chronic renal failure. Br. J. Clin. Pharmacol. 12, 19–45.

Dencker, H., Dencker, S. J., Green, A. and Nagy, A. (1976) Intestinal absorption demethylation and enterohepatic circulation of imipramine studied by catheterization in man. Clin. Pharmacol. Ther. 19, 584–586.

De Vane, C. L., Savett, M. and Jusko, W. J. (1981) Desipramine and 2-hydroxy-desipramine pharmacokinetics in normal volunteers. Eur. J. Clin. Pharmacol. 19, 61–64.

Dingell, J. V. and Bass, A. D. (1969) Inhibition of the hepatic metabolism of amphetamine by desipramine. Biochem. Pharmacol. 18, 1535–1586.

Eschenhof, E. and Rieder, J. (1969) Untersuchungen uber das Schicksal des Antidepressivums Amitriptyline in Organismus der Ratte und des Menschen. Arzneim.-Forsch. 19, 957–966.

Flemenbaum, A. (1971) Methylphenidate: a catalyst for the tricyclic antidepressants. Am. J. Psychiatry 128, 239.

Gottfries, C-G. (1981) Discussion, treatment of depression in the elderly. In: Proceedings of the Corfu Symposium. Acta Psychiatr. Scand. 63 (Suppl. 290), 433.

Gram, L. F. (1974) Metabolism of tricyclic antidepressants: a review. Dan. Med. Bull. 21, 218–231.

Gram, L. F. (1976) Effects of neuroleptics on the metabolism of tricyclic antidepressants. In: Radouco-Thomas (Ed.), Proceedings of 10th CINP, Quebec 1976, Pergamon Press, New York.

Gram, L. F. (1981) Pharmacokinetics of tricyclic antidepressants. In: G. D. Burrows and T. R. Norman (Eds), Psychotropic drugs: Plasma Concentration and Clinical Response. Marcel Dekker, New York, pp. 139–168.

Gram, L. F. and Christiansen, J. (1975) First pass metabolism of imipramine in man. Clin. Pharmacol. Ther. 17, 555–563.

Gram, L. F. and Fredricson Overø, K. (1972) Drug interacton: inhibitory effect of neuroleptics on metabolism of tricyclic antidepressants in man. Br. Med. J. 1, 463–465.

Gram, L. F. and Fredricson Overø, K. (1975) First pass metabolism of nortriptyline in man. Clin. Pharmacol. Ther. 18, 305–314.

Gurland, B. J., Copeland, J. R. M., Kelleher, M. J., Kuriansky, J., Sharpe, L. and Dean, L. (1982) The Mind and Mood of Ageing. The Mental Health Problems of the Community Elderly in New York and London. Haworth Press, New York (in press).

Hammar, C. G., Alexanderson, B., Holmstedt, B. and Sjöqvist, F. (1971) Gas chromatography-mass spectrometry of nortriptyline in body fluids of man. Clin. Pharmacol. Ther. 12, 496–505.

Hammer, W. and Sjöqvist, F. (1967) Plasma levels of monomethylated tricyclic antidepressants during treatment with imipramine-like compounds. Life Sci. 6, 1895–1903.

Hart, P., Farrell, G. C., Cooksley, W. G. et al. (1976) Enhanced drug metabolism in cigarette smokers. Br. Med. J. 2, 147–149.

Heptner, W., Hornke, I., Cavagna, F., Fehlhaber, H. W. et al. (1978) Metabolism of nomifensine in man and animal species. Arzneim.-Forsch. 28, 58.

Hobbs, D. C. (1969) Distribution and metabolism of doxepin. Biochem. Pharmacol. 18, 1941–1954.

Jandhyala, B. S., Steenberg, M. L., Perel, J. M., Marian, A. A. and Buckley, J. P. (1977) Effects of imipramine, chlorimipramine, and its metabolites in the hemodynamics and myocardial contractility of anesthetized dogs. Eur. J. Pharmacol. 42, 403–410.

Jones, R. B. and Luscombe, D. K. (1976) Single-dose study with maprotiline in normal subjects. Paper presented at the Ludiomil Symposium, Malta.

Jørgensen, A. (1977) Comparative bioavailability studies with slow release tablets and ordinary tablets of amitriptyline in human volunteers. Eur. J. Clin. Pharmacol. 12, 187–190.

Kato, R., Chiersara, E. and Vassanelli, P. (1963) Mechanism of potentiation of barbiturates and meprobamate actions by imipramine. Biochem. Pharmacol. 12, 357–364.

Kopera, H. (1975) Aspects of clinical pharmacology and clinical experiences with mianserin. In: T. Vossenaar, (Ed.), Depressive Illness and Experiences with a New Antidepressant Drug GB94. Excerpta Medica, Amsterdam.

Kopera, H., Schenk, H. and Stulemeijer, S. (1978) Phenprocoumon requirement, whole blood coagulation time, bleeding time and plasma gamma-GT in patients receiving mianserin. Eur. J. Clin. Pharmacol. 13, 351–356.

Lewis, P., Rack, P. H., Vaddadi, K. S. and Allen, J. J. (1980) Ethnic differences in drug response. Postgrad. Med. J. 56 (Suppl. 1), 46–49.

Lundström, J., Gosztonyi, T. and de Paulis, T. (1981) Metabolism of zimelidine in rat, dog, and man. Identification and synthesis of the principal metabolites. Arzneim.-Forsch. 31, 486–494.

Luscombe, D. K. and John, V. (1980) Influence of age, cigarette smoking and the oral contraceptive on plasma concentration of clomipramine. Postgrad. Med. J. 56 (Suppl.) 1), 99–102.

Maguire, K. P., Burrows, G. D., Norman, T. R., and Scoggins, B. A. (1981) Metabolism and pharmacokinetics of dothiepin. Br. J. Pharmacol. 12, 405–409.

Maguire, K. P., McIntyre, I., Norman, T. R. and Burrows, G. D. (1982) The pharmacokinetics of mianserin in elderly depressed patients. Psychiatry Res. (in press).

Mattila, M. J., Liljequist, R. and Seppälä, T. (1978) Effects of amitriptyline and mianserin on psychomotor skills and memory in man. Br. J. Clin. Pharmacol. 5 (Suppl. 53).

McIntyre, I. M., Norman, T. R., Burrows, C. D. and Maguire, K. P. (1982) Pharmacokinetics of nomifensine after a single oral dose. Br. J. Clin. Pharmacol. 13, 740–743.

Mellström, B. and Tybring, G. (1977) Ion-pair liquid chromatography of steady-state plasma levels of chlorimipramine and desmethylchlorimipramine. J. Chromatogr. 143, 597–605.

Midgley, I., Hawkins, D. R. and Chasseaud, L. F. (1978) The metabolic fate of the antidepressant agent amitriptyline in man. Arzneim.-Forsch. 28, 1911–1916.

Minder, R., Schnetzer, F. and Bickel, M. H. (1971) Hepatic and extra-hepatic metabolism of the psychotropic drugs, chlorpromazine, imipramine, and imipramine-N-oxide. Naunyn-Schmiedeberg's Arch. Pharmacol. 268, 334–347.

Moldowan, M. and Bellward, G. D. (1974) Studies on ^{14}C-imipramine metabolism in the isolated perfused rat liver. Can. J. Physiol. Pharmacol. 52, 441–450.

Moody, J. P., Tait, A. C. and Todrick, A. (1967) Plasma levels of imipramine and desmethylimipramine druing therapy. Br. J. Psychiatry 113, 183–193.

Nagy, A. and Hansen, T. (1978) The kinetics of imipramine-N-oxide in man. Acta Pharmacol. Toxicol. 42, 58–67.

Nakano, S. and Hollister, L. E. (1978) No circadian effects on nortriptyline kinetics in man. Clin. Pharmacol. Ther. 23, 199–203.

Norman, T. R., Burrows, G. D., Maguire, K. P., Rubinstein, G., Scoggins, B. A. and Davies, B. (1977) Cigarette smoking and plasma nortriptyline levels. Clin. Pharmacol. Ther. 21, 453–456.

Norman, T. R., Burrows, G. D., Scoggins, B. A. and Davies, B. (1979) Pharmacokinetics and plasma levels of antidepressants in the elderly. Med. J. Aust. 1, 273–274.

Norman, T. R., Cheng, H. and Burrows, G. D. (1981) Preliminary studies on the effect of dothiepin and its metabolites on serotonin uptake by human blood platelets in vitro. In: E. Usdin, S. Dahl, L. F. Gram, and O. Lingjaerde (Eds), Proceedings of the 2nd International Meeting on Clinical Pharmacology in Psychiatry, Tromso, June 1980. Macmillan, Basingstoke, U.K.

Ögren, S-O., Lundström, J. and Moore, G. (1981) Zimelidine pharmacology, pharmacokinetics, and clinical response. In: G. D. Burrows and T. R. Norman, (Eds), Psychotropic Drugs: Plasma Concentration and Clinical Response. Marcel Dekker, New York and Basle.

Olivier-Martin, R., Marzin, D., Buschenschutz, E. et al. (1975) Plasma levels of imipramine and desmethylimipramine and antidepressant effect during controlled therapy. Psychopharmacology 41, 187–195.

O'Malley, K., Sawyer, R. R., Stevenson, H. and Turnbull, M. J. (1972) Effects of tricyclic antidepressants on drug metabolism. Br. J. Pharmacol. 44, 372P.

Perel, J. M., Shostak, M., Gann, E., Kantor, S. J. and Glassman, A. H. (1975) Pharmacodynamics of imipramine and clinical outcome in depressed patients. In: L. Gottschalk and S. Merlis (Eds), Pharmacokinetics, Psychoactive Drug Blood Levels and Clinical Outcome. Spectrum, New York, pp. 229–241.

Perel, J. M., Jandhyala, B. S., Steenberg, M. L., Manian, A. A. and Buckley, J. P. (1977) Effects of imipramine, chlorimipramine and its metabolites on the hemodynamics and myocardial contractility of anesthetized dogs. Eur. J. Pharmacol. 42, 403.

Perel, J. M., Irani, F., Hurwic, M., Glassman, A. and Manian, A. A. (1978) Tricyclic antidepressants: relationships among pharmacokinetics, metabolism and clinical outcome. In: S. Garattini (Ed), Depressive Disorders. Schattauer Verlag, Stuttgart and New York, pp. 325–336.

Pinder, R. M., Brogden, R. N., Speight, T. M. and Avery, G. S. (1977) Maprotiline: a review of its pharmacological properties and therapeutic efficacy in mental depressive states. Drugs 13, 321–352.

Plym Forshell, G., Siwers, B. and Tuck, J. R. (1976) Pharmacokinetics of lofepramine in man. Relation to inhibition of noradrenaline uptake. Eur. J. Clin. Pharmacol. 9, 291–298.

Potter, W. Z., Calil, H. M., Manian, A. A., Zavadil, A. P. and Goodwin, F. K. (1979) Hydroxylated metabolites of tricyclic antidepressants: preclinical assessment of activity. Biol. Psychiatry 14, 601–613.

Potter, W. Z., Calil, H. M., Zavadil, A. P., Jusko, W. J., Sutfin, T., Rapaport, J. L. and Goodwin, F. K. (1980) Steady-state concentrations of hydroxylated metabolites of tricyclic antidepressants in patients: relationship to clinical effect. Psychopharmacol Bull. 16, 32–34.

Prange, A. J., Jr., Wilson, I. C., Breese, G. R. and Lipton, M. A. (1976) Hormonal alteration of imipramine response: a review. In: E. J. Sachar, (Ed), Hormones, Behavior and Psychopathology. Raven Press, New York, pp. 41–67.

Pscheidt, G. R. (1962) Demethylation of imipramine in male and female rats. Biochem. Pharmacol. 11, 501–502.

Reidenberg, M. M., (1977) The binding of drugs to plasma proteins and the interpretation of measurements of plasma concentrations of drugs in patients with poor renal function. Am. J. Med. 62, 466–470.

Riess, W., Dubey, I., Funfgeld, E. W., Imhof, P. et al. (1975) The pharmacokinetic properties of maprotiline (Ludiomil) in man. J. Int. Med. Res. 3 (Suppl. 2), 16–41.

Rollins, D. E., Alvan, G., Bertilsson, L., Gillette, J. R. et al. (1980) Interindividual differences in amitriptyline demethylation. Clin. Pharmacol. Ther. 28, 121–129.

Santagostino, G., Facino, R. M. and Pirillo, D. (1974) Urinary excretion of amitriptyline-N-oxide in humans. J. Pharm. Sci. 63, 1690–1691.

Shibuya, T., Matsuda, H., Endo, T., Chen, P. O. et al. (1975) Pharmacological studies of drug action on CNS, with special reference to effects of maprotiline. Int. J. Clin. Pharmacol. 11, 192.

Silverman, G. and Braithwaite, R. A. (1973) Benzodiazepines and tricyclic antidepressant plasma levels. Br. Med. J. 3, 18–20.

Swartz, C. M. (1982) Dependency of tricyclic antidepressant therapy on thyroid hormone potentiation: case studies. J. Nerv. Ment. Dis. 170, 50–52.

Von Bahr, C. (1972) Metabolism of tricyclic antidepressants: pharmacokinetics and molecular aspects. Doctoral thesis, Karolinska Institute, Stockholm.

Wharton, R. N., Perel, J. M., Dayton, P. G. and Malitz, S. (1971) A potential clinical use for methylphenidate with tricyclic antidepressants. Am. J. Psychiatry 127, 1619–1625.

Wilhelm, M. (1972) The chemistry of polycyclic psychoactive drugs – serendipity or systematic investigation? In: P. Kielholz, (Ed.), Depressive Illness, Diagnosis, Assessment, Treatment. Hans Huber, Berne, pp. 129–137.

Wilkerson, R. D. (1978) Antiarrhythmic effects of tricyclic antidepressant drugs in ouabain-induced arrhythmias in the dog. J. Pharmacol. Exp. Ther. 205, 666–674.

World Health Organisation (1981) Health care in the elderly: report of the technical group on use of medicaments by the elderly. Drugs 22, 279–294.

Ziegler, V. E. and Biggs, J. T. (1977) Tricyclic plasma levels. Effects of age, race, sex, and smoking. J. Am. Med. Assoc. 238, 2167–2169.

Ziegler, V. E., Biggs, J. T., Wylie, L. T. et al. (1978a) Protriptyline kinetics. Clin. Pharmacol. 23, 580–584.

Ziegler, V. E., Biggs, J. T., Wylie, L. T. et al. (1978b) Doxepin kinetics. Clin. Pharmacol. Ther. 23, 573–579.

Burrows/Norman/Davies (eds) Antidepressants
© *1983, Elsevier Science Publishers*

Chapter 6

Tricyclic antidepressants plasma level measurement

K. P. MAGUIRE

and

B. A. SCOGGINS

Department of Psychiatry and Howard Florey Institute of Experimental Physiology
and Medicine, University of Melbourne, Parkville, Victoria, Australia

INTRODUCTION

Various methods for the measurement of the tricyclic antidepressants (see Fig. 1) have been reported since 1960. These methods generally involve extraction of the drug from the biological sample prior to analysis by the methods referred to below. Early animal studies involving measurement of these drugs used methods such as spectrophotometry, colorimetry and thin-layer chromatography. None of these methods were of sufficient sensitivity for the analysis of plasma concentrations. Sensitive fluorimetric methods were developed but these lacked specificity. The late 60s saw the development of isotope-derivative assays (IDDA) and gas-chromatography (GC), both being suitable for plasma concentration analysis. More recently, mass fragmentography (GC-MF), high performance liquid chromatography (HPLC), and radioimmunoassay (RIA) have become widely used techniques.

It is beyond the scope of this article to review all the published methodology since 1960. Instead, the requirements of a good assay will be discussed and the techniques mentioned above will be evaluated in that light. For a more comprehensive review the reader is referred to Scoggins et al. (1980).

REQUIREMENTS OF A GOOD ASSAY

A good assay must meet certain criteria. Definitions of analytical parameters to be considered are as follows: Precision (reproducibility) — the closeness of agreement between the results obtained by applying the experimental procedure several times under prescribed conditions. Accuracy — the closeness of agreement between the true value and the mean results obtained by applying the experimental procedure a very large number of times. In practice this should involve as many results as possible, the total number being stated. Limit of detection — the smallest concentration of substance which can be reported with a specified degree of certainty. Sensitivity — the change in measured value resulting from a concentration change of one unit. The sensitivity required for the routine analysis of steady-state plasma concentrations of most of the tricyclic antidepressants is $5-10$ μg/l. The assay should be capable of a precision of approximately $\pm 5-10\%$ (CV) over the total concentration range. A procedure is considered specific if drug metabolites or endogenous plasma constituents do not interfere. In addition, only drugs which do not interfere in the assay procedure should be administered concomitantly.

Several practicalities should also be considered when assessing assay procedures. These are expense, in terms of initial outlay for equipment and running costs, time required to complete the assays, convenience and ease of performing the procedure.

ANALYTICAL TECHNIQUES

Isotope derivative dilution analysis

In 1967, Hammer and Brodie described an isotope-derivative dilution procedure for the analysis of nortriptyline and desipramine. The major drawback to the method was a lack of specificity. More recent methods have incorporated a second isotope (double-isotope derivative dilution analysis, DIDDA) to correct for procedural losses and a chromatographic step to ensure specificity (Maguire et al., 1976).

The procedure involves extraction of the drug, formation of a derivative with (^{3}H)-acetic anhydride, separation of the labelled derivative by thin-layer chromatography and quantitation by liquid scintillation spectrometry. It fulfills the requirements of accuracy, precision, sensitivity and specificity but is expensive initially unless one has access to a liquid scintillation spectrometer and requires 2 days to analyse 24 samples.

Gas-liquid chromatography

Gas-liquid chromatography is now the most widely used approach for the measurement of the tricyclic antidepressants. Initial studies involved flame-ionization detection (Braithwaite and Whatley, 1970) or electron-capture detection (Ervik et al., 1970). Recent advances such as the nitrogen-selective detector and the coupling of GC with mass fragmentography have led to better, more sensitive assays.

The procedure involves extraction from plasma or blood, injection of the extract onto the GC column where separation of compounds takes place and detection of the compounds as they elute (Norman et al., 1977).

77

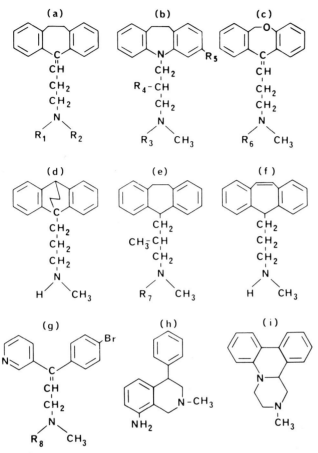

Fig. 1. Structures of tricyclic antidepressants and related drugs. (a) Amitriptyline – R_1 = CH_3; R_2 = CH_3. Nortriptyline – R_1 = CH_3; R_2 = H. Desmethylnortriptyline R_1 = H; R_2 = H. (b) Imipramine – R_3 = CH_3; R_4 = H; R_5 = H. Desipramine – R_3 = H; R_4 = H; R_5 = H. Chlomipramine – R_3 = CH_3; R_4 = H; R_5 = Cl. Desmethylclomipramine – R_3 = H; R_4 = H; R_5 = Cl. Trimipramine – R_3 = CH_3; R_4 = CH_3; R_5 = H. (c) Doxepin – R_6 = CH_3. Desmethyldoxepin – R_6 = H. (d) Maprotiline. (e) Butriptyline – R_7 = CH_3. Norbutriptyline – R_7 = H. (f) Protriptyline. (g) Zimelidine – R_8 = CH_3. Norzimelidine – R_8 = H. (h) Nomifensine. (i) Mianserin.

Internal standardization is necessary to achieve reproducibility and derivatization of the secondary amines following extraction is often needed to facilitate chromatographic analysis. Derivatization is necessary for the majority of drugs if electron-capture is to be the method of detection.

Gas-chromatography techniques have acceptable precision, accuracy and specificity. Better sensitivity is possible with either electron-capture or nitrogen-selective detection compared to flame-ionization detection. Simultaneous quantitation of parent drug and active metabolites is possible with this technique. Care must be taken with these assays in that thoroughly clean glassware and very pure solvents are essential. Depending on the extraction procedure used, 24 samples can be analysed in 1–2 days.

Gas-chromatography mass fragmentography involves the use of a mass spectrometer as an ion-specific detector for the GC. Simultaneous and continuous monitoring of mass spectral ions representing typical fragments of the compounds to be measured provides for a high degree of selectivity. Combining this with the separative powers of GC has produced one of the most powerful analytical techniques available. However, the high cost of the instrumentation will restrict the use of this technique.

An advantage of this procedure is that it can be used for screening of plasma from overdose patients. It is 10–20 times more sensitive than the other GC methods (Borga et al., 1973), hence, is extremely useful for single dose pharmacokinetic studies (Maguire et al., 1981).

Thin-layer chromatography – densitometry

A very simple procedure involving extraction of the sample, separation of components by thin-layer chromatography and detection by either densitometry (Nagy and Treiber, 1973) or by UV reflectance photometry (Breyer and Villumsen, 1976) has been utilized in some studies. Large amounts of plasma were necessary to obtain appropriate sensitivity with this technique.

High performance liquid chromatography

The first report of the application of HPLC to the analysis of the tricyclics appeared in 1975 (Knox and Jurand, 1975). Since then, there has been extensive development of this technique. Following extraction of the sample, either ion-pair partition, adsorption or reversed phase liquid chromatography is performed to separate components and detection is usually by UV absorbance. At present it is not possible to generalize which separation procedure is most suitable for the tricyclic drugs.

The sensitivity of these methods appears to be similar to GC – with flame ionization detection and is adequate for steady-state plasma concentrations. The advantage of HPLC is that it is carried out at room temperature hence stability of drug or metabolites is not a problem, and the sample is not destroyed as occurs with GC. On the other hand, the cost of equipment for HPLC is greater than for GC. Time of analysis and ease of performing the analyses would be similar for the two techniques.

Radioimmunoassay

The basic principle of radioimmunoassays is that of competitive protein-binding where a radioactive and a nonradioactive compound compete for a fixed number of antibody binding sites. The antibodies are generated by raising antisera in animals. The most investigated antiserum to the tricyclic drugs is that raised by Aherne et al. (1976).

The major problem with this type of assay is that most antisera show substantial cross-reactivity between parent drug and metabolites. Furthermore, the cross-reactivity between drug and metabolites is not identical so that an accurate measurement of total drug and metabolites is not obtained. For the secondary amine tricyclics such as nortriptyline, this is not a problem as their major metabolites do not cross-react (Maguire et al., 1978).

TABLE 1

Summary of evaluation of procedures used to measure antidepressant drugs in plasma.

Method	Sensitivity μg/l	Accuracy and precision	Specificity	Convenience	Cost	
					Materials	Equipment
TLC-D	5	++	++	+++	++	+
IDDA	5–10	++	+	+++	++++	+++
DIDDA	5	+++++	++++	+++	++++	+++
GC-FID	10–20	++	+++	+++	+++	++
GC-ECD	1–10	+++	+++	+++	+++	++
GC-NSD	1–10	++++	+++	+++	+++	++
GC-MF	1	+++++	+++++	+++	+++	+++++
HPLC	2–10	+++	+++	++++	+++	+++
RIA	0.1–2	+++	++	+++++	+	+++

Ratings rage from + (poor) to +++++ (excellent).
Abbreviations: TLC-D = thin-layer chromatography densitometry; IDDA = isotope derivative dilution analysis; DIDDA = double-isotope derivative dilution analysis; GC = gas chromatography; FID = flame ionization detection; ECD = electron capture detection; NSD = nitrogen selective detection; MF = mass fragmentography; HPLC = high performance liquid chromatography; RIA = radioimmunoassay.

With the development of more specific antisera, RIA will be a useful technique for pharmacokinetic studies. For clinical studies requiring separate quantitation of drug and active metabolites, RIA has a limited role. As a screening procedure for checking drug compliance or detecting abnormally high or low plasma concentrations, RIA is most suitable as results are available within 24 hours.

SAMPLE COLLECTION AND PREPARATION

Blood is usually collected into heparinized glass or polystyrene tubes, centrifuged as soon as possible and the plasma stored frozen. Plasma may be left at room temperature for several days without a change in tricyclic concentrations (Burch et al., 1979) or when frozen for at least 2 years (Maguire et al., 1976).

A recent practice has been to collect blood samples into Vacutainer tubes (Becton, Dickinson & Co.). It has been shown that this procedure results in lower plasma levels compared to conventional tubes due to inhibition of protein-binding by the plasticiser present in the rubber stopper.

As has been mentioned previously, extraction of the drug from the biological material must be carried out prior to analysis. The only exception to this is that some RIA can be directly performed on plasma samples. Extraction procedures either involve a single extraction into a solvent such as hexane from plasma alkalinized to ph ⩾ 10, or a more complex 3-stage procedure. For the latter, following extraction into solvent, a back extraction into acid and a third extraction into solvent are carried out. This extensive clean up of the sample is necessary to obtain minimum interference by endogenous plasma constituents.

Isotope derivative assays and some RIA methods require only the single extraction but the majority of GC, HPLC and mass-fragmentography assays require the full 3-step procedure.

SUMMARY

A comparison of the analytical techniques in this article is presented in Table 1. The methods of choice for simultaneous quantitation of plasma tricyclic antidepressants and metabolites are GC and HPLC. Gas-chromatography coupled with mass-fragmentography is most useful for overdose analysis, characterization of metabolites and pharmacokinetic studies. Radioimmunoassay has a role in routine screening of plasma samples and with the development of more specific antisera, in pharmacokinetic studies.

REFERENCES

Aherne, G. W., Piall, E. M. and Marks, V. (1976) The radioimmunoassay of tricyclic antidepressants. Br. J. Clin. Pharmacol. 3, 561–565.

Borga, O., Palmer, L., Sjoqvist, F. and Holmstedt, B. (1973) Mass fragmentography used in quantitative analysis of drugs and endogenous compounds in biological fluids. In: Pharmacology and the Future of Man, Proc. 5th Int. Congr. Pharmacol. Karger, Basel 3, 56–68.

Braithwaite, R. A. and Whatley, J. A. (1970) Specific gas-chromatographic determination of amitriptyline in human urine following therapeutic doses. J. Chromatogr. 49, 303–307.

Breyer, U. and Villumsen, K. (1976) Measurement of plasma levels of tricyclic psychoactive drugs and their metabolites by UV reflectance photometry of thin layer chromatograms. Eur. J. Clin. Pharmacol. 9, 457–465.

Burch, J. E., Raddats, M. A. and Thompson, S. G. (1979) Reliable routine method for the determination of plasma amitriptyline and nortriptyline by gas chromatography. J. Chromatogr. 162, 351–366.

Ervik, M., Walle, T. and Erhsson, H. (1970) Quantitative gas-chromatographic determination of nanogram levels of desipramine in serum. Acta Pharm. Suec. 7, 625–634.

Hammer, W. H. and Brodie, B. B. (1967) Application of isotope-derivative technique to assay of secondary amines: estimation of desipramine by acetylation with ^{3}H-acetic anhydride. J. Pharmacol. Exp. Ther. 157, 503–508.

Knox, J. H. and Jurand, J. (1975) Separation of tricyclic psychosedative drugs by high-speed ion-pair partition and liquid-solid adsorption chromatography. J. Chromatogr. 103, 311–326.

Maguire, K. P., Burrows, G. D., Coghlan, J. P. and Scoggins, B. A. (1976) Rapid radio-isotopic procedure for the determination of nortriptyline in plasma. Clin. Chem. 22, 761–764.

Maguire, K. P., Burrows, G. D., Norman, T. R. and Scoggins, B. A. (1978) A radioimmunoassay for nortriptyline (and other tricyclic antidepressants) in plasma. Clin. Chem. 24, 549–554.

Maguire, K. P., Norman, T. R. and Burrows, G. D. (1981) Simultaneous measurement of dothiepin and its major metabolites in plasma and whole blood by gas chromatography-mass fragmentography. J. Chromatogr. 222, 399–408.

Nagy, A. and Treiber, L. (1973) Quantitative determination of imipramine and desipramine in human blood plasma by direct densitometry of thin-layer chromatograms. J. Pharm. Pharmacol. 25, 599–603.

Norman, T. R., Maguire, K. P. and Burrows, G. D. (1977) Determination of therapeutic levels of butriptyline in plasma by gas-liquid chromatography. J. Chromatogr. 134, 524–528.

Scoggins, B. A., Maguire, K. P., Norman, T. R. and Burrows, G. D. (1980) Measurement of tricyclic antidepressants. Part 1. A Review of methodology. Clin. Chem. 26, 5–17.

Burrows/Norman/Davies (eds) Antidepressants
© 1983, Elsevier Science Publishers

Chapter 7

Antidepressants: Receptors, pharmacokinetics and clinical effects

LARS F. GRAM

*Department of Clinical Pharmacology, Odense University School of Medicine, J. B. Winsløws Vej 19,
DK-5000 Odense C, Denmark*

INTRODUCTION

The introduction of imipramine and subsequently other tricyclic antidepressants (TCAs) in the late 50s and early 60s was entirely based on empirical clinical observations. Since then considerable efforts have been made to reach an understanding of the mechanism of action of these compounds.

In the first decade that TCAs were used, clinical observations showed that the compounds not only possessed antidepressant effects, but also had several undesired or toxic effects, in particular on the cardiovascular system, and the compounds could also be useful for other therapeutic purposes, e.g. the treatment of nocturnal enuresis. Experimentally, it was shown that TCAs are potent inhibitors of reuptake of noradrenaline and serotonin from the synaptic cleft, and a possible relationship to the therapeutic effect was postulated (Carlsson et al., 1968a,b).

In the second decade of TCAs use, pharmacokinetic research has shown that the variability in therapeutic effect may very well be explained by interindividual differences in the kinetics, in particular related to the elimination of the parent compound and formation of active metabolites that may act differently from the parent compound (Gram, 1977). The introduction of receptor binding assay techniques by use of radio-labelled ligands has prompted a range of studies showing that TCAs and newer antidepressants interact with several different types of receptors (Hall and Ögren, 1981). The implications of these findings for clinical therapy and future development are still largely unknown, although some preliminary assumptions can be made.

TABLE 1

Influence of antidepressants on different types of receptors.

Receptor	Effect	Relative potency	References
α_1-Adreno-	blockade	DX = AT > CI > IP > NT > DMI	U'Prichard et al., 1978
		DX > AT > MN > CI = NT > IP > DMI	Tang and Seeman, 1980
		AT > CI > MN > NT > IP > DMI	Hall and Ögren, 1981
α_2-Adreno-	stimulation	DMI > IP (low doses)	Svensson and Usdin, 1978
			McMillen et al., 1980
	blockade	MN > AT > DX > NT > IP > CI > DMI	Tang and Seeman, 1980
		MN > AT > NT > IP > CI > DMI	Hall and Ögren, 1981
	down-regulation	DMI	Crews and Smith, 1978
			Johnson et al., 1980
β-Adreno-	down-regulation	IP, DMI	Vetulani et al., 1976
			Banerjee et al., 1977
Cholinergic-muscarinic	blockade	AT > DX > IP > NT > DMI	Richelson, 1978
		AT > NT > CI > IP > MN > DMI	Hall and Ögren, 1981
5-HT-	blockade	MN > AT > DX > NT > CI > IP > DMI	Tang and Seeman, 1980
		MN > NT > AT > CI > DMI > IP	Hall and Ögren, 1981
H_1-histamine	blockade	AT = MN > IP > NT > CI > DMI	Hall and Ögren, 1981
		DX > AT > NT > IP > DMI	Figge et al., 1979,
			Taylor and Richelson, 1980
[3]H-imipramine	high affinity binding	CI > AT > IP > DMI > NT > DX > MN	Langer et al., 1980
		CI > IP > AT > NT > DMI > DX	Paul et al., 1981
		IP > CI > AT > DX > DMI > NT	Rehavi et al., 1981
	down-regulation	IP, DMI	Kinnier et al., 1980
[3]H-desipramine binding	high affinity binding	DMI > NT > IP	Langer et al., 1981
		DMI > NT > IP = AT > DX	Rehavi et al., 1981
Serotonin reuptake	blockade	CI > IP = AT > NT > DX = DMI	Maitre et al., 1980
		CI > IP > AT > NT > DX > DMI	Rehavi et al., 1981
Noradrenaline reuptake	blockade	DMI > NT > IP > CI > DX > AT	Rehavi et al., 1981
		DMI > NT > AT	Langer et al., 1981

Abbreviations: AT = amitriptyline; CI = clomipramine; DMI = desipramine; DX = doxepin; IP = imipramine; NT = nortriptyline; MN = mianserin.

RECEPTOR AFFINITY AND EFFECTS

As shown in Table 1, various antidepressants have been shown to influence a remarkably large number of well defined receptors both associated with the autonomic nerve systems and others. Interference with these receptors has been shown by displacement experiments with specific radio-labelled ligands, as well as demonstration of altered effects specifically related to the individual receptors. In general, most studies have indicated an antagonistic blocking effect of TCAs on the various receptors. The affinity differs for different antidepressants and different receptors, and only few general rules for these differences have, as yet, been established.

Alpha₁-adrenoceptors denote the postsynaptic α-receptor typically found in arteries and veins mediating vasoconstriction following increase of the sympathetic tone, and these receptors are specifically labelled by antagonists such as prazosin (Lees, 1981). Blockade of these receptors by antidepressants has been established by studies with stimulation of selected tissue preparations (Schriabine, 1969; Brown et al., 1980) and by radio-ligand binding studies on cerebral and peripheral tissues (Tang and Seeman, 1980; Hall and Ögren, 1981; Pugsley and Lippman, 1981) Comparison of different antidepressants in these studies has yielded slightly different results, but amitriptyline and mianserin appear to be particularly potent, whereas desipramine is among the least potent of the TCAs.

Alpha₂-adrenoceptors have been indentified as presynaptic receptors modulating (inhibiting) the release of noradrenaline as well as other transmitters (reviews: Starke, 1977; Langer, 1981). These receptors possess distinct ligand binding characteristics different from the α_1-receptors (specific agonist: clonidine; specific antagonist: yohimbine). Alpha₂-adrenoceptors have also been identified on platelets and other nonneuronal tissues (langer, 1981). The CNS effect of clonidine has been related to postsynaptic α_2-adrenoceptors (Langer, 1981).

Various antidepressants have been shown to block the α_2-adrenoceptors resulting in increased noradrenaline release following nerve stimulation (Baumann and Maitre, 1977; Hughes, 1978; Collis and Shepherd, 1980). In these studies mianserin has been found to be a particularly potent antagonist, but also amitriptyline and, to a lesser extent, some other TCAs possess this effect. Interestingly, it has been found, in studies on firing rate from nucleus locus coeruleus, that some TCAs (mainly desipramine) at low doses appear to act agonistically on the α_2-adrenoceptors (Svensson and Usdin, 1978; McMillen et al., 1980). In accordance with these different data, Tang et al. (1979) in studies on brain MHPG concentration found effects compatible with an α_2-antagonistic effect of mianserin and an α_2-agonistic effect of desipramine. Some studies with desipramine have indicated that chronic treatment may be associated with a down-regulation or subsensitivity of the α_2-adrenoceptors (Crews and Smith, 1978; Johnson et al., 1980; Spyraki and Fibiger, 1980). This effect is possibly secondary to the pronounced blockade of noradrenaline reuptake exerted by desipramine.

Beta-adrenoceptors are present in a variety of tissues, such as heart (mediating positive, inotropic, chronotropic and bathmotropic effects), lungs (bronchodilatation), arteries (dilatation) and in relation to various hormonal tissue effects (Lees, 1981).

Binding studies have revealed that a variety of antidepressants are devoid of any immediate effect on β-adrenoceptors (Tang and Seeman, 1980; Hall and Ögren, 1981).

However, several studies, mainly with desipramine and imipramine have demonstrated that chronic administration causes a down-regulation of the β-adrenoceptors (Vetulani et al., 1976; Banerjee et al., 1977; Wolfe et al., 1978; Minneman et al., 1979; Sulser, 1979; Kinnier et al., 1980; Meyerson et al., 1980; Crews et al., 1981). This may, at least partly, be secondary to the increased noradrenaline level in the synaptic cleft following the reuptake inhibition (Banerjee et al., 1977; Crews et al., 1981; Langer, 1981). Bergstrom and Keller (1979) showed that the β-adrenoceptor down-regulation was not accompanied by alteration in the density of α_1-adrenoceptors or serotonin receptors.

The muscarinic acetylcholine receptors are found in the effector cells innervated by the parasympathetic nerve system as well as widely distributed in the CNS (Karczmar and Dun, 1978), and are probably also present as modulatory receptors presynaptically in adrenergic synapses (Muscholl, 1979). Binding studies have shown that antidepressants bind to muscarinic receptors (Snyder and Yamamura, 1977; Innis et al., 1979; Hall and Ögren, 1981), and biochemical studies have shown that this binding results in a blockade of the receptor (Richelson and Divinetz-Romero, 1977). In these studies amitriptyline and doxepin have been found to be the most potent blockers, imipramine, clomipramine and nortriptyline intermediate and mianserin and desipramine fairly weak (Richelson and Divinetz-Romero, 1977; Innes et al., 1979; Hall and Ögren, 1981). Collis and Shepherd (1980) reported results indicating that amitriptyline antagonized presynaptic inhibitory effects of acetylcholine on the release of noradrenaline.

Serotonin (5-HT) receptors are widely distributed in the central nervous system (Pradhan and Bose, 1978), whereas their role in peripheral tissues is poorly understood. Binding studies have indicated that 5-HT receptors might be classified in two subgroups (Peroutka and Snyder, 1979). Behavioural and binding studies have shown that antidepressants are potent blockers of 5-HT receptors (Fuxe et al., 1977; Tang and Seeman, 1980; Hall and Ögren, 1981). Amitriptyline, nortriptyline and mianserin were among the most potent blockers whereas imipramine, clomipramine and desipramine were weaker. Fuxe et al. (1977) underlined that the 5-HT blockade was exerted at doses below those causing blockade of the 5-HT and noradrenaline reuptake.

Histamine receptors have been divided into two subgroups on the basis of the effect of selective antagonists (H_1: mepyramine; H_2: cimetidine). Beyond the well established sites of histamine effect in capillaries in all parts of the body (H_1) and in gastric mucosa (H_2), H_1- and H_2-receptors also appear to be present in the brain (Green et al., 1978; Diffley et al., 1980) and in the heart (Sakai, 1980).

Biological, biochemical, *in vivo* binding, and *in vitro* binding studies on tissues from CNS and the periphery have shown that several antidepressants possess strong H_1-antagonistic properties, doxepin being more potent than any available antihistamine drug (Richelson, 1978; Figge et al., 1979; Diffley et al., 1980; Taylor and Richelson, 1980; Coupet and Szuchs-Myers, 1981; Hall and Ögren, 1981; Tran et al., 1981). Next to doxepin, amitriptyline and possibly mianserin (Hall and Ögren, 1981) are very potent followed by nortriptyline, imipramine, clomipramine and maprotiline. Desipramine was relatively weaker than the other TCAs (Figge et al., 1979; Taylor and Richelson, 1980; Hall and Ögren, 1981).

Green and Maayani (1977) and Kanof and Greengard (1978) reported that antidepressants block H_2-receptors in brain (inhibition of histamine activated adenylate cyclase), but the significance of these findings is presently difficult to assess, since binding studies (using ^{3}H-cimetidine) have revealed no specific high affinity binding of antidepressants for H_2-receptor sites (Coupet and Szuchs-Myers, 1981).

High affinity binding sites of ^{3}H-imipramine and ^{3}H-desipramine have a physiological/pharmacological significance that is not yet fully understood. The binding sites do not represent well-known receptors (Langer and Zarifian, 1981) but as indicated in Table 1, comparison between different antidepressants suggests that the ^{3}H-imipramine and ^{3}H-desipramine high affinity binding sites are associated to the mechanism of presynaptic reuptake of serotonin and noradrenaline, respectively (Langer et al., 1980; Langer et al., 1981; Paul et al., 1981; Rehavi et al., 1981).

The ^{3}H-imipramine binding sites have been demonstrated in a variety of brain regions, but have not been found in many peripheral tissues (Langer and Zarifian, 1981). Blood platelets that also have active serotonin uptake mechanisms (Lingjaerde, 1981) have been shown to be rich in ^{3}H-imipramine binding sites (Briley et al., 1979) with affinity for different compounds similar to that found in brain tissue (Rehavi et al., 1980). It has been shown that repeated administration of imipramine results in a down-regulation of the number of ^{3}H-imipramine high affinity sites, occurring in different parts of the brain than the concurrent down-regulation of β-adrenoceptors (Kinnier et al., 1980).

The ^{3}H-desipramine high affinity binding sites have been demonstrated in brain and in heart and other noradrenaline-rich tissues, and the binding characteristics are quite similar in heart and brain (Langer et al., 1981).

The reuptake inhibition of noradrenaline and serotonin exerted by TCAs was established many years ago (Carlsson et al., 1969a,b) and these findings have heavily influenced the theories about the mode of action of antidepressants, and thereby, the search strategies for development of new compounds with antidepressant effect. As shown in Table 1, the order of potency for ^{3}H-imipramine binding and serotonin reuptake inhibition correlate wel as do the order of potency for ^{3}H-desipramine binding and noradrenaline reuptake inhibition. These correlations were extended beyond the listed drugs and formed the basis for postulating the pharmacological relationships within the two pairs of 'receptors'.

Many antidepressants thus have these relatively specific effects as well as effects on known receptors, where other psychotropic drugs also have effects. For example, neuroleptics are more potent as α_1-adrenoceptor blockers than are the antidepressants (U'Prichard et al., 1978).

The new selective serotonin-reuptake inhibitors such as citalopram and norzimelidine (metabolite of zimelidine) have particularly high affinity to the ^{3}H-imipramine binding sites (Langer et al., 1980), but are almost devoid of effects on the well-known receptors. Among the new antidepressants without clear-cut effects on serotonin or noradrenaline reuptake (mianserin, nomifensine, iprindole), only mianserin shares the profile of multiple receptor effects with the TCAs (Table 1, Tang and Seeman, 1980; Hall and Ögren, 1981).

Hall and Ögren (1981) also tested the affinity of classical and new antidepressants to GABA, benzodiazepine and opiate receptors and found no significant effect of any of the compounds. Some antidepressants (clomipramine, amitriptyline) exhibited some affinity to dopamine receptors however. Among those antidepressants exhibiting effects on several receptors (Table 1), it is striking that the rank order of potency among different compounds is rather similar at different receptors. The only noticeable difference is the weaker antimuscarinic effect of mianserin compared to its other effects. On the other hand, the order of relative affinity for high affinity binding sites (^{3}H-imipramine, ^{3}H-desipramine) was quite different from that of the established receptors (Table 1).

PHARMACOKINETICS

In order to transfer the considerable amount of data on receptor affinity (Table 1) into clinically useful information, it is required that the inherent pharmacokinetics are considered: the primary question being whether the effects observed in the experimental tests occur at drug concentrations that are relevant to the clinical situation.

This problem has only been discussed in a few of the experimental reports (Kanof and Greengard, 1978; Tang and Seeman, 1980). The receptor and binding effects listed in Table 1 were observed at drug concentration ranges of 10–1,000 nM, usually with a 100–300-fold difference between the least and most potent drug. The effects on serotonin and α_2-adrenoceptors occurred generally at somewhat higher concentrations (higher IC_{50}) than on the other receptors.

Clinical studies throughout the last 5–10 years have demonstrated a correlation between therapeutic effect and drug plasma levels for some antidepressants (Gram, 1977; Gram et al., 1982). For imipramine, nortriptyline and amitriptyline the data are sufficiently consistent to permit recommendation of therapeutic drug levels (Table 2). Since the free-drug concentration in plasma can be assumed to be in equilibrium with the tissue water concentration, this concentration probably most closely reflects the concentration at the receptor site. The calculations of free-drug concentrations in Table 2 were based on the assumption of a plasma protein binding of 87–93% for imipramine and desipramine (Kristensen and Gram, 1982; Gram, 1981) and 90–95% for amitriptyline and nortriptyline (Gram, 1981). These free-drug concentrations in patients were of the same magnitude as those being effective in experimental studies, and the receptor effects thus can be expected to be reflected in clinical effects at least for the most potent drugs (Table 1). Furthermore, the concentrations used experimentally are total concentrations where a possible unspecific binding to tissue proteins has not been corrected for. The actual, effective concentrations in the experimental studies thus may have been even lower. In overdose cases, severe toxicity has been observed at total plasma levels 4–10 times higher than the therapeutic levels (Spiker et al., 1975), but due to some degree of saturation of the protein binding, these total levels may even represent relatively higher free concentrations (Kristensen and Gram, 1982).

The other pharmacokinetic problem in transferring experimental data, in particular

TABLE 2

Drug	Compounds assayed in plasma	Therapeutic* concentration (μg/l)	Degree of protein binding (%)	Free concentration (nM)
Imipramine	imipramine + desipramine	250–600	88–92	80–200
Nortriptyline	nortriptyline	60–150	90–95	15–40
Amitriptyline	amitriptyline + nortriptyline	120–300	90–95	30–80

* Editors' Footnote: There is considerable debate concerning the therapeutic concentrations of antidepressants (the reader is referred to chapter 9 of this volume).

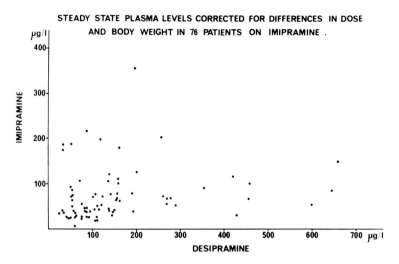

Fig. 1. Corresponding steady-state plasma concentrations of imipramine and the primary metabolite desipramine in 76 hospitalized patients. Concentration levels were corrected for differences in imipramine dose and weight (to 3.5 mg per kg per day). (Data from Gram et al., 1977.)

those from *in vitro* studies, into clinically meaningful information, is the appearance of active metabolites with an effect profile different from that of the parent compound.The most widely discussed difference in this respect is that between imipramine-desipramine, amitriptyline-nortriptyline, respectively (Potter, 1981). As shown in Table 1 the tertiary amines imipramine and amitriptyline are more potent inhibitors of the serotonin reuptake compared to desipramine-nortriptyline, respectively, whereas the latter compounds are more potent inhibitors of noradrenaline reuptake. During administration of imipramine or amitriptyline, the net effect on these systems thus depends on the relative amount of parent compound and metabolite in the body, which – in particular for imipramine – may vary considerably among patients (Fig. 1, Gram et al., 1977). Clinically, differences in effect of parent compound and metabolite have been shown in a study with clomipramine where the parent compound and desmethylclomipramine were assayed in plasma (Reisby et al., 1979). Analysis of some side effects considered to be adrenergic (increased sweating, tremor, palpitations) showed that this effect was pronounced in patients with high desmethylclomipramine levels, and weak in those patients with high clomipramine levels (Fig. 2). The side effects thus were best correlated to the difference in concentration (desmethylclomipramine-clomipramine), indicating that the two compounds have opposite effects in this respect. Desmethylclomipramine thus showed adrenergic effects probably mediated through noradrenaline reuptake inhibition, whereas clomipramine showed adrenolytic effects probably mediated through α_1-adrenoceptor blockade which is usually most pronounced for the tertiary amines (Table 1). Even the parent compound and metabolite have qualitatively the same effect, they may very well differ in potency (cf. Table 1) and their relative concentration in the body may be of importance. For example, plasma level studies have indicated that imipramine is about twice as potent in terms of antidepressant effect as desipramine, relative to the plasma levels (Reisby et al., 1977;

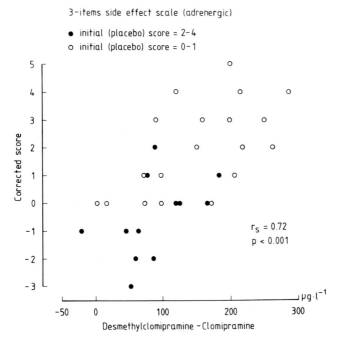

Fig. 2. Correlation between the difference between desmethylclomipramine and clomipramine concentration and change in adrenergic side effect score (3-items scale: palpitations, tremor, sweating). Corrected score = Drug treatment score – placebo score. (Data from Reisby et al., 1979.)

Perel et al., 1978). Unfortunately, most experimental studies comparing the effect obtained after administration of the parent compounds and the metabolites have been done without checking the plasma levels actually obtained.

The hydroxymetabolites of imipramine and nortriptyline have also been shown to possess *in vitro* effects similar to those of their parent compounds (Bertilsson et al., 1979; Potter et al., 1979), and for imipramine the 2-hydroxymetabolites appear to exhibit effect patterns similar to those of the corresponding parent compounds (2-OH-imipramine~imipramine, 2-OH-desipramine~desipramine, Potter et al., 1979).

In patients, a good correlation between the plasma levels of these OH-metabolites and their respective parent compounds seems to exist (Gram, 1978; Potter, 1981). However, the extent to which these compounds reach the CNS is still unclear (Christiansen and Gram, 1973; Potter, 1981).

CLINICAL EFFECTS

The main driving force behind the many experimental studies discussed above has been the search for an explanation of the mode of (antidepressant) action of these compounds. The antidepressive effect has been associated with various experimental effects, the re-uptake inhibition of serotonin and/or noradrenaline being the most strongly favoured hypothesis, although other possibilities such as β-adrenoceptor down-regulation have strong supporters (Sulser, 1979; Leonard, 1980). Most researchers discussing this problem, apparently take it for granted that only one mode or site of action can be expected, although none of the data excludes the existence of more than one site of action, e.g. analogues to antihypertensive treatment.

The introduction of viloxazine, iprindole and mianserin as antidepressant drugs created renewed interest in this field, since these three compounds have no effects on serotonin reuptake and only weak effects on noradrenaline reuptake. However, the true antidepressant effect of these compounds has been seriously questioned (Edwards, 1977; Zis and Goodwin, 1979; Zeersen and Cording-Tömmel, 1981). The possibility exists that the antidepressant effect requires that the drug and/or its metabolites interact with two or more receptors simultaneously. The possible clinical effect of the recently developed specific serotonin reuptake inhibitors (zimelidine, citalopram) thus will be of considerable theoretical as well as practical interest.

Tricyclic antidepressants have a well established therapeutic effect in enuretic children, and a therapeutic plasma level has been established that is 3–4 times lower than those required for the antidepressant effect (Jørgensen et al., 1980; Gram et al., 1981). The therapeutic effect is not entirely associated with the antimuscarinic effect of the drugs, since simple antimuscarinic drugs are devoid of convincing effect (Blackwell and Currah, 1973; Korczyn and Kish, 1979). Antidepressant or antimuscarinic effects thus appear not to explain the enuretic effect. The role of, e.g. adrenergic or adrenolytic effects, is presently difficult to assess, but clinical trials with some of the newer antidepressants might clarify this.

Side effects of antidepressants may be divided into those affecting the central nervous system, the autonomic nervous system and the cardiovascular system.

Sedation is a common effect of at least some antidepressants, although the incidence appears to vary in different studies probably due to differences in treatment schedule, patient characteristics, pharmacokinetics etc. It is well established that amitriptyline, doxepin and mianserin are among the most sedative antidepressants (Perry et al., 1978; Peterson et al., 1978), whereas desipramine and clomipramine usually are considered the least sedative among the TCAs (Gore, 1973; Blackwell et al., 1978). The weak sedative effect of clomipramine may at least partly be explained by the considerable conversion of clomipramine to desmethylclomipramine after oral dose (Beaumont 1973; Mellström and Tybring, 1977). The order of potency for sedation fits well with the potency for histamine H_1-blockade, which has been considered the most likely explanation of the sedative effect (Figge et al., 1979) and is consistent with the well-known sedative effect of many antihistamines. It has also been suggested that α_1-adrenoceptor or muscarinic receptor blockade may be associated with sedation (Hall and Ögren, 1981; Potter, 1981), but the clinical rank orders do not fit quite as well with the *in vitro* studies (Table 1).

Delirious reactions and convulsions, in particular seen in overdose cases, seem to be mainly related to the anticholinergic effects of antidepressants, since these states may be effectively treated with physostigmine (Hall et al., 1981).

Autonomic side-effects such as decreased saliva production (dry mouth), constipation, micturition disturbances, blurred vision, are generally considered as being a result of antimuscarinic effects, whereas other effects such as tachycardia, palpitations, sweating more frequently are considered as being a result of adrenergic effects of antidepressants.

However, most autonomic effects of antidepressants probably represent both antimuscarinic and adrenergic effects (Kolk et al., 1978). Several clinical studies on such antimuscarinic effects in particular reduction in saliva production have revealed rank orders of potency fairly compatible with that depicted in Table 1 (Blackwell et al., 1978, 1980; Peterson et al., 1978; Szabadi et al., 1980; Arnold et al., 1981) and the low antimuscarinic activity of mianserin shown in experimental studies (Table 1) has indeed been confirmed in clinical studies (Coppen et al., 1976).

Cardiovascular effects during antidepressant therapy will usually be limited to changes in heart rate and blood pressure. Orthostatic blood pressure drop is a clinically significant problem that sometimes limits the use of antidepressants in susceptible patients (Glassman et al., 1979; Thayssen et al., 1981). Also, the blood pressure effect appears to be different for different antidepressants. Increased orthostatic blood pressure drop thus has been reported after imipramine and mianserin, but not after nortriptyline or desipramine (Zavadil et al., 1980; Thayssen et al., 1981; Møller et al., in press). The major physiological mechanism by which the cardiovascular system adapts to the standing position is considered to be an increase in sympathetic tone resulting in vasoconstriction and tachycardia, and reflected in a rise in the peripheral plasma level of noradrenaline (FitzGerald and Dollery, 1979). The increased sympathetic tone causing vasoconstriction may be influenced either by a direct blocking effect of the postsynaptic α_1-adrenoceptor (like prazosin) or by a decrease in noradrenaline release following stimulation of the presynaptic α_2-adrenoceptor (like clonidine). The antidepressants listed in Table 1 are all quite potent α_1-adrenoceptor blockers, and with the exception of mianserin, all relatively weak α_2-adrenoceptor blockers. Alpha$_1$-adrenoceptor blockade thus seems to be the most likely explanation of the orthostatic blood pressure drop, but this does not explain the clinical differences between imipramine, nortriptyline and mianserin. Furthermore, a pure α_1-adrenoceptor blockade should result in increased reflex firing with increased plasma noradrenaline levels upon standing as seen in studies with prazosin (Rubin and Blaschke, 1980; Elliott et al., 1981). However, in a recent study, Rokkedal Nielsen et al. (in press) found that imipramine caused orthostatic hypotension, but the rise in plasma noradrenaline was the same in the control period and after imipramine administration. These data may indicate that the hypotensive effect of imipramine is a consequence of α_1-adrenoceptor blockade, in particular affecting the venous part of the vascular bed, and perhaps also central inhibition of sympathetic firing through an α_2-agonistic effect like that of clonidine (Weinshilboum, 1980) (cf. Table 1). The possible significance of other receptors for the hypotensive effects of the antidepressants remains to be examined, however.

The tachycardia seen with some antidepressants may reflect both adrenergic and anticholinergic effects, and the orthostatic tachycardia seen with imipramine in younger subjects may reflect decreased preload due to vein dilatation.

CONCLUSION AND PERSPECTIVES

The recent rapid development in receptor research has considerably increased our knowledge about the possible sites of actions of antidepressants. However, the clinical interpretation and utilization of this information are still difficult. To narrow the gap between experimental and clinical pharmacology in this field, further basic and clinical research is needed. The basic physiological role of various receptors and their mutual interactions both within the CNS and peripherally are still insufficiently known, and the role of various presynaptic modulatory receptors is a field of considerable interest. Clinically, more well-defined effect measurements accompanied by precise monitoring of blood levels of active compounds may improve the value of comparative studies with different antidepressants. The introduction of new antidepressants, with effect profiles clearly different from the classical TCAs, may certainly contribute to a clarification of the problems concerning the receptor and clinical effect relationships.

ACKNOWLEDGEMENTS

Studies from our group discussed in this review have been supported by grants from the Danish Medical Research Council, P. Carl Petersens Found, Fonden til Laegevidenskabens Fremme, F. L. Smidth's Fond and Lundbeck's Psychopharmacology Research Foundation.

We thank Mrs. Gitte Halling Jensen for her excellent assistance in preparation of the manuscript.

REFERENCES

Arnold, S. E., Kahn, R. J., Faldetta, L. L. Laing, R. A. and McNair, D. M. (1981) Tricyclic anti-depressants and peripheral anticholinergic activity. Psychopharmacol. 74, 325–328.

Banerjee, S. P., Kung, L. S., Riggi, S. J. and Chanda, S. K. (1977) Development of β-adrenergic receptor subsensitivity by antidepressants. Nature (London) 268, 455–456.

Baumann, P. A. and Maitre, L. (1977) Blockade of presynaptic α-receptors and of amine uptake in the rat brain by the antidepressant mianserin. Naunyn-Schmiedeberg's Arch. Pharmacol. 300, 31–37.

Beaumont, G. (1973) Oral and intravenous clomipramine (Anafranil) in depression – a review of the work of dr. G. H. Colleüs. J. Int. Med. Res. 1, 361–364.

Bergstrom, D. A. and Kellar, K. J. (1979) Adrenergic and serotonergic receptor binding in rat brain after chronic desmethylimipramine treatment. J. Pharmac. Exp. Ther. 209, 256–261.

Bertilsson, L., Mellström, B. and Sjöqvist, F. (1979) Pronounced inhibition of noradrenaline uptake by 10-hydroxy-metabolites of nortriptyline. Life Sci. 25, 1285–1292.

Blackwell, B. and Currah, J. (1973) The psychopharmacology of nocturnal enuresis. In: I. Kolvin, R. C. MacKeith and S. R. Meadow (Eds), Bladder Control and Enuresis. Spastics International Medical Publications, London and Philadelphia, pp. 231–257.

Blackwell, B. Stefopoulos, A., Enders, P., Kuzma, R. and Adolphe, A. (1978) Anticholinergic acti-vity of two tricyclic antidepressants. Am. J. Psychiatry 135, 722–724.

Briley, M. S., Raisman, R. and Langer, S. Z. (1979) Human platelets possess high affinity binding sites for ^{3}H-imipramine. Eur. J. Pharmacol. 58, 347–348.

Brown, J., Doxey, J. C. and Handley, S. (1980) Effects of α-adrenoceptor agonists and antagonists and of antidepressant drugs on pre- and postsynaptic α-adrenoceptors. Eur. J. Pharmacol. 67, 33–40.

Carlsson, A., Corrodi, H., Fuxe, K. and Hökfelt, T. (1969a) Effect of antidepressant drugs on the depletion of intraneuronal brain 5-hydroxytryptamine stores caused by 4-methyl-α-ethyl-meta-tyramine. Eur. J. Pharmacol. 5, 357–366.

Carlsson, A., Corrodi, H., Fuxe, K. and Hökfelt, T. (1969b) Effects of some antidepressant drugs on the depletion of intraneuronal brain catecholamine stores caused by 4, α-dimethyl-meta-tyra-mine. Eur. J. Pharmacol. 5, 367–373.

Christiansen, J. and Gram, L. F. (1973) Imipramine and its metabolites in human brain. J. Pharm. Pharmacol. 25, 604–607.

92

Collis, M. G. and Shepherd, J. T. (1980) Interaction of the tricyclic antidepressant amitriptyline with prejunctional alpha and muscarinic receptors in the dog saphenous vein. J. Pharmacol. Exp. Ther. 213, 616–622.

Coppen, A., Gupta, R., Montgomery, S., Ghose, K., Bailey, J., Burns, B. and de Ridder, J. J. (1976) Mianserin hydrochloride: a novel antidepressant. Br. J. Psychiatry 129, 342–345.

Coupet, J. and Szuchs-Myers, V. A. (1981) Brain histamine H_1- and H_2-receptors and histamine-sensitive adenylate cyclase: effects of antipsychotics and antidepressants. Eur. J. Pharmacol. 74, 149–155.

Crews, F. T. and Smith, C. B. (1978) Presynaptic alpha-receptor subsensitivity after long-term antidepressant treatment. Science, N. Y. 202, 322–324.

Crews, F. T., Paul, S. M. and Goodwin, F. K. (1981) Acceleration of β-receptor desensitization in combined administration of antidepressants and phenoxybenzamine. Nature (London) 290, 787–789.

Diffley, D., Tran, V. T. and Snyder, S. H. (1980) Histamine H_1-receptors labelled in vivo: antidepressant and antihistamine interactions. Eur. J. Pharmacol. 64, 177–181.

Edwards, J. G. (1977) Viloxazine: assessment of potential rapid antidepressant action. Br. Med. J. 2, 1327.

Elliott, H. L., McLean, K., Sumner, D. J., Meredith, P. A. and Reid, J. L. (1981) Immediate cardiovascular responses to oral prazosin effects of concurrent β-blockers. Clin. Pharmacol. Ther. 29, 303–309.

Figge, J., Leonard, P. and Richelson, E. (1979) Tricyclic antidepressants: potent blockade of histamine H_1-receptors of guinea pig ileum. Eur. J. Pharmacol. 58, 479–483.

FitzGerald, G. A. and Dollery, C. T. (1979) Biochemical indices of sympathetic function in man. Trends Pharmacol. Sci. 1, 84–87.

Fuxe, K., Ögren, S.-O., Agnati, L., Gustafsson, J. Å. and Jonsson, G. (1977) On the mechanism of action of the antidepressant drugs amitriptyline and nortriptyline. Evidence for 5-hydroxytryptamine receptor blocking activity. Neurosci. Lett. 6, 339–343.

Glassman, A. H., Giardina, E. V., Perel, J. M., Bigger, J. T., Kantor, S. J. and Davies, M. (1979) Clinical characteristics of imipramine-induced orthostatic hypotension. Lancet i, 468–472.

Gore, C. P. (1973) Clomipramine (Anafranil), Tofranil, Imipramine and placebo: a comparative study in relation to electroconvulsive therapy. J. Int. Med. Res. 1, 347–351.

Gram, L. F. (1977) Plasma level monitoring of antidepressants. Clin. Pharmacokin. 2, 237–251.

Gram, L. F. (1978) Plasma level monitoring of tricyclic antidepressants; methodological and pharmacokinetic considerations. Comm. Psychopharmacol. 2, 373–380.

Gram, L. F. (1981) Pharmacokinetics of tricyclic antidepressants (Review). In: G. D. Burrows and T. Norman (Eds), Plasma Level Measurements of Psychotropic Drugs and Clinical Response, Marcel Dekker Inc., New York, pp. 139–168.

Gram, L. F., Søndergaard, I., Christiansen, J., Petersen, G. O., Bech, P., Reisby, N., Ibsen, I., Ortmann, J., Nagy, A., Dencker, S. J., Jacobsen, O. and Krautwald, O. (1977) Steady state kinetics of imipramine in patients. Psychopharmacology 54, 255–261.

Gram, L. F., Bech, P., Reisby, N. and Jørgensen, O. S. (1981) Methodology in plasma level/effect studies on tricyclic antidepressants. In: E. Usdin (Ed.), Clinical Pharmacology in Psychiatry. Elsevier/North-Holland, New York, pp. 155–179.

Gram, L. F., Pedersen, O. L., Kristensen, C. B., Bjerre, M. and Kragh-Sørensen, P. (1982) Drug level monitoring in psychopharmacology: usefulness and clinical problems, with special reference to tricyclic antidepressants. Ther. Drug Monit. 4, 17–25.

Green, J. P. and Maayani, S. (1977) Tricyclic antidepressant drugs block histamine H_2-receptor in brain. Nature (London) 269, 163–165.

Green, J. P., Johnson, C. L. and Weinstein, H. (1978) Histamine as a neurotransmitter. In: M. A. Lipton, A. DiMascio and K. F. Killam (Eds), Psychopharmacology, A Generation of Progress. Raven Press, New York, pp. 319–332.

Hall, H. and Ögren, S.-O. (1981) Effects of antidepressant drugs on different receptors in the brain. Eur. J. Pharmacol. 70, 393–407.

Hall, R. C., Feinsilver, D. L. and Holt, R. E. (1981) Anticholinergic psychosis, differential diagnoses and management. Psychosomatics 22, 581–587.

Hughes, I. E. (1978) The effect of amitriptyline on presynaptic mechanisms in noradrenergic nerves. Br. J. Pharmacol. 63, 315–321.

Innis, R. B., Tune, L., Rock, R., Depaulo, R., U'Prichard, D. C. and Snyder, S. H. (1979) Tricyclic antidepressant radioreceptor assay. Eur. J. Pharmacol. 58, 473–477.

Johnson, R. W., Reisine, T., Spotnitz, S., Wiech, N., Ursillo, R. and Yamamura, H. I. (1980) Effects of desipramine and yohimbine on α_2- and β-adrenoceptor sensitivity. Eur. J. Pharmacol. 67, 123–127.

Jørgensen, O. S., Løber, M., Christiansen, J. and Gram, L. F. (1980) Plasma concentration and clinical effect in imipramine treatment of childhood enuresis. Clin. Pharmacokin. 5, 386–393.

Kanof, P. D. and Greengard, P. (1978) Brain histamine receptors as targets for antidepressant drugs. Nature (London) 272, 329–333.

Karczmar, A. G. and Dun, N. J. (1978) Cholinergic synapses: Physiological, pharmacological and behavioural considerations. In: M. A. Lipton, A. DiMascio and K. F. Killam (Eds), Psychopharmacology, A Generation of Progress. Raven Press, New York, pp. 293–305.

Kinnier, W. J., Chuang, D.-M. and Costa, E. (1980) Down regulation of dihydroalprenolol and imipramine binding sites in brain of rats repeatedly treated with imipramine. Eur. J. Pharmacol. 67, 289–294.

Kolk, B. A. v.d., Shader, R. I. and Greenblatt, D. J. (1978) Autonomic effects of psychotropic drugs. In: M. A. Lipton, A. DiMascio and K. F. Killam (Eds), Psychopharmacology, A Generation of Progress. Raven Press, New York, pp. 1009–1020.

Korczyn, A. D. and Kish, I. (1979) The mechanism of imipramine in enuresis nocturna. Clin. Exp. Pharmacol. Physiol. 6, 31–35.

Kristensen, C. B. and Gram, L. F. (1982) Equilibrium dialysis for determination of protein binding of imipramine. Evaluation of a method. Acta Pharmacol. Toxicol. 50, 130–136.

Langer, S. Z. (1981) Presynaptic regulation of the release of catecholamines. Pharmacol. Rev. 32, 337–362.

Langer, S. Z. and Zarifian, E. (1981) High affinity ^{3}H-imipramine binding: a new tool in biological psychiatry. In: E. Usdin, S. G. Dahl, L. F. Gram and O. Lingjaerde (Eds), Clinical Pharmacology in Psychiatry, Neuroleptic and Antidepressant Research. Macmillan Publ. Ltd., London, pp. 63–77.

Langer, S. Z., Briley, M. S., Raisman, R., Henry, J.-F. and Morselli, P. L. (1980) Specific ^{3}H-imipramine binding in human platelets. Naunyn-Schmiedeberg's Arch. Pharmacol. 313, 189–194.

Langer, S. Z., Raisman, R. and Briley, M. (1981) High-affinity ^{3}H-DMI binding is associated with neuronal noradrenaline uptake in the periphery and the central nervous system. Eur. J. Pharmacol. 72, 423–424.

Lees, G. M. (1981) A hitch-hiker's guide to the galaxy of adrenoceptors. Br. Med. J. 283, 173–178.

Leonard, B. E. (1980) Pharmacological properties of some "second generation" antidepressant drugs. Neuropharmacology 19, 1175–1183.

Lingjaerde, O. (1981) Biological assay systems for tricyclic antidepressants. In: E. Usdin, S. G. Dahl, L. F. Gram and O. Lingjaerde (Eds), Clinical Pharmacology in Psychiatry, Neuroleptic and Antidepressant Research. Macmillan Publ. Ltd., London, pp. 27–32.

Maitre, L., Moser, P., Baumann, P. A. and Waldmeier, P. C. (1980) Amine uptake inhibitors: criteria of selectivity. Acta Psychiatr. Scand. 61, (Suppl. 280), 97–110.

McMillen, B. A., Warnack, W., German, D. C. and Shore, P. A. (1980) Effects of chronic desipramine treatment on rat brain noradrenergic responses to α-adrenergic drugs. Eur. J. Pharmacol. 61, 239–246.

Mellström, B. and Tybring, G. (1977) Ion-pair liquid chromatography of steady-state plasma levels of chlorimipramine and demethylchlorimipramine. J. Chromatogr. 143, 597–605.

Meyerson, L. R., Oug, H. H., Martin, L. L. and Ellis, D. B. (1980) Effect of antidepressant agents on β-adrenergic receptor and neurotransmitter regulatory systems. Pharmacol. Biochem. Behav. 12, 943–948.

Minneman, K. P., Dibner, M. D. Wolfe, B. B. and Molinoff, P. B. (1979) β_1- and β_2-adrenergic receptors in rat cerebral cortex are independently regulated. Science 204, 866–868.

Møller, M., Thayssen, P., Kragh-Sørensen, P., Pedersen, O. L., Kristensen, C. B., Bjerre, M., Benjaminsen, S. and Gram, L. F. Mianserin: cardiovascular effects in elderly patients. Psychopharmacology (in press).

Muscholl, E. (1979) Presynaptic muscarine receptors and inhibition of release. In: D. B. Paton (Ed.),

The Release of Catecholamines from Adrenergic Neurons. Pergamon Press, Oxford, pp. 87–110.

Paul, S. M., Rehavi, M., Rice, K. C., Ittah, Y. and Skolnick, P. (1981) Does high affinity ^{3}H-imipramine binding label serotonin reuptake sites in brain and platelets? Life Sci. 28, 2753–2760.

Perel, J. M., Irani, F., Hurwic, M., Glassman, A. H. and Manian, A. A. (1978) Tricyclic antidepressants: relationship among pharmacokinetics, metabolism and clinical outcome. In: S. Garattini (Ed.), Symposium Medicum Hoechst 13, Depressive Disorder, Rome 1977. Schattauer Verlag, Stuttgart and New York, pp. 325–336.

Peroutka, S. J. and Snyder, S. H. (1979) Multiple serotonin receptors: differential binding of ^{3}H-5-hydroxytryptamine, ^{3}H-lysergic acid diethylamide and ^{3}H-spiroperidol. Mol. Pharmacol. 16, 687–699.

Perry, G. F., Fitzsimmons, B., Shapiro, L. and Irwin, P. (1978) Clinical study of mianserin, imipramine and placebo in depression: blood level and MHPG correlations. Br. J. Pharmacol. 5, 35S–41S.

Peterson, G. R., Blackwell, B., Hostetler, R. M., Kuzma, R. and Adolphe, A. (1978) Anticholinergic activity of the tricyclic antidepressants desipramine and doxepin in non depressed volunteers. Comm. Psychopharmacol. 2, 145–150.

Potter, W. Z. (1981) Active metabolites of tricyclic antidepressants. In: E. Usdin, S. G. Dahl, L. F. Gram and O. Lingjaerde (Eds), Clinical Pharmacology in Psychiatry, Neuroleptic and Antidepressant Research. Macmillan Publ. Ltd., London, pp. 139–153.

Potter, W. Z., Calil, H. M., Manian, A. A. Zavadil, A. P. and Goodwin, F. K. (1979) Hydroxylated metabolites of tricyclic antidepressants: preclinical assessment of activity. Biol. Psychiatry 14, 601–613.

Pradhan, S. N. and Bose, S. (1978) Interactions among central neurotransmitters. In: M. A. Lipton, A. DiMascio and K. F. Killam (Eds), Psychopharmacology, A Generation of Progress. Raven Press, New York, pp. 319–332.

Pugsley, T. A. and Lippmann, W. (1981) Affinity of butriptyline and other tricyclic antidepressants for -adrenoceptors binding sites in rat brain. J. Pharm. Pharmacol. 33, 113–115.

Rehavi, M., Paul, S. M., Skolnick, P. and Goodwin, F. K. (1980) Demonstration of specific high affinity binding sites for ^{3}H-imipramine in human brain. Life Sci. 26, 2273–2279.

Rehavi, M., Skolnick, P., Hulihan, B. and Paul, S. M. (1981) High affinity binding of ^{3}H-desipramine to rat cerebral cortex: relationship to tricyclic antidepressant-induced inhibition of norepinephrine uptake. Eur. J. Pharmacol. 70, 597–599.

Reisby, N., Gram, L. F., Bech, P., Nagy, A., Petersen, G. O., Ortmann, J., Ibsen, I., Dencker, S. J. Jacobsen, O. J., Krautwald, O., Søndergaard, I. and Christiansen, J. (1977) Imipramine: clinical effects and pharmacokinetic variability. Psychopharmacology 54, 263–272.

Reisby, N., Gram, L. F., Bech, P., Sihm, F., Krautwald, O., Elley, J., Ortmann, J. and Christiansen, J. (1979) Clomipramine: plasma levels and clinical effects. Commun. Psychopharmacol. 5, 341–351.

Richelson, E. (1978) Tricyclic antidepressants block H_1-receptors of mouse neuroblastoma cells. Nature (London) 274, 176–177.

Richelson, E. and Divinetz-Romero, S. (1977) Blockade by psychotropic drugs of the muscarinic acetylcholine receptor in cultured nerve cells. Biol. Psychiatry 12, 771–785.

Rokkedal Nielsen, J., Johansen, T., Arentoft, A. and Gram, L. F. Effects of imipramine on the orthostatic changes in blood pressure, heart rate and plasma catecholamines. Clin. Exp. Pharmacol. Physiol. (in press).

Rubin, P. C. and Blaschke, T. F. (1980) Studies on the clinical pharmacology of prazosin I. Cardiovascular catecholamine and endocrine changes following a single dose. Br. J. Clin. Pharmacol. 10, 23–32.

Sakai, K. (1980) Role of histamine H_1- and H_2-receptors in the cardiovascular system of the rabbit. J. Cardiovasc. Pharmacol. 2, 607–617.

Schriabine, A. (1969) Some observations on the adrenergic blocking activity of desipramine and amitriptyline on aortic strips of rabbits. Experientia 25, 164–165.

Snyder, S. H. and Yamamura, H. I. (1977) Antidepressants and the muscarinic acetylcholine receptor. Arch. Gen. Psychiatry 34, 236–239.

Spiker, D. G., Weiss, A. N., Chang, S. S., Ruwitch, J. F. and Biggs, J. T. (1975) Tricyclic antidepressant overdose: clinical presentation and plasma levels. Clin. Pharmacol. Ther. 18, 539–546.

Spyraki, C. and Fibiger, H. C. (1980) Functional evidence for subsensitivity of noradrenergic α_2-receptors after chronic desipramine treatment. Life Sci. 27, 1863–1867.

Starke, K. (1977) Regulation of noradrenaline released by presynaptic receptor systems. Rev. Physiol. Biochem. Pharmacol. 77, 1–124.

Sulser, F. (1979) New perspectives on the mode of action of antidepressant drugs. Trends Pharmacol. Sci. 1, 92–94.

Svensson, T. H. and Usdin, E. (1978) Feedback inhibition of brain noradrenaline neurons by tricyclic antidepressants: α-receptor mediation. Science, N. Y. 202, 1089–1091.

Szabadi, E., Gaszner, P. and Bradshaw, C. M. (1980) The peripheral anticholinergic activity of tricyclic antidepressants: comparison of amitriptyline and desipramine in human volunteers. Br. J. Psychiatry 137, 433–439.

Tang, S. W. and Seeman, P. (1980) Effect of antidepressant drugs on serotonergic and adrenergic receptors. Naunyn-Schmiedeberg's Arch. Pharmacol. 311, 255–261.

Tang, S. W., Helmeste, D. M. and Stancer, H. C. (1979) Interaction of antidepressants with clonidine on rat brain total 3-methoxy-4-hydroxy-phenylglycol. Can. J. Physiol. Pharmacol. 57, 435–437.

Taylor, J. E. and Richelson, E. (1980) High affinity binding of tricyclic antidepressants to histamine H_1-receptors: fact and artifact. Eur. J. Pharmacol. 67, 41–46.

Thayssen, P., Bjerre, M., Kragh-Sørensen, P., Møller, M., Petersen, O. L., Bruun Kristensen, C. and Gram, L. F. (1981) Cardiovascular effects of imipramine and nortriptyline in elderly patients. Psychopharmacology 74, 360–364.

Tran, V. T., Lebkovitz, R., Toll, L. and Snyder, S. H. (1981) ^{3}H-doxepin interactions with histamine H_1-receptors and other sites in guinea pig and rat brain homogenates. Eur. J. Pharmacol. 70, 501–509.

U'Prichard, D. C., Greenberg, D. A. Sheenhan, P. P. and Snyder, S. H. (1978) Tricyclic antidepressants: therapeutic properties and affinity for α-adrenergic receptor binding sites in the brain. Science, N. Y. 199, 197–198.

Vetulani, J., Stawarz, R. J., Dingell, J. V. and Sulser, F. (1976) A possible common mechanism of action of antidepressant treatments. Naunyn-Schmiedeberg's Arch. Pharmacol. 293, 109–114.

Von Zeersen, D. and Cording-Tömmel, C. (1981) Is mianserin a potent antidepressant? Paper presented at 3rd World Congress of Biological Psychiatry, Stockholm, Abstract F 534.

Weinshilboum, R. M. (1980) Antihypertensive drugs that alter adrenergic function. Mayo Clin. Proc. 55, 390–402.

Wolfe, B. B., Harden, T. K., Sporn, J. R. and Molinoff, P. B. (1978) Presynaptic modulation of β-adrenergic receptors in rat cerebral cortex after treatment with antidepressants. J. Pharmacol. Exp. Ther. 207, 446–457.

Zavadil, A. P., Ross, R., Blombery, P., Calil, H., Potter, W. and Kopin, I. (1980) Influence of acute and chronic desipramine on blood pressure, pulse, plasma norepinephrine and its deaminated metabolites. Paper presented at the World Conference on Clinical Pharmacology and Therapeutics, London, Abstract 0829.

Zis, A. P. and Goodwin, F. K. (1979) Novel antidepressants and the biogenic amine hypothesis of depression. Arch. Gen. Psychiatry 36, 1097–1107.

Chapter 8

Prediction of steady-state plasma concentrations and individual dosage requirements of tricyclic antidepressants from a single test dose

R. A. BRAITHWAITE

The Regional Laboratory for Toxicology, Dudley Road Hospital, Birmingham, U.K.

and

S. DAWLING

Poisons Unit, Guy's Hospital, London, U.K.

INTRODUCTION

Despite the enormous increase in attention paid to pharmacokinetic theory over the last decade, this science has found very little direct application to the treatment of patients. This is particularly true when one considers the use of drugs in psychiatry. This chapter describes recent investigations which suggest a useful role of pharmacokinetic studies to predict optimum dosage regimes of tricyclic antidepressants early in treatment. This approach has already been successful in the treatment of manic-depressive disorders with lithium (Cooper et al., 1973; Cooper and Simpson 1976). These workers demonstrated that it was possible to make an accurate prediction of individual dosage requirements from a single blood sample collected 24 hours after the ingestion of a single dose of the drug.

Many studies have shown that patients receiving the same daily dose of tricyclic antidepressant display extremely large interindividual differences in steady-state plasma drug

98

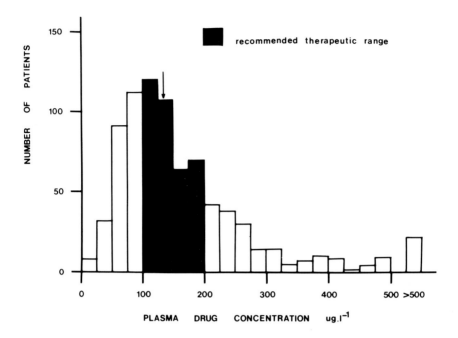

Fig. 1. Plasma amitriptyline plus nortriptyline concentrations in 1,574 patients receiving routine treatment with different daily doses of amitriptyline. The median plasma drug concentration (135 μg/l) is indicated by the vertical arrow.

concentrations (Hammer and Sjöqvist, 1967; Moody et al., 1967. Sjöqvist et al., 1969; Mellström and Tybring, 1977; Braithwaite et al., 1978; Braithwaite, 1980). Figure 1 shows the observed distribution of plasma amitriptyline plus nortriptyline concentrations in a large group (n = 1574) of depressed patients receiving routine treatment with various daily doses of amitriptyline. This variation in plasma drug concentrations is large compared with the suggested therapeutic range (Braithwaite, 1980). Moreover, following treatment with tricyclic antidepressants, the clinical end point is often slow to develop and difficult to measure.

Assessment of clinical response is further complicated by the difficulty in distinguishing between symptoms of depression and those of apparent drug side effects. Variability in plasma drug concentrations appears to be genetically determined and stems mainly from individual differences in rates of drug metabolism, but may also be modified by factors such as age, concurrent disease states and concomitant medication (Alexanderson et al., 1969; Dawling et al., 1980a). One other major factor, often overlooked, is the extent to which patients take the drugs which they are prescribed. The situation in general medical practice, where most of the prescriptions for these drugs are written, appears to be particularly unsatisfactory, and studies have shown that as many as 50% of patients given 'therapeutic' doses of antidepressants may have stopped taking them within a few weeks of their first being prescribed (Johnson, 1974). On any standard dosage regime, a sizeable proportion of patients will have plasma antidepressant levels which are known to

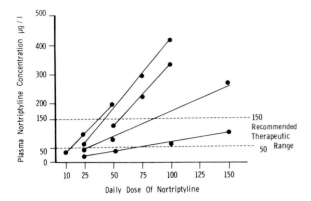

Fig. 2. Mean steady-state plasma nortriptyline (NT) concentrations observed in five patients who received different daily doses of nortriptyline during treatment.

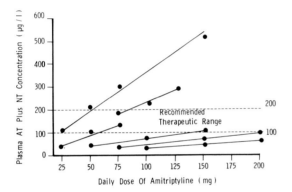

Fig. 3. Mean steady-state plasma amitriptyline (AT) plus nortriptyline (NT) concentrations observed in six patients who received different daily doses of amitriptyline during treatment.

be associated with either a poor therapeutic outcome or an increased incidence of objective side effects.

For these various reasons the arbitrary selection of antidepressant dosage regimes can be a very unreliable guide to plasma drug concentrations achieved during therapy. Furthermore, it has been suggested that both a greater proportion of patients would respond to treatment and the likelihood of toxicity be reduced if drug dosages were adjusted in the light of plasma antidepressant concentrations. This is illustrated in Figures 2 and 3 which show the steady-state plasma concentrations of nortriptyline (Fig. 2) and amitriptyline plus nortriptyline (Fig. 3) observed in patients given three or more different daily doses of nortriptyline and amitriptyline respectively. Although the relationship between dose and plasma drug concentration is linear within an individual patient, and kinetic information obtained at one dose can be directly applied to another, several dosage adjustments may be required in order to achieve optimum drug levels. As shown in Figures 2 and 3, these adjustments in dosage can vary considerably between individuals. Moreover, in some patients, particularly the elderly, plasma antidepressant half-lives in excess of 70 hours have been observed (Dawling et al., 1980a) and true steady-state concentrations may not be reached without a long delay, sometimes as long as 2–3 weeks. There will, therefore, be the risk of patients being exposed to excessively high plasma drug concentrations for some considerable time, which may even prevent natural recovery from the illness (Kragh-Sørensen et al., 1976; Montgomery et al., 1978).

One way in which therapy with these drugs might be improved would be to individualise drug dosage regimes at the onset of treatment. Recent evidence shows that this can be easily achieved using pharmacokinetic data obtained following administration of a single test dose of the drug to be used in treatment.

PHARMACOKINETICS OF PREDICTION

Following administration of a single oral dose (Ds) the total area under the plasma drug concentration versus time curve (AUC_∞) may be described by the equation (Alexanderson, 1972a):

$$AUC_\infty = \frac{F \cdot Ds}{Vd \cdot Kel} \qquad \text{Equation 1}$$

Where F is the fraction of each dose systemically available; Vd the distribution volume and Kel, the elimination rate constant for the removal of drug from plasma.

Following repeated administration plasma drug concentrations will rise until a plateau or steady-state concentration is reached. This is usually achieved by 4–5 times the drug elimination half-life. Using the model described by Wagner et al. (1965) and Alexanderson (1972a,b) the mean steady-state plasma concentration ($\bar{C}ss$) may be described by the equation:

$$\bar{C}ss = \frac{F \cdot Dm}{Vd \cdot Kel \cdot \Delta t} \qquad \text{Equation 2}$$

Where Dm is the maintenance dose and Δt the dosage interval.

By rearranging equations 1 and 2, the following equation is obtained:

$$\bar{C}ss = \frac{AUC_\infty \cdot Dm}{\Delta t \cdot Ds} \qquad \text{Equation 3}$$

Theoretically, therefore, the mean steady-state concentration ($\bar{C}ss$) should be easily predicted from the measurement of the single dose AUC_∞ for any chosen maintenance dose (Dm). Conversely, Dm can also be chosen in order to produce any desired $\bar{C}ss$.

Equation 3 makes a number of assumptions. The most important of these are that the drug obeys a linear pharmacokinetic model and that there is no time dependent kinetic change. Most of these assumptions are valid in the case of the tricyclic antidepressants. In oder to calculate AUC_∞, serial blood samples (usually not less than 10) need to be taken following administration of the single dose. AUC_∞ may be calculated from the expression:

$$ACU_\infty = AUC_{0-t} + \frac{Ct}{\beta}$$

Where AUC_{0-t} represents the area under the plasma level time curve up to the point of the last blood sample (concentration Ct) which can be calculated by the Trapezoid rule. The residual area between time t and ∞ may be calculated from Ct/β, where β is the terminal elimination rate constant. An alternative to the calculation of AUC_{∞} is to determine the value of $AUC\beta$. This is the area under the β slope extrapolated between zero time (Coβ) and ∞. Alexanderson (1972a) first suggested that an individual dosage prediction could be made from several timed blood samples obtained on the drug's β elimination phase so as to calculate $AUC\beta$ instead of AUC_{∞}. He showed that, in a group of six healthy volunteers receiving single doses of nortriptyline AUC_{∞} and $AUC\beta$ were almost identical. This has the advantage that only 4–5 samples are required to describe $AUC\beta$.

In an investigation of our own, AUC_{∞} and $AUC\beta$ were compared in a group of 13 healthy volunteer subjects who received a 75 mg single oral dose of nortriptyline. There was found to be an excellent correlation between these two parameters (Fig. 4) although $AUC\beta$ was a significant overestimate of the value of AUC_{∞} (approximately 30%). In Alexanderson's study (1972a), a solution of nortriptyline was used, whereas in later studies of our own, tablets were used which may have been more slowly absorbed. More recently, using amitriptyline, a good agreement was found between AUC_{∞} and $AUC\beta$ following administration of 75 mg (tablets), to eight healthy volunteers (Fig. 5).

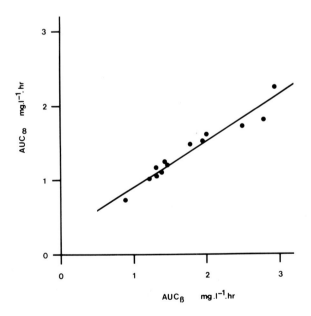

Fig. 4. Relationship between two methods of computation of plasma nortriptyline concentration versus time curve area following the administration of single oral doses of nortriptyline to 13 healthy volunteers. $AUC_{\infty} = 0.61 \, AUC\beta + 0.294$ mg · 1^{-1} · hr (r = 0.97).

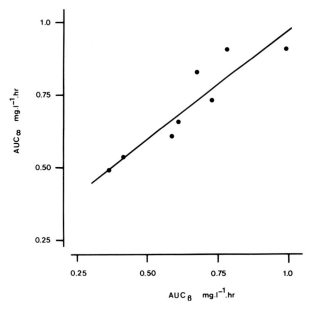

Fig. 5. Relationship between two methods of computation of plasma amitriptyline concentration versus time curve area following the administration of single oral dose of amitriptyline to eight healthy volunteers (AUC_∞ = 0.75 $AUC\beta$ + 0.226 mg · 1^{-1} · hr (r = 0.92).

PREDICTION OF STEADY-STATE PLASMA CONCENTRATIONS FROM PHARMA-COKINETIC DATA

The use of pharmacokinetics in the prediction of plasma antidepressant concentrations was first given serious consideration by Alexanderson (1972 a,b, 1973) in a series of elegant studies carried out in groups of healthy volunteers given single and repeated oral doses of nortriptyline and desipramine. He clearly demonstrated that it was possible to retrospectively predict steady-state plasma nortriptyline concentrations from $AUC\beta$ following administration of a single test dose (Alexanderson, 1973). This finding was later confirmed in a group of depressed patients by our own group (Braithwaite et al., 1978; Montgomery et al., 1978, 1979a). Patients received a single 100 mg oral dose prior to chronic treatment with a once nightly 100 mg dose. There was found to be a good correlation (r = 0.90) between observed mean steady-state plasma concentrations and those predicted from $AUC\beta$ (Fig. 6). However, observed levels were some 30% higher than those predicted, which may have been due to the use of a once nightly dosage regime and a sample time approximately 12 hours following the previous evening dose.

In contrast, a later study using a divided dosage regime showed a good agreement between observed and predicted levels (Dawling et al., 1980b). This latter study was the first prospective prediction study to be successfully carried out on patients. In this study, 16 depressed elderly hospital inpatients received a single oral dose of nortriptyline prior to commencing treatment with the drug. A series of five timed plasma nortriptyline measurements made after the single dose were used to calculate $AUC\beta$. This value was then used to predict from Equation 3 the daily dose required by each patient to achieve a steady-state plasma nortriptyline concentration within the recommended therapeutic range. Predicted optimum dosage regimes were between 20 and 90 mg per day (mean dose 43 mg/day). Using these dosage regimes the mean observed steady-state plasma nortriptyline concentration in each patient showed a highly significant correlation with the predicted value (r = 0.71, p < 0.002), there being no significant difference between

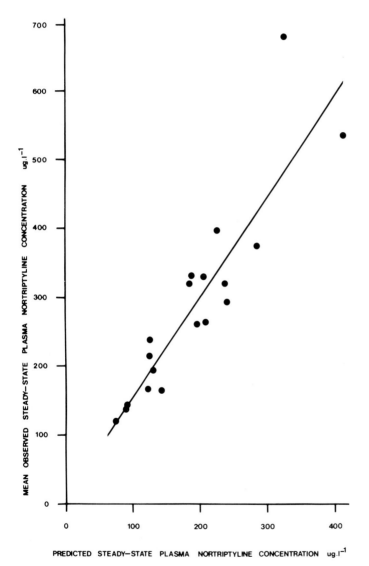

Fig. 6. Relationship between the predicted steady-state and the mean observed steady-state plasma nortriptyline concentration in 19 patients (y = 1.45 × + 10 μg · 1⁻¹; r = 0.90, p < 0.0001) treated with a fixed dose of 100 mg nocte.

observed and predicted values. All patients had steady-state plasma nortriptyline concentrations within or very close to the suggested therapeutic range of 50–150 μg/l (mean 106 μg/l, range 38–157 μg/l). If all patients had received a standard daily dose of 75 mg, over half would have had plasma concentrations above 150 μg/l and in two cases, in excess of 300 μg/l. Thus the possibility of toxic side effects was reduced.

Because of the need to obtain several carefully timed blood samples following administration of the test dose this method of prediction does not easily fit in with routine clinical practice and can only be applied to the treatment of patients in a research situation. Simpler prediction tests are required if this approach to treatment is to have a widespread application.

PREDICTION OF STEADY-STATE CONCENTRATIONS USING A SIMPLIFIED TOLERANCE TEST

Interestingly, Cooper et al. (1973) and Cooper and Simpson (1976) first reported the use of simple tolerance test to predict blood lithium concentrations and optimum dosage regimes. Use of this type of simple tolerance test in the selection of tricyclic antidepressant dosage requirements was first described for nortriptyline in retrospective studies carried out in both healthy volunteers (Cooper and Simpson, 1978) and depressed patients (Braithwaite et al., 1978; Montgomery et al., 1979a). These latter studies in patients demonstrated that it was possible to accurately predict steady-state plasma nortriptyline concentrations from a single blood sample taken 24, 48 or even 72 hours after a single oral test doese (Table 1). Moreover, use of a single timed blood sample was as reliable a predictor of steady-state plasma drug concentrations as were the methods using AUC_∞ or $AUC\beta$, and far superior to plasma half-life.

Similar studies have also been carried out on other tricyclic antidepressants such as desipramine and imipramine (Brunswick et al., 1979; Potter et al., 1980; Rudorpher and Young, 1980) and amitriptyline (Montgomery et al., 1979b, 1980). Because imipramine and amitriptyline are partially converted to their N-desmethyl metabolites, desipramine

TABLE 1

Relationship between steady-state plasma nortriptyline (NT) concentrations and single dose kinetic parameters in 19 depressed patients.[a]

y	x	r	t
Steady-state NT	Reciprocal clearance NT[b]	0.89	8.2[d]
Steady-state NT	Plasma half-life NT	0.65	3.5[c]
Steady-state NT	24 hour level NT	0.80	5.5[d]
Steady-state NT	48 hour level NT	0.97	15.2[d]
Steady-state NT	72 hour level NT	0.94	11.4[d]

[a] Adapted from Montgomery et al., 1979a.
[b] Nortriptyline clearance (clo) calculated from the expression clo = $\dfrac{\text{Dose}}{AUC\beta}$.
[c] $p < 0.005$; r = correlation coefficient.
[d] $p < 0.0001$; t = Student's t-test.

and nortriptyline respectively, the prediction of total effective steady-state plasma concentrations (parent drug plus metabolite) is more complex. Table 2 shows the retrospective correlations obtained between steady-state plasma concentrations of amitriptyline and nortriptyline and single dose kinetic parameters in a group of 18 depressed inpatients receiving treatment with amitriptyline carefully selected for good compliance (Montgomery et al., 1980). Although significant correlations were obtained between individual steady-state plasma amitriptyline and nortriptyline concentrations and respective single dose concentrations of amitriptyline and nortriptyline at 24 hours, a much better correlation was obtained between combined steady-state concentrations and combined single dose 24 hour concentrations (Fig. 7). This latter correlation was almost as good as that obtained between steady-state plasma amitriptyline levels and amitriptyline clearance (Table 2). There was no significant correlation between steady-state plasma amitriptyline concentrations and amitriptyline half-life. Recommended therapeutic ranges are based on the addition of plasma concentrations of parent drug and demethylated metabolite (Glassman et al., 1977; Montgomery et al., 1979c) therefore, a simple prediction test based on a total plasma antidepressant concentration is attractive.

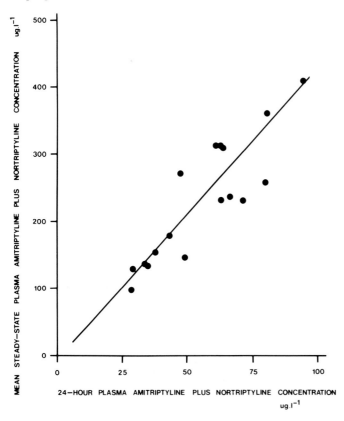

Fig. 7. Relationship between the single oral dose 24 hour plasma amitriptyline plus nortriptyline concentration combined and the mean steady-state plasma concentration of amitriptyline plus nortriptyline in 17 patients (r = 0.88, p < 0.0001).

In the most recent prospective study to be carried out, Dawling et al. (1981) have used a simple nortriptyline tolerance test to successfully predict individual dosage requirements in a group of 10 depressed elderly hospital inpatients. Each patient received a single 50 mg test dose of nortriptyline and blood was taken for measurement of plasma nortriptyline concentration 24 hours later. Using a newly constructed nomogram (Table 3) individual nortriptyline dosages were predicted from the 24 hour plasma nortriptyline value. The predicted dosages ranged between 20 and 100 mg daily (mean 50 mg/day). Observed plasma nortriptyline concentrations were between 76 and 180 μg/l (mean 104 S.D. 30 μg/l) with only one patient outside the recommended therapeutic range (50–150 μg/l).

Other studies are now in progress to extend these findings to the treatment of larger numbers of patients receiving antidepressant therapy with both amitriptyline and nortriptyline. However, it may be possible to extrapolate predictions made on one drug to treatment with a similar drug in the same individual. Studies have shown that there is a good correlation between the rate of metabolism of desipramine and nortriptyline in the same

TABLE 2

Relationship between steady-state plasma concentrations of amitriptyline (AT) and nortriptyline (NT) and single dose kinetic parameters in 18 depressed patients.

y	x	r	t
Steady-state AT	Reciprocal clearance AT[a]	0.90	8.1[c]
Steady-state AT	Plasma half-life AT	0.28	1.2
Steady-state AT	24 hour level AT	0.80	5.4[c]
Steady-state NT	24 hour level NT	0.69	3.7[b]
Steady-state AT + NT	24 hour level AT + NT	0.88	7.1[c]

[a] Amitriptyline clearance (clo) calculated from the expression $clo = \dfrac{Dose}{AUC\beta}$.
[b] $p < 0.005$; r = correlation coefficient.
[c] $p < 0.001$; t = Student's t-test.

TABLE 3

Nomogram for nortriptyline dosage prediction following 50 mg test dose (taken from Dawling et al., 1981).

24 Hr NT concentration (μg/l)	Daily dose (mg)
$\leqslant$10	200
11–13	150
14–18	100
19–22	75
23–31	50
32–37	40
38–50	30
51–75	20
$\geqslant$76	10

individual (Alexanderson, 1972b), similarly between amitriptyline and clomipramine (Mellström et al., 1979). Thus, where similar metabolic reactions are involved, e.g. demethylation or hydroxylation, similar rates of elimination may be expected. More recently, work by Bertilsson et al. (1980) has shown that there is a good correlation between an individual's ability to hydroxylate debrisoquine, an antihypertensive drug, and the clearance of nortriptyline, indicating that both benzylic hydroxylations are controlled by adjacent if not identical genes. Information on an individual's ability to hydroxylate debrisoquine is easily obtained from the ratio of 4-hydroxy debrisoquine to parent drug in urine following administration of a single oral dose.

CONCLUSIONS

It would now seem feasible to apply simple pharmacokinetic prediction tests to the determination of optimum dosage regimes of tricyclic antidepressants and possibly other drugs. However, before such tests can be put into wider use a number of requirements must be met (Table 4). Nevertheless, a simplified pharmacokinetic tolerance tests fits in easily with routine clinical practice and takes only a short time to perform. A patient is given a small test dose of drug at which time a baseline blood sample may be taken. The patient is asked to return to the clinic at the same time the following day, for a second blood sample. The plasma antidepressant concentration measurement is then used to select an appropriate dosage regime. Patients can start treatment with a low standard dose which can be changed to the predicted optimum dose as soon as the test result is available (usually within a few days).

The clinical advantages of such a test are:

1) Ensure that an appropriate starting dosage is prescribed.
2) Reduce the number of dosage alterations.
3) Reduce the risk of toxicity.
4) Check on patient compliance when used in combination with therapeutic monitoring.
5) Improve the likelihood of a satisfactory response.

At the present time the availability of such prediction tests is limited because of the scar-

TABLE 4

Requirements for a simple prediction test.

1)	A rapid and reliable analytical method
2)	The drug obeys a simple and linear pharmacokinetic model
3)	There is no time dependent pharmacokinetic change, e.g. the drug does not stimulate its own metabolism
4)	Absorption is rapid and complete
5)	The drug elimination half-life is not extremely long
6)	Existence of an established therapeutic range
7)	Clinical response is difficult to judge or slow to appear
8)	The ratio of therapeutic to toxic concentrations (the therapeutic index) is low compared to the interindividual variability in concentrations obtained on a standard dosage regime

city of laboratories offering facilities for the measurement of plasma antidepressant concentrations. However, with recent developments in radio- and enzyme-immunoassay techniques, it should be possible in the forseeable future to use such a single dose test procedure routinely for the selection of individual initial dosages.

ACKNOWLEDGEMENT

We would like to thank Mrs. G. Cartwright for her kind help and attention in the preparation of this paper.

REFERENCES

Alexanderson, B. (1972a) Pharmacokinetics of nortriptyline in man after single and multiple oral doses: the predictability of steady-state plasma concentrations from single-dose plasma level data. Eur. J. Clin. Pharmacol. 4, 82–91.

Alexanderson, B. (1972b) Pharmacokinetics of desmethylimipramine and nortriptyline in man after single and multiple oral doses – a cross over study. Eur. J. Clin. Pharmacol. 5, 1–10.

Alexanderson, B. (1973) Prediction of steady-state plasma levels of nortriptyline from single oral dose kinetics: a study in twins. Eur. J. Clin. Pharmacol. 6, 44–53.

Alexanderson, B., Price-Evans, D. A. and Sjöqvist, F. (1969) Steady-state plasma levels of nortriptyline in twins – influence of genetic factors and drug therapy. Br. Med. J. 4, 764–768.

Bertilsson, L., Eichelbaum, M., Mellström, B., Säwe, J., Schulz, H-U. and Sjöqvist, F. (1980) Nortriptyline and antipyrene clearance in relation to debrisoquine hydroxylation in man. Life Sci. 27, 1673–1677.

Braithwaite, R. A. (1980) The role of plasma level monitoring of tricyclic antidepressant drugs as an aid to treatment. In: Drug Concentrations in Neuropsychiatry. Ciba Foundation Symposium 74. Excerpta Medica, Elsevier/North-Holland, Amsterdam, pp. 167–197.

Braithwaite, R. A., Montgomery, S. and Dawling, S. (1978) Nortriptyline in depressed patients with high plasma levels. Clin. Pharmacol. Ther. 23, 303–308.

Brunswick, D. J., Amsterdam, J. D., Mendels, J. and Stern, S. L. (1979) Prediction of steady-state imipramine and desmethylimipramine plasma concentrations from single dose data. Clin. Pharmacol. Ther. 25, 605–610.

Cooper, T. B. and Simpson, G. M. (1976) The 24 hour lithium level as a prognosticator of dosage requirements: a 2 year follow-up study. Am. J. Psychiatry 133, 440–443.

Cooper, T. B. and Simpson, G. M. (1978) Prediction of individual dosage of nortriptyline. Am. J. Psychiatry 135, 333–335.

Cooper, T. B., Bergner, P-E. E. and Simpson, G. M. (1973) The 24 hour serum lithium level as a prognosticator of dosage requirements. Am. J. Psychiatry 130, 601–603.

Dawling, S., Crome, P. and Braithwaite, R. A. (1980a) Pharmacokinetics of single oral doses of nortriptyline in depressed elderly hospital patients and young healthy volunteers. Clin. Pharmacokin. 5, 394–401.

Dawling, S., Crome, P., Braithwaite, R. A. and Lewis, R. R. (1980b) Nortriptyline therapy in elderly patients: dosage prediction after single dose pharmacokinetic study. Eur. J. Clin. Pharmacol. 18, 147–150.

Dawling, S., Crome, P., Heyer, E. J. and Lewis, R. R. (1981) Nortriptyline therapy in elderly patients: dosage prediction from plasma concentration at 24 hours after a single 50 mg dose. Br. J. Psychiatry 139, 413–416.

Glassman, A. H., Perel, J. M., Shostak, M., Kantor, S. J. and Fleiss, J. L. (1977) Clinical implications of imipramine plasma levels for depressive illness. Arch. Gen. Psychiatry 34, 197–204.

Hammer, W. and Sjöqvist, F. (1967) Plasma levels of monomethylated tricyclic antidepressants during treatment with imipramine-like compounds. Life Sci. 6, 1895–1903.

Johnson, D. A. W. (1974) A study of the use of antidepressant medication in general practice. Br. J. Psychiatry 125, 186–192.

Kragh-Sørensen, P., Eggert-Hansen, C., Baastrup, P. C. and Hvidberg, E. F. (1976) Self inhibiting action of nortriptyline's antidepressive effect at high plasma levels. Psychopharmacologia (Berl.) 45, 305–312.

Mellström, B. and Tybring, G. (1977) Ion-pair liquid chromatography of steady-state plasma levels of clomipramine and desmethyl clomipramine. J. Chromatogr. 143, 597–605.

Mellström, B., Bertilsson, L., Träskman, L., Rollins, D., Åsberg, M. and Sjöqvist, F. (1979) Individual similarity in the metabolism of amitriptyline and clomipramine in depressed patients. Pharmacology 19, 282–287.

Montgomery, S., Braithwaite, R. A., Dawling, S. and McAuley, S. (1978) High plasma nortriptyline levels in the treatment of depression. Clin. Pharmacol. Ther. 23, 309–314.

Montgomery, S. A., McAuley, R. Montgomery, D. B., Braithwaite, R. A. and Dawling, S. (1979a) Dosage adjustment from simple nortriptyline spot level predictor tests in depressed patients. Clin. Pharmacokin. 4, 129–136.

Montgomery, S. A., McAuley, R., Rani, S. J., Roy, D., Montgomery, D. B., Dawling, S. and Braithwaite, R. A. (1979b) High levels of amitriptyline and clinical response. In: J. Obiols, C. Ballus, E. G. Monclus and J. Pujol (Eds), Biological Psychiatry Today. Elsevier/North-Holland, Amsterdam, pp. 980–984.

Montgomery, S., McAuley, R., Rani, S. J., Montgomery, D. B., Braithwaite, R. A. and Dawling, S. (1979c) Amitriptyline plasma concentrations and clinical response. Br. Med. J. 1, 230–231.

Montgomery, S., McAuley, R., Montgomery, D. B., Dawling, S. and Braithwaite, R. A. (1980) Pharmacokinetic efficacy of maprotiline and amitriptyline in endogenous depression: a double blind controlled trial. Clin. Therap. 3, 292–310.

Moody, J. P., Tait, A. C. and Todrick, A. (1967) Plasma levels of imipramine and desmethylimipramine during therapy. Br. J. Psychiatry 113, 183–193.

Potter, W. Z., Zavadil, A. P., Kopin, I. J. and Goodwin, F. K. (1980) Single dose kinetics predicts steady-state concentrations of imipramine and desipramine. Arch. Gen. Psychiatry 37, 314–320.

Rudorpher, M. V. and Young, R. C. (1980) Plasma desipramine levels after single dosage and at steady-state in outpatients. Commun. Psychopharmacol. 4, 185–188.

Sjöqvist, F., Hammer, W., Borgå, O. and Azarnoff, D. L. (1969) Pharmacological significance of plasma levels of monomethylated tricyclic antidepressants. Excerpta Med. Int. Congr. Ser. 180, 128–136.

Wagner, J. G., Northam, J. I., Alway, C. D. and Carpenter, O. S. (1965) Blood levels of drug at equilibrium state after multiple dosing. Nature 207, 1301–1302.

Chapter 9

Plasma concentrations of antidepressant drugs and clinical response

TREVOR R. NORMAN

and

GRAHAM D. BURROWS

Department of Psychiatry, University of Melbourne, Parkville, 3052, Victoria, Australia

INTRODUCTION

The introduction of the tricyclic antidepressants in the 1950s provided an effective means of pharmacotherapy for depressive disorders. Based on the imipramine prototype a number of other tricyclic antidepressants followed. Recent developments have seen the modification of the tricyclic nucleus to give mono-, bi- and tetra-cyclic antidepressants and some drugs, e.g. trazodone, which are structurally unrelated to the tricyclics. These drugs share the common property of effective clinical antidepressant action in 70–80% of treated patients.

Recognition of the failure of some patients to respond to adequate doses of drugs, for an appropriate length of treatment, prompted the suggestion that plasma monitoring may improve therapeutic outcome (Brodie, 1967). This would occur by identifying the range of drug concentrations within which the best clinical effect is observed. Such an approach had proven useful in anticonvulsant therapy for example. A brief review of the attempts to provide therapeutic ranges for the antidepressants is presented.

MEASUREMENT OF ANTIDEPRESSANT DRUGS

An essential element in the assessment of pharmacokinetics and plasma level-response relationships is the assay methodology. Detailed reviews of the methods for tricyclic antidepressant assay have been published (see Chapter 6 in this volume; Gupta and Molnar, 1979; Scoggins et al., 1980b; Scoggins and Maguire, 1981). In practical terms the issues of importance are not what methodology is used for an assay, but the accuracy, specificity and precision. Specificity implies that the drug of interest can be detected by the method, free of any interferences by other drugs or metabolites which may be present in the biological fluid of interest, usually blood, plasma or serum. This issue is important for the tricyclic antidepressants since they are extensively metabolised and some of the metabolites are pharmacologically active (Gram, 1974). Precision is a measure of the variation between repeated determinations of the sample, and is most often expressed as the coefficient of variation ($CV\% = \dfrac{\text{Standard Deviation}}{\text{Mean}} \times 100\%$). In a reliable assay this should be low as possible, but less than 10% is generally regarded as acceptable. Most analytical methods display poorer precision at low concentrations than at high concentrations. This is true of gas-liquid chromatography (GLC) and high pressure liquid chromatography (HPLC), but for radioimmunoassay (RIA) the opposite is true. Accuracy should not be confused with precision. Accuracy is the degree to which the determined result agrees with the true value. It is quite possible for an assay to demonstrate excellent precision and poor accuracy. The use of an appropriate quality control scheme within the laboratory or inter-laboratory comparisons should ensure assay accuracy.

For most laboratories, GLC or HPLC assays for the tricyclic antidepressants are available, or could be readily implemented. Both of these techniques are specific, precise and have sufficient sensitivity for the determination of steady-state antidepressant levels. Radioimmunoassays are sensitive and precise but often lack the specificity of a separative technique like GLC. This type of assay would be useful in situations where an approximate plasma concentration is required rapidly, e.g. suspected noncompliance or toxicity. Gas chromatography-mass spectrometry (GC-MS) is available in some laboratories but this very sensitive technique is usually not required for routine monitoring. Other methods such as spectrophotometry, thin-layer chromatography, fluorimetry often lack specificity or are not sensitive enough to quantitate antidepressant concentrations at a sufficient level of precision. There are exceptions, e.g. the combination of thin-layer chromatography and scanning spectrodensitometry which has been used successfully in some clinical studies (Gram et al., 1976).

PHARMACOKINETICS OF ANTIDEPRESSANTS

Some common features of the kinetics of antidepressant drugs have been described by several authors (Braithwaite, 1980; Gram, 1981; Norman et al., 1981a). The drugs are extensively bound to protein and demonstrate a large apparent volume of distribution. Kinetic parameters, particularly elimination half-life, show a wide interindividual variation resulting in large differences in steady-state plasma levels between individuals on the same dose. The drugs are efficiently and almost completely eliminated by metabolism in the liver with a high 'first pass' clearance rate.

Peak plasma concentrations of the drugs are usually seen 2–6 hours after single oral doses (Alexanderson, 1972; Gram and Christiansen, 1975; Nagy and Johansson, 1975). Peaks of plasma concentration are also observed during multiple oral dosing within the same time period, but drug concentrations continue to rise until steady state is achieved (Gram et al., 1977). The absorption of the tricyclics varies markedly depending on the route of drug administration and drug formulation. Absorption of nortriptyline and desipramine was incomplete after single intramuscular injection (Alexanderson et al., 1973; Nagy and Johansson, 1975). Food may also affect the bio-availability of antidepressants (Nakano and Hollister, 1978).

Between 30 and 70% of an oral dose of a tricyclic may be extracted and eliminated from the body by metabolism in the liver (Gram, 1974). This high extraction ratio partly accounts for the low plasma concentrations observed after single oral doses compared with intravenous doses (Gram and Christiansen, 1975; Gram and Fredricson-Overø, 1975). Despite the efficient hepatic elimination ratio, the rate constant of elimination is small and the half-life of elimination long, since very little drug is available in the blood. Very little of the total dose of a tricyclic is eliminated unchanged via the kidneys. The major metabolic pathways of the tricyclics are demethylation, hydroxylation and glucuronide coupling, N-oxidation and dealkylation (Gram, 1974). These pathways are illustrated for imipramine in Chap. 5, p. 59. Some differences between tricyclics are observed, but these are usually related to differences in the appearance of minor metabolites. It has recently been shown that some of these metabolites are pharmacologically active at least in animal and platelet models (Potter et al., 1979; Norman et al., 1981b, Fulton et al., 1982).

A high degree of protein binding has been observed for most tricyclics studied. Generally, the results obtained by ultrafiltration, equilibrium dialysis or the simultaneous measurement of plasma and cerebrospinal fluid concentrations, have consistently shown binding to be more than 80% in healthy adults. Tertiary amines are more highly bound than their corresponding secondary amines (Borga et al., 1969). Interindividual variation in the percent free fraction has been found to be 2–3-fold with a close to normal distribution (Alexanderson and Borga, 1972; Glassman et al., 1973). Tricyclics bind to albumin, lipoproteins and α-acid-glycoprotein (Piafsky and Borga, 1977). Small variations in the degree of protein binding can markedly alter pharmacokinetic parameters, especially the volume of distribution.

FACTORS INFLUENCING TRICYCLIC CONCENTRATIONS

Interindividual variation in the pharmacokinetics and steady-state concentrations of tricyclics is well recognized. Among the factors identified as a probable cause of the variation is genetic variability. Alexanderson (1972, 1973) showed that both half-life of elimination and apparent volume of distribution, following administration of single oral doses of nortriptyline to mono and dizygotic twins, were genetically determined.

Age-related differences in tricyclic antidepressant kinetics have been reported for some drugs (Nies et al., 1977; Ziegler and Biggs, 1977; Henry et al., 1981). No alteration of nortriptyline or desipramine kinetics with age has been observed in other studies (Turbott et al., 1980; Cutler et al., 1981). Steady-state concentrations of nortriptyline are not influenced by age (Norman et al., 1979), while imipramine, amitriptyline and desipramine steady-state concentrations are (Gram et al., 1977; Nies et al., 1977), but this is disputed (Cutler et al., 1981). Clearly, the effects of age on antidepressant pharmacokinetics, steady-state plasma concentrations and clinical response require further investigation.

The influence of co-administered drugs on the steady-state plasma concentrations of tricyclic antidepressants has been investigated for several drugs. Barbiturates lower tricyclic concentrations, probably through stimulation of hepatic microsomal enzyme systems (Alexanderson et al., 1969; Burrows and Davies, 1971; Moody et al., 1977). Several antipsychotic drugs may inhibit the metabolism of the tricyclics, causing steady-state levels of the tricyclic to rise (Gram and Fredricson-Overø, 1972; Gram, et al., 1974a). Most benzodiazepines have no influence on the kinetics of tricyclics (Silverman and Braithwaite, 1973; Gram, et al., 1974b). Preliminary investigations have shown that lorazepam lowers steady-state nortriptyline levels (Burrows et al., 1974). These drug interactions appear to have little clinical significance apart from the obvious alteration in pharmacokinetic parameters. The possibility of pharmacodynamic interactions has not been extensively investigated. Cigarette smoking has been shown to lower steady-state imipramine, desipramine, amitriptyline and nortriptyline plasma concentrations (Perel et al., 1976; Linnoila et al., 1981). In two other studies nortriptyline steady-state concentrations were not influenced by cigarette smoking (Norman et al., 1977; Zeigler and Biggs, 1977). Why such differences should exist is difficult to explain, but may be due to different definitions of smoking or to other variables involved. More studies in this area are required.

RELATIONSHIP BETWEEN PLASMA CONCENTRATION AND CLINICAL RESPONSE

Use has been made of the measurement of antidepressant plasma concentrations in the study of their relationship to clinical improvement. Given that many of the antidepressant drugs have been available for 15—20 years, relatively few studies (about 50 in all) have addressed themselves to this question. In the past this was due to the lack of reliable methods for drug assay, but, as discussed above and in Chapter 6, such assays are available.

The plasma concentration-clinical response issue for antidepressant drugs has been widely debated and reviewed (Burrows, 1977; Burrows et al., 1978; Risch et al., 1979a,b; Norman and Burrows, 1980; Scoggins et al., 1980b; Burrows and Norman, 1981). A summary of the types of relationships found for several drugs is presented in Table 1. A detailed critique of all of the studies is not presented here, rather, some individual examples are discussed and some conclusions drawn concerning the role of monitoring and interpreting plasma concentration data.

Nortriptyline was studied initially in plasma concentration-response relationships and immediately produced two studies with conflicting results. Åsberg et al. (1971) demonstrated a curvilinear relationship between plasma nortriptyline concentration and clinical response as measured by the Cronholm-Ottosson rating scale. These authors proposed a so-called 'therapeutic window' or range of nortriptyline concentrations of 50—140 μg/litre. Kragh-Sørensen et al. (1973, 1974, 1976) confirmed the curvilinear nature of the relationship, but modified the upper limit to 150 μg/litre. On the other hand, Burrows et al. (1972, 1974b, 1977a) were unable to demonstrate any simple correlation between plasma concentration and clinical response for the total group. For 12 patients, in whom plasma levels were alternately raised and lowered, Burrows et al. (1977a) were able to show a correlation for individuals. A number of subsequent studies have supported one or the other of these opposed views. More studies have corroborated a curvilinear than no simple relationship.

Demonstration of a curvilinear relationship for nortriptyline suggests that routine monitoring of plasma concentrations should be undertaken in patients receiving this drug. However, the meaning of a therapeutic range needs some consideration. For example, it is well recognized in psychiatry that the therapeutic range of plasma lithium concentrations is 0.5–1.2 mmol/litre. Above 1.5 mmol/litre toxic symptoms are often experienced. It is also clearly recognized that for some patients, lithium concentrations outside of the 'therapeutic window', at either end, are necessary to achieve satisfactory clinical response. Further, some individuals do not respond to lithium irrespective of plasma concentrations. The therapeutic range is then an initial goal, with any further adjustments of plasma concentration being dictated by the clinical response of the patient. The same may be said of nortriptyline plasma concentrations: some patients outside of the therapeutic range will be satisfactorily managed; some patients (up to 20%) will not respond to antidepressant therapy regardless of the plasma concentration. The upper therapeutic limit of nortriptyline is now regarded as 200 μg/litre. This is based on the findings of Burrows et al. (1977c) that cardiotoxicity is associated with nortriptyline concentrations above 200 μg/litre. Not all patients have conduction defects above this concentration and some patients with plasma concentrations below this figure will experience cardiac changes, i.e. 200 μg/litre should not be regarded as an absolute upper limit. In the majority of patients plasma monitoring is unnecessary since adjustment of dosages will be made on the basis of clinical response. Some specific indications for plasma monitoring are indicated below.

TABLE 1

Plasma concentration response relationships for antidepressant drugs.

Drug	Total no. of studies	Type of relationship			Selected references
		None	Curvilinear	Other	
Nortriptyline	12	4	7	1	Burrows et al. (1972); Asberg et al. (1971); Kragh-Sørensen et al. (1973).
Amitriptyline	11	3	3	5	Braithwaite et al. (1972); Zeigler et al. (1976); Coppen et al. (1978).
Imipramine	11	2	0	9	Ballinger et al. (1974); Glassman et al. (1977).
Maprotiline	4	4	0	0	Angst and Rothweiler (1973); Miller et al. (1977).
Protriptyline	2	0	2	0	Biggs et al. (1975); Whyte et al. (1976).
Clomipramine	2	2	0	0	Miller et al. (1977); Gringas et al. (1977).
Butriptyline	1	1	0	0	Burrows et al. (1977).
Viloxazine	2	2	0	0	Norman et al. (1980); Peet (1978).
Mianserin	2	1	1	0	Coppen et al. (1976); Montgomery et al. (1978).

For other antidepressant drugs the relationship between plasma concentrations and clinical response is as confused as the relationship for nortriptyline. Studies of imipramine have suggested a minimum of 45 μg/litre imipramine and 75 μg/litre desipramine to be necessary for recovery (Gram et al., 1976) with no upper limit detected. Other studies of imipramine have found no correlation (Ballinger et al., 1974) or negative correlations, i.e. suggesting a curvilinear relationship (Bhanji and Lader, 1977). For amitriptyline all of the above types of relationship have been found. Limited studies of maprotiline, protriptyline, butriptyline, doxepin, mianserin, clomipramine, nomifensine, dibenzepin, lofepramine, dothiepin and viloxazine have produced conflicting findings.

In all studies attempting to delineate plasma concentration-clinical response relationships for antidepressants, the data base is as yet small. Fewer than 500 patients have been included in the nortriptyline studies reported in the literature and even less for the other drugs studied. Between-study comparisons are difficult to make because of differing diagnosis, rating scales and criteria of response. Choice of the method of statistical analysis may also be important. For example, reanalysis of Asberg's 1971 data on 29 patients using the Spearman rank correlation gave $r_s = -0.014$, $P > 0.05$ for the association between plasma nortriptyline and amelioration score, i.e. no simple correlation is observed. Grouping the data by plasma concentration gives the curvilinear relationship. The only clear consensus on the plasma level-response issue is that some minimum drug concentration is necessary for response and that high plasma concentrations (probably 200–300 μg/litre) are best avoided because of associated toxicity. Routine monitoring is probably unnecessary in the majority of cases but is of practical utility as discussed below.

MONITORING ANTIDEPRESSANT PLASMA CONCENTRATIONS

Situations in which plasma monitoring is clinically useful have been discussed (Norman et al., 1982). Case of suspected noncompliance are the most obvious example of a use for plasma monitoring, which might act as an aid to patient compliance. Consistently low plasma concentrations would indicate noncompliance or rapid metabolism of the drug.

For all the antidepressant drugs, toxic symptoms (paralytic ileus, acute brain syndrome, delirium) occur at excessively high concentrations. Further, characteristic changes are observed in the electrocardiogram (prolongation of conduction time, nonspecific ST-T wave changes, atrioventricular block, tachycardia, broadening of the QRS width) at high plasma concentratons (Vohra and Burrows, 1974). For patients receiving high doses of tricyclics routine cardiographic monitoring is advisable. In patients with toxic signs a plasma concentration is indicated to confirm the association between high concentrations and symptomatology.

Other indications for plasma monitoring include the management of overdoses; where several drugs are prescribed concomitantly and drug interactions are suspected (see above); and in patients with physical illnesses, especially hepatic and renal disease, where dangerously high plasma levels may appear using recommended doses.

CONCLUSION

In general, it can be concluded that routine monitoring of tricyclic antidepressants is unnecessary in all patients. While there is some evidence for a therapeutic range of tricyclic concentrations, this is equivocal. In practical terms a range of 50–300 μg/litre may be a useful guide for most patients. As with the therapeutic range for lithium some patients outside of it, at either end, have alleviation of symptoms without significant side-effects. Valuable information, aiding clinical judgement, can be obtained from monitoring of tricyclic antidepressant plasma concentrations for the specific indications discussed. Plasma monitoring can never substitute for sound clinical judgement.

REFERENCES

Alexanderson, B. (1972) Pharmacokinetics of nortriptyline in man after single and multiple oral doses: the predictability of steady state concentrations from single dose plasma level data. Eur. J. Clin. Pharmacol. 4, 82–91.

Alexanderson, B. A. (1973) Prediction of steady-state plasma levels of nortriptyline from single oral dose kinetics: a study in twins. Eur. J. Clin. Pharmacol. 6, 44–53.

Alexanderson, B. A. and Borga, O. (1972) Interindividual differences in plasma protein binding of nortriptyline in man – a twin study. Eur. J. Clin. Pharmacol. 4, 196–200.

Alexanderson, B. A., Evans, D. A. P. and Sjöqvist, F. (1969) Steady state plasma levels of nortriptyline in twins: influence of genetic factors and drug therapy. Br. Med. J. 4, 764–768.

Alexanderson, B., Borga, O. and Alvan, G. (1973) The availability of orally administered nortriptyline. Eur. J. Clin. Pharmacol. 5, 181–185.

Angst, J. and Rothweiler, R. (1973) Blood levels and clinical effects of maprotiline (Ludiomil). In: Classification and Prediction of Outcome of Depression. Symposia Medica Hoechst 8. F. K. Schattauer Verlag, Stuttgart, pp. 237–244.

Åsberg, M., Cronholm, B., Sjöqvist, F. and Tuck, D. (1971) Relationship between plasma level and therapeutic effect of nortriptyline. Br. Med. J. 3, 331–334.

Ballinger, B. R., Presley, A., Reid, A. H. and Stevenson, I. H. (1974) The effects of hypnotics on imipramine treatment. Psychopharmacology 39, 267–274.

Bhanji, S. and Lader, M. H. (1977) The electroencephalographic and psychological effects of imipramine in depressed inpatients. Eur. J. Clin. Pharmacol. 12, 349–354.

Biggs, J. T. and Ziegler, V. E. (1977) Protriptyline plasma levels and antidepressant response. Clin. Pharmacol. Ther. 22, 269–273.

Borga, O., Azarnoff, D. L., Forshell, G. P. and Sjöqvist, F. (1969) Plasma protein binding of tricyclic antidepressants in man. Biochem. Pharmacol. 18, 2135–2143.

Braithwaite, R. A. (1980) The role of plasma level monitoring of tricyclic antidepressant drugs as an aid to treatment. In: Ciba Foundation Symposium 74, Drug Concentrations in Neuropsychiatry. Excerpta Medica, Amsterdam, pp. 167–197.

Braithwaite, R. A., Goulding, R., Theano, G., Bailey, J., and Coppen, A. (1972) Plasma concentration of amitriptyline and clinical response. Lancet 1, 1297–1300.

Brodie, B. B. (1967) Physicochemical and biochemical aspects of pharmacology. J. Am. Med. Assoc. 202, 600–609.

Burrows, G. D. (1977) Plasma levels of tricyclics, clinical response and drug interactions. In: G. D. Burrows (Ed), Handbook of Studies on Depression. Excerpta Medica, Amsterdam, pp. 173–194.

Burrows, G. D. and Davies, B. M. (1971) Antidepressants and barbiturates. Br. Med. J. 4, 113.

Burrows, G. D. and Norman, T. R. (1981) Tricyclic antidepressants: plasma levels and clinical response. In: G. D. Burrows and T. R. Norman (Eds), Psychotropic Drugs, Plasma Concentration and Clinical Response. Marcel Dekker, New York, pp. 169–204.

Burrows, G. D., Davies, B. M. and Scoggins, B. A. (1972) Plasma concentration of nortriptyline and clinical response in depressive illness. Lancet 2, 619–623.

Burrows, G. D., Davies, B. M. and Scoggins, B. A. (1974a) Plasma tricyclic levels and drug interactions. Presented at 9th Congress Collegium Internationale Neuropsychopharmacologium. Paris, July, 7–12.

118

Burrows, G. D., Scoggins, B. A., Turecek, L. R. and Davies, B. M. (1974b) Plasma nortriptyline and clinical response. Clin. Pharmacol. Ther. 16, 639–644.

Burrows, G. D., Maguire, K. P., Scoggins, B. A., Stevenson, J. and Davies, B. M. (1977a) Plasma nortriptyline and clinical response – a study using changing plasma levels. Psychol. Med. 7, 87–91.

Burrows, G. D., Norman, T. R., Maguire, K. P., Rubinstein, G., Scoggins, B. A. and Davies, B. M. (1977b) A new antidepressant butriptyline – plasma levels and clinical response. Med. J. Aust. 2, 604–606.

Burrows, G. D., Vohra, J., Dumovic, P., Maguire, K. P., Scoggins, B. A. and Davies, B. (1977c) Tricyclic antidepressant drugs and cardiac conduction. Prog. Neuro-Psychopharmacol. 1, 329–334.

Burrows, G. D., Davies, B., Norman, T. R., Maguire, K. P. and Scoggins, B. A. (1978) Should plasma level monitoring of tricyclic antidepressants be introduced in clinical practice? Commun. Psychopharmacol. 2, 393–408.

Coppen, A., Gupta, R., Montgomery, S., Ghose, K., Bailey, J., Burns, B., and de Ridder, J. J. (1976) Mianserin hydrochloride: a novel antidepressant. Br. J. Psychiatry 129, 342–345.

Coppen, A., Ghose, K., Montgomery, S. A., Rama Rao, V. A., Bailey, J., Christiansen, J., Mikkleson, P. L., van Praag, H. M., Van de Poel, F., Minsker, E. J., Kozulja, V. G., Matussek, N., Kungkunz, G. and Jorgensen, A. (1978) Amitriptyline plasma concentration and clinical effect, a World Health Organisation collaborative study. Lancet 1, 63–66.

Cutler, N. R., Zaradil, A. P., Eisdorfer, G., Ross, R. J., and Potter, W. Z. (1981) Concentrations of desipramine in elderly women. Am. J. Psychiatry 138, 1235–1237.

Fulton, A., Norman, T. R. and Burrows, G. D. (1982) Ligand binding and platelet uptake studies of loxapine, amoxapine and their 8-hydroxylated derivatives. J. Affect. Dis. 4, 113–119.

Glassman, A. H., Hurwic, J. and Perel, J. M. (1973) Plasma binding of imipramine and clinical outcome. Am. J. Psychiatry 130, 1367–1369.

Glassman, A. H., Perel, J. M., Shostak, M., Kantor, S. J. and Fleiss, J. L. (1977) Clinical implications of imipramine plasma levels for depressive illness. Arch. Gen. Psychiatry 34, 197–204.

Gram, L. F. (1974) Metabolism of tricyclic antidepressants. A review. Dan. Med. Bull. 21, 218–231.

Gram, L. F. (1981) Pharmacokinetics of tricyclic antidepressants. In: G. D. Burrows and T. R. Norman (Eds), Psychotropic Drugs, Plasma Concentration and Clinical Response. Marcel Dekker, New York, pp. 139–168.

Gram, L. F. and Christiansen, J. (1975) First-pass metabolism of imipramine in man. Clin. Pharmacol. Ther. 17, 555–563.

Gram, L. F. and Fredricson-Overø, K. (1972) Drug interaction: inhibitory effect of neuroleptics on metabolism of tricyclic antidepressants in man. Br. Med. J. 1, 463–465.

Gram, L. F. and Fredricson-Overø, K. (1975) First-pass metabolism of nortriptyline in man. Clin. Pharmacol. Ther. 18, 305–314.

Gram, L. F., Christiansen, J. and Fredricson-Overø, K. (1974a) Pharmacokinetic interaction between neuroleptics and tricyclic antidepressants in the rat. Acta Pharmacol. Toxicol. 35, 223–232.

Gram, L. F., Fredricson-Overø, K. and Kirk, L. (1974b) Influence of neuroleptics and benzodiazepines on metabolism of tricyclic antidepressants in man. Am. J. Psychiatry 131, 863–866.

Gram, L. F., Reisby, N., Ibsen, I., Nagy, A., Dencker, S. J., Bech, P., Petersen, G. O. and Christiansen, J. (1976) Plasma levels and antidepressive effect of imipramine. Clin. Pharmacol. Ther. 19, 318–324.

Gram, L. F., Sondergaard, I., Christiansen, J., Petersen, G. O., Bech, P., Reisby, N., Ibsen, I., Ortmann, J., Nagy, A., Dencker, S. J., Jacobsen, O. and Krautwald, O. (1977) Steady state kinetics of imipramine in patients. Psychopharmacology 54, 255–261.

Gringas, M., Luscombe, D. K., Jones, R. B., Beaumont, G., Seldrup, J. and John, V. (1977) A clinical trial of a 50 mg formulation of clomipramine (Anafranil) with steady-state plasma level measurements. J. Int. Med. Res. 5 (Suppl.), 119–124.

Gupta, R. and Molnar, G. (1979) Measurement of therapeutic concentrations of tricyclic antidepressants in serum. Drug. Metab. Rev. 9, 79–97.

Henry, J. F., Altamura, C., Gomeni, R., Henry, M. P., Forette, F. and Morselli, P. L. (1981) Pharmacokinetics of amitriptyline in the elderly. Int. J. Clin. Pharmacol. 19, 1–5.

Kragh-Sørensen, P., Äsberg, M. and Eggert-Hansen, C. (1973) Plasma nortriptyline levels in endogenous depression. Lancet 1, 113–115.

Kragh-Sørensen, P., Eggert-Hansen, C., Larsen, N., Naestoft, J. and Hvidberg, E. F. (1974) Long-term treatment of endogenous depression with nortriptyline with control of plasma levels. Psychol. Med. 4, 174–180.

Kragh-Sørensen, P., Hansen, C. E., Baastrup, P. C. and Hvidberg, E. F. (1976) Self inhibiting action of nortriptyline antidepressive effect at high plasma levels. Psychopharmacology 45, 305–312.

Linnoila, M., George, L., Guthrie, S. and Leventhal, B. (1981) Effect of alcohol consumption and cigarette smoking on antidepressant levels of depressed patients. Am. J. Psychiatry 138, 841–842.

Maguire, K. P., Norman, T. R., McIntyre, I., Burrows, G. D. and Davies, B. (1982) Blood and plasma concentrations of dothiepin and its major metabolites and clinical response. J. Affect. Dis. 4, 41–48.

McIntyre, I. M., Burrows, G. D., Norman, T. E., Dumovic, P. and Vohra, J. (1980) Plasma nomifensine concentrations: cardiological effects and clinical response. Int. Pharmacopsychiatry 15, 325–333.

Mendlewicz, J., Linkowski, P. and Rees, J. A. (1980) A double blind comparison of dothiepin and amitriptyline in patients with primary affective disorder: serum levels and clinical response. Br. J. Psychiatry 136, 154–160.

Miller, P., Beaumont, G., Seldrup, J., John, V., Luscombe, D. K., and Jones, R. (1977a) Efficacy, side effects, plasma and blood levels of maprotiline (Ludiomil). J. Int. Med. Res. 5 (Suppl. 4), 101–111.

Miller, P., Luscombe, D. K., Jones, R. B., Seldrup, J., Beaumont, G. and John, V. (1977b) Relationships between clinical response, plasma levels and side effects of clomipramine (Anafranil) in general practitioner trials. J. Int. Med. Res. 5 (Suppl. 1), 108–118.

Modestin, J. (1973) The relationship between the clinical effects of dibenzepin (Noveril) and its plasma concentration. Pharmakopsychiatry 6, 28–38.

Montgomery, S., McAuley, R. and Montgomery, D. B. (1978) Relationship between mianserin plasma levels and antidepressant effect in a double-blind trial comparing a single night-time and divided daily dose regimens. Br. J. Clin. Pharmacol. 5, 71S–76S.

Moody, J. P., Whyte, S. F., MacDonald, A. J. and Naylor, G. J. (1977) Pharmacokinetic aspects of protriptyline plasma levels. Eur. J. Clin. Pharmacol. 11, 51–56.

Nagy, A. and Johansson, R. (1975) Plasma levels of imipramine and desipramine in man after different routes of administration. Naunyn-Schmiedeberg's Arch. Pharmacol. 290, 145–160.

Nakano, S. and Hollister, L. E. (1978) No circadian effect on nortriptyline kinetics in man. Clin. Pharmacol. Ther. 23, 199–203.

Nies, A., Robinson, D. S., Friedman, M. J., Green, R., Cooper, T. B., Ravaris, C. L. and Ives, J. O. (1977) Relationship between age and tricyclic antidepressant plasma levels. Am. J. Psychiatry 134, 790–793.

Norman, T. R. and Burrows, G. D. (1980) Plasma levels of psychotropic drugs and clinical response. In: G. D. Burrows and J. Werry (Eds), Advances in Human Psychopharmacology, Vol. 1. JAI Press, Connecticut, pp. 103–140.

Norman, T. R., Burrows, G. D., Maguire, K. P., Rubinstein, G., Scoggins, B. A. and Davies, B. M. (1977) Cigarette smoking and plasma nortriptyline levels. Clin. Pharmacol. Ther. 21, 453–456.

Norman, T. R., Burrows, G. D., Scoggins, B. A. and Davies, B. M. (1979) Pharmacokinetics and plasma levels of antidepressants in the elderly. Med. J. Aust. 1, 273–274.

Norman, T. R., Burrows, G. D., Davies, B. M., Maguire, K. P. and Wurm, J. M. E. (1980) Viloxazine plasma concentrations and clinical response. J. Affect. Dis. 2, 157–164.

Norman, T. R., Burrows, G. D. and Maguire, K. P. (1981a) Pharmacokinetics of tricyclic antidepressants. In: B. Angrist, G. D. Burrows, M. Lader, O. Lingjaerde, G. Sedvall and D. Wheatley (Eds), Recent Advances in Neuropsychopharmacology. Pergamon Press, Oxford, pp. 339–350.

Norman, T. R., Cheng, H. and Burrows, G. D. (1981b) The effect of tricyclic antidepressant metabolites on the uptake of serotonin by the human blood platelet 'in vitro'. In: E. Usdin, S. Dahl, L. Gram, and O. Lingjaerde (Eds), Clinical Pharmacology in Psychiatry. Neuroleptic and Antidepressant Research. Macmillan, London, pp. 155–160.

Norman, T. R., Maguire, K. P., Scoggins, B. A. and Burrows, G. D. (1982) Monitoring and interpretation of antidepressant plasma concentrations. Aust. N. Z. J. Psychiatry 16, 74–78.

120

Peet, M. (1973) A clinical trial of ICI 58, 834 – a potential antidepressant. J. Int. Med. Res. 1, 624–626.

Perel, J. M., Shostak, M., Gann, E., Kantor, S. J. and Glassman, A. H. (1976) Pharmacodynamics of imipramine and clinical outcome in depressed patients. In: L. Gottschalk and S. Merlis (Eds), Pharmacokinetics, Psychoactive Drug Blood Levels and Clinical Outcome. Spectrum – John Wiley, New York, pp. 229–241.

Piafsky, K. M. and Borga, O. (1977) Plasma protein binding of basic drugs 11. Importance of acid glycoprotein for individual variation. Clin. Pharmacol. Ther. 22, 545–549.

Potter, W. Z., Calil, H. M., Manian, A. A., Zacadil, A. P. and Goodwin, F. K. (1979) Hydroxylated metabolites of tricyclic antidepressants: preclinical assessment of activity. Biol. Psychiatry 14, 601–613.

Risch, S. C., Huey, L. Y. and Janowsky, D. S. (1979a) Plasma levels of tricyclic antidepressants and clinical efficacy: review of the literature, Part 1. J. Clin. Psychiatry 40, 4–16.

Risch, S. C., Huey, L. Y. and Janowsky, D. S. (1979b) Plasma levels of tricyclic antidepressants and clnical efficacy: review of the literature, Part 11. J. Clin. Psychiatry 40, 58–69.

Scoggins, B. A. and Maguire, K. P. (1981) Methods for the measurement of psychotropic drugs. Antidepressants. In: G. D. Burrows and T. R. Norman (Eds), Psychotropic Drugs Plasma Concentration and Clinical Response. Marcel Dekker, New York, pp. 47–82.

Scoggins, B. A., Maguire, K. P., Norman, T. R. and Burrows, G. D. (1980a) Measurement of tricyclic antidepressants. Part 1. A review of methodology. Clin. Chem. 26, 5–17.

Scoggins, B. A., Maguire, K. P., Norman, T. R. and Burrows, G. D. (1980b) Measurement of tricyclic antidepressants. Part 2. Applications. Clin. Chem. 26, 805–815.

Silverman, G. and Braithwaite, R. A. (1973) Benzodiazepines and tricyclic antidepressant plasma levels. Br. Med. J. 3, 18–20.

Siwers, B., Borg, S., D'Elia, G., Lundlin, G., Plym-Forshell, G., Raotman, H. and Roman, G. (1977) Comparative clinical evaluation of lofepramine and imipramine, pharmacological aspects. Acta Psychiatr. Scand. 55, 21–31.

Turbott, J., Norman, T. R., Burrows, G. D., Maguire, K. P. and Davies, B. M. (1980) Pharmacokinetics of nortriptyline in elderly volunteers. Commun. Psychopharmacol 4, 225–231.

Vohra, J. and Burrows, G. D. (1974) Cardiovascular complications of tricyclic antidepressant overdosage. Drugs 8, 432–437.

Whyte, S. F., MacDonald, A. J. Naylor, G. J. and Moody, J. P. (1976) Plasma concentrations of protriptyline and clinical effects in depressed women. Br. J. Psychiatry 128, 384–390.

Ziegler, V. E. and Biggs, J. T. (1977) Tricyclic plasma levels, effect of age, race, sex and smoking. J. Am. Med. Assoc. 238, 2167–2169.

Ziegler, V. E., Co., B. T., Taylor, J. R., Clayton, P. J. and Biggs, J. T. (1976) Amitriptyline plasma levels and therapeutic response. Clin. Pharmacol. Ther. 19, 795–801.

Chapter 10

Clinical application – management of the depressed patient

BRIAN DAVIES

and

GRAHAM D. BURROWS

*Department of Psychiatry, University of Melbourne, Clinical Sciences Building,
Royal Melbourne Hospital, Australia*

MANAGEMENT OF THE DEPRESSED PATIENT

The recognition of depression has been described in Chapter 1.

Once a diagnosis of depression has been made, most doctors today reach for their prescription pad and prescribe their favourite tricyclic compound.

Three separate management plans should be considered for each patient. They are given in the order of importance to the family doctor.

Treatment by supportive care

The doctor spends time listening to the patient's problems. In addition, he gives reassurance about the patient's physical and mental health and may offer advice to the patient. Symptomatic treatment with hypnotics and anti-anxiety medication may also be helpful. This mode of treatment is indicated especially for young patients with recent symptoms and social and personal problems. The patient will be seen several times.

Treatment by supportive care and antidepressants

In addition to the supportive care mentioned above, antidepressant medication is prescribed (see below). Such treatment is specially important for middle-aged and elderly patients whose depressive symptoms have been present for some months.

Referral to a psychiatrist

This is the appropriate management for about 5% of depressed patients seen by their family doctors. These are the severely ill patients who present a suicide risk. Such patients can be:

a) Severely ill, agitated, or retarded patients with marked sleep disturbances, and perhaps ideas that they have cancer, and severe guilt feelings. Such patients have often been in hospital with similar symptoms in the past and have been treated and responded well to electroconvulsive treatment. Such patients will, if given the opportunity, describe their feelings about the worthlessness of their present situation and the hopelessness of the future. A suicide attempt in a previous illness is a particularly important clinical feature.
b) Depressed patients with severe symptoms who live alone.
c) Severe psychiatric symptoms that develop soon after the birth of a child. Important features are lack of feeling and thoughts of hurting the baby when it cries.
d) Patients who have recurring attacks of depression and mania (an elevated mood). Such patients require special psychiatric care.
e) Depressed patients with sexual problems, e.g. depressed homosexuals. These patients often feel guilty and paranoid and need expert care.

Listening to patients with psychiatric symptoms

Time is the problem here for the General Practitioner. Some family doctors, once recognising psychiatric problems, make a special, longer appointment so that the patient can talk, without the General Practitioner having to watch the clock. It need hardly be said that some doctors use the 'time excuse' as a means of avoiding patients with psychiatric problems.

Time given early on is most important

Encouraging the patients to talk about their background, and their present day problems is therapeutic. The doctor must be an interested listener. He must feel that 'being with' the patient and understanding the problems, is more help than 'doing things to' the patient, by prescribing tablets and altering the patient's brain metabolism.

Notes 'on giving advice' to depressed patients

Depressed patients can complain of their health, house, spouse, children or job. It is very important that doctors do not advice patients to do anything drastic in regard to selling their home or leaving their spouse or job until the depression has been treated. Sometimes these problems can disappear when depression is relieved.

Similarly, one should never send a depressed person with sleep disturbance and suicidal thoughts away on a holiday. Symptoms may persist, the patient feels more guilty and suicide can occur.

ANTIDEPRESSANT DRUGS

Two main groups of substances are available that have been shown in controlled trials to be superior to placebo in relieving depressive symptoms.

1) The tricyclic group of antidepressants. These are iminodibenzyl derivatives and are the antidepressants of first choice.
2) The monoamine oxidase inhibitors (MAOI) which are prescribed in less than 1% of prescriptions written in general practice (in Australia).

In general, it can be said that the tricyclic compounds frequently produce uncomfortable, but not dangerous side effects. The MAOI produce fewer unpleasant side effects but occasionally produce dangerous ones, in combination with other drugs or certain food substances. Both compounds take some while (10–21 days) to exert their antidepressant effects.

Both groups are dangerous if taken in overdosage and in this respect tricyclic overdosage is now a serious problem in general hospitals.

For these reasons (despite new antidepressants detailed later) an effective antidepressant without side effects or toxicity problems and that acts quickly, is an important therapeutic need.

TREATMENT WITH ANTIDEPRESSANTS

Introduction

In general practice, most patients treated with antidepressants improve, often improving in the first week of treatment. Such improvement is not due to the antidepressant action of the compound. It is due to the most important ingredients of medical treatment, the doctor's faith in his treatment and the patient's faith in his doctor.

This transactional interpersonal relationship is the basis of all good medicine though it is often called the 'placebo reaction'. In a controlled trial (Blashki et al., 1971) in some general practices in Melbourne, 75 mg or 150 mg of amitriptyline, or 150 mg of amylobarbitone or inert capsules were given to depressed patients each day for 4 weeks. More than 60% of the patients improved, irrespective of the content of the capsules and most improved in the first week of treatment. However, 150 mg of amitriptyline was significantly better than other treatments in relieving anxiety and depressive symptoms over a 4-week period.

The patients who stopped the capsules because of complaints of side effects were equally distributed among the four treatment groups (including the inert capsules).

Practical therapeutics in depression

1) The doctor should begin antidepressant treatment with a tricyclic antidepressant

either imipramine or amitriptyline or his own favourite tricyclic antidepressant. The initial dosage of imipramine or amitriptyline is 50 mg at night. Patients should be told to expect side effects — dry mouth, constipation and sleepiness. They should be told that these symptoms mean the pills are beginning to work but that the depression will not really begin to improve for 7 to 14 days.

2) The patient should be seen again in 4—7 days.

(a) If improvement has already begun and the patient seems well, the medication at the above dose should be continued for a month.

(b) If the patient is still depressed, increase the night dose to 75 mg and add 25 mg in the morning.

3) The patient should be seen again in 4—7 days. If the patient is still depressed increase the dose to 150 mg/day, 100 mg at night and 50 mg in the morning. The whole dose can be given at night.

4) The patient should be seen weekly until improvement is definite. Patients should be given a definite appointment and not told 'come and see me if you are not better'.

At the end of the 4 weeks most patients will have improved. For those who have not, dosage should be continued at 150—250 mg/day for at least another 3 weeks. Clinically, patients who are not experiencing side effects are not having a therapeutic dose of drug (they may not even be taking the drug!). If there is no improvement in this time, patients should be referred to a psychiatrist.

No other drugs should be given with tricyclic drugs if at all possible.

Giving the tricyclic at night usually helps insomnia without adding an hypnotic. If an hypnotic is still needed, never use barbiturates. They affect the metabolism of tricyclics by increasing liver enzyme activity. If needed diazepam, nitrazepam or temazepam can be given as hypnotics.

Practical therapeutic notes

(1) If one tricyclic does not help there is no point in changing to another compound, their metabolites are very similar. It is better to increase the dose of the original compound.

(2) Warnings about alcohol and tricyclics and driving should be given to patients. Patients who have to drive should take all the daily dose at night and none in the day before driving (unless they are driving at night, in which case the drug should be taken in the morning).

(3) The pharmaceutical companies warn doctors not to prescribe tricyclics (or any drugs) in the first trimester of pregnancy. However, if the clinical condition merits tricyclics, there is no hard evidence that they cause fetal abnormalities.

(4) Tricyclics should be continued for some months after moderately depressed patients improve. As a general rule they should be continued for as long as the symptoms had been present before treatment began, before attempting to reduce the dosage. This should be done gradually, one tablet a week to see if a recurrence occurs. If it does the original dosage should be reinstituted.

Generally in general practice drugs need to be continued for about 3 months. In some patients with longer standing symptoms 6 months is needed. Some patients, treated usually by psychiatrists, need to be taking tricyclics for longer than a year.

(5) There is some evidence that at therapeutic dosage, imipramine and amitriptyline can cause cardiac arrhythmias in patients with heart disease. Studies have shown that doxepin and mianserin are less likely to do this, so that these drugs are at present recommended for patients with heart disease and depression. Initial dosage of doxepin is similar to imipramine and amitryptyline but 200–250 mg may be needed in some patients. Ten mg mianserin appears equivalent to 25 mg imipramine.

(6) Patients with glaucoma and depression can be treated with tricyclics but need referral to a psychiatrist and ophthalmologist.

(7) Patients with urinary retention also need referral since tricyclics can aggravate this problem.

(8) Elderly patients with depression usually need energetic treatment with tricyclics. Therapeutic dosage is the same, namely 150 mg/day and while attaining this daily dose may take longer, it should be done. In this respect, the 10 mg tablets often used in the elderly are pharmacologically useless as antidepressants. Mianserin, 40–80 mg a day, is often used in elderly patients because of its relative lack of side effects (including cardiological).

(9) Mixed preparations of an antidepressant and a tranquilliser are available and are widely prescribed. There are some pharmacological grounds for their use, since the phenothiazine tranquilliser increases the amount of tricyclic in the plasma and is an anti-anxiety agent. However, the effective antidepressant dose is still 150 mg/day of the amitriptyline contained in these capsules.

(10) Menopausal women are often depressed and respond well to antidepressants. In the long term however, more than this is usually needed. Often some part time activity outside the home is most helpful while oestrogens may be needed for the specific symptoms caused by oestrogen deficiency (flushes and dyspareunia).

(11) Occasionally, starting tricyclic medication can produce an epileptic fit. Usually if the dosage is reduced then increased gradually, drug treatment can still continue. Depressed epileptics who are receiving barbiturates or barbiturate derivatives as treatment for their epilepsy should be referred for specialist advice, since, as has been mentioned barbiturates interfere with tricyclic metabolism.

(12) Some patients who are being treated with hypotensive drugs also need treatment with antidepressants. Despite occasional problems of blood pressure control, the drugs can be used together, but again, the general practitioner may wish to seek specialist advice. Reserpine and alpha methyl dopa are among hypotensive drugs that can actually cause depression.

(13) Depressed patients with severe liver or kidney disease should be referred for specialist advice about antidepressant treatment.

Monoamine oxidase inhibitors (MAOI)

These substances are not the first line of treatment in depression. Their place in practical therapeutics is still debated. Treatment with these drugs is probably better started by a psychiatrist than a general practitioner. Among psychiatrists there are enthusiastic and

126

cynical reports about these drugs. They are almost certainly underused because of fears about toxic reactions. Paykel has shown that for groups of outpatient depressed patients, nardil and amitriptyline are equally effective and both better than placebo. General practitioners should read the drug information carefully before using them. They are used most often in:

1) Anxious patients who have severe phobic symptoms as well as depressive symptoms;
2) in some depressed patients who have responded to them previously;
3) in some depressed patients who have not responded to tricyclics.

Except for causing difficulty in sleeping, the MAOI do not produce the unpleasant side effects that tricyclics do. 'Marplan', 'Nardil' and 'Parnate' are the drugs of choice.

Dosage. The tablets are best given in the morning, since they tend to keep patients awake if taken after mid-day. 'Marplan' should be given 10 mg 2 tablets in the morning and one added at mid-day after a few days. 'Parnate' should be given in a similar way.

'Nardil' tablets (15 mg) are given as above but dosage should be increased to 60–90 mg/day if improvement does not occur.

All patients treated with these drugs should have a careful explanation given to them about problems that could arise with certain food (mainly cheese) and certain drugs (mainly sympathomimetic drugs and pethidine). A card should be given to each patient that reads:

'*A word of caution.* Your physician has prescribed an effective modern drug for the treatment of your condition. Be sure to follow his instructions carefully. Here are a few things to keep in mind while you are taking his medication:

1) Don't take any other medicine (including cold remedies) without asking your physician.
2) Don't eat cheese (particularly strong or aged varieties), raisins, chocolate, sour cream, pickled herring, chicken livers, canned figs, avocado pears, the pods of broad beans or protein extracts (Marmite, Vegemite, Bonox, etc.). In general, avoid foods in which ageing is used to increase flavour.
3) Do not drink red wine.
4) If you are to receive an anaesthetic for surgical or other purposes, advise the physician or dentist in charge that you are taking this drug.
5) Report promptly to your physician any unusual headache or other symptoms.
6) If you become pregnant or are likely to do so, discuss with your doctor any drugs you are taking.'

New antidepressant compounds

In recent years, new compounds have been introduced as antidepressants. They resemble the tricyclic antidepressants clinically, but are distinct chemically. They include iprindole, dibenzepin, maprotiline, mianserin, nomifensine and viloxazine.

Mianserin is the most widely prescribed of these compounds. Safety on overdose and relative lack of side effects including effects on the heart are the important properties of this drug. For this reason it is often the antidepressant of first choice in patients with heart disease, elderly patients and patients who cannot tolerate imipramine or amitryptyline because of side effects. Ten mg of mianserin appears equivalent to 25 mg of amitriptyline or imipramine. Nomifensine, which appears to be a more stimulant drug than mianserin, also has no effect on cardiac functions. Dosage is as amitriptyline though tablets should all be given early in the day to prevent insomnia.

Lithium

Lithium is used to prevent recurrences of severe illnesses of mood that lead to hospital admission. Lithium prevents recurrences of manic-depression and recurring depression, in 80–90% of such patients. The actual use of this drug is described elsewhere (Schou, 1980; Chapters 18 and 19 in this book).

Two important and common medical problems need mentioning.

Physical illnesses and depression

Patients with chronic diseases of the joints, lungs, heart, kidneys, nervous and blood systems are often significantly depressed. While understanding and help of the physical, social and psychological problems of the chronic condition are needed, antidepressant medication can be most helpful.

Patients recovering from an acute catastrophic physical illness, e.g. myocardial infarction are also often depressed and again the use of antidepressants may help in the overall management.

Chronic pain

Patients with chronic pain for which no relevant physical cause can be found can be very troublesome clinical problems. Antidepressants may be an important part of the total medical care of these patients.

SUMMARY

Effective antidepressant medication causes an improvement in outcome of from 55% with inert medication to 75%. This is important clinically. However, the basic 'understanding' aspects of the doctor/patient interaction should not be forgotten in a chemical assault on the patient.

This book contains chapters about many aspects of depression written by leading authorities. Further references can also be found in this book.

REFERENCES

Blashki, T. G., Mowbray, R. M. and Davies, B. M. (1977) Br. Med. J. 1, 133–138.
Burrows, G. D. (Ed.) (1977) Handbook of Studies on Depression. Excerpta Medica, Amsterdam.
Paykel, G. and Coppen, A. (1979) Psychopharmacology of Affective Disorders. Oxford Medical Publication.
Schou, M. (1980) Lithium Treatment of Manic Depressive Illness. S. Karger, Basel.

Chapter 11

Tricyclic antidepressants and children

ALAN ZAMETKIN

and

JUDITH L. RAPOPORT

Unit on Childhood Mental Illness, NIMH, Bethesda, MD 20205, U.S.A.

INTRODUCTION

The adult type of depression which constitutes the original and main use of the antide-pressants and which gave them their name is rare in childhood (Rapoport, 1976). The antidepressants' use in paediatric psychopharmacology is principally for a variety of other conditions such as enuresis, school phobia, conduct disorders, and attention disorder, which makes the unavoidable name antidepressant incongruous. Most recently, some studies of tricyclics in childhood depression have been carried out, and these will be also discussed here.

Because of the unique considerations due for tricyclic use in pediatric age groups, a brief review of the pharmacology and actions of antidepressants as they relate to child-hood conditions is presented first. Following this, clinical indications and side effects are discussed. With the exception of the rather large number of studies on enuresis, most of the other areas are scanty and so are easily reviewed.

BASIC PHARMACOLOGY OF RELEVANCE TO PEDIATRICS

Peak plasma levels of imipramine occur $1\frac{1}{2}$ to 3 hours after an oral dose on continuous treatment, with a half-life in children that may range from 10 to 17 hours using available methods (Winsberg et al., 1974).

Children differ significantly from adults in pharmacokinetics; children have a smaller adipose compartment, and lipid soluble drugs are not taken up, redistributed and stored in inactive lipid-storage sites to the same extent as in adults. There are also reported differences in children in the degree of drug binding to plasma albumin (Pruitt and Dayton, 1971, Winsberg et al., 1974). Imipramine binding in umbilical cord and adult plasma average 74% and 86% respectively, indicating 26% free drug in the neonate and 14% free medication in the adult. At age 13, adult binding values are obtained. It has been suggested that children are more susceptible to imipramine side effects because of this relatively greater amount of circulating free drug (Winsberg et al., 1974). These authors also suggest that with chronic administration, a single daily dose may have a bolus effect and thus have the pharmacokinetics of an intravenous dose.

Except for newborns, the rate of drug biotransformation by the liver in children tends generally to be enhanced, probably due to a relatively higher amount of liver tissue. This property could result in the enhanced production of some metabolites, but there is little actual information about differential metabolic or excretion rates and patterns for tricyclics for children compared with that for adults. One recent study (Klutch and Hanna, 1976), however, reports that children excrete a higher portion of 2-hydroxylated imipramine which may have relevance to the cardiotoxicity of tricyclics in children, discussed below. Excretion patterns for quadricyclics in adults are similar to those of the tricyclics, but have not been studied in children (Riess et al., 1972, 1975).

Sites and mode of action

The tricyclics are thought to owe their therapeutic effect in the treatment of depression to the inhibition of transmitter reuptake back into monoaminergic neurons in the brain where most of it is normally inactivated, presumably thus increasing transmitter effectiveness (Carlsson et al., 1966).

The tricyclics also have anticholinergic effects both centrally and peripherally. The peripheral anticholinergic effects, generally regarded as unwanted or side-effects in adult patients, have been thought to provide the basis for the efficacy of tricyclics in enuresis (see below). A recent review of the relative potency of the various tricyclics in blocking muscarinic type acetylcholine receptors indicates considerable variation between compounds in this action (Snyder and Yamamura, 1977); amitriptyline is the most potent and desipramine the least potent, with imipramine intermediate between these two.

Both the quadri- and tricyclics also have the property of potentiating peripheral alpha adrenergic activity by sensitizing alpha receptors to the effects of noradrenaline (Sigg, 1959); however, they have some antagonistic effects at alpha-adrenoreceptors as well. The sympathetic nervous system may be critically important in control of urination by providing a balance between detrusor contractility and involuntary urethral sphincter tone. The alpha adrenergic system, in particular, is involved in maintaining the bladder sphincter muscle tone. As imipramine inhibits bladder neck response to noradrenaline in laboratory studies, this action, rather than the anticholinergic one, has been also postulated as the basis for clinical effectiveness in enuresis. Additionally, tricyclics have local anesthetic properties and a resultant direct cocaine-like action on the muscle membrane, decreasing resting muscle tension, has been described for imipramine (Labay and Boyarsky, 1973). It is questionable, however, whether this effect occurs within the therapeutic dose range used in enuresis.

Dose response data

Several studies have addressed the dose response relationship for tricyclics in paediatric conditions, finding some interesting differences from that found with adults. Winsberg et al. (1976, 1977) and Weller et al. (1981) have established that, as with adults, serum levels vary considerably across children after similar doses, but that clinical response in be-haviourally disturbed children parallels roughly the serum level.

Subsequent studies (Linnoila et al., 1979) with conduct disordered children, as well as others with enuretic children (Jorgensen et al., 1980; Rapoport et al., 1980) have documented a significant correlation between steady-state plasma levels and therapeutic effect. Clinical effects were found at concentrations around 50 ng/ml, considerably lower than that needed for antidepressant effect in adult populations.

On the other hand, Puig-Antich (1979) suggests that high plasma concentration of tri-cyclic 150 ng/ml or more, is needed for clinical antidepressant action.

Time response data

The clinical effects of tricyclics in enuresis and behaviour disorders are seen within hours or a few days of the start of treatment (Blackwell and Currah, 1973; Yepes et al., 1977). This is in contrast to the 2–4 week delay in the clinical response of depressed adults, and to the 3–6 week delay in the response of school phobic children (Gittelman-Klein and Klein, 1971). This difference in time response, if replicated in future studies, is important as it suggests different mechanisms of drug action in these different clinical conditions.

CLINICAL EFFECTS

Sleep-EEG

In adults, tricyclics produce a prolonged sustained reduction in REM sleep as seen on the EEG; this is an immediate effect, and though some tolerance to it does develop, this is in-complete (Mendelson et al., 1977). Similar effects have been reported for enuretic children (Ritvo et al., 1969; Mikkelson et al., 1980; Rapoport et al., 1980). Such changes in REM time and associated dreaming and the rebound increase in both upon cessation of the drug could, in theory, be associated with some psychological discomfort. In the largest study of sleep EEG effects of imipramine in enuretic children to date, Rapoport et al. (1980) confirmed the previous findings of decreased REM sleep and increased percentage of stage 2 sleep. There was no relationship, however, between effects on sleep EEG and clinical anti-enuretic response.

Autonomic nervous system

As noted above, tricyclic antidepressants possess cholinergic blocking properties, effective particularly against the muscarinic actions of acetylcholine. Some of the side effects seen clinically, such as blurred vision, dryness of mouth, constipation, and urinary retention, can be attributed to this atropine-like effect. The cholinergic rebound upon stopping these drugs, especially when done suddenly after high doses, may explain the withdrawal symptoms sometimes seen (vomiting, sweating, colic) (Byck, 1975), and may be seen in children (Law et al., 1981).

The peripheral action of imipramine on autonomic control of bladder functioning described above (under site of action) may provide the basis for its therapeutic efficacy in enuresis. There are conflicting reports on the effect of imipramine on the micturition reflex in the treatment of neurogenic bladder. One study (Diokno et al., 1972) found no effect on the cystometrogram 45 minutes after 75 mgm of imipramine was administered intramuscularly. On the other hand, Cole (1972) reported a significant effect of imipramine in a similar population following one week of an oral daily dose of 50 mgm. Mahoney et al. (1973) reported increased involuntary (internal) sphincter tone in the bladder in about 50% of a group of 73 enuretic children who received treatment with 25–50 mg/day of imipramine. The authors cite a slightly higher percentage (59% compared to 44%) in the markedly improved group compared with non-responders. However, these group differences are small, did not reach significance, and do not correspond well with observed clinical outcome. It is possible then that the change in vesical tone simply reflects blood levels of the drug which may vary considerably among children and which may not relate to clinical effect at all. The authors do raise the interesting possibility (which their data fail to support) that imipramine in enuresis may act via its action on alpha adrenergic nerves rather than anticholinergic action. However, a recent study by Shaffer and co-workers (1977) showed that an alpha blocker drug had no deleterious effect on enuresis, suggesting that the therapeutic action of imipramine is unlikely to be due to any alpha adrenergic action.

Two recent studies (Korczyn and Kish, 1979; Rapoport et al., 1980) had failed to show any clinical efficacy of methscopolamine bromide, a peripheral anticholinergic agent, in enuresis. As scopolamine bromide does not cross the blood brain barrier, these findings argue against peripheral anticholinergic action as crucial in enuresis (although a central anticholinergic mechanism is possible).

Cardiovascular system

Imipramine obtunds various cardiovascular reflexes and hence can lower the blood pressure, the degree depending mostly on dosage, but there is also individual variation. Paradoxically, clinical studies of tricyclics in children which have addressed themselves to this issue (Rapoport et al., 1974; Greenberg and Yellin, 1975; Werry et al., 1975a; Lake et al., 1979) have all revealed slight *increases* in blood pressure (as well as the expected increase in heart rate). Toxic doses of imipramine may produce serious cardiac arrhythmias and tachycardia, which can result in death in accidental and deliberate poisoning. The possibility of relatively greater cardiotoxicity of imipramine in the pediatric age group has been suggested in recent reports (Winsberg et al., 1975; Robinson and Barker, 1976; Saraf et al., 1978) in which ECG change of prolonged PR and QR intervals and T wave changes including first degree AV block were observed at doses in the 5 mgm/kg range in children with behaviour disorders.

Activity

Tricyclics and quadricyclics produce depression of spontaneous motor activity in laboratory animals. Tricyclics have been reported useful in the treatment of hyperkinetic behaviour disordered children, but, in contrast to the stimulants, there have been only two studies of effects of tricyclics on motor activity in children. Werry et al. (1975a, 1976) found evidence of reduction in motor overflow during a sedentary task using a specially designed seat. Effects on disruptive behaviour are discussed below.

Central nervous system

The frequent reports of insomnia and euphoria and the occasional induction of seizures in psychiatric patients indicate that tricyclics and quadricyclics can have a stimulant-like action under certain circumstances.

Cognitive functioning

There are few studies of cognitive effects of tricyclics in children compared with the vast literature for the stimulants. However, these studies are of considerable theoretical importance as they may provide indirect evidence for the mechanisms of action of the drugs.

Rapoport et al. (1974) found imipramine in relatively low doses (2–3 mgm/kg), given to behaviour disordered children, to have a stimulant-like effect increasing vigilance (Continuous Performance Task) and decreasing impulsivity as measured by the Porteus Maze test. There was an increase in latency, but not a decrease in errors in the Kagan Matching Familiar Figure test, presumably a test of cognitive 'impulsivity'. This finding, in combination with the side effects (appetite, weight loss, increased blood pressure), suggested a stimulant-like action of tricyclics in children. Similar effects for amitriptyline, also with behaviour disordered children, have been reported (Yepes et al., 1977; Kupietz and Balka, 1976), in which the absolute score and correct detections improved on the CPT and omission errors were decreased to an extent comparable to that for methylphenidate.

The cognitive effects of imipramine (and other tricyclics) have rarely been examined in enuretic children. In the only studies on the subject, Werry et al. (1975a, 1976, 1980) likewise found weak stimulant-like effects on motor overflow and less certainly directly on cognitive function. These latter reports are of particular interest as most of their samples of enuretic children were regarded as normal and so this represents a rare opportunity to observe the effects of tricyclics in normal children; there is need for more such work.

Academic achievement

There have been no reports of beneficial effects of tricyclics on academic achievement in naturalistic settings. One study failed to find any difference between the Wide Range Achievement test scores in Arithmetic or Reading between hyperactive children who had been treated for a year on imipramine and a comparable group of children who had dropped off medication during the year because of adverse side effects (Quinn and Rapoport, 1975). It remains unknown, therefore, whether or not academic improvement can be produced by antidepressant medication. Since laboratory tests, which are assumed to be learning related, have tended to show improvement with tricyclics, these tests are clearly not sufficient measures for predicting adequate scholastic performance.

A study of academic achievement and antidepressant treatment could be of considerable interest in validating the disputed diagnostic entity of 'masked depression' evidenced by learning disability and poor self-esteem (see Rapoport, 1976).

Behaviour

Imipramine has been reported useful for the treatment of school refusal in a double-blind study (Gittelman-Klein and Klein, 1971). Imipramine treatment (mean dose of 152 mgm/day) of nonpsychotic school phobic children in the context of a multidisciplinary treatment program produced significant drug-placebo differences at 6 weeks (not present at 3 weeks). Several points emerge from this study. This is the only study of clinical effects of imipramine in children for which the effects are shown to be delayed as in adults in contrast to immediate effects found in enuresis and conduct disorders. In addition, separation anxiety, but not anticipatory anxiety, was felt to be improved in the phobic children, suggesting a different substrate for those symptoms associated with school phobia.

The authors are careful to point out that they do not interpret the response of these phobic children to antidepressant drug as reflecting an underlying depression in this group (Gittelman-Klein and Klein, 1973). Rather, they feel that a separate biological phenomenon may be involved, i.e. one that related to separation anxiety; this thinking is a continuation of their work on drug responsive anxiety states in adults, also thought to be an independent phenomenon from that for depressive illness.

A recent study (Berney et al., 1981) found no effect of chlorimipramine (doses 40–75 mg/day) in 27 children and adolescents with school phobia in a double-blind placebo-controlled 12-week trial. However, the low doses and absence of plasma drug concentration make this study hard to interpret.

Imipramine has been found to decrease conduct problems such as restless, aggressive, and impulsive behaviour in children (Winsberg et al., 1972; Rapoport et al., 1974; Waizer et al., 1974). In contrast to a true antidepressant effect, this is immediate, occurring within hours after the first dose. In some children, however, there is exacerbated conduct disturbance with hyper-irritability, as discussed below. This has also been noted for quadricyclics (Kuhn and Kuhn, 1972). A recent negative trial of mianserin in six hyperactive aggressive children has been reported (Langer et al., in press).

Mood

Adult-type depression, i.e. disorders characterized by persistent dysphoric mood, self-depreciating thoughts, insomnia, weight loss, and motor retardation, is rare in children. This subject has been reviewed extensively elsewhere and will not be elaborated here (Graham, 1974; Conners, 1976; Rapoport, 1976; Elkins and Rapoport, in press).

The only methodologically adequate studies of tricyclic treatment of childhood depression, those of Puig-Antich (1979) and co-workers, are discussed below under clinical indications.

Few controlled studies have been interested in the effects of imipramine on mood in children with other disorders. Werry et al. (1975a) reported a positive mood effect as rated by psychiatric interview with the mother after 3 weeks of treatment with 25—50 mg of imipramine daily in enuretic children. This study does not conclusively demonstrate a direct effect on mood, however, as a change in mood secondary to achieving continence cannot be entirely ruled out. Indeed, in an attempted replication of this study, Werry et al. (1976) failed to find any mood changes. In their study of school phobia, Gittelman-Klein and Klein (1973) noted universal reports of 'feeling better' which took several weeks to develop.

Several clinical studies with enuretic children report that a minority of children may be restless and irritable even with doses of tricyclics as low as 50 mgm/day (see Blackwell and Currah, 1973; Werry et al., 1975a). In higher doses, the dysphoric effect may be striking, necessitating discontinuation of the drug.

Maprotiline has been reported to improve 'depression' in pediatric populations in two uncontrolled studies, which are discussed in more detail below.

SIDE EFFECTS

Short-term effects

Until recently, the therapeutic use of imipramine was considered safe in children. Di Mascio et al. (1970) found the prevalence and severity of side effects similar to those reported in adults — namely, minor annoyances like dryness of mouth, drowsiness, lethargy, tremors, appetite disturbance, nausea and sweating. While agranulocytosis has been reported in adults, none has yet been reported in children. However, in the past few years, there has been increasing concern about the vulnerability of children to tricyclics, especially as higher doses than those used in enuresis have become more common. Seizure threshold, lower in children in any case, appears to be reduced particularly. Several cases of seizures in children aged 3 to 6 years, previously seizure free, were recently reported with doses ranging from 150 to 225 mgm (about 7—10 mg/kg) of imipramine daily (Brown et al., 1973). This has also been observed in children receiving maprotiline (Kuhn-Gebhardt, 1972).

There has also been particular concern about the possible cardiotoxicity of tricyclics in children. The sudden death of a 6-year old following a bedtime dose of 300 mgm (14 mg/kg) for school phobia (Saraf et al., 1978) may have resulted from cardiotoxicity. Electrocardiogram abnormalities (increased heart rate, increased PR interval and non-specific T wave changes) were found to be produced by imipramine in doses of 5 mgm/kg given over 24 hours (Winsberg et al., 1975). As a result, the Food and Drug Administration in the U.S. has cautioned against the use of doses in excess of 5 mg/kg and advised ECG monitoring as this level is reached (Hayes et al., 1975). As noted previously, it has been speculated that the 2-hydroxy metabolites of imipramine (2-hydroxyimipramine and 2-hydroxydesmethylimipramine) are responsible for this effect as these metabolites show binding affinity to cardiac tissue.

Law et al. (1981) have reported a withdrawal syndrome characterized by gastric symptoms of pain, nausea and vomiting, in children receiving rather low doses of tricyclics. Other symptoms include drowsiness, fatigue, and apathy. The authors feel these symptoms may be the result of cholinergic rebound and suggest long tapering phases, particularly when children have received higher doses.

Weight loss has been reported for children after 3–6 weeks of tricyclic treatment (Rapoport et al., 1974; Waizer et al., 1974; Werry et al., 1975a, 1976, 1980). Two reports have noted mildly increased diastolic blood pressure in behaviour disordered children (Rapoport et al., 1974; Greenberg et al., 1975) and three in enuretic children (Werry et al., 1975a, 1976; Lake et al., 1979).

In contrast to therapeutic uses, poisoning with tricyclics is much more likely to prove life threatening. Delirium, drowsiness, flushing, tachycardia, arrhythmias, coma, and cardiovascular collapse may result. Bickel (1975) has recently discussed reported poisoning with tricyclic drugs in an exhaustive review. The dosages for severe intoxication in adults were found to be a minimum of 7 mgm/kg and maximum of 127 mgm/kg with a mean of 38 mgm/kg. For fatal cases, the values were 10 and 210 respectively, with a mean of 66. The values for children under 7 years were even higher than those for adults, arguing against the assumption that the children *are more sensitive* to the toxic effects of tricyclics than are adults. Nevertheless, it should be pointed out that the smaller body size of young children makes the possible *absolute* fatal dose quite small; the lowest dose reported to result in the death of a child was a mere 250 mg (Sidiropoulos and Bickel, 1971), or only 10 tablets of commonly used antidepressants.

If tetracyclics continue to prove less cardiotoxic than tricyclics, they may find special use in some childhood conditions. There is also some evidence that doxepin may be less cardiotoxic than other tricyclics (Davies et al., 1975).

A particular caution is needed when evaluating and preparing pediatric psychiatric patients for drug treatment. In addition to the more familiar question of suicidal risk, children may also overdose for other reasons less familiar to the general psychiatric practitioner. Impulsive children may be more prone to overdose as an angry gesture in the absence of overt suicidal or depressive mentation. In addition, magical thinking has accounted for overdoses in children believing that larger doses would more quickly 'cure' their problem (Herson et al., 1979). Physicians can prevent needless tragedies by warning both the child and parents of the lethality of imipramine (and other prescription drugs).

Drug interactions of importance for children

Tricyclic antidepressants have clinically important interactions with several agents (Miller, 1975). Combined treatment with methylphenidate increases the serum levels of antidepressant, and there may be a synergistic effect with phenothiazines and other sedatives. Thyroid hormones may increase the antidepressant effect of tricyclics; whether they increase their effectiveness with hyperactive or enuretic children is unknown.

CLINICAL INDICATIONS AND CONTRAINDICATIONS

It is most important that both the child and the parents discuss the indications, side effects, and clinical effects before a drug trial is instituted. Drug non-compliance in children is often due to lack of adequate preparation of the child by the physician.

Established indications

Enuresis. The definitions, diagnoses, and various treatments of enuresis have been extensively reviewed (Blackwell and Currah, 1973; Kolvin et al., 1973). This section addresses only drug treatment of enuresis; there are many instances where no treatment and/or a trial of behavioural treatment are to be recommended.

Following the initial brief report of MacLean (1960) and a controlled clinical trial by Poussaint and Ditman (1965), more than 30 double-blind studies have demonstrated the symptomatic efficacy of tricyclic medication in enuresis in nightly doses ranging from 25–125 mgm. While improvement is noted in 60–80% of most samples, total remissions are reported in only 10–50% in a condition which has a significant spontaneous and placebo remission rate. This literature has been reviewed extensively by Blackwell and Currah (1973), who concluded that the case for *cure* of enuresis by tricyclics is not proven. Most children who appear to be cured resume wetting when medication is stopped.

Studies with enuretic children have not used comparable doses, populations, or even definitions of the condition. For that reason, it is difficult to make a statement about comparability of different tricyclics or to define 'good responders' from the available reports. In general, institutionalized, retarded, older enuretics, and those with daytime wetting seem to show a less favourable response. Interestingly, clinical response to imipramine has been demonstrated in cases with known urinary tract abnormality.

In a study of imipramine and desmethylimipramine treatments of 40 enuretic boys, Mikkelsen et al. (1980) and Rapoport et al. (1980) found that psychiatric status, that is, presence or absence of psychiatric disorder, did not predict clinical efficacy of the tricyclics. However, some behavioural improvement (in addition to anti-enuretic effect) was noted in the behaviourally disturbed subgroup (see Conduct disorders – below).

Conduct and attention deficit (hyperkinetic) disorders. DSM-III has made a clear distinction between Conduct Disorders and Attention Deficit Disorder (Hyperkinetic Disorder). In practice, the distinction is often not clearly made, and most of the studies cited below have populations including both disorders. Controlled trials of tricyclics in childhood conduct and hyperkinetic disorders are summarized in Table I.

Shortly after tricyclics began to be used for enuresis, reports of beneficial effects on hyperactive/aggressive children claimed changes similar to those found with stimulants (Krakowski, 1965; Rapoport, 1965; Huessy and Wright, 1970). More recently, controlled trials have generally confirmed these initial open studies and demonstrated the beneficial effect of tricyclics in doses from 2–5 mg/kg for restless, antisocial behaviour (Winsberg et al., 1972; Waizer et al., 1974; Rapoport et al., 1974; Werry et al., 1977, 1980; Yepes et al., 1977; Garfinkel et al., in press). This response appears to be immediate and, in some cases, dramatic. It should be noted, though, that one study (Greenberg et al., 1975) found no useful clinical effect, and side-effects were prohibitive on 100 mg daily. Most of these studies too have shown methylphenidate to be superior to tricyclics.

All these studies are short-term (4 weeks or less). The long-term usefulness of tricyclics

TABLE 1

Tricyclic antidepressants: controlled clinical trials with hyperactive-aggressive children.

Author and year	N	Age	Drug	Dose	Duration	Comments
Winsberg et al., 1972	32	9.1	IMI Amphetamine	150 mg/day 20 mg/day	10 days	IMI > PL Amphetamine IMI for Hyperactivity
Rapoport et al., 1974	IMI 29 PL 18 M-P 29	9	IMI Methylphenidate	80 mg/day 20 mg/day	6 weeks 6 weeks	IMI > PL Trend for M-P IMI MP > PL
Waizer et al., 1974	19	10	IMI	174 mg/day	8 weeks	IMI > PL Teacher and Parent Ratings
Greenberg et al., 1975	IMI-PL 25 MP-PL 25	9	IMI Methylphenidate	100 mg/day 40 mg/day	2 weeks	IMI > PL M-P > PL IMI = M-P
Kupietz and Balka, 1976	22	9.2	Amitriptyline	92 mg/day	2 weeks	AMI > PL – Attentional Measures and AMI = M-P – Behaviour Ratings (CPT)
Yepes et al., 1977			Methylphenidate	40 mg/day		
Werry et al., 1980	30	8.5	Methylphenidate Imipramine Placebo	0.4 mg/kg 1–2 mg/kg	4 weeks 4 weeks	IMI > PL M-D > PL IMI = M-P
Garfinkel et al., in press	12	7.3	Methylphenidate Desmethylimipramine Chlorimipramine Placebo	18 mg/day 85 mg/day 85 mg/day	2 weeks 2 weeks 2 weeks	MP, CIMI, DMI > PL MP > CIMI, DMI

for these disorders, however, remains controversial. In an open study, Gittelman-Klein (1974) indicated that an initial response to a daily dose of 150–300 mgm of imipramine seen at 2 weeks was not maintained at 12 weeks. Similarly, in a one-year follow-up (Quinn and Rapoport, 1975), significantly more hyperactive children had discontinued tricyclic medication than methylphenidate, even when both groups had shown an initial response after 6 weeks. It is the authors' experience that long-term treatment of conduct disordered and hyperkinetic children with tricyclics is unsatisfactory; this point deserves further study.

Unfortunately, studies to date have not used DSM-III categories and separated out Attention Deficit Disorders from Conduct Disorders sufficiently clearly to be sure in which or how many of these conditions antidepressants may be useful.

If the concept of Adult 'MBD' continues, tricyclics may have a unique role in such individuals for whom the addiction potential of stimulants would cause concern.

Possible indications

Separation anxiety. A single double-blind study has shown that imipramine benefits the separation anxiety associated with school phobia (Gittelman-Klein and Klein, 1971, 1973). This effect was seen at 6 weeks after the rather high average daily dose of 200 mg. The authors stress that the anticipatory anxiety associated with school return did not seem altered. More studies are needed to confirm the usefulness of tricyclics here – and their safety since the doses said to be required are very high and associated with one fatality.

Depressive disorders. The difficulty in defining depressive disorder in childhood has been reviewed elsewhere (Graham, 1974; Conners, 1976; Rapoport, 1976). Several points emerge from these reviews. As the persistent dysphoria, self-recriminations, and psycho-motor retardation characteristic of adult depression are rare in childhood, there is debate as to the existence and nature of childhood depressive disorder. Clinical reports on childhood depression have included heterogeneous populations with temper tantrums, mood swings, learning difficulties, enuresis, and overactivity as presenting problems. The overuse of vague diagnostic labels such as masked depression or depressive equivalent has been detrimental to research in this area.

In uncontrolled studies, imipramine and quadricyclics have been described as useful for a variety of possible depressive symptoms such as learning disabilities, irritability, dysphoria, somatic symptoms such as headaches and stomach aches, insomnia, and nightmares. Some of these studies (Frommer, 1967; Ling et al., 1970; Weinberg et al., 1973) are particularly suggestive of true antidepressant action inasmuch as children, described as having social withdrawal, deteriorating school performance, and self-depreciation of recent onset seem to benefit from tricyclic medication. In an uncontrolled study of 100 children and adolescents (Kuhn-Gebhart, 1972) the quadricyclic maprotiline was also reported to produce good or very good results in 60% of cases when used alone. However, these studies often lack clear clinical description, objective behaviour ratings, independent diagnostic ratings, or proper controls for time and placebo effects.

Selected controlled studies of drug treatment of childhood depressive disorder are summarized in Table 2.

TABLE 2

Selected trials of antidepressant drugs in child affective disorder.

Author and year	Drug	Dose	N	Length	Diagnoses	Comment
Puig-Antich et al., 1978, 1979	Imipramine	5 mg/kg/day	38	5 wks	Maj. Depr. Disorder (RDC)	5 wks parallel pbo (see text)
Weinberg et al., 1973	Amitriptyline Imipramine	min. dose 25 mg	34	3–7 mths	Criteria based on Feighner Criteria	Not double-blind No placebo 40% response of non-treatment gp.
Frommer, 1967, 1968	Phenobarbitone Chlordiazepoxide	30 mgm 20 mgm 30 mgm	32	2 wks	'Phobic gp' 'Mood disorder gp'	No pbo No objective ratings Low dose
Lucas et al., 1965	Amitriptyline	30–75 mg	14	12 wks	Secondary Depression with Schizophrenia and Personality Disorder	Low dose Double blind Placebo crossover

Puig-Antich et al. (1978) have gone on to carry out the best of the few double-blind controlled drug studies. Puig-Antich used the unmodified Research Diagnostic Criteria (RDC) (Spitzer et al., 1978) to identify prepubertal children with a major depressive disorder. In a pilot open clinical study of 13 children, the depressed children all had other difficulties such as separation anxiety, antisocial behaviour or severe familial stress. He treated eight of these children (Puig-Antich et al., 1978) with imipramine after their lack of response to milieu, group, family and individual therapy for at least one month. All were inpatients and continued their non-drug therapy. Six showed a beneficial response after a 4-week period. All three endogenous subtypes were responders. These pilot data stimulated a double-blind, 5-week placebo-controlled study of imipramine in carefully diagnosed depressed children. Preliminary data in 13 nonpsychotic depressed children, of which two were inpatients and 10 outpatients (Puig-Antich et al., 1979) suggested that the degree of improvement in mood is significantly associated with plasma levels of imipramine and metabolites. By the end of 1979, 39 cases had completed the double-blind protocol with 22 assigned to placebo and 16 to imipramine (Puig-Antich, personal communication). To date, there is no difference in clinical response between drug and placebo groups, regardless of method of measurement of the depressive syndrome. However, when the drug group was split into two subgroups by high or low plasma drug levels (above or below the group mean of 165 ngm/ml) and when each subgroup was compared to placebo, it was found that high level cases consistently do better than placebo. Low level imipramine may actually be harmful, as these children do substantially and consistently worse than when on placebo. This is the first study in adults or children that measures plasma levels of drug and placebo-controlled treatment response at the same time. The placebo group of this study was divided into responders and nonresponders. Sixty percent of the placebo group were responders, a figure quoted in other child studies (Eisenberg et al., 1961). The efficacy of imipramine in depression has further been supported by Weller et al. (1981) who reported improvement in all 11 subjects in an open study in which blood levels were monitored.

Puig-Antich's work is the only child study that stands with the best of adult research. Certain problems, however, have to be addressed. Compliance in outpatients is related to the supportive nature of the home. Although there was no significant correlation between maintenance dose and plasma levels, compliance can't be monitored exactly in outpatients. Thus, home environment may have mediated good outcome in this study and needs to be controlled.

The high placebo response and the specific response of anhedonia, depressed mood, and some vegetative signs to drug therapy bring the cited adult work on psychotherapy and medication to mind. In adults, there was a differential effect of the two therapies. Would this be true also in children? Perhaps one explanation of the high placebo response rate is that children, who usually don't have vegetative depressive symptoms, simply may not respond to drugs and may be more like the subgroup of adult depressives who respond to psychotherapy. A comparative study of psychotherapy and drug response in children should be conducted using the Weissman model.

Obsessive-compulsive disorder. Chlorimipramine (Anafranil) has recently been reported useful and specific in the treatment of adult obsessive-compulsive disorder (Thorén et al.,

1980). Many adults report childhood onset of their disorder, and the disorder, though rare in childhood, may, however, be severely disabling (Elkins et al., 1980).

In an ongoing trial of chlorimipramine in children and adolescents with severe primary obsessive-compulsive disorder, Rapoport et al. (1980) did not find a drug effect for nine adolescents treated in a double-blind cross-over study using 150 mg/day of chlorimipramine. However, the study is ongoing and individual responses within that sample suggest that the drug may be useful for some cases.

Contraindications

The tricyclics are not indicated in psychotic and schizophrenic conditions as they may aggravate the underlying psychotic process; although true manic illness in childhood is contentious, presumably tricyclics would also not be indicated for this condition because of possible worsening of the manic process. It might be expected that anxiety states would contraindicate antidepressants but as discussed above the evidence is actually contrary.

Tricyclics should be used with extreme caution or not at all in children with cardiac disease because of their known cardiac toxicity. In children with glaucoma, tricyclic drugs should be used only with ophthalmologic consultation.

Because of a number of reports of collapse, convulsions and hyperpyrexia in adult depressed patients treated with an MAO inhibitor and a tricyclic antidepressant, a 14-day drug-free interval is recommended before discontinuation of either drug and the institution of the other. At the present time, it seems unlikely that paediatric populations will be treated by these agents in combination, but an increase in the use of or indications for these agents with children could make this issue of importance in paediatric psychopharmacology.

CLINICAL ADMINISTRATION, DOSAGES AND PRECAUTIONS

Enuresis

In the treatment of enuresis, a single bedtime dose of 0.5—2.5 mg/kg is the usual therapeutic range. In some instances where the child is likely to wet very early in sleep, it may be advisable to give the medication earlier in the evening (Alderton, 1967). Imipramine should be started at a dose of 10—25 mgm and the dose increased every other night or so until either there is a clinical response (7 out of 10 dry nights is a recommended criterion), side effects appear, or, at the very most, a maximum dose of 5 mgm/kg is reached. The long-term maintenance treatment of enuresis must include periodic withdrawals (in the authors' practice, every 3 months), to ascertain whether medication is still necessary. At low doses graduated withdrawal is not necessary, but at high ones it is necessary to prevent cholinergic rebound symptoms. In treating enuresis, however, it is necessary to titrate the essential benignity of this condition against the risks of medication-discomfort and occasional threat to life in the patient or his small sibs who may gain access to the medication. This calls for good clinical judgment.

Conduct disorder and attention deficit disorders

Tricyclics (like antipsychotics) remain a second line drug in the treatment of these disorders to be used if stimulants have been ineffective. As shown in Table 1, it is rare for doses above 100 mg/day to be used and most studies have seen immediate effects from 50 to 75 mg. A usual starting dose here is around 1 mg/kg increasing in 25 mg increments over 2 weeks.

Long-term tolerance to the drug effect may be handled by increased dosage in some cases and in other cases by drug holidays. An upper daily dose limit of 5 mgm/kg has been recommended for children (Hayes et al., 1975), which for the average grade school child will not exceed 150 mgm. As with most psychotropic drugs, side effects are likely to be most troublesome for a few days immediately after dosage increments after which they often lessen to an acceptable degree.

Separation anxiety disorder (school phobia)

Treatment of school phobia will be largely centered around the family and school co-operation with the treating agency, in supporting early school return. On the basis of a single, double-blind report, doses in the range of 100–200 mg/day produced an effect by 6 weeks; the effect was not seen at 3 weeks. For patients receiving doses of imipramine greater than 3.5 mg/kg, baseline ECG and periodic ECG monitoring are suggested (Saraf et al., 1977).

For children, Kuhn-Gebhardt (1972) recommends that treatment with maprotiline be initiated with 10 mg tablets and gradually increased to a dosage level employed in adults, i.e. 75–150 mg/day, but it is suggested that until more data are available on the use of quadricyclics in children, the same precautions as with the tricyclics be observed.

Depression

Preliminary studies (see Table 2 and Puig-Antich studies) indicate that the higher dose range used for separation anxiety disorders are indicated. Precautions are, of course, the same as indicated above.

REFERENCES

Alderton, H. (1967) Imipramine in childhood nocturnal enuresis: relationship of time of administration to effect. Can. Psychiatr. Assoc. J. 12, 197–203.

Berney, T., Kolvin, I., Bhate, S. R., Garside, R. F., Jeans, J., Kay, B. and Scarth, L. (1981) School phobia: a therapeutic trial with clomipramine and short-term outcome. Br. J. Psychiatry 138, 110–118.

Bickel, M. (1975) Poisoning by tricyclic antidepressant drugs. Int. J. Clin. Pharmacol. 11, 145–176.

Blackwell, B. and Currah, J. (1973) The psychopharmacology of nocturnal enuresis. In: I. Kolvin, R. McKeith and S. Meadow (Eds), Bladder Control and Enuresis, Clinics and Developmental Medicine Nos. 48/49. Heinemann, London, pp. 231–257.

Brown, D., Winsberg, B., Bialer, I. and Press, M. (1973) Imipramine therapy and seizures. Am. J. Psychiatry 130, 210–212.

Byck, R. (1975) Drugs in the treatment of psychiatric disorders. In: L. Goodman and A. Gilman

144

(Eds), The Pharmacological Basis of Therapeutics, 5th Ed. Macmillan, New York, pp. 152–200.

Carlsson, A., Fuxe, K., Hamberger, B. and Lindqvist, M. (1966) Biochemical and histochemical studies on the effects of imipramine-like drugs on central and peripheral catecholamine neurons. Acta Physiol. Scand. 67, 481–497.

Cole, A. and Fried, F. (1972) Favorable experiences with imipramine in the treatment of neurogenic bladder. J. Urol. 107, 44–45.

Conners, C. (1976) Classification and treatment of childhood depression and depressive equivalents. In: D. Gallant and G. Simpson (Eds), Depression: Behavioral, Biochemical, Diagnostic and Treatment Concepts. Spectrum, New York, pp. 181–196.

Conners, C., Eisenberg, L. and Sharpe, L. (1965) A controlled study of the differential application of outpatient psychiatric treatment for children. Jpn. J. Child Psychiatry 6, 125–132.

Davies, B., Burrows, G. D. and Scoggins, B. (1975) Plasma nortriptyline and clinical response. Aust. N. Z. J. Psychiatry 9, 249–253.

DiMascio, A., Soltys, J. and Shader, R. (1970) Psychotropic drug side effects in children. In: R. Shader and A. DiMascio (Eds), Psychotropic Drug Side Effects. Williams and Wilkins, Baltimore.

Diokno, A. C., Hyndman, C. W., Hardy, D. A. and Lapides, J. (1972) Comparison of action of imipramine and propantheline on detrusor contraction. J. Urol. 107, 42–43.

Eisenberg, L., Gilbert, A., Cytryn, L. and Molling, P. (1961) The effectiveness of psychotherapy alone and in conjunction with perphenazine or placebo in the treatment of neurotic and hyperkinetic children. Am. J. Psychiatry 117, 1088–1093.

Elkins, R. and Rapoport, J. Psychopharmacology of adult and childhood depression: an overview. In: D. P. Cantwell and G. Carlson (Eds), Childhood Affective Disorders. Spectrum Publication, Inc., Jamaica, New York (in press).

Elkins, R., Rapoport, J. and Linsky, A. (1980) Obsessive-compulsive disorder in childhood: a review. J. Am. Acad. Child Psychiatry 19, 511–524.

Frommer, E. (1967) Treatment of childhood depression with antidepressant drugs. Br. Med. J. 1, 729–732.

Frommer, E. (1968) Depressive illness in childhood. In: A. Coppen and A. Walk (Eds), Recent Developments in Affective Disorders. Headly Brothers, Kent, pp. 117–136.

Garfinkel, B. D., Wender, P. H., Sloman, L., O'Neill, I. and Golombek, H. Tricyclic antidepressant and methylphenidate treatment of attention deficit disorder in children. J. Am. Acad. Child Psych. (in press).

Gittelman-Klein, R. (1974) Pilot clinical trial of imipramine in hyperkinetic children. In: C. K. Conners (Ed.), Clinical Use of Stimulant Drugs in Children. Excerpta Medica, Amsterdam, pp. 192–201.

Gittelman-Klein, R. and Klein, D. (1971) Controlled imipramine treatment of school phobia. Arch. Gen. Psychiatry 25, 204–207.

Gittelman-Klein, R. and Klein, D. (1973) School phobia: diagnostic considerations in the light of imipramine effects. J. Nerv. Ment. Dis. 156, 199–215.

Graham, P. (1974) Depression in pre-pubertal children. Dev. Med. Child Neurol. 16, 340–349.

Greenberg, L. and Yellin, A. (1975) Blood pressure and pulse changes in hyperactive children treated with imipramine and methylphenidate. Am. J. Psychiatry 132, 1325–1326.

Greenberg, L., Yellin, A., Spring, C. and Metcalf, M. (1975) Clinical effects of imipramine and methylphenidate in hyperactive children. Int. J. Ment. Health 4, 144–156.

Hayes, T. A. (1975) Role of the FDA. In: J. G. Langan (Chair.), Workshop on Psychotropic Drugs and the Mentally Retarded. Symposium presented at the meeting of the American Association on Mental Deficiency, Portland, Oregon.

Hayes, T. A., Panitch, M. L. and Barker, E. (1975) Imipramine dosage in children. A comment on 'Imipramine and Electrocardiographic Abnormalities in Hyperactive Children.' Am. J. Psychiatry 132, 546–547.

Herson, V. C., Schmitt, B. D. and Rumack, B. H. (1979) Magical thinking and imipramine poisoning in two school-aged children. J. Am. Med. Assoc. 241 (18), 1926–1927.

Huessy, H. and Wright, A. (1970) The use of imipramine in children's behavior disorders. Acta Paedopsychiatr. 37, 194–199.

Jorgenson, O. S., Lober, M., Christianson, J. and Gram, L. F. (1980) Plasma concentration and clinical effect in imipramine treatment of childhood enuresis. Clin. Pharmacokinetics 5 (4), 386–393.

Klutch, A. and Hanna, M.   (1976)   The urinary metabolites of imipramine in behavior disordered children (submitted for publication).

Kolvin, I., MacKeith, R. C. and Meadow, S. R.   (1973)   Bladder control and enuresis. J. B. Lippincott, Philadelphia, Pennsylvania.

Korczyn, A. D. and Kish, I.   (1979)   The mechanism of imipramine in enuresis nocturna. Clin. Exp. Pharmacol. Physiol. 6 (1), 31–35.

Krakowski, A.   (1965)   Amitriptyline in treatment of hyperkinetic children, a double-blind study. Psychosomatics 6, 355–360.

Kuhn, V. and Kuhn, R.   (1972)   Drug therapy for depression in children. In: A. Annell (Ed.), Depressive States in Childhood and Adolescence. Halsted Press, New York.

Kuhn-Gebhardt, V.   (1972)   Results obtained with a new antidepressant in children in depressive illness. In: A. Annell (Ed.), Depressive States in Childhood and Adolescence. Halsted Press, New York.

Kupietz, S. S. and Balka, E. B.   (1976)   Alterations in the vigilance performance of children receiving amitriptyline and methylphenidate pharmacotherapy. Psychopharmacology 50, 29–33.

Labay, P. and Boyarsky, S.   (1973)   The action of imipramine on the bladder musculature. J. Urol. 109, 385–386.

Lake, C. R., Mikkelsen, E. J., Rapoport, J. L., Zavadil, A. P., III and Kopin, I. J.   (1979)   Effect of imipramine on norepinephrine and blood pressure in enuretic boys. Clin. Pharmacol. Ther. 26 (5), 647–653.

Langer, D. H., Rapoport, J. I., Ebert, M. H., Lake, C. R. and Nee, L.   (in press)   Pilot trial of mianserin hydrochloride for childhood hyperactivity. In: B. Shopsin and L. Greenhill (Eds), The Psychobiology of Childhood: Profiles of Current Issues. Spectrum Publications, Inc., Jamaica, New York.

Law, W., Petti, T. A. and Kazdin, A. E.   (1981)   Withdrawal symptoms after graduated cessation of imipramine in children. Am. J. Psychiatry 138 (5), 647–650.

Ling, W., Oftedal, G. and Weinberg, W.   (1970)   Depressive illness in childhood presenting as severe headache. Am. J. Dis. Child. 120, 123–124.

Linnoila, M., Gualtieri, C. T., Jobson, K. and Staye, J.   (1979)   Characteristics of the therapeutic response to imipramine in hyperactive children. Am. J. Psychiatry 136 (9), 1201–1203.

Lucas, A. R., Lockett, H. J. L. and Grimm, F.   (1965)   Amitryptyline in childhood depressions. Dis. Nerv. Syst. 26, 105–110.

MacLean, R.   (1960)   Imipramine hydrochloride (Tofranil) and enuresis. Am. J. Psychiatry 117, 551.

Mahoney, D., Laferte, R. and Mahoney, J.   (1973)   Observations on sphincter-augmenting effect of imipramine in children with urinary incontinence. J. Urol. 1, 317–323.

Mendelson, W., Gillin, C. and Wyatt, R.   (1977)   Human Sleep and Its Disorders. Plenum Press, New York.

Mikkelsen, E. J. and Rapoport, J. L.   (1980)   Enuresis: psychopathology, sleep stage, and drug response. Urol. Clin. North Am. 7 (2), 361–377.

Mikkelsen, E. J., Rapoport, J. L., Nee, L. E., Gruenau, C., Mendelson, W. and Gillin, C.   (1980)   Childhood enuresis: sleep pattern and psychopathology. Arch. Gen. Psychiatry 37, 1139–1144.

Miller, R.   (1975)   Clinically important drug interactions. J. Marine Med. Assoc. 66, 18–25.

Poussaint, A. and Ditman, D.   (1965)   A controlled study of imipramine (Tofranil) in the treatment of childhood enuresis. J. Pediatr. 67, 283–290.

Pruitt, A. and Dayton, P.   (1971)   A comparison of the binding of drugs to adult and cord plasma. Eur. J. Clin. Pharmacol. 4, 59–62.

Puig-Antich, J., Blau, S., Marx, N., Breengill, L. and Chambers, S. W.   (1978)   Prepubertal major depressive disorder, a pilot study. J. Am. Acad. Child Psychiatry 17, 695–707.

Puig-Antich, J., Perel, J. M., Lupatkin, W., Chambers, W. J., Shea, C., Tabrizi, M. A. and Stiller, R. L.   (1979)   Plasma levels of imipramine (IMI) and desmethylimipramine (DMI) and clinical response in prepubertal major depressive disorder: a preliminary report. J. Am. Acad. Child Psychiatry 18 (4), 616–627.

Quinn, P. and Rapoport, J.   (1975)   One-year follow-up of hyperactive boys treated with imipramine or methylphenidate. Am. J. Psychiatry 132, 241–245.

146

Rapoport, J. (1965) Childhood behavior and learning problems treated with imipramine. Int. J. Neuropsychiatry 1, 635–642.

Rapoport, J. (1976) Pediatric psychopharmacology and childhood depression. In: D. Klein and R. Gittelman-Klein (Eds), Progress in Psychiatric Drug Treatment, Vol. 2, Brunner/Mazel, New York.

Rapoport, J., Quinn, P., Bradbard, G., Riddle, D. and Brookes, E. (1974) Imipramine and methylphenidate treatments of hyperactive boys: a double-blind comparison. Arch. Gen. Psychiatry 30, 789–793.

Rapoport, J. L., Mikkelsen, E. J., Zavadil, A., Nee, L., Gruenau, C., Mendelson, W. and Gillin, J. C. (1980) Childhood enuresis. II. Psychopathology, tricyclic concentration in plasma, and antienuretic effect. Arch. Gen. Psychiatry 37 (10), 1146–1152.

Rapoport, J., Elkins, R., Mikkelsen, E. and Lipsky, A. (1980) Clinical controlled trial of chlorimipramine in adolescents with obsessive-compulsive disorder. Psychopharmacol. Bull. 16, 61–63.

Riess, W., Rajogopalan, T. and Keberle, H. (1972) The metabolism and pharmacokinetics of ludiomil. In: P. Kielholz (Ed.), Depressive Illness. Williams and Wilkins, Baltimore.

Riess, W., Dubey, L., Funfgeld, E. and Imhof, P. (1975) The pharmacological properties of maprotiline in man. J. Int. Med. Res. 3 (2), 16–41.

Ritvo, E., Ornitz, E., Gottlieb, F., Poussaint, A., Maron B., Ditman, K. and Blinn (1969) Arousal and nonarousal enuretic events. Am. J. Psychiatry 126, 77–84.

Robinson, D. and Barker, E. (1976) Tricyclic antidepressant cardiotoxicity. J. Am. Med. Assoc. 236, 2089–2090.

Saraf, K., Klein, D., Gittelman-Klein, R., Gootman, N. and Greenhill, P. (1978) EKG effects of imipramine treatment in children. J. Am. Acad. Child Psychiatry 17, 60–69.

Shaffer, D. and Stephenson, J. (1977) Studies in enuresis I, alpha blockade in local anesthesia in the control of enuresis with the tricyclic antidepressants (unpublished manuscript).

Sidiropoulos, D. and Bickel, M. (1971) Eine todliche Vergiftung mit Imipramine in Kleiner Dosis bei einem Kleinlind. Schweiz. Med. Wochenschr. 101, 851–855.

Sigg, E. (1959) Pharmacological studies with Tofranil. Can. Psychiatr. Assoc. J. 4 (Suppl.), 75–85.

Snyder, S. and Yamamura, H. (1977) Antidepressants and the muscarinic acetylcholine receptor. Arch. Gen. Psychiatry 34, 236–239.

Spitzer, R., Endicott, J. and Rollins, E. (1978) Research diagnostic criteria: rationale and reliability. Arc. Gen. Psychiatry 35, 773–782.

Thorén, P., Ashberg, M., Cronholm, B., Jornestedt, L. and Traskman, L. (1980) Chlorimipramine treatment of obsessive-compulsive disorder in a controlled clinical trial. Arch. Gen, Psychiatry 37, 1281–1289.

Waizer, J., Hoffman, S., Polizos, P. and Engelhardt, D. (1974) Outpatient treatment of hyperactive school children with imipramine. Am. J. Psychiatry 131, 587–591.

Weinberg, W., Rutman, J., Sullivan, L. et al. (1973) Depression in children referred to an educational diagnostic center: diagnosis and treatment. J. Pediatr. 83, 1065–1072.

Weller, E. B., Weller, R. A., Preskorn, S. H. and Glotzbach, R. (1981) Steady-state plasma imipramine levels in prepubertal depressed children. Presented to Am. Psychiatr. Assoc., New Orleans, Louisiana.

Werry, J. (1976) Medication for hyperkinetic children. Drugs 11, 81–89.

Werry, J., Dowrick, P., Lampen, E. and Vamos, M. (1975a) Imipramine in enuresis: psychological and physiological effects. J. Child Psychol. Psychiatry 16, 289–300.

Werry, J., Sprague, R. and Cohen, M. (1975b) Conners' teacher rating scale for use in drug studies with children. J. Abnorm. Child Psychol. 3, 217–229.

Werry, J., Aman, M. and Lampen, E. (1976) Imipramine and chlordiazepoxide in enuresis. Paper presented to the Annual NIMH ECDEU Conference, Key Biscayne, Florida.

Werry, J. S., Aman, M. and Lampen, E. (1977) The effect of imipramine and methylphenidate in hyperactive aggressive children. Paper presented to the Annual meeting of the Australia and New Zealand College of Psychiatrists, Brisbane.

Werry, J. S., Aman, M. G. and Diamond, E. (1980) Imipramine and methylphenidate in hyperactive children. J. Child Psychol. Psychiatry 21 (1), 27–35.

Winsberg, B., Bialer, I., Kupietz, S. and Tobias, J. (1972) Effects of imipramine and dextroamphet-amine on behavior of neuropsychiatrically impaired children. Am. J. Psychiatry 128, 1425–1431.

Winsberg, B., Perel, J., Hurwic, M. and Klutch, A. (1974) Imipramine protein binding and pharma-cokinetics in children. In: I. Forrest, J. C. Carr and E. Usdin (Eds), The Phenothiazines and Struc-turally Related Drugs. Raven Press, New York.

Winsberg, B., Goldstein, S., Yepes, L. and Perel, J. (1975) Imipramine and electrocardiographic abnormalities in hyperactive children. Am. J. Psychiatry 132, 542–545.

Winsberg, B., Yepes, L. and Bialer, I. (1976) Pharmacological management of children with hyper-active/aggressive/inattentive behavior disorders. Clin. Pediatr. 15, 471–477.

Winsberg, B., Perel, J., Yepes, L. and Botti, E. (1977) Imipramine plasma levels and behavioral res-ponse in hyperkinetic/aggressive children (submitted for publication).

Yepes, L., Balka, E., Winsberg, E. and Bialer, I. (1977) Amitriptyline and methylphenidate treat-ment of behaviorally disordered children. J. Child Psychol. Psychiatry 18, 39–52.

Burrows/Norman/Davies (eds) Antidepressants
© *1983, Elsevier Science Publishers*

Chapter 12

Computer EEG in the discovery of antidepressants

TURAN M. ITIL

Division of Biological Psychiatry, New York Medical College, Valhalla, New York and HZI Research Center, Tarrytown, New York, U.S.A.

INTRODUCTION

The well-known antidepressants, such as imipramine, were discovered by chance. Subsequently, these are tested in different types of animals to determine their pharmacological profile. Then hundreds of compounds are screened through animal pharmacology. Drugs which have similar pharmacological profiles to the accidentally discovered antidepressants are predicted to have similar therapeutic effects, and they are selected for further clinical testing.

The validity and reliability of the animal pharmacological profiles in predicting antidepressants on humans are questionable. This model did not help to discover *brand new antidepressants* with *unusual* therapeutic properties. Instead, it provided many 'me-too' compounds which are a little bit better or worse copies of the antidepressants which are discovered by chance.

The causal treatment of depressive syndromes is not possible as long as the aetiology of the illness is not known. However, most recent theories indicate that the depressive illness is the result of the deviations of the biochemical and/or psychological functions of the brain. Therefore, it is logical to study the human brain function to understand the abnormal deviations of the behaviour and its possible treatment.

As is known, the electroencephalogram (EEG) is the only method to continuously, objectively, easily and economically study the human brain function (Brazier, 1964).

EEG FINDINGS IN DEPRESSION

In the past 40 years, hundreds of EEG studies were conducted in depressive patients.

Lemere (1941) was the first to report that manic-depressive patients tend to have a large amplitude, strongly dominant alpha rhythm. Davis (1941, 1942) confirmed Lemere's finding showing that manic-depressed individuals have more alpha-type EEG's compared with schizophrenics, and that predominantly depressed patients have more alpha-type and mixed alpha and slow activity EEG's, whereas predominantly manic patients have more mixed alpha and fast activity EEG's. Greenblatt et al. (1944) further discriminated the manic patients, based on the large amount of fast activity found in his manic group. Hurst et al. (1954) also found that manic patients have higher alpha frequencies than the depressed patients, but they did not show a shift in alpha frequency accompanying a phase change, whenever a manic-depressive patient shifted from mania to depression or from depression to mania.

Through visual analysis of the EEG's of 73 schizophrenics and 100 endogenous depressed patients, it was shown that there is a significant relationship between alpha dominance and depression, and beta dominance and schizophrenia (Itil, 1964). Brezinova et al. (1966) reported a greater abundance of alpha rhythm in patients with endogenous depression. Volavka et al. (1976) compared the EEG's of five depressed patients during the episodes of depression and during remission. The patients showed significantly more alpha and beta activities during the depressive phase.

Several investigators tried to relate the occurrence of clinical EEG abnormalities to depression. The results were contradictory, and in spite of the fact that this is partly due to the application of different criteria of EEG abnormality by various investigators, it appears that there are no confirmed specific, clinically abnormal EEG findings for depression, at least at a gross visual analysis level. If an increased incidence of EEG abnormalities in depression could be definitely established, it would be an indication of brain dysfunction. However, the clinical significance of the 'abnormal' EEG would still be doubtful since the various abnormalities reported in depressed patients are rather minor and nonspecific. Fehlow (1974), reporting a high incidence of EEG 'abnormality' in 200 depressed patients (45.5%), and an even higher incidence in 100 schizophrenics (57%), includes in the 'abnormalities' an unspecified dysrhythmia and even a reduction of alpha rhythm. This exemplifies the above-mentioned methodological considerations and the validity of reported EEG findings in terms of their clinical significance.

In conclusion, although there is no pathognomonic EEG pattern in depression, it appears that depression is generally related to an increased amount of alpha activity. This is the common finding of various studies both comparative and serial. This, if confirmed in a large study using quantitative EEG analysis, is a very important finding, since many well-controlled studies demonstrate that the EEG pattern of schizophrenia is characterized by a decrease of the amount of alpha waves (Itil et al., 1972a; Itil, 1977). Accordingly, the EEG patterns of schizophrenia and depression may almost be diametrically opposite. This indicates that the electrophysiological correlates of both illnesses are different, suggesting different biochemical bases of schizophrenia and depression. These findings support the fact that drugs effective in depressive illness are ineffective in schizophrenic patients, and they may even exacerbate the schizophrenia symptomatology. From all existing evidence, it seems likely that the decrease of alpha activity induced by the antidepressants has a corrective function, given the commonly found abundance of alpha waves in depression.

CLASSIFICATION OF ANTIDEPRESSANT DRUGS BY EEG EVALUATION

As early as 1937, Berger demonstrated that the drugs effective on human behaviour also produced obvious effects on human EEG. Based on the work of central stimulant and central depressant compounds, he reported that there are close correlations between changes in behaviour and changes in EEG patterns.

The systematic EEG investigations of drugs started with the discovery of the first 'classical' psychotropic compound, chlorpromazine. As early as 1954, it was reported that chlorpromazine, the first classical neuroleptic (major tranquilizer), produces systematic effects on human EEG (Bente and Itil, 1954). It was observed that chlorpromazine-induced changes are different from those of promethazine, a non-psychotropic phenothiazine.

Furthermore, it was demonstrated that piperazine phenothiazines, which have more potent antipsychotic effects than chlorpromazine, produce in quality similar, but in quantity more noticeable, changes in EEG than does chlorpromazine (Itil, 1960). Based on observations with various phenothiazine psychotropic drugs, a new *classification of psychotropics* was done based on scalp recorded, 'visually' evaluated human EEG (Itil, 1961).

It was reported that the drugs which have *'chlorpromazine reaction type'* (decrease of fast activity, increase of slow waves, and increase of slow alpha waves), have antipsychotic (antischizophrenic, or major tranquilizer or neuroleptic) effects in patients. Drugs which produce more alpha waves have more neuroleptic properties *('piperazine reaction type')*. Drugs which produce low voltage slow and fast activity *('promethazine type reaction')* do not have significant antipsychotic properties (Itil, 1961). Soon a 'fourth' type of EEG alteration (decrease of alpha and increase of very slow and fast waves) was found to be characteristic of laevomepromazine as well as thioridazine and imipramine.

In 1964, after studying compounds from the bi- and tricyclic antidepressant groups, the EEG drug classification was expanded. It was found that drugs which have therapeutic effects on depressive patients (antidepressants or thymoleptics) produce characteristic EEG changes (decrease of alpha, increase of both slow and fast waves). These changes were classified as *'laevomepromazine reaction type'*. Amitriptyline, imipramine, laevomepromazine, thioridazine and some experimental compounds (KS-75, Sandoz; WH-1219, Bayer) were included in this group (Itil, 1964). Subsequently, this group was called *'thymoleptic reaction type'*. With the discovery of chlordiazepoxide and diazepam it was established that these drugs, which were called 'minor tranquilizers' or 'anxiolytics', produce another type of EEG which shows significant differences from those of neuroleptics and thymoleptics. Thus, a most comprehensive visual EEG classification of psychotropic drugs was established (Itil, 1968).

While the EEG classification of psychotropic drugs was in agreement with the classification of clinicians (Arnold et al., 1970), it was 'subjective' and was based on visual (eyeball) evaluations of the records. A quantitative approach with scientifically approved techniques and statistically analysable data was required. Subsequently, first the analogue frequency analysis and later the computer methods were used to analyse the EEG (Fink, 1961; Fink et al., 1966; Itil et al., 1968; 1969).

Based on the systematic studies using computer-analysed EEG, we could establish the following:

TABLE 1

HZI selected drug groups correlated with basic study individual thymoleptics.

Basic study	NEUROLEPTICS RR 1 hr	RR 3 hr	RT 1 hr	RT 3 hr	ANXIOLYTICS RR 1 hr	RR 3 hr	RT 1 hr	RT 3 hr	THYMOLEPTICS RR 1 hr	RR 3 hr	RT 1 hr	RT 3 hr	PSYCHOSTIMULANTS RR 1 hr	RR 3 hr	RT 1 hr	RT 3 hr	PLACEBO RR 1 hr	RR 3 hr	RT 1 hr	RT 3 hr
Imipramine	.85	.29	.03	.53	-.46	.33	.29	.18	.43	.92	-.94	.85	.55	-.83	-.52	-.59	.74	-.46	.38	.23
	M = .42				M = .08				M = .78 *1*				M = -.34				M = -.22			
Desipramine	-.53	-.50	-.05	-.06	.30	.38	-.31	.31	-.40	.03	.10	.79	-.35	-.16	-.01	-.63	-.64	-.47	.08	-.29
	M = -.28				M = .17				M = .13				M = -.28				M = -.33			
Amitriptyline	.06	.13	-.21	.32	.65	.61	.50	.36	.37	.86	.94	.98	-.57	-.95	-.68	-.81	-.29	-.56	.12	.02
	M = .07				M = .53				M = .78 *1*				M = -.75				M = -.17			
Nortriptyline	.64	.16	.06	.36	-.11	.53	.52	.36	.63	.92	.22	.93	.23	-.96	.11	-.72	.43	-.55	.53	.11
	M = .30				M = .32				M = .67 *1*				M = -.33				M = .13			
Mianserin	.45	.66	-.43	.15	.02	.11	.46	.27	.87	.84	.88	.77	.35	-.67	-.81	-.60	.01	-.12	.00	-.10
	M = .20				M = .21				M = .84 *1*				M = -.43				M = -.05			

M = mean.

1 First choice: mean is greater than .35 and one or more periods is greater than .75 (no minus correlations).

2 Second choice: mean is greater than .35 or one or more periods is greater than .75 (no minus correlations).

3 Third choice: mean is greater than .35 and minus correlation.

a) The computer EEG drug profiles (CEEG^{TM} t-drug profiles) (Itil, 1974) of the same drugs under standard conditions are almost identical and replicable in the same or in different populations.

b) The *'physiological equivalency'* (the similarity of the computer EEG profiles) of different compounds, independent of their chemical structure or pharmacological properties, is indicative of the *therapeutic (psychotropic) equivalency*. All antidepressants produce similar CEEG effects which are called antidepressant or thymoleptic CEEG profiles. Also, all anxiolytics (anxiolytic CEEG profiles), neuroleptics (neuroleptic CEEG profiles) and psychostimulants (psychostimulant CEEG profiles) induce similar CEEG effects.

c) Drugs with different therapeutic effects (*'therapeutic unequivalent'*) produce also different CEEG effects (*physiological unequivalent*). Computer EEG profiles of clinically well-known antidepressants, for example, are significantly different from neuroleptics.

d) In order to establish whether the well-known antidepressants, neuroleptics, anxiolytics and psychostimulants have indeed 'typical' CEEG profiles and these are significantly different from each other, a computer EEG drug data base was established. HZI Computer Center EEG drug data base includes CEEG profiles of 85 well-established psychotropics, collected in 79 quantitative pharmaco-EEG studies (Itil et al., 1971, 1979; Itil, 1974). The validity and reliability of the data base was demonstrated by classifying the established and marketed psychotropic drugs (Itil 1982; Itil et al., in press).

COMPUTER DATA BASE CLASSIFICATION OF ANTIDEPRESSANTS WHICH ARE ALREADY PREDICTED BY ANIMAL PHARMACOLOGY

According to the CEEG data base classification systems, there are two main types of antidepressant drugs.

'Sedative' type antidepressants

Among the *marketed* compounds in the U.S. studied in our laboratories, amitriptyline (in dosages of 40–75 mg), nortriptyline (50–75 mg), imipramine (50–75 mg), protriptyline (5 mg) and tranylcypromine sulfate (15–20 mg), could clearly be classified as 'sedative' type antidepressants by the computer data base (Tables 1 and 2).

Among the *experimental* compounds which are predicted by animal pharmacology as antidepressants, the computer data base could confirm this prediction on fluotracen (100, 150, 200 mg SKF 28175), TRH (50 mg oral), citalopram (10–50 mg) and fluvoxamine (75 mg). All these compounds were classified by the data base as antidepressant, similar to tricyclic antidepressants (Table 3). Also, sulpiride in 800 mg dose was classified as antidepressant. It is reported that sulpiride has antidepressant properties in addition to its antianxiety and antipsychotic effects. In lower dosages (400 mg), sulpiride was classified by the computer data base as sedative-neuroleptic.

Psychostimulant-type antidepressants

Among the *tricyclics,* desipramine (50–75 mg) and protriptyline (over 5 mg dosages) were classified as 'psychostimulant', similar to dextroamphetamine, phenelzine sulfate,

154

TABLE 2

HZI selected drug groups correlated with basic study individual thymoleptics.

HZI Basic study	NEUROLEPTICS					ANXIOLYTICS					THYMOLEPTICS					PSYCHOSTIMULANTS					PLACEBO				
	RR		RT			RR		RT			RR		RT			RR		RT			RR		RT		
	1 hr	3 hr	1 hr	3 hr		1 hr	3 hr	1 hr	3 hr		1 hr	3 hr	1 hr	3 hr		1 hr	3 hr	1 hr	3 hr		1 hr	3 hr	1 hr	3 hr	
Methyl-phenidate	-.44	-.88	-.36	-.66	M = -.58	.14	.39	.02	.10	M = .16	-.85	-.68	-.76	-.80	M = -.77	.44	.28	.18	.41	M = .32	.08	-.18	-.46	-.16	M = -.17
Phenelzine sulphate	.48	.04	-.11	-.33	M = .02	-.58	-.38	.18	.44	M = .08	.34	-.71	.24	-.29	M = .10	.51	.79	-.46	-.03	M = .20	.41	.64	-.45	.01	M = .15
Dextroamphet-amine	.18	-.27	.47	-.08	M = .07	-.50	-.35	-.58	-.51	M = -.48	-.52	-.84	-.86	-.90	M = -.78	.86	.87	.87	.93	M = .88 *1*	.69	.49	.07	.23	M = .37
Tranylcypro-mine sulphate	.27	.36	-.37	.47	M = .18	-.08	-.03	.47	.05	M = .10	.42	.14	.70	.60	M = .48 *2*	.23	-.06	-.53	-.39	M = -.18	-.36	.33	.18	.14	M = .07
Caffeine	-.70	-.18	-.13	.03	M = -.24	.68	.10	-.04	.03	M = .19	-.55	-.58	-.88	-.63	M = -.66	-.09	.48	.51	.53	M = .35 *2*	-.35	.47	-.30	.54	M = .09

M = mean.

1 First choice: mean is greater than .35 and one or more periods is greater than .75 (no minus correlations).

2 Second choice: mean is greater than .35 or one or more periods is greater than .75 (no minus correlations).

3 Third choice: mean is greater than .35 and minus correlation.

155

TABLE 3

HZI data base / Study drug	N	Proj. no.	SEDATIVE-NEUROLEPTICS				HYPNOTIC-ANXIOLYTICS				SEDATIVE-THYMOLEPTICS				PSYCHOSTIMULANTS				PLACEBO			
			RR 1 hr	RR 3 hr	RT 1 hr	RT 3 hr	RR 1 hr	RR 3 hr	RT 1 hr	RT 3 hr	RR 1 hr	RR 3 hr	RT 1 hr	RT 3 hr	RR 1 hr	RR 3 hr	RT 1 hr	RT 3 hr	RR 1 hr	RR 3 hr	RT 1 hr	RT 3 hr
SKF 28175 150 mg	8	HZI 66	.54	.43	.44	.36	-.10	.47	-.02	.25	.61	.97	.72	.41	-.13	-.94	.50	-.36	.20	-.52	.29	.31
					mean: .44				*.15*				*.68 *1**				*-.48*				*.07*	
SKF 28175 200 mg	8	HZI 66	-.44	.31	.10	.07	.35	.52	.21	.65	.06	.95	.85	.80	-.75	-.94	-.79	-.77	-.75	-.60	.09	-.04
					.01				*.43*				*.67 *1**				*-.81*				*-.32*	
SFK 28175 100 mg	6	NY-147	.80	.35	.21	.04	-.12	.79	.62	.86	.71	.77	.65	.81	-.01	-.69	-.55	-.80	.43	-.25	.08	.00
					.35				*.54*				*.74 *1**				*-.51*				*.07*	
TRH 50 mg	10	HZI 54	-.19	.09	.27	-.22	.14	.44	.34	.56	.60	.62	.90	.83	-.76	-.62	-.75	-.81	-.61	-.54	.32	-.42
					-.01				*.37*				*.74 *1**				*-.74*				*-.32*	
Citalopram 10 mg	12	HZI 122	.69	.22	.67	.31	-.48	.37	.03	.41	.08	.78	.34	.81	.63	-.75	.01	-.58	.65	-.49	.85	.21
					.47				*.08*				*.50 *1**				*-.17*				*.32*	
Citalopram 50 mg	12	HZI 122	.05	.12	-.28	-.41	.13	.43	.50	.20	.58	.78	.70	.40	-.83	-.84	-.15	-.05	.84	-.48	-.23	-.61
					-.13				*.32*				*.62 *1**				*-.71*				*-.48*	
Fluvoxamine 75 mg	12	C14	.79	.58	.11	.18	-.47	-.48	.48	.51	.40	.01	.77	.87	.21	.13	-.74	-.87	.60	.58	.25	-.13
					.41				*.00*				*.51 *1**				*-.32*				*.32*	
Sulpiride 800 mg	12	HZI 76	-.12	.27	.22	.57	.37	.60	.50	.37	.34	.68	.42	.79	-.24	-.68	-.31	-.80	.05	-.30	.28	.14
					.24				*.46*				*.56 *1**				*-.51*				*.04*	

1 First choice: mean is greater than .35 and one or more periods is greater than .75 (no minus correlations).
2 Second choice: mean is greater than .35 or one or more periods is greater than .75 (no minus correlations).
3 Third choice: mean is greater than .35 and minus correlation.

TABLE 4

HZI data base / Study base	N	Proj. no.	SEDATIVE-NEUROLEPTICS				HYPNOTIC-ANXIOLYTICS				SEDATIVE-THYMOLEPTICS				PSYCHOSTIMULANTS				PLACEBO			
			RR 1 hr	RR 3 hr	RT 1 hr	RT 3 hr	RR 1 hr	RR 3 hr	RT 1 hr	RT 3 hr	RR 1 hr	RR 3 hr	RT 1 hr	RT 3 hr	RR 1 hr	RR 3 hr	RT 1 hr	RT 3 hr	RR 1 hr	RR 3 hr	RT 1 hr	RT 3 hr
Desipramine 50 mg	12	NY-117	.33	−.21	−.64	−.25	−.25	−.39	.26	−.31	−.39	−.85	−.41	−.81	.94	.90	.22	.84	.77	.62	−.47	.31
			mean: −.19				*−.17*				*−.62*				*.72 *1**				*.31*			
Protriptyline 40 mg	12	HZI 22	.45	.10	.32	.24	−.60	−.59	.24	.38	−.14	−.73	−.12	.01	.75	.76	.16	−.12	.02	.79	.10	.36
			.28				*−.14*				*−.25*				*.39 *3**				*.31*			
Isocarboxazid 0.5 mg/kg	10	MIP 258	−.25	.01	.29	−.42	.23	−.59	−.27	−.43	−.40	−.80	−.37	−.76	.11	.90	.57	.87	−.18	.71	.38	.04
			−.09				*−.27*				*−.58*				*.61 *1**				*.24*			
Viloxazine 50 mg	12	NY-117	.64	−.15	.02	−.01	−.52	−.71	.63	−.58	−.12	−.90	.82	−.86	.78	.93	−.84	.85	.81	.64	−.01	.27
			−.12				*−.30*				*−.27*				*.43 *3**				*.42*			
Amoxapine 25 mg	10	HZI 24	.14	−.30	.42	.25	−.47	−.75	−.69	−.88	−.58	−.70	−.29	−.71	.93	.66	.55	.75	.57	.28	.54	.16
			.13				*−.70*				*−.57*				*.72 *1**				*.39*			
Amoxapine 50 mg	10	HZI 24	.69	.23	.37	.31	−.78	−.82	−.82	−.80	−.02	−.51	−.62	−.65	.68	.60	.79	.77	.68	.58	.21	.41
			.40				*−.81*				*−.45*				*.71 *1**				*.47*			

1 First choice: mean is greater than .35 and one or more periods is greater than .75 (no minus correlations).
2 Second choice: mean is greater than .35 or one or more periods is greater than .75 (no minus correlations).
3 Third choice: mean is greater than .35 and minus correlation.

caffeine, methylphenidate, etc. (Tables 2 and 4). Isocarboxazid, a MAO inhibitor, was also classified in this group.

Among the *experimental* antidepressants in the U.S.A. viloxazine in low dosage (50 mg) and amoxapine (25 mg) were classified in the psychostimulant group of compounds by the computer EEG data base (Table 4).

CEEG DISCOVERY OF ANTIDEPRESSANTS (not predicted by animal pharmacology model)

A series of compounds which do not have 'typical' pharmacological and biochemical profiles of the classical antidepressants, and therefore could not be predicted by animal pharmacology, were predicted as antidepressant based on their CEEG profiles alone (Itil, 1975, 1978). These compounds were developed, and some even marketed, for uses other than as antidepressant. They were investigated using the methods of QPEEG, either because of the anecdotal informations concerning their behavioural effects or through routine CEEG screening processes. Previously collected data was recently reanalysed and automatically classified by the data base.

Mianserin (GB-94)

Mianserin (GB-94) (Fig. 1) is the first marketed compound of which the antidepressant property was successfully discovered by the computer-analysed EEG (Itil et al., 1972b). Mianserin hydrochloride was developed by structural modification of the phenobenzamine molecule in order to enhance its antiserotonin activity. Based on animal pharmacology, potent, peripheral antiserotonin and antihistamine properties of mianserin were found, but with less central nervous system (CNS) effects than with the control compound, cyproheptadine. Mianserin was predicted to be effective in the treatment of allergic conditions. Since clinical testing did not show any superiority to existing antiallergic compounds, the clinical trials were discontinued. In the search for potent antiserotonin compounds for the treatment of manic patients, we were interested in studying the CNS effects of mianserin. First, a pilot single dose tolerance QPEEG trial and subsequently a

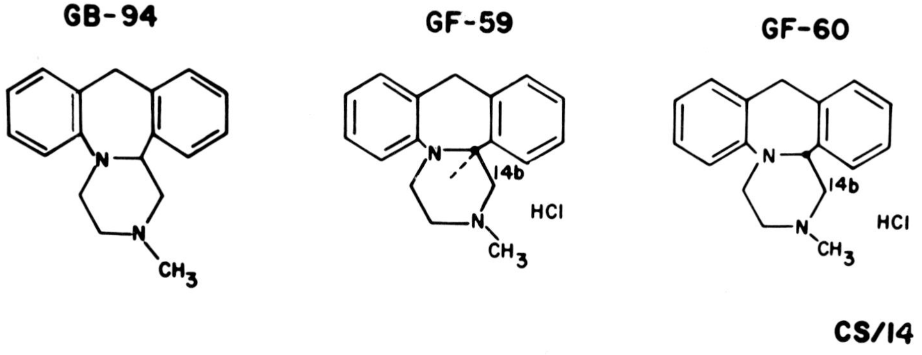

Fig. 1.

double-blind crossover study in healthy volunteers indicated significant CNS effects of this compound. The CEEG profile of mianserin resembled those of tricyclic, sedative-anti-depressants, particularly amitriptyline. Thus, based on the hypothesis that compounds with electrophysiologically 'equivalent' effects (as determined by the scalp-recorded computer-analysed EEG) will also have 'equivalent' psychotropic properties, the antidepressant properties of mianserin were predicted (Itil et al., 1972b). Subsequent clinical trials confirmed the CEEG prediction. Mianserin, which is now marketed as an antidepressant in several countries, does not possess any of the significant biochemical characteristics of the well-known antidepressants.

With the question whether the newly developed computer EEG data base would be able to predict the antidepressant properties of mianserin, the previously collected data from three different studies were reanalysed and classified. As seen in Table 5, the CNS effects of 20 mg and 30 mg mianserin (GB-94) could be classified by our data base as similar to sedative type antidepressants. In higher dosages (40 and 60 mg) mianserin primarily showed sedative type neuroleptic effects. Fifteen milligrams mianserin could not be classified in any psychotropic drug group (sample size was only six subjects). Two-dimensional classification of different dosages of mianserin demonstrated both neuroleptic and anxiolytic properties of this compound in addition to thymoleptic properties (Fig. 2). Also, clinical studies suggested anxiolytic properties of GB-94 (Itil, 1978).

GF-59 and GF-60

Mianserin (GB-94) is comprised of equivalent amounts of optical isomers, GF-59 and GF-60 (Fig. 1). In order to establish whether the biological activities of GB-94 reside in either GF-59 or GF-60, or whether both isomers were equally active, single dose trials were carried out in animals using representative pharmacological tests. As with GB-94, the isomers were found to be less active in rats than they were in mice. GF-60 was somewhat more active as an inhibitor of spontaneous activity than was GF-59 or GB-94. In the test of co-ordinated motor activity, GF-60 was found to be more active than GB-94, and GF-59 was least active. As a serotonin antagonist, GF-60 was more potent than GF-59 as well as GB-94. As a histamine antagonist, all three compounds were found to have the same activity. As anticholinergic, all three compounds also had the same degree of activity, so they were a thousand times less active than atropine. In one test for anticholinergic properties, GF-60 appeared to be less active than GF-59 or GB-94. With respect to the cardiovascular system, however, GF-59 appeared to be more active than both drugs, and GF-60 was similar to GB-94. It was concluded that GF-60 is slightly more toxic than GF-59 and GB-94, and it seems to be somewhat more active centrally as well as peripherally (serotonin, but not histamine), with less effect on the cardiovascular system than GB-94 and GF-59.

Since these data were collected on animals, and no information was available in regard to the effects of the isomers in man, a double-blind crossover study has been carried out in 12 healthy volunteers with 3 doses of GF-59 and GF-60, using the methods of quantitative pharmaco-EEG. As seen in Table 6, the computer data base classified the CNS effects of all three dosages (20 mg, 40 mg, 60 mg) of GF-60 and 60 mg GF-59 as sedative-antidepressant. Twenty and 40 mg GF-59 were classified primarily as sedative-neurolep-

TABLE 5

HZI data base Study drug	N	Proj. no.	SEDATIVE-NEUROLEPTICS RR 1 hr	RR 3 hr	RT 1 hr	RT 3 hr	HYPNOTIC-ANXIOLYTICS RR 1 hr	RR 3 hr	RT 1 hr	RT 3 hr	SEDATIVE-THYMOLEPTICS RR 1 hr	RR 3 hr	RT 1 hr	RT 3 hr	PSYCHOSTIMULANTS RR 1 hr	RR 3 hr	RT 1 hr	RT 3 hr
GB-94 15 mg	10	HZI 1	-.22	-.59	-.22	.16	-.01	.25	.01	-.10	-.16	-.21	.20	.07	-.35	.12	-.23	-.08
					mean: -.22				*.04*				*-.03*				*-.14*	
GB-94 20 mg	10	HZI 33	.74	.67	.46	.74	-.41	-.14	.59	.05	.30	.73	.80	.71	.68	-.67	-.63	-.66
					.65				*.02*				*.64 *1**				*-.32*	
GB-94 30 mg	10	HZI 33	.45	.66	-.43	.15	.02	.11	.46	.27	.87	.84	.88	.77	.35	-.67	-.61	-.60
					.21				*.22*				*.84 *1**				*-.43*	
GB-94 40 mg	10	HZI 33	.54	.50	.43	.66	-.45	-.48	-.36	-.55	-.02	-.34	.23	-.30	.76	.51	.02	.39
					.53 *2*				*-.46*				*-.11*				*.42*	
GB-94 60 mg	10	HZI 33	.72	.81	.79	.78	-.16	-.17	.20	.28	.39	.40	.44	.70	.40	-.27	-.20	-.68
					.78 *1*				*.04*				*.48*				*-.19*	

1 First choice: mean is greater than .35 and one or more periods is greater than .75 (no minus correlations).
2 Second choice: mean is greater than .35 or one or more periods is greater than .75 (no minus correlations).
3 Third choice: mean is greater than .35 and minus correlation.

159

160

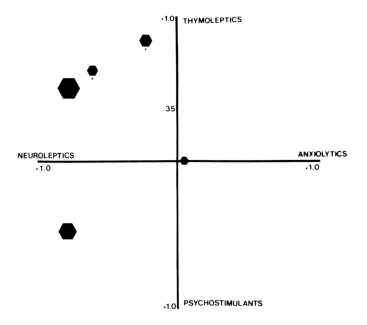

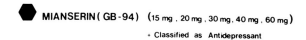 MIANSERIN (GB-94) (15 mg , 20 mg , 30 mg, 40 mg , 60 mg)

+ Classified as Antidepressant

Fig. 2. Two-dimensional classification of mianserin from different studies. If the computer EEG pro-file of a drug is identical to one of the four psychotropic drug groups from the data base, the correla-tion coefficient will be 1.0. In the two-dimensional classification system, the drug is classified based on the highest 2-correlation coefficient. Mianserin, in dosages of 20 and 30 mg, was clearly classified as antidepressant, whereas higher dosages (40 and 60 mg) were classified primarily as neuroleptic. Next to the thymoleptics, 20 and 30 mg mianserin also exhibited neuroleptic properties.

tic. According to the two-dimensional classification system, GF-60 in higher doses (40 mg and 60 mg) was classified between thymoleptics and anxiolytics, whereas GF-59 in all doses (20, 40 and 60 mg) and 20 mg GF-60 were classified between thymoleptics and neuroleptics (Fig. 3). This study indicated that both isomers of GB-94 produce systematic CNS effects on human brain function. One isomer (GF-60) seems to possess more pro-nounced antidepressant (thymoleptic) properties than the other (GF-59). This confirmed the findings of animal pharmacology which suggested that GF-60 is more CNS-effective than GF-59. Like mianserin, GF-59 and GF-60 also do not have the 'classical' animal phar-

TABLE 6

HZI data base Study drug	N	Proj. no.	SEDATIVE-NEUROLEPTICS RR 1 hr	3 hr	RT 1 hr	3 hr	mean	HYPNOTIC-ANXIOLYTICS RR 1 hr	3 hr	RT 1 hr	3 hr	mean	SEDATIVE-THYMOLEPTICS RR 1 hr	3 hr	RT 1 hr	3 hr	mean	PSYCHOSTIMULANTS RR 1 hr	3 hr	RT 1 hr	3 hr	mean	PLACEBO RR 1 hr	3 hr	RT 1 hr	3 hr	mean
GF-59 20 mg	10	HZI 33	.23	.44	.14	.90	*mean: .44*1**	-.14	-.31	.49	-.09	*-.01*	.29	-.32	.93	.46	*.34*	-.27	.44	-.84	-.31	*-.24*	-.06	.72	.16	.60	*.36*
GF-59 40 mg	10	HZI 33	.33	.46	.52	.83	*.54*1**	-.20	-.13	-.21	-.31	*-.21*	.42	.73	.09	.46	*.43*	-.02	-.67	.06	-.34	*-.24*	.05	-.36	.33	.22	*.06*
GF-59 60 mg	10	HZI 33	.76	.87	.22	.61	*.62*	-.20	-.07	.54	.15	*.11*	.78	.24	.94	.74	*.68*1**	.01	-.06	-.85	-.67	*-.39*	.46	.60	.24	.11	*.35*
GF-60 20 mg	10	HZI 33	.44	.79	.23	.66	*.53*	-.53	-.08	.19	.22	*-.05*	.61	.67	.74	.82	*.71*1**	-.16	-.54	-.59	-.78	*-.52*	.08	-.04	.26	.19	*.12*
GF-60 40 mg	10	HZI 33	-.49	.48	-.05	.59	*.13*	.76	.48	.73	-.12	*.46*	.31	.44	.89	.57	*.55*1**	-.82	-.32	-.90	-.41	*-.61*	-.69	.04	-.07	.06	*-.16*
GF-60 60 mg	10	HZI 33	-.52	.40	.08	.46	*.11*	.42	.15	.37	.05	*.25*	.30	.86	.80	.79	*.69*1**	-.89	-.85	-.84	-.69	*-.82*	-.83	-.50	-.04	-.12	*-.37*

1 First choice: mean is greater than .35 and one or more periods is greater than .75 (no minus correlations).
2 Second choice: mean is greater than .35 or one or more periods is greater than .75 (no minus correlations).
3 Third choice: mean is greater than .35 and minus correlation.

162

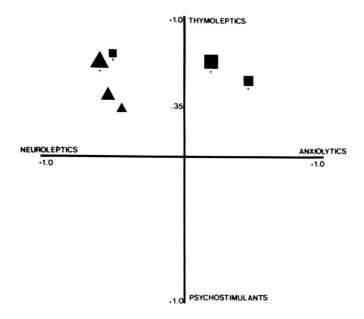

COMPUTER EEG
CLASSIFICATION OF GF-59[(x)] AND GF-60[(x)]
(BASED ON HZI-COMPUTER DATA BASE)

 GF-59 (20, 40, 60 mg)

GF-60 (20, 40, 60 mg)

+ Classified as Antidepressant

(x) Isomers of GB-94 - MIANSERIN

Fig. 3. In two-dimensional classification, all three dosages of GF-60 were primarily classified as anti-depressant (secondarily twice anxiolytic and in one dose neuroleptic). GF-59 was classified in all three dosages between thymoleptics and neuroleptics. In one dose it was primarily classified as antidepressant.

macology and biochemistry profiles of the well-known antidepressants. No clinical studies were conducted with GF-59 or GF-60.

Mesterolone

Mesterolone, a synthetic androgen, is another compound which was predicted by CEEG as having antidepressive properties. Although mesterolone is an active androgen, it does not block LH and FSH secretion of the anterior pituitary up to 100 mg daily. Mestero-lone is considered to be effective in the treatment of disorders due to androgen deficiency. Certain behavioural effects such as increase of mental alertness, mood elevation, improvement of memory, were observed during the mesterolone treatment of patients with androgen deficiency.

Based on the hypothesis that drugs which cause behavioural effects also induce EEG changes, QPEEG trials were conducted with mesterolone in healthy volunteers. In conventional dosage (10–25 mg), mesterolone produced CNS effects similar to psychostimulant compounds such as dextroamphetamine, methylphenidate and isocarboxazid. In high dosages (100–1600 mg), the CEEG profiles of mesterolone resembled sedative type antidepressant drugs (Itil et al., 1974). Thus antidepressant type clinical effects of mesterolone were predicted (Itil and Herrmann 1975).

Preliminary clinical trials confirmed this prediction (Klaiber et al., 1976; Itil et al., 1974, 1978).

Previously collected QPEEG data on mesterolone were reanalysed and classified by the data base. As seen in Table 7, the data base classified the CEEG effects of mesterolone as a first choice sedative type antidepressant.

Oestradiol valerate

Oestradiol valerate, the valeric-acid ester of endogenous female oestrogen, is in daily dosages of 1–2 mg an effective drug in menopausal states. According to the report of Klaiber et al. (1972), conjugated oestrogen in high dosages produced mood elevated effects. Thus we postulated that oestradiol valerate would have significant effects on human brain function. Our QPEEG studies indicated that oestradiol valerate indeed has significant effects on human CNS after single oral dosages (Itil and Herrmann, 1978). The CEEG profiles of oestradiol were classified by the computer data base as thymoleptic (Table 7). Thus, clinical antidepressant effects of oestradiol valerate were predicted (Itil et al., 1977). No systematic clinical studies were conducted with oestradiol valerate in depressed patients.

GC-46

GC-46 (2(n)-methyl-1,3,4,14b-tetrahydro-2H-pyragino (1,2-d) (b,f) (1,4) oxazepine) is a tetracyclic compound, chemically similar to Mianserin, and was developed also as an antiallergic for the treatment of migraine and asthma.

Animal studies with GC-46 demonstrated its capability to diminish the responses to 5-hydroxytryptamine (5-HT) on the bronchi, isolated uterus, blood pressure, and capillary permeability. It also inhibited the oedema-inducing effect of 5-HT in the rat. Furthermore, GC-46 was found to antagonize tryptamine-induced convulsions which are thought to be provoked due to an effect of tryptamine on central 5-HT receptors. In a series of experiments with ganglion-blocked dogs, the anti-adrenaline effect was also examined and this latter effect was found to prevail above the anti 5-HT effect.

Some of the experiments included examination of the anti-histaminic properties of GC-46. The compound decreased the response to histamine of the bronchi and the histamine-induced rat paw oedema. When the cardiovascular activities of GC-46 were studied

164

TABLE 7

HZI data base Study drug	N	Proj. no.	SEDATIVE-NEUROLEPTICS RR 1 hr	RR 3 hr	RT 1 hr	RT 3 hr	mean	HYPNOTIC-ANXIOLYTICS RR 1 hr	RR 3 hr	RT 1 hr	RT 3 hr	mean	SEDATIVE-THYMOLEPTICS RR 1 hr	RR 3 hr	RT 1 hr	RT 3 hr	mean	PSYCHOSTIMULANTS RR 1 hr	RR 3 hr	RT 1 hr	RT 3 hr	mean	PLACEBO RR 1 hr	RR 3 hr	RT 1 hr	RT 3 hr	mean
GC-46 30 mg	6	HZI 5	.35	.46	.34	.32	mean: .38	-.46	-.24	-.20	.00	-.22	.33	.49	.40	.50	.43 *2*	.05	-.47	-.24	-.47	-.28	.28	-.21	.20	-.04	.06
Mesterolone 200 mg	12	NY-093	-.09	.33	.25	.46	.24	.63	.69	.53	.36	.55	.65	.83	.97	.89	.84 *1*	-.63	-.74	-.89	-.83	-.77	-.38	-.41	.16	.00	-.16
Estradiol valerate 5 mg	12	HZI 69	.00	.01	.00	-.12	-.05	.00	.32	.00	.81	.56	.00	.40	.00	.79	.60 *1*	.00	-.81	.00	-.85	-.83	.00	-.48	.00	-.14	-.31

1 First choice: mean is greater than .35 and one or more periods is greater than .75 (no minus correlations).
2 Second choice: mean is greater than .35 or one or more periods is greater than .75 (no minus correlations).
3 Third choice: mean is greater than .35 and minus correlation.

it was found to have a potent α-adrenolytic action. Anti-noradrenaline action was also observed on the perfused hindquarter preparation of the rat.

As to anti-inflammatory properties, the compound GC-46 showed moderate activity in the rat paw oedema test performed with inflammation-inducing agents (kaolin, cobra venom). In the UV erythema test it was feebly active when administered subcutaneously and inactive after oral administration.

The CNS activity was first studied in the reserpine antagonism test. GC-46 showed a tendency to facilitate reserpine-induced hypothermia. This was also found with the reference compound cyproheptadine.

The observation made with GC-46 in the open field behaviour test may indicate sedative properties. The new compound was more active than cyproheptadine in diminishing motor activity in mice. However, as cyproheptadine is known by neuropharmacologists to induce a syndrome of exaggerated reactivity, no conclusions can be drawn as to whether GC-46 is more or less sedative than cyproheptadine. The fact that GC-46 was less active than cyproheptadine in potentiating hexobarbital-induced sleep might indicate that the former compound is less sedative than the latter. In the tremorine test and in the muricide behaviour test, GC-46 was found to be inactive.

Finally, in experimental antimigraine studies, GC-46 was found to exert a strong α-adrenolytic, and a weak anti 5-HT activity. Overall, no significant psychotropic properties could be predicted by animal data.

QPEEG trials indicated that GC-46 has significant CNS effects. The CEEG profiles of GC-46 were found to be similar to tricyclic antidepressants (Itil et al., 1972). Thus antidepressant effects of GC-46 were predicted (Itil, 1975). In reanalysing the previous data, it was demonstrated that the data base classified the CEEG profiles of GC-46 as a first choice antidepressant (Table 7). Two-dimensional classification of these compounds indicated that mesterolone and oestradiol valerate possess anxiolytic properties secondary to their antidepressant effects, whereas GC-46 has secondary neuroleptic effects (Fig. 4).

DISCUSSION AND CONCLUSIONS

As early as 1954, we observed that chlorpromazine produces 'typical' alterations in EEG (Bente and Itil, 1954). In subsequent years we also observed other drugs that are effective for schizophrenia (neuroleptics) do produce similar alterations in EEG as does chlorpromazine.

In the early 60s, we observed that all drugs which have clinical antidepressant effects in depressed patients, produce, after single oral dosages, significant effects on scalp recorded and computer analysed human EEG. These effects are characterized in two different patterns:

a) Antidepressants with primarily sedative properties which produce more slow and fast activities and decrease alpha frequencies. Tricyclic antidepressants such as amitriptyline and imipramine are most representative of this group.
b) Antidepressants with clinically known 'stimulant' properties, which increase slow alpha activity and decrease very slow and very fast activities. Among the tricyclic antidepressants, desmethylimipramine and protriptyline produce these kinds of EEG patterns. Also,

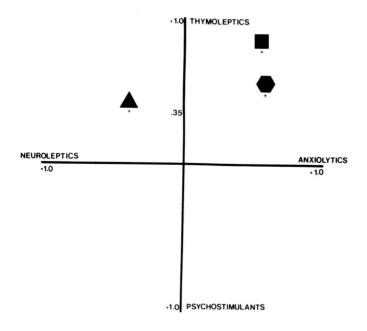

DISCOVERY OF
ANTIDEPRESSANTS BASED ON COMPUTER EEG
(HZI-COMPUTER DATA BASE CLASSIFICATION)

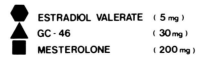

● ESTRADIOL VALERATE	(5 mg)	
▲ GC - 46	(30 mg)	
■ MESTEROLONE	(200 mg)	

. Classified As Antidepressant

Fig. 4. Two-dimensional classification indicated that estradiol valerate and mesterolone primarily have tricyclic type antidepressant effects and secondarily anxiolytic, whereas GC-46 was classified between antidepressants and neuroleptics.

some MAO inhibitors and classical psychostimulants such as dextroamphetamine and caffeine induce similar alterations in human EEG.

It was established that the 'typical' CEEG profiles of antidepressants are observed in both healthy subjects and patient populations after single or multiple dosages. Furthermore, the CEEG profiles of antidepressants are replicable after the same drug is administered in the same population at different times or in different populations. But the most important observation has been the striking similarity between CEEG profiles of clinically well-established antidepressants with different chemical structures. Based on this observation, a hypothesis was made that 'electrophysiologically equivalent effective compounds (as established by computer EEG profiles) shall also have *equivalent psychotropic* (antidepressant) *properties*'.

CEEG predicted a variety of compounds as antidepressant, which were already predicted by animal pharmacology and biochemistry. Thus, the CEEG investigations could only confirm the previous prediction. However, CEEG was also instrumental in the discovery of a series of antidepressants which could not be predicted by animal pharmacology or biochemistry.

While studying the CNS effects of *cyclazocine,* a narcotic antagonist, with Fink, we observed that this compound produces both slow waves and superimposed fast activity and decreases alpha waves. Because of the similarity between cyclazocine induced EEG changes and the EEG pattern of tricyclic antidepressants, antidepressant properties of cyclazocine were predicted (Fink et al., 1969). Subsequent clinical trials supported the EEG prediction (Fink et al., 1970). However, cyclazocine has produced frequent hallucinatory phenomena in dosages effective for depression. Thus, the routine clinical use of this compound as an antidepressant was impossible.

Ditran, an anticholinergic hallucinogen, was reported to have antidepressant effects (Abood et al., 1959). Our EEG investigations demonstrated that Ditran produced both slow and fast activities with the reduction or disappearance of alpha waves (Flugel and Itil, 1962). Since there was a strong resemblance between these kinds of EEG changes induced by tricyclic antidepressants, the prediction of clinical antidepressant effects of Ditran could be supported (Itil, 1964).

The major breakthrough has been the CEEG prediction of the antidepressant properties of GB-94 (Mianserin). Despite several initial sceptics, clinical trials have confirmed the CEEG prediction and GB-94 was eventually marketed as an antidepressant. But even after the confirmed clinical antidepressant properties of GB-94, animal pharmacology and biochemistry investigations were unable to explain why this compound should be an antidepressant. The lack of any 'typical' animal pharmacological profile of mianserin challenged the biochemical hypothesis of depression and the mode of action of antidepressant compounds. Mianserin does not possess strong anticholinergic properties. It is not an MAO inhibitor, and does not inhibit 5-HT or norepinephrine reuptake.

There is a series of important implications concerning Computer Data Base CEEG drug classification for antidepressant drug development.

a) The results of CEEG studies significantly challenge presently existing biogenic amine theories on depressive disorders.

The CEEG profiles of amitriptyline, nortriptyline, imipramine, fluvoxamine, fluotracen, mesterolone and mianserin are very similar to each other. However, according to their effects on biogenic amines, they show marked differences. Amitriptyline and nortriptyline, but particularly fluvoxamine, have predominantly inhibitory effects on 5-HT reuptake. However, fluotracen has almost selective effects on the norepinephrine reuptake, while imipramine has somewhat equal effects on both norepinephrine and 5-HT reuptake. Mesterolone, but particularly mianserin, does not have any significant effect on biogenic amines (if anything, mianserin increases the norepinephrine reuptake).

Accordingly, the common biochemical change which causes a 'typical' antidepressant CEEG profile, and which is closely related to the therapeutic action of an antidepressant, cannot be primarily related to the well-known biogenic amines.

b) Computer EEG may be helpful to discover biochemical aspects of depression.

The similarity of CEEG profiles of two antidepressants indicated that one single dose of these compounds adequately absorbed and metabolized, penetrated through the blood-brain barrier and influenced equal effects of cerebral neurons. Since these effects are most probably the result of *common biochemical changes,* one can postulate that drugs with similar *CEEG profiles* produce similar cerebral biochemical changes. Since the 'shape' of a CEEG profile is closely related to the type of therapeutic effect of a compound, one could further hypothesize that these biochemical changes are *closely related to the therapeutic action of drugs.* The discovery of the nature of biochemical substrate, which is responsible for producing 'typical' bio-electrical effects (CEEG profiles) (after antidepressants), will provide important information on the pathogenesis of this illness and may help to find a causal treatment for certain types of depressive disorders at the very least.

c) The CEEG model may help to develop 'brand new' antidepressant drugs.

Although developed as a retrospective model similar to animal pharmacology models, the CEEG model is successful for the discovery of psychotropic drugs with 'typical' *clinical* effects but without typical animal pharmacology profile. The 'shape' of CEEG profiles is indicative for therapeutic action, but the profiles are independent of chemical structure and the pharmacological properties of drugs. For example, as described above, mianserin, a tetracyclic, does not possess any of the typical pharmacological properties of tricyclic antidepressants.

Mianserin has very little, if any, anticholinergic side effects, but more importantly, almost no cardiotoxic effects of the well-known tricyclic antidepressants. The therapeutic effects seem to begin earlier than tricyclic antidepressants. Mesterolone has no sedative effects of the antidepressants. These examples suggest that the quantitative pharmaco-EEG model may be helpful in developing 'brand-new' antidepressants without well-known side effects.

d) The early human testing of drugs using QPEEG and the computer data base, helps to develop new models for antidepressant drug development.

The classifical model in predicting antidepressant properties of a compound, is retrospective animal pharmacology. This model has not been successful in discovering brand-new antidepressants. However, the development of any other model has been inhibited by the high cost associated with testing the validity and reliability of new models. Early human testing of a compound using QPEEG, and the prediction of antidepressant properties by the computer data base with minimum animal pharmacology and toxicology, can reduce the expense of antidepressant drug development with new models. Among others, compounds predicted to be centrally effective by either the 'physico-chemical' approach, or 'three-dimensional chemical computer models', or 'receptor' models, or the 'enzyme inhibition' model can be economically tested in humans using quantitative pharmaco-EEG. This procedure will not only significantly reduce the time and expense in developing antidepressant drugs, but more importantly, may be helpful in developing 'brand-new' antidepressants with new models.

e) The use of CEEG in early drug trials can speed up *conventional antidepressant drug development without any increase* in cost. Even major drug companies don't have more than one antidepressant tested in humans per year. In conventional drug development, a significant amount of time and money is spent in animal research *before* any effects (and side effects) are seen in man. QPEEG and the data base classification provide an alternative.

When the CNS effect of a chemical is predicted in the animal model (and/or pre-animal models) it should be brought to human trials as soon as possible. Only minimum testing and toxicology are required by the regulatory agencies (for a single rising dose tolerance study, only 2 weeks of toxicology in two species as required). During this first human safety trial, CNS efficacy data can be collected using the QPEEG method. Thus, in very early stages of development, human tolerance and the CNS-effective dosage of a drug, along with the type of psychotropic properties, can be established.

Despite the tremendous progress in the drug treatment of psychiatric syndromes, we all agree that we have significant shortcomings in psychopharmacology. There is a real need to develop a fast-acting antidepressant without potent sedation and/or anticholinergic side effects and/or cardiotoxic properties. Most importantly, we need to develop illness 'specific' drugs and the methods to select the best antidepressant for each patient. Antidepressant drug development requires a major revision. While failing to discover the aetiology of depressive illness, Quantitative Pharmaco-EEG could be an integral part of a new antidepressant drug developmental system.

REFERENCES

Abood, L. G., Ostfeld, A. M. and Biehl, J. H. (1959) Structure-activity relationships of 3-piperidyl benzilates with psychotogenic properties. Arch. Intern. Pharmacodyn. 120, 186–200.

Arnold, O. H., Collard, J., Deniker, P., Ginestet, D., Hippius, H., Itil, T. M., Labhardt, F., Leeds, A., Montanini, R., Morozov, G., Simon, P. and Villeneuve, A. (1976) Definition and classification of neuroleptics. In: The Neuroleptics, Modern Problems of Pharmacopsychiatry, Vol. 5. Karger, Basel, Munich, Paris and New York, pp. 141–147.

Bente, D. and Itil, T. M. (1954) Zur wirkung des phenothiazin korpers megaphen auf das menschliche hirnstrombild. Arzneim. Forsch. 4, 418–423.

Berger, H. (1937) On the electroencephalogram of man. Twelfth report. Arch. Psychiatr. Nervenkr. 106, 165–187.

Brazier, M. A. B. (1964) The effects of drugs on the Electroencephalogram of man. Clin. Pharmacol. Ther. 5, 102–116.

Brezinova, V., Novorna, E., Plzak, M., Soucek, K. and Zaviral, J. (1966) A contribution to the longitudinal study of manic depressive psychosis. Electroencephalogr. Clin. Neurophysiol. 20, 284.

Davis, P. A. (1941) Electroencephalograms of manic-depressive patients. Am. J. Psychiatry 98, 430–433.

Davis, P. A. (1942) A comparative study of the EEGs of schizophrenic and manic-depressive patients. Am. J. Psychiatry 99, 210–217.

Fehlow, P. (1974) EEG-Befunde bei Psychosen mit besonderer Berucksichtigung des depressiven Syndroms. Psychiatr. Neurol. Med. Psychol. (Leip.) 26, 409–415.

Fink, M. (1961) Quantitative electroencephalography and human psychopharmacology: frequency spectra and drug action. Med. Exp. (Basel) 5, 364–369.

Fink, M., Itil, T. M. and Shapiro, D. (1966) Die Anwendung von Digital-Computer Methoden in der Psychopharmakologie. Arzneim. Forsch. 16, 297–299.

Fink, M., Itil, T. M., Zaks, A. and Freedman, A. M. (1969) EEG patterns of cyclazocine, a narcotic antagonist. In: A. Karczmar and W. Koella (Eds), Neurophysiological and Behavioral Aspects of Psychotropic Drugs. Thomas, Springfield, Ill., pp. 62–71.

Fink, M., Simeon, J., Itil, T. M. and Freedman, A. M. (1970) Clinical antidepressant activity of cyclazocine, a narcotic antagonist. Clin. Pharmacol. Ther. 11, 41–48.

Flugel, F. and Itil, T. M. (1962) Klinisch Electroencephalographische Untersuchungen mit 'verwirrtheit' Nervorrufenden Substanzen. Psychopharmacologia 3, 79–98.

Greenblatt, M., Healy, M. M. and Jones, G. A. (1944) Age and electroencephalographic abnormality in neuropsychiatric patients: a study of 1593 cases. Am. J. Psychiatry 101, 82–90.

Hurst, L. A., Mundy-Castle, A. C. and Beerstecher, D. M. (1954) The electroencephalogram in manic-depressive psychosis. J. Ment. Sci. 100, 220–240.

Itil, T. M. (1960) Les modifications electroencephalographiques pendant le traitement chronique par les differents derives de la phenothiazine. Rev. Lyon Med. 74, 171.

Itil, T. M. (1961) Elektroencephalographische Befunde zur Klassifikation neuro- und thymoleptischer Medikamente. Med. Exp. (Basel) 5, 347–363.

Itil, T. M. (1964) Elektroencephalographische Studien bei endogenen Psychosen und deren Behandlung mit Psychotropen Medikamenten unter besonderer Berucksichtigung des Pentothal-elektroencephalogramms. Ahmet Sait Matbaasi, Istanbul.

Itil, T. M. (1968) Electroencephalography and pharmacopsychiatry. In: N. Petrilowitsch, F. A. Freyhan and P. Richot (Eds), Modern Problems of Pharmacopsychiatry. Karger, Basel and New York, pp. 163–194.

Itil, T. M. (1974) Quantitative pharmaco-electroencephalography. In: T. M. Itil (Ed.), Psychotropic Drugs and the Human EEG. Mod. Probl. Pharmacopsciatr., Vol. 8. Karger, Basel and New York, pp. 43–75.

Itil, T. M. (1975) Computer EEG profiles of antidepressants: quantitative pharmaco-EEG in the development of new antidepressive drugs. In: S. Fielding and H. Lal (Eds), Antidepressants (Industrial Pharmacology), Vol. II. Futura, Mt. Kisco, New York, pp. 319–359.

Itil, T. M. (1977) Qualitative and quantitative EEG findings in schizophrenia. Schizophr. Bull. 3, 61–79.

Itil, T. M. (1978a) Quantitative electroencephalography in psychopharmacology-quantitative pharmaco-electroencephalography in the discovery of psychotropic properties of drugs. In: P. Deniker, C. Radouco-Thomas and A. Villeneuve (Eds), Neuropsychopharmacology, Vol. 2. Pergamon Press, New York, pp. 1183–1190.

Itil, T. M. (1978) Tetracyclic Psychotropic Drugs. United States Patent No. 4.128.641, December 5.

Itil, T. M. (1982) The significance of quantitative pharmaco-EEG in the discovery and classification of psychotropic drugs. In: W. M. Herrmann (Ed), EEG in Drug Research. Gustav Fischer, Stuttgart/New York.

Itil, T. M. and Herrmann, W. (1975) Treatment of Mental Depression. United States Patent No. 3,908,007, September 23, 1975. Germany Patent No. 2 345 376. (Appl. published). Assignee: Schering AG, West Berlin (p. 1538).

Itil, T. M. and Herrmann, W. M. (1978) Effects of hormones on computer-analyzed human electroencephalogram. In: M. A. Lipton, A. DiMascio and K. F. Killam (Eds), Psychopharmacology: A Generation of Progress. Raven Press, New York, pp. 729–743.

Itil, T., Shapiro, D. and Fink, M. (1968) Differentiation of psychotropic drugs by quantitative EEG analyses. Agressologie 9, 267–280.

Itil, T. M., Shapiro, D. M., Fink, M., Kiremitci, N. and Hickman, C. (1969) Quantitative EEG studies of chlordiazepoxide, chlorpromazine, and imipramine in volunteer and schizophrenic subjects. In: W. O. Evans and N. S. Kline (Eds), The Psychopharmacology of the Normal Human. Thomas, Springfield, Ill., pp. 219–237.

Itil, T. M., Guven, F., Cora, R., Hsu, W., Polvan, N., Ucok, A., Sanseigne, A. and Ulett, G. A. (1971) Quantitative pharmaco-electroencephalography using frequency analyzer and digital computer methods in early drug evaluations. In: W. L. Smith (Ed.) Drugs, Development and Brain Functions. Charles C. Thomas, Springfield, Ill., pp. 145–166.

Itil, T. M., B. Saletu and S. Davis (1972a) EEG findings in chronic schizophrenics based on digital computer period analysis and analog power spectra. Biol. Psychiatry 5, 1–13.

Itil, T. M., Polvan, N. and Hsu, W. (1972b) Clinical and EEG effects of GB-94, a 'tetracyclic' antidepressant (EEG model in the discovery of new psychotropic drug). Curr. Ther. Res. 14, 395–413.

Itil, T. M., Cora, R., Akpinar, S., Herrmann, W. M. and Patterson, C. (1974) 'Psychotropic' action of sex hormones: computerized EEG in establishing the immediate CNS effects of steroid hormones. Curr. Ther. Res.

Itil, T. M., Herrmann, W. M., Hugue, M. F. and Irrgang, U. (1977) Quantitative pharmaco-EEG with steroidal hormones. Electroenceph. Clin. Neurophysiol. 43, 552.

Itil, T. M., Herrmann, W. M., Blasucci, D. and Freedman, A. (1978) Male hormones in the treatment of depression: effects of mesterolone. In: Progress In Neuro-Psychopharmacology, Vol. 1. Pergamon Press Ltd., Great Britain, pp. 457–467.

Itil, T. M., Shapiro, D. M., Herrmann, W. M., Schulz, W. and Morgan, V. (1979) HZI systems for EEG parametrization and classification of psychotropic drugs. Pharmakopsychiatr./Neuro-Psychopharmakol. 12, 4–19.

Itil, T. M., Shapiro, D. M. and Menon, G. N. (in press) Quantitative Pharmaco-EEG, a new method for early drug screening in man. Presented at the World Conference on Clinical Pharmacology & Therapeutics, London, 3–9 August 1980.

Klaiber, E. L., Broverman, D. M., Vogel, W., Kobayashi, Y. and Moriarty, D. (1972) Effect of estrogen therapy on plasma MAO activity and EEG driving responses of depressed women. Am. J. Psychiatry 12, 1492–1498.

Klaiber, E. L., Broverman, D. M., Vogel, W. and Kobayashi, Y. (1976) The use of steroid hormones in depression. In: T. M. Itil, G. Laudahn and W. M. Herrmann (Eds), The Psychotropic Action of Hormones. Spectrum Publications Inc., New York, pp. 135–154.

Lemere, F. (1941) Cortical energy production in the psychoses. Psychosom. Med. 3, 152–156.

Volavka, J., Matousek, M. and Roubicek, J. (1966) EEG frequency analysis in schizophrenia. An attempt to reconsider the role of age. Acta Psychiatr. Scand. 42, 237–245.

Chapter 13

Clinical studies of antidepressant cardiotoxicity

J. GRAEME SLOMAN

Cardiology Department, Royal Melbourne Hospital, Australia

TREVOR R. NORMAN

and

GRAHAM D. BURROWS

Department of Psychiatry, University of Melbourne, Australia

INTRODUCTION

Antidepressant drugs are the treatment of choice in patients suffering a depressive illness of mild to moderate severity. These drugs are effective treatment in the majority of patients, but they are not without attendant problems. A wide range of side effects following antidepressant treatment has been documented and are well recognized (Burrows and Norman, 1980; Blackwell 1981a, b). The spectrum of effects described reflects the multiplicity of pharmacological actions of the antidepressants. For example, antidepressants block the reuptake of noradrenaline and serotonin into central neurons. Additionally, the antidepressants have effects on muscarinic, cholinergic and histaminergic receptors, to which some of the side effects of treatment can be attributed (Lang, 1981). Of particular importance for the clinical use of the antidepressants are their effects on the cardiovascular system, which arise as a consequence of their anticholinergic action, their effect on adrenergic neurons and a direct myocardial depressant effect (Vohra, 1977).

Despite the extensive use of antidepressants in clinical practice, it should be recognized that the incidence of serious side effects in patients receiving therapeutic doses is low. Generally, these are confined to patients with clinical evidence of heart disease. On the other hand, since depressive illness is frequently associated with suicidal ideas, overdosage with antidepressants occurs too commonly. In these cases, the cardiovascular effects of the drugs represent a serious threat to the patient. A brief review of the effects of antidepressants on the cardiovascular system in therapeutic dose and overdoses is presented, together with some guidelines for the management of antidepressant overdose. The role of monitoring plasma concentrations and their relation to cardiac effects is also discussed.

CARDIAC EFFECTS OF ANTIDEPRESSANTS: THERAPEUTIC DOSES

Haemodynamic effects

The cardiovascular side-effects attributed to antidepressants are postural hypotension, hypotension, occasional hypertension, tachycardia, aggravation of congestive cardiac failure, cardiac arrhythmias, myocardial infarction, atrioventricular block and an increased incidence of sudden death among cardiac patients. These effects have been documented in epidemiological studies and have been the subject of a number of reviews (Coull et al., 1970; Boston Collaborative Drug Surveillance Program, 1972; Moir, 1973; Jefferson, 1975; Stimmel, 1979; Burgess and Turner, 1981; Burrows et al., 1981). Changes in blood pressure can be explained by the action of the tricyclics on the adrenergic neuron.

Orthostatic hypotension was studied in 20 inpatients receiving 50–200 mg/day of imipramine or clomipramine (Hayes et al., 1977). Recordings of supine and standing blood pressure were made 2–5 times daily for the first 14 days of treatment. All patients had falls of diastolic (mean 20 mm Hg) and systolic pressure. Burckhardt et al. (1978) found no significant changes in blood pressure in 62 patients receiving therapeutic doses of various tricyclic and tetracyclic antidepressants. In this study blood pressure was recorded before and after 3 weeks of treatment. These apparently conflicting results can be reconciled by speculation that tolerance to the early falls in blood pressure develops with continued treatment. In studies of mianserin, a tetracyclic antidepressant, administered to healthy male volunteers in doses of up to 60 mg/day for 8 days, no postural hypotension was observed (Kopera, 1978a). Similarly, in depressed patients treated with amitriptyline (150 mg nocte), mianserin (60 mg nocte), zimelidine (200 mg nocte) or nomifensine (150 mg nocte) for 4–6 weeks, none of the drugs affected lying or standing blood pressure (Burgess et al., 1979). These representative studies suggest that the antidepressants have minimal effects on blood pressure in most depressed, but otherwise healthy patients. Such effects that are observed are well tolerated within a few days of the commencement of treatment. In the older patient or patients with pre-existing heart disease, the repercussions of postural hypotension (e.g. cerebrovascular accidents) are serious. Antidepressant drugs should be used carefully in these groups of patients.

Hypertension secondary to the administration of a tricyclic antidepressant has been reported in the literature (Hessov, 1971). In the absence of the concomitant administration of a sympathomimetic drug, this is an unusual occurrence. In patients with cardiac disease, myocardial infarction and congestive heart failure have been reported (Kristiansen, 1961; Muller et al., 1961). Such effects are usually associated with overdosage rather than therapeutic doses.

Electrocardiographic effects

Numerous case studies have been reported in the literature of abnormalities in the electro-cardiogram (ECG) of patients receiving antidepressants (see Burrows et al., 1981). The pattern of ECG changes observed in these studies is summarized in Table 1. Not all patients who receive antidepressants have changes in their ECG. For example, in a study of 32 patients receiving various doses of either amitriptyline, imipramine, nortriptyline or doxepin, four patients had lowering of the T waves, three patients a broadened QRS width and two of these three patients an incomplete right bundle branch block (Vohra et al., 1975b). Heart rate was increased in 26 patients, PR interval increased in all patients. No other changes were noted.

Veith et al. (1980) studied electrocardiographic changes in 26 patients treated with desipramine (up to 200 mg/day) for 3 weeks. Seven patients developed ECG abnormalities during the trial; nonspecific T wave changes in four patients; QRS axis change and P wave abnormalities in two patients and one patient had occasional premature ventricular contractions. Systolic and diastolic blood pressure were not altered during the treatment period. Similar studies with other antidepressants have shown the same pattern of ECG changes.

The electrocardiographic effects of nortriptyline relative to doxepin were examined in a cross-over study conducted in 17 patients (Burrows et al., 1977). Six patients receiving nortriptyline (150 mg/day for 3 weeks) showed a significant prolongation of QRS width, but only one patient on doxepin (150 mg/day for 3 weeks) showed the same effect. It was concluded that doxepin was the less cardiotoxic drug. No other studies have examined the comparative cardiotoxicity of antidepressants using a cross-over design. There is some evidence to suggest that the newer antidepressants may be less cardiotoxic than the older preparations (see section on New antidepressants).

The effects of antidepressants on intracardiac conduction have been studied using His-bundle electrography (HBE). A significant prolongation of the H-V interval occurred in 5 of 12 patients receiving therapeutic doses of nortriptyline, when compared with pre-drug recordings (Vohra et al., 1975b). The effect on AV nodal conduction was variable. The electrophysiological effects observed in this study were similar to those observed in patients receiving quinidine. It was suggested that the increased incidence of sudden death in cardiac patients may be related to drug induced prolongation of distal conduction.

Conventional clinical wisdom dictates that antidepressant drugs should be used with caution in the elderly and patients with pre-existing heart disease. Few studies have sys-

TABLE 1

Therapeutic doses of antidepressants and ECG changes.

Tachycardia
ST-T wave flattening
QRS broadening
Arrhythmias

---

tematically studied electrocardiographic changes in either of these groups. Reed et al. (1980) examined ECG changes in a group of 12 geriatric depressed patients (mean age 68 years) receiving 150 mg/d of nortriptyline. In six of these patients ECG abnormalities (e.g. sinus arrhythmia, Wolff-Parkinson-White syndrome, left and right bundle branch block) were present before the commencement of treatment. Compared with pre-treatment values, heart rate, corrected QT, PR and QRS intervals increased by mean values of 3 beats/minute 6, 11, and 10 milliseconds, respectively. These authors concluded that nortriptyline was safe in regard to cardiotoxicity even in patients with stable pre-existing heart disease. Similarly, no signs of cardiotoxicity were observed in 63 male patients treated with maprotiline following myocardial infarction (Selvini et al., 1976). The dose of maprotiline used in this study was subtherapeutic for the majority of patients (50 mg/day c.f. 150–300 mg/day as the usual dose).

New antidepressants

In recent years a number of new antidepressants have been introduced either as generally available preparations or as investigational agents (see Chapter 14 for a detailed discussion of their clinical pharmacology). The rationale for the development of such agents has been twofold. First, the older drugs are not effective in all patients and have a multiplicity of effects on central receptors. The newer drugs are generally more specific in their mode of action and may be more effective in certain patient subgroups. Secondly, it is claimed that these newer agents are less cardiotoxic than the older drugs. The cardiotoxicity of four of these new agents mianserin, nomifensine, zimelidine and trazodone are discussed. These drugs are chosen because their chemical structures differ from the tricyclics and their mechanism of action is more specific. (For chemical structures, see Chapter 14, Figs. 1, 3 and 6, p. 190.)

Mianserin. Mianserin is a tetracyclic antidepressant and unlike the tricyclic antidepressants has minimal effects on the reuptake of serotonin and noradrenaline. It combines presynaptic α-adrenoceptor blocking activity with antihistamine properties but has no anticholinergic effects (Brogden et al., 1978). It has demonstrated antidepressant properties, the therapeutic efficacy being similar to amitriptyline (Coppen et al., 1976). At therapeutic doses it does not affect the tyramine pressor response nor does it have anticholinergic activity (Ghose et al., 1976). No consistent electrocardiographic effects were noted in 13 depressed patients receiving 80–120 mg of mianserin for 3 weeks (Peet et al., 1977). In a comparative study of mianserin, amitriptyline and placebo administered to healthy volunteers for 7 days, mianserin in doses of up to 60 mg/day lacked the postural hypotension associated with amitriptyline treatment (Kopera, 1978a). Kopera (1978b) also studied the effects of mianserin on cardiological parameters in 54 patients stabilized on phenprocoumon treatment. They were randomly allocated to mianserin 60 mg/day, mianserin 30 mg/day or placebo and treated for a 3-week period. Heart rate, blood pressure and electrocardiogram were monitored throughout the trial. Statistical analysis revealed no significant differences between the three patient groups in heart rate, systolic or diastolic blood pressure or electrocardiographic parameters. Burgess et al. (1979) studied the cardiac effects of mianserin 60 mg nocte in eight depressed inpatients using systolic time intervals (STI) and high speed surface ECG. Cardiac parameters were evaluated during a placebo period and then after 4–6 weeks on drug therapy. No effects on the ECG were noted, but some changes were observed in the STI from the control period. The changes observed seemed to indicate a mixed and paradoxical effect on the heart: a positive inotropic effect (shortening of the QS_2) and decreased contractility (increased PEP:LVET ratio). The authors concluded that mianserin exerted these effects via the peripheral circulation.

Using His-bundle electrography, Burrows et al. (1979) observed no effect of mianserin on cardiac conduction. Mianserin was administered at 60 mg/day for 3 weeks to 10 depressed inpatients. No significant changes in heart rate or blood pressure (supine or standing) were observed.

These studies support the notion that mianserin is without significant cardiological effects and may be useful in the treatment of the depressed patient with heart disease.

Nomifensine. Nomifensine is a tetrahydroisoquinoline derivative chemically distinct from the tricyclic antidepressants and monoamine oxidase inhibitors. It blocks the reuptake of dopamine and noradrenaline, but is a weak inhibitor of serotonin reuptake (Brogden et al., 1979). The drug has been shown to be effective in the treatment of depressive illness (Acebal et al., 1976).

A review of the data from clinical trials of nomifensine revealed that the drug does not have any significant adverse effects on the cardiovascular system and it appears to be well tolerated by patients with pre-existing cardiovascular disease (Stonier and Wittels, 1980). No changes in cardiac output, heart rate, mean arterial pressure or left ventricular filling pressure were observed in seven patients undergoing cardiac catheterisation, who each received 100 mg of nomifensine orally (Biamino, 1977). Nomifensine administered for 3 weeks in doses of up to 200 mg daily to 10 depressed inpatients produced no changes in the His-bundle electrogram compared with pretreatment values (McIntyre et al., 1980). Using STI and high speed surface ECG, Burgess et al. (1979) and Montgomery and Taylor (1980) showed nomifensine, in doses of up to 150 mg/day, to be without cardiovascular effects in 3 and 11 patients respectively. These latter two studies compared nomifensine with amitriptyline and/or imipramine as a standard antidepressant. Both studies concluded that the new antidepressant was safer than the older agents.

Trazodone. Trazodone, a triazolopyridine derivative, is a weak but specific inhibitor of serotonin reuptake. It binds *in vitro* to α-adrenoceptor sites (Clements-Jewery et al., 1980). Clinically the drug is more effective than placebo and as effective as amitriptyline, desipramine, doxepin or dothiepin in the treatment of depressive illness (Brogden et al., 1981). The cardiovascular effects of this agent in man have not been extensively investigated, but trazodone appears less likely to cause important adverse effects on the heart than imipramine. No consistent effects on blood pressure were observed in 30 patients receiving trazodone for 14 days (Mrozikiewicz et al., 1976). Administration of trazodone 150 mg/d to six healthy volunteers did not affect the tyramine pressor response compared to placebo. Response to infused noradrenaline was decreased following trazodone, consistent with an α-adrenoceptor antagonist activity (Larochelle et al., 1979).

Zimelidine.   Zimelidine and its major metabolite norzimelidine are potent inhibitors of serotonin and weaker inhibitors of noradrenaline reuptake (Ross and Renyi, 1977). In an open study the antidepressant efficacy of the drug was confirmed (Benkert et al., 1977). Double-blind comparisons of zimelidine and tricyclics have also shown an antidepressant effect (Montgomery et al., 1978; Coppen et al., 1979). Administration of 200 mg/d of zimelidine to seven depressed patients did not affect cardiac contractility as judged from systolic time intervals. It did tend to slow the heart and prolong the QT_c interval (Burgess et al., 1979). In a study of the cardiovascular effects of zimelidine in six depressed patients assessed by thoracic impedance cardiography, it was suggested that the drug had low cardiotoxicity (Christie and Brown, 1981). Similarly, zimelidine 200 mg/day did not affect the STIs or the ECGs of 21 depressed inpatients treated for 6 weeks, when compared to pre-drug recordings (Montgomery et al., 1981).

These studies suggest a low cardiotoxicity of zimelidine, at least in comparison with the tricyclics. Further studies are required to assess the safety of the drug, on chronic administration, to depressed elderly patients and in patients with pre-existing heart disease.

Drug plasma concentrations and cardiac effects

Some studies have attempted to relate changes in cardiological parameters to concentration of drug in plasma. Freyschuss et al. (1970) studied 40 depressed patients treated with nortriptyline. Heart rate and bood pressure increased in all patients during treatment, but the increase was not correlated with plasma drug concentrations.

Plasma nortriptyline concentrations and ECG were recorded in 20 patients who received the drug for a minimum of 2 weeks (Vohra et al., 1975b). The PR interval and heart rate increased in all subjects after drug administration but this was not correlated with plasma drug concentration.

There is some evidence that plasma nortriptyline concentrations in excess of 200 ng/ml are associated with cardiac effects. Burrows et al. (1977) have shown, using ECG and HBE studies, that significantly more patients receiving nortriptyline had increased H-V intervals and broadened QRS width than patients receiving doxepin. Vohra et al. (1975b) demonstrated that four of five patients receiving nortriptyline, who experienced ECG and HBE changes, had plasma drug levels in excess of 200 ng/ml. In general, this finding of high drug concentrations associated with cardiological effects has been confirmed. Zeigler et al. (1977a, b) have demonstrated an association of plasma nortriptyline or plasma amitriptyline concentrations and increased heart rate in patients receiving either nortriptyline or amitriptyline, respectively. Similarly, Veith et al. (1980) have shown an association between plasma desipramine concentration and heart rate, QRS and QT_c intervals. There were no correlations between plasma concentrations and change in the above variables. Plasma drug concentrations varied over a wide range, 13–882 ng/ml. These authors did not comment on the association of high plasma levels with ECG changes.

It can be concluded from these studies that dosages of the antidepressants within the usual range lead to ECG and HBE changes in some patients. These changes are most likely to be associated with high plasma concentrations of the drug. On the other hand, plasma concentration monitoring is not necessarily a guide to ECG and HBE changes.

CARDIAC EFFECTS OF ANTIDEPRESSANTS: OVERDOSES

Overdosages with the tricyclic antidepressants are a common presentation to hospital casualty wards. Poisoning with the antidepressants whether intentional or accidental, represents a serious threat to the patient's well being. Tricyclic poisoning is unpredictable — serious complications have been observed in some patients who ingest only small amounts of the drug, while mild or no symptoms may occur in others who ingest 2 g or more. Small doses of the antidepressants may produce dangerous side effects in infants and 350 mg of imipramine has produced a fatality (Giles, 1963). Often the tricyclics are combined with other drugs on overdosage and these patients require careful monitoring for cardiovascular complications, especially where the other drug may be a monoamine oxidase inhibitor or an antihypertensive agent (Vohra and Burrows, 1974). It is also common for overdosed patients to present alert and conscious and then to lapse into coma within a few hours.

Electrocardiographic effects and plasma concentrations

The ECG features on overdosage are summarized in Table 2. Some or all of these features are observed on antidepressant overdose. Both ECG and HBE recordings were made in four overdosed patients (two nortriptyline, two imipramine) within 4 hours of admission to hospital (Vohra et al., 1975c). The A-H interval was normal, but in three patients QRS width was broadened to 100–120 msec and H-V interval was 70–90 msec. Both nortriptyline patients had plasma levels in excess of 200 ng/ml. Imipramine levels were not measured. All values had returned to normal 8 days after the overdose. It was suggested that the drugs have a direct effect on His-Purkinje and intraventricular conduction, which could be a potential hazard in patients with impairment of atrioventricular conduction.

ECG parameters and plasma tricyclic levels were determined in a study by Spiker et al. (1975) of 15 patients with overdoses of various tricyclics. Maximum QRS duration showed a strong positive correlation ($r = 0.75$, $p < 0.01$) with total tricyclic levels; excluding one patient with pre-existing bundle branch block. Intraventricular conduction delays were more often associated with plasma levels in excess of 1,000 ng/ml. The QRS width returned to normal as plasma levels fell. This study was confirmed in 36 overdosed patients, all of whom had a QRS width $>$ 100 ms and a total plasma tricyclic level in excess of 1,000 ng/ml (Petit et al., 1976). Spiker and Biggs (1976) found that tricyclic plasma

TABLE 2

Electrocardiographic effects of tricyclic antidepressant overdose.

PR interval prolonged
QRS prolonged
Bundle branch block
Heart block
Impaired cardiac conduction
Dysrhythmias

levels could remain above 1,000 ng/ml for up to 96 hours after overdose; they suggest that sustained plasma levels may play a role in sudden death 3 to 6 days after overdose.

In contrast to Spiker's findings, no relationship between plasma tricyclic concentration and ECG changes was observed in a study of eight patients, six cases of amitriptyline and two cases of imipramine overdose (Hallstrom and Gifford, 1976). Maximum plasma concentration did not exceed 750 ng/ml in any patient. Forty patients ingesting tricyclic antidepressant overdoses were studied by Petit et al. (1977), cases being grouped into those with total plasma tricyclic concentrations above and below 1000 ng/ml. Significantly more patients with major adverse effects had plasma concentrations above 1000 ng/ml, i.e. there was a trend for cardiotoxic symptoms of the tricyclics to be associated with elevated plasma levels. Bailey et al. (1978) studied imipramine and amitriptyline overdosage and the associated ECG changes. There was a significant difference between total tricyclic levels for patients with widened QRS complex and those without widening (821 ng/ml and 396 ng/ml, respectively). There was no correlation between plasma level and the extent of QRS widening. The range of plasma levels observed in this study overlaps with those observed in patients receiving chronic oral doses, making the use of plasma levels alone an unreliable index of tricyclic overdosage.

On the basis of the studies described, the most reliable and readily available clinical index of tricyclic antidepressant overdosage is prolongation of the QRS width by 100 msec or more. This will almost certainly be associated with elevated plasma levels of the drug. Plasma levels are not indicative of cardiotoxicity, but a parent drug-to-metabolite (P/M) ratio may be a better predictor of overdosage. A P/M ratio of less than 2 is more usual in steady-state levels, while a P/M of greater than 2 strongly suggests an overdose, but its absence does not exclude it. Bailey et al. (1978) conclude that QRS widening, arrhythmia, and increased total plasma tricyclic levels represent serious cardiotoxicity.

New antidepressants

Overdoses of some of the new antidepressants have been reported in the literature. In general, these reports have supported the studies in therapeutic doses, that the drugs are less cardiotoxic than the older preparations.

Montgomery et al. (1978) and Vohra et al. (1978) reported overdoses of 1.5 g and 3.5 g, respectively, of nomifensine. In both these patients ECG changes were minor and the QRS width remained within normal limits. The most extensive study of nomifensine overdose concerned 26 patients who took an average dose of 1.15 g (Dawling et al., 1979). Six patients experienced some cardiovascular effects, but these were minor. Nomifensine is apparently without serious cardiovascular effects on overdosage.

On overdosage, mianserin does not cause the severe complications of most other antidepressants. In 21 adults who ingested mianserin alone, Crome et al. (1978) report that there were no serious cardiovascular problems. In another report, no ECG abnormalities were observed in a 53-year-old woman who overdosed on 600 mg of mianserin and 10 g of carbromal-like monoureides (Jansen et al., 1977). Plasma mianserin was 780 ng/ml 5 hours after ingestion. In another case, first degree heart block was observed in a 39-year-old female who overdosed on 580 mg of mianserin, 35 mg diazepam and 30 mg nitrazepam (Green and Kendall-Taylor, 1977). After 9 hours the ECG had returned to normal. One death has been reported in a woman who ingested 600 mg mianserin and a large dose of lorazepam (Crome and Newman, 1977).

Few cases of zimelidine overdosage have been reported. In one case a 38-year-old female took 1.75 g of zimelidine with alcohol and propoxyphene (Georgotas et al., 1981). The ECG showed minor T wave flattening, considered to be insignificant. The patient experienced no adverse effects and was not sedated. The overdose was confirmed from the plasma concentrations of zimelidine and norzimelidine 12 hours after the overdose: 600 ng/ml and 380 ng/ml, respectively. This study indicates that zimelidine may be safer on overdose than the tricyclics. Further observations are required to confirm zimelidine's apparent safety.

Treatment and management of antidepressant overdose

The management of tricyclic overdose has been discussed by Vohra and Burrows (1974) and by Burgess and Turner (1981). It should be noted that there are no specific antidotes for tricyclic poisoning. Treatment of cardiac toxicity or overdose is supportive. Since these drugs have long half-lives, observation over a number of days is essential. Plasma drug levels may remain high for several days and sudden unexpected death can occur.

The immediate treatment of overdosage is to maintain the airways; gastric lavage is likely to be of benefit if the patient is seen within 4 hours of the overdose. Activated charcoal (10 g) to reduce absorption may also be useful. An adequate fluid intake should be maintained. Patients should be monitored for ECG changes. Forced diuresis and haemodialysis are of little or no value, since the drugs are highly protein bound.

Cardiovascular complications should be treated as they occur. Where sinus tachycardia is the only abnormality no specific treatment is required. Supraventricular tachycardia may be managed with physostigmine (1–3 mg). Burgess and Turner (1981) suggest caution in the use of physostigmine since it has been shown to increase the likelihood of seizures. Practolol has proven useful in the treatment of cardiac arrhythmias (Vohra and Burrows, 1974). In order to prevent hypotension practolol should be given in small doses, repeated as required. High degree A-V heart block should be treated with electrical pacing. Ventricular tachycardia can be treated with practolol, phenytoin or lignocaine. Rapid ventricular tachycardia with hypotension or ventricular fibrillation require cardioversion.

Sodium bicarbonate (1–3 mEq/kg) has been reported to be effective in the treatment of cardiac arrhythmias (Brown et al., 1973). Additionally, hyperpyrexia and convulsions as complications of tricyclic overdose should also be treated.

LITHIUM

Lithium is the treatment of choice for manic-depressive disorders (Hollister, 1976). Generally, the effects of lithium on the heart have been regarded as benign (Tilkian et al., 1976). Several effects of lithium have been noted: T wave flattening in the electrocardiogram (Schou, 1962; Hansen and Amdisen, 1978); sinus node abnormalities (Roose et al., 1979); ventricular arrhythmias (Tseng, 1971; Jaffe, 1977); myocarditis (Tseng, 1971) and prolongation of the QT interval during lithium toxicity (Jacob and Hope, 1979).

Weeke (1979) has examined the cause of death in manic-depressive patients and concluded that, apart from suicide, there is an excess mortality from cardiovascular disease compared with an age and sex matched control group. The long-term effect of lithium as a causative factor cannot be excluded. In the short term, lithium appears to be without significant effects on the heart. Dumovic et al. (1980) studied the effects of 2 weeks lithium treatment on the ECG and STIs in six healthy male volunteers. There was a reduction in the T wave amplitude in the ECG of each of the volunteers, which returned to normal after cessation of treatment. Myocardial performance was not significantly affected by lithium treatment.

More systematic studies of the effects of lithium on the heart are required, particularly the effects of long-term administration. The effects of lithium in the elderly and patients with pre-existing heart disease have not been systematically studied and care should be exercised in the administration of lithium to these groups.

MONOAMINE OXIDASE INHIBITORS

The MAO inhibitors consists of two distinct classes: the hydrazides and the nonhydrazides. They exert marked effects on the cardiovascular system, by an as yet unidentified mechanism. Orthostatic hypotension is a common action (Stimmel, 1979). The most studied effect of the MAO inhibitors is the so-called 'cheese effect'. This is a severe headache often secondary to a hypertensive crisis, which may lead to subarachnoid haemorrhage and death may occur. The hypertensive reaction arises due to ingestion of tyramine containing foods of which cheeses contain appreciable amounts. Normally the tyramine has no effect because it is rapidly metabolized by MAO of the liver and intestine. This no longer occurs once MAO inhibitors are administered. Tyramine can replace noradrenaline from its storage granules with subsequent hypertension (Blackwell et al., 1967). Adverse reactions with sympathomimetic agents and MAO inhibitors are also marked by headache, hypertension and pulmonary oedema. Subarachnoid haemorrhage has been demonstrated in post mortem findings in cases resulting in death (Villiers, 1966).

Specific ECG and haemodynamic changes following MAO inhibitor administration have not been studied. More research is required in this area.

CONCLUSIONS

Antidepressant drugs have significant effects on the cardiovascular system of some patients receiving these agents. Characteristic changes are observed in the ECG or can be demonstrated using HBE. Monitoring of the plasma concentrations of antidepressants has not provided a guide to cardiovascular effects, although it has been shown in most studies that high concentrations are associated with electrocardiographic changes. Further studies are required to assess the association between plasma levels and cardiovascular parameters. On overdosage, the antidepressants have been associated with significant cardiotoxicity and represent a serious threat to the patient. The principles of overdosage management have been discribed. Studies with some newer antidepressants suggest that they may be safer agents, particularly in patients with pre-existing heart disease. The risk of suicide by overdose with these agents is markedly reduced. Regular monitoring of cardiovascular status in patients receiving prophylactic treatment is to be recommended.

REFERENCES

Acebal, E., Subira, S., Spatz, J., Faleni, R., Merzbacher, B., Gales, A. and Moizeszowicz, J. (1976) A double blind comparative trial of nomifensine and desipramine in depression. Eur. J. Clin. Pharmacol. 10, 109–113.
Bailey, D. N., van Dyke, C., Langou, A. and Jatlow, P. I. (1978) Tricyclic antidepressant plasma levels and clinical findings in overdose. Am. J. Psychiatry 135, 1325–1328.
Benkert, O., Laakmann, G., Ott, L., Strauss, A. and Zimmer, R. (1977) Effect of zimelidine (H102/09) in depressive patients. Arzneim. Forsch. 27, 2421–2423.
Biamino, G. (1977) In vitro and in vivo studies on cardiovascular side effects of antidepressant drugs. In: S. Garattini (Ed.), Symposia Medica Hoechst 13, Depressive Disorders. F. K. Schattauer Verlag, Stuttgart, pp. 389–399.
Blackwell, B. (1981a) Adverse effects of antidepressant drugs Part 1: Monoamine oxidase inhibitors and tricyclics. Drugs 21, 201–219.
Blackwell, B. (1981b) Adverse effects of antidepressant drugs Part 2: Second generation antidepressants and rational decision making in antidepressant therapy. Drugs 21, 273–282.
Blackwell, B., Marley, E., Price, J. and Taylor, D. (1967) Hypertensive interactions between monoamine oxidase inhibitors and food stuffs. Br. J. Psychiatry 113, 349–365.
Boston Collaborative Drug Surveillance Program (1972) Adverse reactions to tricyclic antidepressant drugs. Lancet 1, 529–531.
Brogden, R. N., Heel, R. C., Speight, T. M. and Avery, G. S. (1978) Mianserin: a review of its pharmacological properties and therapeutic efficacy in depressive illness. Drugs 16, 273–301.
Brogden, R. N., Heel, R. C., Speight, T. M. and Avery, G. S. (1979) Nomifensine: a review of its pharmacological properties and therapeutic efficacy in depressive illness. Drugs 18, 1–24.
Brogden, R. N., Heel, R. C., Speight, T. M. and Avery, G. S. (1981) Trazodone: a review of its pharmacological properties and therapeutic use in depression and anxiety. Drugs 21, 401–429.
Brown, T. C. K., Barker, C. A., Dunlop, M. E. and Loughnan, P. M. (1973) The use of sodium bicarbonate in the treatment of tricyclic antidepressant-induced arrhythmias. Anaesth. Int. Care 1, 203–210.
Burckhardt, D., Raeder, E., Muller, V., Imhof, P. and Neubauer, H. (1978) Cardiovascular effects of tricyclic and tetracyclic antidepressant. J. Am. Med. Assoc. 239, 213–216.
Burgess, C. D. and Turner, P. (1981) Cardiotoxicity of antidepressants: clinical implications. In: D. Wheatley (Ed.), Stress and the Heart, 2nd Edn., Raven Press, New York.
Burgess, C. D., Montgomery, S., Wadsworth, J. and Turner, P. (1979) Cardiovascular effects of amitriptyline, mianserin, zimelidine and nomifensine in depressed patients. Postgrad. Med. J. 55, 704–708.
Burrows, G. D. and Norman, T. R. (1980) Psychotherapeutic drugs: important adverse reactions and interactions. Drugs 20, 485–493.
Burrows, G. D., Vohra, J. Dumovic, P., Maguire, K., Scoggins, B. A. and Davies, B. (1977) Tricyclic antidepressant drugs and cardiac conduction. Prog. Neuropsychopharmacol. 1, 329–334.
Burrows, G. D., Davies, B., Hamer, A. and Vohra, J. (1979) Effect of mianserin on cardiac conduction. Med. J. Aust. 2, 97–98.
Burrows, G. D., Hughes, I. E. and Norman, T. R. (1981) Cardiotoxicity of antidepressants: experimental background. In: D. Wheatley (Ed.), Stress and the Heart, 2nd Edn. Raven Press, New York, pp. 131–171.
Christie, J. E. and Brown, D. (1981) Comparison of the cardiovascular effects of amitriptyline and zimelidine using thoracic impedance cardiography. Acta Psychiatr. Scand. 63 (Suppl. 290), 385–392.
Clements-Jewery, S., Robson, P. A. and Chidley, L. J. (1980) Biochemical investigations into the mode of action of trazodone. Neuropharmacol. 19, 1165–1173.

Coppen, A., Gupta, R., Montgomery, S., Ghose, K., Bailey, J., Burns, B. and de Ridder, J. J. (1976) Mianserin hydrochloride: a novel antidepressant. Br. J. Psychiatry 129, 342–345.

Coppen, A., Rama Rao, V. A., Swade, C. and Wood, K. (1979) Zimelidine: a therapeutic and pharmacokinetic study in depression. Psychopharmacology 63, 199–202.

Coull, D. C., Crooks, J., Dingwall-Fordyce, I., Scott, A. M. and Weir, R. D. (1970) Amitriptyline and cardiac disease. Lancet 2, 590–591.

Crome, P. and Newman, B. (1977) Poisoning with maprotiline and mianserin. Br. Med. J. 2, 260.

Crome, P., Braithwaite, R. A., Newman, B. and Montgomery, S. A. (1978) Choosing an antidepressant. Br. Med. J. 1, 859.

Dawling, S., Braithwaite, R. and Crome, P. (1979) Nomifensine overdose and plasma drug concentration. Lancet 1, 56.

Dumovic, P., Burrows, G. D., Chamberlain, K., Vohra, J., Fuller, J. and Sloman, J. G. (1980) Effect of therapeutic dosage of lithium on the heart. Br. J. Clin. Pharmacol. 9, 599–604.

Freyschuss, U., Sjoqvist, F., Tuck, D. and Asberg, M. (1970) Circulatory effects in man of nortriptyline, a tricyclic antidepressant drug. Pharmacol. Clin. 2, 68–71.

Georgotas, A., Mann, J., Bush, D. and Gershon, S. (1981) Safety data on zimelidine hydrochloride following an overdose. Acta. Psychiatr. Scand. 63 (Suppl. 290), 257–261.

Ghose, K., Coppen, A. and Turner, P. (1976) Autonomic actions and interactions of mianserin hydrochloride (Org. GB94) and amitriptyline in patients with depressive illness. Psychopharmacology 49, 201–204.

Giles, H. McC. (1963) Imipramine poisoning in childhood. Br. Med. J. 2, 844–846.

Green, S. D. R. and Kendall-Taylor, P. (1977) Heart block in mianserin hydrochloride overdose. Br. Med. J. 2, 1190.

Hallstrom, C. and Gifford, L. (1976) Antidepressant blood levels in acute overdose. Postgrad. Med. J. 52, 687–688.

Hansen, H. E. and Amdisen, A. (1978) Lithium intoxication (report of 23 cases and review of 100 cases from the literature). Q.J. Med. 47, 123–144.

Hayes, J. R., Born, G. F. and Rosenbaum, A. H. (1977) Incidence of orthostatic hypertension in patients with primary affective disorders treated tricyclic antidepressants. Mayo Clin. Proc. 52, 509–512.

Hessov, I. (1971) Hypertension during chlorimipramine therapy. Br. Med. J. 1, 406.

Hollister, L. E. (1976) Psychiatric disorders. In: G. S. Avery (Ed.), Drug Treatment. Adis Press, Sydney.

Jacob, A. I. and Hope, R. R. (1979) Prolongation of the Q-T interval in lithium toxicity. J. Electrocardiol. 12, 117–119.

Jaffe, C. M. (1977) First degree atrioventricular block during lithium carbonate treatment. Am. J. Psychiatry 134, 88–89.

Jansen, H., Drykoningen, G. and de Ridder, J. J. (1977) Poisoning with antidepressants. Br. Med. J. 2, 896.

Jefferson, J. W. (1975) A review of the cardiovascular effects and toxicity of tricyclic antidepressants. Psychosom. Med. 37, 160–179.

Kopera, H. (1978a) Anticholinergic and blood pressure effects of mianserin, amitriptyline and placebo. Br. J. Clin. Pharmacol. 5, 29S–34S.

Kopera, H. (1978b) Cardiovascular tolerance of mianserin and interactions of mianserin with other drugs. Acta Psychiatr. Belg. 78, 787–797.

Kristiansen, E. S. (1961) Cardiac complications during treatment with imipramine (Tofranil). Acta Psychiatr. Neurol. 36, 427.

Lang, W. (1981) Pharmacological basis of mechanism of action of psychotropic drugs. In: G. D. Burrows and T. R. Norman (Eds), Psychotropic Drugs: Plasma Concentration and Clinical Response. Marcel Dekker, New York, pp. 1–45.

Larochelle, P., Hamet, P. and Enjalbert, M. (1979) Responses to tyramine and norepinephrine after imipramine and trazodone. Clin. Pharmacol. Ther. 26, 24–30.

McIntyre, I. M., Burrows, G. D., Norman, T. R., Dumovic, P. and Vohra, J. (1980) Plasma nomifensine concentration cardiological effects and clinical response. Int. Pharmacopsychiatry 15, 325–333.

Moir, D. C. (1973) Tricyclic antidepressants and cardiac disease. Am. Heart J. 86, 841–842.

Montgomery, S., Crome, P. and Braithwaite, R. (1978) Nomifensine overdosage. Lancet 2, 828–829.

Montgomery, S. A. and Taylor, D. J. E. (1980) Cardiac effects of nomifesine, imipramine and amitriptyline in depressed patients. In: P. D. Stonier and F. A. Jenner (Eds), Royal Society of Medicine Symposium, No. 25. Nomifensine. Royal Society of Medicine, London, pp. 23–25.

Montgomery, S. A., McAuley, R., Rani, S. J., Roy, D. and Montgomery, D. B. (1981) A double blind comparison of zimelidine and amitriptyline in endogenous depression. Acta Psychiatr. Scand. 63 (Suppl. 290), 314–327.

Mrozikiewicz, A., Strzyzewski, W., Kapelski, Z. and Sydor, L. (1976) The influence of trazodone on the circulatory system in patients with endogenous depression. 1. Basic circulation parameters. Arch. Immunol. Ther. Expt. 24, 459–463.

Muller, O. F., Goodman, N. and Bellet, S. (1961) The hypotensive effect of imipramine hydrochloride in patients with cardiovascular disease. Clin. Pharmacol. Ther. 2, 300–307.

Peet, M., Tienari, P. and Jaskari, M. O. (1977) A comparison of the cardiac effects of mianserin and amitriptyline in man. Pharmacopsychiatry 10, 309.

Petit, J. M., Spiker, D. G. and Biggs, J. T. (1976) Psychiatric diagnosis and tricyclic plasma levels in 36 hospitalised overdosed patients. J. Nerv. Ment. Dis. 163, 289–293.

Petit, J. M., Spiker, D. G., Ruwitch, J. F., Ziegler, V. E., Weiss, A. N. and Biggs, J. T. (1977) Tricyclic antidepressant plasma levels and adverse effects after overdose. Clin. Pharmacol. Ther. 21, 47–51.

Reed, K., Smith, R. C., Schoolar, J. C., Hu, R., Leelavathi, D. E., Mann, E. and Lippman, L. (1980) Cardiovascular effects of nortriptyline in geriatric patients. Am. J. Psychiatry 137, 986–989.

Roose, S. P., Nurnberger, J. I., Dunner, D. L., Blood, D. K. and Fieve, R. R. (1979) Cardiac sinus node dysfunction during lithium treatment. Am. J. Psychiatry 136, 804–806.

Ross, S. B. and Renyi, A. L. (1977) Inhibition of neuronal uptake of 5-hydroxytryptamine and noradrenaline in rat brain by (Z)- and (E)-3-(4-bromophenyl)-N,N-dimethyl-3-(3-pyridyl) allylamines and their secondary analogues. Neuropharmacology 16, 57–63.

Schou, M. (1962) Electrocardiographic changes during treatment with lithium and with drugs of the imipramine type. Acta. Psychiatr. Scand. 38, 331–336.

Selvini, A., Rossi, C., Belli, C., Corallo, S. and Lucchelli, P. E. (1976) Antidepressant treatment with maprotiline in the management of emotional disturbances in patients with acute myocardial infarction: a controlled study. J. Int. Med. Res. 4, 42–49.

Spiker, D. G. and Biggs, J. T. (1976) Tricyclic antidepressants: prolonged plasma levels after overdose. J. Am. Med. Assoc. 236, 1711–1712.

Spiker, D. G., Weiss, A. N., Chang, S. S., Ruwitch, J. F. and Biggs, J. T. (1975) Tricyclic antidepressant overdose: clinical presentation and plasma levels. Clin. Pharmacol. Ther. 18, 529–546.

Stimmel, B. (1979) Cardiovascular Effects of Mood Altering Drugs. Raven Press, New York. pp. 133–166.

Stonier, P. D. and Wittels, P. Y. (1980) A review of the cardiovascular effects of nomifensine. In: P. D. Stonier and F. A. Jenner (Eds), Royal Society of Medicine, Symposium No. 25. Nomifensine. Royal Society of Medicine, London, pp. 17–21.

Tilkian, A. G., Schroeder, J. S., Kao, J. J. and Hultgren, H. N. (1976) The cardiovascular effects of lithium in man. A review of the literature. Am. J. Med. 61, 665–670.

Tseng, H. L. (1971) Interstitial myocarditis probably related to lithium carbonate intoxication. Arch. Pathol. Lab. Med. 92, 444–448.

Veith, R. C., Friedel, R. O., Bloom, V. and Bielski, R. (1980) Electrocardiogram changes and plasma desipramine levels during treatment of depression. Clin. Pharmacol. Ther. 27, 796–802.

Villiers, J. C. (1966) Intracranial haemorrhage in patients treated with monoamine oxidase inhibitors. Br. J. Psychiatry 112, 109–118.

Vohra, J. K. (1977) Tricyclic antidepressants and cardiac function. In: G. D. Burrows (Ed.), Handbook of Studies on Depression. Excerpta Medica, Amsterdam, pp. 405–410.

Vohra, J. K. and Burrows, G. D. (1974) Cardiovascular complications of tricyclic antidepressant overdosage. Drugs 8, 432–437.

Vohra, J. K., Burrows, G. D., Hunt, D. and Sloman, G. (1975a) The effect of toxic and therapeutic doses of tricyclic antidepressant drugs on intracardiac conduction. Eur. J. Cardiol. 3, 219–227.

Vohra, J. K., Burrows, G. D. and Sloman, G. (1975b) Assessment of cardiovascular side effects of therapeutic doses of tricyclic antidepressant drugs. Aust. N. Z. Med. J. 5, 7–11.

Vohra, J. K., Hunt, D., Burrows, G. D. and Sloman, G. (1975c) Intracardiac conduction defects following overdose of tricyclic antidepressant drugs. Eur. J. Cardiol. 2, 453–458.

Vohra, J. K., Burrows, G. D., McIntyre, I. and Davies, B. (1978) Cardiovascular effects of nomifensine. Lancet 2, 902–903.

Weeke, A. (1979) Causes of death in manic-depressives. In: M. Schou and E. Stromgren (Eds), Origin, Prevention and Treatment of Affective Disorders. Academic Press, New York, pp. 289–299.

Ziegler, V. E., Co, B. T. and Biggs, J. T. (1977a) Plasma nortriptyline and ECG findings. Am. J. Psychiatry 134, 441–443.

Ziegler, V. E., Co, B. T. and Biggs, J. T. (1977b) Electrocardiographic findings in patients undergoing amitriptyline treatment. Dis. Nerv. Syst. 38, 697–699.

Burrows/Norman/Davies (eds) Antidepressants
© *1983, Elsevier Science Publishers*

Chapter 14

Newer antidepressants — clinical aspects

ROBERT POHL

and

SAMUEL GERSHON

*Department of Psychiatry, Wayne State University and Lafayette Clinic,
Detroit, Michigan, U.S.A.*

INTRODUCTION

The number of drugs that are thought to have antidepressant effects has dramatically increased over the past decade. This chapter will review a number of the newer antidepressants, with an emphasis on clinical aspects. Because this is a rapidly growing and changing area, and space is limited, we cannot present an encyclopedic analysis of the available data.

Newer antidepressants are of interest because of the inadequacies of the widely and currently available tricyclic antidepressants and monoamine oxidase (MAO) inhibitors. Familiar drawbacks are the slow onset of action of present drugs, anticholinergic side effects, cardiotoxicity and, with MAO inhibitors, potentially lethal interactions with foodstuffs and drugs. New drugs that will be clinically useful must be more than effective; they must have a side effect profile that offers an advantage over currently available drugs. For this reason, we will pay special attention to drugs with advantageous side effect profiles, even if the evidence for a lack of side effects is from animal studies.

Unfortunately, the efficacy of many of the new drugs has been only tested in comparison to standard antidepressants. It is our view that clinicians should be sceptical of claims for efficacy unless a new drug is compared to both a standard drug and placebo. Finding that a new compound is as effective as a standard drug does not insure that either drug is more effective than placebo; standard drugs are simply not more effective than placebo in all studies, often because of methodological weaknesses. Common methodological pitfalls (in addition to lack of placebo controls) are a small number of subjects or a heterogeneous, ill-defined subject group.

'Second generation' antidepressant drugs include compounds that are structurally, and often pharmacologically, different from standard tricyclic antidepressants. These drugs can be categorized by their pharmacological effects into three groups. The first group is selectively serotonergic; the second group is selectively noradrenergic. A third group includes drugs that are neither selectively serotonergic nor adrenergic; they have either mixed effects or an unknown mechanism of action because of an apparent lack of effect on either neurotransmitter. Antidepressant drugs that lack both noradrenergic and serotonergic activity are of great interest because they do not fit current theories of the pathophysiology of depression.

Structurally novel antidepressants are not the only new antidepressants. Tricyclic antidepressants have been modified to get new compounds. Known drugs that are not thought of as antidepressants and naturally occurring substances may also be useful antidepressants. And MAO inhibitors have been modified to get more selective compounds. A list of compounds presented in this chapter, and their classification, is presented in Table 1.

TABLE 1

Non-tricyclics		*Tricyclics*
SEROTONERGIC	**OTHERS**	Amineptine
Fluoxetine	Adinazolam	Amoxapine
Fluvoxamine	Alprazolam	Butriptyline
Trazodone	Bupropion	Clomipramine
Zimelidine	Clovoxamine	Dibenzepine
	Iprindole	Dothiepin
NORADRENERGIC	Pridefine	Lofepramine
Maprotiline	Nomifensine	Melitracen
Nisoxetine	Viloxazine	Noxiptiline
Tandamine	Zometapine	
Drug not usually used for depression		*Monoamine oxidase inhibitors*
Carbamazepine		Clorgyline
Lithium		Deprenyl
Pemoline		Pargyline
Salbutamol		Toloxatone
Naturally occurring substances		
Phenylalanine		
Tryptophan		
SAMe		

NON-TRICYCLIC SEROTONERGIC DRUGS

Trazodone

Trazodone, a triazolopyridine, is a unique new antidepressant with a structure unlike other psychotropic agents. Trazodone is a very selective inhibitor of serotonin uptake. Though less potent than clomipramine, trazodone is four times more selective in its ability to inhibit uptake of serotonin compared to norepinephrine in an animal model (Riblet et al., 1979). It does not potentiate catecholamines and does not inhibit MAO. Although serotonergic centrally, trazodone has peripheral anti-alpha adrenergic and antiserotonergic activity.

Clinical experience with trazodone is extensive; for over a decade it has been tested in more than 200 open and controlled trials involving over 10,000 patients (Ayd, 1979). There is general agreement that trazodone is as effective as standard tricyclic antidepressants and superior to placebo for the treatment of depression. A review of the literature (Saarma, 1974) and recent comparisons to imipramine (Fabre et al., 1979; Feighner, 1980) indicate that trazodone has a rapid onset of action; antidepressant effects may be evident within one week. The usual dosage of trazodone is twice that of standard tricyclic antidepressants.

Trazodone has a sedative effect but remarkably few other side-effects when compared to tricyclic antidepressants. It slows the heart rate but does not appear cardiotoxic; there is no effect on cardiac conduction (Gomoll and Byrne, 1979). Trazodone lacks anticholinergic effects; the incidence of these effects in trazodone patients is the same as for placebo patients and significantly less than the anticholinergic effects of imipramine (Gershon and Newton, 1980). Because of the lack of anticholinergic and cardiovascular effects, trazodone is tolerated much better in the elderly (Gerner et al., 1980).

Fluvoxamine

Fluvoxamine is currently being investigated as a potential antidepressant because both *in vitro* and *in vivo* experiments suggest a potent serotonergic effect. Fluvoxamine interferes with both the neuronal reuptake of serotonin and reduces serotonin turnover in the brain. Unlike tricyclic antidepressants, the reuptake of norepinephrine is either unaffected or only slightly inhibited (Claassen et al., 1977). In addition, fluvoxamine appears to lack anticholinergic or MAO-inhibiting properties.

Although gastrointestinal side effects caused 5 out of 18 patients to drop out of a study that compared fluvoxamine to clomipramine in the treatment of cataplexy (Schachter and Parkes, 1980), fluvoxamine has been well tolerated in two preliminary clinical trials for the treatment of depression. In the first study (Saletu et al., 1977a), depressed patients improved significantly by the end of the first week of a 5-week trial that utilized a mean daily dosage of about 150 mg. In the second open trial (Wright and Denber, 1978) 10 of 12 depressed patients showed moderate to marked improvement with minimal or no side effects.

(1)

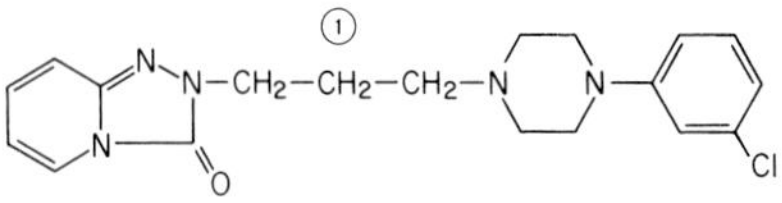

TRAZODONE

(2)

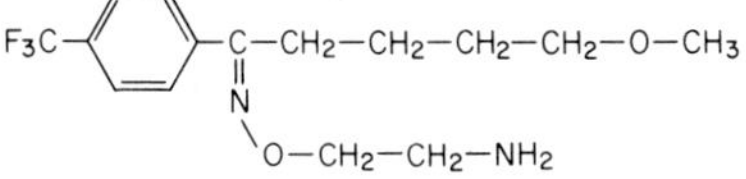

FLUVOXAMINE

(3)

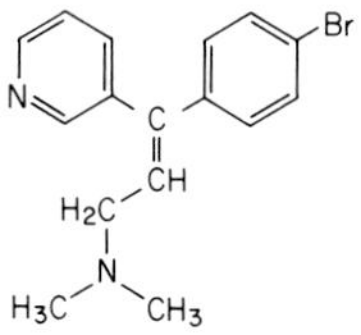

ZIMELIDINE

(4)

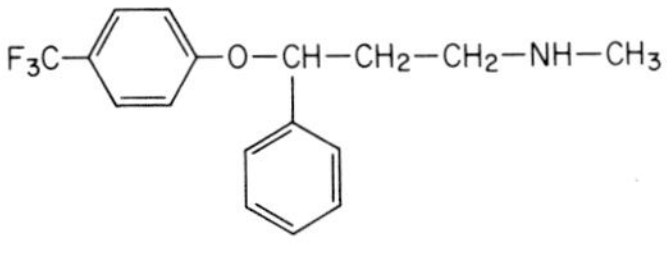

FLUOXETINE

(5)

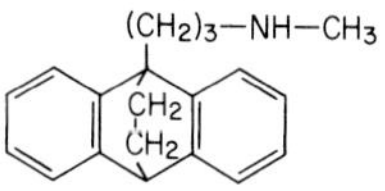

MAPROTILINE

(6)

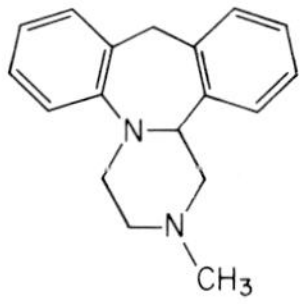

MIANSERIN

(7)

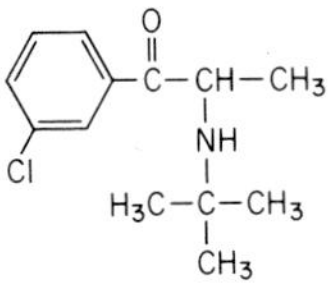

BUPROPION

(8)

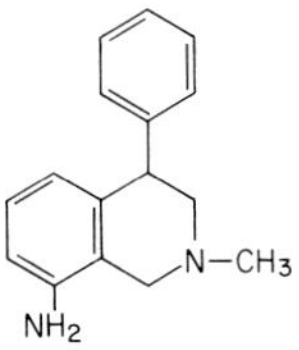

NOMIFENSINE

(9)

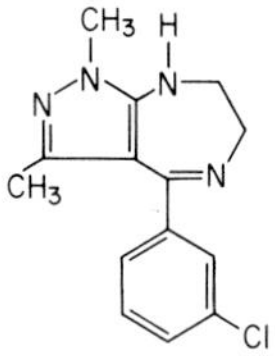

ZOMETAPINE

(10)

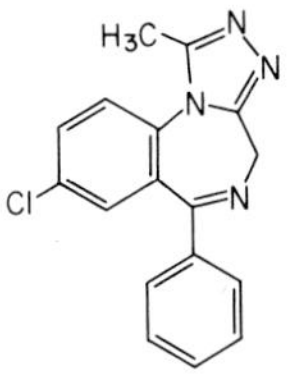

ALPRAZOLAM

(11)

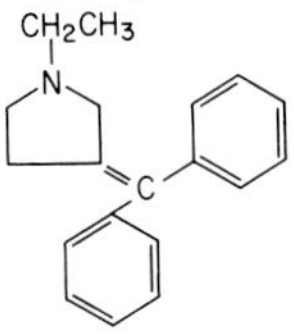

PRIDEFINE

(12)

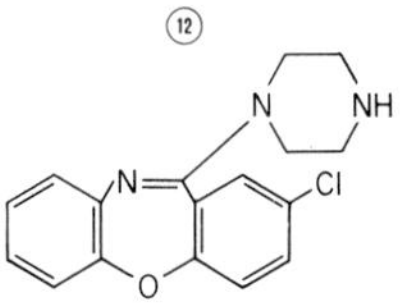

AMOXAPINE

Figs. 1–12.

Zimelidine

Zimelidine, a bicyclic compound, is a highly selective inhibitor of serotonin uptake (Ross and Renyi, 1977) and has only weak anticholinergic and cardiovascular effects. In an open trial (Georgotas et al., 1980) eight of ten depressed patients showed moderate to marked improvement, often beginning the first week. The most common side effects were dry mouth, constipation and drowsiness, but each of these side effects occurred in only two or three patients. The low incidence of these side effects suggest they are symptoms of depressive illness, rather than true side effects. In a double-blind study, 200 mg of zimelidine a day was found to be as effective as 150 mg of amitriptyline (Coppen et al., 1979). Side effects were significantly less with zimelidine, reflecting its weak anticholinergic effect.

Although chemically similar to nisoxetine, a highly selective inhibitor of norepinephrine uptake, *fluoxetine* is instead a highly selective inhibitor of serotonin uptake in both pre-clinical (Fuller et al., 1975) and clinical (Lemberger et al., 1978) studies. The manufacturer reports that preliminary unpublished double-blind studies show that the drug is an effective antidepressant and claims it has fewer anticholinergic effects compared to tricyclics.

NON-TRICYCLIC NORADRENERGIC DRUGS

Maprotiline

Maprotiline, used in Europe for years, has only recently been introduced into the U.S. It is a tetracyclic and differs from tricyclics by having an ethylene bridge across the central ring. Unlike standard tricyclics, maprotiline is a highly selective inhibitor of norepinephrine uptake in peripheral and central neurons without any inhibition of serotonin uptake (Baumann and Maitre, 1979).

Maprotiline appears to be an effective antidepressant based on comparisons to standard drugs. However, there are no placebo-controlled trials to unequivocally show maprotiline to be superior to placebo. Numerous controlled trials have shown it to be as effective as imipramine and amitriptyline, and to have similar side effects (Pinder et al., 1977). A few controlled trials suggest that side effects are less severe when compared to equal doses of imipramine (Singh et al., 1976) and amitriptyline (Botter, 1976). Cardiovascular effects, such as postural hypotension and sinus tachycardia, may be less severe with maprotiline and comparable to the effects of doxepin (Hattab, 1976).

The dose range of maprotiline is the same as for standard tricyclics. In a comparative review of once daily dosage studies and divided dosage studies, once daily dosage is equally effective and well tolerated (Bartholini, 1975). A derivative of maprotiline, oxaprotiline, is currently being tested in clinical trials. At this time it is not clear if oxaprotiline will have any advantage over currently available compounds, including maprotiline.

Tandamine

Tandamine, a thiopyranoindole, also appears to be a potent and selective inhibitor of norepinephrine uptake. In animals, it has no effect on dopamine or serotonin uptake, and only a slight anticholinergic effect (Pugsley and Lippman, 1979). In human volunteers, the drug is sedative, reduces appetite, has anticholinergic effects and may block dopamine as well as norepinephrine uptake (Ehsanullah et al., 1977). However, in an open study of hospitalized depressed patients (Saletu et al., 1977b), tandamine has a pronounced stimulatory effect and only a slight, though significant, antidepressant effect.

Nisoxetine

Nisoxetine is chemically different from tricyclic antidepressants and is also a selective inhibitor of neuronal norepinephrine uptake (Fuller et al., 1979). The manufacturer reports that initial open label and double-blind clinical studies show the drug is effective for the treatment of depression, although an unpublished trial (Gershon et al.) has had negative results. A small number of patients have developed leukopenia on nisoxetine and clinical trials have been discontinued.

OTHER NON-TRICYCLIC ANTIDEPRESSANTS

Mianserin

Another antidepressant with both a novel structure and pharmacology is mianserin, a tetracyclic piperazino-azepine. First synthesized in 1966, mianserin was found to be anti-serotonergic peripherally and a potent antihistamine. Although animal testing did not suggest a possible antidepressant effect, clinical observations of sedative and possible mood-lifting effects and quantitative EEG studies suggested mianserin would have antidepressant properties (Peet and Behagel, 1978).

Mianserin is pharmacologically distinct from tricyclic antidepressants. It is clearly less potent than imipramine or amitriptyline in blocking both serotonin and norepinephrine uptake, although to the extent it does block amine uptake, it is relatively selective for norepinephrine (Zis and Goodwin, 1979). It increases the turnover of norepinephrine without appreciably affecting the turnover of dopamine or serotonin, in contrast to tricyclics which reduce norepinephrine and serotonin turnover (Leonard, 1977).

Mianserin appears to be an effective antidepressant at doses that usually range between 30 mg and 60 mg/day. It is more effective than diazepam (Russell et al., 1978; Hamouz et al., 1980) and comparable in efficacy to amitriptyline (Coppen et al., 1976; Jaskari et al., 1977; Mehta et al., 1980) and to imipramine (Pichot et al., 1978).

A general finding is that mianserin causes fewer side effects than tricyclics. There are no anticholinergic effects and it appears to be free of cardiovascular effects at normal doses. Rather than causing a dry mouth, mianserin actually increases salivary flow (Wilson et al., 1980). It has no consistent effects on the ECG or heart rate (Peet et al., 1977), no effect on cardiac conduction at 60 mg/day (Burrows et al., 1979), and does not cause postural hypotension (Kopera, 1978). Unlike tricyclic antidepressants, there may be little interaction with antihypertensive drugs like guanethidine. Mianserin does seem capable of precipitating mania in bipolar patients (Coppen et al., 1977).

Bupropion

Bupropion also has a novel non-tricyclic structure and pharmacology. In preclinical studies, bupropion does not inhibit MAO. Unlike the tricyclics, bupropion is also a relatively poor inhibitor of norepinephrine and serotonin uptake; for example, it is 60 times less potent as an inhibitor of norepinephrine uptake than amitriptyline. It is without cholinergic effects and is not sympathomimetic. Compared to imipramine and amitriptyline, bupropion is 6 and 20 times more potent in inhibiting dopamine uptake (Soroko et al., 1977).

In a double-blind, placebo-controlled study to investigate the efficacy and tolerance of bupropion (Fabre and McLendon, 1978), antidepressant effects and markedly few side effects were found at dosages of 300–600 mg/day. No patients dropped out of the study due to side effects. There were no clinically significant changes in blood pressure, heart rate, ECG or laboratory values. Bupropion and placebo groups were indistinguishable based on the occurrence of side effects.

In this study and in another placebo-controlled trial, there is a notable absence of anticholinergic, sedative or stimulating side effects, even at higher dose levels. At higher doses a significant antidepressant effect occurs after the first week. This may occur because bupropion's low side effect profile permits a more aggressive dosing regimen compared to tricyclics (Stern and Harto-Truax, 1980).

Bupropion has been extensively reviewed by Maxwell et al. (1981). In inpatient and outpatient studies comparing bupropion to maximally effective doses of amitriptyline, the two drugs show comparable efficacy. Thus, bupropion appears to be an effective antidepressant that would be especially advantageous for patients who are sensitive to sedative, anticholinergic, or cardiovascular side effects. In addition, bupropion is not associated with weight gain. However, convulsions have been reported in several cases. Bupropion's dopaminergic effects may also exacerbate psychotic symptoms in psychotic patients.

Nomifensine

Nomifensine is a tetrahydroisoquinoline antidepressant that is structurally different from tricyclic and tetracyclic antidepressants. Unlike tricyclics, nomifensine inhibits the reuptake of dopamine as well as norepinephrine and is a relatively weak inhibitor of serotonin uptake. In animal studies, it is similar to amphetamine in its ability to produce stereotyped behavior, but does not appear to release stores of epinephrine and dopamine. The usual dose range for nomifensine is 50–200 mg/day.

The therapeutic efficacy of nomifensine has been reviewed by Brogden et al. (1979). Nomifensine is as effective as imipramine, desipramine, amitriptyline, nortriptyline, clomipramine and doxepin at equal or similar doses in double-blind comparisons, and is clearly superior to placebo. The most commonly reported side effects have been sleep disturbances, restlessness, paranoid symptoms, tachycardia and nausea; however, side effects are usually mild and seldom require stopping the drug.

The side effect profile of nomifensine is substantially different from tricyclic antidepressants in several advantageous ways. It produces little or no sedation. Autonomic side effects in general are less severe and less frequent than with tricyclics (Brogden et al.,

1979). Nomifensine has little cardiac effect, and does not appreciably affect cardiac conduction (Burrows et al., 1978).

In a report of 26 cases of probable nomifensine overdosage, there was a low incidence of cardiovascular effects and serious complications (Dawling et al., 1979). Vohra et al. (1978) have noted an absence of ECG changes in a woman who ingested 3.5 g of nomifensine.

Viloxazine

Viloxazine is a bicyclic tetrahydroxazine. In studies that lack placebo controls, it is as effective as amitriptyline for the treatment of endogenous depression at identical doses (Kiloh et al., 1979) and at twice the dosage of amitriptyline (Botter, 1979). Viloxazine's side effect profile is different from tricyclic antidepressants. It has fewer anticholinergic and sedative effects but nausea and vomiting are relatively common side effects. It is as effective as imipramine in moderately depressed patients, and has significantly fewer side effects (Davies et al., 1977).

The half-life of viloxazine is relatively short, in the range of 2–5 hours (Bayliss and Case, 1975). It appears to be less cardiotoxic than tricyclics; in a report of 12 cases of overdose, no ECG abnormalities were observed (Brosnan et al., 1976). Compared to placebo, viloxazine is effective and well tolerated in depressed elderly patients at doses of 100 mg to 200 mg (Von Knorring, 1980). Viloxazine appears to be a useful alternative treatment for some patients.

Zometapine

Zometapine is the first drug in a new class of psychoactive agents, the pyrazodiazepines, that are structurally similar to benzodiazepines. In laboratory studies, zometapine produces effects similar to tricyclic antidepressants; it potentiates amphetamine-induced anorexia, motor activity and electrical self-stimulation (James et al., 1980). Zometapine appears to have a novel mechanism of action. It potentiates and prolongs the effects of pressor amines without blocking the reuptake of norepinephrine or serotonin and without inhibiting MAO. Cardiovascular effects appear to be minimal, and, in animal studies, zometapine has negligible anticholinergic effects.

Initial uncontrolled clinical trials suggest that zometapine is an effective antidepressant at doses that range from 200 to 600 mg/day (James et al., 1980; Tuason et al., 1980). Side effects of zometapine are predominantly gastrointestinal, with nausea, vomiting and abdominal cramps the most common side effects. These effects are dose related and tend to decrease or disappear with continued treatment. More moderate dosage regimens of 200–400 mg/day may be just as therapeutic and minimize the gastrointestinal effects. An antidepressant that produces nausea at higher doses may also help prevent suicide attempts (Tuason et al., 1980).

Triazolobenzodiazepines are characterized by the incorporation of a triazole ring in the basic benzodiazepine structure. *Alprazolam* is a triazolobenzodiazepine with both anxiolytic and antidepressant properties.

In animal studies, it is less toxic in comparison to other benzodiazepine compounds

(Castaner and Chatterjee, 1976). In comparison to diazepam, alprazolam is frequently a more efficacious anxiolytic and has fewer side effects (Fabre and McLendon, 1979). It is better than placebo and as effective as imipramine for the treatment of depressed out-patients, and results in fewer side effects (Fabre and McLendon, 1980). *Adinazolam* is another triazolobenzodiazepine which may have antidepressant activity (Hester, 1979), although no clinical trials have been yet reported.

Iprindole

Iprindole is a relatively weak inhibitor of norepinephrine and serotonin reuptake. A number of studies show that iprindole is as effective as imipramine, but methodological flaws in most of the studies prevent a conclusion that iprindole is effective for the treat-ment of major depression with endogenous features (Zis and Goodwin, 1979).

Pridefine

Pridefine is a pyrrolidine compound that is structurally unrelated to tricyclic antidepres-sants or to any other commercially available compound. According to the manufacturer, early investigations with this drug suggest a low incidence of adverse side effects and a lack of cardiac toxicity. In clinical studies pridefine is superior to placebo and as effec-tive as imipramine for the treatment of depression.

Clovoxamine

Clovoxamine is a novel antidepressant with a structure unlike that of tricyclic antidepres-sants. In animals, it is an active inhibitor of norepinephrine and serotonin uptake, is not sedative, and has no anticholinergic activity. It is a weak MAO inhibitor *in vitro* but not *in vivo* (Claassen et al., 1978). In a preliminary open trial, most patients improved rapid-ly. Side effects were well tolerated and included typical, though mild, anticholinergic symptoms (Wright et al., 1981).

TRICYCLIC ANTIDEPRESSANTS

Amoxapine

Amoxapine is a dibenzoxapine tricyclic with a structure similar to loxapine, an anti-psychotic agent. The recommended maximum and mean dose of amoxapine is twice that of standard antidepressants; the drug has just recently been released in the U.S.

Studies comparing amoxapine to amitriptyline in depressed outpatients show that amoxapine is equally effective and has similar side effects but a quicker onset of action (Hekimian et al., 1978; Donlon et al., 1981). Studies comparing amoxapine to impira-mine have found that amoxapine is as effective, has similar or fewer side effects, and have also found a rapid onset of action (Bagadia et al., 1979; Holden et al., 1979; Taka-hashi et al., 1979). The above studies all lack placebo controls. The need for placebo controls is emphasized by the results of a study by Steinbook et al. (1979) that found that neither amoxapine nor imipramine were superior to placebo.

The structure of *clomipramine* is the same as imipramine with the addition of a chlorine atom. Although not available in the U.S., clomipramine is now used in many countries. It is an effective antidepressant in the same dose range of other tricyclic antidepressants, and has similar side effects. It is of interest because pilot trials suggest it is an effective treatment for obsessive compulsive neurosis. Controlled trials are needed to investigate clomipramine's usefulness for this disorder.

Lofepramine

Lofepramine is an analogue of imipramine that may have fewer side effects (Obermair and Wegener, 1978). In a double-blind study comparing 210 mg of lofepramine to 150 mg amitriptyline, lofepramine was more effective and better tolerated (Marneros and Philipp, 1979). Other studies have suggested that the drug is effective but without appreciable differences in side effects when compared to amitriptyline (McClelland et al., 1979) and imipramine, although in the latter case anticholinergic effects were less intense (d'Elia et al., 1977). Lofepramine does not appear to offer any compelling advantages over currently available drugs.

Butriptyline

Butriptyline is structurally similar to amitriptyline. Like other tricyclics, it is an effective antidepressant but does have anticholinergic side effects (Burrows et al., 1977). It does not block the reuptake of sympathomimetic amines and for that reason may be less likely to interfere with antihypertensive drugs such as guanethidine (Ghose et al., 1977). Otherwise, butriptyline seems to have no advantages over other tricyclic drugs (Drug Ther. Bull., 1977).

Dothiepin

Dothiepin, or dosulepin, is also related to amitriptyline. Dothiepin is as effective as amitriptyline (Lipsedge et al., 1971) and imipramine (Eilenberg, 1980) and better tolerated. Qualitatively, dothiepin has the same side effects as other tricyclic antidepressants, including cardiotoxic effects (Rysanek et al., 1974).

Other tricyclic antidepressants that are not in general use are noxiptiline, dibenzepin, amineptine and melitracen.

Noxiptiline

Noxiptiline is an effective antidepressant with a relatively rapid onset of action and milder side effects when compared to equal doses of amitriptyline (Lingjaerde et al., 1975). *Dibenzepin* is just as effective as amitriptyline and possibly has less intense side effects (Baron et al., 1976; Gowardman and Brown, 1976). There have been no new clinical studies since 1976; dibenzepin does not appear to have any clearcut advantages over classic tricyclics.

Amineptine

Amineptine appears as effective as modest doses (75 mg/day) of trimipramine (Vauterin and Bazot, 1979) and amitriptyline (Van Amerongen, 1979). Amineptine appears to be more arousing and less sedating than classic antidepressants (Bornstein, 1979). Many of the clinical trials with *melitracen* took place in the 60s. The most recent controlled trial compared melitracen to amitriptyline in hospitalized patients (Francesconi et al., 1976). In this study, melitracen was as effective as amitriptyline and side effects, though less intense, were qualitatively the same.

DRUGS NOT USUALLY USED FOR DEPRESSION

Lithium

Lithium is generally recognized as an effective agent for the treatment and prophylaxis of mania and for the prophylaxis of either unipolar or bipolar depression. The effectiveness of lithium as an antidepressant has recently been reviewed by Mendels et al. (1979) and by Gershon and Goodnick (1981). In view of our familiarity with lithium, it is amazing to note that the total published evidence of its acute antidepressant effects rests on data from 11 controlled studies involving only slightly more than 300 patients.

Three of these studies have failed to find an effect while at least eight studies do show a significant antidepressant effect. The studies with negative results have been criticized on methodological grounds, and the results interpreted as equivocal by Mendels et al. (1979). There is a definite trend in the studies for bipolar patients to respond better than unipolar patients. Further work needs to be done to confirm the suggestive evidence that lithium is an effective antidepressant for a subgroup of affectively disordered patients. Obvious potential advantages for lithium as an antidepressant are that lithium does not precipitate mania and lacks anticholinergic or sedative effects.

The anticonvulsant *carbamazepine*, an iminodibenzyl derivative, may also have both antimanic and antidepressant effects. In a double-blind study with an on-off placebo controlled design, Ballenger and Post (1980) found that 7 out of 9 manic patients and 7 out of 13 depressed patients had a positive response to carbamazepine alone at doses that ranged between 600 and 1600 mg/day. Although the antidepressant effect appears to be modest, carbamazepine may have an advantage over other antidepressants if the antimanic effect prevents the induction of mania in the treatment of depressed bipolar patients. The major disadvantage of carbamazepine is that it is associated with bone marrow depression and, rarely, aplastic anemia.

Pemoline

Pemoline is a central nervous system stimulant that has minimal sympathomimetic effects. It is currently used to treat hyperkinetic syndromes (attention deficit disorders) in children. In a clinical trial of pemoline in general practice patients with mild depression and fatigue, pemoline was better than placebo but the difference was significant only for the first 2 weeks of a 4-week crossover trial (Kagan, 1974).

In another controlled trial comparing pemoline to placebo in patients with moderate depression, apathy, fatigue and lack of energy, there was no difference between groups on ratings of global response. Pemoline patients did show significant improvement for some symptoms over baseline (Elizur et al., 1979). Rickels et al. (1970), compared both pemoline and methylphenidate hydrochloride to placebo in mildly depressed patients with fatigue treated in one of three settings. Both drugs produced significant improvement in general practice and psychiatric clinic patients, but no improvement in private psychiatric patients.

The major methodological problem with the above studies is that they preselect patients who would respond to a stimulant drug. The suggestive finding that pemoline works for patients who complain of mild depression and fatigue does not mean that pemoline is effective for major affective disorders. It is possible that caffeine would be just as effective; this would explain the observation by Rickels et al. (1970) that the private psychiatric patients who did not respond to pemoline drank significantly more coffee than other patients.

Salbutamol

Salbutamol is an adrenergic drug that acts primarily on beta-2 receptors. It is therefore a powerful bronchodilator with minimal cardiac effects and for this reason is currently in use for the treatment of asthma. Lecrubier et al. (1980) compared 6 mg/day of salbutamol to 150 mg/day of clomipramine in a controlled study. Eight out of ten salbutamol patients showed clear improvement. Salbutamol's therapeutic effect was superior to clomipramine and more rapid, with improvement often occurring within 2–5 days. Tachycardia and tremor were the most common side effects. The major disadvantage of salbutamol is that it must be given intravenously. However, if larger clinical trials confirm salbutamol's efficacy and rapid onset of action, it may be a useful drug for the initial treatment of hospitalized, actively suicidal patients. And if salbutamol is effective, it seems likely that orally administered beta adrenergic drugs will be effective.

NATURALLY OCCURRING SUBSTANCES

If depressive illness is the result of a deficiency in serotonin, then theoretically the administration of *L-tryptophan* should ameliorate depression. The amount of serotonin synthesized depends in part on the amount of its precursor, tryptophan, rather than on the availability of rate-limiting enzymes. 'Precursor loading' with tryptophan may employ tryptophan as the only active drug, or the use of tryptophan with known antidepressants.

The efficacy of L-tryptophan as the solely active drug in the treatment of depression is controversial. The question of efficacy is further complicated by the fact that additional compounds may be given with tryptophan that may enhance its effect. The addition of pyridoxine, the coenzyme involved in the decarboxylation of 5-hydroxytryptophan to serotonin, and the addition of nicotinamide, which reduces the alternative kynurenine metabolic pathway, may be useful. Combination of tryptophan with allopurinol (Shopsin, 1978) has also been suggested to prevent tryptophan loading activation of liver enzymes.

Comparisons of tryptophan to placebo, with and without pyridoxine, have shown no difference from placebo (d'Elia et al., 1978). In a review of the effects of tryptophan compared to tricyclic antidepressants, d'Elia et al. (1978) concluded that tryptophan is probably inferior to imipramine and to ECT, although some studies show tryptophan to be equal to imipramine. A subsequent study has shown tryptophan combined with nicotinamide may be as effective as imipramine (Chouinard et al., 1979). In an open, preliminary trial, tryptophan combined with allopurinol appears to be an effective and rapid treatment (Shopsin, 1978). Other recent trials suggest that tryptophan alone is not an effective antidepressant (Worrall et al., 1979; Cooper and Datta, 1980). In view of the potential safety of tryptophan as an antidepressant, there is a need for larger, multi-center trials of tryptophan combined with compounds that enhance its effect.

The combination of tryptophan with tricyclic antidepressants appears to offer no advantage over tricyclics alone (d'Elia et al., 1978). One possible exception is that tryptophan may enhance the therapeutic effect of clomipramine (Walinder et al., 1976). Tryptophan does not appear to enhance the effect of zimelidine (Walinder et al., 1980), perhaps because zimelidine is even more strongly serotonergic than clomipramine. In contrast to the tricyclic antidepressant studies, the combination of tryptophan with MAO inhibitor appears to be more effective than a MAO inhibitor alone (d'Elia et al., 1978).

The amino acid *phenylalanine* is decarboxylated *in vivo* to phenethylamine, an amphetamine-like substance. Open trials (Fischer et al., 1975; Beckmann et al., 1977) and one controlled trial with imipramine (Beckmann et al., 1979) have shown phenylalanine to have substantial antidepressant effects. However, a subsequent open trial by Mann et al. (1980) failed to show appreciable antidepressant activity. Phenylalanine needs to be re-evaluated, perhaps at higher doses, in controlled trials.

S-adenosyl-L-methionine (SAMe)

SAMe is a methyl donor involved in the metabolism of central nervous system neurotransmitters. Given parenterally, SAMe may enhance the synthesis of serotonin and norepinephrine (Curcio et al., 1978; Algeri et al., 1979).

In double-blind studies, intramuscularly administered SAMe is superior to placebo (Agnoli et al., 1976) and equal to imipramine (Mantero et al., 1975). Given intravenously, SAMe appears to be as effective as clomipramine and amitriptyline for the treatment of depression (Miccoli et al., 1978). SAMe needs to be investigated further; it appears to be without side effects.

MONOAMINE OXIDASE INHIBITORS

Renewed interest in monoamine oxidase (MAO) inhibitors centers on the differentiation of MAO into two types, type A and type B. MAO-A deaminates tyramine, norephinephrine and serotonin; MAO-B deaminates dopamine and phenethylamine. *Clorgyline* is a relatively specific inhibitor of MAO-A. Another investigational drug, deprenyl, is a relatively specific inhibitor of MAO-B. *Pargyline,* a drug marketed for the treatment of hypertension, is also an MAO inhibitor that preferentially inhibits MAO-B.

In a crossover comparison of clorgyline to pargyline (Lipper et al., 1979), clorgyline

200

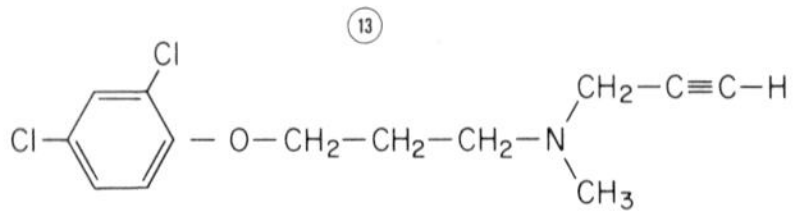

CLORGYLINE

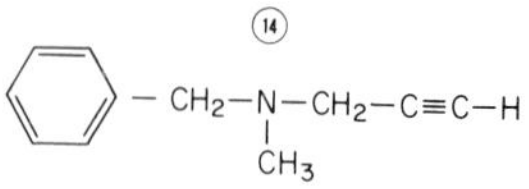

PARGYLINE

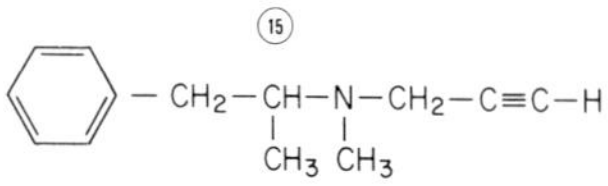

DEPRENYL

Figs. 13–15.

showed significant antidepressant effects and was superior to pargyline. Pargyline showed modest antidepressant effects but was associated with greater activation-related side effects. Both drugs precipitated hypomanic symptoms in predisposed individuals. The results of this study suggest that the inhibition of MAO that deaminates norepinephrine and serotonin (MAO-A) has a greater antidepressant effect than the inhibition of MAO-B.

Toloxatone

Toloxatone, like clorgyline, is a relatively specific inhibitor of MAO-A. Unlike clorgyline and the clinically available MAO inhibitors, toloxatone is a reversible MAO inhibitor (Kan et al., 1978). The lack of irreversible inhibition is of special interest because of the clinical implications; a reversible MAO inhibitor should be safer and easier to use.

However, MAO-B inhibitors, if effective for the treatment of depression, are of interest because they are potentially much safer. *Deprenyl,* at a modest dose of 10 mg for up to 18 months, is not associated with the tyramine pressor response ('cheese effect'). In addition, significant tyramine responses are not seen at higher doses of 40–60 mg daily given for 3 weeks (Stern et al., 1978). L-deprenyl is metabolized to the L-isomers of methamphetamine and amphetamine. Although the L-isomers of these metabolites are only one quarter as active as the D-isomers, the possibility that deprenyl might be abused must be considered (Sandler et al., 1978).

In an open trial in endogenously depressed patients, L-deprenyl was an effective antidepressant for patients who did not respond to placebo (Mann and Gershon, 1980). It produced a broad-range antidepressant effect rather than a nonspecific activating effect. At the dosage used (15 mg daily), there was no postural hypotension and it is unlikely there would be a 'cheese effect'.

Deprenyl needs to be investigated further as a potentially safer, effective, MAO-inhibiting antidepressant. It has been suggested that hysteroid dysphoric patients may preferentially respond to a MAO-B inhibitor (Quitkin et al., 1979). To our knowledge, this hypothesis remains untested.

CONCLUSIONS

A large number of 'second generation' antidepressants will eventually be clinically available. New drugs that have had extensive clinical evaluations appear to be no more effective than currently available drugs. The fact that no drug is 100% effective is consistent with the idea that depression is a heterogeneous disorder. However, newer antidepressants still offer enormous advantages over currently available compounds.

Newer antidepressants cover a pharmacological spectrum. Some compounds may be more effective for particular patients because they are more selective in their effect on noradrenergic or serotonergic systems, or more selective inhibitors of MAO. Other compounds appear to have novel pharmacological effects and are antidepressant without any appreciable effect on noradrenergic and serotonergic systems; examples are mianserin, bupropion and zometapine. Hopefully, these drugs will be useful for treatment-resistant patients, although this hypothesis remains untested.

The major advantage of many newer drugs is the lack of troublesome and dangerous side effects associated with tricyclics. Drugs that lack significant anticholinergic or cardiotoxic effects are especially noteworthy; examples include trazodone, mianserin, bupropion, nomifensine, and zimelidine. As for sedative effects, the clinician is still left with the option of choosing a sedating or non-sedating compound, depending upon the needs of the patient. Newer drugs that lack any appreciable sedative effects include nomifensine, zimelidine, and bupropion.

The newer antidepressants represent a new era in the management of depression. Clinicians will have drugs with fewer side effects, and the atypical mechanism of action of some of the newer drugs will help us to understand the pathophysiology of depression.

REFERENCES

Agnoli, A., Andreoli, V., Casacchia, M. and Cerbo, R. (1976) Effect of S-adenosyl-L-methionine (SAMe) upon depressive symptoms. J. Psychiatr. Res. 13, 43–54.

Algeri, S , Catto, E., Curcio, M., Ponzio, F. and Stramentinoli, G. (1979) In: V. Zappia, E. Usdin and F. Salvatore (Eds), Biochemical and Pharmacological Roles of Adenosylmethionine. Pergamon Press Ltd., Oxford, p. 81.

Ayd, F. J. (1979) Trazodone: a unique new broad spectrum antidepressant. Int. Drug Ther. Newslett. 14, 33–40.

Bagadia, V. N., Shah, L. P., Pradhan, P. V. and Gada, M. T. (1979) A double-blind controlled study of amoxapine and imipramine in cases of depression. Curr. Ther. Res. 26, 417–429.

Ballenger, J. C. and Post, R. M. (1980) Carbamazepine in manic-depressive illness: a new treatment. Am. J. Psychiatry 137, 782–790.

Baron, D. P., Unger, H. R., Williams, H. E. and Knight, R. G. (1976) A double-blind study of the antidepressants dibenzepin (Noveril) and amitriptyline. N.Z. Med. J. 83, 273–274.

Bartholini, E. (1975) Once daily dosage with maprotiline (Ludiomil). J. Int. Med. Res. 3 (Suppl. 2), 101–108.

Baumann, P A. and Maitre, L. (1979) Neurobiochemical aspects of maprotiline (Ludiomil) action. J. Int. Med. Res. 7, 391–400.

Bayliss, P. F. and Case, D. E. (1975) Blood level studies with viloxazine hydrochloride in man. Br. J. Pharmacol. 2, 209–214.

Beckmann, H., Strauss, M. A. and Ludolph, E. (1977) DL-phenylalanine in depressed patients: an open study. J. Neural Trans. 41, 123–134.

Beckmann, H., Athen, D., Olteanu, M. and Zimmer, R. (1979) DL-phenylalanine versus imipramine: a double-blind controlled study. Arch. Psychiatr. Nervenkr. 227, 49–58.

Bornstein, S. (1979) Cross-over trial comparing the antidepressant effects of amineptine and maprotiline. Curr. Med. Res. Opin. 6, 107–110.

Botter, P A. (1976) A clinical double-blind comparison of maprotiline and amitryptyline in depression. Curr. Med. Res. Opin. 3, 634–641.

Botter, P. A (1979) A double-blind comparison of viloxazine and amitriptyline in involutional and endogenous depression. Acta Psychiatr. Belg. 79, 198–209.

Brogden, R. N., Heel, R. C., Speight, T. M. and Avery, G. S. (1979) Nomifensine: a review of its pharmacological properties and therapeutic efficacy in depressive illness. Drugs 18, 1–24.

Brosnan, R. D., Busby, A. M. and Holland, R. P. (1976) Cases of overdose with viloxazine hydrochloride (Vivalan). J. Int. Med. Res. 4, 83–85.

Burrows, G. D., Norman, T. R., Maguire, K. P., Rubinstein, G., Scoggins, B. A. and Davies, B. (1977) A new antidepressant butriptyline: plasma levels and clinical response. Med. J. Aust. 2, 604–606.

Burrows, G D., Vohra, J., Dumovic, P., Scoggins, B. A. and Davies, B. (1978) Cardiological effects of nomifensine, a new antidepressant. Med. J. Aust. 1, 341–343.

Burrows, G. D , Davies, B., Hamer, A. and Vohra, J. (1979) Effect of mianserin on cardiac conduction. Med. J. Aust. 2, 97–98.

Castaner, J. and Chatterjee, S. S. (1976) Alprazolam. Drugs of the Future 1, 551–554.

Chouinard, G., Young, S. N., Annable, L. and Sourkes, T. L. (1979) Tryptophan-nicotinamide, imipramine and their combination in depression. A controlled study. Acta Psychiatr. Scand. 59, 395–414.

Claassen, V., Davies, J. E., Herting, G. and Placheta, P. (1977) Fluvoxamine, a specific 5-hydroxytryptamine uptake inhibitor. Br. J. Pharmacol. 60, 505–516.

Claassen, V., Boschman, T. A. C., Dhasmana, K. M., Hillen, F. C., Vaatstra, W. J. and Zwagemakers, J M. A (1978) Pharmacology of clovoxamine, a new nontricyclic antidepressant. Arzneim.-Forsch./Drug Res. 28, 1756–1766.

Cooper, A. J. and Datta, S. R. (1980) A placebo controlled evaluation of L-tryptophan is depression in the elderly. Can. J. Psychiatry 25, 386–390.

Coppen, A., Gupta, R., Montgomery, S., Ghose, K., Bailey, J., Burns, B. and DeRidder, J. J. (1976) Mianserin hydrochloride: a novel antidepressant. Br. J. Psychiatry 129, 342–345.

Coppen, A., Ghose, K., Rao, V. A. and Peet, M. (1977) Mianserin: the prophylactic treatment of bipolar affective illness. Int. Pharmacopsychiatry 12, 95–99.

Coppen, A., Ramo-Rao, V. A., Swade, C. and Wood, K. (1979) Zimelidine: a therapeutic and pharmacokinetic study in depression. Psychopharmacology 63, 199–202.

Curcio, M , Catto, E., Stramentinoli, G. and Algeri, S. (1978) Effect of S-adenosyl-L-methionine on serotonin metabolism in rat brain. Prog. Neuro-Psychopharmacol. 2, 65–71.

Davies, B., Joshua, S., Burrows, G. and Poynton, C. (1977) A sequential trial of viloxazine (Vivalan) and imipramine in moderately depressed patients. Med. J. Aust. 1, 521–522.

Dawling, S., Braithwaite, R. and Crome, P. (1979) Nomifensine overdose and plasma drug concentration. (letter) Lancet 1, 56.

D'Elia, G., Borg, S., Hermann, L., Lundin, G., Perris, C., Raotma, H., Roman, G. and Siwers, B. (1977) Comparative clinical evaluation of lofepramine and imipramine. Psychiatric aspects. Acta Psychiatr. Scand. 55, 10–20.

D'Elia, G., Hanson, L. and Roatma, H. (1978) L-tryptophan and 5-hydroxytryptophan in the treatment of depression. A review. Acta Psychiatr. Scand. 57, 239–252.

Donlon, P. T., Biertuemphez, H. and Willenbring, M. (1981) Amoxapine and amitriptyline in the outpatient treatment of endogenous depression. J. Clin. Psychiatry 42, 11–15.

Drug. Ther. Bull. (1977) Two more new antidepressives: mianserin and butriptyline. Drug. Ther. Bull. 15, 1–4.

Ehsanullah, R. S., Ghose, K., Kirby, M. J., Turner, P. and Witts, D. (1977) Clinical pharmacological studies of tandamine, a potential antidepressive drug. Psychopharmacology 52, 73–77.

Eilenberg, D. (1980) A double-blind comparative trial of dothiepin and imipramine for the treatment of depressive patients. N.Z. Med. J. 91, 92–93.

Elizur, A., Wintner, I. and Davidson, S. (1979) The clinical and psychological effects of pemoline in depressed patients – a controlled study. Int. Pharmacopsychiatry 14, 127–134.

Fabre, L. F. and McLendon, D. M. (1978) Double-blind placebo-controlled study of bupropion hydrochloride (Wellbatrin) in the treatment of depressed inpatients. Curr. Ther. Res. 23, 393–402.

Fabre, L. F. and McLendon, D. M. (1979) A double-blind study comparing the efficacy and safety of alprazolam with diazepam and placebo in anxious out-patients. Curr. Ther. Res. 25, 519–526.

Fabre, L. F. and McLendon, D. M. (1980) A double-blind study comparing the efficacy and safety of alprazolam with imipramine and placebo in primary depression. Curr. Ther. Res. 27, 474–482.

Fabre, L. F., McLendon, D. M. and Gainey, A. (1979) Trazodone efficacy in depression: a double-blind comparison with imipramine and placebo in day-hospital type patients. Curr. Ther. Res. 25, 827–834.

Feighner, J. P. (1980) Trazodone, a triazolopyridine derivative in primary depressive disorder. J. Clin. Psychiatry 41, 250–255.

Fischer, E., Heller, B., Nachon, M. and Spatz, H. (1975) Therapy of depression by phenylalanine. Preliminary note. Arzneim. Forsch. 25, 132.

Francesconi, G., LoCascio, A., Mellina, S., Fici, F., Bagnoli, M. and Lepore, R. (1976) Controlled comparison of melitracen and amitriptyline in depressed patients. Curr. Ther. Res. 20, 529–540.

Fuller, R. W., Perry, K. W. and Molloy, B. B. (1975) Effect of 3-(p-trifluoromethylphenoxy)-n-methyl-3-phenylpropylamine on the depletion of brain serotonin by 4-chloroamphetamine. J. Pharmacol. Exp. Ther. 193, 796–803.

Fuller, R. W., Snoddy, H. D. and Perry, K. W. (1979) Nisoxetine antagonism of norepinephrine depletion in brain and heart after a-methyl-m-tyrosine administration. Neuropharmacology 18, 767–770.

Georgotas, A., Mann, J., Bush, D. and Gershon, S. (1980) A clinical trial of zimelidine in depression. Commun. Psychopharmacol. 4, 71–77.

Gerner, R., Estabrook, W., Steuer, J. and Jarvik, L. (1980) Treatment of geriatric depression with trazodone, imipramine, and placebo: a double-blind study. J. Clin. Psychiatry 41, 216–220.

Gershon, S. and Goodnick, P. J. (1981) Lithium use in affective disorders. Psychiatr. Annals 11, 143–153.

Gershon, S. and Newton, R. (1980) Lack of anticholinergic side effects with a new antidepressant – trazodone. J. Clin. Psychiatry 41, 100–104.

Ghose, K., Huston, G. J., Kirby, J. J., Witts, D. J. and Turner, P. (1977) Some clinical pharmacological studies with butriptyline, an antidepressive drug. Br. J. Clin. Pharmacol. 4, 91–93.

Gomoll, A. W. and Byrne, J. E. (1979) Trazodone and imipramine: comparative effects on canine cardiac conduction. Eur. J. Pharmacol. 57, 335–342.

Gowardman, M. and Brown, R. A. (1976) Dibenzepin and amitriptyline in depressive states: comparative double-blind trial. N.Z. Med. J. 83, 194–197.

Hamouz, W., Pinder, R. M. and Stulemeijer, S. M. (1980) A double-blind group comparative trial of mianserin and diazepam in depressed out-patients. Pharmacology 13, 79–83.

Hattab, J. R. (1976) The cardiovascular effects of ludiomil in comparison with those of some tricyclic antidepressants. Paper presented at the Ludiomil Symposium (Malta).

Hekimian, L. J., Friedhoff, A. J. and Deever, E. (1978) A comparison of the onset of action and therapeutic efficacy of amoxapine and amitriptyline. J. Clin. Psychiatry 39, 633–637.

Hester, J. B. (1979) New synthesis of 8-chloro-1-(2-(dimethylamino)ethyl)-6-phenyl-4 H-s-triazolo-(4,3-a) (1,4)-benzodiazepine, which has antidepressant properties. J. Org. Chem. 44, 4165–4169.

Holden, J. M. C., Kerry, R. J. and Orme, J. E. (1979) Amoxapine in depressive illness. Curr. Med. Res. Opin. 6, 338–341.

James, N. M., Searle, J. P., Goodman, L. I. and Borgen, L. A. (1980) An early phase II study of zometapine, a new antidepressant. Curr. Ther. Res. 27, 100–108.

Jaskari, M. O., Ahfors, U. G., Ginman, L., Lydecken, K. and Tienari, P. (1977) Three double-blind comparative trials of mianserin (Org GB 94) and amitriptyline in the treatment of depressive illness. Pharmakopsychiatr. Neuropsychopharmakol. 10, 101–103.

Kagan, G. (1974) Clinical trial of pemoline in general practice. B. J. Clin. Pract. 28, 375–378.

Kan, J. P., Malone, A. and Benedetti, M. S. (1978) Monoamine oxidase inhibitory properties of 5-

hydroxymethyl-3-m-tolyloxazolidin-z-one (toloxatone). J. Pharm. Pharmacol. 30, 190–192.

Kiloh, L. G., Bartrop, R. W., Franklin, J. A. and Neilson, M. D. (1979) A double-blind comparative trial of viloxazine and amitriptyline in patients suffering from endogenous depression. Aust. N. Z. J. Psychiatry 13, 357–360.

Kopera, H. (1978) Anticholinergic and blood pressure effects of mianserin, amitriptyline and placebo. Br. J. Clin. Pharmacol. 5 (Suppl. 1), 29–34.

Lecrubier, Y., Peuch, A. J., Jouvent, R., Simon, P. and Widlocher, D. (1980) A beta adrenergic stimulant (salbutamol) versus clomipramine in depression: a controlled study. Br. J. Psychiatry 136, 354–358.

Lemberger, L., Rowe, H., Carmichael, R., Crabtree, R. and Horng, J. S. (1978) Fluoxetine, a selective serotonin uptake inhibitor. Clin. Pharmacol. Ther. 23, 421–429.

Leonard, B. E. (1977) Some effects of mianserin (Org GB 94) on amine metabolism in the rat brain Pharmackopsychiatr. Neuropsychopharmakol. 10, 92–95.

Lingjaerde, O., Asker, T., Bagge, A., Engstrand, E., Eide, A., Grinaker, H., Herlofsen, H., Ose, E. and Ofsti, E. (1975) Noxiptilin (Agedal) – a new tricyclic antidepressant with a faster onset of action? A double-blind multicentre comparison with amitriptyline. Pharmakopsychiatr. Neuro-Psychopharmacol. 1, 26–35.

Lipper, S., Murphy, D. L., Slater, S. and Buchsbaum, M. S. (1979) Comparative behavioral effects of clorgyline and pargyline in man: a preliminary evaluation. Psychopharmacology 62, 123–128.

Lipsedge, M. S., Rees, W. L. and Pike, D. J. (1971) A double-blind comparison of dothiepin and amitriptyline for the treatment of depression with anxiety. Psychopharmacology 19, 153–162.

Mann, J. and Gershon, S. (1980) L-deprenyl, a selective monoamine oxidase type-B inhibitor in endogenous depression. Life Sci. 26, 877–882.

Mann, J., Peselow, E. D., Snyderman, S. and Gershon, S. (1980) D-phenylalanine in endogenous depression. Am. J. Psychiatry 137, 1611–1612.

Mantero, M., Pastorino, P., Carolei, A. and Agnoli, A. (1975) Studio controllato in doppio cieco (SAMe imipramin) nelle sindromi depressive. Minerva Med. 66, 4098–4101.

Marneros, A. and Philipp, M. (1979) A double-blind trial with amitriptyline and lofepramine in the treatment of endogenous depression. Int. Pharmacopsychiatry 14, 300–304.

Maxwell, R. A., Mehta, N. B., Tucker, W. E., Schroeder, D. H. and Stern, W. C. (1981) Bupropion. In: M. E. Goldberg (Ed.), Pharmacological and Biochemical Properties of Drug Substances, Vol. 3. American Pharmaceutical Association Academy of Pharmaceutical Sciences, Washington, D.C. (in press).

McClelland, H. A., Kerr, T. A., Stephens, D. A. and Howell, R. W. (1979) The comparative antidepressant value or lofepramine and amitriptyline. Results of a controlled trial with comments on the scales used. Acta Psychiatr. Scand. 60, 190–198.

Mehta, B. M., Spear, F. G. and Whittington, J. R. (1980) A double-blind controlled trial of mianserin and amitriptyline in depression. Curr. Med. Res. Opin. 7, 14–22.

Mendels, J., Ramsey, A., Dyson, W. L. and Frazer, A. (1979) Lithium as an antidepressant. Arch. Gen. Psychiatry 36, 845–846.

Miccoli, L., Porro, V. and Bertolino, A. (1978) Comparison between the antidepressant activity of S-adenosylmethionine (SAMe) and that of some tricyclic drugs. Acta Neurol. 33, 243–255.

Obermair, W. and Wegener, G. (1978) Lofepramine – a new antidepressant. Resume of international clinical trial results. J. Pharmacotherapy, 1, 108–110.

Peet, M. and Behagel, H. (1978) Mianserin: a decade of scientific development. Br. J. Clin. Pharmacol. 5 (Suppl. 1), 5–9.

Peet, M., Tienari, P. and Jaskari, M. O. (1977) A comparison of the cardiac effects of mianserin and amitriptyline in man. Pharmakopsychiatr. Neuropsychopharmakol. 10, 309–312.

Pichot, P., Dreyfus, J. F. and Pull, C. (1978) A double-blind multicentre trial comparing mianserin with imipramine. Br. J. Clin. Pharmacol. 5 (Suppl. 1), 87–90.

Pinder, R. M., Brogden, R. N., Speight, T. M. and Avery, G. S. (1977) Maprotiline: a review of its pharmacological properties and therapeutic efficacy in mental depressive states. Drugs 13, 321–352.

Pugsley, T. A. and Lippmann, W. (1979) Effect of acute and chronic treatment of tandamine, a new heterocyclic antidepressant, on biogenic amine metabolism and related activities. Naunyn. Schmiedeberg's Arch. Pharmacol. 308, 239–247.

Quitkin, F., Rifkin, A. and Klein, D. F. (1979) Monoamine oxidase inhibitors. A review of antidepressant effectiveness. Arch. Gen. Psychiatry 36, 749–760.

Riblet, L. A., Gatewood, C. F. and Mayol, R. F. (1979) Comparative effects of trazodone and tricyclic antidepressants on uptake of selected neurotransmitters by isolated rat brain synaptosomes. Psychopharmacology 63, 99–101.

Rickels, K., Gordon, P. E., Gansman, D. H., Weise, C. C., Pereira-Ogan, J. A. and Hesbacher, P. T. (1970) Pemoline and methylphenidate in mildly depressed outpatients. Clin. Pharmacol. Ther. 11, 698–710.

Ross, S. B. and Renyi, A. L. (1977) Inhibition of neuronal uptake of 5-hydroxytryptamine and noradrenaline in rat brain by (Z)- and (E)-3-(4-bromophenyl)-N, N-dimethyl-3-(3-pyridyl) allylamines and their secondary analogues. Neuropharmacology 16, 57–63.

Russell, G. F., Niaz, U., Wakeling, A. and Slade, P. D. (1978) Comparative double-blind trial of mianserin hydrochloride (Organon GB 94) and diazepam in patients with depressive illness. Br. J. Clin. Pharmacol. 5 (Suppl. 1), 57–65.

Rysanek, K., Rotrekl, J., Homola, D., Nahunek, K., Rodova, A., Svestka, J. and Srnova, V. (1974) Mechanocardiographical comparison of the cardiotoxic effect of prothiaden and imipramine. Act. Nerv. Super. (Praha) 16, 183–184.

Saarma, J. (1974) Trazodone – a review of the literature. In: T. A. Ban and B. Silverstrini (Eds), Modern Problems of Pharmacopsychiatry, Vol. 9. Karger, Basel, pp. 95–109.

Saletu, B., Schjerve, M., Grunberger, J., Schanda, H. and Arnold, O. H. (1977a) Fluvoxamine – a new serotonin re-uptake inhibitor: first clinical and psychometric experiences in depressed patients. J. Neural Trans. 41, 17–36.

Saletu, B., Kriefer, P., Grunberger, J., Schanda, H. and Sletten, I. (1977b) Tandamine – a new norepinephrine reuptake inhibitor. Clinical, psychometric and quantitative EEG studies in depressed patients. Int. Pharmacopsychiatry 12, 137–152.

Sandler, M., Glover, V., Ashford, A. and Stern, G. M. (1978) Absence of 'cheese effect' during deprenyl therapy: some recent studies. J. Neural Trans. 43, 209–215.

Schachter, M. and Parkes, J. D. (1980) Fluvoxamine and clomipramine in the treatment of cataplexy. J. Neurol. Neurosurg. Psychiatry 43, 171–174.

Shader, R. I. and Greenblatt, D. J. (1981) Antidepressants: the second harvest and DSM-II. J. Clin. Psychopharmacol. 1, 51–52.

Shopsin, B. (1978) Enhancement of the antidepressant response to L-tryptophan by a liver pyrrolase inhibitor: a rational treatment approach Neuropsychobiology 4, 188–192.

Singh, A. N., Saxena, B., Gent, M. and Nelson, H. L. (1976) Maprotilin (Ludiomil, CIBA 34, 276-BA) and imipramine in depressed outpatients: a double-blind clinical study. Curr. Ther. Res. 19, 451–462.

Soroko, F. E., Mehta, N. B., Maxwell, R. A., Ferris, R. M. and Schroeder, D. H. (1977) Bupropion hydrochloride ((+1–) alpha-t-butylamino-3-chloropropiophenone HCl): a novel antidepressant agent. J. Pharm. Pharmacol. 29, 767–770.

Steinbook, R. M., Jacobson, A. F., Weiss, B. L. and Goldstein, B. J. (1979) Amoxapine, imipramine and placebo: a double-blind study with pretherapy urinary 3-methoxy-4-hydroxyphenylglycol levels. Curr. Ther. Res. 26, 490–496.

Stern, G. M., Lees, A. J. and Sandler, M. (1978) Recent observations on the clinical pharmacology of (–) deprenyl. J. Neural Trans. 43, 245–251.

Stern, W. C. and Harto-Truax, N. (1980) Two multicenter studies of the antidepressant effects of bupropion HCl versus placebo. Psychopharmacol. Bull. 16, 43–46.

Takahashi, R., Sakuma, A., Hara, T., Kazamatsuri, H., Mori, A., Saito, Y., Murasaki, M., Oguchi, T., Sakurai, Y., Yuzuriha, T., Takemura, M., Kurokawa, H. and Kurita, H. (1979) Comparison of efficacy of amoxapine and imipramine in a multi-clinic double-blind study using the WHO schedule for a standard assessment of patients with depressive disorders. J. Int. Med. Res. 7, 7–18.

Tuason, V. B., Garvey, M., Goodman, L. I. and Borgen, L. A. (1980) An initial clinical trial of zometapine, a novel antidepressant. Curr. Ther. Res. 1, 94–99.

206

Van Amerongen, P. (1979) Double-blind clinical trial of the antidepressant action of amineptine. Curr. Med. Res. Opin. 6, 93–100.

Vauterin, C. and Bazot, M. (1979) A double-blind controlled trial of amineptine versus trimipramine in depression. Curr. Med. Res. Opin 6, 101–106.

Vohra, J. K., Burrows, G. D., McIntyre, I. and Davies, B. (1978) Cardiovascular effects of nomifensine (letter). Lancet 2, 902–903.

Von Knorring, L. (1980) A double-blind trial: vivalan against placebo in depressed elderly patients. J. Int. Med. Res. 8, 18–21.

Walinder, J., Skott, A., Carlsson, A., Nagy, A. and Bjorn-Erik, R. (1976) Potentiation of the antidepressant action of clomipramine by tryptophan. Arch. Gen. Psychiatry 33, 1384–1389.

Walinder, J., Carlsson, A., Persson, R. and Wallin, L. (1980) Potentiation of the effect of antidepressant drugs by tryptophan. Acta Psychiatr. Scand. 61 (Suppl. 280), 243–249.

Wilson, W. H., Petrie, W. H. and Ban, J. A. (1980) Possible lack of anticholinergic effects with mianserin: a pilot study. J. Clin. Psychiatry 41, 63–65.

Worrall, E. P., Moody, J. P., Peet, M., Dick, P., Smith, A., Chambers, C., Adams, M. and Naylor, G. J. (1979) Controlled studies of the acute antidepressant effects of lithium. Br. J. Psychiatry 135, 255–262.

Wright, J. H. and Denber, H. C. B. (1978) Clinical trial of fluvoxamine: a new serotonergic antidepressant. Curr. Ther. Res. 23, 83–89.

Wright, J. H., McNeely, J. D., Moore, D. P. and Hurst, H. E. (1981) Early clinical trial of clovoxamine: a new antidepressant. Curr. Ther. Res. 29, 148–155.

Zis, A. P. and Goodwin, F. K. (1979) Novel antidepressants and the biogenic amine hypothesis of depression. The case for iprindole and mianserin. Arch. Gen. Psychiatry 36, 1097–1107.

Section III

MONOAMINE OXIDASE INHIBITORS

Chapter 15

Monoamine oxidase inhibitors and monoamine oxidase: Biochemical and physiological aspects relevant to human psychopharmacology

D. L. MURPHY, N.A. GARRICK

and

R. M. COHEN

Clinical Neuropharmacology Branch, National Institute of Mental Health,
Bethesda, Maryland, U.S.A.

INTRODUCTION

The metabolic inactivation of a large number of biogenic amines which serve as neuro-transmitters or modulators of neural activity is accomplished in part by monoamine oxidase (MAO). Inhibition of this enzyme leads to alterations in brain function and behaviour mediated by these amines. Blood pressure regulation, sleep, temperature and endocrine functions as well as many other body systems are affected by changes in MAO activity.

MAO inhibitors are principally used clinically as antidepressants. While mood and behavioural changes are the most prominent features of depression, this disorder is now generally considered to result from an interaction of personality, biological factors and life events, and contributions to its development have been sought in brain biogenic amine metabolic pathways. In the last decade, abnormalities in many monoamine-dependent functions including neuroendocrine responses, cardiovascular regulation, other autonomic functions, sleep, and biological rhythms have been convincingly documented in severely depressed individuals (Post and Ballenger, 1982).

It is by no means clear how MAO inhibitors exert their antidepressant effects. The elevation in brain and other tissue amine concentrations which follow acute, high dose MAO-inhibitor administration to animals constitute a common action of these drugs, but it now seems that clinical behavioural changes may depend upon a series of more subtle, adaptational synaptic events which follow low dose, longer term drug administration.

In the last few years there has been rapid development of new information about MAO and the consequences of MAO inhibition. An especially rapidly expanding area concerns the properties of the substrate-selective subtypes of MAO. Some of this material has been assembled in several symposia volumes dealing with MAO (Wolstenhome and Knight, 1976; Singer et al., 1979; Youdim and Paykel, 1981; Beckmann and Riederer, in press). This chapter will attempt to synthesize some of the recent new findings, emphasizing those in particular that bear upon the mode of action of the MAO inhibitors in man, and those which may have implications for future research on the function of this enzyme.

BIOCHEMICAL CHARACTERISTICS OF THE AMINE OXIDASES

Monoamine oxidase activity is present in most tissues of all vertebrate species and in many invertebrates and some plants as well (Blaschko, 1974). Highest enzyme activities in rodents and primates are found in the liver. Regional variations in MAO activity are found in the brain, with highest activity in the hypothalamus as compared to cortex and cerebellum (Blaschko, 1974). In brain tissue preparations, MAO activity is higher in synaptosomes than in other subcellular fractions, although it is present in glial cells as well. Its localization in presynaptic terminals has been verified by reductions in tissue enzyme activity following chemical lesions produced by 6-hydroxydopamine or 5,6-dihydroxytryptamine in brain, and following surgical sympathectomy or immunosympathectomy in the periphery (Jarrott, 1971; Squires, 1978). MAO is located predominantly in the outer mitochondrial membrane (Schnaitman and Greenawalt, 1968); some of its properties have been suggested to depend upon its topographical position in this membrane, and its interaction with membrane lipids (Houslay and Tipton, 1973; Russell et al., 1979b).

Monoamine metabolizing enzymes were first named for the substrates they attacked: a 'tyramine oxidase' was identified in 1928 by Hare, and an 'adrenaline oxidase' subsequently by Blaschko and coworkers (1937a). As more substrates were studied, general similarities in the process of oxidative deamination led to the suggestion that a single enzyme, amine oxidase, was responsible (Blaschko et al., 1937b). It was later renamed monoamine oxidase to differentiate it from another enzyme, diamine oxidase, which degraded histamine and other diamines and which was sensitive to different classes of inhibitors and utilized a different cofactor, pyridoxal (Zeller, 1938; Blaschko, 1974).

The development of several substrate-selective monoamine oxidase inhibitors in the 1960s moved the scientific pendulum back to a re-emphasis on the plurality of MAO (Johnston, 1968). The existence of an enzyme subtype, MAO-A, was suggested on the basis of the sensitivity of a portion of total MAO activity in rat brain to inhibition by low concentrations of clorgyline or Lilly 51641, and the ability of this subtype to selectively deaminate serotonin and norepinephrine (Fuller, 1968; Johnston, 1968; Goridis and Neff, 1971). The counterpart subtype, MAO-B, was sensitive to inhibition by low concentrations of deprenyl, and selectively degraded benzylamine and phenylethylamine (Knoll and Magyar, 1972; Yang and Neff, 1974). The hydrazine and cyclopropylamine MAO-inhibiting antidepressant drugs such as phenelzine, isocarboxazid and tranylcypromine, which had been developed earlier and have been studied to the greatest extent in animals, are non-selective inhibitors of both MAO-A and MAO-B. A list of selective inhibitors of the MAO subtypes and of the substrates deaminated preferentially by MAO-A and MAO-B is presented in Table 1. The structures of three extensively studied selective inhibitors are provided in Figure 1.

Only very recently has sufficient evidence been obtained to strongly suggest that the two major enzyme subtypes may be different proteins. Hints that this might be the case came from studies that extended the evidence on substrate preferences and differential inhibitor sensitivity to tissues which appeared to possess only MAO-A (human placenta, mouse neuroblastoma, and some other tissue-culture cell lines) or MAO-B (human platelet) (Donnelly et al., 1976; Donnelly and Murphy, 1977; Brown et al., 1980).

Study of the MAO subtype forms by the usual techniques for solubilization and

TABLE 1

Inhibitors and substrates for monoamine oxidase.*

Enzyme subtype	Selectively deaminated substrates	Selective inhibitors
MAO-A	Serotonin (and in rodents, norepinephrine and dopamine)	Clorgyline Lilly 51641 Harmaline Harmine PCO FLA 336 Cimoxatone R011-1163 CGP-11305
MAO-B	Phenylethylamine Phenylethanolamine tele-Methylhistamine Benzylamine o-Tyramine	Deprenyl Pargyline Lilly 54781 MD 780236
MAO-A and MAO-B (non-selective)	Tyramine Tryptamine (and others)	Phenelzine Iproniazid Isocarboxazid Tranylcypromine

* References regarding the inhibitors and the experimental basis for these conclusions can be found in several reviews and symposia volumes (Wolstenhome and Knight, 1976; Fowler et al., 1978; Singer et al., 1979; Beckmann and Riederer, in press).

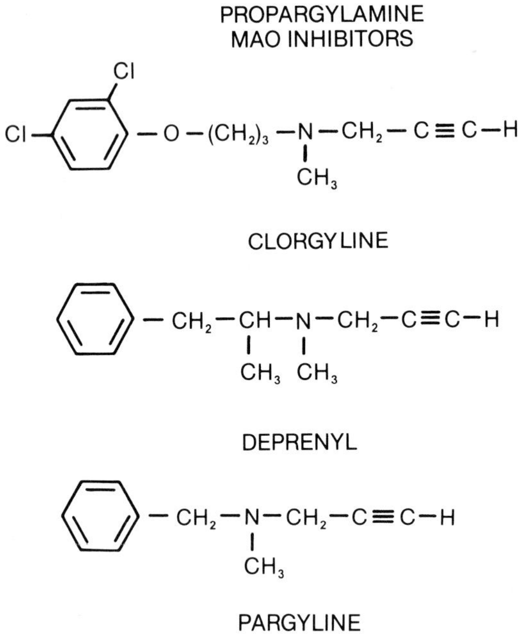

PROPARGYLAMINE
MAO INHIBITORS

Cl—C₆H₃(Cl)—O—(CH₂)₃—N(CH₃)—CH₂—C≡C—H

CLORGYLINE

C₆H₅—CH₂—CH(CH₃)—N(CH₃)—CH₂—C≡C—H

DEPRENYL

C₆H₅—CH₂—N(CH₃)—CH₂—C≡C—H

PARGYLINE

Fig. 1. Structures of three acetylenic MAO inhibitors with substrate-selective properties.

characterization using biochemical and immunological approaches has been difficult because the enzyme is tightly bound to the outer mitochondrial membrane. Solubilization has often been accomplished only by procedures which altered the kinetic characteristics of MAO activity or the qualitative properties distinguishing MAO-A and MAO-B (Houslay and Tipton, 1973; Dennick and Mayer, 1977).

Immunochemical approaches have recently yielded evidence of protein structural differences between the enzyme subtypes. McCauley and Racker (1973) first suggested the existence of two immunologically distinct enzyme forms, using antibodies prepared against bovine liver. These antibodies inhibited the portion of bovine brain MAO which deaminated phenylethylamine (MAO-B) but not that which deaminated serotonin (MAO-A). Using human tissues, Powell and Craig (1977) developed antibodies from placenta (which contains only MAO-A) that yielded a single precipitin line against the placental enzyme, but did not cross-react with the human platelet enzyme, which is solely MAO-B. Another antiserum prepared against enzyme obtained from human liver (which contains both MAO-A and MAO-B) cross-reacted with placental, platelet, liver and brain MAO (Russell et al., 1979a). Work by Cawthon and coworkers (1981) provided more definite evidence for MAO-A and MAO-B being distinct isozymes. ^{3}H-pargyline-labelled human platelet, placental and fibroblast MAO's were studied using electrophoresis and peptide mapping techniques. Different peptide fragments were found in the platelet (MAO-B) compared to placental (MAO-A) preparations. Different molecular weights for MAO-A (63,000) and MAO-B (60,000) were also found. The somewhat higher molecular weight found for MAO-A was consistent with an earlier study (Brown et al., 1980) using different preparative techniques which yielded a higher molecular weight for ^{3}H-pargyline-labelled placental enzyme (67,000) compared to platelet enzyme (63,000). In the first study using the human platelet enzyme as a source of MAO-B, Denney and coworkers (1982) produced a monoclonal antibody which cross-reacted with MAO-B from human liver and platelets but not with MAO-A from human liver or human placenta. The identity of MAO-A in human liver was verified by its preferential deamination of serotonin and its sensitivity to clorgyline. Using immunoaffinity columns to bind MAO-B and separate it from MAO-A in the liver preparation, the molecular weight of the ^{3}H-pargyline-labelled MAO-B fraction was estimated to be 59,000. This monoclonal antibody against human platelet MAO-B did not cross-react with MAO-B from mouse liver, and did not inhibit MAO-B activity in human liver or platelet preparations. While the evidence for two separate proteins is growing stronger, it should be noted that other explanations have been promulgated for the different properties of MAO-A and MAO-B, including conformational changes related to membrane lipids (Fowler et al., 1980) and suggested differences in vectorial locations within the outer mitochondrial membrane (Russell et al., 1979b).

MOLECULAR BASIS FOR INACTIVATION OF MAO BY DIFFERENT CLASSES OF MAO INHIBITORS

As noted above, MAO is an outer mitochondrial membrane protein. A number of studies examining the enzyme without regard to subtype differences have established that the active form is a dimer consisting of two subunits, each having a molecular weight of approximately 60,000. The enzyme active site contains flavin adenine dinucleotide (FAD) as a cofactor and also depends upon the availability of sulfhydryl groups and lipids for full activity (see Singer et al., 1979, for references).

Clinically used, non-selective MAO inhibitors (Table 1) all act by irreversibly inactivating the enzyme. The cyclopropylamines, such as tranylcypromine, alkylate a sulfhydryl group at the catalytic site, thereby blocking access of oxygen to the reduced flavin and preventing its reoxidation (Paech et al., 1979). The selective acetylenic inhibitors such as pargyline, clorgyline and deprenyl covalently bind the 8α-5-cysteine FAD cofactor at the active site, preventing access of substrate to the site. Hydrazines such as phenylhydrazine and phenelzine appear to form an irreversible adduct with the flavin in addition to alkylating sulfhydryl groups (Maycock et al., 1976; Kenney et al., 1979). It is of interest that all of these 'suicide' inhibitors are actually substrates for the enzyme, and initially react competitively before forming the irreversible, covalent linkage.

New experimental work on MAO inhibitors has been in three areas: a) several compounds which are potent reversible inhibitors of the enzyme, including cimoxatone FLA336 and RO11—1163 (Table 1) are being evaluated in animals and man in the anticipation that dose-by-dose control of their effects, and also their toxicities, including tyramine potentiation, may yield a safer drug; b) other reversible MAO inhibitors (e.g. CGP-11305) with amine uptake-inhibiting properties, which may result in a wider spectrum of action among depressed patient subgroups and fewer side effects, are also being investigated; the ability of these drugs to block the uptake of tyramine into noradrenergic nerve endings, thereby preventing the release of accumulated norepinephrine stores, should reduce the risk of hypertensive crises; and c) the largest body of recent experimental work has been directed towards the explication of the properties of substrate-selective, irreversible MAO-inhibiting drugs, clorgyline, pargyline and deprenyl (Table 1) (Singer et al., 1979; Kan and Strolin Benedetti, 1980; Fowler and Oreland, 1981; Youndim and Paykel, 1981; Beckmann and Riederer, in press).

BIOCHEMICAL AND PHYSIOLOGICAL CONSEQUENCES OF MAO INHIBITION IN ANIMALS AND MAN

Several issues are pertinent to a consideration of the principal effect of MAO inhibitors in animals and man. As noted above, much of the literature has resulted from studies examining the immediate consequences of high doses of these drugs in animals. Because low doses given over periods of weeks and months are the conditions under which the therapeutic actions of the MAO inhibitors are obtained in man, special consideration needs to be given to information from chronic studies. There are still only a handful of such studies, especially ones using substrate-selective drugs, and so some of the general conclusions necessarily derived from acute studies summarized below may require re-evaluation when more information is available from chronic studies more closely approximating clinical use of these drugs. Furthermore, while many of the qualitative characteristics and consequences of MAO inhibition seem quite similar between animals and man, extrapolation requires caution because important quantitative differences have been described between the relative proportions of MAO-A and MAO-B in humans, non-human primate and rodent brain (Garrick and Murphy, 1981). Primates, including man, have a higher proportion of MAO-B activity (approximately 70% of the total MAO activity) in brain, whereas the widely studied laboratory rat, as well as other rodents such as the hamster, possess more MAO-A than MAO-B activity. A consequence of this is that certain substrates including dopamine and norepinephrine, which are almost exclusively de-aminated by MAO-A in the rat, are deaminated to a substantial extent by MAO-B in human and monkey brain *in vitro* (Glover et al., 1977; Demarest and Azzaro, 1979; Garrick and Murphy, 1980, 1982).

Neuronal and extraneuronal functions of MAO

There is good evidence that MAO functions in a generally similar fashion within norepinephrine, dopamine and serotonin neurons and possibly other neurotransmitter systems (Wolstenholme and Knight, 1976; Squires, 1978). It deaminates these major monoamines in presynaptic terminals as well as in cell bodies, thereby regulating their free cytoplasmic concentrations within the neuron. In addition, MAO deaminates trace amines not synthesized within the same neuron, which otherwise may have several consequences: these trace amines may be accumulated and stored in vesicles and then released as cotransmitters or false transmitters (e.g. octopamine as a false transmitter); they may induce the release of major monoamines (e.g. tyramine as a releaser of norepinephrine); and they may exert feedback effects on the synthetic enzymes of the major monoamines. Furthermore, MAO, via its effects on intracellular deamination, secondarily regulates the new synthesis of monoamines via a feedback control mechanism dependent on cytoplasmic amine concentration changes; this has been demonstrated for tyrosine hydroxylase in catecholamine neurons, and suggested for tryptophan hydroxylase in serotonergic neurons. MAO also affects the relative production of methylated versus deaminated metabolites, which may be of particular significance for those methylated compounds which have biological activity and, additionally, determines the production of its aldehyde products, some of which have physiological effects. MAO also degrades released monoamine neurotransmitters in the postsynaptic neuron and perineuronal tissue. In addition to these intraneuronal functions, MAO degrades and detoxifies circulating monoamines in liver, lung, kidney, and other vascular beds, and is a component of the blood-brain, gut-blood and other blood-tissue barriers for monoamines (Blaschko, 1974; Squires, 1978).

It should be noted that many MAO-inhibiting drugs have other metabolic effects besides their principal effect on MAO, such as the direct amphetamine-like sympathetic stimulation produced by tranylcypromine and phenelzine. Additional properties of some of these drugs include amine-uptake inhibiting effects, effects on the transport of amines and related substances across various membranes as well as some effects not primarily related to metabolism, including effects on the metabolism of other drugs. Continued caution is therefore necessary in attributing all consequences of the administration of different doses of MAO inhibitors to direct reductions in MAO activity alone.

Neuronal changes resulting from MAO inhibition

Depending on the dose and duration of treatment with an inhibitor, a number of different neuronal effects of MAO inhibition have been described, as outlined in Table 2. The most prominent consequence of MAO inhibition is a rapid increase in the intracellular concentrations of monoamines. Not only are neuron-specific amines increased (e.g. norepinephrine levels in noradrenergic cell bodies and presynaptic processes), but other amines whose concentrations are normally very low in brain (e.g. tryptamine, phenylethylamine) are even more markedly elevated. Brain serotonin concentrations are raised to a greater extent than are those of the catecholamines, norepinephrine and dopamine, following acute, high dose MAO-inhibitor administration. Vesicular concentrations of amines are increased, as are cytoplasmic concentrations which normally are very low.

After amine concentrations have increased, secondary adaptive consequences of MAO inhibition begin to occur. These include a reduction in amine synthesis via an apparent feedback mechanism which has been best demonstrated within the noradrenergic system (Neff and Costa, 1966; Lin et al., 1969). Increased concentrations of norepinephrine, dopamine, and possibly other amines (e.g. octopamine) can block the initial step in the formation of norepinephrine by direct inhibition of tyrosine hydroxylase.

Shortly after the neuron-specific amine concentrations have increased, other amines accumulating in the cytoplasm begin to enter amine storage vesicles from which they may displace the endogenous amines or where they may be released as cotransmitters or partial false transmitters. These changes in vesicular amines available for release are incompletely understood, but depending upon the proportions of the different amines collected in vesicles (e.g. whether phenylethylamine or octopamine are accumulated in noradrenergic neurons, or dopamine or dimethyltryptamine in serotonergic neurons), various tertiary responses may occur.

The specific effects of MAO inhibition outlined above have been studied, for the most

TABLE 2

Changes in monoamine neurons in response to the inhibition of MAO

	Presynaptic neuronal cellular functions				Postsynaptic neuronal cellular functions
	Vesicle amine content	Cytoplasmic amine content	Amine synthesis	Neuronal firing rate	
1) Acute response to treatment with an MAO inhibitor	Increased, with beginning changes in proportions of various amines	Increased	–	–	–
2) Short-term adaptation to acute treatment	Increased, usually with definite changes in amine balances	Increased	Decreased	Decreased	–
3) Longer term adaptation to chronic treatment	Possibly less increased, with changes in amine balances	Possibly less increased	Probably decreased	Decreased	Decreased receptor numbers and decrease in adenyl cyclase response

part, in one or another isolated experimental system, and whether these changes can be extrapolated to all monoamine-related neurons is not clear. The alterations in the functional state of a particular neurotransmitter system vary with duration of treatment and with dosage. For example, with low drug dosages given over a 3-week period to rats approximating the clinical use of these drugs, maximum elevations in brain norepinephrine and serotonin concentrations require approximately one week of treatment instead of the few hours required after single, high-dose drug administration (Campbell et al., 1979b; Waldmeier et al. 1981). With continued treatment, brain serotonin concentrations return towards pretreatment levels by the third week of drug administration; brain norepinephrine levels remain elevated for 3 weeks (Campbell et al., 1979b). Similarly, phenelzine and tranylcypromine given for 6 weeks result in a peak in rat brain norepinephrine, dopamine and serotonin concentrations during the first week of treatment, followed by a gradual decline to control levels. These decrements in brain amine concentrations are not explained by reductions in brain tryptophan hydroxylase or tyrosine hydroxylase activities (Campbell et al., 1979b).

Neuronal receptor changes following MAO inhibition

In addition to these changes in the distribution and balance of amines within neurons, other delayed responses to amine accumulation begin to occur within a period of hours. A slowing of neuronal firing rates has been demonstrated in both serotonin-containing neurons in the median raphe and in norepinephrine-containing neurons in the locus ceruleus (Aghajanian et al. 1972; Campbell et al. 1979a). Both effects are thought to represent a direct consequence of the increased amines available to presynaptic feedback autoreceptors.

After several weeks treatment with MAO inhibitors, a reduction in α_2- and β-adrenoreceptor numbers and in β-receptor functional activity — as measured by norepinephrine stimulated cyclic-AMP formation — as well as in serotonin receptor numbers has been observed in a number of studies (Sulser et al., 1978; Peroutka and Snyder, 1980; Savage et al., 1980; Kellar et al., 1981; Cohen et al., 1982). These changes follow treatment with both nonselective MAO inhibitors (nialamide and phenelzine) and the selective MAO-A inhibitor clorgyline at low doses, but occur only at high, probably nonselective doses of the partially selective MAO-B inhibitor, pargyline. These neurochemical alterations induced by MAO-A inhibition are accompanied by a decrease in the firing rate of noradrenergic neurons in the locus ceruleus and a reduction in the sensitivity of cortical neurons to iontophoretically applied norepinephrine and serotonin, presumably reflecting the changes in amine receptor numbers and function reviewed above (Campbell et al., 1979b; Olpe et al., 1980, 1981). These adaptive neurochemical changes also appear to be reflected in behavioural changes in animals, as chronic, but not acute clorgyline treatment leads to an attenuation of the changes in locomotor activity produced by the α_2-adrenergic agonist clonidine (Cohen et al., in press). Clonidine's effects under these circumstances are believed to be mediated through an α_2-adrenoreceptor presynaptic inhibitor system. These latter results in rodents are in agreement with findings from a recent clinical study indicating that clonidine's hypotensive responses, which are also believed to involve α_2-adrenoreceptors, are significantly reduced after treatment of psychiatric patients with clorgyline for 21 days (Siever et al., 1981).

It is extremely difficult to attribute biological or behavioural changes during MAO inhibition to a particular change in a specific monoamine neurotransmitter system without very extensive studies of the series of changes outlined in Table 2 in several monoamine systems. In addition, treatment with MAO inhibitors in combination with selective antagonists for each neurotransmitter system is usually necessary to examine whether blockade of a specific metabolic change also antagonizes the physiological or behavioural change under investigation. Because of the complex studies required, it is not yet clear how the fairly well-defined neuronal events which follow MAO inhibition can be related to the integrated physiological and behavioural responses of the whole organism to MAO inhibition.

BEHAVIOURAL CHANGES PRODUCED BY MAO INHIBITORS IN ANIMALS

The animal pharmacology of MAO inhibitors has been extensively reviewed by Pletscher, et al. (1966) and more recently by Squires (1978). The most frequently studied behavioural change produced by MAO inhibitors is an increase in locomotor activity, often associated with other signs of behavioural excitation. Studies using large doses of nialamide, iproniazid, tranylcypromine, and other nonselective MAO inhibitors report an increase in locomotion, twitching, stereotypy, and rectal temperature in rodents (Carlsson and Corrodi 1964; Braestrup et al., 1975). Hyperactivity has not been reported in all studies, however, and under some circumstances reduced motor activity and sedation have been observed. Differences between drugs, drug dosage, duration of treatment, species or strain differences, and experimental condition differences contribute to these varying results.

In one animal study, single low doses of clorgyline (0.5–1.0 mg/kg) and deprenyl (0.5–10.0 mg/kg) failed to affect locomotor activity of rats in an open-field test (Smith, 1976). In a second study, the chronic administration of pargyline, isocarboxazid, tranylcypromine, or other MAO inhibitors for 20 days in low, nontoxic doses led to generally increased open-field activity in rats, although different time patterns of response occurred with the different drugs, and longer term treatment with one drug, tranylcypromine, was associated with reduced motor activity (Maickel et al., 1974). Changes in brain amines in this study did not uniformly correspond to the behavioural changes observed with the different drugs, suggesting that intraneuronal adaptive response differences might be involved.

More profound activating effects of MAO inhibitors are seen when animals are pretreated with amine-depleting drugs, especially reserpine and tetrabenazine. MAO inhibitors produce a dramatic reversal of the profound sedation, hypotension, hypothermia, and miosis which follow reserpine administration. Increased spontaneous motor activity, and enhanced irritability and aggressivity are the most frequently reported changes. Other more discrete behavioural alterations have also been noted, including alterations in conditioned avoidance responding, eating, sexual activity, body temperature, stress-related defecation, and brain self-stimulation (Pletscher et al., 1966; Squires, 1978).

Two investigations have indicated that reversal of reserpine sedation, which has been a frequently used animal biochemical model for depression and a useful predictor of drug efficacy in clinical depression, is primarily a consequence of MAO-A inhibition rather than MAO-B inhibition, since doses of clorgyline (1.0 mg/kg) which maintained a selective inhibition of MAO-A *in vivo* restored reserpine-reduced motor activity to control levels, whereas low, selective doses of deprenyl or pargyline (0.5–1.0 mg/kg for both MAO-B inhibitors) did not (Christmas et al., 1972; Fuentes and Neff 1975). In studies of selective and nonselective MAO inhibitors, it was of interest that partial inhibition of enzyme activity (35–75% reduction in serotonin and tyramine deamination, together with a 0–90% reduction in benzylamine deamination) led to a significant antagonism of the tetrabenazine-induced sedation in rodents (Christmas et al., 1972). Studies of this type in other species may be of importance, since, as noted above, there is a considerable difference in the proportion of brain MAO-A to MAO-B in rodents as compared to nonhuman primates and humans (Garrick et al., 1979).

In a group of studies which have attempted to either intensify or ameliorate behavioural responses to MAO inhibitors by altering the serotonergic system, MAO inhibitors have been given together with serotonin precursors, tryptophan hydroxylase inhibitors, or other drugs such as lithium that are known to affect brain serotonin concentrations. Hess and Doepfner (1961) were the first to describe a serotonin-related hyperactivity syndrome with relatively large doses of nialamide or iproniazid together with tryptophan, 200 mg/kg. Similar hyperactivity was also observed following 5-hydroxytryptophan, 160–320 mg/kg, with MAO inhibitor pretreatment. Numerous investigations have followed this paradigm and have obtained similar results in rats as well as mice, guinea pigs, rabbits, and dogs (Corrodi, 1966; Carlsson and Lindqvist, 1969; Himwich et al., 1972; Modigh and Svensson, 1972).

Grahame-Smith (1971) demonstrated that the hyperactivity in rats pretreated with an MAO inhibitor and loaded with L-tryptophan was not correlated with the overall concentration of brain serotonin. However, pretreatment with the decarboxylase inhibitor RO4-4602 was shown to prevent the MAO-inhibitor interaction with tryptophan (Hodge et al., 1964). Others have blocked the syndrome with the serotonin synthesis inhibitor, parachlorophenylalanine. Squires and Buus Lassen (1975) demonstrated that low doses of clorgyline (1.0 mg/kg) along with deprenyl (1.0 mg/kg) followed by L-tryptophan were necessary to produce the syndrome, whereas inhibition of the A or B form of the enzyme by clorgyline or deprenyl alone did not. The necessity for the simultaneous inhibition of MAO-A and MAO-B suggested that the excitation syndrome is not entirely produced by increased serotonin concentration. The direct serotonin receptor agonist, 5-methoxy-N,N-dimethyl-tryptamine leads to a syndrome very similar to that produced by MAO inhibitors plus tryptophan, as do drugs that block serotonin reuptake such as clomipramine combined with an MAO inhibitor (Carlsson and Lindqvist, 1969).

Although unusual, some symptoms which may represent phenomena similar to the serotonin syndrome in animals occurred in two patients who received clorgyline and several weeks later were given single 100 mg doses of the tricyclic antidepressant, clomipramine. Both patients developed brief, acute episodes characterized by tremor, lower extremity myoclonic contractions, hyper-reflexia and signs of autonomic activation. Increased blood pressure and temperature as well as clonus were also observed in the one patient where these features were assessable (Insel et al., in press).

Many other agents interact with MAO inhibitors, some of which are naturally occurring substances. The list includes lithium, rubidium, tricyclic antidepressants, antihistamines, narcotics, hallucinogens (such as tryptamine, bufotenin, dimethyltryptamine, and phenylethylamine), caffeine, theophylline, 6-hydroxydopamine, 5-6-dihydroxytryptamine, and amphetamines and other sympathomimetic drugs.

PHYSIOLOGICAL CHANGES PRODUCED BY MAO INHIBITORS IN ANIMALS AND MAN

The principal effects of MAO inhibition include not only the directly reduced availability of oxidative deamination as a metabolic pathway but, more importantly, impairment of the cellular regulatory functions normally subserved by MAO, with consequent alterations in the synthesis, accumulation, and storage of monoamines, especially in response to metabolic load stresses. Reduced oxidative deamination leads directly to the accumulation of amines in cells, and to the shifts in monoamine metabolism which have been well-documented in studies of amine metabolism in brain, cerebrospinal fluid, and urine of animals and man (Pletscher et al., 1966; Murphy, 1977; Squires, 1978; Major et al., 1979). As noted above, one of the most impressive changes is the disproportionate elevation in trace amine concentrations (including tryptamine, phenylethylamine, phenylethanolamine, tyramine, octopamine, and tele-methylhistamine) which occur during MAO-inhibitor administration. Changes in the catecholamines and even serotonin are relatively small in comparison.

Among the most prominent of the physiologic consequences of MAO inhibition is the essentially total suppression of rapid eye movement (REM) sleep in animals and man. No other class of drugs has an equally profound effect on this phenomenon, although its mechanism remains incompletely understood.

A reduction in blood pressure, especially decreased systolic blood pressure upon standing which is clinically evident as orthostatic hypotension, is another prominent change during MAO-inhibitor administration. Relatively greater reductions in systolic and diastolic blood pressure occur in hypertensive animals and man. A central mechanism of action has been implicated as the basis for the blood pressure reductions.

A summary of some of the major physiological consequences which can occur when certain dietary substances or drugs are ingested during MAO-inhibitor administration is presented in Table 3. Altered pressor responses have been reported within hours of the administration of the first dose of the MAO inhibitor, and this enhanced pressor sensitivity to tyramine and to sympathomimetic drugs has been reported to persist for as long as 2—3 weeks after drug treatment was stopped. This delayed reaction results from the fact that most MAO inhibitors are irreversible inhibitors of the enzyme; their effects persist until new enzyme is synthesized. The other changes listed in Table 3 indicate the wide range of substances whose effects are potentiated by MAO inhibitors, or whose effects may be qualitatively as well as quantitatively altered.

CLINICAL PHARMACOLOGY OF THE SELECTIVE MAO INHIBITORS

MAO inhibitor plasma levels and platelet MAO inhibition

Possible associations in man between the biological consequences of MAO-inhibitor ad-

TABLE 3

Physiological consequences of interactions between MAO inhibitors and dietary constituents or drugs in animals and man.

Substance	Effect of MAO inhibition
1) Many amines and amine precursors (e.g. tyramine, tryptamine, dopamine, L-dopa)	Potentiation of pressor effects
2) Sympathomimetic drugs (e.g. amphetamine, ephedrine, phenylephrine, metaraminol, phenylpropanolamine, and tricyclic antidepressants)	Potentiation of pressor and hyperpyrexic effects
3) Reserpine, methyldopa	Conversion of hypotensive response to hypertensive response
4) Caffeine, theophylline	Conversion of hypokinesia, hypothermic response to hyperkinesia, agitation, and hyperthermic response
5) Insulin, chlorpropamide, tolbutamide	Potentiation of hypoglycaemic response
6) Narcotic analgesics	Toxic interaction with agitation, tremor, twitching, hyperreflexia, hyperpyrexia, and, rarely, coma and death

ministration and the behavioural responses to these drugs have been explored in a number of ways. Unlike the situation for many drugs, including the tricyclic antidepressants, little useful information has been accrued from measurement of the plasma concentrations of these drugs. As noted above, the currently used MAO inhibitors are irreversible inhibitors of this enzyme which, in brain, has a half-life of approximately 12 days (Nelson et al., 1979), while the drugs themselves are quite rapidly cleared from plasma, with estimated half-lives for clorgyline and other drugs measured in hours (Campbell et al., 1979; Robinson et al., 1980). Thus, there is no necessary association between the amount of MAO inhibition present in cellular mitochondria and concentrations of the MAO inhibitor in plasma.

Measurement of platelet MAO inhibition, in contrast, has provided evidence that higher phenelzine doses, on the order of 60–75 mg/day (or 1 mg/kg), yield greater than 80–85% enzyme inhibition (Robinson et al., 1978). This level of inhibition is associated with significantly greater antidepressant and anti-anxiety efficacy than lesser amounts of platelet MAO inhibition (Davidson et al., 1978; Ravaris et al., 1980). No general association between pretreatment platelet MAO activity and response to phenelzine has been observed. It should be noted that the association between reductions in platelet MAO activity and clinical response has only been studied for phenelzine, and does not hold for a selective MAO-A inhibitor with antidepressant properties like clorgyline, as the platelet contains only MAO-B, and it is possible to achieve greater than 85% inhibition of MAO-A (as reflected in changes in urinary amine metabolites) with negligible reductions in platelet MAO-B in clorgyline-responsive depressed patients (Lipper et al., 1979; Murphy et al., 1979). On the other hand, very low doses of pargyline and deprenyl, which have not been demonstrated to consistently lead to antidepressant effects, produce over 95% inhibition of platelet MAO activity in a matter of a few hours (Murphy et al., 1979; Eisler et al., 1981). Similarly tranylcypromine, and to a lesser extent isocarboxazid, yield marked platelet MAO inhibition at clinically subtherapeutic doses (Giller and Loeb, 1980; Giller et al., 1982).

Clinical pharmacologic evidence regarding the mode of antidepressant action of MAO inhibitors

The question of which of the amines affected by MAO inhibition is most likely to be involved in therapeutic responses to these agents has recently been approached in comparative studies using clorgyline, pargyline and deprenyl for their substrate-selective actions. The largest aggregation of evidence from these studies suggests that reductions in depressive symptoms during treatment with MAO inhibitors are most closely correlated with norepinephrine neurotransmitter systems changes, as based on direct measurements of the plasma and cerebrospinal fluid concentrations of norepinephrine and its metabolites and on a series of indirect measures of changes in noradrenergic function, such as blood pressure alterations, during MAO-inhibitor treatment (Murphy et al., 1981; Murphy et al., in press, a). The data suggest that a reduction in a central noradrenergic output, dependent upon longer term drug administration (rather than an acutely produced norepinephrine increase), is most closely associated with clinical improvement (Murphy et al., in press, b). The data from these studies with selective MAO inhibitors argue against the existence of a disorder in phenylethylamine metabolism as an important component of depression, as depressed patients have no evident abnormality in phenylethylamine production (Murphy et al., in press, c).

Furthermore, the 50-fold elevations in phenylethylamine observed in patients treated with pargyline were not associated with clinical improvement, while clorgyline treatment, which did not elevate phenylethylamine, was clinically effective. Dopamine and histamine changes seem unlikely to have a primary role in the antidepressant effects of MAO inhibitors, as their metabolism is also more affected by pargyline than by clorgyline (Hough and Domino, 1979; Major et al., 1979). A role for serotonin has not been clarified (Murphy et al., in press, b). Changes in tyramine sensitivity which are associated with clinical effectiveness seem not to be directly related to clinical change via any selective alteration in tyramine metabolism. Rather, the enhanced sensitivity to tyramine found with MAO inhibition seems to depend upon changes in tyramine-releasable norepinephrine stores in neurons (Pickar et al., 1981). The positive association between clinical antidepressant responses and changes in tyramine sensitivity thus serve to reinforce the conclusion that norepinephrine changes are most likely connected with clinical response.

REFERENCES

Aghajanian, G. K. (1972) Influence of drugs on the firing of serotonin-containing neurons in brain. Fed. Proc. Am. Soc. Exp. Biol. 31, 91–96.

Beckmann, H. and Riederer, P. Monoamine Oxidase and Its Selective Inhibitors: New Concepts in Therapy and Research. Karger, Basel (in press).

Blaschko, H. (1974) The natural history of amine oxidases. Physiol. Biochem. Pharmacol. 70, 83–148.

Blaschko, H., Richter, D. and Schlossmann, H. (1937a) The inactivation of adrenaline. J. Physiol. 90, 1–19.

Blaschko, H., Richter, D. and Schlossmann, H. (1937b) The oxidation of adrenaline and other amines. Biochem. J. 31, 2187–2196.

Braestrup, C., Andersen, H. and Randrup, A. (1975) The monoamine oxidase β-inhibitor deprenyl potentiates phenylethylamine behaviour in rat without inhibition of catecholamine metabolite formation. Eur. J. Pharmacol. 34, 181–187.

Brown, G. K., Powell, J. F. and Craig, I. W. (1980) Molecular weight differences between human platelet and placental monoamine oxidase. Biochem. Pharmacol. 29, 2595–2603.

Campbell, I. C., Murphy, D. L., Gallager, D. W., Tallman, J. F. and Marshall, E. F. (1979a) Neurotransmitter-related adaptation in the central nervous system following chronic monoamine oxidase inhibition. In: T. P. Singer, R. W. Von Korff and D. L. Murphy (Eds), Monoamine Oxidase: Structure, Function, and Altered Functions. Academic Press, New York, pp. 517–530.

Campbell, I. C., Robinson, D. S., Lovenberg, W. and Murphy, D. L. (1979b) The effects of chronic regimens of clorgyline and pargyline on monoamine metabolism in the rat brain. J. Neurochem. 32, 49–55.

Campbell, I. C., Shiling, D. J., Lipper, S., Slater, S. and Murphy, D. L. (1979c) A biochemical measure of monoamine oxidase type A and type B inhibitor effects in man. J. Psychiatr. Res. 15, 77–84.

Carlsson, A. and Corrodi, H. (1964). In dem Catecholamin-metabolismus eingreifende Substanzen. 2,3-Dihydroxyphenylacetamide und Verwandte. Helv. Chim. Acta 47, 1340–1349.

Carlsson, A. and Lindqvist, M. (1969) Central and peripheral monoaminergic membrane-pump blockade by some addictive analgesics and antihistamines. J. Pharm. Pharmacol. 21, 460–464.

Cawthon, R. M., Pintar, J. E., Haseltine, F. P. and Breakefield, X. O. (1981) Differences in the structure of A and B forms of human monoamine oxidase. J. Neurochem. 37, 363–372.

Christmas, A. J., Coulson, C. J., Maxwell, D. R. and Ridel, D. A. (1972) A comparison of the pharmacological and biochemical properties of substrate-selective monoamine oxidase inhibitors. Br. J. Pharmacol. 45, 490–503.

Cohen, R. M., Campbell, I. C., Dauphin, M., Tallman, J. F. and Murphy, D. L. (1982) Changes in α- and β-receptor densities in rat brain as a result of treatment with monoamine oxidase inhibiting antidepressants. Neuropharmacology 21, 293–298.

Cohen, R. M., Aulakh, C. S., Campbell, I. C. and Murphy, D. L. (1982) Functional subsensitivity of alpha 2 adrenoreceptors accompanying reduction in yohimbine binding after clorgyline treatment. Eur. J. Pharmacol. 81, 145–148.

Corridi, H. (1966) Blockade of the psychotic syndrome caused by nialamide in mice. J. Pharm. Pharmacol. 18, 197–199.

Davidson, J., McLeod, M. N. and White, H. L. (1978) Inhibition of platelet monoamine oxidase in depressed subjects treated with phenelzine. Am. J. Psychiatry 135, 470–472.

Demarest, K. T. and Azzaro, A. J. (1979) The association of type A monoamine oxidase with the nigrostriatal dopamine neuron. In: T. P. Singer, R. W. Von Korff and D. L. Murphy (Eds), Monoamine Oxidase: Structure, Function and Altered Functions. Academic Press, New York, pp. 423–430.

Denney, R. M., Fritz, R. M., Patel, N. T. and Abell, C. W. (1982) Human liver MAO-A and MAO-B separated by immunoaffinity chromatography with MAO-B-specific monoclonal antibody. Science 215, 1400–1403.

Dennick, R. G. and Mayer, R. J. (1977) Purification and immunochemical characterization of monoamine oxidase from rat and human liver. Biochem. J. 161, 167–174.

Donnelly, C. H. and Murphy, D. L. (1977) Substrate and inhibitor-related characteristics of human platelet monoamine oxidase. Biochem. Pharmacol. 26, 853–858.

Donnelly, C. H., Richelson, E. and Murphy, D. L. (1976) Properties of monoamine oxidase in mouse neuroblastoma NIE-115 cells. Biochem. Pharmacol. 27, 959–963.

Eisler, T., Teravainen, H., Nelson, R., Knebs, H., Weise, V., Lake, C. R., Ebert, M. H., Whetzel, N., Murphy, D. L., Kopin, I. J. and Calne, D. B. (1981) Deprenyl in Parkinson disease. Neurology 31, 19–23.

Fowler, C. J. and Oreland, L. (1981) Substrate- and stereoselective inhibition of human brain monoamine oxidase by 4-dimethylmino-α-2-dimethylphenethylamine (FLA 336). J. Pharm. Pharmacol. 33, 403–406.

Fowler, C. J., Callingham, B. A., Mantle, T. J. and Tipton, K. F. (1978) Monoamine oxidase A and B: a useful concept? Biochem. Pharmacol. 27, 97–101.

Fowler, C. J., Callingham, B. A., Mantle, T. J. and Tipton, K. F. (1980) The effect of lipophilic compounds upon the activity of rat liver mitochondrial monoamine oxidase-A and -B. Biochem. Pharmacol. 29, 1177–1183.

Fuentes, J. A. and Neff, N. H. (1975) Selective monoamine oxidase inhibitor drugs as aids in evaluating the role of type A and B enzymes. Neuropharmacology 14, 819–825.

Fuller, R. W. (1968) Influence of substrate in the inhibition of rat liver and brain monoamine oxidase. Arch. Intern. Pharmacodyn. Ther. 174, 32–37.

Garrick, N. A. and Murphy, D. L. (1980) Species differences in the deamination of dopamine and other substrates for monoamine oxidase in brain. Psychopharmacology 72, 27–33.

Garrick, N. A. and Murphy, D. L. Monoamine oxidase type A: Differences in selectivity towards L-norepinephrine compared to serotonin. Biochem. Pharmacol. (in press).

Garrick, N. A., Redmond, D. E., Jr. and Murphy, D. L. (1979) Primate-rodent monoamine oxidase differences. In: T. P. Singer, R. W. Von Korff and D. L. Murphy (Eds), Monoamine Oxidase: Structure, Function, and Altered Functions. Academic Press, New York, pp. 351–359.

Giller, E. and Loeb, J. (1980) MAO inhibitors and platelet MAO inhibition. Commun. Psychopharmacol. 4, 79–82.

Giller, E., Bialos, D., Riddle, M., Sholomskas, A. and Harkness, L. (1982) Monoamine oxidase inhibitor-responsive depression. Psychiatry Res. 6, 41–48.

Glover, V., Sandler, M., Owen, F. and Riley, G. J. (1977) Dopamine is a monoamine oxidase B substrate in man. Nature 265, 80–81.

Goridis, C. and Neff, N. H. (1971) Evidence for a specific monoamine oxidase associated with sympathetic nerves. Neuropharmacology 10, 557–564.

Grahame-Smith, D. G. (1971) Studies in vivo on the relationship between brain tryptophan, brain 5-HT synthesis and hyperactivity in rats treated with a monoamine oxidase inhibitor and L-tryptophan. J. Neurochem. 18, 1053–1066.

Hare, M. L. C. (1928) Tyramine oxidase. I. A new enzyme system in liver. Biochem. J. 22, 968–979.

Hess, S. M. and Doepfner, W. (1961) Behavioral effects and brain amine content in rats. Arch. Int. Pharmacodyn. Ther. 134, 89–99.

Himwich, W. A., Davis, J. M., Forbes, D. J., Glisson, S. N., Magnusson, T., Stout, M. A. and Trusty, D. W. (1972) Indole metabolism and behavior in dog. Biol. Psychiatry 4, 51–63.

Hodge, J. V., Oates, J. A. and Sjoerdsma, A. (1964) Reduction of the central effects of tryptophan by a decarboxylase inhibitor. Clin. Pharmacol. Ther. 5, 149–155.

Hough, L. B. and Domino, E. F. (1979) Tele-methylhistamine oxidation by type B monoamine oxidase. J. Pharmacol. Exp. Ther. 208, 433–438.

Houslay, M. D. and Tipton, K. F. (1973) The nature of the electrophoretically separable multiple forms of rat liver monoamine oxidase. Biochem. J. 135, 173–186.

Insel, T. R., Roy, B. F., Cohen, R. M. and Murphy, D. L. An unusual drug interaction: possible development of the 'serotonin syndrome' in man. Am. J. Psychiatry (in press).

Jarrott, B. (1971) Occurrence and properties of monoamine oxidase in adrenergic neurons. J. Neurochem. 18, 7–16.

225

Johnston, J. P. (1968) Some observations upon a new inhibitor of monoamine oxidase in brain tissue. Biochem. Pharmacol. 17, 1285–1297.

Kan, J. P. and Benedetti, M. S. (1980) Antagonism between long acting monoamine oxidase inhibitors (MAOI) and MD780515, a new specific and reversible MAOI. Life Sci. 26, 2165–2171.

Kellar, K. T., Cascio, C. S. and Butler, T. A. (1981) Differential effects of electroconvulsive shock and antidepressant drugs on serotonin-2-receptors in rat brain. Eur. J. Pharmacol. 69, 515–518.

Kenney, W. C., Nagy, J., Salach, J. I. and Singer, T. P. (1979) Structure of the covalent phenylhydrazine adduct of monoamine oxidase. In: T. P. Singer, R. W. Von Korff and D. L. Murphy (Eds), Monoamine Oxidase: Structure, Functions, and Altered Functions. Academic Press, New York, pp. 25–38.

Knoll, J. and Magyar, K. (1972) Some puzzling pharmacological effects of monoamine oxidase inhibitors, Vol. 5. In: E. Costa and M. Sandler (Eds), Advances in Biochemical Psychopharmacology. Raven Press, New York, pp. 393–408.

Lin, R. C., Neff, N. H., Ngai, S. H. and Costa, E. (1969) Turnover rates of serotonin and norepinephrine in brain of normal and pargyline-treated rats. Life Sci. 8, 1077–1084.

Lipper, S., Murphy, D. L., Slater, S. and Buchsbaum, M. S. (1979) Comparative behavioral effects of clorgyline and pargyline in man: a preliminary evaluation. Psychopharmacology 62(2), 123–128.

Maickel, R. P., Rompalo, A. M. and Cox, R. H., Jr. (1974) Differential effects of monoamine inhibitors. Res. Comm. Chem. Pathol. Pharmacol. 8, 727–730.

Major, L. F., Murphy, D. L., Lipper, S. and Gordon, E. (1979) Effects of cloryline and pargyline on deaminated metabolites of norepinephrine, dopamine and serotonin in human cerebrospinal fluid. J. Neurochem. 32, 229–231.

Maycock, A. L., Abeles, R. H., Salach, J. I. and Singer, T. P. (1976) The structure of the covalent adduct formed by the interaction of 3-dimethyamino-1-propyne and the flavine of mitochondrial amine oxidase. Biochemistry 15, 114–125.

McCauley, R. and Racker, E. (1973) Separation of two monoamine oxidases from bovine brain. Mol. Cell. Biochem. 1, 73–81.

Modigh, K. and Svensson, T. H. (1972) On the role of central nervous system catecholamines and 5-hydroxytryptamine in the nialamide-induced behavioural syndrome. Br. J. Pharmacol. 46, 32–45.

Murphy, D. L. (1977) The behavioral toxicity of monoamine oxidase inhibiting antidepressants. Adv. Pharmacol. Chemother. 81, 178–202.

Murphy, D. L., Lipper, S. Slater, S. and Shiling, D. (1979) Selectivity of clorgyline and pargyline as inhibitors of monoamine oxidases A and B in vivo in man. Psychopharmacology 62(2), 129–132.

Murphy, D. L., Pickar, D., Jimerson, D., Cohen, R. M., Garrick, N. A., Karoum, F. and Wyatt, R. J. (1981) Biochemical indices of the effects of selective MAO inhibitors (clorgyline, pargyline and deprenyl) in man. In: E. Usdin, S. Dahl, L. F. Gram and O. Lingjaerde (Eds), Clinical Pharmacology in Psychiatry. Macmillan Press, London, pp. 307–316.

Murphy, D. L., Roy, B., Pickar, D., Lipper, S., Cohen, R. M., Jimerson, D., Lake, C. R., Muscettola, G., Saavedra, J. and Kopin, I. J. Cardiovascular changes accompanying monoamine oxidase inhibition in man. In: E. Usdin, N. Weiner and C. Creveling (Eds), Function and Regulation of Monoamine Enzymes: Basic and Clinical Aspects. Macmillan Press, London, (in press a).

Murphy, D. L., Cohen, R. M., Garrick, N. A., Siever, L. J. and Campbell, I. C. Utilization of substrate selective monoamine oxidase inhibitors to explore neurotransmitter hypotheses of the affective disorders. In: R. M. Post and J. C. Ballenger (Eds), Neurobiology of the Mood Disorders. Williams and Wilkins Co., Baltimore (in press b).

Murphy, D. L., Cohen, R. M., Siever, L. J., Roy, B., Karoum, F., Wyatt, R. J., Garrick, N. A. and Linnoila, M. Clinical and laboratory studies with selective monoamine oxidase inhibiting drugs: implications for hypothesized neurotransmitter changes associated with depression and antidepressant drug effects. In: H. Beckmann and P. Riederer (Eds), Monoamine Oxidase and Its Selective Inhibitors: New Concepts in Therapy and Research. Karger, Basel (in press c).

Neff, N. H. and Costa, E. (1966) The influence of monoamine oxidase inhibition on catecholamine synthesis. Life Sci. 5, 951–958.

226

Nelson, D. L., Herbert, A., Glowinski, J. and Hamon, M. (1979) [³H]Harmaline as a specific ligand of MAO A–II. Measurement of the turnover rates of MAO A during ontogenesis in the rat brain. J. Neurochem. 32, 1829–1836.

Olpe, H.-R. (1981) Differential effects of clomipramine and clorgyline on the sensitivity of cortical neurons to serotonin: effect of chronic treatment. Eur. J. Pharmacol. 69, 375–377.

Olpe, H.-R. and Schellenberg, A. (1980) Reduced sensitivity of neurons to noradrenaline after chronic treatment with antidepressant drugs. Eur. J. Pharmacol. 63, 7–13.

Peach, C., Salach, J. I. and Singer, T. P. (1979) Suicide inactivation of monoamine oxidase by trans-phenylcycloproplamine In: T. P. Singer, R. W. Von Korff and D. L. Murphy (Eds), Monoamine Oxidase: Structure, Function, and Altered Functions. Academic Press New York, pp. 39–50.

Peroutka, S. and Snyder, S. H. (1980) Long-term antidepressant treatment decreases spiroperidol labeled serotonin receptor binding. Science 210, 88–90.

Pickar, D., Cohen, R. M., Jimerson, D. C., Lake, R. L. and Murphy, D. L. (1981) Tyramine infusions and selective MAO inhibitor treatment. II. Interrelationships among pressor sensitivity changes, platelet MAO inhibition and plasma MHPG reduction. Psychopharmacology 74, 8–12.

Pletscher, A., Gey, F. K. and Burkand, W. P. (1966) Inhibitors of monoamine oxidase and decarboxylase of aromatic amino acids. Handb. Exper. Pharmacol. 19, 593–735.

Post, R. M. and Ballenger, J. C. (Eds), Neurobiology of the Mood Disorders, Williams and Wilkins, Baltimore (in press).

Powell, J. F. and Craig, I. W. (1977) Biochemical and immunological studies of the monoamine-oxidizing activities of cultured human cells. Biochem. Soc. Trans. 5, 180–182.

Ravaris, C. L., Robinson, D. S., Ives, J. O., Nies, A. and Bartlett, D. (1980) Phenelzine and amitriptyline in the treatment of depression. Arch. Gen. Psychiatry 37, 1075–1080.

Robinson, D. S., Nies, A., Ravaris, C. L., Ives, J. O. and Bartlett, D. (1978) Clinical pharmacology of phenelzine. Arch. Gen. Psychiatry 35, 629–635.

Robinson, D. S., Nies, A. and Cooper, T. B. (1980) Relationships of plasma phenelzine levels to platelet MAO inhibiton, acetylator phenotype, and clinical outcome in depressed outpatient. Clin. Pharmacol. Ther. 20, 180.

Russell, S. M., Davey, J. and Mayer, R. J. (1979a) Immunochemical characterization of monamine oxidase from human liver, placenta, platelets and brain cortex. Biochem. J. 181, 15–20.

Russell, S. M., Davey, J. and Mayer, R. J. (1979b) The vectorial orientation of human monoamine oxidase in the mitochondrial outer membrane. Biochem. J. 181, 7–14.

Savage, D. J., Mendels, J. and Frazer, A. (1980) Monoamine oxidase inhibitors and serotonin uptake inhibitors: differential effects on [³H] serotonin binding sites in rat brain. J. Pharmacol. Exper. Ther. 212, 259–263.

Schnaitman, C. and Greenawalt, J. W. (1968) Enzymatic properties of the inner and outer membranes of rat liver mitochondria. J. Cell Biol. 38, 158–175.

Siever, L. J., Cohen, R. M. and Murphy, D. L. (1981) Antidepressants and α_2-adrenergic autoreceptor desensitization. Am. J. Psychiatry 138, 681–682.

Singer, T. P., Von Korff, R. W. and Murphy, D. L. (Eds) (1979) Monoamine Oxidase: Structure, Function and Altered Functions. Academic Press, New York.

Smith, D. F. (1976) Effects of tranylcypromine stereoisomers, clorgyline and deprenyl on open field activity during long term lithium administration in rats. Psychopharmacology 50, 81–84.

Squires, R. F. (1978) Monoamine oxidase inhibitors: animal pharmacology. In: L. L. Iversen, S. D. Iversen and S. H. Snyder (Eds), Handbook of Psychopharmacology, Affective Disorders: Drugs Actions in Animals and Man, Vol. 14. Plenum Press, New York, pp. 1–58.

Squires, R. F. and Buus Lassen, J. (1975) The inhibition of A and B forms of MAO in the production of a characteristic behavioural syndrome in rats after L-tryptophan loading. Psychopharmacology 41, 145–151.

Sulser, F., Vetulani, J. and Mobley, P. (1978) Mode of action of antidepressant drugs. Biochem. Pharmacol. 27, 257–261.

Waldmeier, P. C., Felner, A. E. and Maitre, L. (1981) Long-term effects of selective MAO inhibitors on MAO activity and amine metabolism. In: M. B. H. Youdim and E. S. Paykel (Eds), Monoamine Oxidase Inhibitors. The State of the Art. John Wiley and Sons, New York, pp. 87–102.

Wolstenholme, G. E. W. and Knight, J. (Eds)   (1976)   Monoamine Oxidase and Its Inhibition. Ciba Foundation Symposium 39. Elsevier, Amsterdam.

Yang, H.-Y. T. and Neff, N. H.   (1974)   The monoamine oxidases of brain: selective inhibition with drugs and the consequences for the metabolism of the biogenic amines. J. Pharmol. Exper. Ther. 733–740.

Youdim, M. B. H. and Paykel, E. S. (Eds)   (1981)   Monoamine Oxidase Inhibitors. The State of the Art. John Wiley and Sons, New York.

Zeller, E. A.   (1938)   Zur Kenntnis der Diamine-oxydase. 3. Mitteilung uber den enzymatischen Abbau von Poly-aminen. Helv. Chim. Acta 21, 1645–1655.

Burrows/Norman/Davies (eds) Antidepressants
© *1983, Elsevier Science Publishers*

Chapter 16

Clinical applications of MAOIs

ALEXANDER NIES

Dartmouth Medical School, Hanover, New Hampshire, U.S.A.

INTRODUCTION

The psychoactive drugs possessing the property of inhibiting monoamine oxidase (MAO) enzymes have a firm place in the history of what has been called the psychopharmacological revolution. The serendipitous discovery of their 'psychic energizing' and mood-elevating or stabilizing effects (Selikoff et al., 1952; Bloch et al., 1954; Crane, 1957; Kline, 1958) when linked with the earlier discovery that they had a common monoamine oxidase inhibiting (MAOI) effect (Zeller et al., 1952) is a key concept in what have become the biogenic amine hypotheses of affective disorder (Garver and Davis, 1979). Reports of severe hypertensive episodes associated with the use of MAOI antidepressants led to the temporary withdrawal of some of these drugs from clinical usage and virtual abandonment of their use by many clinicians. As a result, their clinical efficacy was in danger of being relegated to mere historical and theoretical interest, even though once the mechanism of the hypertensive effect was clearly established (Blackwell et al., 1967) the means for preventing the occurrence of this toxic manifestation was available.

The first MAOI widely used in psychiatry was iproniazid (Marsilid), originally studied as one of a series of compounds synthesized primarily for anti-tubercular activity. It was noted, however, that global clinical improvement with an increased sense of well-being, and increased energy and appetite occurred before or even without significant bacteriological or pathological improvement. Iproniazid, an extremely clinically effective MAOI antidepressant was later removed from clinical use because of reports of cases, some fatal, of hepatoxicity. The hepatoxicity has been associated with the hydrazine portion of the molecule although the other hydrazine MAOIs have a very low order of reported clinical hepatotoxicity.

Another factor in the fall from grace of the MAOIs was the influential British Medical Research Council (1965) collaborative study comparing phenelzine, imipramine, and ECT in severely ill patients hospitalized for treatment of endogenous depression. This study presented phenelzine as being no more effective than placebo and as a result, a reputation of lack of efficacy was added to that of dangerousness. Accordingly, the MAOIs fell into disrepute although there were already hints of specific indications for their use (West and Dally, 1959). And so, until quite recently the considered body of opinion of most psychiatric and other medical academicians was that these drugs lacked efficacy and were too toxic to warrant clinical utilization, although they obviously remained in limited and selective use by some practitioners, since a small number of MAOIs maintained consistent annual sales without educational or advertising promotion by manufacturers.

Scientific advance waits on advances in technology; one measures what can be measured. Technological developments not only provide means for breaking completely new ground, but also means of looking at old things in new ways. Thus, the availability of a convenient method of reliably measuring mitochondrial MAO activity in the human using platelets (Robinson et al., 1968) served as a stimulus to re-examine the antidepressant and antianxiety effects of the MAOIs. One obvious reason for unreliable clinical effectiveness might be variability in enzyme inhibition among individuals, so the opportunity to serially monitor MAO activity in an effort to guide and adjust treatment offered promise and justification for re-evaluation of the MAOI antidepressants. For these and other reasons, the past decade has seen a resurgence of interest in the MAOIs and they now have a legitimate place in the psychopharmacologic armamentarium (Editorial, Br. Med. J., 1976).

With elucidation of the mechanism of hypertensive reactions during MAOI therapy by Blackwell and colleagues, MAOIs could be used safely, and controlled clinical trials of phenelzine began to appear. These trials were initially all double-blind with placebo controls, but more recent trials have focused on comparisons with tricyclics such as amitriptyline. Our own studies employed a standardized depression interview (SDI) schedule to characterize patient symptoms and to assess change-over time with treatment (Robinson et al., 1973; Nies et al., 1974). Serial monitoring of MAOI activity and plasma drug concentrations were also carried out in order to investigate their relationship to therapeutic outcome and to study the pharmacokinetic properties of phenelzine.

In our initial trial, begun in 1970, phenelzine at a 60 mg per day dose was compared to placebo for a 6-week course of treatment in outpatients with depression (Robinson et al., 1973). These patients were selected for the presence of significant depressive symptoms warranting drug treatment if the index illness met criteria for a primary depressive disorder. Patients with illnesses secondary to alcoholism, organic brain syndromes, drug abuse, persistent character disorder, or schizophrenia were excluded. Findings were that phenelzine, 60 mg per day, was clinically effective and that features of atypical depression showed particularly good improvement.

During this same period, three other studies of phenelzine were reported. Tyrer and coworkers (1973) showed that phenelzine, 60 mg per day, was effective in treating patients with agoraphobia. Johnstone and Marsh (1973) reported that patients who were slow acetylators of phenelzine treated with 90 mg per day showed significantly greater improvement than patients treated with placebo. Solyom and coworkers (1973) also found that phenelzine-behavioural treatment combinations were superior to placebo-behavioural combinations in treating phobic patients.

TABLE 1

Controlled trials of phenelzine in depression.

Source	Drug comparison	Sample size (completing/ entering)	Dose phenelzine (mg/day)	Duration (weeks)	Outcome
Robinson et al. (1973)	Placebo	60/87	60	6	+
Johnstone and Marsh (1973)	Placebo	72/97	45–90	3	+
Kay et al. (1973)	Amitriptyline	45/62	15–45	4	0
Raskin et al. (1974)	Placebo, Diazepam	118/325	45	4–7	0
Ravaris et al. (1976)	Placebo	49/60	30 and 60	6	+[a]
Mountjoy et al. (1977)	Placebo	83/117	45–70	3	+
Ravaris et al. (1980)	Amitriptyline	105/130	60	6	+
Rowan et al. (1981)	Placebo, Amitriptyline	131/176	60–75	6	+

[a] 30 mg/day = 0; 60 mg/day = +.

Two negative studies of phenelzine were also reported. The first compared phenelzine in doses ranging from 15 to 45 mg per day to amitriptyline in a small outpatient sample (Kay et al., 1973). This small variable dose study employed what is now known to be an ineffective or borderline dose of phenelzine. Raskin and coworkers (1974) reported on the results of a large inpatient study conducted in several collaborating mental institutions. In a comparison with diazepam and placebo, phenelzine in a dosage of 45 mg per day for 4 to 7 weeks was no more effective than placebo and less effective than diazepam. Again, a borderline effective dose of phenelzine was employed, and in addition, many of the patients in the sample may have suffered from depressive disorders secondary to personality or other psychiatric disorders as well as severe endogenous depressions, all of which are probably less suitable candidates for MAOI therapy.

In a second study, we explored the issue of optimal phenelzine dosage. Using the same protocol as in the first study, we compared phenelzine 60 mg per day, phenelzine 30 mg per day, and placebo for 6 weeks (Ravaris et al., 1976). The high dosage phenelzine treatment group again showed definite improvement whereas phenelzine 30 mg per day produced improvement no better than placebo treatment. We also noted the empirical finding that patients achieving platelet MAO inhibition of 80% or more showed significantly greater improvement than those with less than 80%. Mean percent MAO inhibition was nearly 90% in the high phenelzine dosage group, but few patients treated with 30 mg per day reached 80% inhibition. The dose effect is clinically important since the manufacturer's recommendations at the time were for a dose of not more than 45 mg per day with lower 'maintenance dosages' suggested. The use of low dosages seemed to explain the reports of lack of efficacy for phenelzine in the earlier literature which not only reported use of borderline doses but also often short treatment periods of 14–28 days. In our placebo controlled studies, while there were significant improvements compared to placebo as early as 14 days, maximum improvement occurred at 6 weeks (Robinson et al., 1978).

TABLE 2

Controlled trials of phenelzine in anxiety.

Source	Drug comparison	Sample size (completing/ entering)	Dose phenelzine (mg/day)	Duration (weeks)	Outcome
Tyrer et al. (1973)	Placebo	32/40	45–90	8	+
Solyom et al. (1973)	Placebo, Behav. R	50/	45	12	+
Sheehan et al. (1980)	Placebo Imipramine	57/78	45–50	6	+
Nies et al. (1982)	Amitriptyline	145/169	60	6	+

Three recent studies have added to our knowledge of the comparative efficacy of phenelzine with tricyclic antidepressant drugs. Sheehan and coworkers (1980) compared phenelzine to imipramine and placebo in agoraphobic outpatients in a double-blind study of 12-weeks duration. While both antidepressant drugs were superior to placebo, the phenelzine treatment group revealed a greater proportion of patients who were completely or markedly improved compared to imipramine, and there was a strong and consistent trend for phenelzine rather than imipramine-treated patients to exhibit better response on the majority of items measured. A subsequent study has confirmed the superiority of phenelzine over imipramine in agoraphobics (Sheehan, unpublished). We have also recently reported a 6-week comparison of phenelzine 60 mg per day with amitriptyline 150 mg per day in outpatients with depression (Ravaris et al., 1980), and on the antianxiety and antiphobic effects of phenelzine (Nies et al., 1982). The two drugs appeared to be equally efficacious overall, with the phenelzine-treated patients showing significantly greater improvement on the anxiety scale of the Symptom Check List-90 at 6 weeks. Clinical predictors of response to the two different antidepressants were also examined and are discussed below. Completion of this trial and further analysis shows a clear superiority of phenelzine over amitriptyline for several measures of anxiety (Nies et al., unpublished).

Paykel and associates have also conducted a controlled trial comparing phenelzine, amitriptyline, and placebo in depressed patients. Preliminary findings from this study are in agreement that the two drugs are remarkably similar in overall therapeutic effect, with suggestions that atypical symptoms improve more with phenelzine and typical symptoms with amitriptyline (Paykel et al., 1979; Rowan et al., 1981).

In summary, a variety of recent controlled and uncontrolled clinical trials clearly support the efficacy of MAOI treatment of diverse affective disorders ranging from agoraphobia, phobic anxiety, and hysteroid dysphoria to atypical depression, depressive neurosis, and nonendogenous depression. Tables 1 and 2 summarize controlled trials of phenelzine, the MAOI whose efficacy is best documented.

PHARMACOLOGICAL CONSIDERATIONS AND CLASSIFICATIONS OF MAO INHIBITORS

The amine oxidases

The amine oxidases are enzymes which are widely distributed in most tissues of the body. Although they are known to play a role in the degradation of intracellular amines thereby contributing to the maintenance of a homeostatic balance in the dynamic equilibrium of amine synthesis and catabolism, this physiological function is as yet poorly understood.

MAO catalyses the oxidative deamination of noradrenaline, adrenaline, dopamine, phenylethylamine, serotonin and other biogenic amines whose aldehyde products are subsequently converted by aldehyde dehydrogenases to pharmacologically inactive acidic derivatives. Treatment by MAO inhibition can result in elevation of brain levels of neurotransmitter amines such as noradrenaline and serotonin, as demonstrated in studies on both animals and humans. The antidepressant actions of amine-pump-inhibiting agents such as the tricyclic antidepressant drugs, the provocation of depression by amine-depleting agents such as reserpine, along with the amine elevations produced by the MAOIs, led to the popular concept of the 1960s and 1970s that such amines play a critical role in the central nervous system mediation of the experience of emotion.

Since MAO enzyme protein is continually generated and degraded, it can be considered to have an elimination half-life analogous to a drug; for mitochondrial (neuronal, platelet, other tissue) MAO, this half-life is estimated to range from 8 to 12 days. This is especially significant when the enzyme is subjected to the irreversible inhibitors of MAO which are firmly attached near active sites on the enzyme molecule, necessitating a 10–20 day waiting period for synthesis of new enzyme protein before tissue MAO activity approximates pretreatment levels.

Reversible and irreversible MAO inhibitors

The naturally occurring reversible MAO inhibitors, the alkaloids yohimbine and harmaline, have been used primarily as tools in biochemical and pharmacological investigation but have had very limited application in clinical studies primarily because they possess undesirable actions such as hallucinogenic and epileptogenic effects. It is possible that if their actions were more fully understood, drugs of this type might be especially useful in the treatment of patients with hepatic impairment in whom it is preferable to avoid exposure to the potentially toxic hydrazine moiety. Reversible MAO-A inhibitors have been developed by several manufacturers and are currently undergoing early clinical trials. It is possible that such compounds will have a significantly lower potentiation of tyramine pressor effects and thereby possess a wider margin of safety and require less stringent dietary precautions (Ögren et al., 1981).

The irreversible inhibitors are further classified into hydrazine and non-hydrazine drugs on the basis of the presence of a hydrazine moiety. The hydrazines are possibly most clinically effective but also have the potential (though rarely) for producing a lupus-like syndrome and chemical hepatotoxicity. Phenelzine is the MAOI for which there is presently the most substantial clinical evidence of efficacy. The non-hydrazine, tranyl-

234

cypromine, appears to have greater stimulant properties which may be attributable to its conversion to significant amounts of amphetamine *in vivo*. Also, it has been suggested, but not confirmed, that the L-form of this compound, a more potent reuptake but less potent MAO inhibitor, may be more clinically effective, but this study included too few patients to establish significance (Escobar et al., 1974).

Selective and non-selective MAO inhibitors

Biochemical pharmacological experimentation based on ease of inhibition by various MAOIs with different amine substrates, has shown that two families or species of tissue MAO may exist. These have been termed MAO-A and MAO-B and the proportion of type A and type B activity varies from tissue to tissue in the same animal species and in the same tissue from different animal species. Although the presently used MAOIs are non-selective inhibitors of MAO-A and MAO-B, the utility of the A versus B distinction for design of MAOI drugs with a more favourable therapeutic index is a possibility which remains to be explored.

The effects and comparative efficacy and safety of the so-called 'selective inhibitors', clorgyline and deprenyl, are currently topics of fairly intense investigation. Although these agents offer the promise of selective inhibition confined to, for example, intraneuronal central nervous system MAO (which currently is thought to be primarily MAO-A in the human), the selective action of these agents established *in vitro* in acute experiments is likely dissipated with chronic treatment, with consequent loss of potential selectivity and limiting clinical advantage (Campbell et al., 1979; Lipper et al., 1979).

Pharmacological actions of MAO inhibitors: role of enzyme inhibition

These drugs, as their classification indicates, all share the common property of inhibiting MAO. In addition, they inhibit other oxidases such as plasma diamine oxidase, and other enzymes such as aldehyde dehydrogenase (Lebsack and Anderson, 1978). In addition to these effects on the monoamine metabolising system, their pharmacological actions may be mediated by other mechanisms which affect amine function. They may block amine reuptake, or act indirectly by discharging amines from storage sites. Some have also been

TABLE 3

Classification of MAOI drugs.

Hydrazine	Non-Hydrazine
Phenelzine (Nardil)	Tranylcypromine (Parnate)
Isocarboxazid (Marplan)	Pargyline (Eutonyl)[b]
Nialamid (Niamid)[a]	Deprenyl[c]
Iproniazid (Marsilid)[a]	Clorgyline[c]

[a] Withdrawn in U.S.A.
[b] Marketed for hypertension.
[c] 'Selective' MAO inhibitors (investigational).

shown to have direct agonist actions (Knoll and Magyar, 1972). The MAO-inhibiting action occurs at low drug concentrations ($10^{-8}-10^{-9}$ M) and continues to be the most studied pharmacological mechanism. The relationship of inhibition of MAO activity to clinical improvement as measured by platelet assay methods (Robinson et al., 1968) is discussed later. It is worth emphasizing at this point, however, that some of the effects of these agents may be related to mechanisms other than MAO inhibition; indeed, the antianxiety effects of the hydrazines may result from alterations in GABA metabolism (Manyam et al., 1980).

Because of the possibility of greater effectiveness and safety, as well as theoretical interest, a number of clinical trials comparing drugs which are more selective against type A or type B MAO are presently being carried out. One of these drugs, deprenyl, is a relatively selective MAO-B inhibitor whose L-isomer has the property of blocking the pressor response to tyramine in animal preparations. L-Deprenyl is said to be effective as an antidepressant but has not had sufficient study in well designed clinical trials to establish efficacy. Nor has it been shown with certainty that the diet and drug restrictions necessary with other MAOI drugs are not required or may be relaxed, although this may be true. Another drug, clorgyline, is a relatively selective MAO-A inhibitor. Preliminary results suggest that it is less effective than existing agents as an antidepressant (Lipper et al., 1979), but this needs confirmation. As mentioned, the facts that selective inhibition may be lost with chronic MAOI treatment and antidepressant treatment requires several weeks, suggest that existing 'selective' MAO-A and -B inhibitors may not offer significantly improved efficacy or reduced toxicity.

Although MAOIs have effects on the autonomic nervous and cardiovascular systems to lower blood pressure, the absence of direct cardiotoxicity and anticholinergic activity has clinical importance. They do not interfere with cardiac conduction, do not alter heart rate and do not frequently induce urinary retention (Robinson et al., 1982). Their actions in producing a reduction in collagen cross-linkage has been advanced, as a mechanism responsible for their effectiveness in treating illnesses as diverse as angina, rheumatoid arthritis and inflammatory bowel disease (Scherbel and Harrison, 1959). However, many of the early studies of MAOI use in chronic medical illnesses lack confirmation.

PREDICTORS OF MAO RESPONSE: CLINICAL AND BIOLOGICAL

It is possible to predict response to MAOI treatment both clinically (e.g. illness patterns) and biologically (e.g. measurement of drug levels or biochemical or physiological measures of drug effects). Further, the clinical predictors may be classified as categorical (type of disorder, personality type) or dimensional (severity, endogenous or non-endogenous).

Clinical predictors

As a result of their clinical experience and a retrospective analysis of patients who had responded to iproniazid, West and Dally (1959) were able to identify a symptom profile of patients who showed good MAOI outcome. Those symptoms, commonly associated with non-endogenous depression, included low incidence of self-reproach, initial insomnia, phobia, worsening of symptoms in either the evening or latter parts of the day, and 'atypical vegetative' signs. While West and Dally's description of patients with 'atypical depression' evolved from uncontrolled studies of iproniazid, review of published controlled clinical trials of phenelzine treatment revealed that the greatest degree of effectiveness was shown in outpatients (Robinson et al., 1973). Later observations by Paykel and coworkers (1979) corroborated these findings. Negative or equivocal results were almost invariably noted in inpatients. Since outpatients are more likely to have less severe and fixed disorders of mood with higher representations of neurotic, non-delusional, non-suicidal and atypical symptoms, treatment location would seem to be partially and at least indirectly related to clinical classification and treatment outcome.

Rather than rely on categorical clinical diagnosis, we used a numerical representation of endogenous-nonendogenous (atypical) depression, similar to Kendell's use of a numerical index to predict ECT response (Kendell, 1968). This Diagnostic Index (DI) used was to match patients and ensure balanced treatment groups and also to examine for predictors of outcome (Nies et al., 1974). When patients from two clinical trials treated with either placebo or phenelzine 60 mg per day are combined, the phenelzine-treated patients with lower DI scores (indicating predominance of nonendogenous or atypical symptoms) improved more than those with high scores (indicating a predominance of endogenous symptoms) on three measures, a scale of depressed mood, an anxiety scale, and the Hamilton Depression Scale. In contrast, the DI did not predict placebo response. Since the DI scores were assigned to each patient before treatment on the basis of the SDI performed by a trained interviewer unaware of the hypothesis, this finding amounts to a prospective evaluation of the hypothesis that atypical (at least nonendogenous) depressive symptoms respond well to a MAOI. Further analysis of data from these two studies has shown that a DI constructed from a patient self-rated questionnaire similarly predicts outcome and that discriminant functions which divide the phenelzine-treated patients into two groups 'markedly improved' and 'minimally improved', contain items similar to those weighted highly negatively on the DI. Several discriminant functions that evolved from the responses contained the items, 'reactivity', 'self-pity', age above 40 years, and absence of diurnal variation A.M. worse.

Paykel and coworkers (1979) in an open study of 64-depressed patients treated with phenelzine for 4 weeks examined the validity of several predictors of phenelzine treatment outcome. Patients with atypical, anxious, neurotic, and less severe symptoms showed a consistent trend of greater improvement while two sets of dimensional predictors — one our DI, and the other, factors derived from a principal component analysis reflecting severity and contrasting anxiety with depressions — correlated with outcome measures. Treatment setting was related to outcome, with most improvement occurring in outpatients and day patients, and least in inpatients. Also, a typology classifying patients into retarded, anxious, agitated and hostile types, showed a relationship to outcome, with hostile and agitated depressive showing the best and retarded depressives the last improvement on two different measures. These investigators interpreted their findings to support the concept of the existence of a MAO inhibitor responsive subgroup of patients consistent with the early clinical experience.

In another recent and large scale comparative study of phenelzine 60 mg per day and amitriptyline 150 mg per day, the overall efficacy of the two drugs is comparable although phenelzine was superior to amitriptyline in improvement on the psychic anxiety, reactivity of mood, symptom fluctuation, and hypomania scales of the SDI. On the other hand, amitriptyline was superior to phenelzine from improvement on all three of the insomnia scales (initial, middle and terminal) (Ravaris et al., 1980).

Furthermore, global assessment of improvement by the psychiatrist at the end of the 6 weeks of treatment also substantiated that phenelzine was superior for depressed mood, anxiety, loss of interest and energy, and level of activity, whereas amitriptyline was superior for vegetative symptoms, particularly improving appetite and sleep. Finally, a patient group with retention of reactivity of mood and absence of terminal insomnia (mean DI of 4.0) showed superior improvement on phenelzine, and a group showing reduced mood reactivity and terminal insomnia (mean DI of 8.0) improved more with amitriptyline.

More recently, studies have been conducted which have systematically examined the efficacy of phenelzine in the treatment of phobic anxiety, testing the early clinical findings of Sargant and Dally (1962). Three well-designed and controlled clinical trials have established the efficacy of phenelzine in the treatment of phobic and agoraphobic patients (Solyom et al., 1973; Tyrer et al., 1973; Sheehan et al., 1980). Furthermore, Sheehan and coworkers found phenelzine superior to imipramine in reducing avoidance and anticipatory anxiety, although not more effective than imipramine in blocking the panic attacks experienced by agoraphobic patients. Finally, in a comparison of the effects of phenelzine and amitriptyline, we have found that phenelzine is superior in antianxiety and antiphobic actions in depressed outpatients (Nies et al., 1982).

Klein and associates also claim that phenelzine is particularly effective in treating patients with Hysteroid Dysphoric Disorder, based on a preliminary uncontrolled study (Quitkin et al., 1979, personal communication). These investigators also report phenelzine to be effective in blocking the panic episodes associated with agoraphobia (Liebowitz and Klein, 1981). Some of the patients exhibiting hysteroid dysphoria resemble the Phobic Anxiety Depersonalization Syndrome of Roth (1959). This syndrome of phobic anxiety, panic attacks, and episodes of depersonalization occurring in young, somewhat hysterical women following a bereavement, has features which overlap with 'atypical' depression. It has also been suggested that hysteroid dysphoria is an adult variant of separation anxiety, occurring in individuals particularly vulnerable to rejection.

Pharmacological predictors

Initial reports suggested that the therapeutic response to phenelzine (Johnstone and Marsh, 1973) and side effects (Evans et al., 1965) were influenced by the acetylator phenotype of the individual, a genetically determined trait. In a subsequent report, Johnstone (1976) showed a relationship of acetylator phenotype and clinical response in patients with depressive neurosis, with greater improvement shown by the slow acetylators of sulphadimidine.

These earlier reports have not been confirmed by subsequent studies by at least three other groups of investigators. Using rate of acetylation of a loading dose of sulfapyridine 10 mg/kg in 40 patients clarifies the content (treated with phenelzine 60 mg per day) after completion of the phenelzine-placebo double-blind trial, we found no significant

238

differences between fast and slow acetylators in either clinical or pharmacological measures (Robinson et al., 1978). Mean improvement on the SDI anxiety and depression scales and the 17-item Hamilton Depression Rating Scale did not differ between the two groups. Furthermore, platelet MAO inhibition with benzylamine as substrate was 83 ± 2% after 14 days and 86 ± 2% after 6 weeks of phenelzine treatment for the fast acetylators and 74 ± 5% at 2 weeks and 87 ± 2% at 6 weeks for the slow acetylators. Plasma phenelzine levels did not differ for the two groups being, if anything, higher at 2, 4, and 6 weeks of phenelzine treatment in fast acetylators. Other investigators who studied acetylator phenotype and clinical response to phenelzine have also recently reported negative findings (Davidson et al., 1978; Marshall et al., 1978). These three negative studies have all employed standard dosage ranges and durations of treatment in well-controlled double-blind clinical trials. The consistent lack of association between acetylator status and either clinical response or pharmacologic differences suggests that rate of acetylation of a sulfa drug is not a useful clinical test. Furthermore, it would appear that acetylation is perhaps not an important metabolic pathway for the degradation of phenelzine and may not represent the primary route of biotransformation of the drug.

Monitoring platelet MAO activity during MAOI treatment has been of considerable recent interest, using a practical and convenient assay of blood platelet MAO activity (Robinson et al., 1968). Such studies have shown that there are consistent differences in clinical response to phenelzine treatment between patients with high and low per cent inhibition (see Fig. 1). Platelet MAO inhibition of at least 80% at 2 weeks with tryptamine as substrate predicted a more favourable response at 6 weeks of treatment in patients from the phenelzine-placebo control clinical trials (Nies et al., 1974; Robinson et al., 1978). Since platelet MAO activity is at best only a very indirect index of brain enzyme activity, this is basically an empirical test of adequate treatment. Hence, the relationship applies only to the use of benzylamine and tryptamine as substrates for MAO in phenelzine-treated patients. The relative potencies and rate of drug uptake by the platelet of other clinically used MAO inhibitors differ from phenelzine so that specific conditions for monitoring MAO inhibition during treatment will have to be established for each drug.

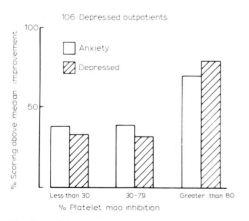

Fig. 1. Antidepressant and antianxiety effects are optimal above a threshhold of 80% platelet MAO inhibition with phenelzine.

The 80% platelet MAOI threshold has recently been confirmed by Georgotas (1981) and colleagues in geriatric depression using a MAO-B substrate, phenylethylamine.

The phenelzine findings are of interest because of the earlier animal studies which showed that no detectable increases in brain monoamines could be confirmed until a critical level of inhibition was achieved in the range of 70–85% (Gey and Pletscher, 1961; Dubnick et al., 1962). Since phenelzine 30 mg per day is no more effective than placebo and MAO inhibition greater than 80% was associated with therapeutic efficacy regardless of dosage, these findings suggest that MAO inhibition is a crucial pharmacologic action of this group of drugs. We have also examined the relationship of baseline platelet MAO activity to treatment outcome. The level of pretreatment MAO activity is not associated with response to MAOI treatment (patients with high MAO are neither more resistant nor more benefited), and the baseline level is not related to the ease of reaching a maximal level of inhibition.

In spite of the interesting relationship of outcome to platelet MAO inhibition, and the more controversial relationship to acetylation, the simple expedient of dosing on a mg/kg basis is sufficient to optimize clinical results (Robinson et al., 1978).

USE OF MAOIs IN CLINICAL PRACTICE

Evidence accumulated from both controlled and uncontrolled studies plus clinical experience indicates that the MAOIs are effective in a heterogeneous group of disorders such as nonendogenous and atypical depression and anxiety states such as agoraphobia. Their effectiveness extends also to the less well recognized disorders such as Klein's Hysteroid Dysphoria and Roth's Phobic-Anxiety Depersonalization Syndrome. Thus far, there is very little systematic evidence suggesting that MAOIs are effective in major depressive illness; for these, tricyclic drugs and ECT remain the treatments of choice.

Based on the presence of such a clinical picture, particularly if there has been no response to a tricyclic such as imipramine, and especially if there has been a dysphoric response to modest or quite low doses of amitriptyline, the clinician may elect treatment with an MAOI, drawing on the symptom profile outlined in Table 4.

Since the previously recommended dose of 45 mg per day is only marginally effective and more recent work from controlled clinical trials suggests that phenelzine 1 mg/kg body weight per day is the optimally effective dose, most adult patients should receive 60 or 75 mg per day. Our standard practice is to administer 1 tablet (15 mg) the initial day, 2 tablets on the second day, and then 30 b.i.d. or the optimal dose, thereafter. After a 2–4 week trial of therapy, it may be indicated to try a higher dose up to 90 mg per day in partial responders or non-responders. Other investigators have employed the higher dose of 90 mg per day routinely but apparently at the expense of a greater incidence of troublesome side effects (Davidson et al., 1978).

We have not found the routine monitoring of platelet MAO activity to be necessary, or indeed useful, for adequately treating most patients. For almost all patients, 60 mg per day of phenelzine is satisfactory, although dosage is adjusted upward or downward on the basis of extremes in body weight, and downward initially in geriatric patients.

For a patient showing a positive response to a MAOI, maintenance drug therapy should be continued for varying periods of time lasting from 4 months to 1 year or more.

240

TABLE 4

Features of symptom profile of MAOI-responsive patients.

Psychopathological symptoms	*Vegetative symptoms*
retained mood reactivity	initial insomnia
irritability	hypersomnia
panic episodes	craving sweets
social fears	hyperphagia
agoraphobia	weight gain
hypochondriasis	lassitude
obsessive preoccupations	tremulousness
Personality features	*Historical features*
self-pity/blaming others	personal loss before intensification
rejection sensitive	dysphoric amitriptyline response
vanity/applause-seeking	liking amphetamines
abandonment fears	alcohol/sedative abuse
communicative suicidal actions	poor prior ECT response

Agoraphobic patients in particular require maintenance on full dose drug treatment for a long enough period to allow spontaneous *in situ* relearning and modification of behaviour to occur. Formal behaviour modification programs are not routinely necessary but can be very helpful once spontaneous panic episodes are pharmacologically ablated. Because the relapse rate of depressive illness is higher if antidepressants are discontinued before 6 months of maintenance drug therapy, treatment should rarely be completely discontinued before this time. Patients with a chronic lingering or recurrent course of several or many years duration before responding to a MAOI often require prolonged maintenance for months or years. Because of rebound effects, as with the tricyclics, treatment should not be terminated abruptly. Trial reductions by one daily dosage unit per fortnight has been found to be a useful procedure for initiating gradual discontinuation.

In addition to the established indications for MAOI treatment of atypical depression (in West and Dally and not the DSM-III concept of atypical), and in agoraphobia and endogenous panic states (Sheehan), there is evidence that the MAOIs may be effective for less conventional indications. Such indications include the treatment of narcolepsy (Wyatt et al., 1971) post-traumatic stress disorders (Hogben and Cornfield, 1981) particularly when visual 'flashbacks' are prominent, inflammatory bowel disease with secondary depression (Rosenthal, personal communication) and irritable bowel (Weiss, unpublished manuscript). Perhaps the area in which MAOIs are most neglected and underutilized is in geriatrics in which, for example, phenelzine shows greater antidepressant effectiveness with increasing age (Nies, Ravaris, Robinson, unpublished) and has been shown safe and effective in depressed geriatric patients (Georgotas et al., 1981) and in a larger series of tricyclic resistant geriatric depression (Georgotas, unpublished). In light of the lack of cardiotoxicity of MAOIs compared to tricyclics (Robinson et al., 1982), a quality which deserves wider recognition, and the absence of the central anticholinergic toxicity of the tricyclics to which the ageing brain seems especially vulnerable (Davies et al., 1971), the increased effectiveness in the aged becomes of greater significance.

SIDE EFFECTS AND TOXICITY OF MAOI TREATMENT

The side effects of MAOIs (Table 5) produce relatively little limitation of treatment, particularly as compared to other classes of psychotropics. The most frequently encountered side effects are mild to moderate insomnia (30–50%), daytime sedation (30%), and dryness of the mouth (30%). Many patients with drug-induced insomnia, often in the form of increased awakenings and reduction in total sleep time, may note some daytime drowsiness and still experience significant improvement in depression. Some patients with insomnia may benefit by concentrating dosage in the latter part of the day (e.g. 30 mg in the evening, 30 mg at bedtime, or 60 mg at bedtime), and paradoxically, other patients show less insomnia when dosage is concentrated earlier in the day (e.g. 30 mg on arising, 30 mg at noon). Some show benefit from addition of a soporific benzodiazepine to a bedtime MAOI dose. Occasionally, a patient will benefit from a bedtime combination with tryptophan, although the latter can produce marked outbursts of sleep-onset myoclonic jerking. In this context, one may mention the exacerbation of myoclonic movements associated with REM rebound when MAOI treatment is abruptly discontinued; further evidence that a gradual reduction in dosage is appropriate to avoid disturbing myoclonic episodes as well as unpleasant nightmares.

Other less frequent side effects include impaired sexual responsiveness. This is somewhat more common in men (10–20%) who note some degree of impotence. About 5–10% of women may experience loss of ability to achieve orgasm. These side effects appear to be dose-related and loss of therapeutic benefit is often the price of dose reduction to avoid this sexual impairment. Another occasionally troublesome side effect is a marked increase in appetite, particularly a craving for sweets leading to excessive weight gain and obesity. This can be managed by dietary counselling but in some cases it may be necessary to reduce MAOI dosage.

The complaint of dry mouth is much less frequent and severe than with tricyclic anti-

TABLE 5

Phenelzine side effects.

Side effects	Estimated frequency	Impairment liability
Insomnia	50%	Usually tolerated
Daytime sedation	30%	Rarely impairing
Dry mouth	40%	Mild
Impaired sexual response	20% (men) 25% (women)	Ceases with dose reduction or discontinuation
Myoclonic jerks	10%	Mild
Gastric irritation	<10%	Responds to taking drug with meals
Hyperphagia and weight gain	10–15%	May require dose reduction or discontinuation
Oedema	<5%	Mild
Orthostatic hypotension	40%	Occasionally requires dose reduction
Postural dizziness	5–10%	Can be impairing with syncope

242

TABLE 6

Toxicities associated with MAOI therapy.

Toxicity	Frequency
Hypertensive crisis	Rare (more common with tranylcypromine)
Hepatotoxicity	Uncommon (hydrazine agents)
Lupus-like syndrome	Rare (hydrazine agents)
Pyridoxine deficiency	Not well documented
Mouth sores	Occasional with hydrazines
Rash	Rare

depressants. Other anticholinergic side effects such as urinary hesitancy and constipation occur infrequently and are considerably less troublesome than with tricyclics.

Although some degree of orthostatic hypotension is common (especially in older age groups), it far less commonly produces symptoms and is only rarely a cause for discontinuing treatment. Patients who obtain improvement only with a MAOI yet experience incapacitating syncope present a rare but vexing problem; resorting to the addition of a potent mineralocorticoid (9-alpha-fluorocortisol) has been successful in such instances.

Furthermore, there is no evidence of a direct cardiotoxic effect of MAO inhibitors as with the tricyclic antidepressants. MAOIs produce no electrocardiographic changes and may be used in the patient with heart disease as long as no contraindicated cardiac drugs are employed (Robinson et al., 1982), and, therefore, are especially advantageous in the elderly.

A potentially lethal but fortunately rare toxicity occurring with MAOI treatment is a hypertensive crisis induced by ingestion of tyramine-containing foods, or the concurrent administration of indirectly acting adrenergic agonist drugs. This hazard has been essentially eliminated by applying the understanding of the mechanisms of this interaction to careful patient instruction to avoid certain foods (Table 7) and medications (including over-the-counter sinus, cold and headache combinations) (Table 8). The recommended treatment for a hypertensive crisis is the intravenous administration of an alpha adrenergic blocker, such as phentolamine. However, oral or intramuscular chlorpromazine is also useful and has the virtue of being more routinely available in emergency rooms and hospital units. In our experience of over 10 years of investigation with phenelzine, we have encountered only three mild hypertensive reactions secondary to unintentional dietary lapses. These patients experienced some headache and were found to have mild elevations of blood pressure which did not require intervention with alpha-blocking drugs such as phentolamine or chlorpromazine. This experience is consistent with that of Raskin and associates who found that among 110 phenelzine treated patients in a nine hospital co-operative study no episodes of hypertensive crisis were encountered (Raskin et al., 1972). This is also consistent with the available evidence which shows that phenelzine is a relatively safe MAOI. Even before the discovery of the 'cheese effect' and the institution of dietary precautions, it was noted that the incidence of hypertensive responses with tranylcypromine was five times that with phenelzine (Blackwell et al., 1967).

The administration of a stimulant drug such as amphetamine to patients receiving a

TABLE 7

MAOI dietary restrictions.

High tyramine content – not permitted

Unpasteurised cheeses (aromatic): cheddar, camembert, stilton, bleu, etc.
Meat extracts: 'Bovril', 'Marmite', etc.
Smoked/pickled protein: herring, sausage
Aged/putrifying protein: chopped chicken liver, tuna salads, etc.
Red wines: chianti, burgundy, sherry, etc.
Italian broad bean (fava) pods

Limited tyramine – limited amounts allowed

Meat extract: bouillon, consomme
Pasteurised light and pale beers
White wines: champagne
Ripe avocado, ripe banana
Sour cream, yogurt

Low tyramine – permissible

Distilled spirits (in moderation)
Pasteurised cheeses: cream, cottage
Chocolate
Yeast breads
Fruits: figs, grapes, raisins
Soy sauce, meat tenderizer
Caffeine containing beverages

MAOI is clearly contraindicated. Recognition of this incompatibility may assume more importance with the increased use of test doses of amphetamine to predict antidepressant response to a tricyclic drug. Another potential problem is switching from another MAOI to tranylcypromine. While we have observed no problems in changing from tranylcypromine to phenelzine, a hypertensive MAOI-MAOI inter-reaction has been observed in patients who have been changed from phenelzine to tranylcypromine. This side effect may be due to the conversion of tranylcypromine to amphetamine in the body, resulting in amphetamine-MAOI interaction. Therefore, when tranylcypromine is prescribed following another MAOI, it is recommended that the first MAOI be discontinued for 2 weeks before starting tranylcypromine. Tables 7 and 8 summarize the dietary restrictions and therapeutic precautions which are observed when prescribing MAOI treatment.

The combination of a tricyclic antidepressant with a MAOI may be indicated in selected cases of resistant depression where single drug therapy has not been successful (White and Simpson, 1981). Almost all of the reported adverse reactions with such combined treatment have occurred with a MAOI combined with imipramine (Schukit et al., 1971; Ananth and Luchins, 1977). The reports of toxic reactions to amitriptyline-MAOI treatment have been very infrequent and involved significant overdoses of amitriptyline. The adverse tricyclic-MAOI interaction seems to be a characteristic of 'noradrenergic' tri-

244

TABLE 8

MAOI drug incompatibilities.

Contraindication

Stimulants: amphetamines, cocaine, anorectic drugs
Decongestants: sinus, hay fever, cold tablets
Antihypertensives: methyldopa, guanethidine, reserpine
Antidepressants: imipramine, desipramine, clorimipramine, trimipramine
MAOIs: tranylcypromine after other MAOIs

Relatively contraindicated (marked potentiation)

Narcotics: meperidine (pethidine)
Sympathomimetics: adrenaline, noradrenaline, dopamine, isoprel
General anaesthetics
Amine precursors: L-dopa, L-tryptophan

Potentiation

Narcotics: morphine, codeine, etc.
Sedatives: alcohol, barbiturates, benzodiazepines
Local anaesthetics: containing vasoconstrictors
Hypoglycaemic agents: insulin, tolbutamide, chlorpropamide

Insufficient knowledge

Antidepressants: maprotiline, amoxapine, trazodone, zimelidine
MAOI-MAOI: new, reversible after irreversible

---

cyclics rather than 'serotonergic' types. This interaction which consists of pyrexia, excitation and delirium without significant hypertension also occurs with desipramine, chlorimipramine, trimipramine and protriptyline.

The hydrazine MAOIs such as phenelzine and isocarboxazid, can produce hepatotoxicity, and a lupus-like syndrome, although these are rare. Because these reactions are infrequent, routine monitoring of liver function tests is unnecessary in the non-alcoholic patient, but in the event of fever or jaundice, documentation by laboratory tests is indicated. Such reactions with these two drugs have been completely reversible. Because of altered acetylation pathways by enzyme induction following repeated heavy alcohol ingestion, there is a more frequent occurrence of elevation of liver transaminases in alcoholics treated with a hydrazine such as phenelzine (Nies, unpublished). One indication for treatment with the non-hydrazine tranylcypromine, is therefore, the presence of recent active alcoholic drinking.

SUMMARY

Recent evidence has clearly established the clinical efficacy of MAO inhibitors in the treatment of a variety of mood disorders ranging from patients with mixed endogenous-nonendogenous symptoms, several forms of atypical depression, and in panic states, phobic anxiety, agoraphobia, and 'hysteroid dysphoria'. Furthermore, phenelzine treatment has been shown to have significantly greater anti-anxiety effects in outpatients with depression whereas amitriptyline is only somewhat superior in relieving insomnia and other endogenous depressive symptoms. Retention of reactivity of mood, absence of terminal insomnia, and presence of somatic symptoms of anxiety are baseline symptoms which predict a better overall response rate to phenelzine (and other MAIOs) compared to tricyclics such as amitriptyline.

The MAOIs have a lower overall incidence of side effects compared to tricyclic antidepressant drugs. Furthermore, the lack of anticholinergic and cardiotoxic effects make them better tolerated, especially in the elderly patient. MAOIs can be prescribed with safety if proper precautions are observed including careful instruction of the patient. Additionally, a list of contraindicated foods and drugs should be provided to patients for use as immediate reference.

REFERENCES

Ananth, J. and Luchins, D. (1977) A review of combined tricyclic and MAOI therapy. Compr. Psychiatry 18, 221–230.

Blackwell, B., Marley, E., Price, J. and Taylor, D. (1967) Hypertensive interactions between monoamine oxidase inhibitors and foodstuffs. Br. J. Psychiatry 113, 349–365.

Bloch, R. G., Dooneief, A. S., Buchberg, A. S. and Spellman, S. (1954) The clinical effects of isoniazid and iproniazid in the treatment of pulmonary tuberculosis. Ann. Intern. Med. 40, 881–900.

Campbell, I. C., Robinson, D. S., Lovenberg, W. and Murphy, D. L. (1979) The effects of chronic regimens of clorgyline and pargyline on monoamine metabolism in the rat brain. J. Neurochem. 32, 49–55.

Crane, G. E. (1957) Iproniazid (Marsilid) phosphate, a therapeutic agent for mental disorders and debilitating disease. Psychiatr. Res. Rep. Am. Psychiatr. Assoc. 8, 142–152.

Davidson, J., McLeod, M. N. and Blum, R. (1978) Acetylation phenotype, platelet monoamine oxidase inhibition, and the effectiveness of phenelzine in depression. Am. J. Psychiatry 135, 467–469.

Davies, R. K., Tucker, G. J., Harrow, M. and Detre, T. (1971) Confusional episodes and antidepressant medication. Am. J. Psychiatry 128, 127–131.

Dubnick, B., Leeson, G. A. and Phillips, G. E. (1962) An effect of monoamine oxidase inhibitors on brain serotonin of mice in addition to that resulting from inhibition of monoamine oxidase. J. Neurochem. 9, 299–306.

Editorial (1976) New look at monoamine oxidase inhibitors. Br. Med. J. 2, 69.

Escobar, J. I., Schiele, B. C. and Zimmermann, R. (1974) The tranylcypromine isomers: a controlled trial. Am. J. Psychiatry 13, 1025–1026.

Evans, D. A. P., Davison, K. and Pratt, R. T. C. (1965) The influence of acetylator phenotype on the effects of treating depression with phenelzine. Clin. Pharmacol. Ther. 6, 430–435.

Garver, D. L. and Davis, J. M. (1979) Biogenic amine hypothesis of affective disorders. Life Sci. 24, 383–394.

Georgotas, A., Mann, J. and Friedman, E. (1981) Platelet MAO inhibition as a potential indicator of favorable response to MAOIs in geriatric depressions. Biol. Psychiatry 16, 997–1001.

Gey, K. F. and Pletscher, A. (1961) Activity of monoamine oxidase in relation to the 5-hydroxytryptamine and norepinephrine content of the rat brain J. Neurochem. 6, 239–243.

Hogben, G. L. and Cornfield, R. B. (1981) Treatment of traumatic war neurosis with phenelzine. Arch. Gen. Psychiatry 38, 440–445.

246

Johnstone, E. C. (1976) The relationship between acetylator status and inhibition of monoamine oxidase, excretion of free drug and antidepressant response in depressed patients on phenelzine. Psychopharmacologia 46, 289–294.

Johnstone, E. D. and Marsh, W. (1973) Acetylator status and response to phenelzine in depressed patients. Lancet 1, 567–570.

Kay, D. W. K., Garside, R. F. and Fahy, T. J. (1973) A double-blind trial of phenelzine and amitriptyline in depressed outpatients: a possible differential effect of the drugs on symptoms: Br. J. Psychiatry 123, 64–67.

Kendell, R. E. (1968) The Classification of Depressive Illness. Maudsley Mono. No. 18. Oxford University Press, New York.

Kline, N. S. (1958) Clinical experience with iproniazid (Marsilid). J. Clin. Exp. Psychopathol. 19 (Suppl. 1), 72–78.

Knoll, J. and Magyar, K. (1972) Some puzzling pharmacological effects of monoamine oxidase inhibitors. Adv. Biochem. Psychopharmacol. 5, 393–408.

Lebsack, M. E. and Anderson, A. D. (1978) Mechanism of inhibition of aldehyde dehydrogenase activity by pargyline. Curr. Alcohol. 3, 351–361.

Liebowitz, M. R. and Klein, D. F. (1981) Interrelationship of hysteroid dysphoria and borderline personality disorder. Psychiatr. Clin. North Am. 4 (1), 67–87.

Lipper, S., Murphy, D. L., Slater, S. and Buchsbaum, M. S. (1979) Comparative behavioral effects of clorgyline and pargyline in man: preliminary evaluation. Psychopharmacology 62, 123–128.

Manyam, N. V. B., Hare, T. A. and Katz, L. (1980) Effect of isoniazid on cerebrospinal fluid and plasma GABA levels in Huntington's disease. Life Sci. 26, 1303–1308.

Marshall, E. F., Mountjoy, C. Q., Campbell, I. C., Garside, R. F., Leitch, I. M. and Roth, M. (1978) The influence of acetylator phenotype on the outcome of treatment with phenelzine in a clinical trial. Br. J. Clin. Pharmacol. 6, 247–254.

Mountjoy, C. Q., Roth, M., Garside, R. F. and Leitch, I. M. (1977) A clinical trial of phenelzine in anxiety depressive and phobic neuroses. Br. J. Psychiatry 131, 486–492.

Nies, A., Robinson, D. S. and Lamborn, K. R. (1974) The efficacy of MAO inhibitor, phenelzine: dose effects and prediction of response. In: J. R. Boissier, H. Hippius and P. Pichot (Eds). Neuropsychopharmacology. Excerpta Medica, Amsterdam, pp. 765–770.

Nies, A., Howard, D. and Robinson, D. S. (1982) Antianxiety effects of MAO inhibitors. In: R. J. Matthew (Ed.), Biology of Anxiety. Brunner/Mazel, New York, pp. 123–133.

Ögren, J. O., Ask, A. L., Holm, A. C., Flarvall, L.-O., Lindbom, J., Lundström, J. and Ross, S. B. (1981) Biochemical and pharmacological properties of a new selective and reversible monoamine oxidase inhibitor FLA 336(+). In: M. B. H. Youdim and E. S. Paykel (Eds), Monoamine Oxidase Inhibitors: The State of the Art. John Wiley and Sons, New York, pp. 103–112.

Paykel, E. S., Parker, R. R., Penrose, R. J. J. and Rassaby, E. R. (1979) Depressive classification and prediction of response to phenelzine. Br. J. Psychiatry 134, 572–581.

Quitkin, F., Rifkin, A. and Klein, D. F. (1979) Monoamine oxidase inhibitors: a review of antidepressant effectiveness. Arch. Gen. Psychiatry 36, 749–760.

Raskin, A. (1972) Adverse reactions to phenelzine: results of a 9-hospital study. J. Clin. Pharmacol. 12, 22–25.

Raskin, A., Schulterbrandt, J. G., Reatig, N., Crook, T. H. and Olde, D. (1974) Depression subtypes and response to phenelzine, diazepam, and a placebo. Arch. Gen. Psychiatry 30, 66–75.

Ravaris, C. L., Nies, A., Robinson, D. S., Ives, J. O., Lamborn, K. R. and Korson, L. (1976) A multiple-dose control study of phenelzine in depressive-anxiety states. Arch. Gen. Psychiatry 33, 347–350.

Ravaris, C. L., Robinson, D. S., Ives, J. O., Nies, A. and Bartlett, D. (1980) A comparison of phenelzine and amitriptyline in the treatment of depression. Arch. Gen. Psychiatry 37, 347–350.

Robinson, D. S., Bovenberg, W., Keiser, H. and Sjoerdsma, A. (1968) The effects of drugs on human blood platelet and plasma monoamine oxidase activity in vitro and in vivo. Biochem. Pharmacol. 17, 109–119.

Robinson, D. S., Nies, A., Ravaris, C. L. and Lamborn, K. R. (1973) The monoamine oxidase inhibitor phenelzine, and the treatment of depressive-anxiety states. Arch. Gen. Psychiatry 29, 407–413.

Robinson, D. S., Nies, A., Ravaris, C. L., Ives, J. O. and Bartlett, D. (1978) Clinical pharmacology of phenelzine. Arch. Gen. Psychiatry 35, 629–635.

Robinson, D. S., Nies, A., Corcella, J., Cooper, T. B., Spencer, C. and Kefover, R. (1982) Cardio-vascular effects of antidepressants: differences between phenelzine and amitriptyline. J. Clin. Psychiatr. 43, 8–5.

Roth, M. (1959) The phobic anxiety-depersonalization syndrome. Proc. R. Soc. Med. 52, 587–595.

Rowan, P. R., Paykel, E. S., Parker, R. R., Gratehouse, J. M. and Rao, B. M. (1981) Tricyclic anti-depressants and MAO inhibitors: are there differential effects? In: M. B. H. Youdim and E. S. Pay-kel (Eds), Monoamine Oxidase Inhibitors: The State of the Art. John Wiley & Sons, New York, pp. 125–139.

Sargant, W. and Dally, P. (1962) Treatment of anxiety states by antidepressant drugs. Br. Med. J. 1, 509.

Scherbel, A. and Harrison, J. (1959) The effects of iproniazid and other amine oxidase inhibitors in rheumatoid arthritis. Ann. N.Y. Acad. Sci. 80, 820–830.

Schukit, M., Robins, E. and Feighner, J. (1971) Tricyclic antidepressants and monoamine oxidase inhibitors. Arch. Gen. Psychiatry 24, 509–514.

Selikoff, I. J., Robitzek, E. H. and Ornstein, G. G. (1952) Toxicity of hydrazine derivatives of isonicotinic acid in the chemotherapy of human tuberculosis. Q. Bull. Sea View Hosp. 13, 17.

Sheehan, D. V., Ballenger, J. and Jacobsen, G. (1980) Treatment of endogenous anxiety with phobic, hysterical, and hypochondriacal symptoms. Arch. Gen. Psychiatry 37, 51–59.

Solyom, L., Heseltine, G., McClure, D., Solyom, C., Ledwidge, B. and Steinberg, D. (1973) Beha-vior therapy versus drug therapy in the treatment of phobic neuroses. Can. Psychiatr. Assoc. J. 18, 25–32.

Tyrer, P., Candy, J. and Kelly, D. (1973) A study of the clinical effects of phenelzine and placebo in the treatment of phobic anxiety. Psychopharmacologia 32, 237–254.

West, E. D. and Dally, P. J. (1959) Effects of iproniazid in depressive syndromes. Br. Med. J. 1, 1491–1494.

White, K. and Simpson, A. M. (1981) Combined MAOI-tricyclic antidepressant treatment: a re-evaluation. J. Clin. Psychopharmacol. 1, 264–282.

Wyatt, R., Fram, D., Buchbinder, R. and Snyder, F. (1971) Treatment of intractable narcolepsy with a monoamine oxidase inhibitor. N. Engl. J. Med. 285, 3–7.

Zeller, E. A., Barksy, J. and Fouts, J. R. (1952) Influence of isonicotinic acid hydrazid (INH) and 1-isonicotinyl-2-isopropyl hydrazid (IIH) on bacterial and mammalian enzymes. Experientia 8, 349–350.

Section IV

STIMULANTS

Burrows/Norman/Davies (eds) Antidepressants
© *1983, Elsevier Science Publishers*

Chapter

Amphetamines and related stimulants as antidepressants

R. FRANCIS SCHLEMMER, JR., LOLITA O. ANG

and

JOHN M. DAVIS

Illinois State Psychiatric Institute, Chicago, Illinois, U.S.A.

INTRODUCTION

The catecholamine depletion hypothesis believed to be the underlying factor for depression has generated extensive studies on the efficacy of the various pharmacological agents for depression. Antidepressants, such as imipramine, act by decreasing the membrane reuptake of specific monoamines resulting in increased availability of the catecholamines in the central nervous system. Amphetamines and the other psychomotor stimulants, on the other hand, block the neuronal reuptake of norepinephrine and dopamine after releasing these catecholamines from presynaptic neurons. We review here the literature on the therapeutic use of the psychomotor stimulants as antidepressants. There has been only a limited number of studies since amphetamine has not been found to be effective as an antidepressant.

HISTORY

Amphetamine was first synthesized in 1887 by Edeleanu, but its potent pharmacological actions were not recognized until more than 40 years later (Piness et al., 1930). The first report of its CNS stimulant action came in 1933 (Alles, 1933) which led to the report that amphetamine had therapeutic value in the treatment of narcolepsy (Prinzmetal and

Bloomberg, 1935). Because of its known mood-elevating property, amphetamine was soon suggested as a treatment for depression (Alles, 1939), the d-isomer being a more potent stimulant than the l-isomer.

Over the years, however, amphetamine has not proven very useful in the long-term management of depression. Although some depressed patients may respond with a rapid, sometimes dramatic, elevation of mood, the effect usually wanes within a few days. Other patients treated with amphetamine may experience little change or even a worsening of their depressed state (Rudolph, 1956). With the introduction and acceptance of more effective tricyclic antidepressants and monoamine oxidase (MAO) inhibitors to the arsenal of antidepressant drugs during the 1960s, the use of amphetamine in the treatment of depression has fallen by the way, resulting in a limited investigation of the psychomotor stimulants as antidepressants.

AMPHETAMINE PHARMACOLOGY

Amphetamine and related compounds exert their potent effects on the central and the peripheral catecholamine systems to which the majority of their pharmacological effects have been attributed. Although amphetamine alters several synaptic processes, the combined effect is the facilitation of transmission in norepinephrine and dopamine systems.

Amphetamine is absorbed well from the GI tract and muscle tissue (Vree and Henderson, 1980). Once in the blood stream, amphetamine readily penetrates the blood-brain barrier as well as other highly perfused tissues (Axelrod, 1954). On the synaptic level, amphetamine acts to facilitate catecholamine transmission by affecting principally the release, and reuptake of norepinephrine and dopamine (Carlsson, 1970; Scheel-Kruger, 1972). Amphetamine also inhibits MAO, thereby slowing catecholamine breakdown, but is considerably weaker in this regard than clinically effective MAO inhibitors such as tranylcypromine and, therefore, this is probably only a minor component of its stimulant action (Glowinski et al., 1966). In addition, amphetamine may have a direct agonist effect on norepinephrine (Hoffer et al., 1971) and dopamine receptors (Feltz and DeChamplain, 1973). Again this effect must be minimal since alpha-methyl p-tyrosine (AMPT), which depletes pre-synaptic stores of catecholamines, effectively antagonizes the behavioural effects of amphetamine (Gunne et al., 1972; Garver et al., 1975; Kelly, 1977). Nonetheless, it should be kept in mind that despite the multiplicity of mechanisms by which amphetamine acts on catecholamine neurons, the end point common to each is a facilitation of norepinephrine and dopamine transmission.

Amphetamine derivatives act in a similar fashion to amphetamine to produce their stimulant effects, i.e., releasing catecholamines and inhibiting reuptake. However, one difference does exist which allows these agents to be divided into two groups – AMPT-sensitive and reserpine-sensitive (Table 1). As mentioned above, AMPT, an inhibitor of catecholamine synthesis, is a potent antagonist of the amphetamine effects (Scheel-Kruger, 1971; Gunne, 1972). This suggests that amphetamine action is dependent upon the availability of newly synthesized catecholamines presynaptically. This is also true for several amphetamine derivatives such as methamphetamine and phenmetrazine. In contrast, AMPT does *not* block the effects of another amphetamine derivative, methylphenidate, and drugs with similar stimulant actions like nomifensine and cocaine (Scheel-

TABLE 1

AMPT-sensitive drugs	Reserpine-sensitive drugs
d-Amphetamine	Methylphenidate
l-Amphetamine	Nomifensine
Methamphetamine	Cocaine
Phenmetrazine	

Kruger, 1971; Scheel-Kruger et al., 1977). Instead, the latter agents are antagonized by reserpine (Scheel-Kruger, 1971; Scheel-Kruger et al., 1977). Conversely, reserpine fails to antagonize the former drugs. Since reserpine acts by depleting presynaptic monoamine storage granules, this finding signifies that methylphenidate releases catecholamines stored in the older pools while amphetamine releases from the newer pools. The clinical significance of this difference is unclear at this time.

At higher doses, amphetamine releases serotonin from its pre-synaptic terminals (Fuxe and Ungerstedt, 1970). Again, the clinical significance of this effect is not known and may be irrelevant except in cases where extremely large doses of amphetamine are used.

CLINICAL APPLICATIONS

The psychomotor stimulants have been used in medicine for a wide variety of purposes. In child psychiatry they are used to treat attention deficit disorders (previously known as hyperactivity or minimal brain dysfunction). They have also been used for the treatment of narcolepsy. The psychomotor stimulants produce a mild euphoria. They are also taken to increase mental alertness during sleep deprivation, for example, by soldiers in combat situations, by truck drivers in long distance driving, or by students staying up at night studying. Because of their euphoriant properties they are also ingested for purposes of abuse. Before the tricyclic drugs and MAO inhibitors were discovered, they were used to some extent for depression.

The review here concerns their antidepressant actions. The pharmacologic parallels to any antidepressant actions would be their property of producing a mild euphoriant effect. However, it is important to keep conceptually distinct the true antidepressant effect from the euphoric effect that occurs in the first few days of the treatment with the psychomotor stimulant. Prior to the discovery of the true antidepressive agents, clinicians used amphetamines on patients with major depressive disorder resulting in some degree of relief of depressive symptoms for a day or two. But these agents did not prove to be effective long-term antidepressants. A new drug is born only after a series of open studies in which clinicians impressed with the efficacy of the drug pursue further by double-blind random studies verifying the efficacy of the drug. In the case of amphetamine, many experienced clinicians observed that amphetamine did not produce the true therapeutic benefit for depressed patients, when given over a course of 2 or 3 weeks. Some clinicians may feel that initial euphoria for a day or two may be helpful to some patients, while others may think that the same effect may not be helpful. Most clinicians, nevertheless, agree that amphetamine did not produce a true antidepressant effect in major depressive disorders analogous to that produced by ECT, tricyclic drug, or the MAO inhibitors. In situations where clinicians do not feel that a drug has any true beneficial effect, an in-depth investigation of that drug is often discontinued. Since the majority of clinicians felt that amphetamine was ineffective as a true antidepressant, it is not surprising that double-blind random assignments were not carried out. There is only a very limited literature on psychomotor stimulants as true antidepressants. We feel that this reflects the fact that clinicians did not feel these drugs were really antidepressants and, hence, were not motivated to carry out more systematic trials. It is important to keep in mind that depression is a heterogeneous disease. ECT and the tricyclics are the classical methods for treating major depressive disorders of a moderate or severe degree either in hospitalized depression, or in severe outpatient depression. Taking this into consideration, we will review the limited evidence of the use of amphetamines as antidepressants.

Overall et al. (1962) investigated the effectiveness of isocarboxazid, dextroamphetamine + amobarbital, and placebo on 204 patients with depressive syndromes in various Veterans Administration Hospitals. Of the 204 patients, 115 had neurotic depressive reactions, 10 with manic depressive psychosis, depressed type, 22 had psychotic depressed reactions, 23 with involutional reactions and 34 schizoaffective, depressed type. A fixed dosage schedule was used initially. In the first 3 days, total daily dosages of dextroamphetamine 10 mg + amobarbital 64 mg, isocarboxazid 10 mg, and imipramine 75 mg were given; in the next 3 days, maximal doses given were dextroamphetamine 20 mg + amobarbital 128 mg, isocarboxazid 20 mg and 150 mg of imipramine. From days 7 to 21, a total of dextroamphetamine 30 mg + amobarbital 192 mg, isocarboxazid 30 mg and imipramine 225 mg were administered. The dosage was flexible in the next 9 weeks. After 3 weeks of treatment, imipramine produced a statistically significant degree of improvement compared to the other treatment groups. The particularly relevant finding is that amobarbital + dextroamphetamine group did not improve to normal level any more than placebo either during the initial 3-week period or at any other time during the study. Thus, this group found the dextroamphetamine + amobarbital combination no better than placebo. Since clinicians have not observed amphetamine to be effective in the major depressive disorders, there have been few questions on this study. It is possible that amphetamine could have an antidepressant effect in a mild variant of the depressive disorder and not on the severe type.

Hare and his coworkers (1962) carried out a double-blind study on primary depressive disease including both endogenous and reactive depressives but excluding patients who had depressive symptoms associated with schizophrenia or organic brain disorder. Most patients were attending a psychiatric day hospital and a few inpatients were included. This was a random assignment double-blind study where patients received either phenelzine, lactose or dextroamphetamine (10 mg). Patients were evaluated for depression, anxiety and agitation. Patients on amphetamine had a slightly poorer response than the placebo group, but this difference was not statistically significant. This study failed to find amphetamine to be effective. Since a low dose of amphetamine was used, the results should be interpreted with caution. It is, indeed, possible that although amphetamine would not benefit classical major depressive disorder it might be of use in some mild depression. Particularly relevant to this are the studies of the British General Practitioner collaborative research group (1964) who evaluated the use of amphetamine in typical

TABLE 2

British general practice study. Acute depression – one week of treatment.

	Amphetamine	Placebo
Complete relief of symptoms	21 (20%)*	20 (25%)
Partial relief	48 (45%)	39 (49%)
No relief	38 (38%)	21 (26%)
Total number of subjects	107	80

* % of subjects

Chronic depression

	Amphetamine	Placebo
Complete relief	3 (16%)	4 (19%)
Partial relief	6 (32%)	8 (38%)
No effect	10 (53%)	9 (43%)
Total number of subjects	19	21

general practice patients. They analyzed their data separately for the acute depressions and for the chronic depressions. The dose was generally 5 mg amphetamine tablets given 2 or 3 times daily. The data on the results of treatment at the end of one week are presented in Table 2. In neither the acute depressive population nor in the chronic depressive population was amphetamine more effective than placebo. These investigators also reported the results for 2 and 4 weeks following treatment but did not observe any overall significant statistical differences between the two even though placebo appeared to be more effective than amphetamine. However, they did not report the effects a day or two after treatment. Therefore, we are uncertain what the acute effects may have been. Thus, these three control studies found no evidence for therapeutic antidepressant efficacy of amphetamine in any population of depressives.

Rickels and his coworkers (1970) investigated 120 mildly to moderately depressed patients who were all characterized as having the target symptoms of fatigue, apathy, or anorexia. Patients were subdivided as to whether they were seen in the clinic, in general practice, or in psychiatric practice. Patients were randomly assigned to methylphenidate, magnesium pemoline, and placebo. His group found a somewhat inconsistent beneficial effect of methylphenidate and magnesium pemoline in comparison to placebo. There was a significant difference seen on some measures but not on others. When a significant effect was seen it was generally an effect of a very modest degree. Insofar as the psychomotor stimulants produced better therapeutic effects than placebo, these effects tended to occur only in the general-practice patients.

Interpretation of this study is somewhat unclear since Rickels used an overall F test for drug differences, but he did not compare the therapeutic differences among the three drugs, such as methylphenidate versus placebo, magnesium pemoline versus placebo or methylphenidate versus magnesium pemoline. For example, in Figure 1 we see that there was a slight degree of improvement produced by methylphenidate and magnesium pemoline in comparison to placebo in the general-practice patients. On the other hand,

256

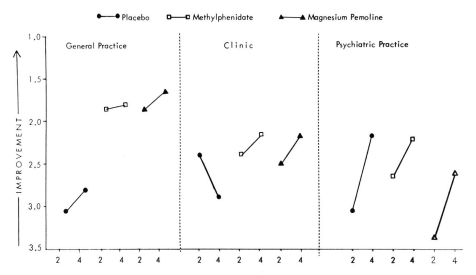

Fig. 1. Clinical improvement (adjusted means) in three populations of depressed patients after 2 and 4 weeks of treatment with methylphenidate, magnesium pemoline, and placebo. The y-axis represents the Physician Questionnaire total score and the x-axis represents weeks of treatment. Data from Rickels et al. (1970, 1972).

these drugs produced no beneficial effect greater than that produced by placebo in the psychiatric patients. The clinic group showed no effect at 2 weeks and a suggestion of an effect at 4 weeks. Rickels et al. (1972) performed a second study comparing methylphenidate against placebo in 101 mildly depressed outpatients suffering from fatigue, apathy, loss of interest or listlessness. In 2 weeks, they found virtually no significant differences. At 4 weeks using end-point analysis, they failed to find any significant differences on the Physicians Questionnaire (PQ) and the Physicians Depressed Scale (PDS) but did find some significant differences on some of the patient self-rating scales. It is of interest that those patients who drank three or more cups of coffee a day while on methylphenidate did produce significantly more improvement than the group on placebo who drank two cups of coffee or less per day. When used as a whole, the evidence that methylphenidate is clearly better than placebo is somewhat uncertain. Robin and Wiseberg (1958) performed a study on outpatient depressives suffering from a mild to moderate degree of depression. All patients had four or more of the following symptoms: a) sleep disturbance; b) loss of appetite and weight; c) impaired interest; d) lack of confidence; e) reduced alertness; or f) retardation or agitation. They did not observe any therapeutic differences between methylphenidate and placebo in a study of 40 depressed patients (the study originally started with 45 patients but 2 dropped out because of unpleasant side effects and 3 failed to complete the expected treatment period of one month). No improvement of depressive symptoms or increase in the rate of performance was observed in these patients who were given 10—20 mg of methylphenidate twice daily.

Some chronic schizophrenics are withdrawn and apathetic, symptoms similar to the negative symptoms of depression. It is reasonable to explore whether amphetamine in combination with neuroleptic can help the apathetic schizophrenics. Casey et al. (1961)

TABLE 3

Comparison of treatment with control groups.

	Methylphenidate	Placebo
Psychiatrists' Rating		
Much improved	2	2
Improved	7	11
No change	9*	10
Worse	2**	0

* Includes one patient who dropped out because the drug produced no effect.
** Includes two patients who developed increased tension.

studied 520 schizophrenics who were characterized as apathetic and withdrawn but physically healthy schizophrenic males. An activator drug was added to the maintenance dose of chlorpromazine. The drugs used were dextroamphetamine (60 mg maximum dose), isocarboxazid and trifluoperazine (30 mg), imipramine (225 mg) and placebo. Baseline measures used were the Inpatient Multidimensional Psychiatric Scale (IMPS) and the Psychotic Reaction Profile (PRP). The same measures were given 4 weeks and 20 weeks after treatment. None of the drug combinations was superior to chlorpromazine + placebo. Dextroamphetamine caused increased hostility. Therefore, adding amphetamine to chlorpromazine did not prove therapeutically helpful, but instead had a negative effect.

AMPHETAMINE AS A TEST TO PREDICT THERAPEUTIC RESPONSE TO IMIPRAMINE AND DESIPRAMINE

Although amphetamine has not been proven useful in the long-term treatment of depression, it may be useful in predicting response to the more effective antidepressant drugs. Tricyclic antidepressant therapy results in a significant improvement in depressive symptomatology in many but not all patients if the sufficient dosage is given for a sufficient length of time. However, several weeks may elapse before a therapeutic response is seen. On the other hand, the mood-elevating effects of amphetamine are rapid, but short-lived, in responding depressed patients. In an intriguing study, Fawcett and coworkers (1971, 1972) found that 7 out of 13 depressed patients who had a positive response to *d*-amphetamine eventually improved with imipramine or desipramine treatment. Of the remaining six patients who failed to respond to *d*-amphetamine, only one improved with imipramine or desipramine treatment. Coincidentally, amphetamine responders had a lower baseline urinary excretion of 3-methoxy-4-hydroxyphenethylene glycol (MHPG) than non-responders. MHPG is a major metabolite of norepinephrine in the brain and urinary levels of MHPG are thought to reflect the activity of noradrenergic neurons in the CNS (Maas and Landis, 1968). Amphetamine increased MHPG excretion in positive responders, but not in non-responders. Although these findings need to be replicated, results suggest that this test may be useful in severely depressed patients where there is an urgent need to immediately predict therepeutic response to tricyclics. In addition, this study suggests a link between noradrenergic mechanisms and the mood-elevating properties of amphetamine in depressed patients and their therapeutic response to two tricyclic antidepressants.

AMPHETAMINE WITHDRAWAL

Interestingly, depression occasionally accompanied by suicidal tendencies may occur during amphetamine withdrawal when large doses have been used (Connell, 1958). Schildkraut and coworkers (1971) have investigated this response in greater detail in four patients who had ingested high doses of amphetamine on a daily basis. While taking amphetamines, these patients were rated hypomanic on a mania-depression rating scale and had elevated levels of urinary MHPG. The patients became depressed within 24–48 hours after abrupt withdrawal, peaking approximately 24 hours later. The changes in urinary excretion of MHPG closely paralleled the clinical state with MHPG decreasing dramatically. These results suggest a decrease in norepinephrine turnover during amphetamine withdrawal. Similar large dose chronic treatment of rats with d-amphetamine results in a severe depletion of both norepinephrine and dopamine (Fuxe and Ungerstedt, 1970).

MECHANISM OF ANTIDEPRESSANT ACTIVITIY

Since amphetamine and its related psychomotor stimulants are not effective antidepressants in the long term, one would at least expect some distinguishing properties between these drugs and the effective antidepressant treatments. Recently, there has been considerable interest in the effect of the latter on beta-adrenergic receptors in the brain. Chronic treatment with clinically effective antidepressants including tricyclic antidepressants, MAO inhibitors, electroconvulsive shock, and newer antidepressant drugs (buproprion, trazodone, etc.) results in a reduction in beta-adrenergic receptor density in animal brain (Charney et al., 1981). Conversely, chronic amphetamine administration to rats fails to reduce the density of beta-adrenergic receptors (Banerjee et al., 1979; Sellinger-Barnette et al., 1980; G. N. Pandey, personal communication). A reduction in beta-adrenergic receptor density is believed to result from chronic potentiation of noradrenergic systems. Therefore, these results provide evidence that *chronic* amphetamine treatment does not result in potentiation of central noradrenergic transmission in animals.

TOLERANCE

Upon repeated administration, tolerance develops to several amphetamine-induced effects within a few days to a few weeks. However, tolerance does not develop to *all* amphetamine-induced effects. This appears to hold for amphetamine derivatives with similar stimulant properties as well. Thus, it is important to distinguish those effects to which tolerance develops from those to which it does not. A review of the literature failed to produce any conclusive evidence that tolerance does or does not develop to the antidepressant effect of psychomotor stimulants. There are anecdotal reports that the improvement seen in some depressed patients who are treated with d-amphetamine or methamphetamine wanes within a few days (Rudolf, 1949; Fawcett et al., 1972). Also, some studies elevate the drug dose during the study (Rudolf, 1949; Koutsky et al., 1960). Both suggest that tolerance may develop. Yet, the few properly controlled studies only report that there is no significant antidepressant activity one or more weeks into treatment. Since no results are given for the first few days of treatment, an acute antidepressant effect may be obscured. The Fawcett and Siomopoulos study (1971) demonstrated an immediate significant improvement in some depressed patients treated with d-amphetamine, but they did not administer amphetamine for more than 3–4 consecutive days. However, some depressed patients *failed* to show a significant improvement with d-amphetamine. In light of these findings, there appear to be two possible explanations for the lack of significant antidepressant activity of the psychomotor stimulants tested in the controlled, chronic studies: 1) there was an initial response to the drug, but tolerance developed prior to the first treatment evaluation one or more weeks into treatement; or 2) there was no significant response at any time during treatment. Therefore, a definitive statement regarding tolerance to the antidepressant effect of psychomotor stimulants cannot be made at this time.

It is also well recognized that amphetamine users desiring the euphoriant effect of this drug find it necessary to progressively increase the dose to maintain this effect upon repeated administration (Kramer et al., 1967). Again, well controlled studies in this area are lacking but there have been numerous reports of amphetamine users administering doses of 300–1,500 mg per day (Connell, 1958; Kramer et al., 1967). In a single-blind study, Rosenberg and coworkers (1963) have reported that tolerance developed to the 'mental activating effect' of d-amphetamine when doses up to 0.6 mg/kg/day were given for 13 days. Since the questionnaire was not detailed in the report it is not possible to assess the contribution of euphoria to this effect.

It is also assumed that tolerance develops to the cardiovascular effects of amphetamines since chronic users have administered up to 1 gram without incurring severe toxicities. There is little question that an acute dose of this magnitude would result in a fatal cardiovascular response. Tolerance even develops to the elevated systolic blood pressure with much lower doses of d-amphetamine (Rosenberg et al., 1963). In addition, tolerance develops to amphetamine-induced hyperthermia in animals (Harrison et al., 1952; Lewander, 1971) and humans (Rosenberg et al., 1963).

On the other hand, tolerance does not develop to some effects of psychomotor stimulants. In a review of the amphetamine psychosis literature, we found no case where a user who developed amphetamine psychosis improved while maintaining the same or greater dose of amphetamine (Davis and Schlemmer, 1980). The same was true for methamphetamine, phenmetrazine, and methylphenidate. Stereotyped behaviour induced in animals by psychomotor stimulants likewise fails to show tolerance (Segal and Mandell, 1974). In addition, children can be maintained on the same dose of methylphenidate and amphetamine for years in the treatment of attention deficit disorder suggesting that tolerance does not develop to this effect (Barkley, 1977).

The mechanism of amphetamine tolerance is uncertain and quite perplexing. Since amphetamine blood and brain levels are unchanged or higher than first dose levels in tolerant animals and human subjects, metabolic or dispositional tolerance can be ruled out (Mitchard et al., 1971, Caldwell et al., 1980). One conspicuous change that does occur upon repeated amphetamine administration is a rapid depletion of catecholamines, particularly norepinephrine, from their storage sites in central neurons (Fuxe and Ungerstedt, 1970). This finding led to the hypothesis that p-hydroxynorephedrine, a metabolite of amphetamine, may displace norepinephrine from its presynaptic storage sites and act as a false neurotransmitter upon release (Lewander, 1971). Therefore, with accumulation of p-hydroxynorephedrine from amphetamine metabolism during chronic treatment, less and less norepinephrine would be available for release and the response to amphetamine would rapidly dissipate over time. This would explain why tolerance develops to amphetamine for some behaviours (those mediated by norepinephrine), but not for others (those mediated by dopamine). Although evidence has been presented to support this hypothesis, further investigation has provided evidence which seriously questions the hypothesis. Guinea pigs who do not metabolize amphetamine to p-hydroxynorephedrine still develop tolerance to amphetamine (Caldwell et al., 1980). Tolerance develops to several amphetamine derivatives (e.g. phenmetrazine) which are not metabolized to p-hydroxynorephedrine. Perhaps the most important consideration is that p-hydroxynorephedrine is only a minor amphetamine metabolite in humans (Davis et al., 1971; Caldwell et al., 1980).

SIDE EFFECTS

The *acute toxic effects* of psychomotor stimulants are essentially extensions of their therapeutic effects and can largely be attributed to massive catecholamine release. Peripherally, the *cardiovascular* effects are prominent. Mild to moderate symptoms include palpitations, headache, pallor, and flushing. More severe toxicities include angina, cardiac arrhythmias, hypertention, hypotension, circulatory collapse, and cerebral haemorrhages. *Central nervous system* toxicities are also quite prominent. Initial toxicities may present as restlessness, talkativeness, irritability, tremor, dizziness, hyperreflexia, and insomnia. In more severe cases, symptoms can include hyperthermia, aggressive behaviour, suicidal or homicidal tendencies, anxiety, panic, paranoia, confusion, delirium, hallucinations, convulsions, coma, and death (Gleason, 1969; Weiner, 1980). Environmental influences can also be an important factor in stimulant toxicity. For example, athletes ingesting amphetamines to enhance performance may experience serious or even fatal heat exhaustion and cardiovascular collapse due to the combination of amphetamine-induced hyperthermia, warm temperature, and the excess body heat generated by physical exertion. Bernheim and Cox (1960) reported a case where a cyclist who had ingested 105 mg of amphetamine collapsed and died of cardiovascular collapse during a strenuous bicycle race. The symptoms closely resembled heat exhaustion.

There is considerable variability between individuals as to the acute toxic dose range, making it difficult to specify the toxic dose ranges. Mild toxicities may occur in some individuals well into the therapeutic dose range of amphetamine (2 mg). Severe toxicities reportedly have been seen at doses just above the therapeutic range (30 mg of amphetamine). One must also consider the state of health of the individual. Thus, persons with compensated cardiovascular function may be more vulnerable to stimulant toxicity. On the same token, there is evidence that persons with a history of endogenous psychosis (Janowsky et al., 1974) or drug-induced psychosis (Bell, 1973) may be particularly vulnerable to the psychotomimetic effects of amphetamines and methylphenidate. Moreover, drugs which enhance amphetamine effects (e.g MAO inhibitors) often lower the acute toxic dose (see section on Drug Interactions).

Treatment of acute intoxication with amphetamine and related compounds includes reduction of environmental stimulation and acidification of the urine with an agent, such as ammonium chloride, to enhance drug excretion (Anggard et al., 1970; Davies et al., 1971). If positive identification of amphetamine has been made, treatment with an anti-psychotic agent such as chlorpromazine will reduce CNS toxicities and help control hypertension (Espelin and Done, 1968). Additional treatment with alpha-adrenergic blockers may be necessary to reduce the elevated blood pressure. Barbiturates do not necessarily alleviate the CNS effects and may accentuate the hypertension induced by amphetamine (Bell, 1973), so are not recommended in the treatment of amphetamine intoxication.

Toxicities appearing later in the course of stimulant treatment present a somewhat different picture. Cardiovascular toxicities and hyperthermia are less likely to occur during chronic treatment since tolerance develops to these effects unless, of course, there is a very large, sudden escalation of dose during treatment. The most troublesome side effects in *chronic treatment* are the progressive symptoms involved in the development of stimulant-induced psychosis. The best known is the amphetamine psychosis (Connell, 1958; Davis and Schlemmer, 1980), but similar schizophreniform psychoses have been reported for methylphenidate (McCormick and McNeel, 1963), phenmetrazine (Evans, 1959) and cocaine (Post, 1975). Symptoms include varying degrees of paranoia and paranoid ideation, delusions of persecution, compulsive behaviour, autistic behaviour, auditory, visual, and tactile hallucinations, and general hyperactivity. Importantly, these persons are not disoriented (Snyder, 1972). The toxicities vary directly in intensity with dose, frequency of administration, and duration of treatment; however, again, there is considerable variability in severity from individual to individual (Davis and Schlemmer, 1980). Apparently, tolerance does not develop to the amphetamine psychosis induced by stimulants (Davis and Schlemmer, 1980) (see discussion in section on Tolerance). Therefore, repeatedly increasing the dose to overcome tolerance to amphetamines increases the risk for a schizophreniform psychosis to develop. This is an important consideration when contemplating a dosage increase to overcome tolerance to therapeutic effects of stimulants. In the case of depression, there is no evidence that depressed patients are less vulnerable or more vulnerable to the psychotomimetic effects of stimulant drugs than the normal population.

As with acute intoxication, the treatment of choice for chronic psychomotor-stimulant intoxication is reduction of sensory input, acidification of the urine, and administration of an antipsychotic agent.

DRUG INTERACTIONS

Because of the profound effects stimulants exert on central and peripheral catecholamine systems, numerous drug-drug interactions involving these agents have been documented. Perhaps the most subtle interaction, yet one that may have significant effect, is with agents that affect the pH of the urine. Drugs which make urine alkaline (e.g. ammonium chloride, acetazolamide) retard amphetamine excretion into the urine, thereby greatly prolonging its action (Davis et al., 1971). Conversely, urinary acidifiers (e.g. sodium bicarbonate) enhance excretion, thereby shortening the duration of action. To exemplify the profound effect this may have, Anggard and coworkers (1970) found that patients with amphetamine psychosis whose urine was made alkaline remained psychotic twice as long as similar patients whose urine was made acidic.

One of the major groups of drugs with which psychomotor stimulants interact is (predictably) agents which affect catecholamine systems. The most serious interaction appears to occur with MAO inhibitors. Since these agents inhibit one of the major deactivation mechanisms, more catecholamines are available presynaptically for release by psychomotor stimulants and are deactivated at a much slower rate because of the inhibition of MAO plus the inhibition of reuptake by the stimulant. Clinically, MAO inhibitors are known to greatly accentuate the effects of the amphetamines, leading to toxicities. Fatalities in patients taking this combination are not uncommon. One patient taking phenelzine died of a cerebral haemorrhage after taking only 20 mg of d-amphetamine (Lloyd et al., 1965). Severe headache, hypertensive crisis, cardiac arrhythmias, and extreme hyperthermia have also been reported (Martin, 1978; Hansten, 1979). MAO inhibitors bearing structural resemblance to amphetamine (e.g. phenelzine, tranylcypromine) may be particularly dangerous when used in combination with amphetamines (Hansten, 1979). It is also important to remember that some antibiotics, such as furazolidine, possess MAO-inhibitor properties.

By far, tricyclic antidepressants are the most frequently used form of drug therapy in the treatment of psychotic depression. The literature is sparse for clinical reports on concomitant use of tricyclics and stimulants. This is undoubtedly because of the theoretically dangerous practice of combining two classes of agents which individually possess potent adrenergic activating properties. However, methylphenidate inhibits the metabolism of the tricyclic antidepressant, imipramine (Perel et al., 1969; Wharton et al., 1971). Some clinicians have used this interaction to advantage. Wharton and coworkers (1971) in an uncontrolled, non-blind study of 7 patients, Flemenbaum (1971) in a preliminary uncontrolled study of 10 patients, and Cooper and Simpson (1973) in a single case report reported clinical improvement in these patients when methylphenidate was given in combination with imipramine or nortriptyline as opposed to the tricyclic alone. For imipramine, this improvement was attributed to increased blood levels of imipramine (Wharton et al., 1971; Cooper and Simpson, 1973). Nevertheless, one should view the concomitant use of psychomotor stimulants and tricyclic antidepressants with extreme caution because of the potential interaction at catecholamine synapses.

Other drugs which facilitate catecholamine transmission could theoretically potentiate the effect of amphetamines. These would include antiparkinsonian agents (e.g. L-dopa, bromocriptine) and certain drugs of abuse (e.g. cocaine, phencyclidine). Unfortunately, studies or reports in this area are lacking or difficult to interpret because of multiple drug use or lack of positive identification of the intoxicants.

On the other hand, drugs which inhibit catecholamine transmission tend to inhibit the action of psychomotor stimulants *provided* they do not rely on the presynaptic uptake mechanism to reach their site of action. Therefore, anti-psychotic agents (e.g chlorpromazine, haloperidol) which block dopaminergic and alpha-adrenergic receptors effectively antagonize the effects of amphetamine (Espelin and Done, 1968; Angrist et al., 1974). Many anti-hypertensive agents (e.g. phentolamine, prazosin) interfere with alpha-adrenergic transmission. Their antihypertensive effect may be compromised by the pressor effect of amphetamines. Amphetamine also antagonizes the effect of another antihypertensive agent, guanethidine, but through a different mechanism. To exert its antiadrenergic effect, guanethidine must be taken up into adrenergic neurons by the presynaptic uptake mechanism. Amphetamines block the uptake pump and, thus, block the uptake of guanethidine (Ober and Wang, 1973).

Lithium carbonate is particularly effective in the treatment of manic-depressive disorders and manic episodes. Since some cases of amphetamine intoxication resemble acute manic episodes or hypomania, the effect of lithium on amphetamine-induced behavioural changes has been studied clinically. Van Kammen and Murphy (1975) in a double-blind, controlled study, examined the effect of lithium on the euphoriant and activating properties of *d*- and *l*-amphetamine in seven depressed patients. Lithium significantly attenuated or antagonized these effects for both amphetamine isomers. Also, Flemenbaum (1974) has reported three cases in which patients undergoing lithium treatment ingested amphetamine or phenmetrazine. All reported diminished amphetamine effect. However, one case is complicated by the fact that the patient was also taking an antipsychotic agent which is also known to antagonize euphoriant and activating effects of amphetamine (Gunne et al., 1972; Angrist et al., 1974).

Finally, some interactions of amphetamines with opiate and opiate-like drugs have been noted. Small doses of amphetamine potentiate the effect of morphine and meperidine (Forrest et al., 1977). On the other hand, amphetamine may precipitate convulsions in cases of propoxyphene overdose (Martin, 1978). The mechanism for these interactions has not been clearly elucidated, but may result from an interaction between catecholamine and opiate peptide systems centrally.

CONCLUSIONS

Soon after amphetamine was introduced as a potentially useful sympathomimetic agent with potent mood-elevating properties approximately 50 years ago, it was used in the treatment of depression. For almost 20 years, only a small number of reports proclaimed the usefulness of amphetamine as an antidepressant. Then, effective antidepressant agents — tricyclic antidepressants and MAO inhibitors — were introduced and since then amphetamine has been seldom used in the treatment of depression. Even more recently introduced amphetamine derivatives have rarely been tested in the treatment of depression with the exception of methylphenidate. Only recently have a few proper randomized controlled studies been conducted on the antidepressant effects of these agents. They have confirmed what practitioners apparently realized years earlier, that amphetamines and related psychomotor stimulants were rarely more effective than placebo on improving depressive symptomatology. The lack of long-term effect and the potential complications arising from drug toxicities result in a low benefit-to-risk ratio for the depressed patient. We can only conclude that psychomotor stimulants are not useful in the treatment of depression.

REFERENCES

Alles, G. A. (1933) The comparative physiological actions of dl-Beta-phenylisopropylamines. I. Pressor effect and toxicity. J. Pharmacol. Exp. Ther. 47, 339–354.

264

Alles, G. A. (1939) Comparative actions of optically isomeric phenisopropylamines. J. Pharmacol. Exp. Ther. 66, 1.

Anggard, E., Gunne, L. M., Jonsson, L. M. and Niklasson, F. (1970) Pharmacokinetic and clinical studies on amphetamine dependent subjects. Eur. J. Clin. Pharmacol. 3, 3–11.

Angrist, B. M., Sathananthan, G., Wilk, S. and Gershon, S. (1974) Amphetamine psychosis: behavioral and biochemical aspects. J. Psychiatr. Res. 11, 13–23.

Axelrod, J. (1954) Studies on sympathominetic amines. II. The biotransformation and physiological disposition of d-amphetamine, d-p-hydroxyamphetamine, and d-methamphetamine, J. Pharmacol. Exp. Ther. 110, 315–326.

Banerjee, S. P., Sharma, V. K., Kung-Chung, L. S., Chanda, S. K. and Riggi, S. J. (1979) Cocaine and d-amphetamine induce changes in central beta-adrenoceptor sensitivity: effects of acute and chronic drug treatment. Brain Res. 175, 119–130.

Barkley, R. A. (1977) A review of stimulant drug research with hyperactive children. J. Child. Psychol. Psychiatry 18, 137–165.

Bell, D. S. (1973) The experimental reproduction of amphetamine psychosis. Arch. Gen. Psychiatry 29, 35–40.

Bernheim, J. and Cox, J. N. (1960) Amphetamine overdosage in an athlete. Br. Med. J. 2, 590.

Caldwell, J., Croft, J. E. and Sever, P. S. (1980) Tolerance to the amphetamines: an examination of possible mechanisms. In: J. Caldwell (Ed), Amphetamines and Related Stimulants: Chemical, Biological, Clinical, and Sociological Aspects. CRC, Boca Raton, pp. 131–146.

Carlsson, A. (1970) Amphetamine and brain catecholamines. In: E. Costa and S. Garattini (Eds), Amphetamine and Related Compounds. Raven Press, New York, pp. 289–300.

Casey, J. F., Hollister, L. E., Klett, C. J., Lasky, J. I. and Caffey, E. M. (1961) Combined drug therapy of chronic schizophrenics: controlled evaluation of placebo, dextroamphetamine, imipramine, isocarboxazid and trifluoperazine added to maintenance doses of chlorpromazine. Am. J. Psychiatry, 117, 997–1003.

Charney, D. S., Menkes, D. B. and Heninger, G. R. (1981) Receptor sensitivity and the mechanism of action of antidepressant treatment. Arch. Gen. Psychiatry 38, 1160–1180.

Connell, P. H. (1958) Amphetamine Psychosis. Maudsley Monographs, No. 5. Oxford University Press, London.

Cooper, T. B. and Simpson, G. M. (1973) Concomitant imipramine and methylphenidate administration: a case report. Am. J. Psychiatry 130, 721.

Davis, J. M. and Schlemmer, R. F., Jr. (1980) The amphetamine psychosis. In: J. Caldwell (Ed.), Amphetamines and Related Stimulants: Chemical, Biological, Clinical, and Sociological Aspects, CRC, Boca Raton, pp. 161–173.

Davis, J. M., Kopin, I. J., Lemberg, L. and Axelrod, J. (1971) Effects of urinary pH on amphetamine metabolism. Ann. N.Y. Acad. Sci. 179, 493–501.

Edeleanu, L. (1887) Ueber einige derivate der phenylmethyl-acrylsaure und der phenylisobutyler-saure. Chem. Ber. 20, 616.

Espelin, D. E. and Done, A. K. (1968) Amphetamine poisoning. Effectiveness of chlorpromazine. N. Engl. J. Med. 278, 1361–1362.

Evans, J. (1959) Psychosis and addiction to phenmetrazine (Preludin). Lancet i, 152–155.

Fawcett, J. and Siomopoulos, V. (1971) Dextroamphetamine response as a possible predictor of improvement with tricyclic therapy in depression. Arch. Gen. Psychiatry 25, 247–255.

Fawcett, J., Maas, J. W. and Dekirmenjian, H. (1972) Depression and MHPG excretion: response to dextroamphetamine and tricyclic antidepressants. Arch. Gen Psychiatry 26, 246–251.

Feltz, P. and DeChamplain, J. (1973) The postsynaptic effect of amphetamine on striatal dopamine-sensitive neurones. In: E. Udsin and S. H. Snyder (Eds), Frontiers in Catecholamine Research. Pergamon Press, New York, pp. 951–956.

Flemenbaum, A. (1971) Methylphenidate: a catalyst for the tricyclic antidepressant? Am. J. Psychiatry 128, 239.

Flemenbaum, A. (1974) Does lithium block the effects of amphetamines? A report of three cases. Am. J. Psychiatry 131, 820–821.

Forrest, W. H., Brown, B. W., Jr., Brown, C. R., Defalque, R., Gold, M., Gordon, E., James, K. E.,

Katz, J., Mahler, D. L., Schroff, P. and Teutsch, G. (1977) Dextroamphetamine with morphine for the treatment of postoperative pain. N. Engl. J. Med. 296, 712–715.

Fuxe, K. and Ungerstedt, U. (1970) Histochemical, biochemical, and functional studies on central monoamine neurons after acute and chronic amphetamine administration. In: E. Costa and S. Garattini (Eds), Amphetamines and Related Compounds. Raven Press, New York, pp. 257–288.

Garver, D. L., Schlemmer, R. F., Jr., Maas, J. W. and Davis, J. M. (1975) A schizophreniform behavioral psychosis mediated by dopamine. Am. J. Psychiatry 132, 33–38.

General Practitioner Research Group (1964) Report Number 51. Dexamphetamine compared with an inactive placebo in depression. Practitioner 192, 151–154.

Gleason, M. N. (1969) Amphetamines. In: Clinical Toxiology of Commercial Products. Williams & Wilkins, Baltimore, pp. 20–23.

Glowinski, J., Axelrod, J. and Iversen, L. L. (1966) Regional studies of catecholamines in the rat brain. IV. Effects of drugs on the disposition and the metabolism of ^{3}H-norepinephrine and ^{3}H-dopamine. J. Pharmacol. Exp. Ther. 153, 30–41.

Gunne, L. M., Anggard, E. and Jonsson, L. E. (1972) Clinical trials with amphetamine-blocking drugs. Psychiatr. Neurol. Neurochir. 75, 255–266.

Hansten, P. D. (1979) Drug interactions, 4th Ed. Lea & Febiger, Philadelphia.

Hare, E. H., Dominian, J. and Sharpe, L. (1962) Phenelzine and dexamphetamine in depressive illness: a comparative trial. Br. Med. J. 1, 9–12.

Harrison, J. W. E., Ambrus, C. M. and Ambrus, J. L. (1952) Tolerance of rats towards amphetamine and methamphetamine. J. Am. Pharm. Assoc., Sci. Ed. 41, 539–549.

Hoffer, B. J., Stiggins, G. R. and Bloom, F. E. (1971) Studies on norepinephrine-containing afferents to Purkinje cells of rat cerebellum. II. Sensitivity of Purkinje cells to norepinephrine and related substances administered by microiontophoresis. Brain Res. 25, 523–534.

Janowsky, D. S. and Davis, J. M. (1974) Dopamine, psychomotor stimulants, and schizophrenia. In: E. Usdin (Ed.), Neuropsychopharmacology of Monoamines and their Regulatory Enzymes. Raven Press, New York, pp. 317–323.

Kelly, P. H. (1977) Drug-induced motor behavior. In: L. L. Iversen, S. D. Iversen and S. H. Snyder (Eds), Drugs, Neurotransmitters, and Behavior, Handbook of Psychopharmacology, Vol. 8. Plenum Press, New York, pp. 295–331.

Koutsky, C. D., Westendorf, F. and Bransford, P. (1960) High dosage methylphenidate for depression. Dis. Nerv. Syst. 21, 275–277.

Kramer, J. C., Fischman, V. S. and Littlefield, D. G. (1967) Amphetamine abuse. J. Am. Med. Assoc. 201, 305–309.

Lewander, T. (1971) A mechanism for the development of tolerance to amphetamine in rats. Psychopharmacology 21, 17–31.

Lloyd, J. T. A. and Walker, D. R. H. (1965) Death after combined dexamphetamine and phenelzine. Br. Med. J. 2, 168–169.

Maas, J. W. and Landis, D. H. (1968) In vivo studies of the metabolism of norepinephrine in the central nervous system. J. Pharmacol. Exp. Ther. 163, 147–162.

Martin, E. W. (1978) Drug Interactions Index 1978/79. Lippincott, Philadelphia.

McCormick, T. C. and McNeel, T. W. (1963) Acute psychosis and Ritalin abuse. Tex. State J. Med. 59, 99–100.

Mitchard, M., Kumar, R., Salmon, J. A. and Shenoy, E. V. B. (1971) Plasma levels and excretion rates of amphetamine in a dexamphetamine tolerant man. Proc. Eur. Soc. Study Drug Toxic. 12, 72–77.

Ober, K. F. and Wang, R. I. H. (1973) Drug interactions with guanethidine. Clin. Pharmacol. Ther. 14, 190–195.

Overall, J., Hollister, L., Pokorny, A., Casey, J. and Katz, G. (1962) Drug therapy in depressions – controlled evaluation of imipramine, isocarboxazid, dextroamphetamine-amobarbital, and placebo. Clin. Pharmacol. Ther. 3, 16–22.

Perel, J. M., Black, N., Wharton, R. N. and Malitz, S. (1969) Inhibition of imipramine metabolism by methylphenidate. Fed. Proc. 28, 418.

Piness, G., Miller, H. and Alles, G. A. (1930) Clinical observations on phenylaminoethanol sulphate.

J. Am. Med. Assoc. 94, 790.

Post, R. M. (1975) Cocaine psychoses: a continuum model. Am. J. Psychiatry 132, 225–231.

Prinzmetal, M. and Bloomberg, W. (1935) The use of benzedrine for the treatment of narcolepsy. J. Am. Med. Assoc. 105, 2051–2054.

Rickels, K., Gordon, P., Gansman, D., Weise, C., Pereira-Ogan, J. and Hesbacher, P. (1970) Pemoline and methylphenidate in mildly depressed out-patients, Clin. Pharmacol. Ther. 11, 698–710.

Rickels, K., Gingrich, R., McLaughlin, F., Morris, R., Sablosky, L., Silverman, H. and Wentz, H. (1972) Methylphenidate in mildly depressed outpatients. Clin. Pharmacol. Ther. 13, 595–600.

Robin, A. and Wiseberg, S. (1958) A controlled trial of methylphenidate (Ritalin) in the treatment of depressive states. J. Neurol. Neurosurg. Psychiatry 21, 55–57.

Rosenberg, D. E., Wolbach, A. B., Jr., Miner, E. J. and Isbell, H. (1963) Observations on direct and cross tolerance with LSD and d-amphetamine in man. Psychopharmacology 5, 1–15.

Rudolf, G., DeM. (1949) The treatment of depression with desoxyephedrine (Methedrine). J. Ment. Sci. 95, 920–929.

Rudolf, G., DeM. (1956) The treatment of depression with methylamphetamine. J. Mental Sci. 102, 358–363.

Scheel-Krüger, J. (1971) Comparative studies of various amphetamine analogues demonstrating different interactions with metabolism of the catecholamines in the brain. Eur. J. Pharmacol. 14, 47–59.

Scheel-Krüger, J. (1972) Behavioral and biochemical comparison of amphetamine derivatives, cocaine, benztropine, and tricyclic antidepressant drugs. Eur. J. Pharmacol. 18, 63–73.

Scheel-Krüger, J., Braestrup, C., Nielson, M., Golembiouska, K. and Mogilinicka, E. (1977) Cocaine: discussion on the role of dopamine in the biochemical mechanism of action. In: E. H. Ellinwood, Jr and M. M. Kilbey (Eds), Cocaine and Other Stimulants. Plenum Press, New York, pp. 373–407.

Schildkraut, J. J., Watson, R., Draskoczy, P. R. and Hartmann, E. (1971) Amphetamine withdrawal: depression and MHPG excretion. Lancet ii, 485–486.

Segal, D. S. and Mandell, A. J. (1974) Long-term administration of d-amphetamine: progressive augmentation of motor activity and stereotypy. Pharmacol. Biochem. Behav. 2, 249–255.

Sellinger-Barnette, M. M., Mendels, J. and Frazer, A. (1980) The effect of psychoactive drugs on beta-adrenergic receptor binding sites in rat brain. Neuropharmacology 19, 447–454.

Snyder, S. H. (1972) Catecholamines in the brain as mediators of amphetamine psychosis. Arch. Gen. Psychiatry 27, 169–170.

Van Kammen, D. P. and Murphy, D. L. (1975) Attenuation of the euphoriant and activating effects of d- and l-amphetamine by lithium carbonate treatment. Psychopharmacology 44, 215–244.

Vree, T. B. and Henderson, P. T. (1980) Pharmacokinetics of amphetamines: in vivo and in vitro studies of factors governing their elimination. In: J. Caldwell (Ed.), Amphetamines and Related Stimulants: Chemical, Biological, Clinical, and Sociological Aspects, Chap. 4. CRC, Boca Raton, pp. 47–68.

Weiner, N. (1980) Norepinephrine, epinephrine, and the sympathomimetic amines. In: A. G. Gilman, L. S. Goodman and A. Gilman (Eds), The Pharmacological Basis of Therapeutics. Macmillan Press, New York, pp. 138–175.

Wharton, R. N., Perel, J. M., Dayton, P. G. and Malitz, S. (1971) A potential clinical use for methylphenidate with tricyclic antidepressants. Am. J. Psychiatry 127, 1619–1625.

Section V

LITHIUM

Chapter 18

Lithium treatment: Problems and precautions

MOGENS SCHOU

and

PER VESTERGAARD

*The Psychopharmacology Research Unit, Aarhus University Institute of Psychiatry
and the Psychiatric Hospital, DK-8240 Risskov, Denmark*

INTRODUCTION

The main aim and art of lithium treatment is to administer the drug in such a way that the patients obtain maximum therapeutic and prophylactic benefit with a minimum of inconvenience and risk. In the present chapter we concentrate on topics which are controversial or in need of emphasis, or which have been brought into focus by recent developments in lithium treatment and research. We shall deal first with special problems and the precautions they necessitate. Thereafter we discuss general safeguards and control measures. At the end there is a list of supplementary reading.

PROBLEMS

Side effects

Side effects which are particularly frequent or may be especially troublesome during lithium treatment include thirst, nycturia, weight gain, hand tremor, diarrhoea, acne, psoriasis, goitre, and myxoedema. No effort should be spared to administer and monitor treatment in such a way that side effects are minimized. We concentrate here on the effect of long-term lithium administration on thyroid and kidney function.

Development of goitre or myxoedema is reported with varying frequency in different

270

studies, but they occur sufficiently often to require attention. Once diagnosed, they are easy to treat through administration of thyroid hormone concurrently with lithium; this leads to complete normalization of thyroid function in spite of continued lithium treatment. It is important, however, that psychiatrists are alert to their possible development, so that an incipient myxoedema is not misdiagnosed as a depressive relapse. Moreover, lithium treatment may lead to elevation of serum TSH which, if it is sufficiently pronounced, may be associated with reduction of serum T_4 and constitute indication for treatment with thyroid hormone even in the absence of clinical signs and symptoms. It is therefore advisable that serum TSH is determined at intervals during long-term lithium treatment, for example, every 6 months.

Lithium effects on the kidneys have attracted particular attention since 6 years ago reports were published of morphological kidney changes in patients given long-term lithium treatment. These reports have been followed by extensive research activity. At the present time kidney morphology has been studied in more than 150 and kidney function in more than 2,000 lithium-treated patients, and it is possible to draw at least tentative conclusions concerning the effects of long-term lithium treatment on the kidneys. Expressed briefly, the studies have shown that morphological kidney changes can be found in perhaps 10–20% of the patients, but similar changes of an unspecific nature seem to occur to almost the same extent in manic-depressive patients who have not yet been started on lithium. The primary functional activity of the kidneys, glomerular filtration, is largely unaffected by long-term lithium treatment; glomerular filtration rates lower than 50% of the normal are extremely rare, and the risk of progressive renal deficiency with terminal azotaemia is remote, even in patients given lithium treatment for many years.

In a number of lithium-treated patients renal water reabsorption is impaired, and this leads to polyuria and polydipsia. These side effects may be troublesome for the patients, but they are not dangerous. They are not in themselves associated with reduction of renal lithium elimination or elevation of the serum lithium concentration. However, because of the lowered renal concentrating ability these patients become dehydrated easily if fluid intake is restricted or if additional fluid is lost. Dehydration may lead to fall of renal lithium clearance and risk of lithium poisoning. Patients in lithium treatment should be instructed to drink amply under conditions which involve risk of negative water balance. Re-establishment of normal concentrating ability after discontinuation of lithium is slow and may be incomplete.

The mechanism underlying lithium-induced polyuria is inhibition of the response of the distal tubules and collecting ducts to the action of the antidiuretic hormone. We are, in other words, dealing with a functional change akin to renal diabetes insipidus, and it is therefore not astonishing that treatment of lithium-induced polyuria with vasopressin or vasopressin analogues has given unsatisfactory results. Administration of diuretic drugs may in this condition, as in other conditions with lowered renal water reabsorption, lead to a reduction of the urine flow, but due to its effects on sodium and water balance such treatment may lower the renal lithium clearance and thereby expose the patients to risk of lithium poisoning. Treatment of lithium-induced polyuria with diuretics should therefore be used with caution.

Lithium-induced impairment of renal water reabsorption seems to increase with increasing duration of the treatment and with the magnitude of the serum lithium concentration. It is accordingly these two factors that must be considered in a discussion of the possible prevention of lithium-induced polyuria. The duration of the lithium treatment is determined by the course of the patients' illness and the risk of relapse if lithium is discontinued; in most cases this variable is therefore not amenable to manipulation. The situation is somewhat different with the serum lithium concentration. It seems as if clinics which maintain their patients at 12-hour serum lithium levels of 0.8–0.9 mmol/l encounter lithium-induced polyuria and polydipsia more frequently than do clinics in which the patients are maintained at levels of 0.6–0.7 mmol/l, and treatment results do not seem to be strikingly less good in the latter than in the former clinics. For the prevention of lithium-induced polyuria and polydipsia it may therefore be important to maintain patients at the lowest lithium dosages and serum lithium levels which are compatible with effective protection against manic and depressive relapses. Use of the lowest effective dosages and serum levels may lead to reduction of also other side effects, those which may be associated with the polyuria/polydipsia (thirst, nycturia with disturbed sleep, weight gain if patients do not avoid calorie-rich drinks, increased blood pressure secondary to weight gain, etc.) as well as others, for example lithium-induced hand tremor.

Lithium poisoning

The main risk to patients in lithium treatment is the development of lithium poisoning. This condition is dangerous; it affects the central nervous system, the kidneys and the fluid/electrolyte balance; and it has in some cases led to death, in others to permanent neurological after-effects. Patients with lithium poisoning must be given the same corrective and supportive therapy that is used for narcotic poisoning, and haemodialysis should be considered in all but the mildest cases.

Two features of lithium poisoning are worth noting: 1) it does not develop capriciously and without reason; and 2) it does not develop suddenly and without warning. There are certain situations and conditions in which there is an increased risk that patients may develop poisoning, and it is important that physicians and patients know them. Lithium is accumulated, and the accumulation may lead to poisoning, if more lithium is administered than can be excreted through the kidneys. The renal lithium clearance may fall as a result of kidney disease, but is may also be lowered in situations with manifest or impending negative sodium balance or negative water balance. These are accordingly the circumstances one should guard against through clinical and laboratory monitoring. Negative sodium and water balance may result from intake of a low-salt diet, start of a slimming diet, start of treatment with diuretic drugs, salt and fluid loss caused by heavy sweating, physical disease with fever and lowered intake of food and fluid, etc.

A fully developed lithium poisoning may resemble cerebral haemorrhage. There is marked apathy or coma, the patients look ill, epileptic seizures may occur, and kidney function and fluid/electrolyte balance may be deranged. This picture of severe lithium poisoning is, however, preceded for some days by more subtle signs and symptoms, and these warning signals of impending intoxication should be memorized by patients, relatives and physicians. They are: apathy, sleepiness, lowered concentrating ability, muscle weakness, heaviness of the limbs, unsteady gait, strong and possibly irregular hand tremor, slight muscle twitchings, indistinct speech, nausea, vomiting, stomach ache, and diarrhoea. The symptoms are rarely present all at once. If one or more of these signs becomes prominent, the patient must contact the doctor as soon as possible for clinical and laboratory examination.

Non-adherence and non-compliance

It has been estimated that 20–30% of patients starting prophylactic lithium treatment stop the treatment again before the end of 6 months. For one reason or another they do not adhere to the treatment. Among patients who do adhere to the treatment some may be negligent about the tablet intake for shorter or longer periods of time without their physician's knowledge or consent. The frequency of such non-compliance is presumably limited to some extent by the patients' knowledge about the blood control, but some patients may take their tablets regularly only during the last days before the control.

Non-adherence and non-compliance may interfere seriously with the efficacy of lithium treatment. If treatment prescribed on weighty psychiatric indication is not taken, the consequences may involve family disrupture, social and occupational disability, need for readmission to hospital, and suicide attempts.

An examination of the factors which characterize non-adhering and non-complying patients may serve to identify those who perhaps should never have been started on lithium or who, if started, should have been given attention over and above that offered in the usual treatment regimen. Such factors may include the diagnosis; schizo-affective patients probably discontinue or neglect treatment more often than do manic-depressive patients without schizophrenic features. The treatment setting may also be of importance, and negative factors may include inconvenient clinic location or clinic hours, inadequate clinical supervision by physician and other health personnel, frequent change of treating physician, etc. Patients may discontinue or neglect treatment because they harbour misconceptions about the disease, or because the family is unstable or fails to give support. The development of side effects may be associated with non-adherence and non-compliance, whereas such demographic factors as age, sex, education, and income seem to be of less importance.

The reasons given by the patients themselves for not taking the medication also merit attention. Patients may, for example, feel bothered by the notion that their mood is controlled by drugs, or they may resent the idea of suffering from a chronic illness which is constantly kept in mind by the daily lithium intake. They may miss hypomanic or manic episodes and in this connection feel less creative and productive and perhaps less attractive sexually. Side effects of lithium treatment are often given as a reason for discontinuation or negligence, the most prominent being weight gain, troublesome hand tremor, and polyuria/polydipsia with nycturia disturbing sleep.

Management of non-adherence and non-compliance has two aspects: patients who are especially prone to this behaviour should not be started on lithium, or they should from the very start of the treatment be given special attention. Furthermore, in the clinical monitoring of lithium treatment patients and physicians should communicate freely, so that developments which might lead the patients to discontinue treatment are made the subject of discussion and joint decision.

Pregnancy and breast-feeding

When the International Lithium Baby Register stopped its information collection in 1979 a total of 217 children had been reported, children born to mothers who had been given lithium during at least the first 3 months of pregnancy. Of these 217 children 25 showed malformations, and in 18 of the children the malformations involved the heart and the big vessels. The data indicate, although they do not prove, that lithium may exert teratogenic action on the human cardiovascular system. It seems therefore in general advisable to discontinue lithium treatment in a woman who plans to become pregnant, to stop treatment as soon as possible after an unplanned pregnancy has been discovered, and not to start the treatment again until after the first third or half of the pregnancy has passed. Decision about stopping lithium treatment must, however, be made with proper regard to the individual patient's situation, including the intensity of the parents' wish to have a child as well as past experiences about the frequency and severity of relapses when lithium was not given. The decision should be made in consultation with the fully informed parents. It is debatable whether the occurrence of conception during lithium treatment may constitute indication for induced abortion. Women in lithium treatment should use contraceptive measures.

It is not known whether the fetus may be exposed to risk if the father is on lithium at the time of conception.

Late pregnancy and delivery are associated with marked changes of glomerular filtration rate and lithium clearance. Lithium treatment should therefore be monitored with particular care during these periods, and it may be wise to discontinue lithium immediately before delivery and start it again a few days after.

Lithium passes from the blood into the milk, and the nursing child's serum lithium concentration is 1/10–1/2 of the mother's. It is not known whether these concentrations expose the infant to risk, but observations on rats nursed by lithium-treated mothers indicate that the kidneys may be particularly sensitive to lithium immediately after delivery. It seems advisable that women in lithium treatment bottle-feed rather than breast-feed their children.

Interactions

Lithium interactions fall into two categories, namely: 1) drug interactions and 2) interactions with situations and drug treatments which may affect sodium and/or water balance. The latter kind of interaction has been dealt with above.

The most frequent combinations are those with neuroleptic drugs and antidepressant drugs. Reports indicate that interaction with neuroleptics may occur and take the form of increased frequency of mild neurological side effects. On the other hand, extensive surveys of large patient groups given lithium together with neuroleptics show that major or lasting neurological damage is extremely rare when moderate doses are administered under proper supervision. The combination of neuroleptics and lithium often offers advantage in the treatment of acute mania and schizo-affective illness.

Combination of lithium and antidepressants is more controversial. Patients who develop depressive relapses during prophylactic lithium treatment are usually treated with antidepressant drugs, and there is evidence that the two drugs do not counteract and may even potentiate each other. But often the antidepressant drugs are continued after disappearance of the depression, in many instances for long periods of time, and this may be disadvantageous. The administration of antidepressant drugs together with lithium may antagonize the stabilizing effect of the latter, may precipitate manic and, secondarily, depressive relapses, and may convert patients into 'rapid' or 'continuous' cyclers. Further systematic studies are required for documentation of this interaction, but suggestive observations have been reported with sufficient frequency to merit serious consideration and to call into question the advisability of administering long-term treatment with lithium and antidepressant drugs concurrently.

Other drug interactions with lithium have been reported. For some drugs (morphine, codeine, dextropropoxyphene, amphetamine, methylphenidate) the reports are based on animal studies, and the clinical significance of the interaction is unclear. For other drugs (digoxin, diazepam, mazindol) the reports are based on a single or a few cases; the occurrences may have been coincidental. Some drugs (indomethacin, phenylbutazone, ketoprofen, oxyphenbutazone, diclofenac) seem to interfere with the renal elimination of lithium, and their use may lead to lithium accumulation. Administration of pancuronium bromide or succinylcholine to lithium-treated patients has occasionally led to prolonged neuromuscular blockade.

Patients who suffer a depressive relapse during lithium treatment are sometimes given additional electric convulsive treatment. Such combination therapy has occasionally led to the development of transitory organic brain syndromes with confusion, restlessness, disorientation, and EEG seizure activity. No systematic studies have yet been carried out to determine the frequency of this occurrence, and it is not clear whether discontinuation of lithium a few days before ECT offers advantage.

CLINICAL AND LABORATORY MONITORING

Safe and effective lithium treatment must be based on close co-operation between patients, relatives and physician. The selection of patients for prophylactic lithium treatment has been discussed earlier in the chapter. Once a patient has been selected, a medical history should be taken for the identification of patients at particular risk, for example, because of disease of the kidneys, the heart, the central nervous system or the thyroid. Appropriate physical and laboratory examinations should be carried out before treatment starts; the latter may include baseline values for serum creatinine, serum TSH and body weight.

In addition to regular consultations for clinical and laboratory examination the patients should seek contact on the occurrence of unwanted developments: manic or depressive relapses, side effects, signs of impending intoxication, etc. Patients and relatives should be given detailed instructions about treatment principles and management so that ineffectual dosages and adverse reactions can be detected early. They should be informed about the risk situations and danger signs mentioned above, and the importance of adequate intakes of salt and water should be emphasized. Patient and physician should jointly cope with problems that might lead to non-adherence or non-compliance.

Instruction of patients must be comprehensive, easily understandable, and readily available; the information should be given both before treatment starts and currently during the treatment; and it should be presented not only verbally but also in written form. Instruction sheets and folders as well as more detailed treatment guide books are available.

There is not general agreement about the kind and number of laboratory tests which should be carried out during long-term lithium treatment. The 'kidney scare' of recent years has led to proposals that patients should be subjected to extensive examinations of glomerular filtration rate and renal concentrating ability at yearly or half-yearly intervals. However, since the lithium-kidney studies did not reveal progressive deterioration of glomerular filtration as a result of the treatment, regular and extensive examinations of glomerular filtration rate are hardly mandatory for the safe use of lithium. On the other hand, glomerular filtration may fall for other reasons, for example, intercurrent kidney disease, use of analgesics, etc., and since a fall of glomerular filtration leads to a fall of lithium clearance, it is important that such changes are detected. A consistent rise of the serum lithium concentration during administration of constant dosage may be an early signal that the kidney function is undergoing change and should lead to closer clinical and laboratory examination. It may be advisable to supplement determinations of the serum lithium concentration with determinations of the serum creatinine concentration, but attention should again be focused on changes of the latter value rather than on absolute levels. A consistently rising serum creatinine can be a danger sign even at levels which are below the upper normal limit.

Proposals have also been made that the patients' renal concentrating ability should be determined at regular intervals, for example, through measurement of urine osmolality or specific gravity after thirst or after administration of vasopressin or vasopressin analogues. Such determinations may admittedly be of interest for clinics doing research on the treatment and prevention of this particular side effect, but we do not think that they provide information of such value for therapeutic decisions that it justifies the effort and inconvenience involved in their use on a routine basis. Even if a patient's maximum urine osmolality falls, this does not constitute ground for discontinuing properly indicated, prophylactically effective, and otherwise well tolerated lithium treatment.

In well instructed patients under adequate clinical control only a limited number of regular laboratory tests would seem strictly required during long-term lithium treatment, and we present here for consideration routine determinations of serum lithium and serum creatinine every 3 months (more frequently in the beginning) and of serum TSH every 6 months. The appearance of unexpected signs and symptoms should lead to closer clinical and laboratory examination.

During lithium treatment determination of the serum lithium concentration serves two purposes. The *absolute* value of the serum concentration is a measure of the degree to which the organism is exposed to lithium, and it is this concentration which should be adjusted to, and then maintained at, a level which in the individual patient provides a maximum of therapeutic and prophylactic benefit and a minimum of inconvenience and risk. In addition, *change* of the serum lithium concentration with unaltered dosage is a sensitive indicator of change in the renal ability to eliminate lithium. A consistent rise of the serum lithium concentration shows that there has been a fall of the lithium clearance and should lead to closer clinical and laboratory examination.

In order to serve these two purposes reliably, the serum lithium concentration must be determined under standardized conditions, for example, in blood samples drawn in the morning 12 hours (± 1 hour) after the last intake of lithium and under steady-state conditions, i.e. at least 4–5 days after start of treatment and after dosage changes. If blood samples are drawn under other conditions, serum lithium values may be grossly misleading and may give rise to unwarranted and possibly harmful dosage changes.

REFERENCES

Amdisen, A. and Schou, M. (1980) Lithium. In: M. N. G. Dukes (Ed.), Meyler's Side Effects of Drugs, 9th Ed. Excerpta Medica, Amsterdam–Oxford–Princeton, pp. 43–50.

Jefferson, J. W. and Greist, J. H. (1977) Primer of Lithium Therapy. Williams and Wilkins, Baltimore.

Johnson, F. N. (1980) Handbook of Lithium Therapy. MTP Press, Lancaster.

Schou, M. (1983) Lithium Treatment of Manic-Depressive Illness: A Practical Guide, 2nd revised edn. Karger, Basel–München–Paris–London–New York–Sydney.

Vestergaard, P. (1981) Clinically important side effects of long-term lithium treatment: a review. Acta Psychiatr. Scand. (in press).

Vestergaard, P., Schou, M. and Thomsen, K. (1982) Monitoring of patients in prophylactic lithium treatment: an assessment based on recent kidney studies. Br. J. Psychiatry 140, 185–187.

Burrows/Norman/Davies (eds) Antidepressants
© *1983, Elsevier Science Publishers*

Chapter 19

Lithium: Clinical applications

RONALD R. FIEVE

Department of Clinical Psychiatry, Columbia Presbyterian Medical Center and Foundation for Depression and Manic Depression, New York, U.S.A.

and

ERIC D. PESELOW

Department of Psychiatry, New York University School of Medicine and Foundation for Depression and Manic Depression, New York, U.S.A.

LITHIUM: CLINICAL USES

Lithium was discovered in 1817 by Arfvedson when he isolated it from the mineral petalite. Over the next 130 years lithium was used as an anti-convulsant, hypnotic, and in the treatment of urinary calculi and gout.

However, in the 1940s lithium was used as a salt substitute in cardiovascular and hypertensive heart disease with extreme toxicity and three deaths (Corcoran et al., 1949, Talbott, 1950). This resulted in lithium being given a notorious reputation throughout the American community and resulted in lithium being withdrawn from the American market in 1950. This unfortunate alarm for lithium tended to dampen the revolutionary discovery of Cade (1949) who, working independently in Australia, noted a marked attenuation of manic symptomatology when he gave lithium to 10 manic patients and noted a relapse in one of the patients when he withdrew the lithium.

Because of the aforementioned toxic hazards, the concurrent discovery of other psychotropic agents (chlorpromazine) for which frequent blood monitoring was not necessary, and the lack of diagnostic precision in psychiatry it took over two decades before lithium received official recognition as an efficacious treatment in psychiatric illness. The American

TABLE 1

Lithium in the treatment of acute mania.

Lithium vs. Placebo

Investigator	Design	No. of patients	Results	Comments
Schou et al., 1954	Double-blind 2 week cross-over (lithium vs. placebo) in 30 'typical' manics and 8 'atypical' manics. Patients were given 900–1,800 mg/day	38	14 patients showed positive response and 18 others showed a possible response. 90% positive or possible response in typical manics (27/30) and 62.5% response in atypical manics (5/8)	8 atypical manics who showed delusions and hallucinations had a significant affective component and would probably be classified manic according to DSM III
Maggs, 1963	Double-blind crossover of lithium vs. placebo over 6 weeks. Patient given lithium or placebo the first 2 weeks then no therapy, weeks 3 and 4 alternate therapy of first 2 weeks for 5 and 6. Patients given fixed dose of 1,500 mg/day	28	Lithium superior to placebo in decreasing scores of manic symptoms on Wittenborn scale	10 of 28 patients did not complete study. Lack of diagnostic criteria and high drop-out rate are main drawbacks of the study
Fieve et al., 1968	Double-blind lithium-placebo crossover	35	28 patients responded completely to lithium (80%) and 2 patients had some improvement (6%)	Study did not report on patients response to placebo, nor did it report the length of time followed
Bunney et al., 1968	Longitudinal double-blind crossover of lithium vs. placebo	2	Improvement in 2 patients while on lithium with corresponding of manic symptoms within 24 hrs of switching to placebo	Increase in symptoms correlated with fall in serum lithium levels

Study	N	Method	Results	Comments
Goodwin et al., 1969	12	Longitudinal double-blind lithium-placebo crossover in 12 acutely manic patients. Patients received 900–1,800 mg/day of lithium maintaining levels of 0.8–1.3 mEq/L	8 of 12 patients had complete response to lithium. One had partial response and 3 became worse. 5 of 8 lithium responders relapsed when switched to placebo	All patients did worse on placebo vs. lithium. Crossover non-random
Stokes et al., 1971	38	Longitudinal non-random crossover in 38 acutely manic patients given lithium or placebo over 7–10 day periods	75% of patients on lithium improved within 7–10 days, whereas 18% worsened	Lack of randomization, lack of washout period between lithium and placebo and short trial period are methodological flaws

Lithium vs. Neuroleptics

Study	N	Method	Results	Comments
Johnson et al., 1968	29	29 manic-depressive patients randomized to lithium or chlorpromazine (CPZ) (lithium level 1.0–2.5 mEq/L. CPZ dose 200–1,800 mg/day) for 21 days after an average 5-day washout	14 of 18 lithium-treated patients showed marked improvement or complete remission while only 4 of 11 manics on CPZ showed marked improvement	The finding of lithium's superiority to CPZ specifically in the area of normalization of affect and ideation was based on clinical impression only
Johnson et al., 1971	21	21 manic-depressive patients randomized to lithium or CPZ (lithium level 1.0 mEq/L, CPZ dose 200–2,000 mg/day) for 21 days after a 5–7 day placebo period; 13 patients were randomized to lithium and 8 to CPZ	Lithium demonstrated trends toward greater improvement in psychopathology than CPZ based on BPRS, CGI, NOSIE, TRAM and SCI scales. CPZ decreased hyperactivity to a greater degree than lithium	Similar finding to previous study
Spring et al., 1970	14	Double-blind randomization of 14 manic patients – 9 on lithium and 5 on CPZ over 3 weeks time. Lithium dose – 1,800–3,000 mg/day, CPZ dose – increased up to 1,600 mg/day. Failures were then crossed over to the other treatment	Intially 6 of 7 patients on lithium improved (2 dropped out) while 3 of 5 on CPZ improved. The 2 CPZ failures subsequently responded to lithium whereas the one lithium failure did not respond to CPZ	Authors' clinical impression was lithium superior to CPZ. Target symptoms of euphoria, hyperactivity, elevated mood and pressured speech responded more to lithium than CPZ
Platman, 1970	23	23 manic patients randomized in a double-blind fashion to	Most of the 13 patients randomized to lithium could be	Though lithium was not statistically superior to CPZ on rating

Lithium vs. Neuroleptics

Investigator	Design	No. of patients	Results	Comments
	lithium (mean dose 1,800 mg/day, mean serum level 0.8 mEq/L) or CPZ (mean dose = 879 mg/day) over 2–3 week period		discharged but 0 of the 10 patients could be discharged on CPZ	scales, the investigators clinical impression was that the state of the lithium-treated group was better
Prien et al., 1972	255 patients were randomized to lithium (avg. dose = 1,800 mg/day) or CPZ (dose range 200–3,000 mg – mean dose 1,000 mg/day) over a 3-week period after a 3–5 day washout period. The 255 patients were divided into 2 groups: a) 125 highly active patients, 59 on lithium, 66 on CPZ b) 130 mildly active patients, 69 on lithium, 61 on CPZ	255	45 early terminators in the study, 26 in highly active group and 19 in mildly active group. 22 early terminators on lithium vs. 4 on CPZ in highly active group. CPZ was more effective than lithium in controlling excitement, grandiosity, hostility, hyperactivity, a psychotic disorganization in the 1st week of treatment. In the mildly active group there was a higher drop-out rate on CPZ. (12 CPZ vs. 7 lithium). Again CPZ was better in controlling inital hyperactivity but lithium did not make the patient feel sluggish and fatigued	In highly active group CPZ decreased excitement by the 4th day vs. the 10th day for lithium. For patients who completed the study lithium was equal to CPZ in highly active group. Both CPZ and lithium were effective in decreasing symptoms in the mildly active group with no significant difference between the 2 groups
Takahashi et al., 1975	Double-blind study in 80 bipolar patients randomly assigned lithium (mean serum level 0.57 mEq/L) or CPZ (avg. dose – 256 mg/day) up to a maximum of 450 mg over a 5-week period following a 7 day washout	80	Of the 71 who completed the 5-week trial, 12 of 37 patients on lithium (32%) improved vs. 4 of 34 (12%) on CPZ as noted on a global scale. Onset of the specific effect was earlier with lithium	Lithium noted to have greater effect on mood, verbal hyper-activity, sleep whereas CPZ was more effective against activity. Doses of both lithium and CPZ about 30–50% of average dose needed to treat acute mania in U.S. This may

TABLE 1 *(continued)*

(continued from previous page) both groups and makes it difficult to draw generalized conclusions concerning comparative efficacy between the 2 drugs

Study	N	Method	Results	Comments
Shopsin et al., 1975	30	30 acutely manic patients randomized in a double-blind fashion to lithium (up to a maximum of 4,500 mg/day), CPZ (up to maximum of 1,800 mg/day) or haloperidol (up to maximum of 26 mg/day) after a one week placebo period over a 3-week period	There was a non-significant trend toward greater improvent in CGI and BPRS scores in the lithium and haloperidol group vs. the CPZ group. SCI profiles indicated a non-significant trend in favour of lithium over the 2 neuroleptics. Though all 3 groups improved, overall 7 of 10 patients on lithium vs. 2 of 10 patients on haloperidol and 1 of 10 on CPZ, were well enough to be discharged from the hospital	Clinical impression of lithium's superiority over Haloperidol and CPZ not supported by rating scale. Overall haloperidol group had improvement in 10 of 18 BPRS items vs. 8 of 18 for lithium-treated group and 4 of 18 for CPZ group. There were no items on BPRS where one group showed statistical superiority over another group
Garfinkel et al., 1980	21	Double-blind control trial of lithium alone (avg. serum level = 1.20 mEq/L) haloperidol alone (avg. dose 28.0 mg/day) and lithium (level 0.81 mEq/L) plus haloperidol (24.2 mg/day) in 21 acutely manic patients over a 3-week period following a 7 day washout period for 81% of the patients	Only 3 of 7 lithium-treated patients completed 3-week study vs. 5 of 7 in the haloperidol group and 6 of 7 in the lithium + haloperidol group. BPRS scores were significantly better for haloperidol and lithium + haloperidol combination vs. lithium alone at days 8 and 15. 3 patients remaining in lithium group were equivalent to haloperidol and haloperidol-lithium group at day 22 in terms of BPRS scores. Globally haloperidol and haloperidol-lithium group superior to lithium alone group at days 8, 15 and 22. Haloperidol alone was not significantly better than haloperidol + lithium on any measure at days 8, 15, and 22	EPS noted in 5 of 7 patients in both haloperidol and haloperidol + lithium group vs. 1 of 7 in lithium alone group. High drop-out rate and small no's make it difficult to evaluate lithium vs. neuroleptic here. It does appear that adding lithium to haloperidol resulted in both little increased toxicity or benefit

282

Food and Drug Administration officially approved it for the treatment of mania in 1970 and also approved it in 1974 for prophylactic use in individuals with histories of recurrent mania. However, lithium has been shown to have some degree of efficacy in a wide variety of psychiatric and non-psychiatric disorders (Jefferson and Griest, 1977). It is the purpose of this chapter to describe the clinical uses of lithium in medical practice.

Lithium in the treatment of mania

Since Cade's initial report (1949) lithium has been the subject of many open and controlled trials. Goodwin and Ebert (1973) reviewed 10 open studies examining the efficacy of lithium in acute mania. When one globally tabulates the results – 334 of 413 patients, or 81%, showed improvement in acute mania as a result of lithium treatment mostly in the first 10 days of treatment.

The initial open reports describing lithium's success in the treatment of acute mania have been confirmed in six double-blind trials comparing the effect of lithium vs. placebo (Table 1). The overall response rate of four of those listed (Schou et al., 1954; Maggs, 1963; Goodwin et al., 1969; Stokes et al., 1971) was 76% (see Goodwin and Zis, 1979). The six studies do have some methodological shortcomings such as high drop-out rate, lack of diagnostic criteria (Maggs, 1963), lack of randomization, washout periods and short lithium trials (Stokes et al., 1971) and small numbers of patients (Bunney et al., 1968). However, despite these flaws and despite methodological differences between studies there seems to be no question that lithium is superior to placebo in the treatment of acute mania.

Further evidence of lithium's use in acute mania comes from studies comparing its efficacy vs. that of a neuroleptic (Table 1). The eight double-blind studies accomplished to date do not conclusively establish the superiority of lithium over a neuroleptic. Five of the six studies comparing lithium against chlorpromazine (Johnson et al., 1968; Platman et al., 1970; Spring et al., 1970; Johnson et al., 1971; Takahashi et al., 1975) observed lithium's superiority over chlorpromazine. For the most part, however, these claims were based on clinical impression and in fact could not be substantiated by clinical rating scales in two instances (Platman et al., 1970; Spring et al., 1970). Prien et al. (1972) in a study that had twice as many patients as the other five combined divided 255 patients into a highly active group of 125 and a mildly active group of 130. They noted an equal effect of lithium vs. chlorpromazine in the mildly active group. They stated that chlorpromazine was superior to lithium in the highly active group basing their findings on the fact that the lithium treated group had a significantly higher drop-out rate than the chlorpromazine group. It is interesting to note that the lithium treated highly active patients who completed the 3-week study did as well as the highly active chlorpromazine group that completed the study.

Two studies have examined the efficacy of haloperidol in acute mania. Shopsin et al. (1975) noted that 7 of 10 lithium treated patients were able to be discharged from the hospital after 3 weeks as compared with 2 of 10 patients on haloperidol and 1 of 10 on chlorpromazine. There were, however, no statistical differences in BPRS or CGI scores among the three treatments. It was the authors' clinical impression that although the neuroleptics initially suppressed hyperactivity they did not affect the underlying thought and mood whereas the effect of lithium although slower initially, eventually was more specific on the manic symptoms.

The most recent study by Garfinkel et al. (1980) compared 21 patients randomized to lithium alone, haloperidol alone and lithium + haloperidol. The results in the study substantiated some of the previous impressions. Only 3 of the 7 lithium patients were able to complete the 3-week trial. All patients remaining at the end of day 22 improved but the haloperidol and haloperidol + lithium group did improve by day 8 and the latter 2 groups were statistically superior to lithium alone on various BPRS items at day 8 and 15. The adding of lithium to haloperidol did not improve symptoms or enhance toxicity. Despite the small number of patients studied the finding of a neuroleptics superiority over lithium in acute mania deserves further attention and argues against Shopsin's view of a specific effect on manic symptoms.

In review, there seems no question of lithium's efficacy in acute mania. However, the findings of efficacy of neuroleptics in acute mania (Prien et al., 1972; Garfinkel et al., 1980) cannot be dismissed. The quality of response for neuroleptics and the question as to whether they are superior, inferior or equal to lithium remains to be resolved.

Lithium in acute depression

Lithium was originally reported by Cade (1949) and Noack and Trautner (1951) to have no antidepressant activity. However, since 1968 data has been accumulating suggesting that the initial impression may have been incorrect. Table 2 lists 13 controlled studies either comparing lithium with placebo (9 studies) or with a reference antidepressant (4 studies). Only three (Fieve et al., 1968; Hansen et al., 1968; Stokes et al., 1971) suggest that lithium was either not superior to placebo or less effective than an antidepressant. Furthermore these three have been criticized as having the more serious methodological flaws in that the treatment period was too short (Hansen et al., 1968; Stokes et al., 1971) and there were lack of rating scales and no reporting of antidepressant doses and lithium levels (Fieve et al., 1968). The other 10 studies suggest an antidepressant effect for lithium. Combining the other 7 lithium-placebo studies − 90 to 200 patients showed a complete response to lithium and another 28 had a partial response. In addition, three studies demonstrated that lithium was as effective as imipramine (Watanabe et al., 1975; Worrall et al., 1979) and norpramin (Mendels et al., 1972).

Shopsin and Gershon (1978) reviewed the literature concerning characteristics that would predict a favourable lithium response. Some of these are: 1) bipolar illness (in the studies that examined these subdivisions 76 of 102 bipolar patients (BP or BP II) but only 30 of 72 unipolar patients responded); 2) family history of bipolar illness; 3) 'endogenous symptom pattern'; 4) high RBC lithium to plasma lithium ratio; 5) increased average evoked response; 6) high baseline plasma calcium/magnesium ratio; 7) initial increase in plasma magnesium and calcium concentration with lithium treatment; 8) low pretreatment MHPG levels; 9) decreased 5-HIAA in the CSF. It must be pointed out that none of the above claims have been adequately replicated.

The APA Task Force on lithium therapy concluded that for the acute depressive episode 'experimental results are not sufficiently conclusive to permit a clear definition of the value of lithium in acute depression'. It was felt that lithium should not be standard treatment but used in selected cases of poor response to other treatments. Nevertheless, there does appear to be a subgroup of patients who respond to lithium and clearly further

TABLE 2

Lithium in acute depression

Lithium vs. Placebo

Investigator	Design	No. of patients	Results	Comments
Hansen et al., 1968	Double-blind crossover in 12 patients given both lithium and placebo over 2 weeks with 'severe endogenous depression'	12	Most patients improved with lithium but only one relapsed with placebo	2 week treatment period
Stokes et al., 1971	Evaluation of 18 bipolar patients treated with lithium or placebo during a period of time the patient was judged to be depressed (overall 38-treatment periods). Data analyzed over a 7–10 day period. Mean lithium level = 0.93 mEq/L	18	For patients treated with lithium there was statistical improvement compared with ratings the day before lithium was started. Trend was toward improvement with lithium but it was not significant to placebo	7–10 day treatment period was too short for an evaluation of lithium effect
Goodwin et al., 1969	Double-blind evaluation of 18 patients — 6 bipolar I 6 bipolar II, 1 unipolar and 5 chronic depressives given lithium alternating with placebo for at least 2 weeks after placebo washout. Lithium level 0.8–1.3 mEq/L	18	10 of 13 cyclic patients improved; 5 complete and 5 partial vs. 2 of 5 chronic depressives with partial response	7 responders (3 complete and 4 partial) relapsed when switched to placebo

Study	Method	N	Results	Comments
Goodwin et al., 1972	Double-blind evaluation in 52 patients – 40 bipolar I or II and 12 unipolar given placebo or lithium for at least 2 weeks on an alternating basis	52	15 complete and 21 partial response. Overall 32 of 40 bipolars (80%) vs. 4 of 12 unipolar (33%) showed a complete or partial response	Better response noted in patients with regular cycles
Noyes et al., 1974	Lithium-placebo substitution in 6 bipolar and 16 unipolar patients over a minimum 2-week course. Lithium level range 0.93–2.15 mEq/L	22	6 of 6 bipolar patients responded vs. 7 of 16 unipolar patients responded	11 unipolar patients and 1 bipolar patient had history of non-response to ECT and antidepressants
Johnson, 1974	Single-blind evaluation of 2 bipolar, 6 unipolar and 3 patients with depressive neurosis given lithium (level = 0.7–1.9 mEq/L) over 21 days after an average 9 day placebo period	11	5 patients showed 'marked improvement' on lithium – 4 of 6 unipolar patients and 1 of 2 bipolar patients responded	Small numbers involved make it difficult to assess efficacy of lithium
Baron et al., 1975	Double-blind placebo substitution in 9 bipolar patients (bipolar I and II) and 14 unipolar patients after 1–2 week placebo washout. Average lithium level = 0.8–1.0 mEq/L	23	5 patients improved on placebo. Out of the remaining 18 who received lithium 7 of 8 bipolar patients and 3 of 10 unipolar patients showed either equivocal or partial response	Statistically greater improvement for lithium in bipolar patients
Mendels, 1976	Lithium placebo crossover in 13 bipolar and 8 unipolar hospitalized patients given lithium for at least 3 weeks preceeded by a 7–15 day placebo period	21	9 of 13 bipolar patients and 4 of 8 unipolar patients achieved 'unequivocal' improvement	7 of the 13 patients relapsed with placebo substitution

TABLE 2 *(continued)*

Lithium vs. placebo

Investigator	Design	No. of patients	Results	Comments
Donnelly et al., 1978	Lithium-placebo cross-over in 53 patients, 16 bipolar I, 17 bipolar II, and 20 unipolar patients. They were given lithium over a 4-week period	53	10 of 16 bipolar I patients responded vs. 11 of 17 bipolar II's vs. 8 of 20 unipolar patients	
Lithium vs. antidepressant				
Fieve et al., 1968	29 bipolar patients randomly assigned to lithium or imipramine over a 3-week period	29	Imipramine was superior to lithium which had only a mild antidepressant effect	Doses of lithium and imipramine and plasma levels of lithium were not recorded. The fact that no statistical tests were done comparing lithium to imipramine limit interpretation of the study
Mendels et al., 1972	24 endogenously depressed patients randomly assigned to lithium or desimipramine on 3-week trial. Patients who did not achieve 50% response were switched to the other drug. Lithium dose average 2,000 mg/day – desimipramine 200 mg/day	24	9 of 12 patients on lithium and 6 of 12 patients on desimipramine improved. 3 of 3 lithium failures improved on desimipramine and 4 of 6 desimipramine failures responded to lithium	Lithium as effective as desimipramine in terms of percentage changes on the depression rating scale scores. No report on unipolar-bipolar distinction
Watanabe et al., 1973, 1975	Double-blind study randomly assigning 64 patients to	64	At 3 weeks lithium was reported as effective as	Severe depressives were excluded. If one were to include 19 early

Reference	n	Design / patients	Results	Comments
		150 mg/day to imipramine or 900 mg/day of lithium over a 3–5 week period. Patients were non-severely depressed – 6 circular manic-depressed, 41 'periodic' depression, 13 involutional, 2 reactive depression and 2 schizo-affective depressed. Lithium level for responders = 0.41 mEq/L and for non-responders 0.45 mEq/L	imipramine. For patients who completed 3 weeks 16 of 26 lithium patients and 12 of 19 imipramine patients improved	terminators, improvement rate would be 54% for lithium and 50% for imipramine – not much higher than a placebo response for mild depression. This plus heterogeneity of depressed group are drawbacks in this study
Worrall et al., 1979	29	3 week double-blind study involving 29 patients with at least 2 previous episodes of depression were randomized to lithium carbonate (serum level average 0.91 mEq/L) or imipramine (plasma level IMI + DMI avg. 4.04 ng/ml). Lithium group included 7 unipolar, 5 bipolar, 2 'indeterminate'. The imipramine group included 10 unipolar, 3 bipolar and 2 indeterminate	Imipramine group improved significantly in the 1st week with little improvement thereafter. The lithium group had more uniform improvement showing improvement by 2nd and 3rd week of treatment	No specific individual responses given

double-blind studies are needed to evaluate the response of lithium in acute depression.

Lithium prophylaxis of bipolar illness and BP I where diagnosed

Early investigators were the first to notice that lithium had an effect not only in treating the acute manic state but in decreasing the frequency and severity of future episodes (Noack and Trautner, 1951). Gershon and Yuwiler (1960) noted that moderate doses of lithium were needed to control recurrences of mania (as opposed to the higher doses during the acute phase). They described that at intervals corresponding to the time a manic episode is scheduled to occur, the patient exhibits symptoms characteristic of manic illness. At that point they stated the maintenance dose of lithium should be increased and by doing this the manic symptoms would be suppressed. The authors called this phase the 'hypomanic alert'. It was the authors' impression that lithium diminished the amplitude of symptoms primarily and secondarily decreased the frequency of episodes. The amplitude of symptoms in some cycles would be decreased to the point where they are clinically unrecognizable – thus decreasing the frequency of episodes.

Investigators from Denmark, Czechoslovakia and Sweden formed an international collaborative study (Angst et al., 1970; Grof et al., 1970; Schou et al., 1970) to investigate the prophylactic efficacy of lithium in recurrent manic-depressive episodes and unipolar depression. For 114 patients with recurrent manic-depressive episodes, there were 329 episodes before lithium treatment and 121 episodes during lithium treatment. (For 58 unipolar patients there were 154 depressive episodes before lithium treatment and 42 episodes during lithium treatment.) The investigators felt that this was conclusive evidence of lithium's prophylactic ability in bipolar disorders. However, Blackwell (1970) presented certain criticisms of this longitudinal study, specifically the non-blind nature of the trial and possible observer bias. He and many others felt that only placebo-controlled double-blind studies would give the answer to lithium's effectiveness in this disorder.

Table 3 presents the controlled studies of lithium prophylaxis in bipolar disorders. All with the exception of Persson (1972) were a double-blind design and all but the study of Coppen et al. (1976) used a placebo control. A total of 514 bipolar patients were involved in these studies. Though the designs varied a total of 271 patients were given lithium and 257 were given placebo (some were given both, some were given other medication). One hundred and one of the 271 patients (37.3%) on lithium suffered an affective relapse as compared with 194 of 257 patients (75.5%) on placebo (p < .001). If one examines the frequency of manic relapses based on the studies that specifically reported this (Baastrup et al., 1970; Coppen et al., 1971; Cundall et al., 1972; Fieve and Mendlewicz, 1972; Persson, 1972; Prien et al., 1973a, b; Stallone et al., 1973; Fieve et al., 1976a, b), there was a cumulative manic relapse for 130 of 202 patients (64.4%) on placebo vs. 54 of 204 (16.5%) on lithium (p < .001). If one considered only depressive relapses (Baastrup et al., 1970; Cundall et al., 1972; Persson, 1972; Prien et al., 1973a, Prien et al., 1973b; Fieve et al., 1976) there was a cumulative depressive relapse for 61 of 180 patients (33.9%) on placebo vs. 31 of 187 patients (16.6%) on lithium (p < .001). If one develops finer criteria for evaluating depressive relapse as in the lithium-prophylaxis studies of Fieve et al. (1976a, b), lithium appears statistically superior to placebo in preventing BP I depression with fewer episodes per patient per year, fewer drop-outs due to depression and a tendency for lithium patients to remain in the study longer. It was the contention of Davis (1976) that lithium's prophylactic effect against bipolar illness was so impressive that the finding was not in need of further replication.

It does appear as Gershon and Yuwiler (1960) pointed out 20 years ago, that lithium clearly decreases the amplitude and severity of both manic and depressive symptoms in bipolar patients.

Lithium prophylaxis of unipolar illness

There have been four double-blind and one controlled study specifically matching the efficacy of lithium vs. placebo in recurrent unipolar depression (see Table 4). These studies all followed patients from a period of time at least 1 month after recovery from a depressive episode. If one combines the data from these five studies, one notes a relapse in 19 of 68 patients on lithium vs. 47 of 71 patients on placebo (p < .001). In one of the studies, Fieve et al. (1975, 1976a, b) studied 28 unipolar patients (25 females and 3 males). They were followed up for 3 months–4 years and randomized in a double-blind fashion to lithium or placebo. Six of 14 lithium patients remained free of depressive episodes vs. 5 of 14 on placebo (not significant). However, lithium-treated patients remained in the study significantly longer (20.5 months to 9.00 months) and had less frequent and less severe depressive episodes.

Quitkin et al. (1976) made a significant point of describing two types of treatment: 1) continuation therapy which involves the use of an agent after the disappearance of acute symptoms and; 2) prophylaxis, which involves treatment instituted when the patient is euthymic in the hope of preventing relapses. For an arbitrary period of time which they defined as 6 months, the agent was considered to have suppressed the underlying pathophysiology without curing it. Quitkin argues that at 6 months continuation therapy ceases and prophylaxis begins. This arbitrary point is supported for unipolar depression by Angst et al. (1979) who noted that the natural course of a unipolar depressive episode is 5.1 months. It is also supported by the recent NIMH multicentered U.S. study of Prien (1980) who noted that the sooner one was taken off imipramine following a depressive episode, the greater the likelihood of a depressive relapse within 3 months after discontinuation.

In addition to the studies involving lithium vs. placebo, four studies have examined lithium vs. antidepressants in prophylaxis of unipolar patients. Prien (1973) evaluated 78 unipolar patients over 2 years who, following a depressive episode, were randomized to lithium (serum average levels 0.8 mEq/L) imipramine (average dose = 125 mg/day) or placebo. Overall, 44% of the lithium-treated patients, 48% of the imipramine treated group and 92 of placebo patients relapsed. Lithium was equal in efficacy to imipramine and both were superior to placebo. If one considered only patients who were still in the study at the beginning of the 5th month the results were the same – 85% of the placebo group relapsed from the 5th month on as opposed to 36% of the lithium group and 29% of the imipramine group.

Three other studies comparing lithium and antidepressants argued for lithium's superiority. In a study involving 27 unipolar patients who had been stable for 6 months on imipramine, Quitkin et al. (1978, 1981) noted depressive relapses in 2 of 7 patients on lithium alone, 2 of 8 on the lithium-imipramine combination, 5 of 6 on imipramine alone

TABLE 3

Lithium in recurrent affective disorders

Controlled studies in bipolar patients

Investigator	Design	No. of patients	Results	Comments
Baastrup et al., 1970	50 bipolar patients well stabilized on lithium for 1 year were randomized to lithium or placebo over a 5-month period	50	0 of the 28 lithium-treated patients relapsed but 12 of the 22 placebo patients relapsed, 6 as a result of a manic episode, 5 as a result of depression and 1 as a mixed manic-depressive syndrome	Lithium equally prophylactic for manic and depressive recurrences vs. placebo
Cundall et al., 1972	13 bipolar patients who had been previously stabilized on lithium carbonate were followed in a double-blind fashion and randomized to lithium alternating with placebo over a 6-month period	13	1 patient dropped out. Of the remaining 12, 9 had less affective episodes on lithium, 1 had more on lithium and 2 had the same no. on lithium and placebo. (The individual who did better on placebo only had a plasma level of 0.21 mEq/L of lithium when he had a hypomanic attack).	9 individuals had a total of 10 manic episodes on placebo vs. only 1 manic episode in 1 patient on lithium. 3 individuals had 1 depressive episode on lithium while 5 individuals had 1 depressive episode on placebo
Melia, 1970	18 patients (16 bipolar 2 unipolar) who had been stabilized on lithium carbonate for 9 months were randomized to lithium carbonate or placebo and followed for either 2 years or until first relapse	18	4 of 9 lithium patients but only 2 of 9 placebo patients went 2 years without an affective episode. Lithium-treated patients remained in remission for 433 days vs. 224 for placebo (p ≤ .1 but p > .05)	Type of relapse was not reported

Study	Description	N	Results	
Coppen et al., 1971	38 bipolar patients (14 males and 24 females) were randomly allocated to lithium (serum levels 0.6–1.2 mEq/L avg. = 0.93 mEq/L) or placebo for an average 74.8 weeks	38	The 17 bipolar patients were ill for 16.7% of the time followed as opposed to 56.7% of the time for the 21 patients on placebo	6 of 17 patients on lithium needed anti-manic drugs to suppress some manic symptomatology vs. 17 of 22 on placebo. Bipolar depression also appeared less frequently on lithium vs. placebo
Hullin et al., 1972	1) Evaluated 43 bipolar patients and 23 unipolar patients followed on lithium for an average of 40 months following a prior 5-year history of at least 1 affective episode	66	1) 28 of the 43 bipolar patients did not relapse (all 15 relapses were manic episodes). 18 of 23 unipolar patients did not relapse	The type of relapse suffered in the placebo-controlled study was not specified
	2) Evaluated 36 combined bipolar and unipolar patients who had been stable for 2 years on lithium and randomized them to lithium (serum levels 0.6–1.6 mEq/L) or placebo over 6 months	36	2) Only 1 of 18 patients on lithium suffered an affective episode which required hospitalization as opposed to 6 of 18 on placebo	
Persson, 1972	Controlled but non-blind study of 12 pairs of bipolar patients – one group treated with lithium and one control group that was seen before the advent of lithium therapy (avg. lithium level 0.7 mEq/L) Groups were matched for age, duration of illness and no. of affective episodes. All were stable for 1 month before evaluation	24	5 of 12 bipolar patients on lithium relapsed vs. 11 of 12 controls. 6 of 12 control patients had at least 1 manic episode vs. 5 of 12 on lithium. 8 of 12 control patients had at least 1 depressive episode vs. 5 of 12 on lithium	If one considers individuals free of an affective episode for 6 months there were 10 bipolar pairs. 5 of 10 lithium patients had affective episodes vs. 7 of 10 control patients. 3 of 10 lithium patients had manic episodes vs. 4 of 10 controls. 4 of 10 lithium patients had depressive episodes vs. 7 of 10 placebo

TABLE 3 *(continued)*

Controlled studies in bipolar patients

Investigator	Design	No. of patients	Results	Comments
Prien et al., 1973a	Multiple hospital study (18 hospitals) involving 205 patients hospitalized for a manic episode who were randomized to lithium cabonate (serum levels 0.5–1.4 mEq/L) or placebo and followed over a 2-year course	205	Of the 104 placebo patients 70 had at least 1 severe relapse, 14 had a moderate relapse and 20 did not relapse Of the 101 lithium patients 31 had severe relapses, 12 moderate relapses and 58 no relapses. 45 placebo patients completed 2 years vs. 74 on lithium – only 11 of 45 placebo patients were episode free vs. 49 of 74 lithium patients. 32 of 101 lithium patients had manic episodes vs. 71 of 104 placebo patients. 16 of 101 lithium patients had depressive episodes vs. 27 of 104 on placebo	If one considers patients still in the study after 3 months only 22 of 94 BPO patients remained episode free vs. 61 of 93 lithium patients
Prien et al., 1973b	Multihospital study involving 44 bipolar patients who were hospitalized for a depressive episode and were randomized to lithium (serum levels 0.5–1.2 mEq/L) imipramine (dose range 50–200 mg/day) or placebo and followed over a 2-year course	44	9 of 18 patients or lithium remained free of an affective episode for 2 years vs. only 2 of 13 on imipramine and 1 of 13 on placebo. 2 of 18 lithium patients had a manic episode vs. 7 of 13 on imipramine and 5 of 13 on placebo. 4 of 18 lithium patients had depressive episodes vs. 4 of 13 on imipramine and 8 of 13 on placebo	If one considers patients still in the study at the end of 4 months, 3 of 17 patients had affective episodes on lithium vs. 6 of 9 on both imipramine and placebo

Reference	N	Study	Results
Fieve et al., 1972 Stallone et al., 1973	52	52 individuals with bipolar illness were randomly assigned to lithium (0.8–1.3 mEq/L) or placebo and followed for periods of up to 28 months	14 of 25 lithium-treated patients removed in remission for 2 years vs. only 2 of 27 placebo patients. 9 lithium patients dropped out (3 because of an acute episode) vs. 22 on placebo (18 because of an acute episode). No. of manic episodes/yr was 0.2 for lithium group vs. 0.593 for placebo group. No. of depressive episodes/yr was 0.239 for lithium group vs. 0.703 for depressive group
Coppen et al., 1976	9	A double-blind controlled study that involved 9 bipolar patients randomized to maprotiline (150 mg/day) vs. lithium carbonate (serum level 0.8–1.2 mEq/L). Patients were followed for up to 1 year after having been maintained on lithium for 1 year	2 of 6 lithium patients dropped out before 1 year (1 due to a manic episode) vs. 2 of 3 maprotiline patients (1 due to a manic episode). Of the patients who completed 1 year, 3 of 4 patients on lithium remained free of a relapse. The 1 patient on maprotiline relapsed
Fieve et al., 1976 a, b	35	A double-blind study of 35 bipolar I patients were randomized to lithium (0.7–1.3 mEq/L) or placebo and followed for 4 years	Lithium was shown to be statistically superior in preventing depressive relapses on multiple indices including fewer episodes per patient per year, fewer drop-outs due to depressive relapse and a tendency to remain in the study longer than placebo patients. Overall, 5 of 17 lithium-treated patients had a depressive episode vs. 8 of 18 on placebo. Ten of 17 lithium patients had a manic episode vs. 17 of 18 on placebo. Overall, 10 of 17 patients had an affective episode on lithium vs. 17 of 18 on placebo. Only three of 17 lithium patients were hospitalized for an affective episode vs. 9 of 18 on placebo

TABLE 4

Lithium prophylaxis in unipolar depression

a) *Lithium vs. placebo*

Investigator	Design	No. of patients	Results	Comments
Baastrup et al., 1970	34 female patients who had been stable for 1 year on lithium were randomized to continued lithium treatment or placebo	34	In the 5 months that the patients were followed 9 of 17 patients on placebo relapsed vs. 0 of 17 on lithium	
Coppen et al., 1971	26 unipolar patients (7 male and 19 female) were randomly allocated to lithium (serum levels 0.6–1.2 mEq/L) or placebo for an average of 78 weeks	26	The 11 unipolar patients on lithium were ill for 4.7% of the time followed vs. 30.3% for the 15 patients on placebo	On the basis of global ratings 10 of 11 lithium patients showed no conspicuous affective disturbance or moderate improvement as compared with the previous 2 years vs. only 3 of 15 placebo patients
Cundall et al., 1972	5 unipolar patients were involved in a lithium-placebo crossover (i.e. 6 months on each regime)	5	2 patients had 1 depressive episode on both placebo and lithium and 1 had an episode on lithium but not placebo. 2 other patients did not complete crossover, 1 had 2 depressive episodes on placebo and 1 had a depressive episode on lithium	
Persson, 1972	Controlled but non-blind study of 21 pairs of unipolar patients, one group maintained on lithium and one group treated	42	6 of 21 lithium-treated patients relapsed requiring outpatient treatment as opposed to 14 of 21 control patients	If one considered patients who had been euthymic for 6 months – there were 16 matched pairs of unipolar patients. 13 of 16

Reference	No.	Methodology	Results
		before the advent of lithium therapy. Average lithium level (0.7 mEq/L). Groups were matched for age, duration of illness and no. of active episodes. All were stable for 1 month before evaluation	relapsed on placebo vs. only 4 of 16 on lithium
Fieve et al., 1975, 1976a, b	28	28 unipolar patients (25 females and 3 males) were followed up for 3 months–4 years and randomized in a double-fashion to lithium or placebo	6 of 14 lithium patients remained free of depressive episodes vs. 5 of 14 on placebo (not significant) However, lithium-treated patients remained in the study significantly longer (20.5–9.00 months) and had less frequent and less severe depressive episodes

b) *Lithium vs. antidepressant*

Reference	No.	Methodology	Results
Prien et al., 1973, 1974b	78	2 year double-blind trial — patients were randomized to lithium carbonate (0.5–1.2 mEq/L, median 0.8 mEq/L), imipramine dose ranges 50–200 mg/day (avg. 125 mg/day) or placebo following a depressive episode	24 of the 26 placebo-treated patients relapsed with a depressive episode as compared with 12 of the 25 imipramine patients and 12 of the 27 lithium-treated patients (lithium = imipramine, both superior to placebo) If one considered individuals followed from the 5 months on (months 5–24) there were depressive relapses in 11 of 13 placebo patients, 8 of 22 lithium-treated patients and 6 of 21 imipramine-treated patients
Coppen et al., 1976	30	A double-blind control study involving 30 patients randomized to maprotiline (150 mg/day) vs. lithium carbonate (serum level 0.8–1.2 mEq/L). Patients were followed for up to 1 year after having been maintained on lithium for 1 year	7 of 15 unipolar patients on maprotiline dropped out (1 became depressed and 6 because of side effects) vs. 3 of 15 on lithium (1 depression, 2 side effects) within 29 weeks. Of the patients who completed 1 year, 6 of 8 maprotiline patients had a relapse vs. only 3 of 12 on lithium

TABLE 4 *(continued)*

b) Lithium vs. antidepressant

Investigator	Design	No. of patients	Results	Comments
Coppen et al., 1978	41 unipolar patients, 38 of whom had previously received lithium were randomized to lithium (serum levels 0.8–1.2 mEq/L) or mianserin 60–90 mg/day. Patients were followed for 1 year	41	8 of 21 patients on mianserin dropped out (3 due to side effects, 5 non-compliance) vs. 5 of 20 on lithium (1 depression, 1 side effect, 3 other). Of the remaining patients 0 of 15 lithium patients relapsed vs. 7 of 13 on mianserin	Of the 7 mianserin patients who relapsed 4 had 1 episode, 1 had 2 episodes and 3 had 3 episodes. 5 patients required ECT for their depressive symptoms
Quitkin et al., 1978, 1981a	Double-blind trial in 27 unipolar patients who following a 6 month euthymia on imipramine after a depressive episode were randomized to lithium carbonate (0.8–1.2 mEq/L), imipramine (100–150 mg/day), lithium + imipramine or placebo. Patients were followed for an average of 11 months	27	6 of the 8 patients on the lithium-imipramine combination remained free of a depressive episode as compared with 5 of 7 on lithium alone, 1 of 6 on imipramine alone and and 0 of 6 on placebo. Lithium was noted to have a prophylactic effect whereas imipramine did not	Of the 12 patients in the 4 groups who did not have a depressive episode 7 did not complete the 2 years that the study was designed for but were 'terminated euthymic'. In addition, lithium-imipramine combination which was reported to have no significant effect did not have enough people followed for statistical significance to have been achieved

and 6 of 6 on placebo. The author's conclusion was that lithium had a prophylactic effect whereas imipramine and the lithium-imipramine combination did not. However, it must be pointed out that not enough patients on the lithium-imipramine combination were followed for statistical significance to have been achieved. In addition, the average length of time followed was only 11 months. It was hoped that patients could be followed for a minimum of 2 years but only a few patients could be followed for this long. Indeed 7 of the 12 patients in the 4 groups who did not relapse were reported as 'terminated euthymic' after an average of 17 months.

In two other studies, Coppen (Coppen et al., 1976; Coppen et al., 1978) compared lithium vs. maprotiline and lithium vs. mianserin in a 1 year follow-up of unipolar depressives. In both instances lithium was statistically superior to the tetracyclics. In the maprotiline study (Coppen et al., 1976) 7 of 15 maprotiline patients dropped out and 6 of the remaining 8 became depressed, whereas only 3 of the 15 lithium patients dropped out and 3 of the remaining 12 became depressed. In the mianserin study, 8 of the 21 mianserin patients dropped out and 7 of the remaining 13 had depressive episodes, whereas only 5 of 20 lithium patients dropped out and 0 of the remaining 15 had depressive episodes.

In an open retrospective evaluation, Peselow et al (1981a) examined unipolar patients treated in two outpatient facilities who were maintained on lithium alone (serum levels = 0.7–1.4 mEq/L) antidepressants alone (imipramine or amitriptyline in doses of 75–300 mg/day), lithium and antidepressants and placebo (or no treatment). The study included patients who had been euthymic for 6 consecutive months. In all 64 patients on antidepressants, 55 on lithium, 47 on a lithium-antidepressant combination, and 24 on either placebo or no medication were followed up for a 4-year period. The life-table method of Fleiss et al. (1976) was utilized. In all 21 of 55 (38%) patients on lithium were known to have suffered a depressive episode in the 4-year period as compared with 14 of 47 on the lithium antidepressant combination (36%), 25 of 64 on antidepressants alone (39%), and 14 of 24 on placebo (58%). The 2 year probability range of remaining free of a depressive episode ranged from the maximum of 48–63% on a lithium-antidepressant combination, to 39–60% on lithium alone, to 35–53% on antidepressants alone, to the minimum of 19–31% on placebo or no treatment. The 4 year probability range of remaining free of a depressive episode ranged from the maximum of 30–43% for the lithium-antidepressant combination, to 26–41% for lithium alone, to 17–26% on antidepressants alone, to the minimum of 6–10% on placebo (or no treatment). There was a non-significant overall trend in favour of lithium and lithium + antidepressants vs. antidepressants alone but the trend did not reach statistical significance. Both lithium and the lithium-antidepressant combination were statistically superior to placebo (or no treatment) overall, whereas the trend did not reach statistical significance in the case of the antidepressant vs. placebo.

The American Food and Drug Administration, while giving endorsement to lithium in the prophylaxis of bipolar illness does not give it for unipolar disease. This is interesting in view of the fact that several of the studies we reported on found lithium effective in unipolar illness to a similar degree as bipolar illness (Baastrup et al., 1970; Coppen et al., 1971; Persson, 1972; Prien et al., 1973b) and the F.D.A. accepted the findings for bipolar patients in initiating its approval. In addition, three of four studies comparing lithium and antidepressants found statistical superiority in favour of lithium in preventing unipolar illness and there is no restriction in the use of antidepressants for prophylactic maintenance. This is very impressive in view of the fact that six studies (Seager and Bird, 1962; Kay et al., 1970; Mindham et al., 1973; Klerman et al., 1974; Coppen et al., 1978; Stein et al., 1980) argue for the superiority of antidepressants over placebo in continuation therapy. (In these six continuation studies there was a relapse rate of 16.4% on amitriptyline or imipramine – 29 of 177 vs. 48.6% on placebo – 106 of 218.) The F.D.A. and APA Task force on Lithium Therapy (1975) cited two reasons for failing to recommend the use of lithium in long-term maintenance treatment. One was the fact that the definition of unipolar illness is inexact and because of this lack of specificity it was feared by both the F.D.A. and APA Task Force that this could lead to an unwarranted prescribing of lithium in any recurrent disorder in which depressive symptoms might present. The second was the fact that the number of patients studied is small. If one includes all the studies listed (including the controlled but open study of Persson, 1972) lithium has been given to 128 unipolar patients and placebo was given to 103 unipolar patients.

Despite the warnings of these two committees at this point, there is persuasive evidence from the studies done that lithium is effective in the prophylaxis of depression in unipolar illness. It is hoped that future studies such as the NIMH collaborative study currently in progress can give us the definite answer.

Lithium in bipolar II and cyclothymic patients

The literature we have reviewed on bipolar and unipolar patients predominantly included patients with a history of hospitalizations for mania and depression. However, with the advent of DSM III and RDC criteria (Spitzer et al., 1978) psychiatrists have become more sensitive and aware of the diagnosis of affective disorders. Many clinicians have become more sensitive to the milder forms of bipolar illness. The definitions of bipolar illness have undergone some degree of variation since they were originally defined by Leonhard (1962), Fieve and Dunner (1975) divided the bipolar group into the following categories: *Bipolar I* – individuals with a history of hospitalizations for mania and/or either hospitalization or outpatient treatment for depression. *Bipolar II* – individuals with a history of hospitalization for depression and episodes of hypomania. *Bipolar Other* – individuals who have episodes of depression and hypomania which were never severe enough to have required hospitalization, but did require outpatient treatment.

The Fieve-Dunner criteria were very sensitive to 'mild highs' and required individuals who were classified as unipolar to have never met research criteria for even mild hypomania. RDC criteria combined the Fieve-Dunner bipolar II and bipolar other into a single bipolar II group. While many of the bipolar II and some of the bipolar other patients would fit into the DSM III category of atypical bipolar disorder, it is not clear if the two groups should be combined. Akiskal et al. (1979) validated a cyclothymic group that they noted was equivalent to the Fieve-Dunner bipolar other group. Akiskal noted that his cyclothymic group was not equivalent to the bipolar II group but on a continuum with it and bipolar I disorders noting 30% of cyclothymics had an episode severe enough to later be reclassified bipolar II and 6% had an episode severe enough to be reclassified bipolar I.

The clinical characteristics of bipolar II and cyclothymic patients have not been extensively reported on. Akiskal et al. (1977, 1979) noted that the hypomania for some of these patients was characterized by irritability, explosive outbursts, episodic promiscuity and occasional drug and alcohol abuse. Fieve (1973) described a slightly different pattern for the hypomania. Some of the bipolar II and cyclothymic patients had high energy levels and high drive during their periods of hypomania. When one actually examined these hypomanic periods one notes that they were categorized by a high degree of productivity. These periods for some are often seen as positive by both the individual and his associates. Usually the individual does not seek psychiatric treatment for the hypomanic state which he does not see as 'pathologic'. Recent reports suggest that only 20–25% of bipolar II's (Peselow et al., 1980b) and 23% of cyclothymics (Peselow et al., 1981b) had ever received pharmacologic treatment for the hypomanic phase of their illness prior to entrance into an affective disorder clinic. Usually the diagnosis of a history of hypomania for these people is made for the first time on referral to clinicians familiar with 'atypical bipolar disorder'. Even then it is difficult to assess if these brief periods of hypomania truly meet research criteria for hypomania or represent a skewed segment of normal personality variation.

There is considerable controversy as to the best way to classify atypical bipolar disorders (bipolar II and cyclothymic). Though the bipolar II and cyclothymic distinction is tentative and based on verbal criteria in the absence of definitive laboratory validation (which is usually required in other medical specialities), there is pharmacologic and genetic evidence for both the bipolar II (Dunner et al., 1972, 1976b; Goodwin et al., 1972) and cyclothymic group (Akiskal et al., 1977, 1979) though it is not clear if these groups are distinct or part of the bipolar spectrum (Endicott et al., 1980; Fieve et al., 1981).

There have been three double-blind studies comparing lithium's effectiveness in bipolar II patients (Table 5). Dunner et al. (1976a) examined 32 bipolar II patients – 12 on lithium and 20 on placebo over an average 16.5 months. They noted that only 1 of 12 lithium patients had a hypomanic episode as compared with 6 of 20 placebo patients (mean hypomanic episodes/year – 0.11 for lithium treated group vs. 0.34 for placebo group, $p < .001$). There was no difference in the number of depressive episodes between the lithium and placebo groups during this short period of evaluation as 8 of 12 lithium-treated patients had depressive episodes vs. 10 of 20 on placebo (mean depressive episodes/year – 0.97 for lithium group vs. 0.79 for placebo group). However, there was a non-significant trend for the lithium-treated group to have less severe depressive episodes as measured by a decreased percentage of hospitalizations for the lithium-treated group. A second study of the 18 BP II patients by Fieve et al. (1976a, b) showed that lithium was superior to placebo on multiple indices including mean number of months in the study (30 vs. 21), mean number of depressive episodes per patient per year (.212 vs. .367), and mean duration of depressive episodes (57 vs. 194 days). A subsequent study by Quitkin (Quitkin et al., 1978, 1981) measured the prophylactic effect of lithium, imipramine, lithium and imipramine and placebo in 22 bipolar II patients over an average 11-month period. Three of the 4 lithium-treated patients remained free of a depressive episode as compared with 5 of 6 on the lithium-imipramine combination, 2 of 5 on imipramine alone and 2 of 7 on placebo. The authors suggested a prophylactic effect for lithium but the small numbers of patients studied and the fact that 10 of the 12 patients who did not have depressive episodes were 'terminated euthymic' before they completed the 2-year trial the authors had originally planned, make it difficult to draw conclusions. In a recent open evaluation, Kukopulos

TABLE 5

Lithium prophylaxis for hypomanic individuals (i.e. Bipolar II and cyclothymic patients)

Bipolar II

Investigator	Design	No. of patients	Results	Comments
Dunner et al., 1976a	32 individuals who met criteria for bipolar II disorder were randomized to lithium carbonate (0.8–1.2 mEq/L) or placebo. Patients were followed an avg. 16.4 months	32	With respect to hypomania 11 of 12 individuals followed remained entirely free of a depressive episode on lithium vs. 14 of 20 on placebo. Mean no. of hypomanic episodes/yr on lithium was 0.11 vs. 0.34 on placebo (p < .001). With respect to depression only 4 of 12 patients on lithium remained free of a depressive episode vs. 10 of 20 on placebo (not significant). Mean no. of depressive episodes/yr 0.97 on lithium and 0.79 on placebo. 4 of the 10 depressed patients on placebo were hospitalized vs. only 1 of the 8 depressed lithium patients needed hospitalization	
Fieve et al., 1976 a, b	Double-blind randomization of 18 patients followed from 3–52 months on lithium carbonate (0.7–1.3 mEq/L) vs. placebo	18	4 of 7 lithium-treated patients vs. 7 of 11 placebo patients had depressive episodes. However, lithium-treated patients had less episodes per year and were ill for shorter periods of time	3 of 7 lithium-treated patients remained entirely free of depressive episodes for 52 consecutive months vs. 2 of 11 on placebo

Quitkin et al., 1978, 1981a	22 individuals who met RDC criteria for bipolar II illness were randomized to lithium carbonate (serum levels = 0.8–1.2 mEq/L), imipramine (100–150 mg/day), lithium and imipramine or placebo. Patients followed over an average 17 months following 6 months euthymic mood	22	3 of 4 patients on lithium and 5 of 6 patients on the lithium-imipramine combination remained free of a depressive episode vs. 2 of 5 on imipramine alone and 2 of 7 on placebo. Lithium was noted to have a prophylactic effect against depression whereas the antidepressant did not	Only 1 patient (on imipramine alone) had a hypomanic episode. 10 of the 12 patients who did not have a depressive episode 'terminated euthymic' before the end of the 2-year trial

Cyclothymic (bipolar other)

Dunner et al., 1976a	Bipolar II study also included 8 individuals termed bipolar other (individuals with histories of hypomania and depression which were never severe enough to be hospitalized) which is equivalent to Akiskal's defined cyclothymic group (Akiskal et al., 1977, 1979). Bipolar others or cyclothymics were followed an avg. 13.6 months	8	All 4 lithium-treated patients and all 5 placebo-treated patients were free of hypomania. 1 of the 4 patients treated with lithium and 2 of the 4 patients treated with placebo had a depressive episode	Sample size too small to draw conclusions

and Reginaldi (1980) reported a 'good response' to lithium prophylaxis in 33% of 91 bipolar II patients and a 'partial response' in another 42%.

There has been only one controlled study of bipolar other or cyclothymic patients. Dunner (1976a) examined 8 patients over an average 13.6 months and noted that 1 of 4 lithium-treated patients had a depressive episode as compared with 2 of 4 on placebo. (None of the patients had a hypomanic episode over this time period.) The small numbers of patients studied make it difficult to draw conclusions regarding lithium's effectiveness. In an open observation, Akiskal et al. (1979) observed that 9 of 15 patients exhibited a decrease in: verbal abusiveness, aggressive outbursts, and recurrent substance abuse while on lithium over a 1-year period.

Using a longitudinal life-table design, Peselow et al. (1981c) examined lithium's prophylactic effect against depression in cyclothymic and bipolar II patients. Peselow noted that 38% of 102 bipolar II patients and 29% of 69 cyclothymic patients remained entirely free of a depressive episode on lithium in the 1−36-month period in which they were followed. Thirty-four percent of bipolar II patients and 37% of the cyclothymic patients had one known depressive episode on lithium, 9% of the bipolar II, and 14.5% of the cyclothymic patients had two known depressive episodes on lithium over a 5-year period. The prophylactic utility of lithium in individuals with mild bipolar disorder requires further evaluation in the form of placebo controlled double-blind studies.

Lithium in the treatment of schizophrenic and schizo-affective illness

Before one can begin to answer the question of lithium's effectiveness in schizophrenia and schizoaffective illness, one must examine the changing verbal criteria for mania. Appendix (see p. 314) indicates Feighner (Feighner et al., 1972) RDC (Spitzer et al., 1978) and DSM III (1980) criteria for mania. The Feighner criteria note that individuals who exhibit 'a massive or peculiar alteration of perception or thinking (i.e. delusions or hallucinations)' do not have mania but have a schizophreniform illness. Indeed many of the studies of lithium's effectiveness in mania before 1970 did not include any individuals with delusions or hallucinations. This is important because RDC criteria seemed to allow for delusions and hallucinations to be part of a manic syndrome. However, the RDC criteria noted that if an individual had certain pathognomonic Schneiderian symptoms such as thought control, thought broadcasting, thought insertion, or thought withdrawal, this ruled out mania. However, recent evidence (Pope and Lipinski, 1978) concluded that there were no pathognomonic symptoms of schizophrenia. With this in mind, recent DSM III criteria (1980) noted that as long as the traditional affective symptoms were present this was the diagnosis even if delusions, hallucinations, or Schneiderian symptoms were present. Because of the ever changing diagnostic criteria for mania and schizophrenia it is difficult to interpret the studies examining lithium's effect in schizophrenia and schizo-affective illness.

Lithium in the treatment of schizophrenics. Cade's (1949) original report commented on six schizophrenic patients in whom there was no improvement in the thought disorder with lithium. However, he did note that there was some decrease in agitation, restlessness and excitement in three of those patients. Gershon and Yuwiler (1960) indicated that while lithium decreased excitement it was without effect on cognitive symptoms, in schizophrenics.

There were four double-blind studies concerning the effectiveness of lithium in schizophrenia (Table 6). Shopsin et al. (1971) noted that chlorpromazine was superior to lithium on several rating scales with regard to efficacy. More significantly they indicated that 6 of the 11 lithium patients developed a severe toxic confusional state. Alexander et al. (1979) followed 13 patients in a placebo lithium crossover, where all individuals were given lithium over a 3-week period. Seven of the 13 patients improved while on lithium, 4 of the 7 patients subsequently relapsed on placebo. In an open evaluation, Van Putten and Sanders (1975) noted that 15 schizophrenics who had not responded to phenothiazine treatment subsequently responded to lithium.

Two controlled studies examined the efficacy of lithium plus neuroleptics in chronic schizophrenics. Small et al. (1975) reported on 22 chronic schizophrenic patients (8 with a diagnosis of schizo-affective illness) who had been hospitalized for an average of 9 years in a neuroleptic + lithium, neuroleptic + placebo crossover study. Ten of the 22 patients were felt to have responded to lithium and of these 7 were well enough to leave the hospital on this combination. In contrast, Growe et al. (1979) noted that when lithium was added to a neuroleptic in eight patients the only area of improvement noted on the rating scales was in the area of psychotic excitement. There was no distinct advantage of a neuroleptic-lithium combination vs. neuroleptic alone on items such as hostile belligerence, paranoid projection, psychotic disorganization and social care needed.

The initial neurotoxicity findings of Shopsin et al. (1971) were not replicated in the other studies. Because of the small groups of patients followed little can be concluded but it does appear that a subgroup of schizophrenic patients may benefit from lithium therapy. This subgroup needs further definition and hopefully future double-blind studies will give us the answer as to lithium's role in schizophrenics.

Lithium in the treatment of schizo-affective illness. There have been numerous open studies concerning the efficacy of lithium in schizo-affective illness. Procci (1976) compared six studies examining lithium's effectiveness in schizo-affective illness vs. lithium's effectiveness in mania. Overall, there was improvement in 130 of 149 manics (87.2%) vs. improvement in 73 of 94 schizo-affective patients (77.7%).

There are five controlled studies involving lithium's effectiveness in schizo-affective illness (Table 7). Johnson et al. (1968) reported on a group of schizo-affectives given chlorpromazine (CPZ) or lithium in a 3-week double-blind study. Eight of the 10 patients on CPZ improved whereas only 1 of 17 lithium patients responded with the other 6 lithium patients showing a clinical worsening with manifestations of neurotoxicity. The lithium levels in these patients ranged from 1.16–1.97 mEq/L. A 1971 study by this group yielded similar findings (Johnson et al., 1971). Prien et al. (1972b) studied 83 excited schizo-affective patients and in a design similar to their study of mania evaluated lithium vs. chlorpromazine in highly active and midly active schizo-affectives. Chlorpromazine was found to be statistically superior to lithium with respect to reduction of symptomatology in the highly active group (as measured by BPRS scores). There was equal efficacy for lithium and CPZ in the mildly active schizo-affectives. Brockington et al. (1978) evaluated both schizo-affective manics and schizo-affective depressives in a controlled fashion. Chlorpromazine was compared with lithium in schizo-affective manics. Three of 6 lithium patients who completed the 1-month trial were rated recovered versus 2 of 5 on chlorpromazine.

TABLE 6

Lithium in schizophrenia

Investigator	Design	No. of patients	Results	Comments
Shopsin et al., 1971	21 acute schizophrenic patients (4 of whom were diagnosed as schizo-affective) were randomized to lithium carbonate (0.65–1.28 mEq/L) or chlorpromazine (maximum dose 1,200 mg/day). Patients spent 1 week on placebo, 3 weeks on active medication and 1 week post-study on placebo	21	11 patients were randomized to lithium and 10 to chlorpromazine (CPZ), BPRS, CGI, IMPS, SCI, NOSIE and SRCS rating scale measures all favoured CPZ over lithium on many items to a statistically significant level	6 of 11 patients on lithium developed symptoms of a toxic confusional state
Small et al., 1975	22 hospitalized chronic schizophrenic patients were stabilized on the best neuroleptic and after stabilization were randomized to lithium-placebo-lithium-placebo or placebo-lithium-placebo-lithium + the neuroleptic over a 4-week period. Patients had been continuously or intermittently hospitalized for 9 years	22	15 of the 22 patients completed the 4-week trial. 10 of the remaining 15 patients were felt to have responded to lithium and 7 were able to have been discharged on a lithium-neuroleptic combination	

| Alexander et al., 1979 | 13 acutely psychotic patients (5 schizophrenic, 3 schizo-affective-manic and 3 schizo-affective depressed) were evaluated in a placebo-lithium crossover. Patient given placebo for 1 week, lithium for 3 weeks and placebo for 2 weeks. Serum lithium levels 0.7–1.2 mEq/L (avg. 0.9 mEq/L) | 13 | 7 of the 13 patients responded to lithium and 4 of the 7 responders relapsed within 2 weeks after lithium withdrawal |
| Growe et al., 1979 | 8 patients (6 schizophrenics and 2 schizo-affectives) who did not respond to neuroleptics alone were randomized to neuroleptic and placebo or neuroleptic and lithium (serum level 0.5–1.0 mEq/L) in a double-blind crossover trial that lasted 16 weeks | 8 | Behavioural ratings as measured by the PIP scale noted only a statistical decrease in psychotic excitement on lithium. There was no difference in hostile belligerence, paranoid projection, anxious depression, care needed and psychotic disorganization on neuroleptic-lithium vs. neuroleptic-placebo |

TABLE 7

Lithium in schizo-affective disorder

Investigator	Design	No. of patients	Results	Comments
Johnson et al., 1968	17 schizo-affective patients were randomized double-blind following an average 5 day washout period to lithium carbonate (avg. serum levels 1.0–2.55 mEq/L) or chlorpromazine in doses of 200–1,800 mg/day. Patients were maintained on active medication for a mean duration of 3–4 weeks	17	All 10 schizo-affective patients on chlorpromazine showed some improvement (3 marked, 5 moderate and 2 mild) 6 of 7 lithium patients showed clinical worsening and 1 had moderate improvement	In the 6 lithium schizo-affective patients, 3 developed a toxic confusional state (disorientation and reduced comprehension). Lithium blood levels were 1.16–1.97 mEq/L
Johnson et al., 1971	11 schizo-affective patients were randomized double-blind following a 5 day washout period to lithium (average serum level 1.0 mEq/L) or chlorpromazine (initial dose 200–400 mg) and dose t.i.d. until therapeutic response or toxicity	11	There was a significant decrease in psychopathology in the chlorpromazine group vs. the lithium group as measured by items on BPRS, TRAM, NOSIE, CGI and SCI rating scales	
Prien et al., 1973	Multihospital study in 83 schizo-affective patients who were randomized double-blind to lithium carbonate (serum levels ranged from 0.6–2.0 mEq/L, median 1.3 mEq/L) or chlorpromazine (200–3,000 mg/day – avg. dose 1,100 mg/day) over a 3-week period. Patients were divided into a highly active or mildly active group	83; 42 highly active patients; 41 mildly active patients	Chlorpromazine (CPZ) was superior to lithium in highly active group in 10 of 19 BPRS items, 10 of 17 highly active lithium patients terminated early as opposed to 1 of 25 highly active CPZ patients. CPZ was equal to lithium in mildly active patients (improvement in 9 of 19 BPRS items on CPZ vs. 7 of 19 BPRS items on lithium) 7 of 21 mildly active CPZ patients did not complete the study vs. 3 of 20 mildly active lithium patients	

Brockington et al., 1978	In a double-controlled study 19 schizo-affective manics were randomized to lithium (minimum serum level 0.8 mEq/L) or chlorpromazine (minimum dose 400 mg/day for 1 month).	19 schizo-affective manic	2 of the lithium patients and 6 of the CPZ patients dropped out. Of those left 3 of 6 lithium patients made a complete recovery and 2 made a partial recovery. 2 of 5 CPZ patients made a complete recovery and 2 made a partial recovery	Conclusion was that lithium was not specific for discrete manic symptoms
	41 schizo-affective depressed individuals were randomized to CPZ (avg. dose 600 mg/day) or CPZ + amitriptyline (450 mg/day CPZ + 150 mg/day amitriptyline) or amitriptyline (avg. 182 mg/day)	41 schizo-affective depressed	1 amitriptyline patient, 3 CPZ patients and 1 patient on amitriptyline-CPZ dropped out. Of those remaining 1 of 13 amitriptyline patients responded (with 5 partial responses). 4 of 11 CPZ patients (2 partial response) vs. 2 of 12 on the combination (7 partial responses). CPZ alone was better in decreasing depressive and schizophrenic symptomatology	
Biederman et al., 1979	5 week double-blind trial involving 36 patients randomized to lithium carbonate (avg. lithium levels 0.82–1.08 mEq/L) and haloperidol (avg. dose 27.38 mg/day) or placebo and haloperidol (26–36 mg/day) over a 5-week period. Patients were divided into a schizophrenic schizo-affective group (predominance of schizophrenic symptoms) vs. an affective schizo-affective group (predominance of affective symptoms)	36	The 18 patients treated with lithium haloperidol combination improved to a significantly greater degree than individuals on the haloperidol-placebo group as measured by BPRS, manic and CGI rating scales. This improvement was true for both the affective schizo-affectives and schizophrenic schizo-affectives	

The improvement scores in both manic and schizophrenic items on BPRS and PSE rating scales were approximately equal for lithium and chlorpromazine. In a 1-month evaluation of schizo-depressed patients these investigators noted that 1 of 13 patients given amitriptyline completely recovered as opposed to 4 of 11 on chlorpromazine and 2 of 12 on a chlorpromazine-amitriptyline combination. Improvement in depressive schizophrenics and total symptomatology was more prominent for the chlorpromazine alone patients as opposed to the other two groups.

One of the reasons for suspecting lithium's efficacy in schizo-affective patients is the clinical impression that lithium might work specifically on the target affective symptoms (elation and hyperactivity) that these patients show. In a recent study involving schizo-affective patients, Biederman et al. (1979) subdivided schizo-affectives into schizophrenic schizo-affectives (predominance of schizophrenic symptoms) vs. affective-schizo-affectives (predominance of affective symptoms). They then followed 36 patients over 5 weeks and compared the efficacy of haloperidol and placebo vs. haloperidol and lithium. Lithium and haloperidol were statistically superior to haloperidol + placebo in both the affective and schizophrenic schizo-affectives.

Two open studies have examined the prophylactic efficacy of lithium in schizo-affectives. Angst et al. (1970) in examining the effectiveness of long-term lithium in 114 bipolar, 58 unipolar and 72 schizo-affectives, found a decrease in the frequency of episodes in 67% of the bipolars ($p < .001$), 57% of the unipolars ($p < .001$) and 49% of the schizo-affectives ($p < .02$) in a mirror image evaluation (patients being given lithium, and comparing their course with a corresponding time period before lithium therapy). Smulevich et al. (1974) followed 49 schizo-affective manic patients over a 1-year period and noted a complete disappearance of episodes in 32 patients and a reduction in number or decrease in severity in 9 others.

The above studies seem to suggest that lithium has a beneficial effect in some schizo-affective patients either alone or in combination with a neuroleptic. The recent study of Biederman et al. (1979) would seem to indicate that the response of lithium is more than against specific affective symptoms.

Lithium in psychotic disorders

Open and anecdotal reports have suggested the utility of lithium in catatonia (Abrams and Taylor, 1976) and paranoid disorders (Forssman and Wallender, 1969; Lipkin et al., 1970). A recent study by Perris (1978) looked at lithium's effectiveness in 'cycloid psychosis'. Though this is not an official RDC or DSM III diagnosis it is described as categorized by: 1) confusion with agitation or retardation; 2) paranoid and/or hallucinations not syntonic with levels of mood; 3) motility disturbances (hypokinesia and hyperkinesia); 4) elevated mood; 5) pan-anxiety. In between these 'episodic periods of psychosis' was complete remission. Perris (1978) followed 30 patients (who probably met RDC criteria for schizo-affective illness) for a period of 1–8.5 years and noted less morbidity in patients who took lithium as opposed to those who did not. Perris' conclusion which may have important clinical utility was that lithium may have usefulness in decreasing the frequency, severity, and duration of 'episodic remitting psychotic disturbances'.

Lithium in other psychiatric disorders

Lithium has been examined in individuals with recurrent alcoholism (Kline et al., 1974; Merry et al.,1976) and amphetamine abuse (Flemenbaum,1974; Van Kammen and Murphy, 1975; Angrist and Gershon, 1979) with some reported success. Double-blind placebo controlled studies have suggested efficacy for lithium in individuals with episodic aggression (Sheard, 1976) and in behavioural disturbances of mental retardates (Naylor et al., 1974). There also seems to be some evidence for lithium's efficacy in a variety of childhood behaviour disorders (Campbell and Fish, 1977; Youngerman and Canino, 1978; Davis, 1979). Though further studies need to be carried out to fully evaluate lithium's effectiveness in these syndromes it is clear that there may be uses for lithium in psychiatric syndromes other than affective disorders.

Lithium in non-psychiatric disorders

Lithium has been used in granulocytopenic states (Gupta et al., 1976) inappropriate ADH (Baker et al., 1977), hyperthyroidism (Temple et al., 1972; Kristensen et al., 1976), Meniere's disease (Thomson et al., 1976), Huntington's chorea (Mattsson and Persson, 1973; Leonard et al., 1974; Vestergaard et al., 1977), and epilepsy (Erwin et al., 1973; Morrison et al., 1973). (For a complete description of the non-psychiatric uses of lithium see Prien and Schou, 1979.) For the most part these observations are anecdotal but they clearly require further systematic investigation to fully evaluate the utility and range of lithium's efficacy.

CLINICAL MANAGEMENT

The treatment of the acutely manic patient is usually accomplished in a hospital setting. The acutely manic patient usually has a high degree of elation or irritability and increased psychomotor agitation with accompanied poor judgement and insight. Such individuals exhibit grandiose delusions and severe agitation and as a result deny their illness and tend to be uncooperative toward treatment. Such patients tend to be a danger to themselves and others often require involuntary hospitalization.

Some patients exhibiting mild elevation of mood, mild irritability and mild increase in motor activity (hypomanic) can be treated as outpatients but before this can be accomplished the physician must be assured that the patient has a strong social network and active family involvement so as to insure supervision and dispension of medication for the patient.

Treatment of acute (severe) mania

The goal of treatment is to produce a therapeutic blood level of a minimum of 0.9 mEq/L. Usually control of a manic episode occurs when the serum lithium level is in the range of 0.9–1.4 mEq/L (Prien et al., 1972) but while these levels serve as guidelines both dose and blood level should be individually titrated against therapeutic response and toxicity.

Lithium is usually started on a 300 mg b.i.d.–t.i.d. regimen. Lithium can be increased at the rate of 300 mg every 1 to 2 days until an average 1,200–3,000 mg of lithium/day is needed to control the manic symptoms. The reason for the slow rise of lithium is that side effects of lithium therapy appear to correlate with the steepness of the absorptive rise rather than the actual peak of blood lithium levels. During the early stages of treatment (the first 2 weeks) serum lithium levels should be routinely monitored (with samples obtained 9–12 hours after the last dose) approximately three times per week in hospital if severe mania is being treated.

In an effort better to approximate the lithium dosage needed to achieve serum levels of 0.9–1.4 mEq/L and thus alleviate manic symptoms, Cooper and Simpson (1976) developed a technique whereby a lithium-free patient is given 600 mg of lithium, a lithium level is drawn 24 hours later, and from this individual dosage requirements are predicted.

24 hour serum level	*Dosage required*
Less than 0.05*	1,200 mg t.i.d.
0.05–0.09*	900 mg t.i.d.
.10– .14	600 mg t.i.d.
.15– .19	300 mg t.i.d.
.20– .23	300 mg t.i.d.
.24– .30	300 mg b.i.d.
More than .30*	300 mg b.i.d.

* Patient should be monitored closely

It must be pointed out that these are general guidelines and good clinical observation in terms of therapeutic efficacy and toxicity is required in addition to monitoring of lithium levels.

Lithium has a latent period of between 5–14 days before becoming clinically effective. For this reason it is useful to start with an antipsychotic agent on the first day of treatment particularly if the patient is extremely active (Prien et al., 1972). Typical agents for acute mania include chlorpromazine 300–1200 mg/day or haloperidol 10–60 mg/day but in theory any neuroleptic may be used. Though initial reports suggested severe adverse reaction between lithium and neuroleptics (Cohen and Cohen, 1974) the combination has been found to be safe and effective in the acute treatment of mania (Baastrup et al., 1976). It is felt by some (Shopsin et al., 1975) that neuroleptics merely suppress manic hyperactivity whereas lithium's action is specific but this requires further validation. At any rate, as soon as the patient's symptoms have come under control from the neuroleptic-lithium combination the neuroleptic dosage can be titrated downward at the rate of 10% per 1–2 days until it is withdrawn (usually by the 3rd–4th week of treatment) to avoid exposing the patient to additional side effects.

Maintenance therapy

Maintenance therapy is an extension of treatment initiated to suppress an acute affective episode. Once a manic episode is controlled the patient is usually not able to tolerate such high dosage and toxicity can develop. Doses can generally be reduced after the alleviation of acute manic symptoms to 900–1800 mg/day maintaining serum levels of 0.8–1.2 mEq/L. The natural course of a bipolar episode is approximately 4.4 months (Angst et al., 1979) so it seems reasonable that following an acute episode lithium should be continued for at least a 6–9 month period so as to insure that the disruptive and possibly life-threatening manic episode has run its course.

The question of long-term prophylaxis for both bipolar and unipolar patients remains. About 30% of patients who suffer one affective episode will never have another one (Peselow and Gershon, 1980a). In addition, the mean interval between episodes is long (bipolar patients – 35 months; unipolar patients – 57 months) (Angst et al., 1979). Treating someone for an illness that will not recur for years exposes the patient to the side effects of a drug (lithium) that may not be altogether innocuous. Though there is no specific rule that guides lithium prophylaxis we suggest the following: if the individual has had only a single episode of illness or if he has widely spaced intervals (as suggested by Angst et al., 1979) long-term prophylaxis need not be indicated. In addition, some intervals have seasonal variation to their illness and it may eventually be possible for those people to receive lithium only for that part of the year for which they are vulnerable (if seasonal cycling is clearly documented). In addition, some individuals suffer minor mood swings and for some of these patients the benefits of prophylactic medication may not exceed the risks. However, if the patient does have several affective episodes (i.e. 3 episodes for a bipolar patient every 2 years or 2 episodes for a unipolar patient every 2–3 years) prophylaxis is indicated.

For the bipolar patient the treatment of choice is lithium. Though no absolute minimum levels have been established it seems clear that individuals should receive enough lithium levels to have at least a minimum serum level of greater than 0.4 mEq/L (Hullin, 1980). The usual recommendation in common practice is a dose of 600–1800 mg of lithium per day achieving blood levels of 0.6–1.2 mEq/L. If the individual starts to exhibit a recurrence of hypomanic symptomatology the lithium dose can be increased (as a general rule 300 mg of lithium raises the blood level 0.2 mEq/L) or a neuroleptic may be added. If the individual exhibits a recurrence of depression an antidepressant may be added. In bipolar patients in whom lithium does not provide adequate protection a neuroleptic or antidepressant (to prevent manic and depressive episodes respectively) may provide adequate protection although there are few controlled studies to support this (Quitkin et al., 1981b).

For the unipolar patient the choice is not as clear cut, despite the evidence presented that lithium may be superior to antidepressants in long-term prophylaxis. Whether one uses lithium or antidepressants depends upon the clinical situation. Generally if an individual has responded acutely to a tricyclic the same agent should be used for maintenance therapy. If the tricyclic proves inadequate to alleviate future depressive episodes, lithium should be employed. Few controlled studies suggest adequate serum lithium levels for prophylaxis in unipolar illness (Prien and Caffey, 1976; Decina and Fieve, 1981) but it is suggested that lithium levels should be maintained between 0.8–1.2 mEq/L or doses of 600–1800 mg of lithium a day.

Lithium can be started at any phase of affective illness and if it is started for prophylaxis one can begin at 300 mg b.i.d. and increase at the rate of 300 mg every 3–4 days until adequate serum levels are obtained. Lithium levels for prophylaxis should be check-

312

ed at least weekly over the first month of treatment. Once the level is stable (i.e. two consecutive levels yielding values within .05 mEq/L) the lithium serum level can be checked less frequently. A good recommendation is to have it checked every 4–6 weeks although some clinicians feel subsequent tests can be done every 2 months. The FDA package insert recommends every 1–2 months for maintenance-lithium monitoring.

Side effects of lithium therapy

The side effects of lithium therapy have been described by Reisberg and Gershon (1979). A lithium toxicity checklist developed by Gershon and Shopsin (1973) is shown (Fig. 1). Brown (1980) noted that side effects such as diarrhoea, nausea, fine tremor (unresponsive to antiparkinsonism medication), thirst, increased urination, abdominal discomfort, fatigue,

LITHIUM TOXICITY CHECKLIST (LTCL)*

Gastrointestinal symptoms
1. Anorexia
2. Nausea
3. Vomiting
4. Diarrhoea
5. Constipation
6. Dryness of the mouth
7. Metallic taste

Neuromuscular symptoms and signs
1. General muscle weakness
2. Ataxia
3. Tremor
4. Muscle hyperirritability
   a) Fasciculation (increased by tapping muscle)
   b) Twitching (especially of facial muscles)
   c) Clonic movements of whole limbs
5. Choreoathetotic movements
6. Hyperactive deep tendon reflexes

Central nervous system
1. Anesthesia of skin
2. Incontinence of urine and feces
3. Slurred speech
4. Blurring of vision
5. Dizziness
6. Vertigo
7. Epileptiform seizures
8. Electroencephalographic (EEG) changes

Mental symptoms
1. Difficulty concentrating
2. Slowing of thought
3. Confusion
4. Somnolence
5. Restlessness, disturbed behavior
6. Stupor
7. Coma

Cardiovascular system
1. Pulse irregularities
2. Fall in blood pressure
3. Electrocardiographic (ECG) changes
4. Peripheral circulatory failure
5. Circulatory collapse

Miscellaneous
1. Polyuria
2. Polydipsia
3. Glycosuria
4. General fatigue
5. Lethargy and a tendency to sleep (drowsiness)
6. Dehydration
7. Skin rash-dermatitic lesions
8. Weight loss
9. Weight gain
10. Alopecia
11. Quincke's edema

* Prepared by S. Gershon and B. Shopsin (1973).

Fig. 1.

lethargy, and muscle weakness may appear within the first week of treatment. Recent evidence seems to suggest that they are most prominent within the first 2 months of treatment and are independent of lithium serum level (Peselow et al., 1981d). They seem to disappear with continued lithium treatment and are possibly related to the steepness of the rise in lithium level as opposed to the absolute lithium level. Other side effects, hypothyroidism and goitre, polydipsia and polyuria, weight gain, oedema, leukocytosis and mild memory impairment may be present during maintenance therapy at average serum levels. For the most part they are reversible. Though they may be present and troublesome to some, they usually represent minor symptoms toward which the patient can accustom himself and are in a sense inconvenience rather than true hazards for him.

In some patients severe lithium toxicity can occur. This is usually only if the serum lithium level approaches 2.0 mEq/L but can occur occasionally with lithium levels in the therapeutic range. The onset is usually (but not necessarily) gradual and usually preceded by prodromal symptoms. These symptoms may include sluggishness, lassitude, drowsiness, confusion, slurred speech, ataxia, fine and coarse tremor or muscle twitching, anorexia, vomiting and diarrhoea. Severe lithium poisoning primarily affects the CNS. Consciousness is impaired, coma may develop, the muscles may be hypertonic and rigid with hyperactive deep tendon reflexes and muscle tremor and fasciculations may be seen. Cerebellar symptoms such as tremor, ataxia, slurred speech + Romberg sign and nystagmus may occur.

The initial treatment of lithium poisoning is to discontinue lithium. Melia (1970) indicated that lithium levels decrease by 50% every 1–2 days after lithium is discontinued and Allgen (1969) demonstrated that lithium levels of 2.6–3.0 mEq/L drop to zero in 10–12 days. In severe cases adjunction measures such as forced lithium diuresis (20 g I.V. urea 2–5 times daily or 50–100 g I.V. mannitol) may be used. Lithium clearance can be increased with 0.5 g aminophylline or alkalinization of the urine. If the poisoning is severe the patient should be dialyzed. Most patients who recover from states of lithium poisoning including those who were comatose may show no permanent sequelae.

CONCLUSION

In the 30 years since its introduction, it is clear that lithium has revolutionized the acute and prophylactic treatment of affective disorders and as such its reputation has been firmly established thoughout the scientific community. However, reports of efficacy in other psychiatric and non-psychiatric disorders indicate that lithium may not be specific for manic-depressive illness. It is clear that lithium's utility in disease states other than affective disorders requires further systematic double-blind trials. It is hoped that these further studies can distinguish psychopathological features and specific biochemical and physiological mechanisms which are common to lithium-responding cases.

ACKNOWLEDGEMENTS

The authors gratefully acknowledge the assistance of Mrs. Louise Mussolini in the preparation of this manuscript.

This study was supported in part by the Columbia-Millhauser Depression Center Fund,

The Columbia-Presbyterian Medical Center Depression Research Fund, The Foundation for Depression and Manic Depression, Inc., the Marmot Fund, Federal Grant MH21586 and the New York State Department of Mental Hygiene.

APPENDIX

Feighner-RDC

A.   Euphoria or irritability.

B.   Other features; at least three of the following:
1) Hyperactivity (social, motor, and/or sexual)
2) Push of speech
3) Flight of ideas
4) Grandiosity
5) Decreased sleep
6) Distractability

MANIA

C.   Duration: At least 2 weeks with no other pre-existing, non-affective psychiatric disorder or concomitant disorder that could account for manic symptomatology.

D.   There are patients who fulfill the above criteria, but who also have a massive or peculiar alteration of perception and thinking as a major manifestation of their illness. These patients are currently classified as having a schizo-affective phychosis.

Manic Disorder (may immediately precede or follow Major Depressive Disorder).

A through E are required for the episode of illness being considered.

A.   One or more distinct periods with a predominantly elevated, expansive, or irritable mood. The elevated, expansive, or irritable mood must be a prominent part of the illness and relatively persistent although it may alternate with depressive mood. Do not include if apparently due to alcohol or drug use.

B.   If mood is elevated or expansive, at least three of the following symptom categories must be definitely present to a significant degree, four if mood is only irritable. (For past episodes, because of memory difficulty, one less symptom is required.) Do not include if apparently due to alcohol or drug use.
1) More active than usual — either socially, at work, at home, sexually, or physically restless.
2) More talkative than usual or felt a pressure to keep talking.
3) Flight of ideas (as defined in this manual) or subjective experience that thoughts are racing.
4) Inflated self-esteem (grandiosity, which may be delusional).
5) Decreased need for sleep.
6) Distractibility, i.e. attention is too easily drawn to unimportant or irrelevant external stimuli.
7) Excessive involvement in activities without recognizing the high potential for painful consequences, e.g. buying sprees, sexual indiscretions, foolish business investments, reckless driving.

C.   Overall disturbance is so severe that at least one of the following is present:
1) Meaningful conversation is impossible.
2) Serious impairment socially, with family, at home, at school, or at work.
3) In the absence of (1) or (2), hospitalization.

D.   Duration of manic features at least one week beginning with the first noticeable change in the subject's usual condition (or any duration if hospitalized).

E.   None of the following which suggest Schizophrenia is present. (Do not include if apparently due to alcohol or drug use.)
1)   Delusions of being controlled (or influenced), or thought broadcasting, insertion, or withdrawal (as defined in this manual).
2)   Non-affective hallucinations of any type (as defined in this manual) throughout the day for several days or intermittently throughout a 1-week period.
3)   Auditory hallucinations in which either a voice keeps up a running commentary on the subject's behaviours or thoughts as they occur, or two or more voices converse with each other.
4)   At some time during the period of illness had more than one week when he exhibited no prominent depressive or manic symptoms but had delusions or hallucinations.
5)   At some time during the period of illness had more than one week when he exhibited no prominent manic symptoms but had several instances of marked formal thought disorder (as defined in this manual), accompanied by either blunted or inappropriate affect, delusions or hallucinations of any type, or grossly disorganized behaviour.

DSM III

Manic Episode

Differential diagnosis. Organic Affective Syndromes; Schizophrenia, Paranoid Type; Schizo-affective Disorder; Cyclothymic Disorder.

Diagnostic criteria

A.   One or more distinct periods with a predominantly elevated, expansive, or irritable mood. The elevated or irritable mood must be a prominent part of the illness and relatively persistent, although it may alternate or intermingle with depressive mood.

B.   Duration of at least one week (or any duration if hospitalization is necessary), during which, for most of the time, at least three of the following symptoms have persisted (four if the mood is only irritable) and have been present to a significant degree:
1)   Increase in activity (either socially, at work, or sexually) or physical restlessness.
2)   More talkative than usual or pressure to keep talking.
3)   Flight of ideas or subjective experience that thoughts are racing.
4)   Inflated self-esteem (grandiosity, which may be delusional).
5)   Decreased need for sleep.
6)   Distractibility, i.e. attention too easily drawn to unimportant or irrelevant external stimuli.
7)   Excessive involvement in activities that have a high potential for painful consequences which is not recognized, e.g. buying sprees, sexual indiscretions, foolish business investments, reckless driving.

C.   Neither of the following dominates the clinical picture when an affective syndrome is absent (i.e. symptoms in criteria A and B above):
1)   Preoccupation with a mood-incongruent delusion or hallucination (see definition below).
2)   Bizarre behaviour.

D.   Not superimposed on either Schizophrenia, Schizophreniform Disorder, or a Paranoid Disorder.

E.   Not due to any Organic Mental Disorder, such as Substance Intoxication.

(Note: A hypomanic episode is a pathological disturbance similar to, but not as severe as, a manic episode.)

316

Fifth-digit code numbers and criteria for subclassification of manic episode:

6-In Remission. This fifth-digit category should be used when in the past the individual met the full criteria for a manic episode but now is essentially free of manic symptoms or has some signs of the disorder but does not meet the full criteria. The differentiation of this diagnosis from no mental disorder requires consideration of the period of time since the last episode, the number of previous episodes, and the need for continued evaluation or prophylactic treatment.

4-With Psychotic Features. This fifth-digit category should be used when there apparently is gross impairment in reality testing, as when there are delusions or hallucinations or grossly bizarre behaviour. When possible specify whether the psychotic features are mood-congruent or mood-incongruent. (The non-ICD-9-CM fifth-digit 7 may be used instead to indicate that the psychotic features are mood-incongruent; otherwise, mood-congruence may be assumed.)

Mood-congruent Psychotic Features: Delusions or hallucinations whose content is entirely consistent with the themes of inflated worth, power, knowledge, identity, or special relationship to a deity or famous person; flight of ideas without apparent awareness by the individual that the speech is not understandable.

Mood-incongruent Psychotic Features: Either (a) or (b):

(a)   Delusions or hallucinations whose content does not involve themes of either inflated worth, power, knowledge, identity, or special relationship to a deity or famous person. Included are such symptoms as persecutory delusions, thought insertion, and delusions of being controlled, whose content has no apparent relationship to any of the themes noted above.

(b)   Any of the following catatonic symptoms: stupor, mutism, negativism, posturing.

2-Without Psychotic Features. Meets the criteria for manic episode, but no psychotic features are present.

0-Unspecified.

REFERENCES

Abrams, R. and Taylor, M.   (1976)   Catatonia, a prospective clinical study. Arch. Gen. Psychiatry 83, 579–581.

Akiskal, H. S., Djenderedjian, A. H. and Rosenthal, R. H.   (1977)   Cyclothymic disorder validating criteria for inclusion in the bipolar affective group. Am. J. Psychiatry 134, 1227–1233.

Akiskal, H. S., Khani, M. S. and Strauss, A. S.   (1979)   Cyclothymic temperamental disorders. In: H. S. Akiskal (Ed), Psychiatric Clinics of North America. W. B. Saunders, Philadelphia, pp. 527–554.

Alexander, P. E., Van Kammen, D. and Bunney, W. E.   (1979)   Antipsychotic effects of lithium in schizophrenia. Am. J. Psychiatry 136, 283–287.

Allgen, L. G.   (1969)   Laboratory experience with lithium toxicity in man. Acta Psychiatr. Scand. (Suppl. 207), 98–104.

American Psychiatric Association   (1980)   Diagnostic and Statistical Manual for Mental Disorders (DSM III). APA Press, Washington, D.C.

Angrist, B. and Gershon, S.   (1979)   Variable attenuation of amphetamine effects by lithium. Am. J. Psychiatry 136, 806–810.

Angst, J., Weis, P. and Graf, P.   (1970)   Lithium prophylaxis in recurrent affective disorders. Br. J. Psychiatry 116, 604–614.

Angst, J., Felder, W. and Frey, R.   (1979)   The course of unipolar and bipolar affective disorders. In: M. Schou and E. Stromgren (Eds), Origin, Prevention and Treatment of Affective Disorders. Academic Press, London, pp. 215–226.

Annell, A. (1972) Lithium in the treatment of children and adolescence. In: J. Mendels and S. Secunda (Eds), Lithium in Medicine. Gordon and Breech, London, pp. 85–96.

APA Task Force (1975) Current status of lithium therapy. Am. J. Psychiatry 132, 997–1001.

Baastrup, P. C., Poulsen, K. O. S., Schou, M., Thomsen, K. and Amdisen, A. (1970) Prophylactic lithium double-blind discontinuation in manic depressive and recurrent depressive disorders. Lancet ii, 326–330.

Baastrup, P. C., Hollnagel, P. and Sorensen, R. (1976) Adverse reactions in treatment with lithium carbonate and haloperidol. J. Am. Med. Assoc. 236, 2645–2646.

Baker, R. S., Hurley, R. M. and Feldman, W. (1977) Treatment of recurrent syndromes of inappropriate secretion of antidiuretic hormone with lithium kidney function. Lancet ii, 379.

Baron, M., Gershon, E. S. and Rudy, V. (1975) Lithium carbonate response in depression prediction by unipolar/bipolar illness average evoked response, catechol-o-methyl transferase and family history. Arch. Gen. Psychiatry 32, 1107–1111.

Biederman, J., Lerner, Y. and Belmaker, R. (1979) Combination of lithium carbonate and haloperidol in schizo-affective disorder. Arch. Gen. Psychiatry 36, 327–333.

Blackwell, B. (1970) Lithium. Lancet ii, 875–876.

Brockington, I. F., Kendell, R. E., Kellett, J. M., Curry, S. H. and Wainwright, S. (1978) Trials of lithium, chlorpromazine and amitriptyline in schizo-affective illness. Br. J. Psychiatry 133, 162–168.

Brown, W. T. (1980) The pattern of lithium side effects and toxic reactions in the course of lithium therapy. In: F. N. Johnson (Ed), Handbook of Lithium Therapy. MTP Press, Lancaster, Pa. pp. 279–288.

Bunney, W. E., Goodwin, F. K., Davis, J. M. and Fawcett, J. A. (1968) A behavioral biochemical study in lithium therapy. Am. J. Psychiatry 125, 91–103.

Cade, J. F. (1949) Lithium in the treatment of psychotic excitement. Med. J. Aust. ii, 349.

Campbell, M. and Fish, B. (1977) Lithium and chlorpromazine. A controlled crossover study of hyperactive severely disturbed young children. J. Autism. Child. Schizophr. 2, 234–263.

Cohen, W. J. and Cohen, N. H. (1974) Lithium carbonate, haloperidol and irreversible brain damage. J. Am. Med. Assoc. 230, 1283–1287.

Cooper, T. B. and Simpson, G. M. (1976) The 24 hour lithium level as a prognisticator of dosage requirement – a 2 year followup study. Am. J. Psychiatry 133, 440–443.

Coppen, A., Noguera, R. and Bailey, J. (1971) Prophylactic lithium in affective disorder. Lancet ii, 275–279.

Coppen, A., Montgomery, S. A., Gupta, R. K. and Bailey, J. E. (1976) A double-blind comparison of lithium carbonate and maprotiline in the prophylaxis of affective disorders. Br. J. Psychiatry 128, 479–485.

Coppen, A., Ghose, K., Rao, R., Bailey, J. and Peet, M. (1978a) Mianserin and lithium in the prophylaxis of depression. Br. J. Psychiatry 133, 206–210.

Coppen, A., Ghose, I., Montgomery, S., Rao, R., Bailey, J. and Jorgensen, A. (1978b) Continuation therapy with amitriptyline in depression. Br. J. Psychiatry 133, 28–33.

Corcoran, A. C., Taylor, R. D. and Page, I. H. (1949) Lithium poisoning from use of salt substitutes. J. Am. Med. Assoc. 139, 685–688.

Cundall, R. L., Brooks, P. W. and Murray, L. G. (1972) A controlled evaluation of lithium prophylaxis in affective disorders. Psychol. Med. 2, 308–311.

Davis, J. M. (1976) Overview – maintenance therapy in psychiatry. II. Affective disorders. Am. J. Psychiatry 133, 1–11.

Davis, R. (1979) Manic-depressive variant syndrome of childhood – a preliminary report. Am. J. Psychiatry 136, 702–705.

Decina, P. and Fieve, R. R. (1981) Prophylactic serum lithium levels in recurrent unipolar depression. J. Clin. Psychopharmacol. 1, 150–151.

Donnelly, E. F., Goodwin, F. K., Waldman, I. N. and Murphy, D. L. (1978) Prediction of antidepressant response to lithium. Am. J. Psychiatry 135, 552–556.

Dunner, D. L., Goodwin, F. K. and Gershon, E. S. (1972) Excretion of 17-OH corticosteroids in unipolar and bipolar depressed patients. Arch. Gen. Psychiatry 26, 360–363.

318

Dunner, D. L., Stallone, F. and Fieve, R. R. (1976a) Lithium carbonate and affective disorders. Arch. Gen. Psychiatry 33, 117–120.

Dunner, D. L., Gershon, E. S. and Goodwin, F. K. (1976b) Heritable factors in severity of affective illness. Biol. Psychiatry 11, 31–42.

Endicott, J., Andressen, N. C. and Clayton, P. J. (1980) Bipolar II – combine or keep separate. Sci. Proc. of 133rd American Psychiatric Convention, San Francisco p. 183.

Erwin, C. W., Gerber, W. and Morrison, S. D. (1973) Lithium carbonate and convulsive disorders. Arch. Gen Psychiatry 26, 57–63.

Feighner, J. P., Robins, E., Guze, S. G., Woodruff, R. A., Winokur, G. and Munoz, R. (1972) Diagnostic criteria for use in psychiatric research. Arch. Gen Psychiatry 25, 57–63.

Fieve, R. R. (1973) Overview of the therapeutic and prophylactic trials. In: S. Gershon and B. Shopsin (Eds), Lithium – its Role in Psychiatric Research and Treatment. Plenum Press New York, pp. 317–350.

Fieve, R. R. and Dunner, D. L. (1975) Unipolar and bipolar affective states. In: F. Flach and S. Draghi (Eds), The Nature and Treatment of Depression. John Wiley and Sons New York, pp. 147–160.

Fieve, R. R. and Mendlewicz, J. (1972) Lithium prophylaxis in bipolar manic-depressive illness. Psychopharmacology 26, 93.

Fieve, R. R., Platman, S. R. and Plutchik, R. R. (1968) The use of lithium in affective disorders. I – Acute endogenous depression. Am. J. Psychiatry 125, 487–491.

Fieve, R. R., Dunner, D. L., Kumbarachi, T. and Stallone, F. (1975) Lithium carbonate in affective disorders. Am. J. Psychiatry 82, 1541–1544.

Fieve, R. R., Kumbarachi, T. and Dunner, D. L. (1976a) Lithium prophylaxis of depression in bipolar I, biopolar II and unipolar patients. Am. J. Psychiatry 133, 925–929.

Fieve, R. R., Dunner, D. L., Kumbarachi, T. and Stallone, F. (1976b) Lithium carbonate prophylaxis of depression in three subtypes of primary affective disorder. Pharmakopsychiatry 9, 100–107.

Fieve, R. R., Go, R. and Dunner, D. L. (1981) A multi-center morbid risk family study of 433 affectively ill patients and their 2717 relatives. Paper presented at 3rd World Congress Biological Psychiatry, Stockholm, Sweden, July, 1981.

Fleiss, J. L., Dunner, D. L., Sallone, F. and Fieve, R. R. (1976) The life table – a method for analyzing longitudinal studies. Arch. Gen. Psychiatry 33, 107–112.

Flemenbaum, A. (1974) Does lithium block the effect of amphetamines – a report of 3 cases. Am. J. Psychiatry 131, 820–821.

Forssman, H. and Wallender, J. (1969) Lithium treatment on atypical indications. Acta Psychiatr. Scand. 207 (Suppl.), pp. 41–48.

Garfinkel, P. E., Stancer, H. C. and Persad, E. (1980) A comparison of haloperidol, lithium carbonate and their combination in the treatment of mania. J. Affect. Dis. 2, 279–288.

Gershon, S. and Shopsin, B. (1973) Toxicology of the lithium ion. In: S. Gershon and B. Shopsin (Eds), Lithium – its Role in Psychiatric Research and Treatment. Plenum Press, New York, pp. 237–757.

Gershon, S. and Yuwiler, A. (1960) Lithium ion – a specific pharmacological approach to the treatment of mania. J. Neuropsychiatry 1, 229–241.

Goodwin, F. K. and Ebert, M. H. (1973) Lithium in mania-controlled trials. In: S. Gershon and B. Shopsin (Eds), Lithium – its Role in Psychiatric Research and Treatment. Plenum Press, New York, pp. 237–252.

Goodwin, F. K. and Zis, A. (1979) Lithium in the treatment of mania. Arch. Gen Psychiatry 36, 840–844.

Goodwin, F. K., Murphy, D. L. and Bunney, W. E. (1969) Lithium carbonate in the treatment of mania and depression – a longitudinal double-blind study. Arch. Gen. Psychiatry 21, 486–496.

Goodwin, F. K., Murphy, D. L. and Dunner, D. L. (1972) Lithium response in unipolar vs. bipolar depression. Am. J. Psychiatry 129, 44–47.

Goodwin, F. K., Post, R. H. and Sack, R. L. (1974) Cerebrospinal fluid MHPG in affective illness. Sci. Proc. Am. Psychiatr. Assoc. 127, 100–101.

Grof, P., Schou, M. and Angst, J. (1970) Methodological problems of prophylactic trials in recurrent affective disorders. Br. J. Psychiatry 116, 599–603.

Growe, G., Crayton, J. W. and Kloss, D. (1979) Lithium in chronic schizophrenics. Am. J. Psychiatry 136, 454–455.

Gupta, R. C., Robinson, W. A. and Kurnick, J. E. (1976) Felty syndrome. Effect of lithium on granulocylopolesis. Am. J. Med. 61, 29–32.

Hansen, C. J., Retboll, K. and Schou, M. (1968) Lithium in psychiatry. A review. J. Psychiatr. Res. 6, 67–95.

Hullin, R. P. (1980) Minimum serum levels for effective prophylaxis. In: F. N. Johnson (Ed), Handbook of Lithium Therapy. MTP Press, Lancaster, England, pp. 243–247.

Hullin, R. P., McDonald, R. and Allsop, M. N. E. (1972) Prophylactic lithium in recurrent affective disorders. Lancet i, 1044–1046.

Jefferson, J. W. and Griest, J. H. (1977) Primer of Lithium Therapy. Williams and Wilkins, Baltimore.

Johnson, G. (1974) Antidepressant effect of lithium. Compr. Psychiatry 15, 43–47.

Johnson, G., Gershon, S. and Hekiman, L. J. (1968) Controlled evaluation of lithium and chlorpromazine in the treatment of acute manic states. An interim report. Compr. Psychiatry 9, 563–573.

Johnson, G., Gershon, S. and Burdock, E. I. (1971) Comparative effects of lithium and chlorpromazine in the treatment of manic states. Br. J. Psychiatry 119, 267–276.

Kay, D. W. K., Fahy, T. and Barside, R. F. (1970) A seven month double-blind trial of amitriptyline and diazepam in ECT-treated depressed patients. Br. J. Psychiatry 117, 667–671.

Klerman, G. L., DiMascio, A., Weissman, M., Prusoff, B. and Paykel, E. S. (1974) Treatment of depression by drugs and psychotherapy. Am. J. Psychiatry 131, 186–191.

Kline, N. S., Wren, J. C. and Cooper, T. B. (1974) Evaluation of lithium therapy in acute and chronic alcoholism. Am. J. Med. Sci. 268, 15–22.

Kristensen, O., Andersen, A. H. and Pallisgaard, G. (1976) Lithium carbonate in the treatment of thyrotoxicosis. A controlled trial. Lancet i, 603–605.

Kukopulos, A. and Reginaldi, D. (1980) Recurrences of manic-depressive episodes during lithium treatment. In: F. N. Johnson (Ed), Handbook of Lithium Therapy. MTP Press, Lancaster, pp. 109–177.

Leonard, D. P., Kidson, M. A., Shannon, P. J. and Brown, J. (1974) Double-blind trial of lithium carbonate and haloperidol in Huntington's chorea. Lancet ii, 1208–1299.

Leonhard, K., Korff, I. and Shulz, H. (1962) Die temperamente in der famillier der monopolaren und bipolaren phasischen psychosen. Psychiatr. Neurol. 134, 416–434.

Lipkin, K., Dyrud, J. and Meyer, G. (1970) The many faces of mania. Arch. Gen. Psychiatry 22, 262–267.

Maggs, R. (1963) Treatment of manic illness with lithium carbonate. Br. J. Psychiatry 109, 56–65.

Mattsson, B. and Persson, S. A. (1973) Huntington's chorea, lithium and GABA. Lancet ii, 684.

Melia, P. I. (1970) Prophylactic lithium – a double-blind trial in recurrent affective disorders. Br. J. Psychiatry 116, 621–624.

Mendels, J. (1976) Lithium in the treatment of depression. Am. J. Psychiatry 133, 373–377.

Mendels, J., Secunda, S. K. and Dyson, W. C. (1972) A controlled study of the antidepressant effects of lithium. Arch. Gen. Psychiatry 26, 154–157.

Merry, J., Reynolds, C. M., Bailey, J. and Coppen, A. (1976) Prophylactic treatment of alcoholism by lithium carbonate. Lancet ii, 481–482.

Mindham, R. H. S., Howland, C. and Shepherd, M. (1973) An evaluation of continuation therapy with tricyclic antidepressants in depressive illness. Psychol. Med. 3, 5–17.

Morrison, S. D., Erwin, C. W. and Gianturco, D. T. (1973) Effect of lithium carbonate on combative behavior in humans. Dis. Nerv. Syst. 34, 186–189.

Naylor, G. J., Donald, J. M. and LePoidevin, D. (1974) A double-blind study of long-term lithium in mental defectiveness. Br. J. Psychiatry 124, 52–57.

Noack, C. H. and Trautner, E. (1951) Lithium treatment of maniacal psychosis. Med. J. Aust. 38, 219–222.

Noyes, R., Dempsey, G. M. and Blum, A. (1974) Lithium treatment of depression. Compr. Psychiatry 15, 187–193.

Perris, C. (1978) Morbidity suppressive effect of lithium carbonate in cycloid psychosis. Arch. Gen. Psychiatry 35, 328–331.

Persson, G. (1972) Lithium prophylaxis in affective disorders. An open trial with matched controls. Acta Psychiatr. Scand. 48, 462–479.

Peselow, E. D. and Gershon, S. (1980) Update on depression. Res. House Staff Phys. Vol. 26, No. 11, 82–100.

Peselow, E. D., Dunner, D. L., Fieve, R. R., Deutsch, S. I. and Lautin, A. (1980) The use of the life table in evaluating lithium prophylaxis in bipolar II and other affective subtypes. IRCS Med. Sci. 8, 680–682.

Peselow, E. D., Dunner, D. L., Fieve, R. R., Deutsch, S. I. and Kaufman, M. (1981a) Psychopharmacology in clinical practice. The prophylaxis of unipolar depression. Paper presented at the American Psychiatric Convention, New Orleans, Louisiana, May 12, 1981.

Peselow, E. D., Dunner, D. L., Fieve, R. R. and Lautin, A. (1981b) Lithium prophylaxis against depression in cyclothymic patients – a life table analysis. Compr. Psychiatry 22, 257–264.

Peselow, E. D., Dunner, D. L., Fieve, R. R. and Lautin, A. (1981c) Lithium prophylaxis of depression in unipolar, bipolar II and cyclothymic patients. Am. J. Psychiatry (in press).

Peselow, E. D., Dunner, D. L., Fieve, R. R. and Rubinstein, M. E. (1981d) Course and relationship of lithium side effects to plasma lithium level. Psychiatr. Clin. (in press).

Platman, S. R. (1970) A comparison of lithium carbonate and chlorpramazine in mania. Am. J. Psychiatry 127, 351–353.

Pope, H. G. and Lipinski, J. F. (1978) Diagnosis of schizophrenia and manic depressive illness. Arch. Gen. Psychiatry 35, 811–826.

Prien, R. F. (1980) Continuation therapy in depression: observations from a multihospital collaborative study. Am. Coll. Neuropsychopharmacol. p. 66.

Prien, R. F. and Caffey, E. M. (1976) Relationship between dosage and response to lithium prophylaxis in recurrent depression. Am. J. Psychiatry 133, 567–570.

Prien, R. F. and Schou, M. (1979) Nonpsychiatric uses of lithium. In: T. B. Cooper, S. Gershon, N. S. Kline and M. Schou (Eds), Lithium: Controversies and Unresolved Issues. Excerpta Medica, Amsterdam, pp. 157–167.

Prien, R. F., Caffey, E. M. and Klett, C. J. (1972a) A comparison of lithium carbonate and chlorpromazine in the treatment of mania. Arch. Gen. Psychiatry 26, 146–153.

Prien, R. F., Caffey, E. M. and Klett, C. J. (1972b) Comparison of lithium carbonate and chlorpromazine in excited schizo-affectives. Arch. Gen. Psychiatry 27, 182–187.

Prien, R. F., Caffey, E. M. and Klett, C. J. (1973a) Prophylactic efficacy of lithium carbonate in manic-depressive illness. Report of the Veterans Administration and National Institute of Mental Health Collaborative Study Group. Arch. Gen. Psychiatry 28, 337–341.

Prien, R. F., Klett, C. J. and Caffey, E. M. (1973b) Lithium carbonate and imipramine in the prevention of affective episodes: a comparison of recurrent affective illness. Arch. Gen. Psychiatry 29, 420–425.

Procci, W. (1976) Schizo-affective illness. Fact or fiction. Arch. Gen. Psychiatry 33, 1167–1177.

Quitkin, F., Rifkin, A., Klein, D. and Davis, J. M. (1976) On prophylaxis of unipolar illness. Am. J. Psychiatry 133, 1091–1092.

Quitkin, F., Rifkin, A., Kane, J., Ramos-Lorenzi, J. and Klein, D. F. (1978) Prophylactic effect of lithium and imipramine in unipolar and bipolar II patients. A preliminary report. Am. J. Psychiatry 135, 570–572.

Quitkin, F., Kane, J., Rifkin, A., Ramos-Lorenzi, J., Saraf, K., Howard, A. and Klein, D. F. (1981a) Lithium and imipramine in the prophylaxis of unipolar and bipolar II depression. A prospective placebo controlled comparison. Psychopharmacol. Bull. 17, 1, 142–144.

Quitkin, F., Kane, J., Rifkin, A., Ramos-Lorenzi, J. and Nayak, D. V. (1981b) Prophylactic lithium carbonate with and without imipramine for bipolar I patients. Arch. Gen. Psychiatry 38, 902–909.

Reisberg, B. and Gershon, S. (1979) Side effects associated with lithium therapy. Arch. Gen. Psychiatry 36, 879–887.

Schou, M., Juel-Nielson, N. and Stromgren, E. (1954) The treatment of manic psychoses by the administration of lithium salts. J. Neurol. Neurosurg. Psychiatry 17, 250–260.

Schou, M., Baastrup, P. C. and Grof, P.   (1970)   Pharmacological and clinical problems of lithium prophylaxis. Br. J. Psychiatry 116, 615–619.

Seager, C. E. and Bird, R.   (1962)   Imipramine with electrical treatment in depression. A controlled trial. J. Ment. Sci. 108, 704–707.

Sheard, M.   (1976)   The effect of lithium on impulsive aggressive behavior in man. Am. J. Psychiatry 133, 1409–1413.

Shopsin, B. and Gershon, S.   (1978)   Lithium-clinical consideration. In: L. L. Iverson, S. D. Iverson and S. H. Snyder (Eds), Handbook of Psychopharmacology, Vol. 14. Plenum Publishing Corp., New York, pp. 275–325.

Shopsin, B., Kim, S. S. and Gershon, S.   (1971)   A controlled study of lithium vs. chlorpromazine in acute schizophrenics. Br. J. Psychiatry 119, 435–440.

Shopsin, B., Gershon, S., Thompson, H. and Collins, P.   (1975)   Psychoactive drugs in mania. A controlled comparison of lithium carbonate, chlorpromazine and haloperidol. Arch. Gen. Psychiatry 32, 32–42.

Small, J. G., Kellams, J. J. and Milstein, V.   (1975)   A placebo controlled study of lithium combined with neuroleptics in chronic schizophrenic patients. Am. J. Psychiatry 132, 1315–1317.

Smulevich, A. B., Zavidowskaya, G. I. and Igonia, A. L.   (1974)   The effectiveness of lithium in affective and schizo-affective disorders. Br. J. Psychiatry 125, 65–72.

Spitzer, R. L., Endicott, J. and Robins, E.   (1978)   Research Diagnostic Criteria (RDC) for a seleceted group for functional disorders. NY State Psychiatric Institute, New York.

Spring, G., Schrveid, D. and Gray, C.   (1970)   A double-blind comparison of lithium and chlorpromazine in the treatment of manic states. Am. J. Psychiatry 126, 140–144.

Stallone, F., Shelley, E., Mendlewicz, J. and Fieve, R. R.   (1973)   The use of lithium in affective disorders III. A double blind study in prophylaxis in bipolar illness. Am. J. Psychiatry 130, 1006–1010.

Stein, M. K., Rickels, C. and Weise, C. C.   (1980)   Maintenance therapy with amitriptyline. A controlled trial. Am. J. Psychiatry 137, 370–371.

Stokes, P. E., Stoll, P. M., Shamorian, C. A. and Patton, M. J.   (1971)   Efficacy of lithium in the acute treatment of manic depressive illness. Lancet i, 1319–1325.

Takahashi, R., Sakuma, A. and Itoh, K.   (1975)   Comparison of the efficacy of lithium carbonate and chlorpromazine in mania. Arch. Gen. Psychiatry 32, 1310–1318.

Talbott, J. H.   (1950)   Use of lithium salts as a substitute for sodium chloride. Arch. Int. Med. 85, 1.

Temple, R., Berman, M., Robbins, J. and Woff, J.   (1972)   The use of lithium in the treatment of thyrotoxicosis. A controlled trial. Lancet i, 603–605.

Thomsen, J., Bech, P., Geisler, A., Prytz, S., Rafaelsen, O. J., Vendksborg, P. and Zilstorff, K.   (1976)   Lithium treatment of Meniere's disease. Acta Otolaryngol. (Stockholm) 83, 294–296.

Van Kammen, D. and Murphy, D. L.   (1975)   Attenuation of the euphoriant and activating effects of d and l-amphetamine by lithium carbonate. Psychopharmacologia 44, 215–224.

Van Putten, T. and Sanders, D. G.   (1975)   Lithium in treatment failures. J. Nerv. Ment. Dis. 161, 255–264.

Vestergaard, P., Baastrup, P. C. and Petersson, H.   (1977)   Lithium treatment of Huntington's chorea – a placebo controlled clinical trial. Acta Psychiatr. Scand. 56, 183–188.

Wald, D. and Lerner, J.   (1979)   Lithium in the treatment of periodic catatonia – a case report. Am. J. Psychiatry 135, 751–752.

Watanabe, S., Taguchi, K. and Nakoya, K.   (1973)   Clinical effects of lithium carbonate in depression. Folia Psychiatr. Neurol. (Japn.) 27, 173–181.

Watanabe, S., Ishino, H. and Otsuki, S.   (1975)   Double-blind comparison of lithium carbonate and imipramine in treatment of depression. Arch. Gen. Psychiatry 32, 659–668.

Worrall, E. P., Moody, J. P., Peet, M., Dick, P., Smith, A., Chambers, C., Adams, M. and Naylor, G.   (1979)   Controlled studies of the acute antidepressant effects of lithium. Br. J. Psychiatry 135, 255–262.

Youngerman, J. and Canino, I.   (1978)   Lithium carbonate use in children and adolescence. Arch. Gen. Psychiatry 35, 216–224.

Section VI

ENDORPHINS

Burrows/Norman/Davies (eds) Antidepressants
© *1983, Elsevier Science Publishers*

Chapter 20

Endorphins and depression: Potential for new approaches

JACK D. BARCHAS, JOHN MADDEN, IV, ECKARD WEBER,
CHRISTOPHER J. EVANS

and

PHILIP A. BERGER

Nancy Pritzker Laboratory of Behavioral Neurochemistry and Stanford Mental Health Clinical Research Center, Department of Psychiatry and Behavioral Sciences, Stanford University School of Medicine, Stanford, California, CA 94305, U.S.A.

INTRODUCTION

An entirely new approach to the study of depression may be afforded by the recently discovered neuropeptides, particularly the endorphins (opioid-like peptides). A variety of neuropeptides have been described and these materials are now believed to function as neuroregulators (Barchas et al., 1978). Previously associated as peripheral hormones and as pituitary hormones and releasing factors, neuropeptides are now recognized as extremely important for brain function and believed to be potentially of considerable significance to psychiatry and mental health.

The history of the discovery of the opioid peptides, those whose actions are similar to opiates such as morphine, is a fascinating study of the development of a scientific area. Briefly, two routes both led to the discovery. One was the finding of the opiate receptor, postulated by Goldstein (Goldstein et al., 1971) and described later by three groups in an independent research effort in which the findings were described essentially simultaneously (Pert and Snyder, 1973, Simon et al., 1973; Terenius, 1973). Those studies demonstrated that there was a stereospecific receptor for opiate substances in brain. The intellectual approach that was used in those efforts has been quite important to the development of neurosciences in general for it has been applied to other potential transmitters. The other intellectual approach came from behavioural observations that there are areas within the brain which when stimulated result in analgesia. The striking observation was made (Akil et al., 1972) that the opiate antagonist, naloxone, would block the pain relief from electrical stimulation. This finding was a strong stimulus to Kosterlitz in suggesting that the brain might have its own opiate substances, as was subsequently reported (Hughes et al., 1975).

The finding of opiate substances in the brain has electrified the neurosciences. At a basic research level it has profoundly altered the views of the brain and led to an immediate increase in our concept of the complexity of neuronal systems and their interactions. There are now recognized to be several different opioid-like systems in the brain. The two most generally studied to date are those related to the enkephalins and those related to β-endorphin. As we shall discuss, there are other neuropeptide systems in the brain which may also prove of interest and importance to the study of mental processes and of depression.

ENDORPHINS IN BRAIN

The term endorphin refers to the entire group of endogenous opioid peptides. There are six major opioid peptides which are now known to be present in brain tissue (Table 1). These include the pentapeptides met-enkephalin and leu-enkephalin, as well as a heptapeptide related to met-enkephalin (Hughes et al., 1975; Lewis et al., 1979; Boarder et al., 1982b, c); β-endorphin (Li and Chung, 1976); dynorphin (Goldstein et al., 1979); and α-Neo-endorphin (Kangawa et al., 1981). These materials are found with different distribution patterns and there is reason to believe that some may share origins while others have different origins.

Although met-enkephalin can be shown to be represented in β-endorphin, it has now been shown that the two enkephalins and β-endorphin have different precursors. Certainly anatomically these peptides are present with quite different distribution patterns. The enkephalins are extensively distributed throughout the neuraxis while β-endorphin is found in a very confined projection pathway which originates in the arcuate nucleus of the hypothalamus and terminates mainly in the limbic forebrain areas and brain stem structures (Barchas et al., 1978). β-Endorphin is made from a large molecular weight precursor which also contains adrenocorticotropic hormone (ACTH) and some melanotropin-like peptides (Mains et al., 1977; Roberts and Herbert, 1977a, b; Chang et al., 1980). Enkephalins are made from a different precursor which has multiple copies of the enkephalins within it (Comb et al., 1982a, b; Gubler et al., 1982; Noda et al., 1982). With regard to dynorphin and α-Neo-endorphin, very recent evidence suggests that the two materials are found in the same neuronal pathways and in the same neurons (Weber et al., 1981b; Weber et al., 1982). The precursor for the two materials may be the same and future studies addressing this problem are of special importance since these materials are very active opioids. Therefore, at least two separate opioid peptide neuronal systems exist; namely the β-endorphin systems and the enkephalin pentapeptide systems. How these relate to the α-Neo-endorphin/dynorphin system has yet to be determined.

The work that has been done to date has derived from isolation of the peptides and their characterization. Yet other aspects of our knowledge involving these systems have come from studies using the tools of molecular biology which take advantage of a new

TABLE 1

β-ENDORPHIN

β-LPH (61–91) (human)
Tyr–Gly–Gly–Phe–Met–Thr–Ser–Glu–Lys–Ser–Gln–Thr–Pro–
Leu–Val–Thr–Leu–Phe–Lys–Asn–Ala–Ile–Ile–Lys-Asn–Ala–Tyr–Lys–Lys–Gly–Glu

THE ENKEPHALINS

methionine-enkephalin
Tyr–Gly–Gly–Phe–Met
leucine-enkephalin
Tyr–Gly–Gly–Phe–Leu
methionine-enkephalin–Arg–Phe (heptapeptide)
Tyr–Gly–Gly–Phe–Met–Arg–Phe

DYNORPHIN-RELATED PEPTIDES

dynorphin (1–17) (porcine)
Tyr–Gly–Gly–Phe–Leu–Arg Arg–Ile–Arg–Pro–Lys–Leu–Lys–Trp–Asp–Asn–Gln(OH)
α-neo-endorphin (porcine)
Tyr–Gly–Gly–Phe–Leu–Arg–Lys–Tyr–Pro–Lys

methodology allowing the cloning in bacteria and nucleotide sequencing of messenger RNAs coding for these neuropeptides. Through these powerful techniques it has been possible to surmise the existence of putative peptide hormones not previously isolated and to know their structure prior to their isolation. While this methodology gives invaluable information as to the amino acid sequence of neuroactive peptides, only limited information can be obtained as to the post-translational processing and covalent modifications. For studying these final post-translational products other more classical techniques of peptide chemistry and biochemistry are required. For example, in the rat pituitary β-endorphin is now known to be present in multiple forms of varying chain lengths (Evans et al., 1981; Weber et al., 1981a) many of which are much less bioactive than the parent molecule as opioids but which may have other activities. It will be necessary to determine not only the exact structure of these post-translational variants of neuropeptides but also to determine the roles of these modified substances in terms of the differential effects physiologically and behaviourally. A fruitful field of studies will be to determine whether they are present in brain or pituitary in differential patterns in various psychiatric disorders.

STUDIES SUGGESTING AN ALTERATION IN BRAIN AND CSF OPIOID PEPTIDES IN RELATION TO DEPRESSION

The literature dealing with the possible relationship of endogenous opioids to patients with affective disorders is still at a very early stage of development. Particularly interesting are the pharmacological investigations of the effects of endogenous opioids and their derivatives in relation to depression. One could anticipate that opioid peptides might alter depression. Opioid alkaloids have long been recognized at a clinical level as having anti-depressant-like activity, although there is no double-blind controlled study of such effects.

Recently, the mixed opioid agonist-antagonist buprenorphine has been reported to have antidepressant effects in a preliminary double-blind investigation (Emrich et al., 1981). Further, clinical observations suggest that cessation of opioid administration in some individuals who have received opioid alkaloids for medical reasons, such as pain, may be associated with striking depressive symptoms.

A series of studies has been conducted which bear on the effects of endogenous opioids in relation to depression. A series of investigations have centred about administration of β-endorphin, a major endogenous opioid. When given peripherally, β-endorphin does appear to have physiological effects centrally in terms of hormonal responses and EEG changes (Pfefferbaum et al., 1979; Berger et al., 1980). An important study (Angst et al., 1979) reported that in three of six depressed patients there was a change from depression to hypomania after a 10 mg intravenous injection of β-endorphin. Two other studies have had a similar suggestion although with fewer controls: one (Kline et al., 1977), which stimulated considerable interest, used varying doses in a design that was not double-blind and reported some transient improvement. Another study (Catlin et al., 1980) also suggested a transient decrease in depressive symptoms in depressed patients. A study using appropriate controls (Gerner et al., 1980) was performed involving nine patients in a placebo-controlled double-blind crossover design. This group has provided evidence that transient improvement was noted in depressive symptoms each time β-endorphin was administered. Another double-blind study has also noted transient symptomatic improvement in a group of depressed patients using a double-blind paradigm (Pickar et al., 1981).

A different approach to the study of opioid peptides in relation to depressive disorders is to be found in the studies of changes in CSF in relation to manic-depressive disorder. A provocative and important observation was made (Terenius et al., 1976) involving a set of opioid-like substances the identity of which is not yet clear. These materials, which the investigators labelled Fraction I and Fraction II are not identical to β-endorphin or the enkephalins. Fraction I was reported to be elevated in three of four manic subjects and Fraction II was increased during normal mood states in these patients. It will be important for these studies to be replicated and to determine the chemical nature of these fractions. In light of the variety of opioid substances in the CSF, a number of studies are underway. For example, it has been suggested (Almay et al., 1978) that there is a significant correlation between opiate binding activity and depth of depressive symptomatology.

A pharmacological approach from another direction involves the use of opioid agonists in relation to psychiatric disorders. In particular, following on the positive studies dealing with hallucinations seen in schizophrenia (Gunne et al., 1977; Watson et al., 1978, 1979, 1981), has come investigation of the effects of naloxone in manic patients. Generally, investigators are not finding changes following high doses (Pickar et al., 1982), although an early study in a different population was suggestive (Judd et al., 1978). An approach to the β-endorphin system using another neuroregulator system is suggested by studies with physostigmine, a drug known to inhibit cholinesterase and thereby to increase acetylcholine. When the drug is given it can dramatically alter mania and convert the symptoms to depression (Janowsky et al., 1973, 1974; Davis et al., 1978). At such times it has been found (Risch et al., 1980) that β-endorphin is elevated in the plasma, although a cause and effect relationship cannot be demonstrated.

Studies such as those described raise the question as to whether there is an absolute or relative decrease in endorphin-like activity in association with depression. An endorphin hypothesis of mental disorders would postulate either a change in one or another endorphin-like substance and need not refer to β-endorphin itself; thus, the hypothesis could be valid in terms of β-endorphin, one of the enkephalins, or the dynorphin/α-Neo-endorphin system. Each of these systems has opioid-like activity and the nature of their receptor interactions is sufficiently poorly understood that there could be cross reactivities between receptors for them. If a hypothesis of a relative deficiency were to be correct, there might well be a pivotal or critical change in another system. There are striking interactions between endogenous opioid systems and other neuroregulators. For example, opioid-peptide-containing cell innervate the locu coeruleus and could thereby alter the noradrenergic system (Watson et al., 1980). Involvement of the opioid systems might still be related to a balance between systems such as the serotonergic, dopaminergic, or noradrenergic system — to each of which there has been demonstrated an endogenous opioid link.

STUDIES OF OPIOID-LIKE MATERIALS IN HUMAN PLASMA

Endorphin-like activity has been reported by several investigators to be present in the plasma. Such materials are probably derived from the pituitary gland. It is known that there are endorphins in the pituitary and the release of these would thereby account for the presence of β-endorphin or a related substance from the pituitary. In rats (Guillemin et al., 1977) evidence has been presented that a β-endorphin-like material is released at the same time that ACTH is released. The same group also reported that both β-endorphin-like activity and ACTH release were inhibited by dexamethasone. The implication is that in rodents the two are always released together and controlled by similar mechanisms. Recent work in humans and non-human primates suggests a complex mechanism in which the two systems may be separately activated, for dexamethasone fails to suppress release of endorphin-like materials in the plasma (Kalin et al., 1980).

A limited number of studies have been performed dealing with plasma β-endorphin-like substances. These studies are particularly difficult because of the problem of lack of specificity of the assays and the fact that β-LPH, the immediate precursor of β-endorphin, which has no opioid activity, will cross react with β-endorphin in the assays. Further, even the most essential effort to determine the identity of the materials under study, such as the use of column chromatography separation, is rarely undertaken and only immunoreactive substances are determined. This caveat suggests that careful scrutiny is essential in assessing publications and reports dealing with β-endorphin activity in plasma because while very tempting such reports may be misleading.

There have been studies which attempted to determine the concentration of β-endorphin-like substance in plasma in psychiatric patients. For example, a study has been performed (Emrich et al., 1979) in which the concentration of β-endorphin-like materials was determined in patients before and after electroconvulsive therapy. Increased immunoreactivity activity was demonstrated after the electroconvulsive therapy sessions. These studies are suggestive and of interest for future research must determine whether the change is involved in any aspects of the improvement in the depressive state. It will be especially important to determine whether there is an alteration in the pattern of release of endorphin-like materials into the plasma that would be analogous to that revealed by the dexamethasone

330

suppression test for the pituitary-adrenal axis involving ACTH and steroids.

In order to consider the relationship between plasma opioid substances and depression disorder, a series of studies (Boarder et al., 1982a) has been undertaken to determine the nature of the opioid active substances in blood. While still in their earliest stages, those studies are demonstrating that the situation is indeed quite complex and that there are many different substances that will need to be considered, some of which had not previously been recognized. Four forms of opioid peptides have been described in human blood: β-endorphin (Sarne et al., 1980), β-endorphin immunoreactive plasma factor sized between β-endorphin and met-enkephalin (Ho et al., 1979), and a humoral endorphin of molecular weight 1,000–4,000 (Hexum et al., 1980). A report has also been published that met-enkephalin circulates in human plasma (Clement-Jones et al., 1980).

To approach the issue of opioid-like materials in human plasma, acid acetone extracts of plasma have been analysed using column chromatography. Evidence has been obtained for the existence of opioid peptides of several different molecular weights and a large number of peptides and small proteins which generate opioid activity following tryptic digestion (Boarder et al., 1982a). One strong candidate for opioid activity would be dynorphin since it is present in the secretory terminals in the neural lobe of the pituitary. The results obtained to date demonstrate that dynorphin-like immunoreactivity may indeed be present in human plasma in more than one molecular weight form. In addition, two other peptides which are not accounted for by any of the others described and which seem to constitute the major amount of opioid-like material in human blood can also be noted. The concentration is substantially higher than that of dynorphin or of β-endorphin. These materials could be β-endorphin or dynorphin products not picked up by our radio-immunoassays. The evidence to date suggests that materials may be released which are related to enkephalins and may be slightly larger than met-enkephalin. It has been reported by several workers that the adrenal medulla is able to form opioid peptides related to enkephalins (Lewis et al., 1979). Indeed the adrenal medulla, traditionally viewed as an organ involved in the formation of catecholamines, may also be extremely important as an organ forming and releasing opioid peptides.

It is most likely then that the circulating opioids in the plasma consists of various forms of β-endorphin from the pituitary, various forms of dynorphin most likely from the pituitary, and various forms of enkephalins which may arise from the adrenal medulla. It is of interest that the circulating opioid peptides may be rapidly altered by stress. A doubling in apparent concentration was noted (Boarder et al., 1982a) within minutes with mild stress which may parallel the change in plasma adrenaline that occurs with mild stress. The circulating levels of these peptides are many times greater than the amounts of methionine-enkephalin reported in the literature and the apparent concentration of C-terminal β-endorphin immunoreactivity.

It will be critical to find out exactly what the structure is of the various opioid-like peptides that are present in the plasma and to study their release and turnover. The concentrations of the substances may not reflect their release as they may be utilized and metabolized at different rates. However, the significant levels of the larger enkephalin-containing forms raises the possibility that they may have roles other than as precursors for enkephalin. An area of future research will be the role of these various substances in relation to psychiatric states and particularly in relation to depression.

THE LEARNED HELPLESSNESS AND OTHER ANIMAL MODELS OF DEPRESSION

The concept of learned helplessness is proving to be an important approach to the study of depression. As early as the second century A.D., Aretaeus had advanced the view that depression is characterized by hopelessness, powerlessness, and a sense of futility. Psychological conceptions of depression were developed into a coherent framework by Freud (Freud, 1957) and extended by many others (Bibring, 1953). Today, several theoretical viewpoints have dominated the recent empirically oriented literature on depression and included among them is Seligman's helplessness model of depression. These views on depression (Seligman, 1974, 1975) are rooted in early laboratory findings that dogs given inescapable shock were subsequently poorer at escaping shock than were dogs given prior escapable shock or no shock at all (Overmier and Seligman, 1967; Seligman and Maier, 1967).

Such prior experience with uncontrollable, noxious stimulation is said to result in learned helplessness. This is manifested in motivational deficits and in interference with learning of new response contingencies. The helpless organism is said to have learned that response and outcome are independent. It was proposed (Seligman, 1975) that this laboratory phenomenon of learned helplessness modelled reactive depression in man. In particular, it was argued that beliefs in the uncontrollability of outcomes resulted in depression, irrespective of the correspondence of such beliefs to objective states.

In summary, Seligman's theory proposed that when individuals learn that there is no contingency between responses and outcomes, they not only refrain from admitting adaptive responses but also evidence salient cognitive-affective features of depressive-states, hopelessness, and helplessness. Such characteristics are consistent with, and in a general way, parallel behaviours observed in the earlier animal studies from which Seligman's initial views on depression developed.

Recently, Maier and his colleagues have observed an additional proactive effect of inescapable stress, that is, heightened analgesia in animals previously exposed to inescapable stress when tested 24 hours later following a mild reactivation stress. Study of the neurochemical substrates of this long-term analgesic reaction to inescapable stress has been initiated (Maier et al., 1980a, b). The behaviour has implications for depressive disorders. Initially it was hypothesized that if this form of analgesia was mediated by the endogenous opioid system that it may be sensitive to opiate antagonists. Administration of opiate antagonists was investigated in terms of their effects on the analgesic response which occurs 24 hours after the inescapable shock, an analgesia which is activated by exposure to very mild shock that would otherwise have no analgesic effect had the animal not previously had inescapable shock. The findings to date have revealed that naltrexone, administered prior to inescapable shock or prior to analgesic testing, can completely prevent or reverse the long-term analgesic response and that this pharmacological action occurs in a dose-dependent manner. Naloxone administration can also completely reverse the long-term analgesia, further suggesting that this long-term analgesic effect is mediated by an opiate sensitive system. Interestingly, short-term analgesia, that the authors (Madden et al., 1977) and others have studied, is also blocked by a prior naltrexone administration suggesting that the short-term and long-term analgesia may be mediated by similar neurochemical systems.

These observations may have relatively important implications to depressive disorders when it is recognized that not only have inescapable stressors been shown to also produce analgesic reactions in man but more importantly it has been reported (Davis et al., 1979) that patients with either bipolar or unipolar affective illness like animals which had received prior inescapable stress demonstrate a heightened analgesic reaction in response to subsequent stress when compared to their respective controls. There is suggestive but not conclusive evidence that endogenous opioid systems may play a role in the mediation of both affective states and pain reactivity in affective illness. The implications of these findings to various aspects of depression await further investigation.

Other animal models may also prove worthy of further investigation. Certainly investigation of the effects of opioids and opioid antagonists in the separation induced depression model in nonhuman primates (Suomi and Harlow, 1977; Colotla, 1979) will also be worthy of investigation. These studies will also require the determination of changes in endogenous opioids.

Another animal model, potentially related to depression but requiring further development, involves the use of separation distress vocalization as seen in juvenile and adult guinea pigs. These vocalizations are increased by naloxone, suggesting that endogenous opioids may decrease them (Herman and Panksepp, 1978; Panksepp et al., 1978).

DIRECTIONS FOR FUTURE STUDY

We have described a variety of approaches to the study of endorphins and efforts to link the substances to depression. There is a need for more knowledge regarding the variety of neuroactive peptides, including endorphins, in the brain and hormonal systems. Recent evidence of multiple forms of endogenous opioid peptides and evidence that post-translational modification may be important suggest the need for basic information. It is essential to establish what peptides are present and what biological activities they have. In addition, as highlighted for several peptides discussed in this chapter, it is important to develop information regarding the nature of the substances, their neural pathways and intracellular localization, metabolic pathways of formation, genetic controls on those mechanisms, and metabolic processing including post-translational alterations including covalent modifications. Related to such information are molecular genetic approaches which may permit the diagnosis of disease process by recognition of the alterations produced with genetic variation. These approaches through broad genetic screening might provide basic information and at the same time permit the chemical definition of subtypes of disorders (Barchas and Sullivan, 1982).

Regulation of the inactivation mechanisms of the endorphins will also be important information. There is currently limited information regarding the conversion of larger peptides, active or inactive, to smaller substances which may have biological activity or represent a means of inactivation (Sullivan et al., 1980). Enzymes involved in these pathways tend to be nonspecific at a biochemical level, obtaining their specificity through the geometry of the cells. There is need for more information regarding these enzymes, and about possible pharmacological inhibitors. One could imagine treatment methods oriented to drugs which might alter the ratio of opioid peptides by modifying their enzymatic processing.

Receptors for opioid peptides appear to be differentially sensitive to varying endogenous ligands (Hewlett et al., 1981). Characterization of the receptors could result in the definition of more specific agents interacting with only a cluster of the possible receptors. Such agents, if they could be used with safety, would permit a degree of greater specificity of treatment.

Studies of the role of endorphins in depression must include evaluation of the ways in which pharmacological agents or somatic agents, which are used for the treatment of depression, alter endorphins. There is already substantial evidence that endorphins in brain can be altered by electroconvulsive shock (Hung et al., 1979).

Investigations into the relationships between the endorphins and other neuroregulator systems should prove to be a significant area of research. If, as now seems to be the case, there are multiple neuroregulators within a single neuron, then it will be essential to learn what substances are in that category and the ways in which they act in a combined way either with synergy or antagonism. Further, the balance between systems of neuroregulators involving different nerve cells will be an important direction of basic research and may be an important direction of future clinical hypotheses. A variety of other peptides may also be profitably investigated (Cohen and Cohen, 1981).

The combining of biochemical and behavioural studies, in essence determining the behavioural neurochemistry of the endorphins, will be a long-term task in which it is already clear that the materials have direct roles in behaviour and are modified by behaviours. The ways in which these inter-relationships are controlled and the limits imposed on both the biochemical and behavioural systems will be an important area of research. Particularly as it relates to animal models of depression, studies of endorphins may provide a sense of interactions which are significant for the specific behaviours under inquiry as well as for more generalized models.

Clinical studies must build upon the basic information — we cannot search for a substance clinically until we know what the possible substances may be. Using appropriate controls on a Clinical Research Center it should be possible to determine the pattern of changes associated with mania and depression and the return to the normal state. At the present level of knowledge it is clear that there may be changes in endorphins associated with the depressive disorders, the nature of those substances must be specified. Trials with agonists and antagonists, enzyme inhibitors and receptor-active agents, may provide new diagnostic and clinical treatment modalities.

While the study of the endorphins is in its earliest phases there is reason to believe that these materials will be important for the study of depressive disorders (Berger et al., 1982). Endorphins may be important in only some forms of depressive illness or even in only some symptoms of the illnesses. Several avenues of approach and interdisciplinary efforts will be essential for unravelling the relationships between this intriguing class of bioactive neuroregulators and the profound cluster of feelings and emotions we label as the depressive disorders.

ACKNOWLEDGEMENTS

We are deeply appreciative to the editors of this volume for their gracious encouragement in the preparation of this chapter. We thank Sue Poage for her thoughtful secretarial assis-

334

tance. Our work has been supported by a Program-Project Grant MH 23861 from NIMH; a Clinical Research Center Grant MH 30854 from NIMH; and an award from the MacArthur Foundation.

REFERENCES

Akil, H., Mayer, D. J. and Liebeskind, J. C.   (1972)   Comparison chez le rat entre l'analgesie induite par stimulation de la substance grise periaqueducale et l'analgesie morphinique. C.R. Acad. Sci. Ser. D: 274, 3603.

Almay, B. G. L., Johansson, F., Von Knorring, L., Terenius, L. and Wahlstrom, A.   (1978)   Endorphins and chronic pain: 1. Differences in CSF endorphin levels between organic and psychogenic pain syndrome. Pain 5, 153–162.

Angst, J., Autenrieth, V., Brem, F., Koukkou, M., Meyer, H., Stassen, H. and Storek, U.   (1979)   Preliminary results of treatment with β-endorphin in depression. In: E. Usdin, W. E. Bunney, Jr. and N. S. Kline (Eds), Endorphins in Mental Health Research. Macmillan, New York, pp, 518–528.

Barchas, J. D. and Sullivan, S.   (1982)   Opioid peptides as neuroregulators: potential areas for the study of genetic-behavioral mechanisms. Behav. Genet. 12, 69–91.

Barchas, J. D., Akil, H., Elliott, G. R., Holman, R. B. and Watson, S. J.   (1978)   Behavioral neurochemistry: neuroregulators in relation to behavioral states and mental disorders. Science 200, 964–973.

Berger, P. A., Watson, S. J., Akil, H., Elliott, G. R., Rubin, R. T., Barchas, J. D. and Li, C. H.   (1980)   β-Endorphin and schizophrenia. Arch. Gen. Psychiatry 37, 635–640.

Berger, P. A., Akil, H., Watson, S. J. and Barchas, J. D.   (1982)   Behavioral pharmacology of the endorphins. Ann. Rev. Med. 33, 397–415.

Bibring, E.   (1953)   The mechanism of depression. In: P. Greenacre (Ed.), Affective Disorders. International Universities Press, New York.

Boarder, M. R., Erdelyi, E. and Barchas, J. D.   (1982a)   Opioid peptides in human plasma: evidence for multiple forms. J. Clin. Endocrinol. Metab. 54, 715–720.

Boarder, M. R., Lockfeld, A. J. and Barchas, J. D.   (1982b)   Measurement of methionine-enkephalin-[ARG⁶,PHE⁷] in rat brain by specific radioimmunoassay directed at methionine-sulphoxide enkephalin[ARG⁶,PHE⁷]. J. Neurochem. 38, 299–304.

Boarder, M. R., Lockfeld, A. J. and Barchas, J. D.   (1982c)   Met-enkephalin[Arg⁶,Phe⁷] immunoreactivity in bovine caudate and bovine adrenal medulla. J. Neurochem. 39, 149–154.

Catlin, D. H., Gorelick, D., Gerner, R. H., Gui, K. K. and Li, C. H.   (1980)   Clinical effects of β-endorphin infusion. In: E. Costa and E. M. Trabucchi (Eds), Advances in Biochemical Pharmacology: Regulation and Function of Neuropeptides, Vol. 22. Raven Press, New York, pp. 465–472.

Chang, A. C. Y., Cochet, M. and Cohen, S.   (1980)   Structural organization of human genomic DNA encoding the pro-opiomelanocortin peptide. Proc. Natl. Acad. Sci. USA 77 (8), 4890–4894.

Clement-Jones, V., Lowry, P. J., Rees, L. H. and Besser, G. M.   (1980)   Development of a specific extracted radioimmunoassay for methionine-enkephalin in human plasma and cerebrospinal fluid. J. Endocrinol. 86, 231.

Cohen, R. M. and Cohen, M. R.   (1981)   Peptide challenges in affective illness. J. Clin. Psychopharmacol. 1, 214–222.

Colotla, V. A.   (1979)   Experimental depression in animals. In: Psychopathology in Animals, Academic Press, New York, pp. 223–238.

Comb, M., Herbert, E., and Crea, R.   (1982a)   Partial characterization of the mRNA that codes for enkephalins in bovine adrenal medulla and human pheochromocytoma. Proc. Natl. Acad. Sci. USA 79, 360–364.

Comb, M., Seeburg, P. H., Adelman, J., Eiden, L. and Herbert, E.   (1982b)   Primary structure of the human met- and leu-enkephalin precursor and its mRNA. Nature 295, 663–666.

Davis, G. C., Buchsbaum, M. S. and Bunney, W. E.   (1979)   Analgesia to painful stimuli in affective illness. Am. J. Psychiatry 136, 1148–1151.

Davis, K., Berger, P. A., Hollister, L. E. and De Fraites, E. G.   (1978)   Physostigmine in mania. Arch. Gen. Psychiatry 35, 119–222.

Emrich, H. M., Hollt, V., Kissling, W., Fischer, M., Heinemann, H., Von Zerssen, D. and Herz, A.   (1979)   Measurement of β-endorphin-like immunoreactivity in CSF and plasma of neuropsychiatric patients. Adv. Exp. Med. Biol. 116, 307–317.

Emrich, H. M., Vogt, P. and Herz, A.   (1981)   Possible antidepressive effects of opioids – action of buprenorphine. Presented at the New Academy of Sciences Conference on Opioids, October, 1981, New York.

Evans, C. J., Weber, E. and Barchas, J. D.   (1981)   Isolation and characterization of α-N-acetyl β-endorphin (1–26) from the rat posterior/intermediate pituitary lobe. Biochem. Biophys. Res. Commun. 102, 897–904.

Freud, S.   (1957)   Mourning and melancholia. In: J. Strachey (Ed.), The Complete Psychological Works of Sigmund Freud, Vol. 14. Translator: Hogarth Press, London. (Originally published, 1917.)

Gerner, R. H., Catlin, D. H., Gorelick, D. A., Hui, K. K. and Li, C. H.   (1980)   beta-Endorphin intravenous infusion causes behavioral change in psychiatric patients. Arch. Gen. Psychiatry 37, 642–647.

Goldstein, A., Lowney, L. I. and Pal, B. K.   (1971)   Stereospecific and nonspecific interactions of the morphine congener levorphanol in subcellular fractions of mouse brain. Proc. Natl. Acad. Sci. USA 68, 1742–1747.

Goldstein, A., Tachibana, S., Lowney, L. I., Hunkapiller, M. and Hood, L.   (1979)   Dynorphin-(1–13), an extraordinarily potent opioid peptide. Proc. Natl. Acad. Sci. USA 76, 6666–6670.

Gubler, U., Seeburg, P., Hoffman, B. J., Gage, L. P. and Udenfriend, S.   (1982)   Molecular cloning establishes proenkephalin as precursor of enkephalin-containing peptides. Nature 295, 206–208.

Guillemin, R., Vargo, T., Rossier, J., Minick, S., Ling, N., Rivier, C., Vale, W. and Bloom, F.   (1977)   β-Endorphin and adrenocorticotropin are secreted concomitantly by the pituitary gland. Science 197, 1367–1369.

Gunne, L. M., Lindstrom, L. and Terenius, L.   (1977)   Naloxone-induced reversal of schizophrenic hallucinations. J. Neural Trans. 40, 13–19.

Herman, B. H. and Panksepp, J.   (1978)   Effects of morphine and naloxone on separation distress and approach attachment: evidence for opiate mediation of social affect. Pharmacol. Biochem. Behav. 9 (2), 213–220.

Hewlett, W. A., Akil, H. and Barchas, J. D.   (1981)   Differential interactions of dynorphin(1-13), β-endorphin, and enkephalin-related peptides at μ and δ sites in different brain regions. In: Advances in Endogenous and Exogenous Opioids. Elsevier Science Publ. Co., New York.

Hexum, T. D., Yang, H-YT, and Costa, E.   (1980)   Biochemical characterization of enkephalin-like immunoreactive peptides of adrenal glands. Life Sci. 27, 1211.

Ho, W. K. K., Kwok, K. Y. and Lam, S.   (1979)   Characterization of a plasma factor having opiate and immunoactivity like β-endorphin. Biochem. Biophys. Res. Commun. 87, 448.

Hughes, J., Smith, T. W., Kosterlitz, H. W., Fothergill, L. A., Morgan, B. A. and Morris, H. R.   (1975)   Identification of two related pentapeptides from the brain with potent opiate agonist activity. Nature 258, 577–579.

Hung, J. S., Gillin, J. C., Yang, H. T. Y. and Costa, E.   (1979)   Repeated electro-convulsive shocks and the brain content of endorphins. Brain Res. 77, 273–278.

Janowsky, D. S., El-Yousef, K., Davis, J. M. and Sekerke, H. I.   (1973)   Parasympathetic suppression of mania by physostigmine. Arch. Gen. Psychiatry 28, 542–547.

Janowsky, D. S., Khales, M. K. and Davis, J. M.   (1974)   Acetylcholine and depression. Psychosom. Med. 36, 248–257.

Judd, L. L., Janowsky, D. S., Segal, D. S. and Huey, L. Y.   (1978)   Naloxone related attenuation of manic symptoms in certain bipolar depressives. In: J. van Ree and L. Terenius (Eds), Characteristics and Function of Opioids, Vol. 4. Elsevier/North-Holland, Amsterdam, pp. 173–174.

Kalin, N. H., Risch, S. C., Cohen, R. M., Insel, T. and Murphy, D. L.   (1980)   Dexamethasone fails to suppress β-endorphin plasma concentrations in humans and rhesus monkeys. Science 209, 827–828.

Kangawa, K., Minamino, N., Chino, N., Shabakibara, S. and Matsuo, H. (1981) The complete amino acid sequence of α-Neo-endorphin. Biochem. Biophys. Res. Commun. 99, 871–878.

Kline, N. S., Li, C. H., Lehmann, H. E., Lajtha, A., Laski, E. and Cooper, T. (1977) β-Endorphin-induced changes in schizophrenic and depressed patients. Arch. Gen. Psychiatry 34, 1111–1113.

Lewis, R. V., Stern, A. S., Rossier, J., Stein, S. and Udenfriend, S. (1979) Putative enkephalin precursors in bovine adrenal medulla. Biochem. Biophys. Res. Commun. 89, 822–829.

Li, C. H. and Chung, D. (1976) Isolation and structure of an untriakontapeptide with opiate activity from camel pituitary glands. Proc. Natl. Acad. Sci. USA 73, 1145–1148.

Madden, J., Akil, H., Patrick, R. L. and Barchas, J. D. (1977) Stress-induced parallel changes in central opioid levels and pain responsiveness in the rat. Nature 266, 1358–1360.

Maier, S. F., Davies, S., Grau, J. W., Jackson, R. L., Morrison, D. H., Moye, T., Madden, J. IV and Barchas, J. D. (1980a) Opiate antagonists and the long-term analgesic reaction induced by inescapable shock. J. Compr. Physiol. Psychol. 94, 1172–1183.

Maier, S. F., Drugan, R., Grau, J. W., Hyson, R., MacLennan, A. J., Moye, T., Madden, J. IV and Barchas, J. D. (1980b) Learned helplessness, pain inhibition, and the endogenous opiates. In: M. D. Zeiler and P. Harzem (Eds), Advances in Analysis of Behavior, Vol. 4, John Wiley and Sons, New York.

Mains, R. E., Eipper, B. A. and Ling, N. (1977) Common precursor to corticotropins and endorphins. Proc. Natl. Acad. Sci. USA 74, 3014–3018.

Noda, M., Furutani, Y., Takahashi, H., Toyosato, M., Hirose, T., Inayama, S., Nakanishi, S., and Numa, S. (1982) Cloning and sequence analysis of cDNA for bovine adrenal preproenkephalin. Nature 295, 202–206.

Overmier, J. B. and Seligman, M. E. P. (1967) Effects of inescapable shock upon subsequent escape and avoidance learning. J. Compr. Physiol. Psychol. 63, 23–33.

Panksepp, J., Herman, B., Conner, R., Bishop, P. and Scott, J. P. (1978) The biology of social attachments: opiates alleviate separation distress. Biol. Psychiatry 13, 607–618.

Pert, C. B. and Snyder, S. H. (1973) Opiate receptor: demonstration in nervous tissue. Science 179, 1011–1014.

Pfefferbaum, A., Berger, P. A., Elliott, G. R., Tinklenberg, J. R., Kopell, B. S., Barchas, J. D. and Li, C. H. (1979) Human EEG response to β-endorphin. Psychiatry Res. 1, 83–88.

Pickar, D., Davis, G. C., Schulz, C., Extein, I., Wagner, R., Naber, D., Gold, P. W., van Kammen, D. P., Goodwin, F. K., Wyatt, R. J., Li, C. H. and Bunney, W. E., Jr. (1981) Behavioral and biological effects of acute β-endorphin injection in schizophrenic and depressed patients. Am. J. Psychiatry 138 (2), 160–166.

Pickar, D., Vartanian, F., Bunney, W. E., Jr., Maier, H. P., Gastpar, M. T., Prakash, R., Sethi, B. B., Lideman, R., Belyaev, B. S., Tsutsulkovskaja, M. V. A., Jungkunz, G., Nedopil, N., Verhoeven, W. and van Praag, H. (1982) Short-term naloxone administration in schizophrenic and manic patients. Arch. Gen. Psychiatry 39, 313–319.

Risch, S. C., Cohen, R. M., Janowsky, D. S., Kalin, N. H. and Murphy, D. L. (1980) Mood and behavioral effects of physostigmine on humans are accompanied by elevations in plasma β-endorphin and cortisol. Science 209, 1545–1546.

Roberts, J. L. and Herbert, E. (1977a) Characterization of a common precursor to corticotropin and β-lipotropin: cell-free synthesis of the precursor and identification of corticotropin peptides in the molecule. Proc. Natl. Acad. Sci. USA 74, 4826–4830.

Roberts, J. L. and Herbert, E. (1977b) Characterization of a common precursor to corticotropin and β-lipotropin: identification of β-lipotropin peptides and their arrangement relative to corticotropin in the precursor synthesized in a cell-free system. Proc. Natl. Acad. Sci. USA 74, 5300–5304.

Sarne, Y., Gothilf, Y. and Weissman, B. A. (1980) Humoral endorphin: endogenous opiate in blood, cerebrospinal fluid and brain. In: E. L. Way (Ed), Endogenous and Exogenous Opiate Agonists and Antagonists. Pergamon Press, New York, p. 317.

Seligman, M. E. P. (1974) Depression and learned helplessness. In: R. J. Freidman and M. M. Katz (Eds), The Psychology of Depression: Contemporary Theory and Research. V. H. Winston, Washington D.C., pp. 83–125.

Seligman, M. E. P. (1975) Helplessness: On Depression, Development and Death. Freeman, San Francisco.

Seligman, M. E. P. and Maier, S. F. (1967) Failure to escape traumatic shock. J. Exp. Psychol. 74, 1–9.

Simon, E. J., Hiller, J. M. and Edelman, I. (1973) Stereospecific binding of the potent narcotic analgesic (3H) etorphine to rat brain homogenate. Proc. Nat. Acad. Sci. USA 70, 1947–1949.

Sullivan, S., Akil, H., Blacker, D. and Barchas, J. D. (1980) Enkephalinase: selective inhibitors and partial characterization. Peptides 1, 31–35.

Suomi, S. J. and Harlow, H. F. (1977) Production and alleviation of depressive behaviours in monkeys. In: J. D. Maser and M. E. P. Seligman (Eds), Psychopathology: Experimental Models. Freeman, San Francisco.

Terenius, L. (1973) Characteristics of the 'receptor' for narcotic analgesics in synaptic plasma membrane fraction from rat brain. Acta. Pharmacol. Toxicol. 33, 377–384.

Terenius, L., Wahlstrom, A., Linstrom, L., and Widerlov, E. (1976) Increased CSF levels of endorphines in chronic psychoses. Neurosci. Lett. 3, 157–162.

Watson, S. J., Berger, P. A., Akil, H., Mills, M. J. and Barchas, J. D. (1978) Effects of naloxone on schizophrenia: reduction in hallucinations in a subpopulation of subjects. Science 201, 73–75.

Watson, S. J. Akil, H., Berger, P. A. and Barchas, J. D. (1979) Some observations on the opiate peptides and schizophrenia. Arch. Gen. Psychiatry 36, 35–41.

Watson, S. J., Akil, H., Berger, P. A. and Barchas, J. D. (1979) Some observations on the opiate peptide and noradrenalin systems: light microscopic studies. Peptides 1, 23–30.

Watson, S. J., Akil, H., Berger, P. A. and Barchas, J. D. (1981) The endorphins and psychosis. In: S. Arieti and H. K. H. Brodie (Eds), American Handbook of Psychiatry. Basic Books, New York, pp. 3–24.

Weber, E., Evans, C. J., Chang, J-K. and Barchas, J. D. (1981a) Acetylated and nonacetylated forms of β-endorphin in rat brain and pituitary. Biochem. Biophys. Res. Commun. 103, 982–989.

Weber, E., Roth, K. A. and Barchas, J. D. (1981b) Colocalization of α-Neo-endorphin and dynorphin immunoreactivity in hypothalamic neurons. Biochem. Biophys. Res. Commun. 103, 951–958.

Weber, E., Roth, K. A. and Barchas, J. D. (1982) Immunohistochemical distribution of α-Neo-endorphin/dynorphin neuronal systems in rat brain: evidence for colocalization. Proc. Natl. Acad. Sci. USA 79, 3062–3066.

Subject index

340

342

344

346

348

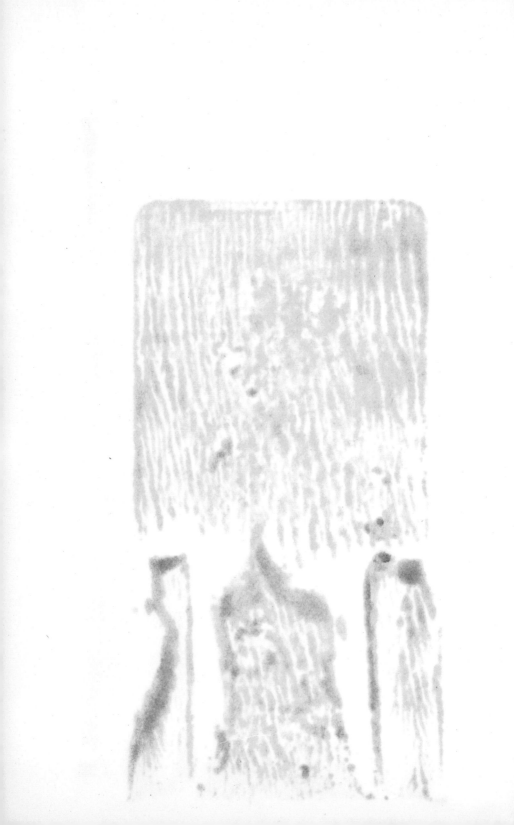

INTRODUCTION TO

Electrical Engineering

THIRD EDITION

INTRODUCTION TO

Electrical Engineering

ROBERT P. WARD

Professor of Electrical Engineering
Agricultural and Mechanical College of Texas

PRENTICE-HALL, INC.

Englewood Cliffs, New Jersey

Library of Congress Catalog Card No. 60-7337

First Printing . . . .*March, 1960*
Second Printing . . . . . .*September, 1960*
Third Printing . . . . .*February, 1964*

PRINTED IN THE UNITED STATES OF AMERICA

48165 — C

PREFACE

This book is intended to be an introduction to electrical science in engineering, and to bridge the gap between the study of electricity and magnetism in physics and the circuits and field courses in engineering. While written primarily for electrical engineering majors, it has been successfully used as an introductory text for students not majoring in the field. The subject matter is, essentially, that traditionally covered in beginning courses in electrical engineering. In keeping with the present trend toward giving the student an earlier and more thorough understanding of the electric circuit, however, proportionately more emphasis has been placed on this phase of the subject.

Following the development of the fundamental concepts and laws in the first three chapters, the fourth chapter is devoted to the steady-state analysis of simple networks containing d-c sources and linear resistances only. The concepts of inductance and capacitance are developed in later chapters, and the final chapter of the book is devoted to the transient response of simple circuits containing these elements and energized by step-voltage or step-current sources. While there is no treatment of the sinusoidal steady state, a method is developed which has proved to be particularly effective for marking the directions selected as positive for the various electromotive forces, current, and voltage drops encountered in sinusoidal circuit analysis. This method is extended to include magnetic fluxes and magnetomotive forces, and in every case the mathematical analysis is closely related to these positive directions. The student learns from the outset that an arrow represents the direction in which a quantity is to be considered positive, and not the actual direction of the quantity.

The mathematical level of the present edition is somewhat above that of previous editions, though this is not apparent in the early chapters of the book. It is expected that, by the time the magnetic field concepts are considered in Chapter VII, the student will be reasonably familiar with the methods of calculus. The use of Δ and Σ followed in the earlier editions is, however, retained even here, in the belief that the mathematical analysis is thereby better related to the physical problem.

The order in which the magnetic concepts are defined has been altered, and the definitions rephrased to conform to the existing standards. Similar changes have been made in the chapter on the electric field. Some descriptive material and some material pertaining to practical applications has been omitted. The material on electronics now appears to be beyond the scope of an introductory course, and, except for certain parts incorporated in Chapter XIII, has been omitted.

Robert P. Ward

CONTENTS

Chapter I

INTRODUCTORY

A note to the student. Much of what follows in this book belongs in one or another of the following categories:

1. Experimental facts — things the truth of which has been determined by observation and experiment.

2. Definitions — things that are true because everybody concerned agrees on their truth.

3. Derived relationships — things that are shown to be true by beginning with experimental facts and definitions, and reasoning logically to a conclusion.

4. Discussion — things that occur to the writer as pertinent to the subject under consideration and that should make for a better understanding on the part of the student.

The student is urged to keep this classification constantly in mind as he reads and to try to place every statement in its proper category. To aid him in this, definitions are either plainly marked *definition* or else the new word or term is in boldface type where it is defined and used for the first time in this book.

The student is warned against falling into the habit of regarding every mathematical expression as a "formula" into which he can substitute numbers and obtain answers. Every such expression is either a definition (defining equation) or a derived relationship and should be recognized as such. In working problems, a conscientious effort should be made to see what has to be done rather than trying to "find a formula." A pretty safe rule to follow is never to use a defining equation unless you can quote the definition, and never to use a derived relationship unless you can derive it yourself. If you know enough about the equation to do that, then as far as you are concerned, it is not a "formula."

1. The place of electrical science in engineering. Engineering is the art of utilizing for the good of mankind the sources of energy and materials that are found in nature. It does not include any of the processes of utilizing energy or materials that involve living organisms, but with these processes excepted, little remains with which engineering is not concerned. Because it is an art, engineering cannot be mastered in the four years of a college curriculum. This first phase of becoming an engineer must be devoted largely to acquiring a strong foundation in mathematics and physics, and to the engineering sciences in which the basic principles are related to the problems of engineering. There follow the years of practice and experience through which the engineer reaches professional status. Electrical engineering is particularly concerned with the conversion, transmission, and utilization of energy through the medium of electricity, and, as a corollary, with the storing, transmission, recall, and processing of information. This does not mean that electrical engineers are not concerned with materials; but they are concerned with materials only as these are useful in building the apparatus needed in the handling of energy and information by electrical means.

Electrical science applies and relates the principles of electricity and magnetism to the solution of problems involving electric circuits, electric and magnetic fields, and electronics. In this book there will naturally be some repetition of material already covered, sometimes from a slightly different point of view. While some of the problems undertaken will be directly from engineering practice, most of them will not be. Since, however, most problems in electrical engineering practice, when reduced to their simplest terms, turn out to be circuit problems or field problems, the electrical engineer needs to be highly proficient in these areas.

2. The beginnings. The earliest recorded electrical phenomenon is the attraction of bits of chaff by a piece of amber that has been rubbed. That discovery was made by the ancient Greeks, and was recorded by Thales in 600 B.C. The word **electricity** comes from the Greek word ēlektron, which means amber.

Over two thousand years later, Sir William Gilbert, who was court physician to Queen Elizabeth I, found that other substances than amber could be electrified, as he called it, and he prepared lists of those which could be electrified and those which could not. During the next hundred and fifty years, the methods of electrifying objects by friction were improved and the results studied by several investigators, among whom were Von Guericke,

Stephen Gray, Charles François de Cisternay Du Fay, and Benjamin Franklin.

Von Guericke arranged to rotate a sphere of sulphur by using a machine, and so produced charges much larger than had his predecessors. He also found that after an attracted particle had touched the sphere, it was repelled. Gray found that substances could be classified as conductors or nonconductors according to whether they would or would not permit the escape of the charge from an electrified body. Du Fay discovered that bodies that had been electrified by friction would, in some instances, exert forces of attraction upon one another, and in other instances forces of repulsion.

To explain these observed facts, Du Fay put forward the theory that there were two mysterious fluids which were subtle enough to permeate all substances. One of these he called *vitreous,* and the other *resinous,* electricity. A body that was electrified contained an excess of one kind or the other of these fluids. If two bodies each contained an excess of the same kind of electricity, they repelled, but if one contained an excess of vitreous electricity and the other an excess of resinous electricity, they attracted each other.

Benjamin Franklin, besides being a statesman, was an electrical experimenter of note. His experiment which proved that lightning was identical with the electricity produced by friction is known to every schoolboy. Franklin proposed a one-fluid theory of electricity, according to which a neutral body always contained a certain normal amount of the fluid. An excess of the fluid then corresponded to one kind of charge and a deficiency of the fluid, to the other kind. The experiments of Gilbert and Guericke, Du Fay and Franklin can be reperformed in our laboratory today, or even with whatever materials are at hand in almost any place. They constitute the basis of **electrostatics,** that phase of the subject which deals with electricity at rest.

Natural magnets (lodestone) must have been known since ancient times, and the magnetic needle was in use by European navigators by the twelfth century. The first work that might be called a study of magnetism was done by Gilbert, who in 1600 published a treatise on the subject called *De Magnete.* Gilbert was a scientific investigator of the first rank, and working both with electricity and with magnets, he made important discoveries concerning each. He evidently did not suspect, however, that the two phenomena were in any way related.

Throughout the eighteenth century, electrical experimenters were severely limited in what they could do, for the reason that frictional machines were the only sources of charge available. These machines were constantly being improved upon, and the invention of the Leyden jar about 1745 made it possible to store considerable charges of electricity. Gray and

Franklin had both demonstrated the possibility of conducting electricity for considerable distances, using wet linen thread as the conductor. But the currents that flowed in these conductors were only momentary, ceasing as soon as the accumulated charge had been neutralized.

The first electric battery was devised by Alessandro Volta, an Italian physicist, who was led to his discovery through results obtained by his friend, Luigi Galvani, in stimulating the muscles of a frog's leg by touching the nerves with metal wires. Galvani evidently thought the stimulus was caused by "animal electricity." Volta was at first inclined to agree with him, but further study and experimenting convinced Volta that the effect was due to electricity caused by the metals. In 1799, he invented his battery, which consisted of alternate disks of copper and zinc arranged in pairs, each pair being separated from the next by paper soaked in acid. This discovery made it possible to send steady currents of electricity through wires and to observe and study two phenomena that are of tremendous practical importance in present-day electrical engineering — namely, the heating of the wires and forces that act between wires carrying currents.

It was not immediately realized that electricity produced by Volta's battery was identical in nature with that produced by friction. We had thus at the close of the eighteenth century three phenomena that were not known to be related: current electricity, frictional electricity, and magnetism. Volta by showing that the two kinds of electricity produced the same effects soon proved them to be identical. The relation between electricity and magnetism was first demonstrated by the Danish physicist, Hans Christian Oersted, in 1820. Oersted discovered that a magnetic needle, when placed beneath a wire carrying current, was acted on by forces which caused it to be oriented in the direction perpendicular to the wire. Conversely, a wire carrying current would be acted on by forces when placed in the vicinity of a magnet. From Oersted's discovery, the advancement of electrical knowledge proceeded with ever-increasing speed. A Frenchman by the name of André-Marie Ampère repeated Oersted's experiments, and in an incredibly short while had discovered the laws which are the basis of **electrodynamics,** which deals with currents and the forces they produce. A few years later Michael Faraday, an Englishman, showed that a current could be caused in a loop of wire by passing a magnet through it. This discovery was also made by Joseph Henry, an American, working independently. Thus by 1832 the relationship between electricity and magnetism had been established, and by 1837 a number of workable motors and generators had been constructed.

The first practical applications of electricity, however, were in the field of communications. Samuel Morse's telegraph was put into commercial use in 1844, and for a long time was the most important electrical industry. Several of our present-day electrical units were chosen to suit the convenience of the telegraphers. The development of the electric-light and power industry can be said to have begun about 1880, with the invention by Thomas Edison and his associates of the incandescent lamp and practical means of supplying energy to large numbers of lamps simultaneously.

The modern theory of electricity came as the result of new discoveries about the nature of matter during the closing years of the last century by J. J. Thomson, H. A. Lorentz, E. Rutherford, and others. With this brief historical outline by way of preface, let us now consider the modern theory.

3. The electrical nature of matter. The molecules and atoms of which all material substances are composed are not elemental, but are themselves made up of simpler entities. We know this because we have, to a certain extent, been able to break up atoms and study the resulting products. For instance, if a piece of tungsten wire be heated, as in the filament of an incandescent lamp or vacuum tube, there are driven out of it particles which are not atoms of tungsten, but are much smaller and lighter, and which have the peculiar property of repelling one another with considerable force. Exactly similar particles are obtained by causing ultraviolet light to fall on cold metal surfaces. They are spontaneously ejected from certain radioactive elements. Since these particles are obtained from many different substances under such widely varying conditions, it is believed that they are one of the elemental constituents of all matter. They are called **electrons.** The size and mass of an electron are so small as to be inconceivable, the mass being 1/1837 the mass of a hydrogen atom, which is 1.67×10^{-24} g, and the diameter being 1/50,000 the diameter of a hydrogen atom, which is about 10^{-8} cm. Electrons may be given velocities approaching the velocity of light, and at these tremendous velocities, may be shot through thin sheets of metal. Their most striking property, however, is the force of repulsion which they exert on one another. These forces are called **electric forces** and the property of the electron which gives rise to these forces is called **electricity** or **electric charge.** What this is, or how the force is exerted we cannot explain, for the reason that there are no simpler terms in which to explain electricity. We do know, however, that the charge does not vary from one electron to another. Every electron has exactly the same charge as every other electron. Atoms, when they lose or gain electrons, become charged accordingly, and are called **ions.** Anything, provided it is insulated from its surroundings, can become charged by having electrons taken away or by receiving electrons above its normal quota. The charge of the electron is arbitrarily designated as negative; consequently, a body with an excess of electrons is said to be negatively charged and one with a deficiency of electrons, positively charged. This seems to be substantially in accord with the theory of Benjamin Franklin, except that Franklin's fluid was an idea only, while we have concrete evidence for the existence of the electron. Although we have spoken of the electron as a particle, it does not always behave as we would expect a particle to behave, and the advanced student may have to modify his idea of what it is. But for the present, we may regard the electron as a hard, round particle with the added property of repelling every similar particle with a definite, invariable force.

Several other kinds of particles have been driven or spontaneously ejected from matter. Of these, the first to be discovered was the **proton** which, like the electron, is endowed with the property of repelling particles similar to itself, but which, instead of repelling electrons, attracts them with the same force with which it would repel another proton. We say, therefore, that the proton carries a charge equal in magnitude to that on an electron but opposite in sign. We arbitrarily designate the charge of the proton as a + charge, and the charge of the electron as a − charge. The mass of the proton is almost identical with the mass of the hydrogen atom. In 1932 came the discovery of the **neutron,** a particle with the mass of a proton but no charge. These three entities: electrons, protons, and neutrons are, according to our present knowledge, the basic building blocks of which atoms are made. Other entities such as the positron and the alpha particle are encountered in atomic research, but these are to be regarded as transitory and not stable components of the atom.

All of the protons and neutrons are bound together into a compact nucleus, which may be thought of as a central sun, about which the electrons revolve in orbits. Figure 1.1 shows a helium atom, the nucleus of which consists of two protons and two neutrons,* with two electrons moving

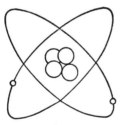

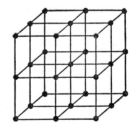

Fig. 1.1. Structure of the helium atom.

Fig. 1.2. Space lattice of copper. Atoms are located at corners of cubes and also (not shown) at centers of cube faces.

in orbits. The nuclei of atoms, for the purposes of this text, may be regarded as stable and unchanging, though it is now well known that the nuclei

---

*Every atom of a given element has the same number of protons in its nucleus, but the number of neutrons may vary. About one helium nucleus in a million has only one neutron.

of atoms of radioactive elements undergo spontaneous changes in their structure, and that the nuclei of atoms of other elements may be changed by bombardment by subatomic particles moving at certain velocities. In most solids, the nuclei are arranged in space according to some definite geometrical pattern. The structure thus formed is known as the **space lattice,** because this name implies finite quantities of matter, symmetrically placed, and separated from one another by intervals that are considerable as compared to their own dimensions. The apparently solid substance is, after all, mostly space. Figure 1.2 shows the space lattice of copper.

Most of the electrons associated with the atom are detached only with some difficulty. In the metals, however, at least some of the electrons appear to leave the atom spontaneously, and to wander about within the space lattice. Such electrons are known as **free electrons,** or **conduction electrons,** and it is in terms of them that electric current, or the conduction of electricity, in metals is explained.

4. Some remarks on energy. Practically every physical and chemical phenomenon, such as the lifting of a weight, the burning of fuel, the turning of a wheel, the utterance of a sound, involves the exchange between bodies of that which we call **energy.** Such exchanges are continually going on in nature whether we will them or not, and our control of them is never complete, yet by promoting certain exchanges and delaying others, we bring about results which we believe to be for the "good of mankind."

Energy is often defined as the capability for doing work. Thus, when a weight is lifted to a certain height above the earth, it becomes able to drive a nail or smash another object simply by falling. It is said to possess **potential energy** by virtue of its position. To lift the weight in the first place, of course, work had to be done, and the potential energy may be regarded as stored work. Now, let us consider the weight as having fallen. It is nearing the earth, and its energy of position is gone. Energy has not been destroyed, however, because the weight is still capable of doing work when it strikes the earth. What has happened is that the weight has gained speed as it fell, and its energy of position has been changed into energy of velocity, or **kinetic energy.** These are the two forms of energy with which we deal in mechanics.

A body may also possess energy by virtue of its temperature — that is, **thermal energy,** or heat energy. Kinetic energy can be readily transformed to thermal energy by friction, as when a meteor burns away because of air friction upon entering the earth's atmosphere, or a cutting tool becomes hot. The transfer in the other direction (from thermal to kinetic energy) is accomplished by heat engines of various kinds. Thermal energy is most often obtained by the burning of fuel, but here again we are dealing with a transformation. The fuel itself is the repository of energy in the **chemical** form, and the process of burning is simply the conversion to the heat form.

It might seem from what has been said that the outstanding fact about energy is that it can readily be changed from one form to another, and this is true. Most of the energy with which we deal in engineering can be traced from the sun, and reaches the earth in the form of radiation, or **radiant energy.** For instance, some of this energy on reaching the earth appears as heat, and evaporates water from the oceans and lakes. This water vapor rises until it is condensed in the cooler upper atmosphere, and falls as rain or snow, some of it eventually finding its way into the reservoirs of hydro-electric plants. The potential energy of the stored water is in due time converted into mechanical energy by hydraulic turbines, and the mechanical energy in turn is converted into **electrical energy** by electric generators.

The great storehouse of energy in our universe is in the nuclei of the atoms of which it is composed. The release of this **nuclear energy,** however, involves the destruction of mass, a thing which was regarded as not possible in nineteenth century physics. About 1905, Albert Einstein showed it to be theoretically possible, and by 1932 experimental proof existed. Used first in the atomic bomb in 1943, nuclear fission processes have been perfected for peace-time uses to the point where sizable commercial plants are now being built.

The radiant energy from the sun is believed to come from a nuclear process (fusion) by which hydrogen nuclei are being converted to helium, with an attendant loss of mass. This process has been duplicated on a small scale in weapons technology, but is not yet developed for peace-time uses. In what follows we will deal only with systems in which the total amount of energy remains fixed, or in other words, systems to which the principle of conservation of energy applies.

One of the principal uses of electricity is to furnish a means of transmitting energy from one place to another. Electricity itself is not energy any more than the weight used in the foregoing illustration is energy. The free electrons may possess energy by virtue of their position or velocity, just as the weight possesses energy by virtue of its position or its velocity, but to say that electricity itself is a form of energy is confusing rather than enlightening.

We have reasonably efficient devices for changing kinetic to electrical energy (generator, velocity microphone) and electrical to kinetic energy (motor, loud speaker, electromagnet), and these are the changes most often made. Devices for changing chemical energy to electrical (batteries) and electrical energy to chemical (storage batteries) are less economical and less used. Devices for changing heat energy to electrical (thermocouples) exist, but their low efficiency limits their use to extremely small amounts of energy. Devices for changing electrical to heat energy (irons, toasters) are probably the most familiar of all. Several of the devices mentioned (generators, storage batteries, thermocouples) are reversible, and at least one of them (the storage battery) is useful precisely for this reason.

As already mentioned, it is possible for energy to reside in, or be propagated through, empty space from one body to another. Devices exist for making the transformation from the heat to the radiant form (radiant heaters, incandescent lamps) and from the electrical to the radiant form (antennas). Radiant energy manifests itself as heat or light, which are recognizable, if in sufficient amount, by the physical senses, and also (depending on the nature of the radiator) as radio waves or other waves or rays, detectable only by special devices which convert it to the heat form or electrical form again. The importance of radiant energy in electrical engineering, particularly in radio and in illumination, is hard to exaggerate.

5. Measuring and units. Physics differs from the other sciences not in its subject matter alone, but also in its methods. We might venture so far as to say that physics is the science of measurement, or, whereas in other fields of science we are content to observe and describe phenomena, in physics we go further and *measure* the effects we observe. Measuring involves, first, the choice of a **unit,** or standard, of the same sort as the quantity to be measured, and second, the comparison of the unit with the quantity to be measured — to find how many times the former is contained in the latter. The choice of a unit depends upon the use that is to be made of the measurement. If an experimenter in an electrical laboratory wishes to cut a piece of wire of the correct length to connect two terminals together, he may choose as his unit of measurement any piece of wood or metal rod that happens to be handy. But if he wishes to place an order for the piece of wire or to record its length in his notes for the use of others, then it becomes necessary to choose a unit that is familiar to all those who may be called upon to interpret the order or the notes. Such a unit might be the foot or the meter or any of a number of other units that are recognized as units of length. Our experimenter could not choose the pound or the quart as his unit, because these are not standards of length, and we are all so perfectly familiar with length that there is no danger of our confusing it with any other quantity. But when we begin to deal with the less familiar units of electricity and magnetism, we shall have to be careful that we choose a unit always of the same sort as the quantity which we attempt to measure.

Having found out how many times our chosen unit is contained in the quantity measured, we must not, in our haste to set down this number and get on with something else, forget to write along with it the name of the unit which was used. To state that a length is seven is meaningless. We must write 7 feet or 7 meters or whatever it is. The student should see clearly that the magnitude of the number depends upon the unit used. If we measure a given quantity in small units, we may obtain a very large number, whereas if we measure the same quantity in large units, we would obtain a much smaller number. Good judgment dictates that we choose units of such size that our measurements will yield numbers that are convenient to manipulate, whenever this is possible. Some of the quantities with which we shall have to deal are so minute or so large that no units so far devised will measure them in convenient numbers.

The student is already familiar, through his everyday experience and his previous studies, with such quantities as length, mass, time, velocity, acceleration, force, energy, and power, and doubtless knows that each of these may be measured in various units of the appropriate sort. He may not be familiar with the fact that there are several comprehensive *systems of units*, any particular system comprising units for each of the quantities mentioned above (and others as well). These systems differ in the quantities that are selected as fundamental and in the units used to measure the fundamental quantities.

6. The mks system of units. The International Electrotechnical Commission, in June 1935, adopted the system of units known as the Giorgi, or mks system, based on the meter, the kilogram, and the second as fundamental units. The meter was first conceived as a unit of length in France toward the end of the eighteenth century, and was arbitrarily taken as being one ten millionth of the distance from the earth's equator to either pole, measured at sea level. This length, as carefully determined as was possible, was marked off on a platinum-iridium bar which is preserved by the International Bureau of Weights and Measures at Sèvres in France. The kilogram, chosen as the unit of mass at the same time the meter was chosen as the unit of length, was arbitrarily taken as the mass of one one-thousandth of a cubic meter of pure water at a temperature of 4° C. It, too, is preserved at Sèvres in the form of a platinum-iridium cylinder, and the standard meters and kilograms of other laboratories are compared to these rather than to the things which they were made to represent. They are the standards for the whole scientific world.

The second is 1/86,400 part of a mean solar day, which is the average time between successive transits of the sun over the meridian. Clocks have been built which approximate this time very closely, and intervals of time may be measured by comparison with these clocks.

From these three fundamental units are derived all the others used in measuring the quantities of mechanics. The velocity of a body is measured by taking the quotient of length traversed, in meters, over the time required to traverse it, in seconds — that is, in meters per second. If we let V stand for velocity, L for length, and T for time, we may write

$$V = \frac{L}{T}, \tag{1.1}$$

which is known as the **defining equation** for velocity. From velocity, we may proceed to define acceleration, then force, then work, and so forth, each definition being based logically on the one before it. Some of the more important mks units used in mechanics are given in Table I, together with their definitions, defining equations, and symbols.

Table I. MKS MECHANICAL UNITS

Quantity Measured	Unit	Symbol	Definition	Defining Equation
Length	Meter (m)	L	Fundamental	
Mass	Kilogram (kg)	M	Fundamental	
Time	Second (sec)	T	Fundamental	
Velocity	Meter per second (m per sec)	V	One meter per sec is the velocity when distance is traversed at the rate of 1 m in 1 sec.	$V = \frac{L}{T}$ (1.1)
Acceleration	Meter per second per second (m per sec per sec)	A	One meter per sec per sec is the acceleration when velocity is being changed at the rate of 1 m per sec in 1 sec.	$A = \frac{V}{T}$ (1.2)
Force	Newton	F	One newton is that force which gives an acceleration of 1 m per sec per sec to a mass of 1 kg.	$F = MA$ (1.3)
Work or energy	Joule	W	One joule is the work done when a force of 1 newton moves a body through a distance of 1 m in the direction of the force.	$W = FL$ (1.4)
Power	Watt (w)	P	One watt is the power when work is done at the rate of 1 joule per sec.	$P = \frac{W}{T}$ (1.5)

7. Conversion from one system of units to another. The mks system of units, as was pointed out in Section 5, is one of a number of systems which have come into use for measuring physical quantities. In the literature of science and engineering, we find all these systems in use, and for satisfactory understanding and use of knowledge contained in this literature, we must be able to take a quantity expressed in given units and express it in any of the other units used for measuring that quantity. Length, for example, may be expressed in angstrom units, in microns, in millimeters, in centimeters, in inches, in feet, in yards, in kilometers, in miles, in light-years, as well as in meters. There are two ways of stating the relation that exists between units of the same quantity. We may write

$$\text{number of inches} = \text{number of meters} \times 39.37, \qquad (1.6)$$

which is an equation, and tells us how to operate on a given length expressed in meters in order to obtain the corresponding length expressed in inches.

Example: A piece of wire is 50 m long. Express this length in inches.

SOLUTION: Substituting 50 for "number of meters" in Equation (1.6), we have

$$\text{number of inches} = 50 \times 39.37 = 1968.5.$$

The number of inches is greater than the number of meters in expressing this same length. Therefore, the inch must be a smaller unit of length than

Fig. 1.3. Measurement of length.

the meter. The use of units of different size for measuring a length is illustrated in Figure 1.3. Or we may write

$$1 \text{ meter} \equiv 39.37 \text{ inches,} \qquad (1.7)$$

which is an identity and tells us how many inches is the same as 1 m. We cannot substitute a number of meters or a number of inches into this expression as we could in (1.6), which was an equation. Either of these expressions gives us the essential information: it tells us which is the larger unit and what the relative size of the units is, but in making conversions we must be certain whether the expression we are reading or writing is an identity, like (1.7), or an equation, like (1.6). That we have taken the meter as our basic unit of length does not mean that we are committed to using the meter to the exclusion of all other units, even in a book like this. We shall use centimeters or microns or kilometers, whichever yields numbers most convenient to manipulate. The same applies to units of other quantities as well. A few conversion factors are listed in Table II for the convenience of the student in solving the problems at the end of this chapter. The student, if he has not already done so, should commit to memory a few of the most essential conversion factors to enable him to solve problems when no books are available. He should know also the usual prefixes used in connection with units, shown in Table III.

Table II. CONVERSION FACTORS

number of pounds =	number of kilograms ×	2.205	(1.8)
number of miles per hour =	number of meters per second ×	2.237	(1.9)
number of newtons =	number of pounds force ×	4.448	(1.10)
number of dynes =	number of newtons ×	10^5	(1.11)
number of joules =	number of foot-pounds ×	1.356	(1.12)
number of ergs =	number of joules ×	10^7	(1.13)
number of joules =	number of gram-calories ×	4.186	(1.14)
number of joules =	number of Btu × 1054.8		(1.15)
number of joules =	number of kilowatt-hours ×	3.6×10^6	(1.16)
number of watts =	number of horsepower × 745.7		(1.17)

Table III. PREFIXES

Prefix	Meaning	
micro................................	a millionth	(10^{-6})
milli................................	a thousandth	(10^{-3})
centi................................	a hundredth	(10^{-2})
deci................................	a tenth	(10^{-1})
deka................................	ten	(10)
hekta................................	a hundred	(10^2)
kilo................................	a thousand	(10^3)
mega................................	a million	(10^6)

Note: The prefix micro is abbreviated μ; milli, m; kilo, k; and mega, M. Thus μw would stand for microwatts, mw for milliwatts, kw for kilowatts, Mw for megawatts, and so forth.

PROBLEMS

(1-I) A high-speed passenger elevator in an office building rises 190 ft in 11.4 sec. What is the average velocity in feet per minute? In meters per second?

(2-I) How long a time would be required for a Diesel-electric train traveling at a speed of 29.1 m per sec to cover a distance of 240 miles?

(3-I) The acceleration of passenger elevators is limited to about 7 fps² in order to avoid discomfort to the passengers. At this rate, how long a time would be required to reach a speed of 1100 fpm, starting from rest?

(4-I) An electron starts from rest and reaches a velocity of 5000 miles per sec in 10^{-8} sec. What is the velocity in mks units? What is the acceleration in mks units?

(5-I) A Diesel-electric train, starting from rest, reaches a speed of 70 mph in 63.6 sec. What is the acceleration in miles per hour per second? In meters per second per second?

(6-I) Derive an expression for calculating the distance covered by a body that is undergoing uniform acceleration in terms of acceleration and time. Use this expression to determine the distance covered by the train of Problem 5-I by the time it reaches a speed of 70 mph.

(**7-I**) What force must have acted upon the electron in Problem 4-I to accelerate it? How far will it be from the starting position when it reaches the stated velocity?

(**8-I**) A force of 1.47×10^5 newtons is applied to the drawbar of a train weighing 452 tons. The train is on a straight level track and friction will be neglected. What is the acceleration in meters per second per second?

(**9-I**) Calculate the work done in lifting an elevator weighing 2500 lb through a distance of 310 ft against the force of gravity. Express the answer in foot-pounds, in joules, and in kilowatt-hours. How much potential energy does the elevator possess at a height of 310 ft above the ground?

(**10-I**) Derive an expression for calculating the kinetic energy of a body in terms of its mass and velocity. Use this expression to calculate the kinetic energy of the electron of Problem 4-I.

(**11-I**) If the elevator of Problem 9-I is lifted 310 ft in 30 sec, find the power required in watts and also in horsepower. Repeat the calculations using a time of 30 min.

(**12-I**) The reservoir of a certain hydroelectric power plant contains 800,000 acre-feet of water at an average elevation above the turbines of 270 ft. Calculate the potential energy in the reservoir in kilowatt-years.

(**13-I**) How long would the potential energy in the reservoir of Problem 12-I operate a 20,000-kw (output) generator? Assume the efficiency of the generator and turbine combined is 80 per cent.

(**14-I**) An electron is acted upon by a force of 9×10^{-21} newton. If the electron starts from rest, find the acceleration, time, final velocity, and kinetic energy when it is 1 cm from the starting point.

STUDY QUESTIONS

1. What was the contribution of each of these men to the store of knowledge of electricity: Gilbert, Von Guericke, Gray, Du Fay, Franklin, Volta, Galvani, Oersted, Ampère, Faraday, Morse?

2. What distinguishes electrostatics from electrodynamics?

3. Explain the electrification of a body by friction, using the modern theory of the electrical nature of matter. How does this theory differ from that advanced by Du Fay?

4. How long a time elapsed from the first recorded discovery in electrostatics until the beginning of electrodynamics? How do you account for this?

5. Why is it more difficult to answer the question "what is electricity," than the question "what is iron"? Which is the more elemental?

6. What evidence is there that such a particle as the electron actually exists? What are some of its properties?

7. The statement is sometimes made that "matter is mostly empty space." What justification is there for such a statement?

8. List by pairs all of the various forms of energy mentioned in the text, pairing each form with all of the others. By each pair list a device by which conversion from one form to the other may be accomplished.

9. Criticize the statement "electricity is a form of energy."

10. What are the two essential things to be done in measuring anything? What are the two essential things to be given when the result of a measurement is stated?

11. A tank is emptied by bailing out the water with a quart measure, and 2312 measures are counted. Had a gallon measure been used, how many would have been counted? Which is the larger unit of measure?

12. Prepare a table of cgs mechanical units similar to Table I.

13. Prepare a table of English mechanical units similar to Table I.

14. For each of the equations in Table II, state which is the larger unit and write the corresponding identity.

15. For each of the following identities, state which is the larger unit and write the corresponding equation.

(a) 1 acre $\equiv 4.356 \times 10^4$ sq ft.
(b) 1 sq cm $\equiv 1.973 \times 10^5$ cir mils.
(c) 1 radian $\equiv 57.3$ degrees.
(d) 1 abampere $\equiv 10$ amperes.
(e) 1 statvolt $\equiv 300$ volts.

Chapter II

FUNDAMENTAL ELECTRICAL
CONCEPTS AND UNITS

---

1. Electrons in motion — current. As was stated in the preceding chapter, there are believed to exist in all metals a number of electrons which are not definitely associated with any particular atomic nucleus and which are free to wander about through the space lattice of the metal. No experimental procedure has ever been devised for determining how many of these free, or conduction, electrons exist in a given conductor, but there is some reason to believe that there may be as many as one free electron per atom. Since it is possible to determine how many atoms there are in a given piece of metal, we can make use of the above assumption of one free electron per atom, and determine the number of free electrons present in any certain piece of metal. For example, in a piece of No. 10 copper wire (0.102 in. diam) 100 ft long, there would be 1.36×10^{25} free electrons.

As was also stated in Chapter I, the interstices in the space lattice are enormously wide when compared with the dimensions of an electron. Within the conductor, then, we may picture the free electrons behaving very much like the molecules of a gas inclosed in a tube. They are continually in motion in every direction. The individual electrons dart about in a random manner, the violence of their motions depending upon the absolute temperature of the conductor. If we now cause these electrons to be acted upon by suitable forces, they can be caused to move consistently in some definite direction. This motion is aptly termed a **drift,** for although the individual electrons experience all sorts of interference with their motion, and are buffeted about in every conceivable direction, there is on the average, provided proper forces act, a certain electron velocity in the required direction. This velocity itself is not directly measurable, but basing our calculations on the foregoing assumption of one free electron per atom, it appears that ordinarily it does not exceed a few hundredths of a centimeter per second.* This drift of free electrons through the space lattice is an **electric current.**

The nature of the electric current, as might be expected, depends upon the nature of the forces which act upon the electrons. The simplest case of all would be that in which the conductor is made part of a **circuit,** or closed loop, which also contains a battery, as in Figure 2.1. The forces which act

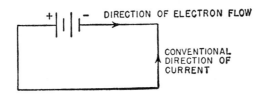

Fig. 2.1. Simple electric circuit.

upon the free electrons tend to cause them to drift always in one direction around the circuit, and given enough time, individual electrons may complete the trip around and get back whence they started.

While metal wires are the most commonly used conductors of electricity, they are by no means the only conductors. Many other solid substances are fair conductors of electricity. The earth itself forms part of countless electric circuits, while carbon and graphite have important uses as conductors for special purposes.

Liquids and gases may also be conductors of electricity. The moving particles here are not electrons, but charged molecules or atoms, known as **ions.** The charge on such particles may be either positive or negative, according to whether there is a deficiency or an excess of electrons. Ions of both signs are usually present, and conduction of electricity in a liquid or a gas involves movement of positive ions in one direction and of negative ions in the opposite direction.

Finally, it is possible to have a stream of electrons move across empty space, as from the cathode to the plate in a vacuum tube. This also is current. In general, any flow or motion of charged particles, either positive or negative, is a current.

*The velocity of 186,272 miles per sec sometimes given for electricity is the velocity at which waves or impulses are propagated in free space. The velocity of the electrons in wires is something else altogether.

2. Direction of current. In the early days of the study of electricity, it was the rule to think of the current as being the flow of positive electricity around the circuit. This was long before the discovery of the electron, and the rule may have had its origin in the experiments of Faraday with conduction in liquids. As the science developed and electricity began to find practical uses, this rule was accepted without question. By the time the electron was discovered and the nature of the electric current in metal wires became known, the conventional assumption that current was the flow of positive electricity had become so firmly rooted in electrical literature and so many other conventions and rules depended upon it that it could not readily be changed, even if that were desirable. As we have seen, positive electricity as well as negative is actually in motion in liquid and gaseous conductors, though the electrons account for most of the current in gaseous conductors.

We therefore have to remember that the direction of current is the direction of the movement of positive electricity in those conductors in which movement of positive electricity occurs. In metal wires the direction of current is the direction opposite to that in which the electrons move, as indicated in Figure 2.1.

This need not be confusing, because the current direction and the direction of electron movement are always opposite. There is no case in which they are the same.

3. Measurement of current — the ampere. Two phenomena that occur when currents flow in conductors are readily demonstrated in the laboratory: (1) The conductors get hot, and (2) if two current-carrying conductors lie parallel, they exert forces on each other, of attraction if the currents are in the same direction, of repulsion if the currents are in opposite directions. These phenomena are of tremendous practical importance; the first is the basis of the incandescent lamp and electrical heating appliances

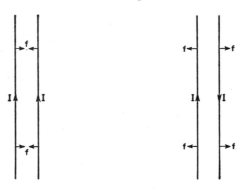

Fig. 2.2. Forces due to currents in parallel conductors.

of every sort. The second is the underlying principle of the electric motor. The forces exerted between current-carrying conductors are called **electromagnetic forces,** and are not to be confused with the electrostatic forces that act between electrons or charged bodies regardless of whether these bodies are in motion or not (Figure 2.2).

Experiments show that the electromagnetic force which acts between very long current-carrying conductors which lie parallel to each other in air or in free space depends upon: (1) the magnitude of the current in the first wire (directly), (2) the magnitude of the current in the second wire (directly), (3) the length of the parallel parts (directly), and (4) the distance between the wires (inversely). These experiments give us a clue as to how current can be measured. If we can measure the distance between the wires, their parallel length, and the force of attraction or repulsion that acts between them when they are located in a certain medium and are each carrying the same current, then the current is determined. It remains only for us to define the unit, which is called the **ampere:** *One ampere (amp) is that current which will cause a force of attraction of 2×10^{-7} newton per meter between two infinitely long parallel conductors placed 1 m apart in free space.*

It can be seen from this definition that for conductors in free space, the forces are rather feeble unless the currents are large. For parallel conductors a meter apart, a current of 4750 amp would be required to give an attractive force of 1 pound per meter length. Currents of this magnitude (and larger) are encountered in power systems when short circuits occur, in certain applications, especially the electro-chemical industries, and in lightning strokes.

As everyday examples of current magnitudes, about 15 to 30 amp flows when an automobile generator is charging the storage battery, while operation of the starter may require from 100 to 300 amp. The current through the filament of an ordinary 100-w lamp is about 0.8 amp.

The heating effect of a given current depends upon the nature of the conductor through which the current flows. The current (0.8 amp) which raises the lamp filament to a temperature of about 2700° absolute would scarcely cause enough heating in a No. 14 copper wire to be perceptible to the touch. A copper wire of this size with Type R (rubber) insulation and located in the open air can carry a current of 20 amp with a temperature rise of about 10° C.

It may be noted in passing that the human body is a conductor of electricity and that currents of more than about 0.1 amp are likely to prove fatal. The smallest current that can be felt is about 1 milliampere, and for currents larger than about 10 milliamperes, muscular contraction occurs and pain begins to be felt.

4. Defining equation for the ampere. The definition of the ampere can be stated in equation form as

$$F = \frac{(2 \times 10^{-7})I^2L}{S},\tag{2.1}$$

where F is force in newtons;

I is current in amperes;

L is parallel length in meters for which force is to be computed;

S is distance in meters between the parallel wires.

It is important to note that Equation (2.1) holds exactly only when the conductors are infinitely long — that is, when the end connections and other parts of the circuit are so remote that they have no effect. It is approximately correct, however, in any case where L is large compared to S, or in any case where the effect of other parts of the circuit can be ignored. It should also be pointed out that, while the equation holds exactly only if the conductors are in free space, the error is negligible if the conductors are in air or are surrounded by any substance other than iron or a ferromagnetic material. The factor 2×10^{-7} is a result of the choice of units in the definition of the ampere. A further consideration of this matter will be found in Chapter VII.

Example: Two conductors run parallel for a distance of 40 m surrounded by air. They are 10 cm apart on centers and carry equal currents. What is the direction and magnitude of the current in each conductor if they are mutually repelled by a force of 1 lb?

SOLUTION: Since

$$F = \frac{(2 \times 10^{-7})I^2L}{S},\tag{2.1}$$

$$I = \sqrt{\frac{FS}{(2 \times 10^{-7})L}}$$

$$= \sqrt{\frac{(1 \times 4.44)(10 \times 0.01)}{(2 \times 10^{-7})(40)}} = 236 \text{ amp.}$$

Since the conductors are repelled, the currents must be in opposite directions.

PROBLEMS

(1-II) What force will act between the parallel wires of a power line, when the wires are 2 ft apart and carrying currents of 50 amp each, in opposite directions? Express the result in pounds per foot.

(2-II) The wires of a twin-conductor cable are each 0.25 in. diam and covered with 0.125 in. of insulation. With what force would the wires repel each other if they carried their normal current of 75 amp? Express the result in pounds per foot.

(3-II) With what force would the wires of Problem 2-II repel each other at the instant a short circuit caused the current to increase to 10 times normal?

5. Absolute measurement of current. The definition of the ampere has to be restated in order to make it a workable one. The forces that act between very accurately built coils which carry current can be reduced to terms of the force between long parallel wires carrying the same current. Such an arrangement, known as a *current balance*, is shown in Figure 2.3, and

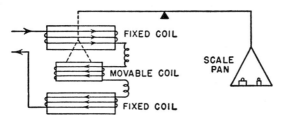

Fig. 2.3. Absolute current balance.

is part of the equipment of some standardizing laboratories such as the United States Bureau of Standards at Washington. By means of it, currents are actually measured in terms of the forces which they cause to act between the coils. Such a measurement is called **absolute,** because current is measured in terms of the fundamental mechanical quantities which are used to define it.

6. Alternating current. If the battery in Figure 2.1 be replaced by a suitable device (an alternating-current generator or an oscillator) the electrons will be urged first in one direction around the circuit and then in the other direction, and as a consequence, instead of drifting steadily in one certain direction, the electrons will simply oscillate about their mean positions. This pattern of electron motion gives rise to the same effects as does the steady drift in one direction — that is, the conductor gets hot and forces of attraction or repulsion act between parallel conductors. Conductors in which this pattern of electron motion occurs are said to carry **alternating current,** as distinguished from **direct current,** when the electron drift is unidirectional.

We may think of the electrons as being acted upon by forces that cause them to start to move in one direction, and which accelerate them until their average velocity reaches a maximum. The current at that instant is maximum. The forces then decrease, and the electrons slow down until their average velocity is again zero. At this instant, the current is zero. Forces then act to set them in motion in the opposite direction, and they reach maximum velocity in this direction. The forces diminish, and the av-

erage electron velocity again falls to zero. This series of events, which is repeated again and again, is called a **cycle.** The time that elapses during a
cycle is called a **period,** and the number of cycles which take place per
second is called the **frequency.**

An alternating current may vary with time in various ways, depending
upon the forces that act upon the free electrons. Some of the possible
modes of variation, or **wave forms,** are shown in Figure 2.4. The graph in

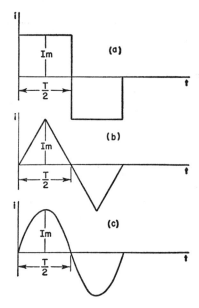

Fig. 2.4. Alternating-current wave forms: (*a*) rectangular; (*b*) triangular; (*c*) sinusoidal.

Figure 2.4*a* represents the current as starting at zero, increasing instantaneously to a certain positive value I_m, remaining constant at this value for a
time $T/2$, then changing instantaneously to a negative value $-I_m$, remaining constant at this value for a time $T/2$, and changing instantaneously to
zero to complete a cycle. This is called a rectangular, or square, wave and is
typical of the currents in some radio circuits. The graph in Figure 2.4*b*
represents the current beginning at zero and increasing at a uniform rate to
$+I_m$ at time $T/4$, then decreasing uniformly to zero at time $T/2$, then
increasing uniformly to $-I_m$ at $3T/4$, then decreasing again to zero at time
T. This is a triangular wave. The graph in Figure 2.4*c* represents the most
common of all wave forms, the sine wave. Commencing at zero, the current
increases to $+I_m$, decreases to zero, increases to $-I_m$, and decreases to zero
again according to the law,

$$i = I_m \sin 2\pi ft, \qquad (2.2)$$

where i is the instantaneous value of the current;

I_m is the maximum value attained by the current at any time;

f is the frequency in cycles per second;

t is the time in seconds since the current was zero increasing in the positive direction.

It will be seen that the product ft is always a number of cycles

$$ft = \frac{\text{cycles}}{\text{seconds}} \times \text{seconds} = \text{cycles}, \qquad (2.3)$$

and $2\pi ft$ is an angle that is zero when t is zero and increases uniformly as t increases. Thus, we see that i varies as the sine of some angle that increases with time. The symbol T is used to denote the period of the current (that is, the time required for the current to go through a complete cycle). Since

$$f \text{ is } \frac{\text{cycles}}{\text{seconds}} \quad \text{and} \quad T \text{ is } \frac{\text{seconds}}{\text{cycles}},$$

it is evident that f and T are reciprocals and

$$fT = 1. \qquad (2.4)$$

An alternating current is said to have an effective value of 1 amp when it produces the same heating effect in a given resistance as would a direct current of 1 amp. Unless there is a statement or indication to the contrary, the effective value is meant whenever an alternating current is given in amperes. It can be shown that for sine waves the effective value is $1/\sqrt{2}$ times the maximum value.

Example: A sinusoidal current has a frequency of 60 cps and a maximum value of 1 amp. (a) What is the value of the current 0.001 sec after it is zero and begins increasing toward maximum positive? (b) How long after the current is zero and increasing toward maximum positive will it be -0.5 amp?

SOLUTION:

$$i = I_m \sin 2\pi ft, \qquad (2.2)$$

(a)
$$i = 1 \sin 2\pi \times 60 \times 0.001$$
$$= 1 \sin 21.6° = 0.368 \text{ amp.}$$

(b)
$$-0.5 = 1 \sin 2\pi \times 60 \times t = \sin 377t.$$

$377t$ is any angle which has a sine of -0.5 — that is, $210°$, $330°$, $570°$, **and so forth.** Therefore, i will first reach -0.5 amp when

$$377t = 210° = 3.67 \text{ radians,}$$
$$t = 3.67/377 = 0.00974 \text{ sec.}$$

PROBLEMS

(4-II) A sinusoidal current has a frequency of 1000 cps and a maximum value of 5 amp. Calculate and plot one cycle of this current using a scale 1 in. = 0.0005 sec and 1 in. = 2 amp.

(5-II) A sinusoidal current has a frequency of 1150 kilocycles (kc) per sec and a maximum value of 20 amp. What is the period? How long a time elapses between zero increasing toward + maximum and + maximum? Between zero increasing toward + maximum and +17.32 amp?

7. Frequency. Frequency is an all-important quantity in electrical engineering. In the various phases of the art we work with frequencies ranging from zero (direct current) up to at least 3×10^{10} cps (cycles per second). For the generation, transmission, and distribution of electrical energy, except in aircraft applications, a frequency of 60 cps is used more than any other (in the United States). Frequencies in this neighborhood are spoken of as "power frequencies." Many aircraft electric power systems use alternating current, the most common frequency being 400 cps. For special applications of electric power in industry, such as induction heating, 300 kcps (kilocycles per second) is a typical frequency.

In the field of communications, frequencies are classified as

audio frequencies, ranging from 15 to 15,000 cps;
radio frequencies, ranging from 10,000 to 3×10^{10} cps.

Radio frequencies are further classified as

Low:	30 to 300 kcps;
Medium:	300 to 3000 kcps;
High:	3 to 30 mcps (megacycles per second);
Very high:	30 to 300 mcps;
Ultra high:	300 to 3000 mcps;
Super high:	3000 to 30,000 mcps.

Within these classifications certain bands of frequencies are set aside for certain purposes, as the familiar radio broadcast band from 535 to 1600 kcps, and the vhf (very high frequency) television bands 54 to 88 and 174 to 216 mcps.

Phenomena that are not present, or are so feeble as to escape notice, at certain frequencies, become important at higher frequencies. Thus, the energy radiated from a 60-cps power system might not be detected a mile away, but the energy radiated from an antenna at 60 kcps might be detected on the opposite side of the earth. Much of the progress in electrical engineering has come about through discoveries of high frequency phenomena and the invention of apparatus for their application.

8. Positive direction. It is obvious that in alternating-current circuits, we cannot say that the current flows in one direction any more than in the other direction. We can, however, select and mark one direction as the **positive direction,** which means that at any time the current is actually in that particular direction we will speak of it and write it as positive; otherwise, we will speak of it and write it as negative. Thus, in Figure 2.5, an arrow pointing to the right has been placed on the upper conductor. This is the positive-direction arrow for the current in the circuit. If we now say that at a certain instant the current is +5 amp, it means 5 amp in the direction indicated by the arrow. At another

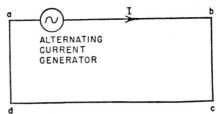

Fig. 2.5. Simple a-c circuit.

instant, the current may be −2 amp — that is, 2 amp in the direction opposite to the arrow. It should be obvious that unless some direction is marked as positive, then +5 and −2 are meaningless so far as the signs are concerned. It is exactly like saying to a man lost in a strange city, "Go two blocks north." His next question will very likely be, "Which way is north?"

Instead of designating the positive direction by an arrow, some books use a double-subscript method of notation. Thus, if we mark a point a and a point b on a circuit, as in Figure 2.5, then, to say that at a certain instant I_{ab} is 5 amp conveys a definite meaning as to direction as well as magnitude. I_{ab} is equal to I_{ba} in magnitude, but is opposite in direction.

The marking of positive directions is essential not only in alternating-current circuits, but in many direct-current circuits as well. In direct-current circuits, the current will be always in one direction, but which direction may not be known when the solution of a problem is begun. A direction is, therefore, assumed, and is marked with an arrow or by double subscripts. As the solution proceeds, the current may be found to be either positive or negative; positive meaning that the current is actually in the arrow direction; negative, that the current is actually opposite in direction to the arrow.

9. Quantity of electricity — the coulomb. As we have seen, current in a wire is the drift of electrons through the space lattice. Each electron carries a certain invariable charge. Hence, when a wire carries a steady current for a given length of time, a definite **quantity of electricity** will pass any fixed reference point on the wire, and we can, therefore, define unit quantity of electricity in terms of current and time. The unit is called the **coulomb,** for Charles Augustus de Coulomb, who in 1785 discovered the law of forces between charged bodies. *One coulomb is that quantity of electricity which passes a reference point on a conductor in 1 sec when the conductor carries a steady current of 1 amp.* We may state this definition in equation form as follows:

$$Q = IT, \tag{2.5}$$

where Q is quantity of electricity in coulombs;

   I is current in amperes;

   T is time in seconds.

Determinations of quantity of electricity, when a steady current flows in a complete circuit as in Figure 2.1, can be readily made by using Equation 2.5 directly.

> **Example:** The current in an ordinary 100-w lamp is about 0.833 amp. What quantity of electricity passes through the filament in 1 hr when the lamp is connected to direct-current mains?
>
> SOLUTION:
>
> $$Q = IT, \tag{2.5}$$
>
> $I = 0.833$ amp,
>
> $T = 1$ hr $= 3600$ sec,
>
> $Q = (0.833)(3600) = 3000$ coulombs.

We see from this example that the coulomb is not a particularly large unit for such measurements.

In electrostatics, however, and in determining charges on particles, the coulomb is immensely larger than the quantities of electricity usually dealt with. For example, if two spheres each 1 cm diam were placed 1 m apart and given opposite charges of 1 coulomb each, they would attract each other with a force of 9×10^9 newtons, or about one million tons. No such experiment has ever been carried out, for the reason that long before the charge on the spheres amounted to anything like 1 coulomb, any known substance used to insulate them would have broken down. The charges usually used in electrostatic experiments are of the order of a few microcoulombs. The largest electrostatic charges known are those which occur on thunderclouds, believed to reach magnitudes of several hundred coulombs.

The charge of an electron was determined by Robert Andrews Millikan in one of the most famous experimental procedures ever devised, the "oil-drop experiment." He found the value of the electronic charge to be 1.60×10^{-19} coulomb, from which it can be seen that a quantity of electricity of 1 coulomb would be equivalent to the charge on $1/(1.60 \times 10^{-19})$, or 6.25×10^{18} electrons.

PROBLEMS

(**6-II**) What quantity of electricity passes a reference point on a conductor in 1 hr if the current is 200 amp? In 0.05 sec, if the current is 0.002 amp?

(**7-II**) Electrons are passing a reference point on a conductor at the rate of 5×10^{21} electrons per min. What is the current in amperes?

10. Resistance. It was pointed out in Section 3 that one of the effects of current was to heat the conductor. In other words, the movement of electrons through the conductor cannot take place without the expenditure of some energy, which appears in the form of heat. The rate of expenditure of energy can be shown to be proportional to the square of the current. That is, doubling the current would result in the rate of heating being increased to four times as much. *The property of a conductor which requires the expenditure of energy by the moving electrons is called* **resistance.** Just what takes place in the space lattice of the conductor to bring about the heating effect is not easily explainable; the most obvious thing to say would be that the moving electrons collide with the atomic nuclei and with one another, each collision resulting in the liberation of a minute quantity of heat. Although this explanation gives a crude picture of the phenomenon that will serve our purpose for the present, it needs a great deal of modification and refinement to make it accurate.

Some simple facts about resistance, however, may be stated with certainty. First, resistance depends upon the material used for the conductor. Metals, particularly silver, copper, and aluminum, make the best conductors. That is, wires made of these metals have less resistance, and they are, therefore, used in preference to others where it is desirable to conduct current with as little energy loss as possible, as in power-station bus bars and in transmission lines. Other metals and metal alloys make much poorer conductors — that is, conductors offering much more resistance, and, therefore, well-suited for use where energy loss and heating effects are wanted, as in incandescent lamps and electric heating appliances.

Resistance also depends upon the temperature of the material. In general, the resistance of any metal conductor increases with increasing temperature and decreases with decreasing temperature. It is found that as the temperature approaches absolute zero ($-273°$ C), the resistance approaches zero, and in some instances, it becomes possible for a conductor to carry current without any loss of energy. We can now begin to improve our explanation of the nature of resistance. As the temperature is reduced, the random darting-about of the electrons becomes less and less. At absolute zero, it stops entirely, and all that is left is the orderly drift of the electrons in the required direction when the conductor carries current. This involves no loss in energy. In some way then, the heating and loss in energy are the result of superimposing the drift motion upon the random motion of the electrons.

Resistance depends also upon the dimensions of the conductor. For a conductor of constant cross section, the resistance varies directly as the length. For a conductor of constant length, the resistance varies inversely with the cross section. Thus, if the length and cross section of a wire were each doubled, the resistance would be the same.

11. Unit of resistance — the ohm. A unit of resistance can now be defined in terms of current and the rate of energy loss. The mks unit of resistance is called the **ohm,** and is defined as follows: *One ohm is the resistance of a conductor in which energy is lost at the rate of 1 joule per sec (1 w) when the current is 1 amp.*

Since the rate of energy loss is found to be proportional to the square of the current, the defining equation of resistance is

$$R = \frac{P}{I^2},\qquad(2.6)$$

where R is resistance in ohms;
   P is rate of energy loss in joules per second;
   I is current in amperes.

The resistance of a piece of No. 10 copper wire 1000 ft long is approximately 1 ohm. This is a convenient fact to remember as a basis for the quick calculation of the resistances of other sizes and lengths (see Chapter VI). An aluminum wire of the same size and length would have a resistance of about 1.6 ohms, an iron wire 5.6 ohms, a nichrome alloy wire 65 ohms.

PROBLEMS

(8-II) Electrical energy is converted to heat in a certain conductor at the rate of 50 joules per sec when the current is 2.24 amp. What is the resistance of the conductor?

(9-II) What is the resistance of a conductor which will absorb 10 w of power when the current is 100 amp?

(10-II) What current flowing in a conductor having a resistance of 50 ohms will cause heating at the rate of 500 w?

12. How energy is supplied to the free electrons. In order that the free electrons may continue to move through the space lattice of the conductor at a constant rate, it is obvious from the law of conservation of energy that we must supply energy to them at the same rate at which the year losing energy in the resistance of the conductor. In order to do this, we include in the circuit some device, such as a battery or generator, that can convert chemical or mechanical energy into the electrical form, so that the energy may be assimilated by the electrons. If a battery is used, the energy comes from a chemical reaction such as

$$Zn + 2HCl$$
$$= ZnCl_2 + H_2 + 166,000 \text{ joules per gram molecule of zinc.} \quad (2.7)$$

This liberated energy, or some part of it at least, is supplied to the electrons.

If a steam-turbine-driven generator is used, the energy still comes from a chemical reaction. Fuel is burned, but instead of the energy passing directly from the chemical into the electrical form, it first appears as heat, which is converted into mechanical energy by the turbine, and this in turn is supplied to the electrons by the generator. We may think of a battery or generator as a device in which the "suitable forces," described as being *required* in Section 1, act upon the free electrons and tend to force them around the circuit. The nature of the forces themselves and how they act upon the electrons will be considered in some detail in the following chapters.

A device which can convert heat energy to electrical energy exists in what is called a thermocouple (Chapter XIII). At present, thermocouples cannot be made efficient enough to be economically feasible for commercial energy conversion, though some progress in this direction is being made. A means by which nuclear energy can be converted directly to electrical energy may eventually be found.

13. Potential difference — the volt. Instead of speaking of the energy gained or lost by the electrons as they move around the circuit, a more convenient concept is that of **potential difference.** *Potential difference is the gain or loss of energy per unit quantity of electricity.* Thus, instead of saying that a number of electrons whose total charge amounts to Q coulombs receive energy in the amount of W joules in a certain part of the circuit (the battery or generator), we divide W by Q and say that, in this part of the circuit, there exists a potential difference of W/Q joules per coulomb.

To be consistent with the definition of direction of current as the direction in which positive charges move, we will suppose in what follows that it is the positive charges, not the electrons, which move around the circuit in Figure 2.6, and that they move in the direction a–b–c–d. In passing from a to b through the battery, the moving positive charges receive energy, and thus possess more energy at b than at a. We say, then, that point b is at

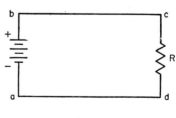

Fig. 2.6

a higher potential than point a, or that there is a rise in potential as we go from a to b. The terminal at point a is the negative $(-)$ terminal of the battery; the terminal at point b is the positive $(+)$ terminal. These signs indicate the **polarity** of the battery. The rise in potential associated with a battery, generator, or other device in which energy is imparted to moving charges will, in what follows, be called an **electromotive force** (emf), and will be designated by the symbol E or e.

In passing from c to d, through the resistance R, the moving positive charges give up energy, and thus possess less energy at d than at c. We say, then, that point d is at a lower potential than point c, or that there is a fall in potential as we go from c to d. The fall in potential associated with a resistance, in which energy is given up by the moving positive charges, will be called a **voltage drop** and will be designated as V or v.*

The term "potential difference" is thus a general term which includes both electromotive forces (rises in potential) and voltage drops (falls in potential).

The unit of potential difference is the joule per coulomb, or **volt,** and is defined as follows: *One volt is the potential difference between two points on a circuit when the energy involved in moving 1 coulomb from one point to the other is 1 joule.*

Potential difference is defined by the equation

$$E \text{ (or } V) = \frac{W}{Q}, \qquad (2.8)$$

where E (or V) is potential difference in volts;

$\qquad W$ is energy in joules;

$\qquad Q$ is quantity of electricity in coulombs

The name **electromotive force** was originally meant to imply that it is the force that causes the electricity to move — that is, causes the current. This is not strictly correct because, as we have just seen, electromotive force is not a force at all but is the energy supplied per unit quantity of electricity moved. Nevertheless, it is convenient to think of electromotive force as being the cause of current, and ordinarily this viewpoint will not lead to any error. On the other hand, voltage drop is usually thought of as being a consequence of current flow.

One thing further is required. We must have some means of designating the points between which the electromotive force or the voltage drop is being considered and of designating which point is at the higher potential.

---

*Unfortunately there is no generally accepted standard notation for potential differences. Some writers use E regardless of whether a rise or a fall of potential is meant. Others use V regardless of which is meant. Others use both E and V but without regard to whether a rise or fall of potential is meant. When reading a textbook or technical paper the student will need to inform himself as to the notation used.

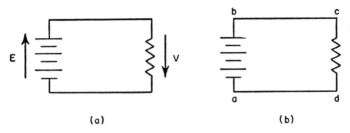

Fig. 2.7

In this book use will be made of arrows placed alongside the circuit with the tail opposite one of the points and the tip opposite the other point. Thus, in Figure 2.7a, the arrow marked E designates the positive direction of an electromotive force (rise of potential) from the lower terminal of the battery to the upper terminal, and the arrow marked V designates the positive direction of a voltage drop (fall of potential) from the upper terminal of the resistor to the lower terminal. Double subscripts are used in many books for designating electromotive forces and voltage drops. Thus, in Figure 2.7b, E_{ab} or V_{ab} would refer to the potential difference between point a and point b, and E_{cd} and V_{cd} would refer to the potential difference between point c and point d.*

The potential difference of an ordinary flashlight cell is about 1.5 volts. Automobile storage batteries are usually designed for an emf of 12 volts. Most generators in large power stations produce (alternating) potential differences of about 13,000 volts between terminals. The generator voltages are stepped up by means of transformers for long-distance transmission of energy and stepped down for distribution to consumers. Transmission voltages as high as 345,000 are in use in the United States, and distribution voltages are commonly 115-230 volts for residential and commercial lighting service. In experimental and test facilities in laboratories, potential differences of several million volts are sometimes used.

14. Meaning of potential difference. Difference in electrical potential can be aptly compared with difference of elevation on the earth's surface. To lift a mass to the top of a hoist requires the conversion of some form of energy by the hoisting engine to potential energy, or energy of

*To know which point is at the higher potential it is necessary to know the system of notation being used. Some (including this writer) would use E_{ab} to designate the positive direction of a voltage rise from point a to point b, and V_{ab} to designate the positive direction of a voltage drop from point a to point b. Other writers use either E_{ab} or V_{ab} to designate the positive direction of a voltage drop from point a to point b. Still others use either E_{ab} or V_{ab} to designate the positive direction of a voltage rise from point a to point b. For a complete account of the possible conventions see "Voltage Notation Conventions," by Myril B. Reed and W. A. Lewis, in *Electrical Engineering*, January 1948.

position, which is acquired by the mass. To lift positive charge to the positive terminal of a battery requires the conversion of chemical energy by the battery to potential energy, or energy of position, which is acquired by the charge. The difference in elevation from the foot of the hoist to the top is comparable to the difference in potential from the negative terminal of the battery to the positive. Once at the top of the hoist, the mass is capable of doing work by falling, as in a drop hammer or pile driver. Once at the positive terminal of the battery, positive charge is capable of doing work by falling through the resistance of the circuit and producing heat. These two phenomena are comparable, but not identical. The energy possessed by the positive charge does not depend upon its mass, and the "height" to which it has been lifted is an electrical height (or potential) and is measured in volts, not meters.

We can compare the trip of a hypothetical positive charge around an electrical circuit to a traverse by a hiker on a path which takes him to the top of a hill, down the other side, and back to his starting point. At the top of the hill the hiker has increased his elevation, as the charge has had its electrical level, or potential, increased by being lifted through the battery from the negative terminal to the positive terminal. Just as the hiker descends to the lower level again, the moving charge falls to points of lower and lower potential as it passes from the positive terminal of the battery around the circuit. Eventually the hiker is back at his starting point, at the same elevation at which he was originally. His increases and decreases in elevation exactly offset each other, and his net change in elevation is zero. Similarly, the rises in potential and falls in potential experienced by the charge as it travels around the circuit must be equal, since the charge comes back to the same potential at the starting point.

In the foregoing paragraphs we have talked about charge as though it were possible to tag one particular group of electrons, or positive particles, as constituting "the charge," and follow its progress around the circuit as we followed the hiker's progress around the traverse. Actually, charge-carrying particles are drifting along in all parts of the circuit simultaneously. It is characteristic of the flow of charge in circuits that it is continuous: the charge passing any reference point on the circuit in a given time is the same as that passing any other reference point in the same time. Charge does not "pile up" at any point on the circuit. But since the drift motions of the charge-carrying particles are superimposed upon their random darting-about within the space lattice, the particles do not progress around the circuit in any definite order. They continually collide with each other, and in doing so exchange energy and thus render inaccurate our concept of a bundle of charge receiving a discrete amount of energy upon which it must make its trip around the circuit. This concept serves a useful purpose: the definition of potential difference is just as valid as if charge did move in bundles, but it can now be seen that it is more accurate to think of the energy gained or lost as belonging to the whole moving stream of free charges rather than to any particular segment of it. While the stream is receiving energy in one part of the circuit (the battery) it is giving up energy in another part (the resistance). The law of conservation of energy requires that the energy received by the stream of charge in any given time shall be equal to the energy given up by the charge in this same time. Likewise, the rate at which charge is moving is the same for all parts of the circuit: just as much charge passes through the battery as through the resistance during any given period of time. Thus, our definition of potential difference as energy gained or lost per unit quantity of electricity is still valid.

    Example: Positive charge moves at a constant rate around the circuit shown in Fig. 2.8 in the direction a–b–c–d. In a given time 100 coulombs passes a reference point on the circuit. During this time, between d and a, energy in the amount of 1500 joules is supplied to the charge by the battery; between a and b 250 joules is converted to heat in the resistor; and between b and c 1000 joules is converted into chemical energy in the battery. Between c and d energy conversion must be such that the system satisfies the law of conservation of energy. Find E_D, V_A, E_B, V_C, V_{ab}, V_{ba}, E_{db}, and V_{ac}.

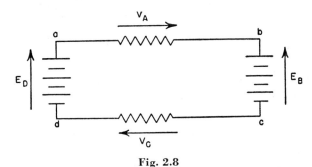

Fig. 2.8

SOLUTION:

$$E_D = \frac{1500}{100} = 15 \text{ v},$$

$$V_A = \frac{250}{100} = 2.5 \text{ v},$$

$$E_B = \frac{1000}{100} = 10 \text{ v}.$$

Energy lost by the charge as heat in the resistor between c and d is

$$W = 1500 - 1000 - 250 = 250 \text{ joules},$$

$$V_c = \frac{250}{100} = 2.5 \text{ v}.$$

With reference arrows as shown E_D, V_A, E_B and E_C are positive

$$V_{ab} \equiv V_A = +2.5 \text{ v},$$

$$V_{ba} \equiv -V_{ab} = -2.5 \text{ v}.$$

In passing from d to b, the net amount of energy supplied to the charge is

$$W = 1500 - 250 = 1250 \text{ joules}.$$

Therefore point b is at a higher potential than point d and

$$E_{db} = \frac{1250}{100} = +12.5 \text{ v}.$$

In passing from a to c, the net amount of energy given up by the charge is

$$W = 250 + 1000 = 1250 \text{ joules}.$$

Therefore point a is at a higher potential than point c and

$$V_{ac} = \frac{1250}{100} = +12.5 \text{ v}.$$

PROBLEMS

(11-II) Positive electricity moves around the circuit shown in Fig. 2.8 in the direction d–c–b–a. The rate of flow is constant, and 100 coulombs passes a reference point on the circuit in a given time. From d to c, during this time, 200 joules is converted to heat; from c to b, 1000 joules is supplied to the charge by the battery; from b to a, 300 joules is converted to heat in the resistor. The energy conversion from a to d must be such that the law of conservation of energy is satisfied for the system. Find V_A, V_C, E_B, E_D, V_{ba}, E_{ad}, V_{ca}, and E_{db}.

(12-II) Positive charge moves at a constant rate in the direction a–b–c–d around a circuit made up of four pieces of apparatus as shown in Fig. 2.9. A charge of 50 coulombs passes a reference point on the circuit in a given time. During this time the energy supplied to the charge is 250 joules in A and 200 joules in B. The energy lost by the charge is 150 joules in C and 300 joules in D. Mark the polarities of A,

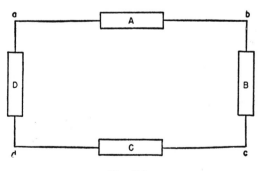

Fig. 2.9

B, C, and D, and place E or V arrows for each. Calculate the electromotive orce or voltage drop for each piece of apparatus.

(13-II) Four pieces of apparatus are connected into a circuit as shown in Fig. 2.9. Free electrons circulate at a constant rate in the direction a–b–c–d. The quantity of electricity passing a reference point on the circuit in a given time is 50 coulombs. During this time, in A, the electrons receive energy in the amount of 600 joules. In B, energy of 200 joules is given up by the electrons, and in C, 300 joules is supplied to the electrons. In D, energy is given up as required by the law of conservation of energy. Redraw the circuit, showing batteries or resistors instead of the rectangles A, B, C, and D. Mark polarities and place E and V arrows. Calculate the electromotive force or voltage drop for each piece of apparatus.

(14-II) Four pieces of apparatus are connected as shown in Fig. 2.9, and a current of 10 amp flows in the direction a–b–c–d. In A, electrical energy is converted to heat at the rate of 60 w. In B, chemical energy is converted to electrical energy at the rate of 140 w. In C, chemical energy is converted to electrical energy at the rate of 30 w. In D, electrical energy is converted to heat at the rate required by the law of conservation of energy. Redraw this circuit, showing batteries or resistors instead of rectangles A, B, C, and D. Mark polarities and place E and V arrows. Calculate the electromotive force or voltage drop for each piece of apparatus.

15. Alternating potential difference. In direct-current circuits, the polarities of batteries and generators will usually be known and will remain unchanged. Hence an electromotive force arrow can readily be placed alongside each battery or generator with the tail opposite the negative terminal and the tip opposite the positive terminal, and the electromotive force treated as a positive quantity throughout.

In alternating-current circuits the polarity of the generator or oscillator changes from instant to instant. An alternating-current generator can be thought of as imparting energy to the free electrons in its windings, momentarily raising the potential of first one terminal and then the other. In most alternating-current generators an effort is made to have the electromotive force vary according to the equation

$$e = E_m \sin 2\pi ft, \tag{2.9}$$

where e is the instantaneous value of the electromotive force;
   E_m is the maximum value of the electromotive force;
   f is the frequency in cycles per second;
   t is the time in seconds since the electromotive force was zero, increasing in the positive direction.

Thus, in Figure 2.10 the electromotive force designated as e would be positive for values of $2\pi ft$ from 0 to 180° and there would be a rise of potential from the lower terminal to the upper terminal. For values of $2\pi ft$ from 180° to 360° the rise of potential would be from the upper terminal to the lower terminal, and the electromotive force designated as e would be negative. Thus, instead of indicating the actual direction of the electromotive force, we see that the arrow marks a positive, or reference direction.* When there is actually a rise of potential from the point designated by the tail of the arrow to the point desig-

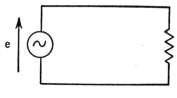

Fig. 2.10

nated by the tip, the electromotive force e is positive; otherwise the electromotive force e is negative.

The remarks above apply also to voltage drops, and it may be added further that since a voltage drop is to be thought of as a consequence of current flow, it is convenient (though not necessary) to place the reference arrow for a voltage drop to agree with the reference arrow for current. Then, if at a certain instant the current is positive, there is actually a drop in potential from the terminal designated by the tail of the voltage drop arrow to the terminal designated by the tip.

It can be seen that for alternating potential differences, the defining equation

$$E \text{ (or } V) = \frac{W}{Q} \tag{2.8}$$

would be meaningless because, when considered over a complete cycle, the quantity of electricity moved from one point to the other would be zero. An alternating potential difference is said to have an effective value of one volt when it is equal to the voltage drop caused by an alternating current of 1 amp in a resistance of 1 ohm.

STUDY QUESTIONS

1. Describe the behavior of the free electrons in conductors.

2. Reconcile the statements "electricity moves with the speed of light" and "the velocity of the free electrons in current-carrying conductors is of the order of a few hundredths of a centimeter per second."

3. How does it happen that the conventional current direction is opposite to the direction of electron flow? Why not change the convention?

4. Two very long parallel wires spaced S meters apart in free space, and each carrying a current of I amp in the same direction, are attracted by a force of F

---

*Strictly speaking, it is not correct to refer to the direction of an electromotive force or a voltage drop (or for that matter, a current). A vector quantity, such as force, has direction, but a scalar quantity, such as potential difference, does not. So long as the discussion is limited to circuits, however, no misunderstanding is likely to arise from speaking of the direction of an electromotive force or voltage drop with reference to the circuit, and the word will be used in this way throughout the book.

newtons. What would be the effect on the force of (a) increasing the spacing to $2S$, (b) increasing the current to $2I$, (c) reversing the current in one conductor?

5. What is an "absolute" measurement of current? Why are such measurements necessary?

6. What is the significance of a current arrow on a circuit diagram?

7. What is the significance of the statement "the current in this part of the circuit is -1.23 amperes"?

8. Would it be practical to store quantities of electricity to be withdrawn gradually to furnish the current for operating electric motors or lamps? Why?

9. Why does the filament of an incandescent lamp become white hot while the wires leading to the lamp, and which carry the same current, remain cool enough to handle?

10. Criticize these statements, and write statements which convey the intended meaning more precisely:

    (a) "Electricity is produced by generators."

    (b) "The light company charged me $6.00 for current last month."

11. Distinguish between electromotive force and voltage drop.

12. What quantity in mechanics would be analogous to potential difference? Explain.

13. Consider the following names as to whether they might be more appropriate than "generator": (a) separator, (b) energizer, (c) electron hoist.

14. What factors do you think may have caused automobile manufacturers to change from 6-v to 12-v electrical systems?

15. Why was 120 v (rather than 12 v or 1200 v) chosen as standard for lighting and appliances?

Chapter **III**

THE LAWS OF THE
ELECTRIC CIRCUIT

---

1. Power and energy in electric circuits. In the preceding chapters we developed the concepts of current, quantity of electricity, resistance, and potential difference, and we defined each concept by an equation and named and defined a unit of each. We will now develop some relationships which will enable us to calculate power and energy in electric circuits in terms of electrical quantities.

Our equation defining potential differences was

$$E \text{ (or } V) = \frac{W}{Q}, \tag{2.8}$$

where E is potential difference in volts;
   W is energy in joules;
   Q is quantity of electricity in coulombs.

We then defined quantity of electricity by the equation

$$Q = IT, \tag{2.5}$$

where I is current is amperes;
   T is time in seconds.

To obtain an equation for the electrical energy supplied by a source in terms of potential difference, current, and time we now substitute (2.5) in (2.8) to obtain

$$W = EIT \text{ joules.} \tag{3.1}$$

38

In like manner the energy absorbed by a resistance is found to be

$$W = VIT \text{ joules.} \tag{3.2}$$

Now since power is defined as the time rate of doing work

$$P = \frac{W}{T} \text{ watts;} \tag{1.5}$$

it follows that

$$P = \frac{VIT}{T} = VI \text{ watts.} \tag{3.3}$$

The power, or rate of absorbing electrical energy by a resistance carrying direct current, is thus found to be the product of current and voltage drop.

Where resistance is known, power can be calculated directly from the defining equation

$$R = \frac{P}{I^2}, \tag{2.6}$$

or $\qquad\qquad\qquad P = I^2R \text{ watts.} \tag{3.4}$

By solving (3.3) for I and substituting in (3.4), it can be shown that

$$P = \frac{V^2}{R} \text{ watts.} \tag{3.5}$$

Equations (3.3), (3.4), and (3.5) are equally valid for calculation of power in direct-current circuits. Which one is to be used depends simply on which quantities are known, or most easily determined.

In general, Equations (3.1),(3.2), (3.3), and (3.5) are not applicable to alternating-current circuits. This is because the current is changing from instant to instant in both magnitude and direction, as is the potential difference; and the time which elapses between the change in direction of the current and the change in direction of the potential difference must be taken into account in calculating power or energy. Expressions for doing this are developed in any text book on alternating currents.

2. Ohm's law. A further consequence of the definitions of resistance, potential difference, and current as formulated in the last chapter becomes evident if we equate the right-hand side of Equation (3.3) to the right-hand side of Equation (3.4) and divide through by I. Thus,

$$VI = I^2R$$

or $\qquad\qquad\qquad V = IR \tag{3.6}$

or $\qquad\qquad\qquad R = \dfrac{V}{I} \tag{3.7}$

or
$$I = \frac{V}{R}. \tag{3.8}$$

This relationship is probably better known and more used than any other in electrical engineering. It is not, in general, valid for alternating-current circuits, but for direct-current circuits it makes possible the ready calculation of any one of the three quantities V, R, or I if the other two are known.

If we consider only metal conductors at constant temperature, the potential difference will always be proportional to the current in the conductor and the resistance will therefore be constant and independent of either potential difference or current. This fact was discovered by George Simon Ohm in 1826 and is known as **Ohm's law.** The law may be concisely stated as follows: *The current in a metal conductor which is maintained at a constant temperature is proportional to the potential difference between its terminals.*

It can be seen that neither Equation (3.6), (3.7), nor (3.8) is a complete mathematical statement of Ohm's law. These equations state the relationship between potential difference, current, and resistance, but say nothing about the constancy of the resistance. A complete mathematical statement of Ohm's law would be

$$R = \frac{V}{I} = \text{a constant.} \tag{3.9}$$

Strictly speaking we may use Equation (3.9) only for metal conductors at constant temperature. Actually there are many other conductors for which the proportionality of V to I is approximately constant and to which we may therefore apply Ohm's law.

Circuits which consist entirely of conductors and devices to which Ohm's law applies are called **linear circuits.** Those circuits to which Ohm's law does not apply are called **nonlinear circuits** and must usually be solved by graphical methods.

3. Nonlinear circuits. The filament of an ordinary incandescent lamp is a very good example of a nonlinear circuit element. The cold resistance of a 100-w lamp is about 10 ohms. When first connected to 120-v mains the current will be

$$I = \frac{V}{R} = \frac{120}{10} = 12 \text{ amp.}$$

The current raises the temperature of the filament very rapidly, and its resistance increases with increased temperature. By the time the normal operating temperature of the lamp is reached, the resistance will have increased to about 144 ohms, reducing the current to

$$I = {}^{120}\!/_{144} = 0.833 \text{ amp}$$

and making the power input to the lamp

$$P = VI = 120 \times 0.833 = 100 \text{ w.}$$

At its normal operating temperature the lamp is able to dissipate energy at the rate of just 100 w, so that no further increase in temperature takes place. It can be seen that if the resistance of the filament did not increase the power input would remain

$$P = 120 \times 12 = 1440 \text{ w,}$$

and the lamp would be destroyed by its own heat before an equilibrium temperature could be reached. It is also obvious that if the cold resistance were used as the basis for calculating normal current and power, the results would be very seriously in error. If the resistance at normal operating temperature were used to calculate the current and power when operating at some voltage close to normal (say 110 or 125 v) the results would not be precise, but would be within the tolerance usually allowed in such calculations.

A number of conducting substances, notably carbon, decrease in resistance as the temperature is increased. Resistors, made of metallic oxides held together with some sort of ceramic binder, have the property of decreasing in resistance by as much as 4 or 5 per cent for one degree increase in temperature. Such resistors are called **thermistors** and have numerous applications based upon the fact that increasing the current raises the temperature and brings about a decrease in resistance.

There are other conductors in which the nonlinearity is inherent in the nature of the material itself and exists even if the temperature remains unchanged. Such a material called *thyrite*, a carborundum-like solid, has the property of decreasing its resistance as the current through it is increased. A piece of thyrite which has a resistance of 15,000 ohms for a current of 5 milliamperes might show a resistance of only 300 ohms at a current of 5 amp. Thyrite was originally developed as a lightning-arrester material and has since found many additional applications.

The contact resistance between two dissimilar substances, such as a carbon brush on a copper commutator, or a copper plate on a layer of copper oxide in a rectifier, is nonlinear as is the resistance of any device, such as an electric arc, or a fluorescent lamp, where the carriers are gaseous ions rather than electrons. A further discussion of conduction in gases will be found in Chapter XIII.

While it is usually possible to find a way of mathematically expressing the relationship between current and potential difference in a nonlinear circuit, such expressions offer little or no advantage over graphical methods for most purposes.

PROBLEMS

(1-III) What is the potential difference between the terminals of a 5-ohm resistance which carries a current of 20 amp?

(2-III) What is the current in a 0.02-ohm resistance if the potential difference across its terminals is 0.1 v?

(3-III) What is the resistance of a wire that has a potential difference of 2.07 v between its terminals when carrying a current of 500 amp?

(4-III) The following data were taken on an ordinary 40-w tungsten-filament incandescent lamp:

V (volts)	I (amp)	V	I
5	0.105	65	0.25
20	0.155	80	0.275
35	0.19	95	0.3
50	0.22	115	0.325

Plot a curve showing potential difference (ordinate) as a function of current. Also plot a curve showing resistance (ordinate) as a function of current. At what voltage does the lamp take 0.215 amp? By what percentage must the voltage be increased to increase the current by 50 per cent?

(5-III) An experimenter measures the current taken by the lamp in Problem 4-III for a potential difference of 5 v. Assuming that Ohm's law applies in this instance, he takes no other readings, but proceeds to find the resistance of the lamp from the data he has taken and then to calculate the current that it would take at a potential difference of 115 v. What current would he find? How much in error would his result be? Why is his result in error?

(6-III) The following data were taken on a 50-cp, metallized, carbon-filament lamp:

V (volts)	I (amp)	V	I
0	0		
5	0.016	65	0.295
20	0.07	80	0.38
35	0.14	95	0.478
50	0.21	115	0.595

Plot a curve showing potential difference (ordinate) as a function of current. Also plot a curve showing resistance (ordinate) as a function of current. At what voltage does this lamp take 0.4 amp? By what percentage must the voltage be increased to increase the current by 50 per cent?

(7-III) The following data were taken on a thyrite disk, $\frac{3}{4}$ in. thick and 6 in. diam (thyrite is a ceramic material developed for use in lightning arresters):

V (volts)	I (ma)	V	I
0	0		
50	3.2	200	42
100	9.8	250	82
150	22.4	300	147

Plot a curve showing potential difference (ordinate) as a function of current. Also plot a curve showing resistance (ordinate) as a function of voltage. For what voltage will the resistance be 10,000 ohms? At how many times this voltage will the resistance be ¼ as much?

(8-III) The following data were taken on a small thermistor (thermally sensitive resistor):

I (ma)	V (volts)	I	V
1	15	6	9.4
2	13.4	7	8.8
3	11.9	8	8.3
4	10.8	9	7.9
5	10	10	7.4

Plot a curve showing the potential difference (ordinate) as a function of current. Also plot a curve showing resistance (ordinate) as a function of current. At what current will the resistance be 5000 ohms? By what per cent does the voltage decrease if the current is increased by 100 per cent from 2.5 milliamperes?

(9-III) The voltage drop across a resistor is 50 v, and the current through it is 5 amp. What is the power absorbed by the resistor?

(10-III) The current through a 10-ohm resistor is 5 amp. What power is absorbed?

(11-III) The voltage drop across a 10-ohm resistor is 50 v. How much power is absorbed?

(12-III) What should be the resistance of an electric heater that is to absorb 600 w when connected to 120-v mains?

(13-III) A heater absorbs 500 w from 230-v mains. What power would it take from 208-v mains?

(14-III) An electric heater absorbs 1000 w from 120-v mains. By how much should its resistance be increased to reduce the power to 900 w?

(15-III) An electric heater takes 450 w from mains of a certain voltage. If the voltage is increased 10 per cent, the current through the heater is 5 amp. What is the original voltage?

(16-III) Plot curves showing power (ordinate) as a function of voltage for each of the lamps for which data are given in Problems 4-III and 6-III. At what voltage does the carbon-filament lamp take 50 w? By what percentage must the voltage be increased in order to increase the power by 10 per cent? At what voltage does the tungsten-filament lamp take 30 w? By what percentage must the voltage be increased in order to increase the power by 10 per cent?

(17-III) A watt-hour meter is installed on the premises of nearly every electric power and light consumer, to measure the energy used. In one type commonly used, the disk makes 2 rev per whr. If a customer having such a meter finds the disk making 19 rev in 1 min, at what rate (in watts) is energy being used?

(18-III) A certain lighting installation consists of twenty 200-w lamps, ten 100-w lamps, and four 40-w lamps. If energy costs 4 cents per kw-hr, what would be the monthly bill for operating this installation 6 hr per day?

(19-III) A direct-current motor takes a current of 5.8 amp when operating at a voltage of 119.5. If energy costs 5 cents per kwhr, what would be the cost per hour of operating this motor?

(20-III) If the motor of Problem 19-III operates at an efficiency of 81.2 per cent, what is its horsepower output?

(21-III) The cost of operating an electric grill is 9 cents per hr with energy at 3.5 cents per kwhr. The operating voltage is 230. What current does the grill take? What is the resistance of the heating element?

(22-III) An electric water heater is required to raise the temperature of 15 gal of water per hr from 50° F to 180° F. The supply voltage is 230. Determine the watt rating and resistance of the heating element.

4. Series circuits — Kirchhoff's voltage law. An electric circuit may contain more than one source of emf and more than one conductor, each with its own particular resistance. If all the parts are arranged to form a single complete loop, as in Figure 3.1, they are said to comprise a **series circuit.** In the battery in Figure 3.1, energy is being imparted to the elec-

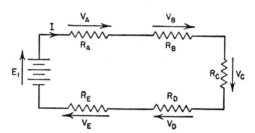

Fig. 3.1. Series circuit.

trons, whereas in each of the resistances, energy is being given up by the electrons and dissipated in the form of heat. Let us consider what happens as a number of electrons whose combined charges total Q coulombs pass a reference point on the circuit. As explained in Section 14 (Chapter II), this same number of electrons, and therefore the same total charge Q, will pass every other reference point on the circuit in the same time. In other words, the current is the same in every part of a series circuit. Let the energy gained by the electrons in passing through the battery be W, and let the energy lost in the various resistances be W_a, W_b, W_c, W_d, and W_e, respectively. Then, from the law of conservation of energy,

$$W = W_a + W_b + W_c + W_d + W_e. \tag{3.10}$$

Dividing by the quantity of electricity Q, we get

$$\frac{W}{Q} = \frac{W_a}{Q} + \frac{W_b}{Q} + \frac{W_c}{Q} + \frac{W_d}{Q} + \frac{W_e}{Q}. \tag{3.11}$$

But W/Q is, by definition, the electromotive force of the battery, W_a/Q is the voltage drop across resistance R_a, W_b/Q is the voltage drop across resistance R_b, and so forth. Therefore

$$E_1 = V_a + V_b + V_c + V_d + V_e. \tag{3.12}$$

Or, substituting for V_a, V_b, and so forth, their equivalents IR_a, IR_b, and so forth, according to Equation 3.5, we get

$$E_1 = IR_a + IR_b + IR_c + IR_d + IR_e. \tag{3.13}$$

This relationship is known as **Kirchhoff's voltage law** and may be stated as follows: *Around any complete circuit, the algebraic sum of the electromotive forces equals the algebraic sum of the voltage drops.*

Kirchhoff's voltage law is much more widely applicable than can be seen from the above. It is essentially a restatement of the law of conservation of energy as applied to electric circuits. If a charge, in moving around a circuit, experiences rises of potential, corresponding to gains of potential energy, and falls of potential, corresponding to loss of potential energy, and eventually returns to the starting point, then the net total of the rises (algebraic sum of the emf's) must be equal to the net total of the falls (algebraic sum of the voltage drops).

Attention is called to the fact that the sum that has to be taken is, in each case, the algebraic sum. This means that the sign, as well as the magnitude, of each electromotive force and each voltage drop must be considered. In the circuit of Figure 3.1, the signs are all positive, and the algebraic sum is no different from the arithmetic sum. In general, however, this will not be true, as we shall see in the following sections.

Example: The battery in Fig. 3.1 has an electromotive force of 30 v, and the resistances R_a, R_b, and so forth, are each 6 ohms. What is the current and what is the voltage drop across each resistance?

SOLUTION: By Kirchhoff's voltage law, we have

$$30 = 6I + 6I + 6I + 6I + 6I = 30I,$$

from which we get

$$I = 1 \text{ amp.}$$

By Ohm's law, the voltage drops V_a, V_b, and so forth, are each

$$V = IR = 1 \times 6 = 6 \text{ v.}$$

PROBLEMS

(23-III) A signaling circuit consists of 18 relays and a battery connected in series. Each relay has a resistance of 30 ohms and the resistance of the connecting lines is 44 ohms. It requires a current of 40 milliamperes to operate the relays.

What should be the electromotive force of the battery? What is the voltage drop across the terminals of each relay? What is the voltage drop in the line?

(24-III) The lamps of street-lighting circuits are sometimes connected in series and the current maintained constant at 6.6 amp. How many lamps, each having a resistance of 7.2 ohms at rated current and connected by lines having a total resistance of 24 ohms, can be operated from a generator which supplies an electromotive force of 5000 v? What is the power taken by each lamp? What is the power loss in the line? What is the power output of the generator?

(25-III) Three resistances of 7, 10, and 12 ohms, respectively, are connected in series, and the group connected to a battery having an electromotive force of 200 v. What is the current in the circuit? What is the voltage drop across each resistance?

(26-III) A battery of unknown electromotive force and resistances of 8, 11, and 14 ohms, respectively, are connected in series. The voltage drop across the 8-ohm resistance is 15 v. What is the current? What is the electromotive force of the battery? What is the voltage drop across each of the other resistors?

(27-III) How much resistance must be put in series with a coil connected to a generator which has an electromotive force of 110 v in order to reduce the current from 2.18 to 1.84 amp?

(28-III) The tungsten-filament lamp described in Problem 4-III and the carbon-filament lamp described in Problem 6-III are connected in series across the terminals of a 200-v generator. Find the current and the voltage drop across each lamp. *Suggestion:* Plot curve showing the sum of the voltage drops for various values of current.

(29-III) The thermistor of Problem 8-III is connected in series with a 3000-ohm wire-wound (linear) resistor and a potential difference of 25 v is applied to the circuit. What is the voltage drop at the terminals of the thermistor? What would happen to the drop across the thermistor if the circuit potential difference were increased to 30 v? *Suggestion:* Plot curve showing the sum of the voltage drops for various values of current.

5. Equivalent resistance of a series circuit. Since the current is the same through all parts of a series circuit, we may factor out I in Equation (3.13) thus:

$$E = I(R_a + R_b + R_c + R_d + R_e).$$ (3.14)

There is some resistance,

$$R_0 = R_a + R_b + R_c + R_d + R_e,$$ (3.15)

that will exactly replace the five resistances in series by permitting exactly the same current to flow when connected to the same electromotive force. This resistance R_0 is called the total resistance or the **equivalent resistance** of the series circuit. The rule for calculating it may be stated as follows: *The equivalent resistance of a series circuit is the sum of the individual resistances.*

PROBLEMS

(30-III) What is the equivalent resistance of a circuit consisting of three coils in series, the resistances of the individual coils being 60.5, 1.45, and 910 ohms, respectively?

(31-III) What is the equivalent resistance of the street-lighting circuit in Problem 24-III?

(32-III) The thyrite disk described in Problem 7-III and a 4000-ohm wire-wound (linear) resistor are connected in series across the terminals of a 200-v generator. What is the equivalent resistance at this particular voltage? *Suggestion:* Plot a curve showing sum of the voltage across the thyrite and voltage across the linear resistor for various values of current.

6. Internal resistance of emf sources. It was stated in Chapter II that an ideal source of emf would maintain a finite difference of potential between its terminals regardless of current through it. Since it is impossible to construct a battery, generator, or other emf source without resistance, the **terminal voltage,** or potential difference between the terminals, of an actual source will depend upon the current. In Figure 3.2 the battery

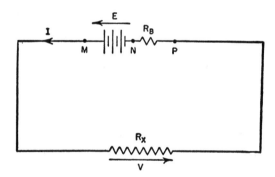

Fig. 3.2. Battery internal resistance.

resistance R_B is in series with whatever additional resistance, R_X, is placed in the circuit. The terminals of the battery are M and P and the terminal voltage is V. The point N is not accessible. Applying Kirchhoff's voltage law to the series circuit

$$E = IR_X + IR_B \qquad (3.16)$$
or
$$E = V + IR_B \qquad (3.17)$$
or
$$V = E - IR_B. \qquad (3.18)$$

The terminal voltage of an emf source wherever the source is delivering energy to the circuit is less than the emf by the voltage drop IR_B.

The equivalent resistance of the series circuit in Figure 3.2 is $R_X + R_B$ and the current is

$$I = \frac{E}{R_X + R_B}.$$ (3.19)

It can be seen from (3.19) that if R_X were very large, the current would be small. Then according to (3.18), the terminal voltage of the source would be only slightly less than the emf. If the circuit were not closed, R_X could be considered infinite, and the terminal voltage would be equal to the emf. On the other hand, if R_X were reduced to zero, the drop in the internal resistance would be equal to the emf and the terminal voltage would be zero. This condition is called **short circuit.** The internal resistance of a battery is ordinarily not constant, but depends somewhat on the condition of the battery and the current that is flowing. It may, however, be treated as constant in problems that do not involve the use of the battery over long periods of time.

Example: A battery has an electromotive force of 6 v and will deliver a current of 5 amp through a resistance of 1 ohm connected to its terminals. What is the internal resistance of the battery?

Solution: By Kirchhoff's voltage law, we have

$$6 = 5R_b + (5 \times 1),$$
$$5R_b = 6 - 5 = 1,$$
$$R_b = 0.2 \text{ ohm.}$$

PROBLEMS

(33-III) The terminal voltage of a battery is found to be 30.65 v when an external resistance of 2 ohms is connected to its terminals. The electromotive force of the battery is 32 v. What is its internal resistance?

(34-III) A storage battery having an electromotive force of 6 v and an internal resistance of 0.006 ohm is connected to an external circuit having a resistance of 0.04 ohm. What is the terminal voltage of the battery?

(35-III) A battery whose electromotive force is 18 v will maintain a current of 8.8 amp through a resistance of 1.95 ohms connected to its terminals. What is the internal resistance of the battery? What current will it supply if the external circuit resistance is reduced to 1.14 ohms?

(36-III) A battery which gives 32.5 amp on short circuit (that is, external resistance equal to zero) will supply a current of 7.5 amp to a resistance of 1.2 ohms connected to its terminals. What is the electromotive force of the battery? What is its internal resistance?

7. Series circuits — energy transmission. Kirchhoff's voltage law and the calculation of power may be further illustrated by consideration of some problems in electric energy transmission. Figure 3.3 shows an emf source E_s connected to a two-wire transmission line, over which energy is delivered to some device at the far end, called the **load.** It will be convenient to think of the source as a direct-current generator and to think of the load as simply a resistance. The resist-

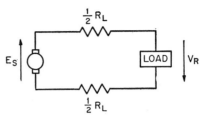

Fig. 3.3. Transmission line.

ance of each wire is designated as $\frac{1}{2} R_L$, or the total line resistance as R_L. The subscripts S and R refer to the sending end (where the generator is located) and the receiving end (where the load is located), respectively. For convenience we will consider the emf source to have no internal resistance, so that its emf, E_S, and its terminal voltage have the same magnitude. By Kirchhoff's voltage law:

$$E_S = V_R + IR_L. \tag{3.20}$$

The voltage drop in the line is

$$E_S - V_R = IR_L \text{ v.} \tag{3.21}$$

The power supplied to the sending end of the line by the source is

$$P_S = E_S I \text{ w.} \tag{3.22}$$

The power delivered by the line to the load at the receiving end is

$$P_R = V_R I \text{ w.} \tag{3.23}$$

The power loss in the line is

$$P_S - P_R = E_S I - V_R I \tag{3.24}$$

$$= (E_S - V_R)I \tag{3.25}$$

$$= (IR_L)I \tag{3.26}$$

$$= I^2 R_L. \tag{3.27}$$

The following examples are typical of the problems that may have to be solved.

Example 1: Power is transmitted over a line having a resistance of 1.07 ohms to a load requiring 1 kw. The voltage at the receiving end is to be 120. Calculate the current, the power loss in the line, and the voltage at the sending end.

SOLUTION: Applying the power equation to the load,

$$I = \frac{P_R}{V_R} = \frac{1000}{120} = 8.33 \text{ amp.}$$

Applying the power equation to the line resistance,

$$P_{\text{loss}} = I^2 R_L = (8.33)^2 \times 1.07 = 74.2 \text{ w.}$$

Applying Kirchhoff's voltage law around the circuit,

$$E_S = V_R + IR_L = 120 + (8.33 \times 1.07) = 128.9 \text{ v.}$$

Example 2: Power is to be transmitted over a line to a load which requires 60 amp at a voltage of not less than 115. The voltage at the sending end is 125. What is the maximum resistance which the line may have? What is the power lost in the line? What is the efficiency of transmission?

SOLUTION: By Kirchhoff's voltage law,

$$R_L = \frac{E_S - V_R}{I} = \frac{125 - 115}{60} = 0.166 \text{ ohm.}$$

Power lost in line is

$$I^2 R_L = (60)^2 \times 0.166 = 600 \text{ w.}$$

Power input to line at sending end is

$$P_S = E_S I = 125 \times 60 = 7500 \text{ w.}$$

Power output of line at receiving end is

$$P_R = V_R I = 115 \times 60 = 6900 \text{ w.}$$

Efficiency of line is

$$\frac{\text{output}}{\text{input}} = \frac{6900}{7500} = 0.92 \text{ or } 92 \text{ per cent.}$$

8. Maximum power transfer. It can be shown that for a transmission line having a certain resistance, maximum receiving-end power will be obtained when the load resistance is made equal to the line resistance.

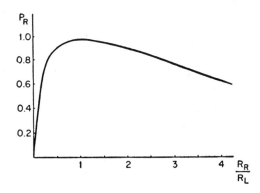

Fig. 3.4. Maximum power transfer occurs when load resistance equals line resistance.

If we let R_R be the load resistance, then the circuit resistance (Figure 3.3) is $R_R + R_L$ and the current is

$$I = \frac{E}{R_R + R_L}.$$ (3.28)

The receiving-end power is then

$$P_R = I^2 R_R = \frac{E^2 R_R}{R_R^2 + 2R_R R_L + R_L^2}.$$ (3.29)

If we plot P_R against R_R/R_L, letting this ratio be zero, $\frac{1}{2}$, 1, 2, etc., we find that the maximum value of P_R is $0.25E^2/R_L$ and that it occurs when $R_R/R_L = 1$.* See Figure 3.4.

The load resistance to obtain maximum receiving-end power is of no particular interest in power engineering because if the load resistance were made equal to the line resistance, the power lost in the line would be equal to the power delivered to the load, and the efficiency of the line would be exactly 50 per cent. Power lines must operate at much higher efficiencies than this in order to be economically feasible. In communications engineering, however, we deal with relatively small amounts of power, and the efficiency of the line is of secondary importance.

The result obtained in this article is valid whenever power is supplied from a source to a load through a resistance. The resistance may be the internal resistance of the source, or the combined resistance of the source and line. For example, an emf source having an internal resistance of R ohms would deliver maximum power to a load connected directly to its terminals if the resistance of the load were also R ohms.

PROBLEMS

(37-III) A generator delivers 1500 w to the sending end of a transmission line. The electromotive force of the generator is 125 v, and voltage at the receiving end is to be 113 v. Determine the current, the voltage drop in line, and the power received by the load.

(38-III) How much power can be delivered over a line having a resistance of 1.5 ohms if the voltage drop in the line resistance is not to exceed 5 per cent of the voltage at the load, which is to be 250 v? What will be the sending-end voltage?

*This result may be obtained by differentiating the expression for P_R with respect to R_R and setting the derivative equal to zero. Thus,

$$\frac{dP_R}{dR_R} = E^2 \left[\frac{(R_R^2 + 2R_R R_L + R_L^2) - R_R(2R_R + 2R_L)}{(R_R^2 + 2R_R R_L + R_L^2)^2} \right].$$ (3.30)

$$E^2(-R_R^2 + R_L^2) = 0.$$ (3.31)

$$R_R^2 = R_L^2.$$ (3.32)

$$R_R = R_L.$$ (3.33)

(**39-III**) The power lost in a line must not exceed 10 per cent of the power supplied to the line. The power required at the receiving end is 5000 w, and the potential difference at the sending end is 250 v. What is the maximum value the line resistance may have? What will be the voltage at the receiving end?

(**40-III**) The power delivered to the sending end of a line is 808 w, and that taken from the receiving end is 727 w. The line resistance is 2 ohms. What is the current? What is the voltage drop at the load? What is the electromotive force at the generator?

(**41-III**) Two transmission lines have the same resistance and deliver the same power to the load, but line B operates at twice the receiving-end voltage of line A. The loss in line A is 600 w. What is the loss in line B?

(**42-III**) Two transmission lines, A and B, operate at the same receiving-end voltage, and the loss in each line is to be the same. Line B has twice as much resistance as line A. If the power delivered to the load by line A is 4000 w, how much power can be delivered by line B?

(**43-III**) Two transmission lines, A and B, have the same resistance and are to operate so that the loss in each line is the same. The receiving-end voltage of line A is twice that of line B. The power delivered to the load by line A is 4000 w. How much power can be delivered to the load by line B?

(**44-III**) Two transmission lines, A and B, operate at the same receiving-end voltage and deliver the same power to the load, but line B has twice the resistance of line A. The efficiency of line A is 80 per cent. What is the efficiency of line B?

(**45-III**) The power input to a transmission line is 3600 w. The sending-end voltage is 240, and the receiving-end voltage is 226. Calculate the current, power output of the line, line loss, and efficiency.

(**46-III**) The power received by the load at the end of a transmission line is 1115 w. The potential difference at the sending end is 160 v, and the line resistance is 0.835 ohm. Find the current, the potential difference at the load, and the line loss. *Note:* This problem requires the solution of a quadratic equation. Obtain both roots and find both possible values of current, potential difference, line loss, and load resistance. Which would be the more practical set of values?

(**47-III**) The sending-end voltage of a transmission line is maintained constant at 125 v. The resistance of the line is 1 ohm. The load resistance is first set at infinity (open circuit) and gradually reduced to zero (short circuit). Calculate and plot the receiving-end power against load resistance for load resistances of infinity, 100 ohms, 10 ohms, 2 ohms, 1 ohm, 0.5 ohm, 0.1 ohm, 0.01 ohm, and zero. For what load resistance is receiving-end power a maximum? What is receiving-end power when V_R is maximum? When I is maximum?

9. Parallel circuits — Kirchhoff's current law. An electric circuit that contains a number of branches, each with its own particular resistance, arranged as in Figure 3.5, is known as a **parallel circuit.** Each of the branches, the resistance of which is designated as R_A, R_B, and R_C, offers a possible path through which current may flow. The electrons arriving at point n split up into three streams, one stream taking the path through R_A,

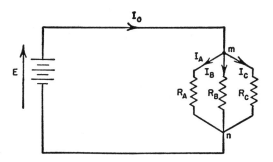

Fig. 3.5. Parallel circuit.

another through R_B, and the third through R_C. At the point m, the streams reunite and continue on around the circuit. We may say the same thing in another way: the current I_0 splits into three currents at the point m, and these three currents I_A, I_B, and I_C reunite at point n to again make up the current I_0. Now, unless electrons can accumulate at point m or point n, the rate at which electrons leave such a point must be exactly equal to the rate at which they enter it. There is no evidence that electrons do accumulate at the points m and n, and we are, therefore, forced to the conclusion that they enter a point and leave it at the same rate. Stated in terms of currents, this is **Kirchhoff's current law**: *At any junction point, the sum of the currents entering the point equals the sum of the currents leaving the point.*

Stated in equation form, we would have, for either junction in Figure 3.5,

$$I_0 = I_A + I_B + I_C. \tag{3.34}$$

Example: In the circuit shown in Fig. 3.5, I_A is 5 amp, I_B is 6 amp, and I_C is 11 amp. Find the current I_0.

SOLUTION:

$$I_0 = 5 + 6 + 11 = 22 \text{ amp.}$$

10. Equivalent resistance of a parallel circuit — conductance. We may apply Kirchhoff's voltage law to the circuit shown in Figure 3.5 to obtain the following equations:

$$E = I_A R_A, \tag{3.35}$$

from which

$$I_A = \frac{E}{R_A};$$

$$E = I_B R_B, \tag{3.36}$$

from which

$$I_B = \frac{E}{R_B};$$

$$E = I_C R_C, \tag{3.37}$$

from which

$$I_C = \frac{E}{R_C}.$$

We may then substitute these values of I_A, I_B, and I_C into Equation (3.34) to obtain

$$I_0 = \frac{E}{R_A} + \frac{E}{R_B} + \frac{E}{R_C}. \tag{3.38}$$

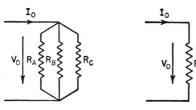

Let R_0 be a single resistance which will replace all of the individual resistances in the sense that it will permit the same current to flow when connected to the battery, so that

Fig. 3.6. Equivalent of a parallel circuit.

$$I_0 = \frac{E}{R_0}. \tag{3.39}$$

Equating the right-hand side of Equation (3.39) to the right-hand side of Equation (3.38) and dividing through by E, we have

$$\frac{1}{R_0} = \frac{1}{R_A} + \frac{1}{R_B} + \frac{1}{R_C}. \tag{3.40}$$

The resistance R_0 is called the *group resistance* or the *equivalent resistance* of the parallel circuit. The rule for calculating it may be stated in words as follows: *The equivalent resistance of a parallel circuit is the reciprocal of the sum of the reciprocals of the individual resistances.* Each term in Equation (3.40) is of the form $1/R$, and is called a **conductance.** Thus, $1/R_0$ is the conductance of the parallel group, $1/R_A$ is the conductance of conductor A, and so forth. The symbol for conductance is G, and its unit is the **mho** (ohm spelled backward). Conductance of any conductor may be found by taking the reciprocal of its resistance, or more directly, by taking the ratio of current to potential difference. Resistance was shown to be

$$R = \frac{V}{I}, \tag{3.7}$$

and we now define conductance as

$$G = \frac{I}{V}. \tag{3.41}$$

Equation (3.40) may now be rewritten as

$$G_0 = G_A + G_B + G_C, \tag{3.42}$$

and our procedure for finding the equivalent resistance of a group of parallel conductors may be restated thus: Find the conductance of each branch; add the individual conductances to find the group conductance; take the reciprocal of the group conductance to find the equivalent resistance.

Example 1: Three conductors that are connected in parallel have resistances of 10, 20, and 30 ohms, respectively. What is the conductance of each branch? What is the group conductance? What is the equivalent resistance?

SOLUTION:

$$G_A = \frac{1}{R_A} = \frac{1}{10} = 0.1 \text{ mho,}$$

$$G_B = \frac{1}{R_B} = \frac{1}{20} = 0.05 \text{ mho,}$$

$$G_C = \frac{1}{R_C} = \frac{1}{30} = 0.0333 \text{ mho,}$$

$$G_0 = G_A + G_B + G_C$$
$$= 0.1 + 0.05 + 0.033 = 0.183 \text{ mho,}$$

$$R_0 = \frac{1}{G_0} = \frac{1}{0.183} = 5.46 \text{ ohms.}$$

Example 2: How would a current of 15 amp divide among the branches of the circuit in the foregoing problem?

SOLUTION: Our first step will be to find the voltage drop across the group. (Refer to Fig. 3.6.)

$$V_0 = I_0 R_0 = 15 \times 5.46 = 81.9 \text{ v.}$$

The divided currents may then be found by Ohm's law:

$$I_A = \frac{81.9}{10} = 8.19 \text{ amp,}$$

$$I_B = \frac{81.9}{20} = 4.09 \text{ amp,}$$

$$I_C = \frac{81.9}{30} = 2.73 \text{ amp.}$$

We can check the correctness of our work by applying Kirchhoff's current law:

$$I_0 = I_A + I_B + I_C$$
$$15 = 8.19 + 4.09 + 2.73 = 15.01.$$

Instead of dividing the voltage by resistance to find current, we may multiply the voltage by conductance:

$$I_A = G_A V = 0.1 \times 81.9 = 8.19 \text{ amp,}$$
$$I_B = G_B V = 0.05 \times 81.9 = 4.09 \text{ amp,}$$

$$I_C = G_C V = 0.0333 \times 81.9 = 2.73 \text{ amp,}$$

$$I_0 = G_0 V = 0.183 \times 81.9 = 15 \text{ amp.}$$

PROBLEMS

(48-III) Conductors of 3, 5, and 8 ohms resistance, respectively, are connected in parallel. What is the conductance of each conductor? What is the resistance of the group? What is the group conductance?

(49-III) Conductors of 5, 11, 13, and 21 ohms resistance, respectively, are connected in parallel, and a current of 10 amp flows in the 13-ohm conductor. What is the current in each of the others, and what is the total current?

(50-III) The total current through a group made up of a 10-ohm, a 15-ohm, and a 30-ohm conductor in parallel is 10 amp. What is the current in each conductor?

(51-III) A 12-ohm and a 17-ohm conductor are in parallel, and a third conductor is to be added to make the group resistance 5 ohms. What should be the resistance of the third conductor?

(52-III) Three conductances of 0.003, 0.005, and 0.0075 mho, respectively, are connected in parallel across a potential difference of 100 v. What is the current in each conductance and in the line?

(53-III) Two parallel conductors carry currents of 12.5 and 15.5 amp, respectively, and the conductance of the first is 0.023 mho. What is the conductance of the other conductor? What is the resistance of the two conductors in parallel?

(54-III) Derive an equation for calculating power in terms of conductance and voltage drop. Using this equation, find the power for each conductance of Problem 52-III.

(55-III) Show that if two resistances R_A and R_B are in parallel the equivalent resistance is given by

$$R_0 = \frac{R_A R_B}{R_A + R_B}. \tag{3.43}$$

(56-III) Derive the corresponding expression for equivalent resistance of three resistances R_A, R_B, and R_C connected in parallel.

(57-III) The tungsten-filament lamp described in Problem 4-III and the carbon-filament lamp described in Problem 6-III are connected in parallel, and a total current of 0.3 amp is sent through the group. What is the voltage drop? What is the current through each lamp? Recalculate for a total current of 0.7 amp. *Suggestion:* Plot a curve showing the sum of the currents for various values of voltage.

(58-III) The thyrite disk described in Problem 7-III and a 4000-ohm wire-wound (linear) resistor are connected in parallel, and a current of 60 milliamperes is sent through the group. What is the voltage drop? What is the current in each conductor? (See the suggestion in Problem 57-III.)

11. Series-parallel circuits. There is a great variety of possible ways in which conductors may be connected to form what may be termed series-parallel, or parallel-series, circuits. There are no additional laws or rules to learn in dealing with such circuits. It is only necessary to remember and intelligently apply Ohm's law, the two laws of Kirchhoff, and the rules for finding equivalent resistance of series and parallel groups. It may be well to point out, however, that the laws of Kirchhoff are more broadly applicable than might be inferred from what has been said heretofore concerning them.

Kirchhoff's voltage law can be applied, not only to simple series loops, but to any loop or circuit through which the student can trace his way back to the starting point. This loop may be part of a more extensive circuit, and it is not necessary that the current be the same in every part of the loop. It is necessary, though, to remember that it is the *algebraic sum* of the voltage drops that must be taken and, therefore, in tracing, strict attention must be paid to whether a particular voltage drop is in the direction traced or in the opposite direction.

Kirchhoff's current law can be applied to any junction point, no matter how extensive the circuit. One of the simplest possible series-parallel circuits is shown in Figure 3.7. Two branches of resistance R_2 and R_3, re-

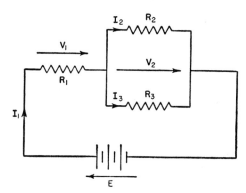

Fig. 3.7. Series-parallel circuit.

spectively, are connected in parallel, and a third branch of resistance R_1 is connected in series with this group. This arrangement is then connected to the terminals of the source. It should be obvious that the current in each of the parallel branches will be different from the current in R_1. These currents are designated I_1, I_2, and I_3, and the directions selected as positive are marked by arrows. Positive directions for the voltage drops are also selected (the same as the current direction in each case) and designated V_1 and V_2. The voltage drop across each parallel branch is, of course, the same.

Let us assume first that the electromotive force of the battery and the three resistances are known, and that we have to find the current in each part of the circuit and the voltage drops. Our first step will be to find the equivalent resistance of the parallel group, and thus, in effect, to reduce the circuit to that shown in Figure 3.8. We then find the equivalent resistance of this circuit, or else apply Kirchhoff's voltage law directly and find the current. We can then find the voltage drops, V_1 and V_2, and knowing V_2, we can find the branch currents, I_2 and I_3.

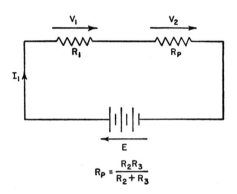

$$R_P = \frac{R_2 R_3}{R_2 + R_3}$$

Fig. 3.8. Equivalent of a series-parallel circuit.

Example: In the circuit shown in Fig. 3.7, let $E = 22$ v, $R_1 = 10$ ohms, $R_2 = 20$ ohms, and $R_3 = 30$ ohms. Then,

$$R_P = \frac{20 \times 30}{20 + 30} = 12 \text{ ohms},$$

$$R_0 = 10 + 12 = 22 \text{ ohms}.$$

By Kirchhoff's voltage law,

$$22 = 22 I_1,$$

$$I_1 = 1 \text{ amp.}$$

Then, $$V_1 = 1 \times 10 = 10 \text{ v},$$

$$V_2 = 1 \times 12 = 12 \text{ v},$$

$$I_2 = {}^{12}\!/_{20} = 0.6 \text{ amp},$$

$$I_3 = {}^{12}\!/_{30} = 0.4 \text{ amp}.$$

Let us now assume that, instead of the emf and all of the resistances being known, we know one or more currents, one or more resistances, one or more voltage drops, and that we have to solve for the remaining currents, resistances, and voltage drops. In such problems, it is not expedient to try to reduce the network to a single equivalent resistance, but rather to apply Ohm's law and Kirchhoff's laws as needed, proceeding a step at a time until the required results are found. In general, we must start with that part of the network about which the most information is given. If we know the resistance and current, or current and voltage drop, or voltage drop and resistance for a certain branch, then that is the logical starting point. In other problems, the first step may be to apply Kirchhoff's current law at some junction point immediately, or Kirchhoff's voltage law around some loop.

Example: Suppose in the circuit of Fig. 3.7, V_1 is 28 v, R_2 is 8 ohms, I_2 is 3 amp, and I_3 is 4 amp. We are to find R_1, R_3, I_1, V_2, and E.

SOLUTION: From Kirchhoff's current law,

$$I_1 = 3 + 4 = 7 \text{ amp.}$$

From Ohm's law,

$$V_2 = 3 \times 8 = 24 \text{ v,}$$
$$R_3 = {}^{24}\!/_4 = 6 \text{ ohms,}$$
$$R_1 = {}^{28}\!/_7 = 4 \text{ ohms.}$$

From Kirchhoff's voltage law,

$$E = 28 + 24 = 52 \text{ v.}$$

PROBLEMS

(59-III) How many different values of resistance can be obtained with three resistors of 10, 20 and 30 ohms, respectively, by connecting them in various ways? Show diagrams and calculate resistances.

(60-III) How many different values of resistance can be obtained with four 10-ohm resistors by connecting them in different ways? Show diagram and calculate resistances.

(61-III) The resistances of the branches of the network shown in Fig. 3.7 are $R_1 = 5$ ohms, $R_2 = 8$ ohms, and $R_3 = 12$ ohms. The electromotive force of the battery is 50 v. Calculate all the currents and voltage drops.

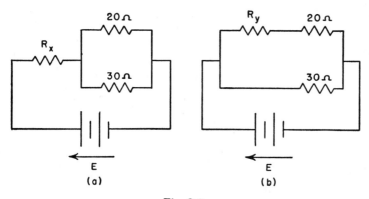

Fig. 3.9

(62-III) In the network shown in Fig. 3.7, E is 40 v, R_1 is 2 ohms, R_2 is 4 ohms, and I_1 is 8 amp. Calculate the other voltage drops, resistances, and currents.

(63-III) In the network shown in Fig. 3.7, E is 75 v, V_1 is 40 v, R_1 is 5 ohms, and I_2 is 2 amp. Calculate the other voltage drops, resistances, and currents.

(64-III) In the network shown in Fig. 3.7, E is 21 v, I_1 is 7 amp, I_2 is 5 amp, and R_3 is 5 ohms. Calculate the other voltage drops, resistances, and currents.

(65-III) It is desired to replace the network in Fig. 3.9a with the network in Fig. 3.9b, so choosing R_Y that the battery current will be the same as before. Calculate R_Y.

(66-III) It is desired to replace the network in Fig. 3.9a with the network in Fig. 3.9b, so choosing R_Y that the current in the 20-ohm resistor will be the same as before. Calculate R_Y.

(67-III) The resistances of the branches of the network in Fig. 3.10 are $R_1 = 11$ ohms, $R_2 = 17$ ohms, $R_3 = 12$ ohms, $R_4 = 30$ ohms, $R_5 = 24$ ohms, and $R_6 = 55$ ohms. The electromotive force of the battery is 100 v. Solve for all currents and voltage drops, and power in each part of the circuit.

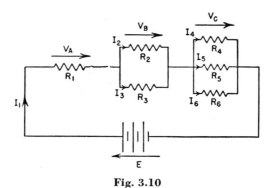

Fig. 3.10

(68-III) In the network in Fig. 3.11a, the resistances are $R_1 = 5$ ohms, $R_2 = 6$ ohms, $R_3 = 7$ ohms, $R_4 = 3$ ohms, $R_5 = 4$ ohms, and $R_7 = 1$ ohm. The battery electromotive force is 10 v. Find currents and voltage drops. *Suggestion:* Reduce the network by successive steps as shown in Fig. 3.11b, c, d, e, and f.

(69-III) In the network shown in Fig. 3.10, E is 80 v, V_A is 20 v, R_1 is 5 ohms, R_2 is 11 ohms, I_3 is 1 amp, R_4 is 44 ohms, and I_5 is 2 amp. Determine the other voltage drops, resistances, and currents.

(70-III) In the network shown in Fig. 3.10, E is 60 v, I_1 is 6 amp, I_4 is 2 amp, I_5 is 3 amp, R_2 is 7 ohms, R_3 is 5 ohms, and R_6 is 12 ohms. Find the other voltage drops, currents, and resistances.

(71-III) In the network of Fig. 3.11a, $V_3 = 35$ v, $V_1 = 25$ v, $V_4 = 10$ v, $R_5 = 3$ ohms, $I_2 = 9$ amp, $R_3 = 8$ ohms, and $R_7 = 7$ ohms. Find the other currents, resistances, and voltage drops.

(72-III) A lamp bank is used as a rheostat, as shown in Fig. 3.12, to regulate the current through a 20-ohm coil. There are 10 lamps in the bank, each having a

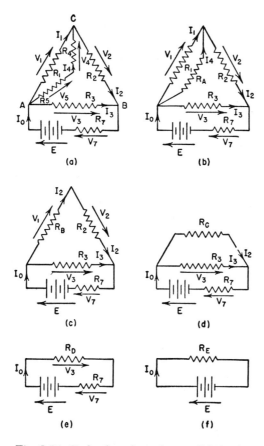

Fig. 3.11. Reduction of a series-parallel circuit.

resistance of 240 ohms, and the current is changed by changing the number of lamps in parallel. The voltage drop across the entire circuit is 115 v. Over what range may the current be varied? Assume the resistance of each lamp to remain constant at 240 ohms.

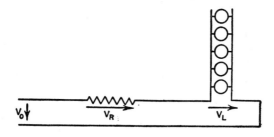

Fig. 3.12. Lamp bank used as a rheostat.

(73-III) For the arrangement described in Problem 72-III, plot the following curves, using as abscissa the number of lamps in parallel: (a) current, (b) V_R, and (c) V_L.

(74-III) A slide-wire rheostat having a maximum resistance of 2800 ohms variable in 2-ohm steps is connected so as to control the last lamp of the bank shown in Fig. 3.12. Over what range may the current now be varied? Can the current be set at exactly 2 amp? Explain how to do this.

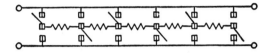

Fig. 3.13. A "load rack" rheostat.

(75-III) Figure 3.13 shows a special rheostat, or "load rack," used in the machinery laboratories. By manipulating the single-pole, double-throw switches, all the resistance units may be put in series, all in parallel, or they may be put into a great many series-parallel combinations. If each unit has a resistance of 25 ohms, what range of resistance may be obtained with a 10-unit rack? Can the resistance be set at 10 ohms?

(76-III) The slide-wire rheostat in Fig. 3.14 is used as a three-point rheostat, or "potentiometer." It permits the voltage V_3 to be varied from zero to maximum, which is a wider range than could be obtained by using the same rheostat in series with R_3 and the generator. What is the current in each part of the network if $E = 100$ v, $R_1 = R_2 = 400$ ohms, and $R_3 = 800$ ohms. What is V_3? What power is consumed in each part of the circuit?

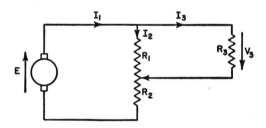

Fig. 3.14. A three-point rheostat.

(77-III) Recalculate Problem 76-III for R_3 equal to 80 ohms.

(78-III) A resistance rack like the one shown in Fig. 3.13 is made up of 10 units of 30 ohms each. What are the maximum and minimum resistances which may be obtained? Show by diagram how to set the switches in each case. What is the maximum and the minimum power when the rack is connected directly to 120-v mains?

(79-III) A resistance rack like the one shown in Fig. 3.13 is made up of 25 units of 30 ohms each. It is desired to adjust this rack for a resistance of 80 ohms. How nearly can this be done? Show by diagram how to set the switches.

(80-III) A resistance rack like the one shown in Fig. 3.13 is made up of 25 units of 30 ohms each. It is desired to connect this rack to 120-v mains and to adjust it to take 2 kw. How nearly can this be done? Show by diagram how to set the switches.

(81-III) A three-point rheostat, like the one shown in Fig. 3.14 and having a resistance of 200 ohms, is connected across the terminals of a 110-v generator. A resistance equal to 200 ohms is connected from one line to the sliding contact. How should the sliding contact be set to make the voltage across the resistance 100 v?

(82-III) A three-point rheostat, like the one shown in Fig. 3.14 and having a resistance of 600 ohms, is connected across the terminals of a 100-v generator. A resistance of 400 ohms is connected from one line to the sliding contact. How should the sliding contact be set to make the power absorbed in the resistance equal to 25 w? What would be the power lost in the rheostat when so set?

12. The delta-wye transformation. We have seen that it is often possible by use of the series and parallel circuit rules to reduce formidable looking circuits to very simple ones. However, there are some networks in

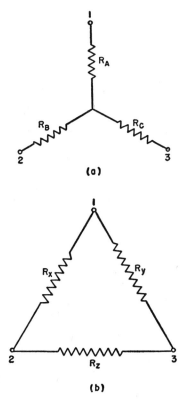

(a)

(b)

Fig. 3.16. Wye and delta networks. Any delta network may be replaced by an equivalent wye network and vice versa.

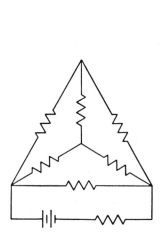

Fig. 3.15. A circuit which cannot be simplified by use of series- and parallel-circuit rules.

which the resistances are neither in series nor parallel. For example, if we add one resistance to the network of Figure 3.11a we have the arrangement shown in Figure 3.15 and its reduction by the series and parallel circuit rules becomes impossible.

It is always possible to find three resistances R_A, R_B, and R_C which, if they be connected in **wye**, as in Figure 3.16a, will be exactly equivalent to three other resistances R_X, R_Y, and R_Z, which are connected in **delta**, as in Figure 3.16b. By *equivalent*, we mean that the resistance, as measured between corresponding terminals, is the same for either arrangement. To prove this theorem, let us begin by writing down the resistances which we would expect to find between the various pairs of terminals. For the wye,

$$R_{12} = R_A + R_B. \tag{3.44}$$

$$R_{23} = R_B + R_C. \tag{3.45}$$

$$R_{31} = R_C + R_A. \tag{3.46}$$

For the delta,

$$R_{12} = \frac{R_X(R_Y + R_Z)}{R_X + (R_Y + R_Z)}. \tag{3.47}$$

$$R_{23} = \frac{R_Z(R_X + R_Y)}{R_Z + (R_X + R_Y)}. \tag{3.48}$$

$$R_{31} = \frac{R_Y(R_Z + R_X)}{R_Y + (R_Z + R_X)}. \tag{3.49}$$

Then, for equivalence,

$$R_A + R_B = \frac{R_X(R_Y + R_Z)}{R_X + (R_Y + R_Z)}. \tag{3.50}$$

$$R_B + R_C = \frac{R_Z(R_X + R_Y)}{R_Z + (R_X + R_Y)}. \tag{3.51}$$

$$R_C + R_A = \frac{R_Y(R_Z + R_X)}{R_Y + (R_Z + R_X)}. \tag{3.52}$$

Solving for R_A, R_B, and R_C, we find

$$R_A = \frac{R_X R_Y}{R_X + R_Y + R_Z}. \tag{3.53}$$

$$R_B = \frac{R_X R_Z}{R_X + R_Y + R_Z}. \tag{3.54}$$

$$R_C = \frac{R_Y R_Z}{R_X + R_Y + R_Z}. \tag{3.55}$$

The wye arrangement made up of R_A, R_B, and R_C is equivalent to the delta, provided R_A, R_B, and R_C are given the values calculated by Equations

(3.53), (3.54) and (3.55). It is important to note that in each of these
equations, the two resistances in the numerator of the right-hand side are
the two that are connected to the same terminal as is the wye resistance
being calculated.

The usefulness of this theorem becomes apparent when it is noticed how
many networks include one or more groups of resistances that form deltas.

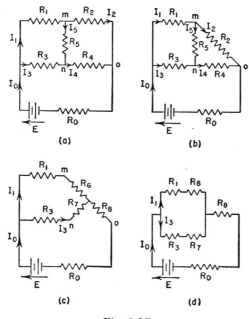

Fig. 3.17

Example: The resistances in Fig. 3.17a are as follows:

$$R_1 = 40 \text{ ohms}, \; R_3 = 10 \text{ ohms, and } R_5 = 50 \text{ ohms},$$

$$R_2 = 20 \text{ ohms}, \; R_4 = 30 \text{ ohms, and } R_0 = \; 5 \text{ ohms}.$$

The emf of the battery is 15 v, and it is required to find the currents in the
various branches.

Solution: It is seen (Fig. 3.17b) that the resistances R_2, R_4, and R_5 form a
delta with corners at points m, n, and o, and that these three resistances may be
replaced by the three resistances R_6, R_7, and R_8 which form a wye, as shown in
Fig. 3.17c. We calculate R_6, R_7, and R_8 by Equations (3.53), (3.54), and (3.55).

$$R_6 = \frac{R_2 R_5}{R_2 + R_4 + R_5} = \frac{20 \times 50}{20 + 30 + 50} = 10 \text{ ohms},$$

$$R_7 = \frac{R_4 R_5}{R_2 + R_4 + R_5} = \frac{30 \times 50}{20 + 30 + 50} = 15 \text{ ohms},$$

$$R_8 = \frac{R_2 R_4}{R_2 + R_4 + R_5} = \frac{20 \times 30}{20 + 30 + 50} = 6 \text{ ohms.}$$

We have thus reduced a three-mesh network to an ordinary series-parallel circuit (Fig. 3.17d), and we proceed with the solution as follows:

$$R_{\text{parallel}} = \frac{(R_1 + R_6)(R_3 + R_7)}{(R_1 + R_6) + (R_3 + R_7)} = \frac{(40 + 10)(10 + 15)}{(40 + 10) + (10 + 15)} = 16.67 \text{ ohms,}$$

$$R_{\text{circuit}} = R_{\text{parallel}} + R_8 + R_0 = 16.67 + 6 + 5 = 27.67 \text{ ohms,}$$

$$I_0 = \frac{E}{R_{\text{circuit}}} = \frac{15}{27.67} = 0.542 \text{ amp,}$$

$$V_{\text{parallel}} = I_0 R_{\text{parallel}} = 0.542 \times 16.67 = 9.04 \text{ v,}$$

$$I_1 = \frac{V_{\text{parallel}}}{R_1 + R_6} = \frac{9.04}{40 + 10} = 0.1805 \text{ amp,}$$

$$I_3 = \frac{V_{\text{parallel}}}{R_3 + R_7} = \frac{9.04}{10 + 15} = 0.361 \text{ amp.}$$

I_1 and I_3 are the currents through the resistances R_1 and R_3, respectively, and are the same in the original network (Fig. 3.17a) as in its series-parallel equivalent. We can now find I_5 by applying Kirchhoff's voltage law around the mesh consisting of R_1, R_5, and R_3.

$$0 = R_1 I_1 + R_5 I_5 - R_3 I_3,$$

$$0 = (40 \times 0.1805) + (50 I_5) - (10 \times 0.361), \tag{3.56}$$

$$50 I_5 = -3.61,$$

$$I_5 = -0.0722 \text{ amp.}$$

Then, by Kirchhoff's current law,

$$I_1 = I_5 + I_2, \tag{3.57}$$

$$I_2 = I_1 - I_5 = 0.1805 - (-0.0722) = 0.253 \text{ amp.}$$

$$I_3 + I_5 = I_4,$$

$$I_4 = 0.361 - 0.0722 = 0.289 \text{ amp.}$$

To check the results, we apply Kirchhoff's voltage law around the loop containing the battery, R_1, R_2, and R_0,

$$E = R_1 I_1 + R_2 I_2 + R_0 I_0, \tag{3.58}$$

$$15 = (40 \times 0.1805) + (20 \times 0.253) + (5 \times 0.542),$$

$$15 = 14.99.$$

PROBLEMS

(83-III) Show that the set of wye-connected resistances R_A, R_B, and R_C

(Fig. 3.16a) may be replaced by the set of delta-connected resistances R_X, R_Y, and R_Z according to the equations

$$R_X = \frac{R_A R_B + R_B R_C + R_C R_A}{R_C}.$$

$$R_Y = \frac{R_A R_B + R_B R_C + R_C R_A}{R_B}.$$

$$R_Z = \frac{R_A R_B + R_B R_C + R_C R_A}{R_A}.$$

(84-III) In the network shown in Fig. 3.18, $R_A = 50$ ohms, $R_B = 250$ ohms, $R_C = 500$ ohms, $R_D = 2000$ ohms, $R_E = 200$ ohms, $R_F = 100$ ohms, and $E = 5$ v. Reduce the network to the simplest possible equivalent circuit, using a delta-wye transformation and parallel-circuit rule.

(85-III) In the network shown in Fig. 3.18, and using the data given in Problem 84-III, calculate the current in the resistance R_E.

(86-III) In the network in Fig. 3.19, $R_1 = 500$ ohms, $R_2 = 400$ ohms, $R_3 = 800$ ohms, $R_4 = 50$ ohms, $R_5 = 1000$ ohms, $R_6 = 1000$ ohms, $R_7 = 900$ ohms, and $R_8 = 20$ ohms. The electromotive force of the battery is 15 v. Reduce the network to the simplest possible equivalent circuit, using the delta-wye transformation and parallel-circuit as necessary.

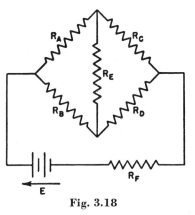

Fig. 3.18

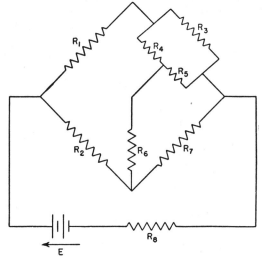

Fig. 3.19

STUDY QUESTIONS

1. During the life of a tungsten-filament lamp, metal is gradually evaporated from the filament, decreasing its cross section. How would this affect the luminous output of a lamp operated at constant voltage? Of a lamp operated at constant current? Ignore the effect of the evaporated metal blackening the bulb.

2. One element of a circuit is nonlinear, showing an increase of resistance with increase of current. What might be done to give linear characteristics to the circuit as a whole?

3. The measurement of the electromotive force of a battery is not a valid test of its condition. For instance, a 6-v battery might be found to have an electromotive force of 6.0 v exactly and still be incapable of delivering any appreciable current. Explain.

4. A storage battery is connected into a circuit as in Fig. 3.20. The polarity of the battery is not known and there is no means of determining the actual direction of the current, but it is observed that the terminal voltage of the battery decreases when the circuit is closed. Is the battery connected for charge or discharge?

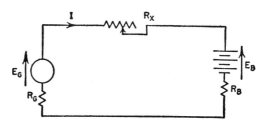

Fig. 3.20. Battery charging circuit.

5. Two batteries having different electromotive forces but equal internal resistances are connected in parallel (positive to positive and negative to negative). What will happen?

6. A storage battery is connected into a circuit, as in Fig. 3.20, and the current is found to be 18 amp. The battery is taken out of the circuit and reconnected with its terminals in the opposite order. The current is now 21 amp. Which is the correct connection for charging the battery?

7. The electrical method of power transmission is, of course, not the only method. A mechanical gear train transmits power and the shipping of coal by rail is, in effect, power transmission. List as many alternative methods as you can think of and for each method, indicate if it is practical or might be practical under certain conditions.

8. When the load at the receiving end of a transmission line has grown to the point where satisfactory service can no longer be rendered, one solution is to operate the line at a higher voltage. For instance, the operating voltage of a certain line might be increased from 120 v to 2400 v. (a) What would be the indications that such a change was necessary? (b) How would increasing the operating voltage remedy the situation?

9. Would it be practical to connect two rheostats in parallel to secure more precise control of current? What should be the relative resistances for the best results?

10. What advantage would there be in operating lamps in series (as is sometimes done for street lighting) rather than in parallel (as is usually done for interior lighting)? What disadvantages?

11. Kirchhoff's voltage law is based upon the principle of conservation of energy. Upon what principle might Kirchhoff's current law be said to be based?

12. A number of lamps are operated in parallel from a generator of constant emf. What would be the effect on these lamps of connecting another lamp in parallel? What would be the effect on the generator?

13. A number of lamps are operated in series from a generator of constant electromotive force. What would be the effect on these lamps of connecting another lamp in series? What would be the effect on the generator?

14. A generator is so modified that it maintains a constant current regardless of the load resistance. A number of lamps in parallel are operated from this generator. What would be the effect on these lamps of adding another lamp in parallel? What would be the effect on the generator?

15. A generator is so modified that it supplies a constant current regardless of the load resistance. A number of lamps in series are operated from this generator. What would be the effect on these lamps of adding another lamp in series? What would be the effect on the generator?

Chapter **IV**

ELECTRICAL NETWORKS

---

1. Terminology. Any arrangement of electrical energy sources, resist-ances, and other circuit elements may be called an electrical network. The terms **circuit** and **network** are used synonymously in electrical literature, any of the circuits, so called, in Figures 3.1 to 3.19 could be properly referred to as networks. Some of the terminology pertaining to networks has already been introduced in the preceding chapter. Referring to Figure 4.1 we

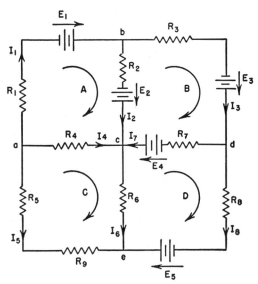

Fig. 4.1. Four-mesh electrical network.

70

should be able to see that there are five **junction points:** a, b, c, d, and e. A part of the network that connects one junction point with another is called a **branch.** In Figure 4.1 there are eight branches: ab, ac, ae, bc, bd, dc, de, and ec. A branch may contain more than one **element.** For instance, branch ab contains one **active** element, the emf source E_1, and one **passive** element, the resistance R_1. Besides resistance, passive elements include inductance and capacitance. A network which contains only passive elements is called a **passive network.**

Points at which two or more elements are joined together are called **nodes.** In Figure 4.1 there are eleven nodes, including the five junction points a, b, c, d, and e. The nodes with which we are most frequently concerned are the junction points, and these are often referred to as "the nodes," as though they were the only ones.

The most elementary of the closed loops which we can trace out in a network are called meshes. In Figure 4.1 there are four meshes, designated A, B, C, and D.

The energy sources in a network may be direct or alternating. The passive elements may be either linear or nonlinear (see Chapter III). In subsequent chapters we will consider energy sources and resistance elements in some detail, and furthermore, we will introduce inductance and capacitance, the other circuit elements mentioned above. For the present we will concern ourselves with networks containing direct sources of emf and linear resistances only.

2. Network graphs. There are certain features of networks that do not depend upon the nature of the elements of which they are made up, but only upon their geometry. In Figure 4.2a the branches and principal nodes of the network of Figure 4.1 are represented by lines and points without regard to what elements any branch may contain. This is called the **graph** of the network. If the lines which make up the graph are thought of as elastic, Figure 4.2a can be distorted into Figure 4.2b, which does not look

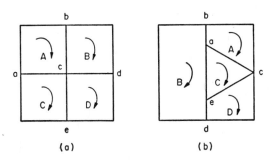

Fig. 4.2. Network graphs.

much like the original graph, but which represents the same nodes, connected in exactly the same way by the same branches. The network in Figure 4.2b is said to be **topologically** the same as the one in Figure 4.2a. There are some things which are different, however. The contour of mesh A is made up of the same branches as before, as is that of mesh C and mesh D. But the contour of mesh B, which in Figure 4.2a was made up of branches bd, dc, and cb, in Figure 4.2b is made up of branches bd, de, ca, and ab. This was the outer contour of the network in Figure 4.2a.

A useful concept in studying the graphs of networks is that of the tree. If branches are removed until barely enough remain to tie the nodes together, the resulting diagram is called a **tree.** There are usually several ways in which the branches to be removed may be chosen, each choice resulting in a different tree. Figure 4.3 shows three possible trees for the

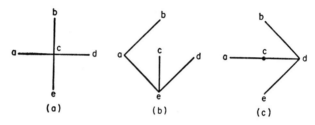

Fig. 4.3. Three possible trees of the network of Fig. 4.1.

graph of Figure 4.2a. The tree has no closed loop around which current could possibly flow. Such loops can be formed by restoring one or more of the branches, or **links,** which were removed. Thus, by restoring branch bd in Figure 4.3a, we would establish mesh B in Figure 4.2a. By restoring one at a time the branches which were removed, we would establish meshes or loops around which current could flow, and around which we could apply Kirchhoff's voltage law to obtain equations with assurance of their being independent. This is a matter about which confusion can easily arise. In the network of Figure 4.1 there are at least twelve loops to which Kirchhoff's voltage law can be applied. Not all of the resulting equations will be independent. For example, if equations are written for meshes A, B, C, and D, then any of the other possible equations could be obtained by combining two or more of the ones already written, and would not, therefore, be independent. By using the procedure described above of starting with a tree, restoring a branch, applying Kirchhoff's voltage law to the loop so formed, removing the branch to get back to the tree, restoring another branch and applying Kirchhoff's voltage law to the loop so formed, and so on, until all the missing branches have been restored one at a time, one can be sure that the resulting equations are independent. Furthermore, the number of equations obtained (which is equal to the number of link branches restored) is the number required for the solution. This will be better understood after reading Section 3.

3. Network analysis — method of branch currents. In most of the circuits or networks considered thus far there was only one source of emf. In those which contained more than one source of emf, these sources were elements of a simple series circuit and could readily be taken into account by applying Kirchhoff's voltage law to the circuit. We now wish to consider networks made up of resistance elements arranged in various ways and including one or more sources of emf. A simple network of this sort, containing two emf sources and three resistances is shown in Figure 4.4.

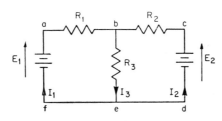

Fig. 4.4

We will suppose that the emf's E_1 and E_2 and the resistances R_1 and R_2 and R_3 are known, and that we are required to find the currents in the various parts of the network. This is a kind of problem that we very often have to solve. We begin by assuming a positive direction for the current in each branch and placing an arrow and symbol on the diagram accordingly. In the beginning we may have no idea as to the actual directions of the currents in the network. Our current arrows, therefore, are not intended to indicate actual directions, but rather the directions in which currents will be considered positive. If the solution of the equations we are about to write yields a positive value for the current I_1, for example, we will know the current is actually in the direction of the arrow. If the value of I_2 turns out to be negative, this means that the current is actually in the direction opposite to that selected as positive. The directions marked as positive for currents on Figure 4.4 seem natural choices, but any other choices would serve as well.

The emf arrows E_1 and E_2 are placed beside the emf sources, pointing in the direction of rise in potential, from the negative to the positive terminal. Since we know the actual directions of the emf's, it would be rather pointless to choose the opposite direction as positive (but not, strictly speaking, incorrect).

Let us now apply Kirchhoff's current law at junction point b, giving

$$I_1 + I_2 = I_3. \qquad (4.1)$$

Applying the current law at the other junction point e gives

$$I_3 = I_1 + I_2, \tag{4.2}$$

which is obviously the same relationship expressed by (4.1) and tells us nothing we did not know already. What we are looking for are *independent* relationships between currents, emf's, and resistances. We therefore turn to Kirchhoff's voltage law. Applying it around the left-hand mesh *abef* we get

$$E_1 = R_1 I_1 + R_3 I_3. \tag{4.3}$$

Around the right-hand mesh *bcde* we get

$$E_2 = R_2 I_2 + R_3 I_3. \tag{4.4}$$

The only other loop to which we might apply the voltage law is the outside loop *abcdef*, and the resulting equation is

$$E_1 - E_2 = R_1 I_1 - R_2 I_2. \tag{4.5}$$

This equation, however, could have been obtained by subtracting (4.4) from (4.3) and it is, therefore, not an independent equation. We are able to get, by use of Kirchhoff's laws, three independent equations (4.1), (4.3), and (4.4). Since we have three unknown currents to be found, the number of independent relationships is just sufficient. This will generally be the case.

    Example 1: In the network of Fig. 4.4, E_1 is 12 v, E_2 is 10 v, R_1 is 4 ohms, R_2 is 2 ohms, and R_3 is 8 ohms. Calculate the current in each branch of the network.

    SOLUTION: Putting numerical values in (4.3)

$$12 = 4I_1 + 8I_3, \tag{4.3}$$

from which $I_1 = 3 - 2I_3.$

Putting numerical values in (4.4)

$$10 = 2I_2 + 8I_3, \tag{4.4}$$

from which $I_2 = 5 - 4I_3.$

Substituting these values for I_1 and I_2 in (4.1)

$$(3 - 2I_3) + (5 - 4I_3) = I_3 \tag{4.1}$$

$$7I_3 = 8$$

$$I_3 = 1.143 \text{ amp.}$$

Substituting this result in (4.3) and (4.4)

$$I_1 = 3 - (2 \times 1.143) = 0.714 \text{ amp,}$$

$$I_2 = 5 - (4 \times 1.143) = 0.428 \text{ amp.}$$

To check the solution we may substitute the results back into (4.1)

$$0.714 + 0.428 = 1.143$$

$$1.142 = 1.143.$$

The positive numbers obtained for I_1, I_2, and I_3 mean that these currents are in the direction selected as positive, that is, in the arrow direction in Fig. 4.4.

The procedure explained above may be extended to networks of any number of branches. The network shown in Figure 4.5 is made up of six

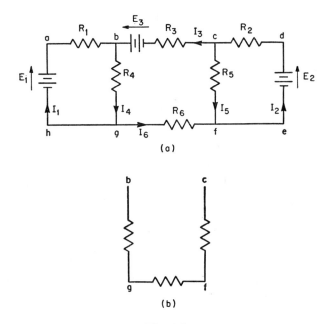

(a)

(b)

Fig. 4.5

branches, containing three sources of emf designated E_1, E_2, and E_3. It is necessary to designate six currents, one for each branch, and to select a positive direction for each current. As before, the selection of the direction to be called positive for a current is arbitrary. The directions indicated on the diagram were chosen as positive in this case. As before, we will assume that the electromotive forces and resistances are known and that our problem is to find the current in each branch. Since there are six such currents to be found, we must use Kirchhoff's laws to obtain six independent equations.

Beginning with the current law, we apply it at the junction points to obtain

$$\text{at } b \qquad I_1 + I_3 = I_4, \qquad (4.6)$$

$$\text{at } c \qquad I_2 = I_3 + I_5, \qquad (4.7)$$

$$\text{at } f \qquad I_5 + I_6 = I_2. \qquad (4.8)$$

Thus far it is impossible to obtain either of these equations by combining the other two. They are therefore independent. If we write the equation at the remaining junction point, however,

$$\text{at } g \qquad I_4 = I_1 + I_6, \qquad (4.9)$$

this equation could have been obtained by adding (4.6), (4.7), and (4.8), and therefore is not independent. Any three of the above equations could have been combined to obtain the fourth one, and thus only three of the four can be regarded as independent. Generally speaking, if a network contains j junction points, then the number of independent current law equations that can be written is $j - 1$.

We now need three additional equations, which we can obtain by use of Kirchhoff's voltage law. Generally speaking, if a network is made up of b branches, the number of equations to be obtained by using the voltage law is $b - (j - 1)$. Actually, there are six possible loops in the network of Figure 4.5 to any one of which Kirchhoff's voltage law can be applied to obtain equations. The three equations we need, however, must be independent equations. One way to be sure that the voltage equations are independent is that explained in Section 1. Branches are removed until we are left with a tree of the network. Thus, we might remove branches $ghab$, bc, and $cdef$, leaving us with the tree shown in Figure 4.5b. Now by replacing branch $ghab$ we form a loop to which we apply Kirchhoff's voltage law to obtain

$$E_1 = R_1 I_1 + R_4 I_4. \qquad (4.10)$$

Removing branch $ghab$ and replacing branch bc, we form a loop which yields the equation

$$E_3 = R_3 I_3 + R_4 I_4 + R_6 I_6 - R_5 I_5. \qquad (4.11)$$

Finally, by removing branch bc and replacing branch $cdef$, we form a loop which yields the equation

$$E_2 = R_2 I_2 + R_5 I_5. \qquad (4.12)$$

Thus, we have the required number of voltage equations, and we are assured that they are independent by the fact that each equation contains at least one term peculiar to the branch that completed the loop around which the equation was written. Thus, none of the equations could be obtained by combining the others.

The choice of loops can usually be made by inspection so that each loop will include at least one branch not included in any loop already traced.

This can best be done by choosing the shortest possible paths, which are the meshes such as $abgh$, $bcfg$, and $cdef$ in Figure 4.5a. As can readily be seen, the application of Kirchhoff's voltage law to these loops will yield Equations (4.10), (4.11), and (4.12). We now have the six required equations from which the currents can be found.

The solution of the equations may be carried out by any of the various methods for solving simultaneous equations. It will usually be found expedient to first study the current law equations with the intention of making substitutions from them into the voltage law equations, thus reducing the number of unknowns. Thus, from (4.7) and (4.8) it is at once obvious that

$$I_3 = I_6.$$

From (4.6) $$I_1 = I_4 - I_3 = I_4 - I_6.$$
From (4.8) $$I_5 = I_2 - I_6.$$

Thus, we may substitute for I_3, I_1, and I_5 in Equations (4.10), (4.11), and (4.12), leaving us with three equations and three unknown currents to be found.

Example 2: The electromotive forces and resistances in the network of Fig. 4.5 are as follows:

$$E_1 = 25 \text{ v} \qquad R_1 = 40 \text{ ohms}$$
$$E_2 = 15 \text{ v} \qquad R_2 = 20 \text{ ohms}$$
$$E_3 = 10 \text{ v} \qquad R_3 = R_6 = 10 \text{ ohms}$$
$$R_4 = R_5 = 100 \text{ ohms}$$

Find the currents in each branch of the network.

SOLUTION: Making the substitutions indicated above for I_3, I_1, and I_5 and putting in the numerical values for the emf's and resistances in Equations (4.10), (4.11), and (4.12), we have

$$25 = 40(I_4 - I_6) + 100I_4. \tag{4.10}$$
$$10 = 10I_6 + 100I_4 + 10I_6 - 100(I_2 - I_6). \tag{4.11}$$
$$15 = 20I_2 + 100(I_2 - I_6). \tag{4.12}$$

Collecting terms

$$25 = \qquad\quad 140I_4 - 40I_6. \tag{4.10}$$
$$10 = 100I_2 + 100I_4 + 120I_6. \tag{4.11}$$
$$15 = 120I_2 \qquad\quad - 100I_6. \tag{4.12}$$

Solving $$I_3 = I_6 = 0.0711 \text{ amp},$$
$$I_1 = 0.128 \text{ amp}, \qquad I_2 = 0.184 \text{ amp},$$
$$I_4 = 0.199 \text{ amp}, \qquad I_5 = 0.113 \text{ amp}.$$

PROBLEMS

(**1-IV**) Construct all the possible trees for the network shown in Fig. 4.4. Write the Kirchhoff's voltage law equations corresponding to each tree. Are the equations independent in each case?

(**2-IV**) Calculate the current in each branch of the network used in Example 1 if E_1 is 6 v and the other values are unchanged.

(**3-IV**) Calculate the current in each branch of the network used in Example 1 if R_3 is 4 ohms and the other values are unchanged.

(**4-IV**) Obtain the literal solution for the current in each branch of the circuit shown in Fig. 4.4.

(**5-IV**) The network shown in Fig. 4.6 is set up in the laboratory for a study of Kirchhoff's laws. The numerical values are as follows: $E_G = 120$ v, $E_B = 30$ v, $R_A = 12$ ohms, $R_B = 8$ ohms and $R_C = 20$ ohms. Find the current in each branch of the network.

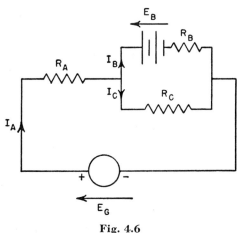

Fig. 4.6

(**6-IV**) The following numerical values are given for the network of Fig. 4.6. $E_G = 75$ v, $E_B = 25$ v, $R_A = 30$ ohms, $R_B = 15$ ohms, $R_C = 5$ ohms. Find the current in each branch of the network.

(**7-IV**) In studying the network shown in Fig. 4.6, it is desired to cause the current I_B to reverse in direction by varying the magnitude of E_G, all the other quantities remaining fixed. If E_G can be varied from 50 to 100 v, and E_B is fixed at 10 v, what relationship should exist among the resistances R_A, R_B, and R_C in order to have I_B reverse at $E_G = 75$ v? Which resistance appears to be of the least significance? *Suggestion:* Make a literal solution for the current I_B.

(**8-IV**) Construct three of the possible trees for the network shown in Fig. 4.5. Write the Kirchhoff's voltage law equations corresponding to each tree. Are the equations independent in each case?

(**9-IV**) Calculate the current in each branch of the network used in Example 2 if $E_1 = 15$ v, $E_2 = 10$ v, and $E_3 = 15$ v. The resistances are unchanged.

(10-IV) Calculate the numerical value of E_3 in the network used in Example 2 which would make $I_3 = 0$. All other emf's and resistances are unchanged.

(11-IV) Calculate the current in each branch of the network shown in Fig. 4.1, taking the numerical values to be as follows:

$$E_1 = 18 \text{ v}, \quad R_1 = 6 \text{ ohms}, \quad R_6 = 13 \text{ ohms},$$

$$E_2 = 5 \text{ v}, \quad R_2 = 3 \text{ ohms}, \quad R_7 = 8 \text{ ohms},$$

$$E_3 = 11 \text{ v}, \quad R_3 = 9 \text{ ohms}, \quad R_8 = 12 \text{ ohms},$$

$$E_4 = 7 \text{ v}, \quad R_4 = 17 \text{ ohms}, \quad R_9 = 2 \text{ ohms}.$$

$$E_5 = 15 \text{ v}, \quad R_5 = 4 \text{ ohms},$$

4. The method of loop currents. The branch currents which have been used up to this point are the actual currents in the branches of the network. In a physical network these currents can be measured by connecting ammeters into the branches, and after a few exercises in the laboratory the student begins to feel that these currents are real. The concept now to be introduced is that of a **loop current,** or a current identified with a particular loop of a network. A loop current cannot be measured, except in those instances where it happens to be identical with a particular branch current, and it therefore is a concept rather than a reality. However, it is a very useful concept in the study of networks, as will be seen.

While the loops to be used may be chosen by the method explained in Section 1, it is expedient to use the simplest possible loops, which are the contours of the meshes. The term *mesh current* is used to mean the loop current identified with a particular mesh.

In Figure 4.7 the mesh currents are designated I_1, I_2, and I_3 for meshes *abgh*, *bcfg*, and *cdef*, respectively. The directions selected as positive are des-

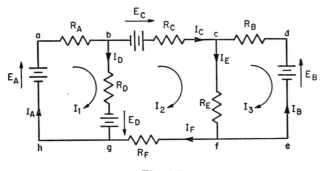

Fig. 4.7

ignated by the curved arrows within the meshes. There is a certain advantage in choosing the positive directions for mesh currents as all clockwise, or all counterclockwise, as will become apparent.

It is obvious that in a single-mesh network, the mesh current and the branch current are either identical, or one is the negative of the other, depending upon the directions selected as positive. In a network of two or more meshes, any particular branch may be part of one mesh only, if it forms part of the outside contour of the network, or it may be common to two or more meshes. If the branch is part of one mesh only, the branch current will be identical with the mesh current (or the negative of it). If the branch is common to two or more meshes, the branch current will be the algebraic sum of the mesh currents. Thus, for the network of Figure 4.7.

$$I_A = I_1. \tag{4.13}$$

$$I_B = -I_3. \tag{4.14}$$

$$I_C = I_2. \tag{4.15}$$

$$I_D = I_1 - I_2. \tag{4.16}$$

$$I_E = I_2 - I_3. \tag{4.17}$$

$$I_F = I_2. \tag{4.18}$$

One advantage of using mesh currents is that the number of unknowns in a network problem is thereby reduced. For the network of Figure 4.7 six branch currents are required, but only three mesh currents. To determine these three mesh currents, three independent equations are needed. These may be obtained by applying Kirchhoff's voltage law to each mesh in succession. The independence of the equations is assured by the presence in each mesh of at least one branch not previously traced through. Thus, no combination of two voltage equations written around meshes would yield the voltage equation for the third mesh.

In applying Kirchhoff's voltage law, two voltage drops will be taken into account in every branch that is common to two meshes, provided the branch has a resistance other than zero. This fact should be obvious when it is considered that the current in any such branch is made up of two mesh currents. The voltage drops due to the mesh currents are to be considered algebraically. Thus, if one traces around a particular mesh in the direction selected as positive for the current in that mesh, the voltage drops caused by that current would all be written as positive. But the voltage drops caused by currents in adjoining meshes might be either positive or negative according to whether, in the common branch, the positive direction of the current in the adjoining mesh agrees with the direction of tracing the mesh under consideration. Since an electromotive force is not considered a consequence of current flow, an electromotive force will appear only once in any voltage equation. For the network of Figure 4.7 the voltage equations will be as follows:

$$E_A + E_D = R_A I_1 + R_D I_1 - R_D I_2. \tag{4.19}$$

$$E_C - E_D = R_C I_2 + R_E I_2 - R_E I_3 + R_F I_2 + R_D I_2 - R_D I_1. \quad (4.20)$$

$$-E_B = R_B I_3 + R_E I_3 - R_E I_2. \quad (4.21)$$

Collecting terms

$$E_A + E_D = (R_A + R_D)I_1 - R_D I_2. \quad (4.22)$$

$$E_C - E_D = -R_D I_1 + (R_C + R_D + R_E + R_F)I_2 - R_E I_3. \quad (4.23)$$

$$-E_B = \qquad\qquad -R_E I_2 + (R_B + R_E)I_3. \quad (4.24)$$

The terms which make up the right-hand side of each of these equations are of two kinds. In Equation (4.22) the term $(R_A + R_D)I_1$ is the product of the mesh current in mesh 1 by the sum of all the resistances, included in mesh 1. This resistance is known as the **self-resistance** of mesh 1, and it may be represented by the symbol R_{11} (read as R one-one, not R eleven). Similar terms appear in each of the other equations. These are the self-resistances of meshes 2 and 3, respectively, and may be represented as R_{22} and R_{33}. The other kind of term in Equation (4.22) is $R_D I_2$, which is the product of the mesh current in mesh 2 by the resistance which is common to mesh 1 and mesh 2. This resistance is known as the **common resistance** of meshes 1 and 2, and may be represented by the symbol R_{12}. Similar terms appear in each of the other equations.

On the left-hand side of each equation is the algebraic sum of emf's of all sources in the mesh. These sums may be represented by E_1, E_2, and E_3.

We may now write Equations (4.22), (4.23), and (4.24) in symbolic form as

$$E_1 = R_{11}I_1 - R_{12}I_2. \quad (4.25)$$

$$E_2 = -R_{21}I_1 + R_{22}I_2 - R_{32}I_3. \quad (4.26)$$

$$E_3 = \qquad\qquad -R_{32}I_2 + R_{33}I_3. \quad (4.27)$$

Note that the equations are arranged in the same order in which the meshes are numbered and the terms on the right are arranged in this same order.

Since there is no resistance common to mesh 1 and mesh 3, no terms involving I_3 appear in (4.25). For like reason, no terms involving I_1 appear in (4.27).

It will be observed that the sign of each term involving a self-resistance is plus, while the sign of each term involving a common resistance is negative. This results from the fact that the positive directions for the mesh currents in Figure 4.7 were all chosen clockwise. Had all been chosen counterclockwise the same consistency in signs would be observed. If some had been chosen clockwise and some counterclockwise, there would be no consistency in the signs for Equations (4.25), (4.26), and (4.27). The choice of uniform positive directions and the resulting consistency of signs tends to reduce the chance of a mistake.

5. Solution by determinants. The solution of the simultaneous equations resulting from the application of Kirchhoff's laws to a network may be systematized by the use of determinants, and any unknown current can be written at once as the quotient of two determinants. Thus, for the group of equations (4.25), (4.26), and (4.27) obtained in Section 4, the mesh current I_1 is given by

$$I_1 = \frac{\begin{vmatrix} E_1 & -R_{12} & 0 \\ E_2 & R_{22} & -R_{32} \\ E_3 & -R_{23} & R_{33} \end{vmatrix}}{\begin{vmatrix} R_{11} & -R_{12} & 0 \\ -R_{21} & R_{22} & -R_{32} \\ 0 & -R_{23} & R_{33} \end{vmatrix}}. \tag{4.28}$$

The denominator of (4.28) is seen to be an array made up of elements which are coefficients of I_1, I_2, and I_3 in Equations (4.25), (4.26), and (4.27). Each coefficient stands in a row and column in the array exactly as it stood in the equations. Each element carries the same sign as it did in the equations. The denominator of (4.28) is called the **determinant of the system,** and is the same regardless of which mesh current is being calculated. The determinant of the system is observed to be symmetrical with respect to the principal diagonal. That is, the element that stands in the first row and second column is identical with the element in the second row and first column ($R_{12} = R_{21}$).

The numerator of (4.28) is identical with the denominator, except that the elements in the first column, which are the coefficients of the mesh current I_1 in Equations (4.25), (4.26), and (4.27), have been replaced by the electromotive forces E_1, E_2, and E_3 which stand on the left-hand side in the equations. The numerator must be recalculated for each mesh current to be found. In each case the electromotive forces E_1, E_2, and E_3 replace the elements of the column made up of coefficients of the mesh current to be found.

Example: In the network shown in Fig. 4.7, the electromotive forces have the following values: $E_A = 30$ v, $E_B = 20$ v, $E_C = 5$ v, and $E_D = 10$ v. The resistances are

$$R_A = 20 \text{ ohms} \qquad R_D = 40 \text{ ohms}$$
$$R_B = 10 \text{ ohms} \qquad R_E = 50 \text{ ohms}$$
$$R_C = 30 \text{ ohms} \qquad R_F = 25 \text{ ohms}$$

Calculate the mesh currents I_1, I_2, and I_3. From the mesh currents calculate the branch currents I_A, I_B, I_C, I_D, I_E, and I_F.

SOLUTION: Putting numerical values in Equations (4.22), (4.23), and (4.24),

$$30 + 10 = (20 + 40)I_1 - 40I_2. \tag{4.22}$$

$$5 - 10 = -40I_1 + (30 + 40 + 50 + 25)I_2 - 50I_3. \qquad (4.23)$$

$$-20 = \qquad\qquad\qquad -50I_2 + (10 + 50)I_3. \qquad (4.24)$$

Collecting terms as in Equations (4.25), (4.26), (4.27),

$$40 = \quad 60I_1 - \quad 40I_2. \qquad (4.25)$$

$$-5 = -40I_1 + \quad 145I_2 - 50I_3. \qquad (4.26)$$

$$-20 = \qquad\qquad -50I_2 + 60I_3. \qquad (4.27)$$

Setting up and evaluating determinants

$$I_1 = \frac{\begin{vmatrix} 40 & -40 & 0 \\ -5 & 145 & -50 \\ -20 & -50 & 60 \end{vmatrix}}{\begin{vmatrix} 60 & -40 & 0 \\ -40 & 145 & -50 \\ 0 & -50 & 60 \end{vmatrix}} = \frac{196{,}000}{276{,}000} = 0.710,$$

$$I_2 = \frac{\begin{vmatrix} 60 & 40 & 0 \\ -40 & -5 & -50 \\ 0 & -20 & 60 \end{vmatrix}}{\begin{vmatrix} 60 & -40 & 0 \\ -40 & 145 & -50 \\ 0 & -50 & 60 \end{vmatrix}} = \frac{18{,}000}{276{,}000} = 0.0652 \text{ amp},$$

$$I_3 = \frac{\begin{vmatrix} 60 & -40 & 40 \\ -40 & 145 & -5 \\ 0 & -50 & -20 \end{vmatrix}}{\begin{vmatrix} 60 & -40 & 0 \\ -40 & 145 & -50 \\ 0 & -50 & 60 \end{vmatrix}} = \frac{-77{,}000}{276{,}000} = -0.279 \text{ amp}.$$

$$I_A = I_1 = 0.710 \text{ amp}, \qquad I_D = I_1 - I_2 = 0.645 \text{ amp},$$

$$I_B = -I_3 = 0.279 \text{ amp}, \qquad I_E = I_2 - I_3 = 0.344 \text{ amp},$$

$$I_C = I_2 = 0.0652 \text{ amp}, \qquad I_F = I_2 = 0.0652 \text{ amp}.$$

PROBLEMS

(12-IV) In the network shown in Fig. 4.8, E_1 is 12 v, E_2 is 8 v, and E_3 is 4 v. R_1 is 2 ohms, R_2 is 7 ohms, R_3 is 3 ohms, R_4 is 8 ohms, R_5 is 5 ohms, and R_6 is 4 ohms. Calculate the mesh currents.

(13-IV) In the network shown in Fig. 4.8, E_1 is 4 v, E_2 is 12 v, and E_3 is 8 v. R_1 is 11 ohms, R_2 is 9 ohms, R_3 is 5 ohms, R_4 is 15 ohms, R_5 is 2 ohms, and R_6 is 6 ohms. Calculate the mesh currents.

(14-IV) In the network shown in Fig. 4.9, E_1 is 16 v, E_2 is 5 v, R_1 is 30 ohms, R_2 is 22 ohms, R_3 is 45 ohms, R_4 is 35 ohms, R_5 is 75 ohms, and R_6 is 10 ohms. Calculate the mesh currents.

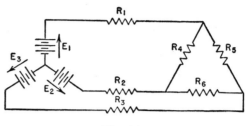

Fig. 4.8

(15-IV) In the network shown in Fig. 4.9, E_1 is 5 v, E_2 is 20 v, R_1 is 5 ohms, R_2 is 7 ohms, R_3 is 10 ohms, R_4 is 3 ohms, R_5 is 8 ohms, and R_6 is 12 ohms. Find the mesh currents.

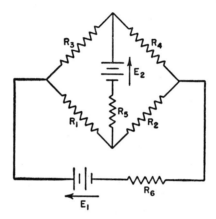

Fig. 4.9

(16-IV) In the network shown in Fig. 4.1,

$E_1 = 10$ v,	$R_1 = 100$ ohms,	$R_6 = 90$ ohms,
$E_2 = 20$ v,	$R_2 = 50$ ohms,	$R_7 = 120$ ohms,
$E_3 = 30$ v,	$R_3 = 150$ ohms,	$R_8 = 180$ ohms,
$E_4 = 40$ v,	$R_4 = 200$ ohms,	$R_9 = 30$ ohms.
$E_5 = 50$ v,	$R_5 = 40$ ohms,	

Calculate the mesh currents.

(17-IV) In the network shown in Fig. 4.10, the resistances R_1 and R_2 are each 2 ohms; R_3 and R_4 are each 50 ohms; R_5, R_6, and R_7 are each 3 ohms; R_8 is 50 ohms; E_G is 600 v; and E_B is 550 v. Calculate the current in each branch of the network.

(18-IV) In the network shown in Fig. 4.10, the resistances R_1 and R_2 are each 5 ohms; R_3 and R_4 are each 100 ohms; R_5, R_6, and R_7 are each 10 ohms; R_8 is

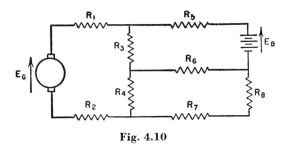

Fig. 4.10

75 ohms; and E_G is 200 v. Find the value of E_B which will make the current zero through the resistance R_5.

6. Current sources. We have made use of sources of emf in practically every circuit considered thus far. A source of emf has meant a battery or other device which normally delivers energy to the circuit and which maintains at its terminals a potential difference that is more or less constant. An ideal source of emf would be one which would maintain at its terminals, regardless of what might be connected to them, a perfectly constant potential difference. This means that an ideal source of emf must deliver a current which depends entirely upon the resistance of the external circuit. The emf of the ideal source shown in Figure 4.11a is 10 volts. At open

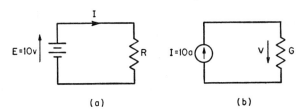

(a)　　　　　　　　　(b)

Fig. 4.11. (a) Simple circuit with ideal emf source. (b) Simple circuit with ideal current sources.

circuit (R = infinity) it would deliver no current. For R = 10 ohms, I = 1 amp; for R = 1 ohm, I = 10 amp; and if R were reduced to zero (short circuit), I would be infinite. A practical emf source is saved from ever having to deliver infinite current by the fact that it has series internal resistance.

A **current source** is a device which normally supplies energy to the circuit, and which delivers a current that is more or less constant. An ideal current source would maintain an exactly constant current regardless of what is connected to its terminals. This means that an ideal current source will have a terminal voltage which depends entirely upon the resistance of the external circuit. The current of the ideal source in Figure 4.11b is 10 amp. At short circuit (G = infinity) its terminal voltage would be zero. For G = 10 mhos, V = 1 v; for G = 1 mho, V = 10 v; and at open circuit V would have to be infinitely large. A practical current source is saved from ever having such a voltage at its terminals by the fact that it has parallel internal conductance.

Most actual energy sources used in electric circuits closely approximate emf sources, or constant-voltage sources, as they are called. Actual sources of electrical energy may, however, be treated as either constant-voltage sources or constant-current sources in network problems. Any constant-voltage source which has internal resistance, or which has resistance in series, may be replaced by an equivalent constant-current source. In many network problems it is advantageous to make this change. A constant-current source, together with whatever parallel conductance it has associated with it, may likewise be replaced by an equivalent constant-voltage source.

7. Equivalence of voltage and current sources. A voltage source and a current source are equivalent if, when delivering equal currents,

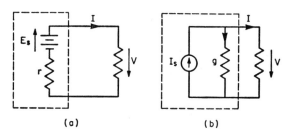

Fig. 4.12. (*a*) Voltage source with series resistance. (*b*) Current source with parallel conductance.

they have equal terminal voltages. For the constant-voltage source in Figure 4.12*a*

$$E_S = V + Ir \tag{4.29}$$

or
$$I = \frac{E_S - V}{r} = \frac{E_S}{r} - \frac{V}{r}. \tag{4.30}$$

For the constant-current source in Figure 4.12*b*

$$I_S = I_g + I \tag{4.31}$$

or
$$I = I_S - I_g = I_S - gV. \tag{4.32}$$

The two sources will therefore be equivalent if

$$I_S = \frac{E_S}{r} \tag{4.33}$$

and
$$gV = \frac{V}{r} \tag{4.34}$$

or
$$g = \frac{1}{r} \tag{4.35}$$

It is important to understand that the two sources are equivalent at their terminals. The equivalent sources in Figure 4.12 are enclosed by the dotted lines. There is no current source which will replace an ideal voltage source.

Example 1: A No. 6 dry cell has an emf of 1.5 v and an internal resistance of 0.05 ohm. Calculate the constants of a current source which will replace the cell.

SOLUTION:

$$I_S = \frac{E_S}{r} = \frac{1.5}{0.05} = 30 \text{ amp},$$

$$g = \frac{1}{r} = \frac{1}{0.05} = 20 \text{ mhos}.$$

Example 2: A branch containing an emf source of 1500 v and a series resistance of 30,000 ohms is to be replaced by a constant-current source. What should its constants be?

SOLUTION:

$$I_S = \frac{E_S}{r} = \frac{1500}{30,000} = 0.05 \text{ amp},$$

$$g = \frac{1}{r} = \frac{1}{30,000} = 0.0000333 \text{ mho}.$$

8. Method of node-pair voltages. In much network analysis, it is expedient to find the potential difference between certain nodes directly, then to find the branch currents. This is especially true if the number of nodes is less than the number of meshes in the network. Let us consider the four-mesh network shown in Figure 4.13. This network has only two nodes, a and b, and we may designate V as the voltage drop from node a to node b. At either node we have, by Kirchhoff's current law,

$$I_1 + I_2 + I_3 + I_4 = I_5. \tag{4.36}$$

Each current can now be expressed in terms of the emf in the branch, the voltage drop V, and the resistance (or conductance) of the branch.

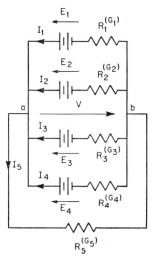

Fig. 4.13

Each current can now be expressed in terms of the emf in the branch, the voltage drop V, and the resistance (or conductance) of the branch.

$$I_1 = \frac{E_1 - V}{R_1} = (E_1 - V)G_1. \tag{4.37}$$

$$I_2 = \frac{E_2 - V}{R_2} = (E_2 - V)G_2. \tag{4.38}$$

$$I_3 = \frac{E_3 - V}{R_3} = (E_3 - V)G_3. \tag{4.39}$$

$$I_4 = \frac{E_4 - V}{R_4} = (E_4 - V)G_4. \tag{4.40}$$

$$I_5 = \frac{V}{R_5} = VG_5. \tag{4.41}$$

We can now substitute the expressions for the currents into (4.36) to obtain

$$(E_1 - V)G_1 + (E_2 - V)G_2 + (E_3 - V)G_3 + (E_4 - V)G_4 = VG_5, \tag{4.42}$$

from which

$$V = \frac{E_1G_1 + E_2G_2 + E_3G_3 + E_4G_4}{G_1 + G_2 + G_3 + G_4 + G_5}. \tag{4.43}$$

The branch currents can now be found by substituting the value obtained for V into Equations (4.37) – (4.41).

We may now consider a network such as the one in Figure 4.14 in which the number of nodes equals the number of meshes. Here we have to give some consideration to which node-pair voltages we can best use. Obvious-

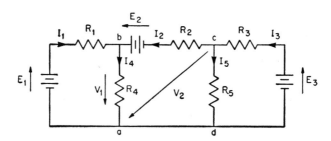

Fig. 4.14

ly, point d is at the same potential as point a, and therefore need not be considered as a node. The connection from R_5 could be made directly to point a without affecting the circuit, which would make point d and point a coincide. There are then actually three nodes, and as we have seen, we can apply Kirchhoff's current law at two of these to obtain independent equations. For reasons much the same as those upon which we based our choice of positive directions for mesh currents, we ordinarily choose one of these nodes as a common, or reference, node, and then designate the node-pair voltages as drops from the remaining nodes to the reference node. In Figure 4.14, point a has been selected as the reference node and the node-pair voltages are designated V_1 and V_2. The current equations at nodes b and c are

$$I_1 + I_2 = I_4; \tag{4.44}$$

$$I_3 = I_2 + I_5. \tag{4.45}$$

Each current can now be expressed in terms of emf's, resistances (or conductances), and the node-pair voltages V_1 and V_2. Thus,

$$E_1 = V_1 + I_1 R_1. \tag{4.46}$$

$$I_1 = \frac{E_1 - V_1}{R_1} = (E_1 - V_1)G_1. \tag{4.47}$$

$$E_3 = V_2 + I_3 R_3. \tag{4.48}$$

$$I_3 = \frac{E_3 - V_2}{R_3} = (E_3 - V_2)G_3. \tag{4.49}$$

$$E_2 = V_1 - V_2 + I_2 R_2. \tag{4.50}$$

$$I_2 = \frac{E_2 - V_1 + V_2}{R_2} = (E_2 - V_1 + V_2)G_2. \tag{4.51}$$

$$I_4 = \frac{V_1}{R_4} = V_1 G_4. \tag{4.52}$$

$$I_5 = \frac{V_2}{R_5} = V_2 G_5. \tag{4.53}$$

Substituting these expressions for currents into (4.44) and (4.45)

$$(E_1 - V_1)G_1 + (E_2 - V_1 + V_2)G_2 = V_1 G_4. \tag{4.54}$$

$$(E_3 - V_2)G_3 = (E_2 - V_1 + V_2)G_2 + V_2 G_5. \tag{4.55}$$

Collecting terms

$$E_1 G_1 + E_2 G_2 = V_1(G_1 + G_2 + G_4) - V_2 G_2. \tag{4.56}$$

$$E_3 G_3 - E_2 G_2 = -V_1 G_2 + V_2(G_2 + G_3 + G_5). \tag{4.57}$$

The simultaneous solution of Equations (4.56) and (4.57) will enable us to find the node-pair voltages V_1 and V_2. We can then find the branch currents by use of Equations (4.47) – (4.53).

The use of node-pair voltages in this particular network does not actually save much of the labor of solution as compared with the use of mesh currents. While there are only two simultaneous equations to be solved, there is more preliminary work to be done. If the node voltages themselves, and not the branch currents, are the quantities wanted, the above method is the more direct.

Example: The emf's in the network of Fig. 4.14 are $E_1 = 12$ v, $E_2 = 4$ v, $E_3 = 8$ v. The resistances are $R_1 = 2$ ohms, $R_2 = 4$ ohms, $R_3 = 16$ ohms, $R_4 = 10$ ohms, and $R_5 = 20$ ohms. The problem is to determine the node-pair voltages V_1 and V_2 and then to find the branch currents.

SOLUTION: First the conductances are calculated and found to be $G_1 = 0.5$ mho, $G_2 = 0.25$ mho, $G_3 = 0.0625$ mho, $G_4 = 0.1$ mho, $G_5 = 0.05$ mho. Putting numerical values in Equations (4.56) and (4.57) we have

$$(12 \times 0.5) + (4 \times 0.25) = V_1(0.85) - V_2(0.25). \tag{4.56}$$

$$(8 \times 0.0625) - (4 \times 0.25) = -V_1(0.25) + V_2(0.362). \tag{4.57}$$

$$7 = 0.85V_1 - 0.25V_2.$$

$$-0.5 = -0.25V_1 + 0.362V_2.$$

Solving
$$V_1 = 9.82 \text{ v,}$$

$$V_2 = 5.40 \text{ v,}$$

$$I_1 = (E_1 - V_1)G_1 = (12 - 9.82)0.5 = 1.09 \text{ amp,}$$

$$I_2 = (E_2 - V_1 + V_2)G_2 = (4 - 9.82 + 5.40)0.25 = -0.105 \text{ amp,}$$

$$I_3 = (E_3 - V_2)G_3 = (8 - 5.40)0.0625 = 0.162 \text{ amp,}$$

$$I_4 = V_1G_4 = 9.82 \times 0.1 = 0.982 \text{ amp,}$$

$$I_5 = V_2G_5 = 5.40 \times 0.05 = 0.27 \text{ amp.}$$

9. Method of node-pair voltages using current sources. Application of the node-pair voltage method is often facilitated if the network contains current sources only. Thus, Equations (4.56) and (4.57) could have been arrived at more directly by first replacing the voltage sources in the network (Fig. 4.14) by equivalent current sources as explained in Section 7. The network with replacements made is shown in Figure 4.15.

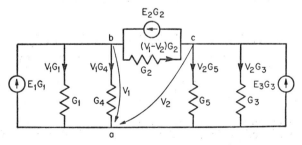

Fig. 4.15

The currents in terms of voltages and conductances are written beside the arrows on the diagram. At node b the currents directed toward the node are E_1G_1 and E_2G_2. The currents directed away from the node are V_1G_1, V_1G_4, and $(V_1 - V_2)G_2$. At node c the currents toward the node are E_3G_3 and $(V_1 - V_2)G_2$. The currents away from the node are E_2G_2, V_2G_5, and V_2G_3. Thus, Equations (4.56) and (4.57) can be obtained by inspection from Figure 4.15.

The terms which make up the right-hand side of these equations are of two kinds. In Equation (4.56) the term $V_1(G_1 + G_2 + G_4)$ is the product of the node-pair voltage V_1 (the drop from node b to the reference node) by the sum of all of the conductances connected to node b (Fig 4.15). A similar term appears in Equation (4.57), and both terms have positive signs. The other kind of term in Equation (4.56) is V_2G_2, which is the product of the other node pair voltage V_2 by the conductance connecting node c to node b. A similar term appears in Equation (4.57), and both terms carry negative signs.

We may put Equations (4.56) and (4.57) in symbolic form as we did Equations (4.22), (4.23), and (4.24) as follows:

$$I_1 = G_{11}V_1 - G_{12}V_2. \tag{4.58}$$

$$I_2 = -G_{21}V_1 + G_{22}V_2. \tag{4.59}$$

PROBLEMS

(19-IV) In the network shown in Fig. 4.4, E_1 is 10 v, E_2 is 12.5 v, R_1 is 30 ohms, R_2 is 20 ohms, and R_3 is 15 ohms. Calculate the node-pair voltage V_{be} and use it to find the branch currents.

(20-IV) In the network shown in Fig. 4.14, E_1 is 18 v, E_2 is 12 v, and E_3 is 6 v. The resistances are $R_1 = 3$ ohms, $R_2 = 5$ ohms, $R_3 = 6$ ohms, $R_4 = 8$ ohms, $R_5 = 4$ ohms. Calculate the node-pair voltages V_1 and V_2 and use them to find the branch currents.

(21-IV) In the network shown in Fig. 4.14, R_2 is zero. The other resistances and the emf's have the values given in Problem 20-IV. Find the node-pair voltages V_{ba} and V_{bc} and use them to find the branch currents.

(22-IV) In the network shown in Fig. 4.16, calculate the node-pair voltages V_1, V_2, and V_3. Calculate the current in each branch.

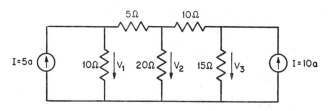

Fig. 4.16

(23-IV) Calculate the branch currents in the circuit shown in Fig. 4.17 by each of the following methods: (a) replace the current source by an equivalent voltage source and use mesh currents, (b) replace the voltage source by an equivalent current source and use node voltages, (c) use mesh currents in the circuit as it is (note that one mesh current is known), (d) use node voltages in the circuit as it is.

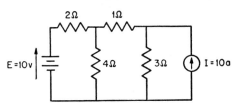

Fig. 4.17

10. The superposition theorem. In a network made up of linear resistances and containing two or more sources of emf, the current in any particular branch may be found by considering the sources of emf to act one at a time, finding the current in the specified branch due to each, and then superimposing, or adding algebraically, these component currents in order to find the current in the branch if all the sources of emf acted simultaneously. While the current due to a particular source of emf is being calculated, all the other electromotive forces are considered to be zero for the time being. All branches are considered to remain intact; that is, the sources of emf are not disconnected, they are merely treated as though their emf's were zero.

Example 1: Let us consider the network shown in Fig. 4.18a. If E_A were zero, we could consider R_A and R_C to be in parallel and this group in series with R_B (Fig. 4.18b). If E_B were zero, we could consider R_C and R_B in parallel and in series with R_A (Fig. 4.18c).

Suppose $E_B = 120$ v, $E_A = 30$ v, $R_A = 5$ ohms, $R_C = 15$ ohms, and $R_B = 20$ ohms, and that we are to find all currents.

SOLUTION: In Fig. 4.18b,

$$R_{\text{parallel}} = \frac{R_A R_C}{R_A + R_C} = \frac{5 \times 15}{5 + 15} = 3.75 \text{ ohms,}$$

$$R_{\text{circuit}} = 3.75 + 20 = 23.75 \text{ ohms,}$$

$$I_B' = \frac{E_B}{R_{\text{circuit}}} = \frac{120}{23.75} = 5.05 \text{ amp,}$$

$$V_{\text{parallel}} = R_{\text{parallel}} \times I_B' = 3.75 \times 5.05 = 18.95 \text{ v,}$$

$$I_A' = -\frac{V_{\text{parallel}}}{R_A} = -\frac{18.95}{5} = -3.79 \text{ amp,}$$

$$I_C' = \frac{V_{\text{parallel}}}{R_C} = \frac{18.95}{15} = 1.262 \text{ amp.}$$

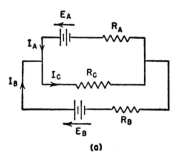

(a)

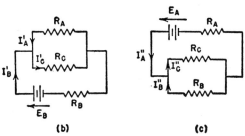

(b)   (c)

Fig. 4.18

In Fig. 4.18c,

$$R_{\text{parallel}} = \frac{15 \times 20}{15 + 20} = 8.58 \text{ ohms,}$$

$$R_{\text{circuit}} = 8.58 + 5 = 13.58 \text{ ohms,}$$

$$I_A{}'' = \frac{E_A}{R_{\text{circuit}}} = \frac{30}{13.58} = 2.21 \text{ amp,}$$

$$V_{\text{parallel}} = 8.58 \times 2.21 = 18.95 \text{ v,}$$

$$I_C{}'' = \frac{18.95}{15} = 1.263 \text{ amp,}$$

$$I_B{}'' = -\frac{18.95}{20} = -0.947 \text{ amp.}$$

Then, superimposing the results,

$$I_A = I_A{}' + I_A{}''$$
$$= (-3.79) + 2.21 = -1.58 \text{ amp,}$$
$$I_B = I_B{}' + I_B{}''$$
$$= 5.05 + (-0.947) = 4.1 \text{ amp,}$$
$$I_C = I_C{}' + I_C{}''$$
$$= 1.262 + 1.263 = 2.52 \text{ amp.}$$

To check, apply Kirchhoff's voltage law to the loop containing both batteries:

$$E_B - E_A = I_B R_B - I_A R_A,$$

$$120 - 30 = (4.1 \times 20) - (-1.58 \times 5),$$

$$90 = 89.9.$$

The superposition theorem is applicable as well if current sources are present in the network. While the current in the specified branch due to a particular current source is being calculated, all the other current sources (but not their parallel conductances) are disconnected.

Example 2: Consider the network in Fig. 4.19a, in which $I_A = 4$ amp' $I_B = 8$ amp, $G_A = 0.3$ mho, $G_B = 0.4$ mho, and $G_C = 0.1$ mho. If we disconnect the current source I_B, the network is reduced to that shown in Fig. 4.19b.

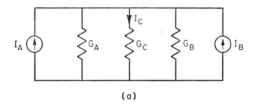

(a)

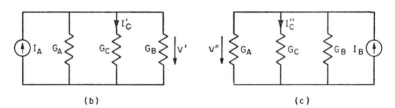

(b)   (c)

Fig. 4.19

$$G_0 = G_A + G_C + G_B$$

$$= 0.3 + 0.1 + 0.4 = 0.8 \text{ mho},$$

$$V' = \frac{I_A}{G_0} = \frac{4}{0.8} = 5 \text{ v},$$

$$I_C' = V'G_C = 5 \times 0.1 = 0.5 \text{ amp}.$$

If we disconnect the current source I_A, the network is reduced to that shown in Fig. 4.19c:

$$V'' = \frac{I_B}{G_0} = \frac{8}{0.8} = 10 \text{ amp},$$

$$I_C'' = V''G_C = 10 \times 0.1 = 1 \text{ amp}.$$

Then superimposing the results,

$$I_C = I_{c'} + I_{c''}$$

$$= 0.5 + 1 = 1.5 \text{ amp.}$$

The use of the superposition principle is not limited to electrical networks. It is applicable wherever physical effects bear a linear relationship to the forces which caused them. However, the linear relationship is essential, and wrong results will be obtained if the superposition theorem is applied where it does not exist.

Note that the superposition theorem applies to currents and voltages; it does not mean that powers from two sources can be superimposed. Consider the calculation of power in a linear network containing two or more sources of emf. As we have seen, we may properly calculate the current in a given branch due to each of the sources, then superimpose these results. Suppose we try to go a step further and calculate the power absorbed in the branch under consideration due to each of the emf sources in turn, then superimpose these amounts of power. The result is obviously less than the power absorbed in the branch when all the emf sources act simultaneously. This is because the relationship between emf and power is not a linear one. Thus, in Example 1 above, the correct power in the resistance R_C is

$$P_C = (I_C)^2 R_C = 2.52^2 \times 20 = 127 \text{ w.}$$

The calculation of power using the currents due to each emf source separately would give

$$P_C = (I_C')^2 R_C + (I_C'')^2 R_C = 1.262^2 \times 20 + 1.263^2 \times 20 = 63.6 \text{ w.}$$

PROBLEMS

(24-IV) Use the superposition theorem to find the current in each branch of the network shown in Fig. 4.20. E_A is 9 v, E_B is 15 v, R_A is 2.5 ohms, R_B is 3.25 ohms, and R_C is 5 ohms.

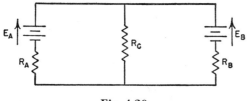

Fig. 4.20

(25-IV) Use the superposition theorem to find the current in each branch of the network shown in Fig. 4.21. E_A is 20 v, E_B is 30 v, E_C is 40 v, R_A is 15 ohms, R_B is 10 ohms, and R_C is 20 ohms.

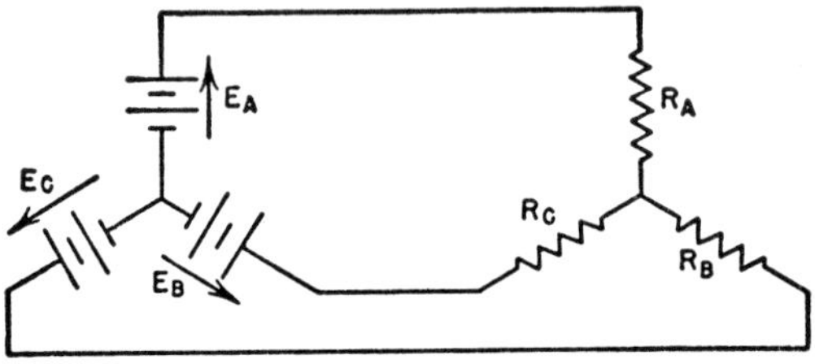

Fig. 4.21

(26-IV) The resistances of the network shown in Fig. 4.18 are $R_A = 10$ ohms, $R_B = 15$ ohms, and $R_C = 5$ ohms. The emf's are unknown, but the current in R_C is 1 amp. By how much would this current be increased if E_A were increased by 5 v?

(27-IV) Use the superposition theorem to calculate the current in each branch of the network in Fig. 4.16.

(28-IV) Use the superposition theorem to find the current in each branch of the network in Fig. 4.17.

11. Thevenin's theorem. It is often desirable in network analysis to study the effect in a network of changing some one branch, all the other branches and the sources which they may contain remaining unchanged. If the entire network, except for this one branch, can be reduced to the simplest equivalent circuit possible, the amount of computation which we have to do each time a change is made will be greatly reduced. This simplification is made possible by **Thevenin's theorem,** which says that: *Any two-terminal network, made up of linear resistances and of voltage and current sources, can be replaced by a single voltage source and a series resistance so chosen that (a) the emf of the source is equal to the voltage which would be measured at open circuit at the network terminals, and (b) the series resistance is equal to the resistance which would be measured at the network terminals at open circuit, all voltage sources and current sources in the network being inactive.* A voltage source is rendered inactive or "dead" by short-circuiting E and reducing it to zero. The branch with its series resistance remains intact. A current source is rendered inactive by open-circuiting the branch containing I. The parallel conductance remains intact.

A demonstration of the truth of this theorem can be made as follows: A network made up of sources and linear resistances is represented by the rectangle in Fig. 4.22a. The only accessible parts of the network are the terminals A and B, between which is measured an open circuit voltage V_{oc}. A branch of resistance R is now connected to terminals A and B (Fig. 4.22b), and due to the network sources, a current I' flows in the branch. Next, a voltage source E_X is connected into the external branch (Fig.

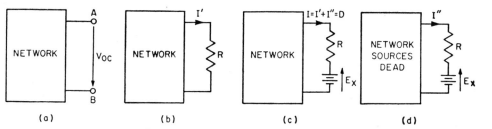

Fig. 4.22. Thevenin's theorem.

4.22c). The magnitude and polarity of E_X are such that the current in the branch is reduced to zero. Then

$$E_X = V_{OC}. \qquad (4.60)$$

The zero current in the external branch, according to the superposition principle, is made up of two parts. One part is due to the external emf E_X (Fig. 4.22d), and is

$$I'' = -\frac{E_X}{R + R_X}, \qquad (4.61)$$

where R_X is the resistance of the network with its sources dead, looking in at the terminals A and B. The second part of the current, (in Fig. 14.22c) is due to the sources within the network, and since the two parts must add up to zero, the second part must be

$$I' = +\frac{E_X}{R + R_X} = \frac{V_{OC}}{R + R_X}. \qquad (4.62)$$

The current which the network will supply to a branch of resistance R connected to its terminals is therefore the same that would be supplied by a single source of emf, $E_X = V_{OC}$ and a series resistance R_X as explained above.

Example 1: In the network shown in Fig. 4.23a, the source emf's are $E_1 = 10$ v and $E_2 = 15$ v. The resistances are $R_1 = 4$ ohms, $R_2 = 6$ ohms, while R_3 is variable. It is desired to find the effect of R_3 upon the current in that branch.

SOLUTION: Our first step is to isolate the branch containing R_3, leaving the rest of the network to be replaced by Thevenin's theorem (Fig. 4.23b). We then need to find the open-circuit voltage V_{AB} between the network terminals. By Kirchhoff's voltage law

$$E_2 - E_1 = R_2 I_2 - R_1 I_1 = I_2 (R_2 + R_1) \qquad (4.63)$$

from which $I_2 = \dfrac{E_2 - E_1}{R_2 + R_1} = \dfrac{15 - 10}{6 + 4} = 0.5$ amp.

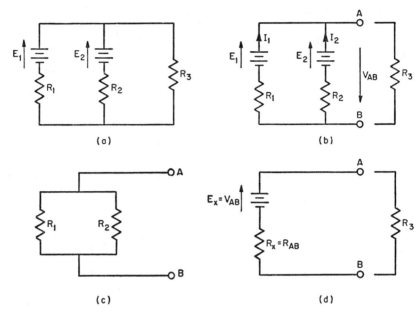

Fig. 4.23

$$E_2 = V_{AB} + I_2 R_2, \qquad\qquad (4.64)$$

from which $V_{AB} = E_2 - I_2 R_2 = 15 - (0.5 \times 6) = 12$ v.

Now we proceed to inactivate the voltage sources E_1 and E_2 and to find the resistance of the network looking in at the terminals A and B (Fig. 4.23c). Since R_1 and R_2 are in parallel, the required resistance is

$$\frac{R_1 R_2}{R_1 + R_2} = \frac{4 \times 6}{4 + 6} = 2.4 \text{ ohms.}$$

The network (not including R_3) can thus be replaced by a voltage source having an emf $E_X = 12$ v (Fig. 4.23d) and a series resistance of $R_X = 2.4$ ohms. The current in the R_3 branch would then be calculated as

$$I_3 = \frac{E_X}{R_X + R_3} = \frac{12}{2.4 + R_3}.$$

Example 2: It is desired to use Thevenin's theorem to replace the Wheatstone bridge network in Fig. 4.24 by its equivalent circuit, maintaining the identity of the galvanometer branch R_G.

SOLUTION: We begin by removing the galvonometer branch R_G and calculating the open-circuit voltage at terminals A and B (Fig. 4.24b):

$$0 = R_1 I_1 + V_{AB} - R_3 I_3. \qquad\qquad (4.65)$$

$$V_{AB} = R_3 I_3 - R_1 I_1. \qquad\qquad (4.66)$$

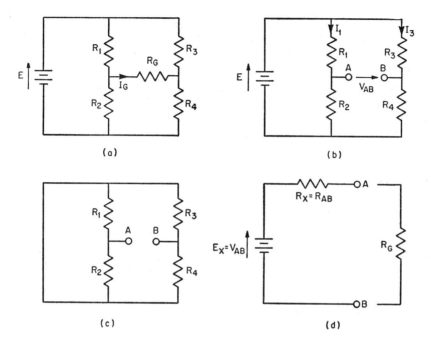

Fig. 4.24

$$V_{AB} = \frac{ER_3}{R_3 + R_4} - \frac{ER_1}{R_1 + R_2}. \tag{4.67}$$

This is the value to be assigned to E_X in the equivalent circuit. Let us now inactivate the voltage source by considering E to be reduced to zero and calculate the resistance of the network looking into the open-circuit terminals A and B. (Fig. 4.24c). Resistances R_1 and R_2 are seen to form a parallel group, as do resistances R_3 and R_4, and these parallel groups are in series between the terminals. Therefore

$$R_{AB} = \frac{R_1 R_2}{R_1 + R_2} + \frac{R_3 R_4}{R_3 + R_4}. \tag{4.68}$$

This is the value to be assigned to R_X in the equivalent circuit (Fig. 4.24d). The current I_G can now be calculated as

$$I_G = \frac{E_X}{R_X + R_G} = \frac{E\left(\dfrac{R_3}{R_3 + R_4} - \dfrac{R_1}{R_1 + R_2}\right)}{\left(\dfrac{R_1 R_2}{R_1 + R_2} + \dfrac{R_3 R_4}{R_3 + R_4}\right) + R_G}. \tag{4.69}$$

This equation enables us to study the effect of any of the resistances in the bridge network, including R_G, upon the galvonometer current.

12. Norton's theorem. It has been shown (Section 7) that a practical voltage source (constant electromotive force and associated series resistance) can always be replaced by an equivalent practical current source (constant current and associated parallel conductance). Now, having demonstrated Thevenin's theorem, which says in effect that we can always replace a two-terminal network by a single voltage source and a series resistance, it follows that such a network can also be replaced by a single current source and a parallel conductance. This is Norton's theorem. The theorem may be stated specifically in these words: *Any two-terminal network, made up of linear resistances and of voltage and current sources, can be replaced by a single current source and a parallel conductance so chosen that (a) the current of the source is equal to the current which would be measured at short circuit at the network terminals, and (b) the parallel conductance is equal to the conductance which would be measured at the network terminals, all voltage sources and current sources in the network being inactive.* This statement is seen to parallel that of Thevenin's theorem. The current which would be measured at the network terminals at short circuit is the same current which would be found in the process of converting a voltage source into an equivalent current source by dividing open-circuit voltage by network resistance with sources inactive.

Example 1: The network shown in Fig. 4.25a contains current sources $I_1 = 10$ amp and $I_2 = 15$ amp. The conductances are $G_1 = 0.2$ mho, $G_2 = 0.3$ mho, and G_3 which is variable. It is desired to use Norton's theorem to simplify the network in order to find the effect of G_3 upon the current in that branch.

SOLUTION: We proceed to disconnect branch G_3 and to short circuit the terminals A and B (Fig. 4.25b). Since the short circuit has infinite conductance, the total of 25 amp supplied by the two sources would be measured through the short-circuited terminals. No current would flow through G_1 or G_2, which

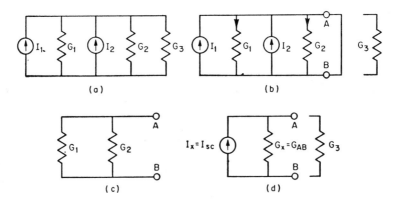

(a)   (b)

(c)   (d)

Fig. 4.25 Norton's theorem.

have finite conductances. Next, the short circuit is removed, and with the current sources inactive (I_1 and I_2 open-circuited), the conductance at the network terminals is determined (Fig. 4.25c). This is obviously the conductance of G_1 and G_2 in parallel, which is 0.5 mho. The equivalent circuit (Fig. 4.25d) consists of a 25-amp current source paralleled by a 0.5-mho conductance.

Example 2: The circuit shown in Fig. 4.26a consists of a current source $I = 10$ amp paralleled by $G = 0.1$ mho, and a voltage source $E = 200$ v with 10 ohms series resistance. Let us first use Thevenin's theorem, then Norton's theorem to find the equivalent networks.

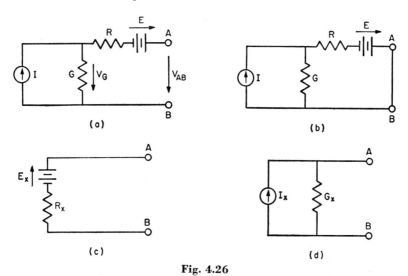

Fig. 4.26

SOLUTION: With terminals A and B open-circuited, the current source will supply 10 amp through the 0.1-mho conductance, the voltage drop across which is thus $V_G = 100$ v. The voltage across the terminals is

$$V_{AB} = E + V_G = 200 + 100 = 300 \text{ v.}$$

With E inactivated (short-circuited) and I inactivated (open-circuited) the resistance as measured between the terminals is

$$R_{AB} = R + \frac{1}{G} = 10 + \frac{1}{0.1} = 20 \text{ ohms.}$$

The equivalent circuit, by Thevenin's theorem, is thus found to be a 300-volt source E_X, in series with a 20-ohm resistance R_X (Fig. 4.26c).

With terminals A and B short-circuited (Fig. 4.26b) the current through the conductance G is found to be 5 amp (upward), and the current through the short-circuited terminals is 15 amp. The conductance as measured between the terminals with the sources inactivated is the reciprocal of R_{AB} as found above:

$$G_{AB} = \frac{1}{R_{AB}} = \frac{1}{20} = 0.05 \text{ mho.}$$

The equivalent circuit by Norton's theorem is thus found to be a 15-amp current source I_X in parallel with a 0.05-mho conductance G_X (Fig. 4.26d).

Obviously, the same results could have been obtained by converting the current source and its parallel conductance (Fig. 4.26a) to an equivalent voltage source, then applying Thevenin's theorem to obtain the equivalent circuit in Fig. 4.26c, and finally converting back to the equivalent current source in Fig. 4.26d.

PROBLEMS

(29-IV) Use Thevenin's theorem to replace the network shown in Fig. 4.20, maintaining the identity of R_C. E_A is 15 v, E_B is 9 v, R_A is 2.5 ohms, and R_B is 3.25 ohms. Calculate the current in R_C as R_C is varied from zero to 10 ohms.

(30-IV) Use Thevenin's theorem to replace the network shown in Fig. 4.21, maintaining the identity of R_A. E_A is 20 v, E_B is 30 v, E_C is 40 v, R_B is 10 ohms, and R_C is 20 ohms. Calculate the current in R_A as R_A is varied from zero to 100 ohms.

(31-IV) Use Thevenin's theorem to replace the network shown in Fig. 4.27, maintaining the identity of R. The battery electromotive force is 50 v. Calculate the current in R as R is varied from 0 to 100 ohms.

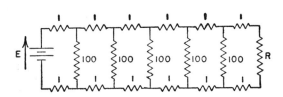

Fig. 4.27

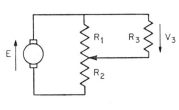

Fig. 4.28

(32-IV) Use Thevenin's theorem to replace the source and three-point rheostat shown in Fig. 4.28, maintaining the identity of R_3. Obtain the general solution for E_X and R_X. For $E = 100$ v and $R_1 = R_2 = 100$ ohms, calculate V_3 for values of R_3 from 0 to 1000 ohms.

(33-IV) Using the general solution obtained in Problem 32-IV, and for $E = 100$ v, $R_3 = 100$ ohms, and $R_2 = 200$ ohms, calculate V_3 for values of R_1 from 0 to 200 ohms.

(34-IV) By use of Thevenin's theorem replace the network shown in Fig. 4.29 with reference to terminals A and B. *Suggestion:* Cut the network at the dotted line and use the theorem to find the equivalent of the part on the left. Then join this equivalent to the part on the right and use the theorem again.

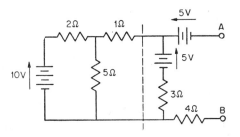

Fig. 4.29

(**35-IV**) Use Norton's theorem to replace the network described in Problem 29-IV, maintaining the identity of R_C.

(**36-IV**) Use Norton's theorem to replace the network described in Problem 34-IV with reference to the terminals A and B.

13. Duality. Let us compare the voltage equations written for the meshes of the two-mesh network in Fig. 4.30a and the current equations

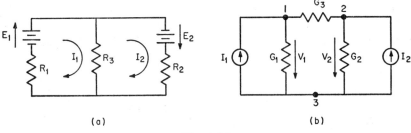

(a)   (b)

Fig. 4.30

written for the nodes of the two-node-pair network in Fig. 4.30b. The voltage equations are

$$E_1 = (R_1 + R_3)I_1 - R_3I_2. \tag{4.70}$$

$$E_2 = -R_3I_1 + (R_2 + R_3)I_2. \tag{4.71}$$

The current equations are

$$I_1 = (G_1 + G_3)V_1 - G_3V_2. \tag{4.72}$$

$$I_2 = -G_3V_1 + (G_2 + G_3)V_2. \tag{4.73}$$

The voltage equations are seen to correspond term for term with the current equations so far as form is concerned. By substituting I for E, G for R, and I for V, Equations (4.70) and (4.71) become Equations (4.72) and (4.73). When this can be done, one network is said to be the **dual** of the other.

In the dual of a network it is possible to find the counterpart of each branch (or node). Thus, the conductance G_3, which connects nodes 1 and 2, corresponds to the resistance R_3, which is the boundary between meshes 1 and 2. The current source I_1 and its associated parallel conductance G_1, which join nodes 1 and 3, correspond to the voltage source E_1 and its associated series resistance R_1, which is the boundary between mesh 1 and the surrounding space (which may be thought of as mesh 3). The current source I_2 and its associated parallel conductance G_2, which join nodes 2 and 3, correspond to the voltage source E_2 and its associated series resistance R_2, which is the boundary between mesh 2 and the surrounding space.

It is, in general, possible to construct the dual of a network by locating nodes to correspond to the various meshes, and then to connect the nodes by parallel branches containing current sources and conductances corresponding to the voltage sources and resistances which are present in the appropriate branches of the original network.

PROBLEMS

(37-IV) It is desired to replace the series-parallel network in Fig. 4.31a with that shown in Fig. 4.31b. The 5-ohm resistance is to be retained in the upper branch and resistances R_A and R_B are to be chosen so that (1) the total current I_0 is the same, and (2) the ratio of I_1 to I_2 is the same. Find R_A and R_B.

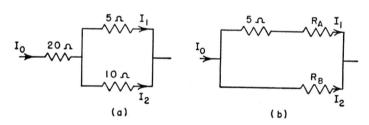

Fig. 4.31

(38-IV) Develop a general equation for replacing a network, in which R_X is in series with a parallel group made up of R_Y and R_Z, with a network in which R_A and R_C are in series and in parallel with this group is R_B. The conditions are the same as called for in Problem 37-IV.

(39-IV) The reciprocity theorem states that if, in any network made up of linear resistances, an electromotive force of E volts in branch X causes a current of I amp in branch Y, then an electromotive force of E volts in branch Y will cause a current of I amp in branch X. Verify this for the network shown in Fig. 4.32 by moving E from branch X to branch Y. Take $E = 10$ v, $R_X = 20$ ohms, $R_Y = 5$ ohms, $R_Z = 30$ ohms.

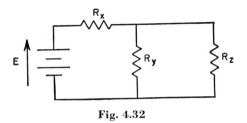

Fig. 4.32

(40-IV) For the lattice-type network shown in Fig. 4.33, the following values are given: $E = 10$ v; R_1, R_3, R_4, R_6 each 50 ohms; R_2 and R_5 each 100 ohms; $R_7 = 200$ ohms; R_8 and R_9 each 500 ohms. Calculate the current in each branch of the network.

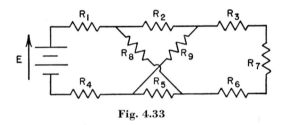

Fig. 4.33

(41-IV) For the network shown in Fig. 4.34, the following values are given: $E = 15$ v; R_1, R_2, R_3, R_4, R_5, and R_6 are each 15 ohms; R_7, R_8, and R_9 are each 75 ohms. Calculate the current in each branch of the network.

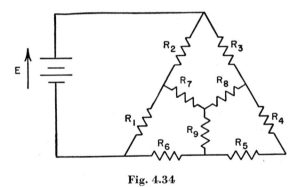

Fig. 4.34

(42-IV) The battery in the network shown in Fig. 4.35 has an electromotive force of 10 v. Calculate the voltage drop in (a) the 20-ohm resistance, (b) the 30-ohm resistance, (c) the 40-ohm resistance.

(43-IV) Twelve identical pieces of wire, each having a resistance of 6 ohms, are welded together to form a cube. Calculate the resistance of the cube: (a) between corners which lie on an edge; (b) between corners which lie on the diagonal of a face; (c) between corners which lie on a diagonal of the cube.

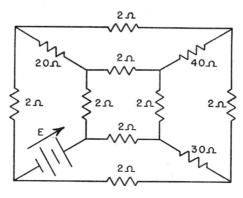

Fig. 4.35

(44-IV) Two resistances of 30 ohms and 50 ohms, respectively, are connected in series, and this group is connected in parallel with a resistance of 70 ohms and with a series group made up of a battery having an electromotive force of 15 v and a resistance of 20 ohms. A resistance of 100 ohms is now connected from the junction of the 30-ohm and 50-ohm resistances to the junction point of the battery and the 20-ohm resistance. There is no direct connection from the 20-ohm resistance to the 30-ohm resistance. Calculate the current in the 70-ohm resistance.

(45-IV) The following data are furnished for the network shown in Fig. 4.36: $E = 30$ v; $R_1 = 15$ ohms; $R_2 = 25$ ohms; R_4, R_5, and R_6 are each 30 ohms; $R_3 = 55$ ohms. Calculate a value of R_7 for which the current through R_5 will be independent of the value of R_5.

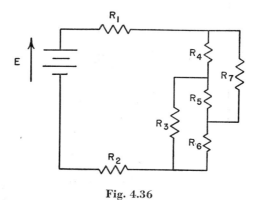

Fig. 4.36

(46-IV) For the network shown in Fig. 4.37 the resistances are as follows: $R_1 = 73.2$ ohms, $R_2 = 19.5$ ohms, $R_3 = 56.4$ ohms, $R_4 = 91.1$ ohms, $R_5 = 66.2$ ohms, $R_6 = 11.9$ ohms, $R_7 = 33.3$ ohms, $R_8 = 85.6$ ohms, $R_9 = 90.5$ ohms. $E_1 = 17.6$ v, and $E_2 = 8.8$ v. Calculate the current in R_9.

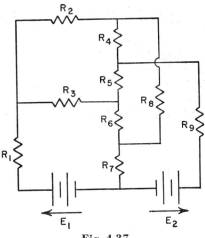

Fig. 4.37

(47-IV) The power system shown in Fig. 4.38 comprises two generators and two loads, connected by lines with resistances as shown. The voltage at the terminals of each generator is maintained constant at 130 v. The current I_1 taken by load No. 1 is 50 amp, and the current I_2 taken by load No. 2 is 40 amp. Calculate the voltage at each load, the current supplied by each generator, and the current in the middle line section.

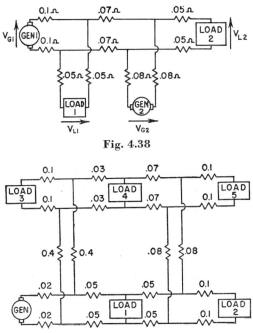

Fig. 4.38

Fig. 4.39

(**48-IV**) (a) The power system shown in Fig. 4.39 is made up of five loads and a single generator connected by lines with resistances as shown. The current taken by each load is 15 amp and the generator voltage is maintained constant at 250 v. Calculate the voltage at each of the five loads.

(b) The power system shown in Fig. 4.39 is made up of five loads and a single generator connected by lines with resistances as shown. The current taken by each load is 15 amp and the voltage at load No. 4 is maintained constant at 225 v. Calculate the voltage at each of the other four loads and at the generator.

Chapter **V**

MEASUREMENT OF
ELECTRICAL QUANTITIES

---

1. Indicating instruments. Current and potential difference are most often determined by reading them directly from the scales of indicating instruments known, respectively, as **ammeters** and **voltmeters.** An ammeter is connected directly into the circuit, as in Figure 5.1, so that the

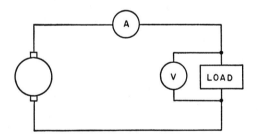

Fig. 5.1. Ammeter and voltmeter connections.

current to be measured or a certain fraction of it passes through the instrument itself. It is thus in *series* with the other parts of the circuit. It must, therefore, be capable of carrying this current without injury to itself and without abnormally increasing the resistance of the circuit into which it is inserted.

A voltmeter is used by connecting its terminals to the two points between which it is desired to measure the potential difference. It is thus in *parallel* with the circuit or some part of the circuit. The voltmeter in Figure 5.1 measures the potential difference at the terminals of the load. To be used in this way, a voltmeter must have enough resistance so that it will not be injured by the current that flows through it, and so that it will not materially affect the current in the circuit to which it is connected.

The basic principle of the ammeter and of the voltmeter is the same. The moving element is actuated by current in either case. In the ammeter, the element is actuated by the current we wish to measure, or a certain fraction of that current. In the voltmeter, the moving element is actuated by a current which is proportional to the potential difference we wish to measure, since the current through the instrument is

$$I_V = \frac{V}{R},\tag{5.1}$$

where I_V is current through the instrument;

V is the potential difference to be measured;

R is the resistance of the instrument itself.

For accurate measurements in direct-current circuits, meters of the D'Arsonval type are generally used. These depend upon the forces acting upon the sides of a movable coil carrying the current, and situated in the field of a permanent magnet. For alternating-current measurements, the **iron-vane** type is most used. It depends upon the forces which act upon a light, movable piece of iron in the field of a fixed coil that carries the current. The **electrodynamometer** type is suitable for either direct-current or alternating-current measurements, and depends upon the forces that act between fixed and movable coils, both of which carry current.

In each of these types, the moving element is caused to rotate by a **torque,** or moment, resulting from the forces mentioned above. This is known as the **deflecting torque** and is always dependent upon current, but not always directly proportional to it. As the coil rotates, it tightens a spiral spring, or twists a suspension strip, thereby setting up a **restoring torque** that tends to restore the coil to its original position. When a current is passed through the meter, the movable element will rotate, carrying the pointer over the scale, until the restoring torque becomes equal to the deflecting torque for that particular current. This represents a condition of equilibrium, and the movable element and pointer will come to rest in a certain position and indicating a certain figure on the scale. It is evident that the position of rest depends as much upon the spring as upon the electrical element of the meter.

Any voltmeter or ammeter is a **secondary** instrument; it reads voltage or current correctly only because it has been **calibrated** — that is, its scale has been made by applying known voltages to its terminals or passing known currents through it, and marking on the scale the position taken by the pointer for each voltage or current. Calibrating of one meter can be done by comparing it with another similar meter already calibrated, but it should be evident that this procedure eventually leads back to an absolute determination in a standards laboratory.

The element of a D'Arsonval type meter is shown in Figure 5.2. The U-shaped permanent magnet is fitted with specially designed pole pieces, between which is mounted a cylindrical iron core. In the uniform air gap

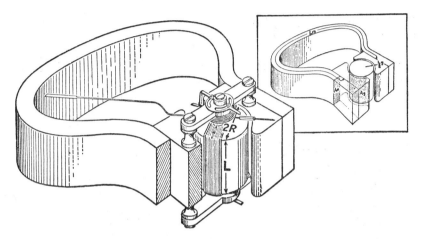

Fig. 5.2. Permanent-magnet moving-coil movement utilizing the D'Arsonval principle. (Courtesy, Weston Electrical Instrument Corporation.)

thus formed the magnetic field is radially directed, and the forces that act on the sides of the moving coil are always perpendicular to the radius of the coil. The coil is rectangular in form and may consist of from 20 or 30, up to several hundred, turns of small-diameter wire. It is fitted with steel pivots top and bottom, which work in jeweled bearings mounted on supporting bridges which, in turn, are carried on the pole pieces. Spiral springs serve the double purpose of furnishing the restoring torque and making the connections to the coil.

2. Ammeters. In a practical current-measuring instrument of the permanent-magnet moving-coil type, a **shunt,** or by-pass, is nearly always provided, so that only a fraction of the current to be measured flows through the moving coil, the remainder taking the parallel path through the shunt. The resistance of the shunt must, of course, be properly adjusted, taking into account the current to be measured, the current required for full-scale deflection of the movable coil, and the resistance of the movable coil itself. In milliammeters and low-range ammeters, the shunts are usually built into the instrument itself. For the measurement of larger currents, however, external shunts are used and connected to the meter by special leads.

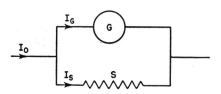

Fig. 5.3. A shunt in parallel with the moving element of an ammeter.

If desired, the meter may be placed some distance from the shunt. In Figure 5.3, G represents the meter element and S the shunt. The resistance of the meter element including the movable coil, springs, leads, and so forth, is designated R_G, and the resistance of the shunt is designated R_S. The current to be measured is I_0 and the currents through the meter element and the shunt are I_G and I_S, respectively. By Kirchhoff's laws,

$$I_0 = I_G + I_S. \tag{5.2}$$

$$I_G R_G = I_S R_S. \tag{5.3}$$

These equations enable us to make the necessary calculations of shunt resistance.

> **Example:** The resistance of a meter element of the permanent-magnet moving-coil type is 1.6 ohms, and it is deflected full scale by a current of 25 ma. What should be the resistance of a shunt to give this instrument a range of 0 to 200 ma?
>
> SOLUTION: The shunt (when I_0 is 200 ma) must carry a current of
>
> $$I_S = I_0 - I_G = 200 - 25 = 175 \text{ ma} = 0.175 \text{ amp.}$$
>
> The voltage drop across the shunt and meter in parallel must be
>
> $$I_G R_G = 0.025 \times 1.6 = 0.04 \text{ v} = I_S R_S.$$
>
> The resistance of the shunt must, therefore, be
>
> $$R_S = \frac{0.04}{0.175} = 0.228 \text{ ohm.} \tag{5.4}$$

PROBLEMS

(1-V) The movable coil of a milliammeter has a resistance of 60 ohms and is deflected full scale by a current of 1 ma. Calculate the shunt resistance to make the range of the meter (a) 0 to 5 ma; (b) 0 to 10 ma; (c) 0 to 25 ma.

(2-V) The resistance of a meter element can be adjusted by putting additional resistance in series in order to make it work with a certain shunt. How much resistance should be connected in series with a milliammeter which requires 10 ma for full-scale deflection in order that it may be used with a 0.5-ohm shunt to measure currents over a range 0 to 500 ma? The resistance of the milliammeter is 7.5 ohms.

(3-V) The moving coil of an ammeter has a resistance of 2.14 ohms including leads. The current for full-scale deflection is 26.7 ma. What should be the shunt resistance if the range of the meter is to be 0 to 100 ma? 0 to 1 amp? 0 to 5 amp? 0 to 100 amp? 0 to 1000 amp?

(4-V) What should be the resistance of the moving coil of an ammeter which requires 30 ma for full-scale deflection so that it may be used with a shunt having a resistance of 0.0005 ohm for a range of 0 to 100 amp?

(5-V) A millivoltmeter may be used in conjunction with a number of different shunts for the measurement of current by designing all the shunts to have a voltage drop of, say, 50 mv across their terminals when they carry their rated current, and the meter to give full-scale deflection when the drop across its terminals is 50 mv. On this basis, what should be the resistance of a 1-amp shunt? A 10-amp shunt? A 50-amp shunt? A 500-amp shunt? Ignore the current through the meter coil.

(6-V) The shunts in the three-range ammeters used in the college laboratories are arranged as is shown in Fig. 5.4. The ranges are 0 to 1 amp, 0 to 2.5 amp, and 0

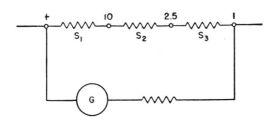

Fig. 5.4

to 10 amp, as marked. If the moving element is deflected full scale when the potential difference across its terminals is 50 mv, what should be the resistance of each part of the shunt? Ignore the current through the meter coil.

(7-V) Recalculate the shunt resistances in Problem 5-V, taking into account the current through the meter coil. Assume that the meter resistance (including leads) is 1 ohm.

(8-V) Recalculate the shunt resistances in Problem 6-V, taking into account the current through the meter coil. Assume that the current for full-scale deflection is 50 ma.

(9-V) An ammeter having a resistance of 1.11 ohms is used with an external shunt to measure currents in the range 0 to 500 amp. The shunt resistance is 0.0001 ohm, and the leads which connect the shunt to the meter have a resistance of 0.05 ohm. Assuming the meter now reads correctly for a current of 500 amp through the shunt, what would be the effect of changing the lead resistance to 0.1 ohm?

(10-V) The emf of a No. 6 dry cell is 1.5 v, and its resistance is 0.05 ohm. What current would flow if the cell were short-circuited by a copper strap of negligible resistance? What current would be read by a 0 to 30 ammeter having a resistance of 0.0015 ohm inserted in the strap?

3. Voltmeters. In a voltmeter, it is necessary to have in series with the meter element enough resistance so that when the greatest voltage to be measured is applied to the meter terminals, exactly enough current to give full-scale deflection will flow through the meter element. The necessary series resistance is usually mounted inside the meter case, but all or part of it may be placed in a separate unit, known as a **multiplier.** Additional series-resistance units, or multipliers, are used when it is desired to measure voltages beyond the nominal range of the instrument.

Example: A meter element of the permanent-magnet, moving-coil type has a resistance of 5 ohms and requires 1 ma for full-scale deflection. What series resistance should be used to give the instrument a range of 0 to 15 v?

SOLUTION: To get a current of 1 ma through the meter with 15 v applied, the total resistance must be

$$R = \frac{V}{I} = \frac{15}{0.001} = 15,000 \text{ ohms.}$$

Fig. 5.5. Resistance in series with the moving element of a voltmeter.

We need, therefore, to add

$$15,000 - 5 = 14,995 \text{ ohms.}$$

PROBLEMS

(11-V) The three-range voltmeters used in the college laboratories are arranged as shown in Fig. 5.6. The ranges are 0 to 3 v, 0 to 15 v, and 0 to 50 v, as marked. If the current for full-scale deflection is 10 ma, what should be the resistance of R_1, R_2, and R_3? The resistance of the moving element is 5 ohms.

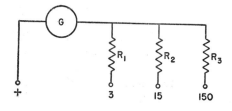

Fig. 5.6

(12-V) It is desired to rebuild a 0 to 1.5-scale voltmeter to measure voltage from 0 to 75 mv. On going into the meter, it is found that the movement itself has a resistance of 2 ohms and that it is in series with a wire-wound resistance of 1480 ohms. How may the change be made?

(13-V) A 0 to 3 voltmeter has a resistance of 2910 ohms. Design a multiplier to be used with this meter so that its range is increased from 0 to 3 to 0 to 75. By what number will the readings then have to be multiplied?

(14-V) Two voltmeters, one having a resistance of 13,500 ohms and the other a resistance of 15,200 ohms, are connected in series across a 115-v line. Both are 0 to 150 range. Calculate the reading of each meter.

(15-V) A 0 to 15-scale voltmeter having a resistance of 1290 ohms is connected in series with a resistance of 10,000 ohms across the terminals of a d-c generator, and shows a reading of 12 v. What is the terminal voltage of the generator?

(16-V) Resistances of 10,000, 20,000, and 40,000 ohms are connected in series and a difference of potential of 150 v is applied. What is the voltage across each resistor? What voltage would be measured across each resistor if a 0 to 150-scale voltmeter having a resistance of 15,000 ohms were used?

4. Measurement of resistance by the voltmeter-ammeter method. Since resistance is the ratio of potential difference to current, its measurement is readily accomplished by taking readings with voltmeter and ammeter and using Equation (3.7),

$$R = \frac{V}{I},$$

to calculate resistance. The accuracy which may be attained by this method depends, of course, on the accuracy with which the potential difference and current can be measured. Besides the inaccuracies that are inherent in the meters themselves, there is always an error in the measurement of the current or voltage owing to the presence of the other meter. The method gives fairly accurate results in the measurement of resistances that are neither extremely small nor extremely large — in the range, say, from 1 to 100 ohms. If measurement of resistances outside this range is attempted, or if better accuracy is wanted, corrections may be applied as explained in Section 6.

5. Measurement of power. Power measurements in d-c circuits involve the use of a voltmeter and an ammeter to obtain potential difference between the terminals of the circuit and the current through it. Power is then found by Equation (3.3),

$$P = VI.$$

This method is subject to the same errors mentioned in the preceding section, which are discussed more fully below.

6. Simultaneous measurement of current and potential difference. Measurements of resistance by the voltmeter-ammeter method and measurements of power require the determination simultaneously of potential difference and current. The meters may be arranged either as in Figure 5.7a or 5.7b. In neither case, however, will both the voltmeter and the

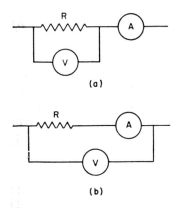

(a)

(b)

Fig. 5.7. Connections for simultaneous measurement of voltage and current.

ammeter give correct indications: the reading of one or the other is affected by the presence of the other meter.

If connected as in Figure 5.7a, the voltmeter reads the potential difference across R, but the ammeter reads the sum of the current through R and the current through the voltmeter. If the resistance of the voltmeter is known, the current through it may be calculated by dividing its reading by its resistance. The true current through R is then found by subtracting the calculated current through the voltmeter from the reading of the ammeter. If the resistance of R is very small compared with the resistance of the voltmeter, the correction will, obviously, be very small and may ordinarily be ignored. If, however, the resistance of the voltmeter and the resistance of R are nearly equal, the correction will be approximately 50 per cent of the measured current. This connection is, therefore, best adapted to measurements of resistance or power when the resistance of R is small compared to the resistance of the voltmeter.

If connected as in Figure 5.7b, the ammeter reads the current through R, but the voltmeter reads the potential difference across R and the ammeter in series. If the resistances of the ammeter and of the connection between the ammeter and R are known, the potential difference across them may be calculated by multiplying resistance by current. The true potential difference across R is then found by subtracting the potential difference calculated from the reading of the voltmeter. If the resistance of the ammeter and of the connecting wire is small compared to the resistance of R, the correction may be negligible. On the other hand, if the resistance of the connecting wire and ammeter were equal to the resistance of R, the correction would amount to approximately 50 per cent of the measured potential difference. This connection is to be recommended only if the resistance of R is large as compared to the resistance of the ammeter connection.

The above recommendations as to which connection is preferable apply only to approximate measurements. If corrections are to be made, the best connection to use depends upon which meter resistance is most accurately known. This will generally be the resistance of the voltmeter, making the connection as in Figure 5.7a the best choice.

PROBLEMS

(17-V) A resistance of the order of 0.01 ohm is to be measured by the voltmeter-ammeter method. There are available a 0 to 25 ammeter having a resistance of 0.004 ohm including the connecting wire, and a 0 to 1 voltmeter having a resistance of 100 ohms. When connected as in Fig. 5.7a the readings are $V = 0.39$ v, $I = 20$ amp. Find the approximate resistance, the current taken by the voltmeter, the true current through R, the corrected resistance, error in ohms, and percentage of error.

(18-V) The resistance described in Problem 17-V is remeasured, using the same instruments connected as in Fig. 5.7b. The readings are $V = 0.353$ v, $I = 15$ amp. Find the approximate resistance, potential difference across ammeter and connecting wire, true potential difference across R, corrected resistance, error in ohms, and percentage of error.

(19-V) A resistance of the order of 10,000 ohms is measured by the voltmeter-ammeter method, using a 0 to 150-scale voltmeter having a resistance of 15,000 ohms, and a 0 to 25-scale milliammeter having a resistance of 10 ohms. With the meters connected as in Fig. 5.7a, the readings are $V = 60$ v, $I = 10.64$ ma. Connected as in Fig. 5.7b, the readings are $V = 90$ v, $I = 9.99$ ma. For each set of readings, calculate approximate resistance, true resistance, error in ohms, and percentage of error.

(20-V) A 0 to 150-scale voltmeter having a resistance of 13,500 ohms and a 0 to 10-scale ammeter having a resistance of 0.0045 ohm are connected as in Fig. 5.7a to measure the power taken by a resistor. The readings are $V = 145$ v, $I = 1.55$ amp. What is the approximate power, power taken by voltmeter, true power, error in watts, and percentage of error?

(21-V) A 0 to 5-scale voltmeter having a resistance of 508 ohms and a 0 to 10-scale ammeter having a resistance of 0.05 ohm are connected as in Fig. 5.7b to determine the power taken by a resistor. If the voltmeter reads 3.63 v and the ammeter reads 9.11 amp, find the approximate power, power taken by ammeter, true power, error in watts, and percentage of error.

7. Use of polarity marks. The direction in which energy flows in a circuit can be determined by reference to the polarity markings on the voltmeter and ammeter.

The actual direction of current in a conductor can be told by using an ammeter having polarity marks on its terminals. For the meter to read up-scale, current must flow in at its positive ($+$) terminal and out at its negative ($-$) terminal.

Likewise, the actual direction of a potential difference can be told by using a voltmeter with polarity markings. For the meter to read up-scale, its positive terminal must be at a higher potential than its negative terminal. In other words, if the meter reads up-scale, there is a positive voltage drop from the point to which its positive terminal is connected to the point to which its negative terminal is connected.

By using both an ammeter and a voltmeter having polarity markings, it is possible to determine the direction of power (that is, the direction in which energy flows) in a circuit. The rule may be stated as follows: *If the meters show there is a voltage drop across a circuit or any part of a circuit in the same direction as the current, then electrical energy is being absorbed. If the meters show there is a voltage drop in the opposite direction to current, then electrical energy is being delivered to the circuit.*

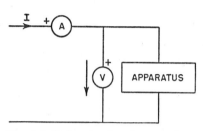

Fig. 5.8. Determination of energy flow by use of polarity marks.

Example: In Fig. 5.8, the ammeter and voltmeter, connected as shown, both read up-scale. Is the apparatus absorbing or delivering electrical energy?

SOLUTION: Since the ammeter is reading up-scale, current is flowing in at its positive terminal — that is, in the direction of the arrow. Since the voltmeter is reading up-scale, there is a voltage drop from its positive to its negative terminal — that is, in the direction of the arrow. Since the voltage drop across the apparatus is the same as the direction of current through it, it is absorbing energy.

PROBLEM

(22-V) In each of the diagrams in Fig. 5.9, the ammeter and voltmeter both read up-scale as connected. For each diagram, state in which direction current

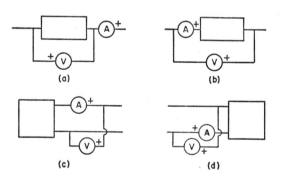

Fig. 5.9

flows, which is direction of voltage drop, and whether the apparatus absorbs or delivers electrical energy.

8. Measurement of resistance by the voltmeter method. A voltmeter of known resistance may be used in conjunction with a source of electromotive force to measure resistance. Suppose we first connect the voltmeter which has a resistance R_G to the terminals of a battery, as in Figure 5.10a. The voltmeter will draw a small current I_1 and will read the voltage drop across itself, which is

$$V_1 = I_1 R_G = E. \qquad (5.5)$$

If we ignore the small voltage drop in the internal resistance of the battery, the voltmeter reading is equal to the battery electromotive force.

Now, suppose we connect a resistance R_X in series with the voltmeter, as in Figure 5.10b. The current will decrease to some new value I_2 because of the increased circuit resistance, and the reading of the voltmeter will also decrease to some new value

$$V_2 = I_2 R_G. \qquad (5.6)$$

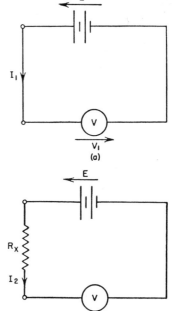

Fig. 5.10. Voltmeter method of measuring resistance.

Now, assuming that the electromotive force of the battery is equal to V_1 and that it remains constant, we can see that

$$I_2 = \frac{V_1}{R_G + R_X}. \qquad (5.7)$$

Substituting (5.7) in (5.6), we have

$$V_2 = \frac{V_1 R_G}{R_G + R_X}, \qquad (5.8)$$

and solving for R_X, we have

$$R_X = \frac{V_1 - V_2}{V_2} R_G. \qquad (5.9)$$

By using Equation (5.8), we can calculate the values of V_2 that correspond to certain values of R_X, and so obtain the necessary data to mark off an ohm scale for the voltmeter. A voltmeter thus adapted to read ohms directly is known as an **ohmmeter.** An ohmmeter, as a rule, does not read resistance with the precision obtainable by the voltmeter-ammeter method or by the Wheatstone bridge. However, the ohmmeter is much easier to use, and resistances can be determined rapidly and with a fair degree of accuracy. This makes it the favorite instrument of the radio serviceman.

Example 1: A voltmeter having a resistance of 15,000 ohms reads 120 v when connected to a certain battery. An unknown resistance is now connected in series with the voltmeter and battery and the reading drops to 112.5 v. What is the unknown resistance?

SOLUTION:

$$R_X = \frac{120 - 112.5}{112.5} \times 15,000 = 1000 \text{ ohms.}$$

Example 2: If it is desired to make an ohm scale for the voltmeter in the above example, where should the 1000-ohm mark be placed? Under what circumstances would the instrument give correct ohm readings?

SOLUTION: From Example 1, it is obvious that the 1000-ohm mark should coincide with the 112.5-v mark on the volt scale. The ohm readings would be correct only if the instrument were used with a 120-v battery, since the calculations were based on that value of V_1.

PROBLEMS

(23-V) A voltmeter having a resistance of 300 ohms reads 3 v across two dry cells that are connected in series. An unknown resistance is connected in series with the voltmeter and battery, and the reading becomes 1.65 v. What is the unknown resistance?

(24-V) Calculate an ohm scale for the voltmeter-and-battery combination described in Example 1. Try ohm values from zero to infinity. What are the practical limits between which resistances can be measured? What establishes these limits?

(25-V) Calculate an ohm scale for the voltmeter-and-battery combination described in Problem 23-V. Try ohm values from zero to infinity. What are the practical limits between which resistances can be measured? What establishes these limits?

9. The D'Arsonval galvanometer. The sensitivity of the permanent-magnet, moving-coil type of meter can be greatly increased by increasing the number of turns in the coil and suspending the coil between the poles of the permanent magnet rather than mounting it in bearings. Such an instrument, known as a **galvanometer,** usually has a scale marked off in arbitrary divisions rather than in amperes or volts. Galvanometers are used not only for measuring small currents and voltages, but also as indicators to show when the current in a certain part of a network has been adjusted to zero, as in bridge and potentiometer networks. For this use, the instrument need not be calibrated. When it is to be used for measurements of current or voltage, the usual procedure is to determine its constant (in amperes or volts per scale division) experimentally. Readings are then taken in scale divisions, and the required current or voltage is found by multiplying the reading by the constant.

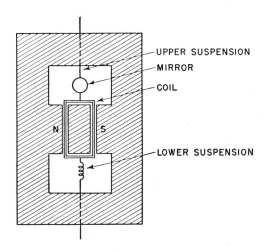

Fig. 5.11. Wall-type D'Arsonval galvanometer.

Galvanometers are made in portable form, and also for wall or pedestal mounting. The latter can be made extremely sensitive, but are also extremely delicate, requiring great care in leveling, protection from vibration, and so forth. The suspension strip, which supports the coil in the wall-type instrument, and which also serves as a connection, is commonly of gold or bronze, two or three thousandths of an inch thick and five inches long. This strip is twisted as the coil rotates and furnishes the restoring torque. The other connection to the coil is made through the spiral strip attached to its lower end.

In place of a pointer, a mirror is mounted upon the coil, and reflects a scale mounted some distance in front of the galvanometer. The observer looks at the mirror through a telescope mounted just below the scale and reads the scale division which coincides with a hairline in the eyepiece of the telescope. Thus, in effect, a beam of light serves as the pointer, which can be quite long and at the same time, weightless.

In portable galvanometers, the suspension strip is much shorter and is held in tension by a flat spring, making the instrument as rugged as the ordinary voltmeter or ammeter. The light-beam pointer of the wall-type instrument is here replaced by a short metal pointer attached to the coil.

PROBLEMS

(26-V) To determine the constant of a wall-type galvanometer having a resistance of 200 ohms, it is connected to a dry cell (emf = 1.5 v) through a series resistance of 0.8 megohm. A deflection of 180 scale divisions is obtained. What is the constant in microamperes per scale division?

(27-V) The galvanometer of Problem 26-V is connected in series with an unknown resistance to the terminals of a 100-v battery. A deflection of 14.5 scale divisions is obtained. What is the unknown resistance?

(28-V) A wall-type galvanometer having a resistance of 1750 ohms is shunted by a resistance of 1000 ohms. This parallel circuit is then connected in series with a 2-megohm resistance to the terminals of a 1.5-v dry cell, and a deflection of 22 scale divisions is obtained. What is the constant of the galvanometer and shunt combination? What would be the constant of the galvanometer used without the shunt?

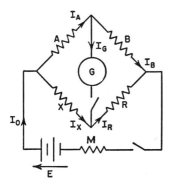

Fig. 5.12. Wheatstone bridge.

10. The Wheatstone bridge. Measurement of resistance is often carried out by means of an arrangement known as a **Wheatstone bridge.** Four resistances, a battery, and a galvanometer are connected as in Figure 5.12. Three of the resistances, A, B, and R, are known; the fourth is the unknown resistance X. At least one of the known resistances must be adjustable. In practice, A and B, which are called **ratio arms,** are usually adjustable to either 1, 10, 100, or 1000 ohms, and R, which is called the **rheostat arm,** is adjustable from 0.1 to 9999.9 ohms in 0.1-ohm steps. It is seen that the bridge constitutes a three-mesh network, and any problem concerning it depends upon the solution of Kirchhoff's law equations as follows:

$$I_A = I_B + I_G, \tag{5.10}$$

$$I_X + I_G = I_R, \tag{5.11}$$

$$I_0 = I_A + I_X, \tag{5.12}$$

$$E = I_0 M + I_R R + I_X X, \tag{5.13}$$

$$0 = I_A A + I_G G - I_X X, \tag{5.14}$$

$$0 = I_B B - I_R R - I_G G, \tag{5.15}$$

where M and G are the resistances of the battery branch and the galvanometer branch, respectively.

To use the bridge, the ratio arms and rheostat arm are adjusted so that the galvanometer shows no deflection, indicating that the current I_G is zero.

Equations 5.10 through 5.15 may then be modified as follows:

$$I_A = I_B. \tag{5.16}$$

$$I_R = I_X. \tag{5.17}$$

$$I_0 = I_A + I_R. \tag{5.18}$$

$$E = I_0 M + I_R R + I_X X. \tag{5.19}$$

$$I_A A = I_X X. \tag{5.20}$$

$$I_B B = I_R R. \tag{5.21}$$

Substituting I_A for I_B and I_X for I_R in (5.21),

$$I_A B = I_X R. \tag{5.22}$$

Dividing (5.20) by (5.22),

$$\frac{A}{B} = \frac{X}{R},$$

or

$$X = \frac{A}{B} R. \tag{5.23}$$

It is essential in using a Wheatstone bridge to choose suitable values for the ratio-arm resistances A and B. Usually, the operator will have some idea of the magnitude of the unknown resistance, and he should choose A and B so that X can be determined to three significant figures.

Example: A resistance believed to be between 1 and 10 ohms is to be measured. Assuming that A or B can be set at either 1, 10, 100, or 1000, and that R can be set at any value from 1 to 10,000 in 1-ohm steps, what values of A and B will be the most satisfactory?

Solution: Suppose we consider first $A = 1$, $B = 1$. Then, to balance the bridge, R must be set equal to X. Since R can be varied only in 1-ohm steps, it will be impossible to balance the bridge unless X happens to be an integral number of ohms. X can be determined only to one significant figure, which is not satisfactory.

Now, suppose we make $A = 1$, $B = 100$. To balance the bridge, R must now be set at $100X$. It may still be impossible to balance the bridge exactly, but out nearest value of R will be, say, 973, and we can determine X to three significant figures, which usually is sufficient. Ratios of $A = 10$, $B = 1000$, or $A = 1$, $B = 1000$ would also be satisfactory.

In case the operator has no idea at all of the magnitude of X, the best procedure is to choose some ratio at random, say, $A = 10, B = 10$, and then in succession to try the minimum and the maximum values of R. If both these settings of R deflect the galvanometer in the same direction, then there is no setting of R that will balance the bridge, and some other ratio must be tried. When a ratio has been found which permits the galvanometer current to be reversed by going from a minimum to a maximum setting of R, the next step is to vary R by 1000-ohm steps, leaving it finally on the 1000-ohm step just below the one which reverses the galvanometer current. This procedure is then repeated, using 100-ohm steps, and so forth, until balance is obtained.

It is seen that the Wheatstone bridge measures a resistance in terms of other resistances, and the accuracy of the method is, therefore, limited by the accuracy of the resistances A, B, and R, and by the sensitivity of the galvanometer. Problems concerning accuracy usually call for a general solution of the bridge equations.

PROBLEMS

(29-V) A Wheatstone bridge connected as in Fig. 5.12 is balanced when $A = 10$ ohms, $B = 1000$ ohms, and $R = 7932$ ohms. What is the value of X?

(30-V) (a) If A had been set at 1 ohm and the maximum setting of R is 9999 ohms, could the bridge in Problem 29-V have been balanced? Why? (b) Would $A = 1000$, $B = 1000$ have served as well as the ratio that was used in Problem 29-V? How precisely could X have been measured?

(31-V) What is the theoretical range of resistances that may be measured with a bridge that permits A or B to be set at either 1, 10, 100, or 1000 ohms, and R at any value from 1 to 9999? Would the practical range be the same? Why?

(32-V) What would be the best choice of ratio for measuring resistances known to lie between 1 and 10 ohms? 10 and 100 ohms? 100 and 1000 ohms? 1000 and 10,000 ohms? 10,000 and 100,000 ohms?

11. The Kelvin bridge. Resistances below 1 ohm cannot be measured with sufficient accuracy by the Wheatstone bridge because the resistance of the leads used to connect them into the bridge network introduces considerable error. The Kelvin bridge obviates this difficulty and makes possible the accurate measurement of resistances as low as 0.0001 ohm.

The resistance to be measured, X, is connected into a series circuit shown by the heavy line in Figure 5.13, containing also an adjustable stand-

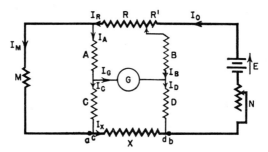

Fig. 5.13. Kelvin bridge.

ard of low resistance R, a battery, and a rheostat. The current in this circuit is much higher than that in any part of a Wheatstone bridge network, and may amount to several amperes. The network is completed by the ratio resistances A, B, C, and D and the galvanometer. The part of the standard of low resistance to the left of the slider is designated as R, the remainder as R'. In use, the ratio resistances and the standard of low resistance are adjusted to make the galvanometer current zero, always keeping $A = B$ and $C = D$. The connections from C and D are joined to the resistance to be measured at points c and d, which are inside the terminals a and b, at which the resistance is connected into the main circuit. Thus, the resistance measured does not include the lead resistance nor the contact resistance at a and b. The effect of contact resistance at points c and d is negligible because the ratio resistances, with which it is in series, are of the order of several hundred ohms. The equations for the general solution of the network are as follows:

$$I_0 = I_R + I_B. \tag{5.24}$$

$$I_B + I_G = I_D. \tag{5.25}$$

$$I_D + I_X = I_0. \tag{5.26}$$

$$I_R = I_A + I_M. \tag{5.27}$$

$$I_A = I_G + I_C. \tag{5.28}$$

$$E = I_0R' + I_0N + I_BB + I_DD. \tag{5.29}$$

$$0 = I_RR + I_AA + I_GG - I_BB. \tag{5.30}$$

$$0 = I_GG + I_DD - I_XX - I_CC. \tag{5.31}$$

$$0 = I_AA + I_CC - I_MM. \tag{5.32}$$

For the special case of the bridge balanced ($I_G = 0$), Equations (5.25), (5.28), (5.30), and (5.31) are modified as follows:

$$I_B = I_D. \tag{5.33}$$

$$I_A = I_C. \tag{5.34}$$

$$0 = I_RR + I_AA - I_BB. \tag{5.35}$$

$$0 = I_DD - I_XX - I_CC. \tag{5.36}$$

Adding Equations (5.24) and (5.26) gives

$$I_D + I_X = I_R + I_B, \tag{5.37}$$

and since $I_B = I_D$ (5.33), we have

$$I_X = I_R. \tag{5.38}$$

Substituting A for B in Equation (5.35) and transposing,

$$I_RR = (I_B - I_A)A. \tag{5.39}$$

Substituting I_R for I_X, I_A for I_C, I_B for I_D, and C for D in Equation (5.36) and transposing,

$$I_R X = (I_B - I_A)C. \tag{5.40}$$

Dividing (5.39) by (5.40), we obtain

$$\frac{R}{X} = \frac{A}{C},$$

or

$$X = R\frac{C}{A}. \tag{5.41}$$

PROBLEMS

(33-V) A Kelvin bridge is balanced when $A = B = 100$ ohms, $C = D = 1000$ ohms, and $R = 0.00852$ ohm. What is the value of X?

(34-V) What is the theoretical range of a Kelvin bridge with provisions for making A, B, C, or D either 100, 550, or 1000 ohms, and R any value from 0.0001 to 0.01 ohm?

12. The potentiometer. A potential difference may be measured by comparing it with a known potential difference by use of a device known as a **potentiometer.** A simple form of the potentiometer, shown in Figure 5.14, consists of a long, uniform resistance wire W along which a sliding

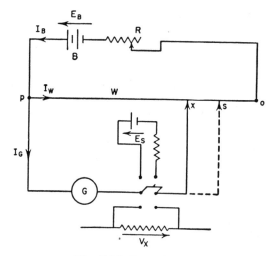

Fig. 5.14. Potentiometer.

contact may be moved. A steady current I_W is sent through the wire by the auxiliary battery B, the current being adjustable by means of the rheostat R. A double-pole, double-throw (dpdt) switch makes it possible to connect either the known potential difference, E_S, or the potential difference to be measured, V_X. A galvanometer G serves as an indicator to show when a balance is attained. In practice, the known potential difference is usually the electromotive force of a Weston standard cell. To use the potentiometer, the current I_W is adjusted to any convenient value by means of the rheostat R, and the dpdt switch is thrown to the standard cell. The slider is then adjusted until the current $I_G = 0$ (indicated by no deflection of the galvanometer), and the distance L_S from the point p to the slider is noted. Around the mesh containing the standard cell, we may then apply Kirchhoff's voltage law to obtain

$$E_S = I_W K_W L_S, \tag{5.42}$$

where E_S is the emf of the standard cell in volts;

I_W is the current in the slide wire in amperes;

K_W is the resistance per unit length of slide wire;

L_S is the distance from point p to the slider.

The dpdt switch is now thrown to the unknown potential difference, and the slider again is adjusted until $I_G = 0$. Then, by Kirchhoff's voltage law,

$$0 = I_W K_W L_X - V_X, \tag{5.43}$$

where L_X is the new distance from point p to the slider;

V_X is the unknown potential difference in volts.

Dividing (5.42) by (5.43), we get

$$\frac{E_S}{V_X} = \frac{L_S}{L_X},$$

or

$$V_X = E_S \frac{L_X}{L_S}. \tag{5.44}$$

It should be noted that no current flows in the potentiometer network from the circuit under test when balance is obtained. This eliminates one error that is always present if a voltmeter is used, and enables one, for example, to measure the true emf of a cell. The circuit is not modified by the introduction of the potentiometer, as it would be by the introduction of a voltmeter.

It may be that the random setting of the current I_B will not permit I_G to be made zero by moving the sliding contact. In this case, I_B must be increased until the potential difference between p and o is at least as great as the potential difference to be measured. The particular value of I_B is of no interest, nor is it necessary to know K_W. It is essential, however, that I_B remain constant during both settings of the slider and that the wire be perfectly uniform in resistance per unit length.

The potentiometer wire may be marked off in volts instead of units of length, thus making the scale direct-reading. If this is done, it is obvious that the marking will be correct for only one particular value of I_W, and the procedure as given above must be modified. The sliding contact is first set at the scale reading that corresponds to the emf of the standard cell, and the rheostat is adjusted until the current $I_G = 0$. The potentiometer is then said to be standardized, and is direct-reading so long as the current I_W does not change. In using a standard cell, the operator must take precautions to insure that the current through it never exceeds 0.0001 amp; otherwise, the cell will be ruined as a standard. This makes it necessary to insert a large resistance, say, 10,000 ohms, in series with the cell and to keep it there until an approximate balance is obtained. The resistance may then be cut out, and the balance perfected.

The range of the potentiometer is limited to potential differences of the order of 1 to 3 v. It may be increased, however, by using an accessory known as a **volt box.** A volt box is simply a series arrangement, as shown in Figure 5.15, of two accurately known resistances. The voltage to be meas-

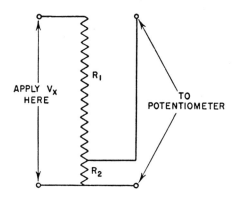

Fig. 5.15. Volt box.

ured is applied to both resistances in series, and since the potentiometer, when balanced, draws no current, the current will be the same in R_1 and R_2. Therefore, the voltage drops will be proportional to the resistances, and the voltage applied to the potentiometer will be

$$\frac{R_2}{R_1 + R_2} V_X. \tag{5.45}$$

A potentiometer may be used in conjunction with a standard resistance to measure current. The current to be measured is sent through the standard resistance, and the potential difference between its terminals is then measured by means of the potentiometer.

PROBLEMS

(35-V) A potentiometer wire is 1 m long and has a resistance of 20 ohms. If the auxiliary battery has an emf of 6 v and the rheostat is adjusted to 40 ohms, what is the current in the wire? What range of voltages may be balanced against the drop in the wire? How would you design a scale to make the wire read directly in volts? At what distance from the zero end would balance be obtained for a standard cell having an emf of 1.0183 v?

(36-V) What should be the resistance of a potentiometer wire to give a drop of 2 v at a current of 1.5 ma? What rheostat resistance would be needed if the battery consisted of 2 dry cells in series? Does the accuracy of the instrument depend upon knowing the rheostat resistance and the emf of the battery accurately?

(37-V) A volt box has a total resistance of 100,000 ohms and is tapped at 2000 ohms. By what factor should the potentiometer readings be multiplied?

(38-V) Could the volt box described in Problem 37-V be used in conjunction with a 0 to 3-scale voltmeter having a resistance of 300 ohms? What would be the multiplying factor if this were done?

ADDITIONAL PROBLEMS

(39-V) A D'Arsonval type voltmeter has a range 0 to 300 v and a resistance of 60,000 ohms, 5 ohms of which is the resistance of the coil itself. It is desired to convert this instrument into an ammeter of range 0 to 50. Explain what must be done, show diagrams of connections before and after the change, and make all necessary calculations.

(40-V) A D'Arsonval type ammeter has a range 0 to 10 amp, and a resistance of 0.0025 ohm. The resistance of the coil itself is 2 ohms. It is desired to convert this instrument into a voltmeter of range 0 to 60 v. Explain what must be done, show diagrams of connections before and after the change, and make all necessary calculations.

(41-V) A voltmeter has a 0 to 75 range and a resistance of 6000 ohms. What should be the resistance of a series multiplier to extend the range to 0 to 300? By what factor would the readings be multiplied?

(42-V) A D'Arsonval ammeter has a 0 to 5 range and a resistance of 0.0125 ohm. What should be the resistance of a shunt to extend the range to 0 to 25? By what factor would the readings be multiplied?

(43-V) Show that, when a millivoltmeter is used with a shunt as an ammeter as explained in Problem 5-V,

$$I = R\frac{A}{S},$$ (5.46)

where I is the current in amperes;
   R is reading in scale divisions;
   A is the ampere rating of the shunt;
   S is the number of scale divisions on the meter.

(44-V) Prove that for a galvanometer of resistance G, paralleled by a shunt of resistance S as in Fig. 5.3,

$$I_G = I_0 \frac{S}{S + G}. \tag{5.47}$$

(45-V) In order to find the resistance G of a galvanometer, it is connected in series with a resistance r and a battery having an emf of E volts, so as to obtain a deflection of d scale divisions. The resistance is then changed to a value R such that the deflection is reduced to $\frac{1}{2} d$. Show that

$$G = R - 2r. \tag{5.48}$$

(46-V) In order to find the resistance G of a galvanometer, it is connected in series with a large resistance R to a battery of emf E and the deflection d observed. It is then shunted by a resistance S of such value that the deflection is reduced to $d/2$. Show that, if $R > > G$, then

$$G = S. \tag{5.49}$$

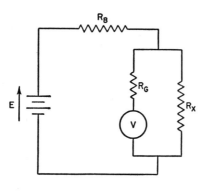

Fig. 5.16

(47-V) Ohmmeters are sometimes designed to have the unknown resistance act as a shunt, as in Fig. 5.16. When R_X is zero, the voltmeter is short-circuited and reads zero. As R_X is increased, the reading of the voltmeter increases, reaching a maximum when R_X is infinity. Assuming $E = 4.5$ v, $R_B = 150$ ohms, and the voltmeter is 0 to 3 range with resistance $R_G = 300$ ohms, calculate the ohm scale for the meter.

(48-V) In a certain Wheatstone bridge, A is 100 ohms, B is 1000 ohms, and R is 400 ohms for balance. The resistances in each arm of the bridge are guaranteed by the manufacturer to be accurate to within 0.2 of 1 per cent. Between what limits is X certain to be? Within what percentage is X certainly determined?

(49-V) It is often impossible to say exactly what setting of R balances the bridge. Owing to lack of sensitivity, the galvanometer may show no deflection when R is varied appreciably. Assume that, in Problem 48-V, the setting of R to give a barely perceptible plus deflection is 399 ohms and the setting to give a barely perceptible minus deflection is 401 ohms. Between what limits is X certain to be? Within what percentage is X certainly determined?

(50-V) Derive the equation of the Wheatstone bridge shown in Fig. 5.12 if the battery and galvanometer are interchanged.

(51-V) In a certain Wheatstone bridge arrangement, as in Fig. 5.12, $A = 10$ ohms, $B = 1000$ ohms, $R = 2000$ ohms, $X = 20.2$ ohms, $G = 250$ ohms, M is negligible, and the battery emf is 3 v. Calculate the galvanometer current.

(52-V) By what percentage is the bridge in Problem 51-V unbalanced? How sensitive must the galvanometer be to detect this amount of unbalance? Assume that the operator can detect a movement of the galvanometer pointer of 0.1 scale division.

(53-V) Show that, for the Kelvin bridge as shown in Fig. 5.13, if $A \neq B$ and $C \neq D$, the equation of the bridge becomes

$$X = \frac{RD}{B} + \frac{M(DA - BC)}{(A + C + M)B}.$$

(54-V) A Kelvin bridge as shown in Fig. 5.13 is balanced for $A = 100$, $B = 100$, $C = 200$, $D = 200$, $M = 0.1$ and $R = 0.005$. (a) What is the value of X? (b) If B is actually 101 ohms instead of 100 as marked, what is the value of X? By what per cent would the value calculated in (a) be in error? Use the expression developed in Problem 53-V.

(55-V) An instructor gives a student a resistance to measure by the volt-meter-ammeter method. The instructor knows the resistance to be exactly 0.01 ohm. The voltmeter to be used has a resistance of 2.25 ohms, including leads, and a range of 0–100 millivolts. The ammeter has a resistance of 0.0075 ohm, including one lead, and a range of 0–10 amp. Show the two possible connections the student may use, and calculate the resistance he will find in each case if he makes no corrections.

(56-V) A volt box used in connection with a potentiometer has a total resistance of 100,000 ohms and is tapped at 2000 ohms. With the volt box connected to the potentiometer in the normal way, an unknown voltage V_X is measured and a reading of 1.055 v is obtained on the potentiometer. Calculate V_X. (b) Suppose an error had been made in connecting and the unknown voltage had been applied to the potentiometer terminals of the volt box and the V_X terminals to the potentiometer. Calculate V_X for a potentiometer reading of 1.055 v.

STUDY QUESTIONS

1. What would happen if an alternating-current measurement was attempted with a D'Arsonval instrument?

2. What is the relative magnitude of the deflecting torque and the restoring torque of a D'Arsonval meter (a) at the instant the meter is connected, (b) when a reading is being taken, (c) at the instant the meter is disconnected, (d) when the meter is on the shelf?

3. Is the cylindrical iron core in a D'Arsonval meter stationary or part of the moving system? Why?

4. How can a D'Arsonval ammeter of one range most readily be converted to a different range?

5. How can D'Arsonval voltmeters of one range be converted to a different range?

6. The resistance of a voltmeter divided by its range gives "ohms per volt," which is an indication of whether the instrument is suitable for a certain use.

D'Arsonval voltmeters are often "100 ohms per volt" or "1000 ohms per volt." Which would be the better instrument from the standpoint of disturbing least the circuit to which it is connected? Why?

7. Why are simultaneous measurements of current and potential difference necessary? Why not, using connection as shown in Fig. 5.7a, take current reading with the voltmeter disconnected, then connect the voltmeter and read potential difference?

8. Ohmmeters usually are provided with a zero adjustment (in addition to the zero adjustment on the moving element itself). With the terminals short-circuited, a rheostat is adjusted until the pointer indicates zero on the ohm scale. Why is such an adjustment necessary? How does it work?

9. Two identical boxes are known to contain, one a source of electromotive force, the other, a resistance. The boxes are connected by two wires to form a circuit. The circuit must not be opened, even momentarily. A voltmeter and an ammeter of suitable range and with polarity marks are provided. Explain how you would proceed to find out which box contains the source of electromotive force.

10. Formulate a general rule for making the connections when resistance is to be measured by the voltmeter-ammeter method, so that the results will be subject to as little error as possible. Assume no corrections are to be made.

11. In using a Wheatstone bridge what would be the first remedy to try if these difficulties arose: (a) R cannot be set high enough to balance the bridge, (b) R cannot be set low enough to balance the bridge, (c) R can vary over a wide range without disturbing the balance, (d) unbalance (as indicated by galvanometer deflection) changes from positive to negative with the slightest change that can be made in R.

12. It is desired to use a Kelvin bridge set-up in the laboratory to measure the resistance of a steel rail outside in the yard. Would this be practical? How many wires would have to be run? Draw a diagram.

13. (a) How could a potentiometer be used to check the correctness of a voltmeter at various readings? Draw a diagram, using a three-point rheostat to vary the voltage. (b) How could a potentiometer be used in connection with a standard resistance to check the correctness of an ammeter at various readings? Draw a diagram.

Chapter VI

CHARACTERISTICS OF
METALLIC CONDUCTORS

---

1. Factors which affect resistance. Let us consider a metal conductor of length L meters and constant cross-sectional area A sq m. A steady potential difference of V volts is established between the ends of the conductor. The voltage drop per unit length is then

$$\frac{V}{L} \text{ volts per meter.}$$

The free electrons in the conductor are given a drift velocity of γ meters per second in the direction from the negative toward the positive end of the conductor. This velocity depends upon the voltage drop per unit length, and we define the **mobility** of the electrons as

$$u = \frac{\gamma}{V/L} = \frac{\gamma L}{V} \text{ meters per sec/volts per meter} \tag{6.1}$$

or
$$\gamma = \frac{uV}{L} \text{ meters per sec.} \tag{6.2}$$

Mobility is the velocity which the electrons would acquire if the voltage drop were one volt per meter. It depends primarily upon how many obstacles the moving electrons encounter. The fewer the collisions the greater the mobility.

Now if the number of free electrons per cu m is N and each carries a charge of e coulombs, the current, which is the charge passing a reference point on the conductor in unit time, is

$$I = NA\gamma e. \tag{6.3}$$

Substituting (6.2) in (6.3)

$$I = NA\frac{uV}{L}e \tag{6.4}$$

or
$$\frac{V}{I} = \frac{L}{NAue}. \tag{6.5}$$

By Ohm's law, $V/I = R$, and therefore

$$R = \frac{L}{NAue}. \tag{6.6}$$

Equation (6.6) would enable us to calculate the resistance of a metal conductor from its dimensions, provided we knew N, the number of free electrons per unit volume; u, the steady velocity acquired by the electrons under standard conditions (a voltage drop of 1 volt per meter along the conductor); and e, the charge carried by an electron. Of these quantities, only the last is precisely known. Even if we did have precise values for N and u, the resistance found by using Equation (6.6) would be for ideal conditions and would not take into account imperfections in the lattice structure due to the presence of impurities and to the boundaries of the crystals.

The equation does tell us, however, that resistance depends directly upon the length L and inversely upon the cross-sectional area A. We therefore can combine N, u, and e into a single constant ρ (rho), so that Equation (6.6) becomes

$$R = \frac{\rho L}{A}. \tag{6.7}$$

The constant ρ depends upon the material used and upon the units chosen for R, L, and A. It is called **resistivity** or **specific resistance.** Since it is a quantity which, when multiplied by a length and divided by an area, gives resistance, it must have the dimensions of resistance times length. The mks unit of resistivity would be the **ohm-meter.** This unit, however, is of such inconvenient size that it is seldom used, and resistivity is measured in (a) microhm-centimeters or (b) ohm-circular mils per foot. The microhm-centimeter is used almost exclusively for laboratory or purely scientific investigations, and it is also well-suited for calculations which involve conductors of square or rectangular cross section. The ohm-circular mil per foot is particularly convenient for calculations involving round conductors, and is, therefore, much used in industry. In any event, the resistivity is found by test. The resistance of a specimen of known length and known cross-sectional area is measured, and the value of ρ is found by substituting in (6.7). The following examples illustrate the use of the ohm-meter.

Example 1: The resistance of a copper bar 50 cm long and having a constant cross-sectional area of 2 sq cm is measured and found to be 4.31×10^{-5} ohm. What is the resistivity in ohm-meters?

Solution: Expressing length in meters and cross-sectional area in square meters, we have

$$L = 50 \text{ cm} = 0.5 \text{ m},$$

$$A = 2 \text{ sq cm} = 2 \times 10^{-4} \text{ sq m.}$$

Substituting in (6.7),

$$4.31 \times 10^{-5} = \frac{\rho(0.5)}{2 \times 10^{-4}},$$

$$\rho = 1.724 \times 10^{-8} \text{ ohm-m.}$$

Example 2: What is the resistivity in microhm-centimeters of the copper bar described in Example 1? What would be the resistance of a bar of the same material 62.5 in. long and having a cross-sectional area of 0.5 sq in.?

Solution: Resistance of the bar is

$$4.31 \times 10^{-5} \text{ ohm} = 43.1 \text{ microhms;}$$

$$L = 50 \text{ cm},$$

$$A = 2 \text{ sq cm.}$$

Substituting in (6.7),

$$43.1 = \frac{\rho(50)}{2},$$

$$\rho = 1.724 \text{ microhm-cm.}$$

Expressing the length and cross section of the second bar in centimeters and square centimeters, respectively,

$$L = 62.5 \text{ in.} = 159 \text{ cm},$$

$$A = 0.5 \text{ sq in.} = 3.225 \text{ sq cm.}$$

Substituting in (6.7),

$$R = \frac{(1.724)(159)}{3.225} = 84.9 \text{ microhm}$$

$$= 8.49 \times 10^{-5} \text{ ohm.}$$

2. Resistance calculations for round conductors. The calculation of the resistances of round conductors is simplified by measuring the cross-sectional area in **circular mils.** The circular mil is a unit of area, and is a

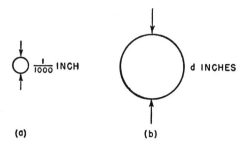

Fig. 6.1. Measurement of area in circular units. The small circle $\frac{1}{1000}$ in. in diameter is a unit of area — a circular mil.

circle one mil ($\frac{1}{1000}$ of an inch) in diameter. The principle of measuring with this unit is the same as always — we simply find how many times the unit is contained in the thing to be measured. Let us apply it to the measurement of the area of a circle d inches in diameter. The area of our unit is

$$A_1 = \frac{\pi(0.001)^2}{4} \text{ sq in.}$$

The area of the circle to be measured is

$$A_2 = \frac{\pi d^2}{4} \text{ sq in.}$$

To find how many times the unit is contained in the area to be measured, we take

$$\frac{A_2}{A_1} = \frac{\pi \dfrac{d^2}{4}}{\pi \dfrac{(0.001)^2}{4}} = \frac{d^2}{(0.001)^2} = (1000d)^2.$$

Thus, to find the area of a circle in circular mils, we simply take its diameter in inches, multiply it by 1000, and square the product. This eliminates the use of the factor π, thereby saving a step in calculating such areas.

Example: The resistance of a round copper wire 100 ft long and 0.1 in. in diameter is 0.1042 ohm. What is the resistivity of the copper in ohm-circular mils per foot? What would be the resistance of a piece of the same wire 0.08 in. in diameter and 1 mile long?

SOLUTION:

$$\text{Area} = (0.1 \times 1000)^2 = 10{,}000 \text{ cir mils,}$$

$$0.1042 = \frac{\rho(100)}{10{,}000},$$

$$\rho = 10.42 \text{ ohm-cir mils per ft.}$$

$$\text{Area of second piece} = (0.08 \times 1000)^2 = 6400 \text{ cir mils,}$$

$$R = \frac{10.42(5280)}{6400} = 8.6 \text{ ohms.}$$

Resistivity may be thought of as being numerically equal to the resistance of a piece of material of unit length and unit cross-sectional area. Resistivity in microhm-centimeters, for example, is numerically equal to the resistance of a piece of material 1 cm in length and 1 sq cm in cross-sectional area, or in other words, to the resistance of a centimeter cube of the material. For this reason, we sometimes see the expression "microhms per centimeter cube," instead of the correct "microhm-centimeters." Similarly, the resistivity in ohm-circular mils per foot is numerically equal to the resistance of a piece of material 1 cir mil in cross-sectional area and 1 ft long, and the expression "ohms per circular mil-foot" is sometimes used in place of "ohm-circular mils per foot." These substitute expressions are dimensionally incorrect and, furthermore, they imply that resistance is a function of volume, which is not the case. It is, therefore, recommended that the correct expressions, microhm-centimeters and ohm-circular mils per foot be used, though thinking of resistivity as being numerically equal to the resistance of a certain piece of material is often useful.

The resistivities of some materials commonly used in the electrical industries are given in Table IV.

3. Conductivity. As stated in Section 10 of Chapter III, conductance G is the reciprocal of resistance. Any factor that tends to make resistance large would, therefore, make conductance small, and vice versa. Thus, we can see that the conductance would decrease with length,

$$G \text{ is proportional to } \frac{1}{L}, \tag{6.8}$$

and that it would increase with cross-sectional area,

$$G \text{ is proportional to } A; \tag{6.9}$$

combining (6.8) and (6.9), we have

$$G \text{ is proportional to } \frac{A}{L}. \tag{6.10}$$

Introducing a proportionality constant σ (sigma),

$$G = \frac{\sigma A}{L}. \tag{6.11}$$

The constant σ is called **conductivity.** Since it is a quantity which, when multiplied by an area and divided by a length, gives conductance, it must have the dimensions of conductance divided by length. From (6.2) and (6.11), and since

$$G = \frac{1}{R},$$

it can be seen that $\qquad\qquad \sigma = \frac{1}{\rho}.$ $\qquad\qquad$ (6.12)

Conductivity is the reciprocal of resistivity. The mks unit of conductivity is the **mho per meter.**

Conductivity is often expressed as a percentage, the conductivity of standard annealed copper being taken as 100 per cent:

$$\text{percentage of conductivity} = \frac{\sigma \text{ of material}}{\sigma \text{ of standard annealed copper}} \times 100, \quad (6.13)$$

or, replacing σ by ρ according to (6.12),

$$\text{percentage of conductivity} = \frac{\rho \text{ of standard annealed copper}}{\rho \text{ of material}} \times 100. \quad (6.14)$$

Example: What is the percentage of conductivity of a material having a resistivity of 2 microhm-cm?

Solution: The resistivity of standard annealed copper from Table IV is 1.724 microhm-cm. By (6.14),

$$\text{percentage of conductivity} = \frac{1.724}{2} \times 100 = 86.2.$$

Copper of greater purity than standard annealed copper and, hence, having more than 100 per cent conductivity is obtainable. Aluminum has about 60 per cent conductivity, steel wire about 10 per cent.

In general the combining of pure metals to form alloys, or even the presence of a small percentage of impurity, results in a material of greatly lowered conductivity. Nichrome, which is an alloy of copper, iron, and nickel, all of which are good conductors, has a conductivity of only about 1.5 per cent. Such alloys are of considerable practical importance, because it is often desirable, as in rheostats and heating elements, to obtain considerable resistance in a relatively short length of conductor.

The ratio of the heat conductivity of a metal to its electrical conductivity at the same temperature is approximately the same for all metals. This is the Wiedemann-Franz relation, and it implies that the medium of heat conduction must be the same as the medium of electrical conduction, the electron.

Table IV. Resistivity and Resistance — Temperature Coefficients

Material	Resistivity (microhm-cm at 20° C)	Resistivity (ohms-cir mils per ft at 20° C)	Resistance — temperature coefficient at 20° C
Advance (alloy)...........	....	298	.00002
Aluminum...............	2.828	....	.0039
Brass..................	....	40	.0017
Carbon.................	3000		
Copper (std annealed).....	1.724	10.37	.00393
Copper (hard drawn)......	....	10.78	.00382
Graphite................	800		
Manganin...............	44	....	.000006
Nichrome...............	100	....	.0004
Silver..................	1.63	....	.0038
Steel (Siemens-Martin)....	....	98.1	
Steel (4% silicon).........	50		
Steel (rails)..............	21.55	....	.0059
Tungsten...............	....	33.2	.0045

PROBLEMS

(1-VI) What is the area in circular mils of a circle 1 in. in diam? What is the diameter of a conductor having a cross-sectional area of 500,000 cir mils?

(2-VI) What is the diameter of a conductor having a cross-sectional area of 1021 cir mils? What is the area in circular mils of a conductor 0.005 in. in diam?

(3-VI) What is the resistance of 1 mile of No. 4 hard-drawn copper wire (diam 0.204 in.)?

(4-VI) What is the resistance of a two-wire line, 20 miles in length, built of No. 8 Siemens-Martin steel wire (diam 0.129 in.)?

(5-VI) What is the resistance of a steel rail, 8.83 sq in. in cross section and 30 ft long?

(6-VI) What is the resistance of a bus bar, 82 ft long, ¼ by 4 in. cross section, of standard annealed copper?

(7-VI) What is the resistivity in microhm-meters of a material the resistivity of which is 3 microhm-cm? What is the resistivity in microhm-centimeters of a material that has a resistivity of 3 microhm-in.?

(8-VI) What is the resistivity in ohm-circular mils per foot of a material that has a resistivity of 3 microhm-cm?

(9-VI) What is the resistivity in microhm-meters of a material that has a resistivity of 40 ohm-cir mils per ft?

(10-VI) What is the percentage of conductivity of silver? of brass? of nichrome?

(11-VI) What is the resistance of a piece of copper wire of 101.8 per cent conductivity 1 mm in diam and 100 m long?

(12-VI) What is the resistance per mile of ASCR (aluminum steel core reinforced) made up of 1 steel strand 0.102 in. diam and 6 aluminum strands 0.102 in. diam? Assume the resistance of each aluminum strand to be increased by 2 per cent owing to spiral effect.

(13-VI) A copper wire bar, 0.875 in. diam and 60 ft long, is hard-drawn into No. 14 copper wire (diam 0.064 in.). What is the resistance of the wire?

(14-VI) What should be the diameter of the steel core of a No. 0 (0.325 in. diam) copper-clad steel conductor in order for the conductivity to be 40 per cent?

(15-VI) What would be the percentage of conductivity of a copper-clad steel conductor of which the over-all diameter is 0.46 in. and the diameter of the steel core is 0.411 in.?

(16-VI) Show that the percentage of conductivity of a copper-clad steel conductor is given by

$$\%\sigma_0 = \frac{\%\sigma_s \%S}{100} + \frac{\%\sigma_c \%C}{100}, \tag{6.15}$$

where $\%\sigma_s$ = percentage of conductivity of steel;

$\%S$ = percentage of steel in make-up of conductor;

$\%\sigma_c$ = percentage of conductivity of copper;

$\%C$ = percentage of copper in make-up of conductor.

4. Variation of resistance with temperature. The resistance of any metal conductor increases with temperature. In the temperature interval from $-50°$ to $+200°$ C, the temperature-resistance graph is found to be so nearly a straight line that we may regard it as such with negligible error. This embraces the range of temperature at which electrical conductors (except heating elements) are required to operate, and in practical problems, we may conveniently make use of the straight-line graph in calculating changes of resistances with temperature. Let D and E (Figure 6.2) be points on the straight portion of the graph. If this line be projected back until it intersects the temperature axis at T_0, and perpendiculars be erected at T_1

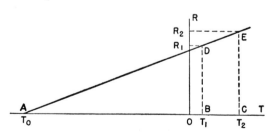

Fig. 6.2. Graph showing the resistance of a metal conductor as a function of temperature.

and T_2, similar triangles ABD and ACE will be formed. From geometry, we may set up the proportionality.

$$\frac{AB}{AC} = \frac{BD}{CE} \tag{6.16}$$

$$\frac{T_1 - T_0}{T_2 - T_0} = \frac{R_1}{R_2} \tag{6.17}$$

From this relation, it can be seen that if the resistance of a conductor is known at one temperature, it can be found at any other temperature, provided that T_0 is known and that both temperatures lie within the interval for which the graph is a straight line. The T intercept, T_0, may be found experimentally by measuring the resistance of a specimen of the conductor material at two different temperatures and plotting the graph, or substituting in (6.17). It need be determined but once for a given material; all T-R graphs for conductors of that material have the same T intercept regardless of their dimensions.

PROBLEMS

(17-VI) A specimen of standard annealed copper wire is found to have a resistance of 1 ohm at 20° C and 1.276 ohms at 90° C. Plot the graph and determine the T intercept.

(18-VI) A piece of standard annealed copper wire has a resistance of 12.5 ohms at 15° C. What will be its resistance at 31° C?

(19-VI) A coil of standard annealed copper wire having a resistance of 10 ohms at 20° C is imbedded in the core of a large transformer. After the transformer has been in operation several hours, the resistance of the temperature coil has become 11.08 ohms. What is its temperature?

It must be made plain that the T-R graph is not a straight line except within reasonable limits of temperature. One of the most interesting parts of the graph from the standpoint of theoretical physics is the interval just above absolute zero ($-273°$ C). As the specimen is cooled down, its resistance decreases consistently, until at a temperature a few degrees above absolute zero, there is a sharp break in the graph, and the resistance drops abruptly to zero. This phenomenon, known as **superconductivity,** is found in some metals, such as lead (at 7° C above absolute zero); not in others, such as gold.

5. Temperature coefficient of resistance. The slope of the T-R graph (Fig. 6.2) by analytic geometry is

$$m = \frac{R_2 - R_1}{T_2 - T_1}. \tag{6.18}$$

This slope has a physical significance, it being the change in resistance per degree change in temperature for a particular piece of wire. If the slope be divided by the resistance of the specimen at any particular temperature, we have the change of resistance per degree change in temperature per ohm.

$$\alpha_1 = \frac{\dfrac{R_2 - R_1}{T_2 - T_1}}{R_1}. \tag{6.19}$$

This quantity is called the **temperature coefficient of resistance** and is designated by the symbol α (alpha). It is obvious that the value obtained for alpha will depend upon the resistance by which the slope is divided, which in turn depends upon the temperature. In other words, the temperature coefficient is different for every temperature.

PROBLEMS

(20-VI) Calculate the temperature coefficient of resistance for standard annealed copper at 20° C, using the data from Problem 17-VI.

(21-VI) Calculate the value of α_{90} for standard annealed copper, using data from Problem 17-VI. Calculate α_0, α_{55}, and α_{100}. *Suggestion:* First use Equation (6.17) to find the resistance at each temperature.

Equation (6.19) may be put into the form

$$R_2 = R_1[1 + \alpha_1(T_2 - T_1)], \tag{6.20}$$

which is more convenient for solving problems. It can be seen that if the resistance of a conductor is known to be R_1 at temperature T_1, its resistance at any other temperature, T_2, may be found, provided α_1 is known. Or, more generally, if any three of the quantities, R_1, R_2, T_1, and T_2 are known, the other can be found provided α_1 is known. It is important that all the quantities subscripted 1 must correspond. That is, if α_1 is the temperature coefficient at 20° C, then T_1 must be 20° C, and R_1 must be the resistance at 20° C.

Example: A brass conductor has a resistance of 50 ohms at 20° C. What would be its resistance at 0° C?

SOLUTION: From Table IV, the temperature coefficient of brass is 0.0017 at 20° C. Substituting in (6.20),

$$R_0 = R_{20}[1 + \alpha_{20}(0 - 20)]$$
$$= 50[1 + 0.0017(0 - 20)] = 48.3 \text{ ohms.}$$

It is sometimes necessary to start with the resistance of a conductor at a given temperature, and find resistance at some new temperature when the only temperature coefficient available corresponds to a third temperature.

In such cases, we may calculate a new value for temperature coefficient, using the relation

$$\alpha_2 = \frac{\alpha_1}{1 + \alpha_1(T_2 - T_1)}, \tag{6.21}$$

and then proceed to use Equation (6.20). An alternate method would be to make use of the relation

$$\alpha_1 = \frac{1}{T_0 + T_1} \tag{6.22}$$

to find the T intercept of the temperature-resistance graph, and then use Equation (6.17).

Example: A brass conductor has a resistance of 50 ohms at $0°$ C. What would be its resistance at $50°$ C?

SOLUTION 1: The resistance-temperature coefficient corresponding to $0°$ C may be found from Equation (6.21), using the value 0.0017 at $20°$ C taken from Table IV,

$$\alpha_0 = \frac{0.0017}{1 + 0.0017(0 - 20)} = 0.00176.$$

Then, from (6.20),

$$R_{50} = R_0[1 + \alpha_0(50 - 0)]$$
$$= 50[1 + 0.00176(50 - 0)]$$
$$= 54.4 \text{ ohms.}$$

SOLUTION 2: The T intercept for brass may be found from Equation (6.22),

$$0.0017 = \frac{1}{T_0 + 20},$$
$$T_0 = 568.$$

Then, from (6.17),

$$\frac{568 + 0}{568 + 50} = \frac{50}{R_{50}},$$
$$R_{50} = 54.4 \text{ ohms.}$$

Most pure metals have positive temperature coefficients ranging from 0.003 to 0.006 at $20°$ C. Alloys in general show much smaller values, and carbon has a negative temperature coefficient (its resistance decreases with increasing temperature). The temperature coefficients for several materials are to be found in Table IV.

PROBLEMS

(22-VI) The resistance of an aluminum conductor is 150 ohms at 20° C. What will its resistance be at 75° C?

(23-VI) The resistance of a steel cable is 80 ohms at 50° C. What will its resistance be at 20° C?

(24-VI) The resistance of a hard-drawn copper conductor is 1.48 ohms at 70° C. What will be its resistance at 40° C?

(25-VI) The resistance of a railroad track is 0.031 ohm per mile at 80° F. What will be its resistance at 0° F?

(26-VI) The resistance of a silver conductor is 3.5 ohms at 130° F. What will be its resistance at 150° F?

(27-VI) Show that

$$\alpha_2 = \frac{\alpha_1}{1 + \alpha_1(T_2 - T_1)}.$$ (6.21)

(28-VI) Show that

$$\alpha_1 = \frac{1}{T_0 + T_1}.$$ (6.22)

6. Other factors affecting resistance. It is found that the resistance of a metal conductor varies slightly with pressure, some metals showing an increase in resistance with increasing pressure, others a decrease in resistance. One element, selenium, shows a change in resistance with illumination, the resistivity being quite large in the dark and decreasing as the intensity of the light is increased. This property of selenium was at one time regarded as possibly having some important practical applications, as for light-sensitive relays, and for measuring light intensity. Photoelectric cells have proved superior for these purposes, however, and selenium is little used.

The boundary surface formed between a layer of selenium and a layer of iron, or between a layer of copper and a layer of copper oxide, has the property of offering much greater resistance to current in one direction than in the other. This is an example of the class of conductors known as *unilateral*, as distinguished from *bilateral* conductors which offer the same resistance in either direction. This property is the basis of the selenium-iron and the copper-oxide rectifiers which are being employed in a wide variety of applications.

7. Commercial wire sizes. The most commonly used conductor material in the electrical industry is copper. Copper conductors may be obtained in sizes running from less than 10 cir mils up to 2,000,000 cir mils cross-sectional area. Certain standard sizes are most often used, though conductors not of standard size are produced for special jobs, such as the winding of armatures. Some standard sizes are designated by gage numbers, the system used in the United States being known as AWG (American Wire Gage) or B&S (Brown & Sharpe). This system originally included forty sizes, numbered from 0000 (the largest) with a diameter of 0.46 in., to 36 (the smallest) with a diameter of 0.005 in. The diameters of the intermediate gage numbers were to form a geometrical progression, and since there were 39 intervals, this fixed the ratio of the diameter of one size to the diameter of the next as

$$\sqrt[39]{\frac{0.46}{0.005}} = \sqrt[39]{92} = 1.123.$$

The system has since been extended to take in gage numbers 37 to 40, the diameters of these sizes being determined according to the ratio indicated above. If the resistivity of the copper is known, we may calculate the resistance per unit length for wire of any specified gage number, but for convenience, the results of such calculations for standard annealed copper wire are made available in **wire tables.** Table V gives data on some commonly used sizes. Complete tables may be found in any electrical handbook.

Table V. COPPER-WIRE DATA

AWG Number	Area (cir mils)	Resistance* (ohms/1000 ft)	Weight** (lb/1000 ft)	Allowable Current†
0000	212,000	0.0490	640	358
000	168,000	0.0618	508	310
00	133,000	0.0779	402	267
0	106,000	0.0983	319	230
1	83,700	0.124	253	196
2	66,400	0.156	201	170
3	52,600	0.197	159	146
4	41,700	0.248	126	125
5	33,100	0.313	100	110
6	26,300	0.395	79.5	94
8	16,500	0.628	50	69
10	10,400	0.999	31.4	50
12	6,530	1.59	19.8	37
14	4,110	2.52	12.4	29
16	2,580	4.01	7.82	
18	1,620	6.38	4.92	
20	1,020	10.1	3.09	
24	404	25.7	1.22	
28	160	64.9	0.484	
32	63.2	164	0.191	
36	25	415	0.0759	
40	9.89	1049	0.0299	

*Std annealed copper at 20° C.
**Bare copper.
†National Electric Code figures for Type RH insulation in open air.

Larger conductors than No. 0000 are specified by area, certain sizes such as 250,000 cir mil, 300,000 cir mil, and so forth being standard. The larger sizes are usually stranded for convenience in handling, the number of strands and the cross section of the strands being selected to give the required total cross-sectional area.

Electrical conductors other than copper are also made in AWG sizes, with the exception of iron and steel wires, which are measured by Birmingham wire-gage numbers. Tables for other materials may be found in handbooks and in manufacturers' literature.

8. Heating of conductors. In any conductor that carries current, we have seen that electrical energy is being converted into heat energy at a rate equal to I^2R watts. The effect of this conversion is a tendency to raise the temperature of the conductor, and any increase in the temperature of the conductor results in the increased transfer of heat from the conductor to its surroundings. Sometimes, as in electrical heating appliances, this transfer of heat from the conductor to its surroundings is exactly the purpose of the installation. In most instances, however, such as electric wiring and the windings of electrical machinery, heating is an undesirable but unavoidable consequence of having the current. In any case, the size of the conductor must be so selected that the rate of heat production will not cause an excessive rise in its temperature.

What constitutes an excessive temperature rise naturally depends on the purpose for which the conductor is used and on what its surroundings are. Bare wire mounted in open air on mica insulators might safely be operated at a temperature of 600° C, or at any temperature at which the rate of oxidation of the wire does not proceed too rapidly. Insulated wire in the windings of a machine or in a building, however, could never be operated at any such temperature because the material used as insulation would be destroyed. Good practice requires that the temperature of such conductors never exceed 90° to 130° C, depending on the material used as insulation.

Let us consider further what happens when heat is produced in a current-carrying conductor. Assuming that the conductor is at room temperature to begin with, it is not able to transfer any heat to its surroundings either by conduction, convection, or radiation, and, consequently, heat is stored in the conductor at the same rate as it is being produced (I^2R). Temperature rise is an inevitable consequence of heat storage, and the temperature of the conductor begins to go up.

Now, as soon as the temperature of the conductor exceeds the temperature of its surroundings, heat transfer begins. At first the rate of transfer is small because it is a function of temperature difference. Small temperature difference means small rate of heat transfer. Most of the heat produced continues to be stored and the temperature continues to rise. But the greater the temperature difference between the conductor and its surroundings becomes, the greater becomes the rate of heat transfer. The greater the rate of heat transfer, the smaller is the rate of heat storage (assuming the rate of heat production is constant), and the less rapid is the temperature rise. Finally a temperature will be reached where the conductor will be able to transfer heat at the same rate at which heat is produced, and heat storage and temperature rise cease. This is called **steady-state temperature.** As we have seen, one of the most important problems before the designer of electrical apparatus or wiring is to be sure the steady-state temperature does not exceed the safe temperature for the grade of insulation used.

The determination of steady-state temperature by theoretical calculations is not a simple matter. In fact, it is so difficult that it is seldom undertaken in practice, except in the simplest cases. In a multilayer coil, for example, heat has to be conducted to the surface through successive layers of copper and insulation, and dissipated from the surface to the surrounding air by conduction, convection, and radiation. The inner layer of the coil will reach a higher equilibrium temperature than the second layer, which will reach a higher temperature than the third layer, and so forth. Obviously, the temperature of the inner layer will be the determining factor in the design of the coil, and this temperature is not readily calculated from theory. Designers make considerable use of accumulated test data, and new designs are constructed and tested to find out whether the steady-state temperature is within the safe limits.

Assuming that a given design gives too high a steady-state temperature, there are several things that may be done. First, we may substitute a grade of insulation that will stand higher temperature — that is, enameled wire in place of cotton-covered wire in a coil, or asbestos-insulated wire for rubber-covered wire in a building. Second, we may seek some means of increasing the rate of heat transfer away from the conductor, such as redesigning a coil so as to have more surface area exposed to the air, or using a blower to force air over the coil at a greater rate. Third, we may select a conductor of larger cross section and, therefore, of less resistance, so that the I^2R loss will be less.

In designing wiring for a building, the National Electric Code must be consulted. This Code, which has the force of law in most localities, specifies the allowable current in conductors of all sizes permitted in wiring installations, for various methods of installation, and for the different grades of insulation available. The Code is based on test data, and aims to limit the heating of conductors so that in no case will the steady-state temperature exceed the value at which deterioration of the insulation begins. Some data on allowable currents are given in Table V.

Example: A circuit in a certain wiring installation must carry a current of 65 amp. What wire size is required by the National Electric Code?

SOLUTION: Assuming that the circuit is not in conduit, and that Type RH insulation is used, Table V shows the allowable current for No. 8 is 69 amp, and it would, therefore, be suitable. If the wiring is to be installed in conduit or if another type of insulation is to be used, reference must be had to the complete tables given in electrical handbooks, or in the Code itself.

For rheostats, resistors, and so forth, it is common practice to give the device a watt rating according to the rate (determined by test) at which it can dissipate heat without exceeding a safe temperature. The user must then assure himself that the device is never installed in a circuit where the I^2R loss will exceed the watt rating.

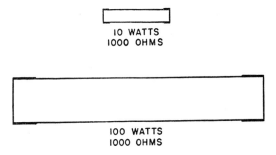

IO WATTS
1000 OHMS

100 WATTS
1000 OHMS

Fig. 6.3. Relative sizes of 10-watt and 100-watt resistors.

Example: A 500-ohm resistor is required in a circuit where it will carry a current of 15 ma. What should be the watt rating of the resistor?

SOLUTION:

$$P = I^2R = (0.015)^2 \times 500 = 1.125 \text{ w}.$$

A 2-w resistor is the nearest commercial size which will answer the purpose.

PROBLEMS

(**29-VI**) What wire size is required in a wiring installation (open wiring Type RH insulation) for a current of 25 amp? 90 amp? 200 amp?

(**30-VI**) Consult the tables in an electrical handbook to determine the effect on allowable current of placing wires in conduit. By what percentage is the allowable current decreased? Explain.

(**31-VI**) Consult the tables in an electrical handbook to determine the allowable currents for various types of insulation for a given size of wire, say No. 4. Explain.

(**32-VI**) Consult an electrical handbook, catalogue, or display board for information on standard watt ratings of resistors. List the standard ratings. How does a 1-w, 1000-ohm resistor differ from a 100-w, 1000-ohm resistor as regards size? As regards cost? Explain.

(33-VI) It is desired to insert 1000 ohms resistance in a circuit which is to carry a current of 0.2 amp. There are available a number of 10-w, 1000-ohm resistors. What combination of these resistors would serve the purpose?

(34-VI) A D'Arsonval type instrument having a resistance of 5 ohms and requiring 10 ma for full-scale deflection is to be adapted for use as a 0 to 500-range voltmeter. What must be the watt rating of the series resistor used?

(35-VI) A D'Arsonval type instrument having a resistance of 5 ohms and requiring 10 ma for full-scale deflection is to be adapted for use as a 0 to 500-range ammeter. What must be the watt rating of the resistor used as a shunt?

(36-VI) The tubular-type rheostats used in the electrical engineering laboratories are 10 in. long and 2 in. in diam. Assume these rheostats can dissipate 7 w per sq in. of winding surface and still remain at safe temperature, and that they are wound with bare Advance alloy wire with the turns in contact. What would be the resistance and ampere rating of a rheostat wound with No. 28 AWG?

(37-VI) Using the data furnished in Problem 36-VI, find the proper size of wire for a 50-ohm rheostat. What would its ampere rating be?

9. Current density. For some purposes, the current per unit cross-sectional area has more significance than the current itself. This quantity, called **current density,** is defined by the equation

$$J = \frac{I}{A},$$ (6.23)

where J is average current density, I is current, and A is cross-sectional area of the conductor. In the mks system, I is measured in amperes and A in square meters, making the unit of current density the **ampere per square meter.** Since practical conductors are never as large as 1 sq m in cross section, the mks unit is not convenient in size, and current density is more often expressed in amperes per square centimeter or amperes per square inch.

The maximum current density which may be used in a given conductor depends, of course, on the purpose for which the conductor is used, on whether it is insulated, and, if so, upon the material used for insulation. In coils and in the windings of electrical machinery, such as motors, generators, and transformers, current densities are usually from 1000 to 2500 amp per sq in. In electric wiring, current densities range from less than 1000 amp per sq in. in large conductors to as high as 10,000 amp per sq in. in No. 14, the smallest size permitted. In electric heating elements and in the filaments of incandescent lamps, current densities may sometimes be as great as 2×10^5 amp per sq in.

In conductors which carry alternating current, the current density is not uniform over the cross-sectional area of the conductor, but is greatest in the elements nearest the surface, and least in an element at the center. This phenomenon is known as **skin effect.** It is negligible at power frequencies, except in large conductors. At radio frequencies and ultra high frequencies, it becomes such an important factor that the resistance of a hollow tube may be not much greater than that of a solid conductor of the same diameter. This is the basis for the statement often heard that current flows along the surface of the conductor. As seen from the foregoing, the statement is not generally correct.

PROBLEM

(38-VI) Determine the maximum current density allowed by the National Electric Code for each wire size listed in Table V. How does the maximum allowable current density vary with cross-sectional area? Explain.

STUDY QUESTIONS

1. Of what would each of the following be a unit: (a) mho-ft per circular mil; (b) feet per ohm-circular mil; (c) ohm-inches; (d) (feet)^2 per mho-circular mil?

2. What would be the T intercept of the extended straight part of the T-R graph for Advance alloy? (See Table IV.) What does this imply as to the shape of the lower part of the graph?

3. From the data given in Table IV, select the material that would be best suited for making shunts for ammeters and series resistances for voltmeters. State the reasons for your choice.

4. Aluminum conductors are extensively used for transmission lines, but practically not at all for wiring installations and windings. By comparing the physical properties of copper and aluminum and their current market prices, can you justify the practice?

5. Does it seem likely that the efficiency of electrical apparatus and wiring installations may be improved by the discovery of a new low-resistivity conductor material? Why?

6. Since the ratio of the diameter of a copper wire to the diameter of the next gage number is 1.123, the ratio of the cross-sectional areas (and therefore of the weights and resistances) will be $(1.123)^2 = 1.26$. The ratio of the areas, weights, and resistances will be $(1.26)^2 = 1.59$ for the next gage number but one, and it will be $(1.26)^3 = 2$ for the third gage number. If these numbers be memorized, together with the data on one particular wire size, say No. 10, as a starting point, the entire wire table or any portion of it can readily be constructed. For instance, No. 13, the third gage number from No. 10, would have half the cross-sectional area, half the weight, and twice the resistance of No. 10 (5200 circular mils, 15.7 lb per 1000 ft, and 2 ohms, approximately). Without consulting the wire table, compute the approximate: (a) cross section of No. 16; (b) weight of No. 11; (c) resistance of No. 8; (d) cross section of No. 4; (e) weight of No. 27; (f) resistance of No. 0.

7. The cross-sectional area of No. 4 copper wire is about 10 times that of No. 14, but the allowable current (for Type RH insulation) is only about four times as much. Why is this?

8. Which would be the larger (as regards space occupied), a 1000-ohm, 10-w resistor or a 1-ohm, 50-w resistor? Why?

9. The average temperature rise of a coil is determined by measuring the increase in its resistance after several hours of operation, and is found to be within the limits regarded as safe for the type of insulation used. Is this sufficient assurance that the coil will not be damaged by over-heating? Explain.

10. In making a "heat-run" on an electrical machine it is operated, usually at rated output, until its temperature becomes steady. The temperature rises fairly rapidly during the first hour or two, then less rapidly until at the last the machine may have to be operated several hours during which the rise is almost imperceptible. Explain.

11. The power loss in a certain conductor carrying 10 amp direct current is measured and found to be 100 w. The loss in the same conductor when carrying 10 amp alternating current is measured as 115 w. What is one factor that might account for the difference? (Several factors may actually be involved.)

12. For which feeders and branches in a wiring installation would it be the heating rather than the voltage drop which determined the minimum wire size?

Chapter **VII**

MAGNETIC CONCEPTS
AND UNITS

---

1. Magnetic fields. Any region in space in which a current-carrying conductor is acted upon by a force is said to be a **magnetic field.** An extensive magnetic field is found surrounding the earth itself. It is not a particularly strong field by comparison with some that have been produced by man, but it has strength enough to cause a measurable force on a delicately suspended current-carrying coil, or to line up the magnetic needle of a pocket compass. The magnetic fields with which we are concerned in electrical engineering are usually produced by (a) a current-carrying conductor, or coil, or (b) a permanent magnet. Both these means of producing fields have already been mentioned in describing electrical measuring instruments, the permanent magnet being an essential part of the D'Arsonval type, and the current-carrying coil, of the soft-iron and electrodynamometer types.

The action of a force on a current-carrying conductor in a magnetic field is in reality the same phenomenon that was described in Chapter II, and which served as our basis for defining unit current. Then we spoke of the force as acting between the two conductors directly. Now we regard one of the conductors as producing a magnetic field and the force as being caused by the interaction of this field and the second conductor. The magnetic field has been made an intermediate agency.

The magnetic field is of the general type referred to as **vector fields.** A vector field differs from a scalar field in that it has direction as well as magnitude. Any scalar field, such as temperature, can be completely described by giving a numerical value for each point in space throughout the region occupied by the field, but to describe completely a particular magnetic field it is necessary to specify for every point a numerical value (either field intensity or flux density), and a direction as well. The direction of a magnetic field at any point may be defined in terms of the orientation of a small current-carrying coil, so suspended that it is free to turn. Such a coil, known as an **exploring coil,** is shown in Fig. 7.1a, where it is being used to determine the direction of the field at various points in the vicinity of a straight vertical conductor that carries current. If we send current through the suspended coil, one of its sides will be attracted and the other

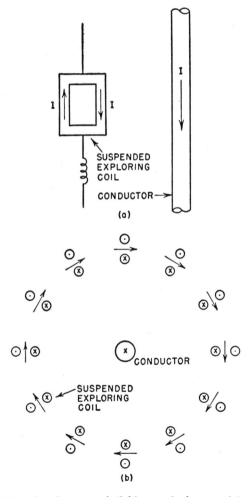

Fig. 7.1. Mapping the magnetic field around a long straight conductor by means of an exploring coil: (*a*) side view; (*b*) top view.

repelled by the conductor, and the coil will take up a position such that the conductor lies in the plane of the coil. *The positive direction of the field is conventionally taken as perpendicular to the plane of the coil, and away from the observer when he faces the coil, so that the positive direction of the current in it appears clockwise to him.*

If we suspend the coil in a new position, it again aligns itself so that the conductor lies in its plane, and we may continue this procedure to investigate the direction of the field at any number of points required. For each point investigated, we may show the direction of the field on a plot or map by means of a small arrow, or **vector,** placed according to the definition above. A number of coil positions and the corresponding arrows are shown in Fig. 7.1*b*. It must be made clear, however, that the field is not confined to any one plane or to any finite distance from the conductor. As we investigate points at greater and greater distances, we find that our exploring coil is aligned with less and less force, until it becomes too insensitive to give any indication.

The suspended coil presents some difficulties in use. For one thing, it is difficult to conduct any considerable current into the coil and out, and still have it perfectly free to turn. Another objection is that it cannot be used if the direction of the field is not horizontal, or more precisely, it indicates only the horizontal component of the field. In practical field mapping, it is much more convenient to use magnetic needles mounted so that they can be used in either horizontal or vertical positions. It is readily demonstrated that the north-seeking end of the needle points in the direction of the field as defined above, and thus the needle may take the place of the coil.

Fundamentally, the suspended-coil method and the magnetic-needle method are the same. The needle may be regarded as containing concealed currents which account for its behavior in exactly the same way as the basic principle of forces of attraction and repulsion between current-carrying conductors accounts for the way in which the suspended coil orients itself.

2. The right-hand rule. The exploring coil and the compass needle enable us, by the rules laid down in the preceding section, to determine the direction of a magnetic field, irrespective of how the field is produced. If the field is produced by a conductor or coil in which the direction of the current is known, the direction of the field can be readily found by the following rule: *Grasp the conductor with the right hand so that the thumb points in the positive direction of the current. The fingers then encircle the wire in the positive direction of the magnetic field.*

This rule can readily be verified by applying it to the conductor shown in Fig. 7.1*b*. The rule works both ways — that is, we may use it to determine which direction current must flow in the conductor to produce a field in a given direction. In applying the rule to a coil, it is easier to let the fingers of the right hand encircle the turns in the direction of current. The thumb then points in the direction of the field inside the coil.

3. Magnetic flux lines. In seeking for a relation between electricity and magnetism, Faraday, in 1831, wound two coils of insulated wire upon an iron ring. One of these coils he connected to a battery, including in the circuit a key for opening and closing it, as shown in Fig. 7.2. The other coil

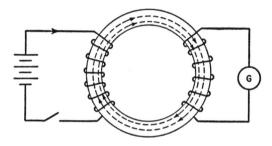

Fig. 7.2. Induction of electromotive force by changing current in a neighboring circuit.

he connected to a galvanometer. When he closed the battery key, he noted a momentary deflection of the galvanometer, which proved that current flowed in that circuit. Upon opening the key, a deflection in the opposite direction resulted. To explain this phenomenon, Faraday made use of what are called **magnetic lines of flux.** When any conductor or coil carries current, we may consider to exist in and around it, and interlinked with it, a number of these magnetic lines of flux. They may also interlink with any other coil or conductor in the region. So long as the current in the first coil remains unchanged, the number of lines is constant, and no effect is produced. But any change in the current in the first coil results in a change in the number of lines, and an emf is set up in the second coil.

Obviously, what we are dealing with here is another aspect of the magnetic field. We first described the field in terms of the forces which act upon current-carrying conductors introduced into it. We are now describing the field in terms of something we call *magnetic lines of flux*, which, when they change in number, are able to induce an emf in a coil or conductor with which they are interlinked.

The direction of the lines of flux is at any point the same as the direction of the field as defined in Section 1. Thus, if we use the exploring coil or magnetic needle to determine field direction at a large number of points, *being careful always to move the coil or needle in the indicated direction of the field,* and marking down an arrow to represent the field direction at each point, we may draw in the lines of flux as smooth lines which coincide at each point with the direction arrows. In the case of a toroidal coil, this procedure would yield circles parallel to the axis of the toroid, as indicated by the dotted lines in Fig. 7.2. In general, magnetic flux lines are closed lines, having no beginning and no end.

The lines, of course, are purely imaginary; they do not exist in the sense that a line on the blackboard exists. Yet there are few, if any, concepts that are more useful. In working with the problems of magnetism, we soon fall into the habit of referring to the lines as though they were real and as if they were the true underlying cause of forces on current-carrying conductors and emf's induced in coils. No harm is likely to come of this habit, and the concept greatly helps in clarifying our thinking, speaking, and writing about magnetic fields.

4. Magnetic flux density. The forces which act upon the sides of the exploring coil, or upon any current-carrying conductor in a magnetic field, depend upon a characteristic of the field called **magnetic flux density.** If the conductor is placed perpendicular to the magnetic lines, we can define magnetic flux density by the equation

$$F = BLI, \tag{7.1}$$

where F is force in newtons;
  B is magnetic flux density in mks units;
  L is length of conductor in meters;
  I is current in amperes.

Rewriting Equation (7.1) as

$$B = \frac{F}{LI}, \tag{7.2}$$

it is obvious that one name for the unit of flux density would be the newton per ampere-meter. For reasons that will presently appear it is called, instead, the **weber per square meter.**

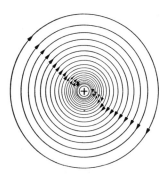

Fig. 7.3. Magnetic lines around a current-carrying conductor.

To get a better conception of what magnetic flux density is, we may think of the lines of magnetic flux which surround a long straight wire carrying current. These are concentric circles about the wire as a center, and we may think of the lines as being highly concentrated in the immediate vicinity of the conductor, becoming less so as the distance from the conductor becomes greater (Fig. 7.3). There are less lines per unit area (measured in a plane perpendicular to the lines), and thus the flux density is less.

Based upon the defining Equation (7.1),

we can word a definition as follows: *The flux density in a magnetic field is* 1 *weber per square meter when a straight conductor* 1 *meter lon⁻, carrying a current of* 1 *ampere and placed perpendicular to the magnetic lines, experiences a force of* 1 *newton.*

5. Forces between current-carrying conductors — permeability. The forces which act between current-carrying conductors (Chapter II) depend not only upon the length and spacing of the conductors and upon the currents which they carry, but also upon the medium in which they are situated. It will be recalled that in the definition of the ampere it was specified that the conductors lie "in free space." Had they been in air, or almost any other substance, the force which repelled or attracted them would have been very slightly different. Had they been separated and surrounded by iron or any of the metals or alloys known as ferromagnetic, the force would have been many times as great. The property of space and air and iron which influences the force between current-carrying conductors is called **permeability.**

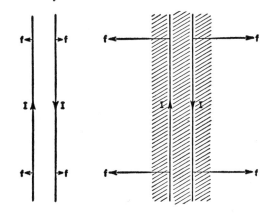

Fig. 7.4. Electromagnetic forces in space and in iron.

Taking into account the medium in which the conductors lie, we can now write a more general equation for the forces between long parallel conductors which carry current:

$$F = \frac{\mu L I_1 I_2}{2\pi S},\qquad(7.3)$$

where F is force in newtons;
  μ (mu) is permeability of the medium in mks units;
    L is parallel length of the conductors in meters;
    I_1 is current in the first conductor in amperes;
    I_2 is current in the second conductor in amperes;
    S is the separation of the conductors in meters.

The value assigned to the permeability of free space in the mks system is $4\pi \times 10^{-7}$. The name of the unit is the henry per meter, which at this point can have very little meaning to the student.

When the value $4\pi \times 10^{-7}$ is substituted for μ in Equation (7.3) we have

$$F = \frac{(2 \times 10^{-7})LI_1I_2}{S},$$

which will be recognized as Equation (2.1) which served as the defining equation for current.

Other substances have permeabilities greater or less than free space, according to whether the forces between current-carrying conductors increase or decrease when immersed in the substance. The permeabilities of most substances differ so little from the permeability of free space that the value $4\pi \times 10^{-7}$ can be used with but little error. The steel used in transformers and electrical machinery may have permeabilities as high as 10^4 times the permeability of free space, and for some alloys used for special purposes this figure may be as high as 10^6.

The symbol for permeability is the Greek letter mu (μ), and for free space the symbol is followed by a subscript zero (μ_0). It is often convenient to express the **relative permeability** (μ_R) of a substance as the ratio of its absolute permeability to the permeability of free space:

$$\mu_R = \frac{\mu}{\mu_0} = \frac{\mu}{4\pi \times 10^{-7}}. \tag{7.4}$$

The absolute permeability of a substance which has a relative permeability μ_R is therefore

$$\mu = \mu_R\mu_0. \tag{7.5}$$

In all calculations involving permeability it is the absolute value which must be used.

6. The Biot-Savart law — flux density due to a long straight current-carrying conductor. Consider a long straight conductor carrying a current I_1, which establishes a magnetic field in which the flux density at a distance of S meters from the axis of the conductor is B webers per sq m. Parallel to the first conductor at a distance of S meters is a second conductor carrying a current I_2. Let us suppose that the medium surrounding these conductors has a permeability μ, and let us consider a section L meters long. By Equation (7.1) the force acting on the second conductor (and the reaction on the first conductor) is

$$F = BLI_2 \text{ newtons.}$$

By Equation (7.3), the force of repulsion (attraction) between the two conductors is

$$F = \frac{\mu L I_1 I_2}{2\pi S} \text{ newtons.}$$

Equating these two expressions and solving for B,

$$BLI_2 = \frac{\mu L I_1 I_2}{2\pi S}. \tag{7.6}$$

$$B = \frac{\mu I_1}{2\pi S} \text{ webers per sq m.} \tag{7.7}$$

This expresses in equation form a relationship known as the **Biot-Savart law.** By use of this law we are able to calculate the magnetic flux density at any specified distance from a long straight current-carrying conductor.

We now have two ways of calculating the forces between current-carrying conductors provided they are straight and that their length is great compared with their distance apart. We may use Equation (7.3) to calculate the force directly. As an alternative method, we may use Equation (7.7) to determine the flux density due to the current in the first conductor and then use Equation (7.1) to find the force upon the second conductor.

7. Ampère's law — magnetic field intensity. A magnetic field can be described by specifying, for certain points in the field, its direction and the magnetic flux density. How many points are necessary depends upon the extent and complexity of the field. In uniform fields one point may suffice; in other instances we need equations that relate the flux density to the coordinates of the point in some way.

Flux density, as we have seen, depends upon the medium in which the current-carrying conductors are situated and in which the field exists. For the field established in the vicinity of a long straight conductor we showed that

$$B = \frac{\mu I}{2\pi S} \text{ webers per sq m.} \tag{7.7}$$

We shall now define another concept, called **magnetic field intensity,** in terms of which we may describe a field. This concept may be defined by the equation

$$B = \mu H, \tag{7.8}$$

where B is flux density in webers per sq m;
$\quad \mu$ is permeability in mks units;
$\quad H$ is magnetic field intensity in mks units.

Substituting (7.8) in (7.7) we have

$$H = \frac{I}{2\pi S} \tag{7.9}$$

for the magnetic field intensity in the vicinity of a long straight wire. Since H is a current divided by a length, it can be seen at once that the unit is the ampere per meter.*

Since magnetic field intensity is related to magnetic flux density in a very simple manner, it makes little difference which is calculated first. If we can find the equation for magnetic field intensity in a certain region, we can get magnetic flux density at once by simply multiplying by permeability. Let us therefore develop an equation by which magnetic field intensity can be calculated from a knowledge of the geometry of the conductors which establish the field.

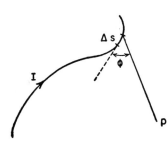

Fig. 7.5. The magnetic field intensity at the point p is found by summing up the effect of every segment ΔS of the current-carrying conductor.

A general method that is applicable whenever the field is produced by an arrangement of current-carrying conductors, and when the field lies entirely in one medium (for example, in free space), depends upon the use of certain assumptions made by Ampère and proved by him to be valid. We begin by dividing the conductor into short segments each of length ΔS (Fig. 7.5). Then we may assume that at any specified point p there will be a magnetic field intensity ΔH due to the current in a particular segment, and further that

ΔH is proportional to the current I in the segment;

ΔH is proportional to ΔS, the length of the segment;

ΔH is inversely proportional to the square of X, the distance from the segment to the point;

ΔH is proportional to the sine of the angle ϕ made with the segment by a line joining the segment to the point.

Combining these proportionalities we obtain

$$\Delta H \quad \text{is proportional to} \quad \frac{I\,\Delta S\,\sin\,\phi}{X^2}, \tag{7.10}$$

or, introducing a proportionality constant,

$$\Delta H = \frac{KI\,\Delta S\,\sin\,\phi}{X^2}. \tag{7.11}$$

*More generally, the unit is the ampere-turn per meter. Since number of turns is dimensionless, amperes per meter and ampere-turns per meter are the same so far as dimensions are concerned.

In the rationalized mks system of units used in this book, the value to be assigned to K is $1/4\pi$. Thus,

$$\Delta H = \frac{I\,\Delta S\,\sin\phi}{4\pi X^2}. \qquad (7.12)$$

In order to find the magnetic field intensity at the specified point, it is then necessary to sum up the ΔH's for every segment of the conductor which contributes to the field:

$$H = \sum_{0}^{S} \frac{I\,\Delta S\,\sin\phi}{4\pi X^2}. \qquad (7.13)$$

The above expression for magnetic field intensity is often referred to as **Ampère's law.**

Example: It is required to find the magnetic field intensity at a point 5 cm distant from the midpoint of a straight wire 20 cm long and carrying a current of 10 amp. As an approximation, let us divide the wire into ten equal segments and find ΔH at the point caused by each segment (Fig. 7.6).

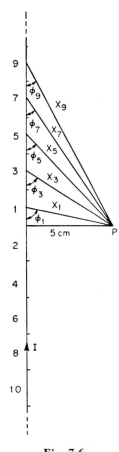

SOLUTION: The distance from the segment to the point will be measured from the middle of the segment. Thus, for segment 1

$$X_1^2 = (1^2 + 5^2)10^{-4} = 0.0026,$$

$$\phi_1 = \tan^{-1}\frac{5}{1} = 78.6°,$$

$$\sin\phi_1 = 0.98,$$

$$\Delta H_1 = \frac{(10)(0.02)(0.98)}{4\pi(0.0026)} = 6.01 \text{ amp per meter.}$$

The direction of the vector is found by the right-hand rule to be perpendicularly into the paper at point P. The contribution of segment 1 is exactly matched by the contribution of segment 2 on the other side of the midpoint. The calculations for segments 1, 3, 5, 7, and 9 are tabulated below:

Segment	X^2	ϕ	$\sin\phi$	H
1	0.0026	78.6°	0.98	6.01
3	0.0034	59.1°	0.858	4.02
5	0.005	45°	0.707	2.25
7	0.0074	35.5°	0.581	1.25
9	0.0106	29.1°	0.485	0.72

Fig. 7.6

Taking into account the contributions of segments 2, 4, 6, 8, and 10, we next find the summation of ΔH as:

$$H = \Sigma \, \Delta H = 2(6.01 + 4.02 + 2.25 + 1.25 + 0.72) = 28.5 \text{ amp per m.}$$

In the above example we were able to add the ΔH's directly because they are all in the same direction at the point P. This will be true only in cases where the point at which H is being calculated lies in the same plane as do the conductors. It is also important to remember that the method used is an approximation. A better approximation could have been made by dividing the wire into 20 segments, a still better approximation by using 40 segments, and so forth. The more segments we use the more laborious the solution becomes, and it remains an approximation. However, it is not practicable to make rigorous mathematical solutions in any except the simplest problems, and the method of approximation illustrated above is often the only one that can be used.

PROBLEMS

(1-VII) What is the magnetic flux density in free space at a distance of 10 cm from a long straight conductor carrying a current of 25 amp?

(2-VII) What is the magnetic flux density in a material having a relative permeability of 1240 if the magnetic field intensity is 5000 ampere-turns per meter?

(3-VII) What is the relative permeability of a material in which (a) a magnetic flux density of 1 weber per sq m corresponds to a magnetic field intensity of 400 ampere-turns per m? (b) a magnetic flux density of 0.5 weber per sq m corresponds to a magnetic field flux density of 5000 ampere-turns per m? (c) a magnetic flux density of 0.875 weber per sq m corresponds to a magnetic field intensity of 35 ampere-turns per in.?

(4–VII) The magnetic field intensity is to be found at a point 1 meter distant from the midpoint of a long straight wire carrying a current of 100 amp. As a first approximation, consider the conductor to be divided into 1-meter segments and compute ΔH for each of the four segments nearest the point. Measure the distance from the midpoint of the segment. Then take the summation, and compare with the magnetic field intensity calculated by Equation (7.9). Is the difference what you might expect? Why?

(5-VII) Compute the magnetic field intensity at a point 1 meter distant from the midpoint of a long straight wire carrying a current of 100 amp by the procedure explained in Problem 4-VII, but taking into consideration the eight 1-meter segments of wire nearest the point. Is this a better approximation than that in Problem 4-VII?

(6-VII) Compute the magnetic field intensity at a point 1 meter distant from the midpoint of a long straight wire carrying a current of 100 amp by the procedure explained in Problem 4-VII, but consider the conductor to be divided into ½-meter segments and take the summation of the 16 segments nearest the point. Is this a better approximation than that in Problem 5-VII?

8. Calculation of magnetic field intensities. If ΔS is allowed to approach zero, the summation in Equation (7.13) becomes the definite integral

$$H = \int_{S_1}^{S_2} \frac{I \sin \phi \, dS.}{4\pi x^2} \qquad (7.14)$$

In problems where S is the only variable, or where ϕ and x are also variables and it is possible to express two of these quantities in terms of the third, it may be possible to evaluate the integral in Equation (7.14) to determine magnetic field intensity.

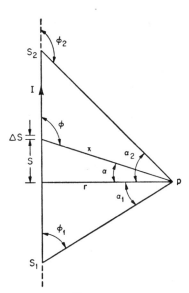

Let us now consider a straight conductor carrying a current of I amperes (Fig. 7.7), and suppose we wish to find the magnetic field intensity at point P. From the geometry of the figure

$$S = r \tan \alpha. \qquad (7.15)$$

$$\frac{dS}{d\alpha} = r \sec^2 \alpha. \qquad (7.16)$$

$$x = r \sec \alpha. \qquad (7.17)$$

$$\phi = 90° + \alpha. \qquad (7.18)$$

$$\sin \phi = \sin (90° + \alpha) = \cos \alpha. \qquad (7.19)$$

Fig. 7.7

We are thus able to express S, x, and ϕ, all of which are variables, in terms of the angle α. We now substitute these expressions in Equation (7.14), and since the variable is now an angle, the limits of the integration must also be expressed as angles.

$$H = \frac{I}{4\pi} \int_{\alpha_1}^{\alpha_2} \frac{r \cos \alpha \sec^2 \alpha \, d\alpha}{r^2 \sec^2 \alpha}. \qquad (7.20)$$

$$H = \frac{I}{4\pi r} [\sin \alpha]_{\alpha_1}^{\alpha_2}. \qquad (7.21)$$

$$H = \frac{I}{4\pi r} (\sin \alpha_2 - \sin \alpha_1).* \qquad (7.22)$$

Equation (7.22) is valid for any point in the vicinity of a straight current-carrying conductor of any length. Obviously, in order to carry current, the conductor must be part of a circuit and attention must be given to the contributions to the magnetic field intensity of the other conductors which

---

*Note that $\sin \alpha_1$ is negative in Fig. 7.7.

are included in the circuit. If the straight conductor is very long and P is opposite the midpoint, the effect of the other parts of the circuit may be negligible. Thus, if $S_1 = S_2 = 10r$, $\sin \alpha_2 = (-\sin \alpha_1) \approx 1$, and the magnetic field intensity becomes

$$H = \frac{I}{2\pi r} \text{ amp per m.} \tag{7.23}$$

This is the same result as that obtained in Section 6 from the Biot-Savart law.

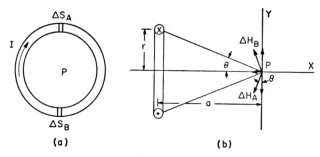

(a)   (b)

Fig. 7.8

In order to get a better understanding of magnetic field intensity as a vector quantity, let us calculate it for a point on the axis of a one-turn circular coil of radius r meters. Let the current in the coil be I amp and let the point be at a distance a meters from the plane of the coil as shown in Fig. 7.8. By use of Equation (7.12) the magnetic field intensity at point P due to the segment ΔS_A is

$$\Delta H_A = \frac{I \Delta S \sin 90°}{4\pi (r^2 + a^2)} = \frac{I \Delta S}{4\pi (r^2 + a^2)}. \tag{7.24}$$

Since ΔS_A is a very short segment it may be regarded as straight and perpendicular to a line joining it to point P. The distance from the segment to the point is $P = \sqrt{r^2 + a^2}$. The field intensity at point P due to segment ΔS_A is represented in Fig. 7.8b by the vector ΔH_A, the direction of which is tangent to a circle drawn through the point with the axis of ΔS_A as a center, and is related to the current direction by the right-hand rule. The angle between the vector and the y axis is

$$\theta = \tan^{-1} \frac{r}{a}. \tag{7.25}$$

In order to add the ΔH's due to the various segments it is convenient to resolve each ΔH into x and y components. Thus,

$$\Delta H_{Ax} = \Delta H_A \sin \theta. \tag{7.26}$$

$$\Delta H_{Ay} = \Delta H_A \cos \theta. \tag{7.27}$$

Now, diametrically opposite to ΔS_A is a segment ΔS_B which produces, at point P, a magnetic field intensity represented by the vector ΔH_B. It can be seen that the component ΔH_{By} of this vector is equal and opposite to ΔH_{Ay}, and therefore the two vectors add up to zero. Likewise, any segment of the conductor may be paired with an opposite segment, the y components of the magnetic field intensities of the two adding to zero in each case. Therefore the magnetic field intensity at point P has no y component and is directed to the left along the x axis, which is the axis of the coil.

We can now find the resultant field intensity by summing up the contributions of all the segments around the coil.

$$\Delta H_x = \Delta H_A \sin \theta = \frac{I\,\Delta S}{4\pi(r^2 + a^2)} \times \frac{r}{(r^2 + a^2)^{1/2}}. \tag{7.28}$$

$$\Delta H_x = \frac{Ir\,\Delta S}{4\pi(r^2 + a^2)^{3/2}}. \tag{7.29}$$

$$H_R = \sum_0^S \frac{Ir\,\Delta S}{4\pi(r^2 + a^2)^{3/2}}. \tag{7.30}$$

In the limit as ΔS approaches zero

$$H_R = \frac{Ir}{4\pi(r^2 + a^2)^{3/2}} \int_0^{2\pi r} ds = \frac{Ir}{4\pi(r^2 + a^2)^{3/2}}(2\pi r - 0). \tag{7.31}$$

$$H_R = \frac{2\pi r^2 I}{4\pi(r^2 + a^2)^{3/2}} = \frac{r^2 I}{2(r^2 + a^2)^{3/2}}$$

$$= \frac{I \sin^3 \theta}{2r} \text{ ampere-turns per m.} \tag{7.32}$$

For the special case of the point at the center of the coil $a = 0$ and

$$H = \frac{I}{2r} \text{ ampere-turns per m.} \tag{7.33}$$

For a concentrated coil of N turns, the result would be

$$H = \frac{NI}{2r} \text{ ampere-turns per m.} \tag{7.34}$$

Example 1: Calculate the correct value of the magnetic field intensity the approximate value of which was found in the example in Section 7.

SOLUTION: Refer to Fig. 7.8.

$$\phi_1 = \phi_2 = \tan^{-1} \frac{5}{10} = 26.57°,$$

$$\cos \phi_1 = -\cos \phi_2 = 0.894,$$

$$H = \frac{10}{4\pi(0.05)}(0.894 + 0.894) = 28.5 \text{ amp per m.}$$

Example 2: Find the magnetic field intensity at a point 1 meter distant from the midpoint of a very long wire carrying a current of 100 amp.

SOLUTION:

$$H = \frac{I}{2\pi r} = \frac{100}{2\pi(1)} = 15.9 \text{ amp per m.}$$

Example 3: Find the magnetic field intensity at the center of a concentrated circular coil of 100 turns, 50 cm in diameter and carrying a current of 1 amp.

SOLUTION:

$$H = \frac{NI}{2r} = \frac{100(1)}{2(0.25)} = 200 \text{ ampere-turns per m.}$$

PROBLEMS

(7-VII) A conductor is formed into a rectangular loop 50 cm by 50 cm and carries a current of 10 amp. Calculate the magnetic field intensity at a point in the center of the loop.

(8-VII) A conductor is formed into a rectangular loop 50 cm by 50 cm and carries a current of 10 amp. Calculate the magnetic field intensity at a point 10 cm in from the left-hand side and 10 cm up from the bottom of the loop.

(9-VII) A concentrated circular coil which has 50 turns and is 25 cm in diameter carries a current of 10 amp. Calculate the magnetic field intensity at a point on the axis of the coil and 40 cm from the plane of the coil. Note that the H vectors in this case do not coincide and will have to be resolved into components before they can be added.

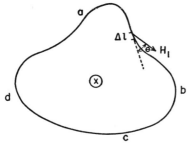

Fig. 7.9. The summation of $H \cos \theta \, \Delta l$ around the closed path a–b–c–d is equal to the number of ampere-turns linked by the path.

9. The circuital form of Ampère's law — magnetomotive force. In general, magnetic field intensity is a vector quantity which varies from point to point, both in direction and in magnitude. Consider a path a-b-c-d (Fig. 7.9) arbitrarily drawn in a magnetic field. At every point on the path, there will be a magnetic field intensity which can be represented by a vector such as H_1 in the figure. Now suppose the path to be divided up into short segments Δl so short that, for the accuracy desired, H may be considered the same in magnitude and direction all along a segment. Let us then form products by multiplying the length of each segment by the component of H that lies along the segment. One such product, for example, would be $H_1 \cos \theta_1 \, \Delta l$, where θ_1 is the angle made by H_1 with the segment Δl. There would be a similar product for each segment. Now let us sum up all of the products around the path and equate this to the number of ampere turns which happen to be linked by the path.

$$\sum_0^L H \cos \theta \, \Delta l = NI. \qquad (7.35)$$

As Δl approaches zero the summation becomes the definite integral

$$\oint H \cos \theta \, dl = NI. \qquad (7.36)$$

The symbol $\oint$ denotes that the integration is to be around the closed path.

To illustrate this relationship, choose for the path a circle of radius r meters, concentric about a long straight conductor, which carries a current of I amperes. By Equation (7.9) the magnetic field intensity at any point along the path is then

$$H = \frac{I}{2\pi r}.$$

Since the direction of the field is tangent to the circle at every point, it will always coincide with Δl, and $\cos \theta$ will be unity. The product $H \cos \theta \, \Delta l$ thus becomes

$$\frac{I}{2\pi r} \Delta l. \qquad (7.37)$$

These products must be summed up all the way around the path, the length of which is $L = 2\pi r$.

As Δl approaches zero, the summation becomes the definite integral

$$\oint H \cos \theta \, dl = \int_0^{2\pi r} \frac{I}{2\pi r} \, dl = I. \qquad (7.38)$$

In case the path links N conductors, each carrying a current of I amperes, the equivalent current is NI amperes, and (7.38) becomes

$$\oint H \cos \theta \, dl = NI. \qquad (7.39)$$

The summation of the products $H \cos \theta \, dl$ around a closed path

$$\oint H \cos \theta \, dl \qquad (7.40)$$

is called **magnetomotive force,** and Equation (7.39) tells us that it is equal to the product of current times turns linked by the path. The unit of magnetomotive force is therefore the ampere-turn.

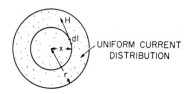

Fig. 7.10

Example 1: A long straight conductor of radius r meters carries a current of I amperes. The current density is assumed to be uniform over the cross section of the conductor. It is required to find the magnetic field intensity of a point within the conductor, x meters from the center.

SOLUTION: Draw a circle of radius x with the axis of the conductor as a center (Fig. 7.10). Because of the symmetry of the field, the magnetic field intensity at every point on this circle is the same. Its direction is tangent to the circle at any point. Let us take the circle as a path, and apply the circuital law —Equation (7.38). The path is linked by a single turn, carrying a current which is

$$\frac{\pi x^2}{\pi r^2} I. \tag{7.41}$$

Application of the law therefore gives

$$\int_0^{2\pi x} H \, dl = \frac{\pi x^2}{\pi r^2} I, \tag{7.42}$$

$$2\pi x H = \frac{x^2}{r^2} I, \tag{7.43}$$

$$H = \frac{x}{2\pi r^2} I. \tag{7.44}$$

Example 2: A uniformly wound toroidal coil (Fig. 7.11) has N turns and carries a current of I amperes. The toroid has a mean radius of R meters. It is required to find the magnetic field intensity at a point on the axis of the toroid.

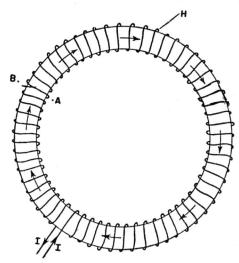

Fig. 7.11. The magnetic field produced by a toroidal coil.

SOLUTION: The magnetic field in a toroid is tangent to the axis. This can be seen by imagining a magnetic needle or an exploring coil to be placed inside the winding. From the symmetry of the winding it can be seen that the magnetic field intensity is the same at every point along the axis. If we take the axis as a path and apply the circuital law, we have

$$\int_0^{2\pi R} H\, dl = NI, \tag{7.45}$$

$$H = \frac{NI}{2\pi R}. \tag{7.46}$$

In this instance the magnetic field intensity is simply the magnetomotive force NI per unit length of path.

PROBLEMS

(**10-VII**) For a long straight conductor 1 cm in diameter and carrying a current of 75 amp. calculate the magnetic field intensity at points from 0 to 10 cm distant from the axis of the conductor. Plot H against distance.

(**11-VII**) A long straight tubular conductor has an inside diameter of 1 in. and an outside diameter of 1.4 in. Calculate the magnetic field intensity at a point (a) 0.4 in. from the axis, and (b) 0.6 in. from the axis when the current is 50 amp.

(**12-VII**) A uniformly wound toroid of circular cross section has a mean diameter of 0.6 m and a cross-sectional diameter of 0.1 m. There are 750 turns carrying a current of 2 amp. Calculate the magnetic field intensity on the axis of the toroid. Also calculate the maximum and the minimum field intensity at any point within the toroid, and the per cent by which these differ from the value on the axis.

10. Magnetic flux — the weber. Magnetic flux density, like magnetic field intensity, is a vector quantity which may vary from point to point, both in direction and in magnitude. Consider a surface a-b-c-d, Fig. 7.12, which lies in a magnetic field and which is penetrated by the lines of magnetic flux. At every point there will be a magnetic flux density which can be represented by a vector such as B. The direction of the vector is the direction of the field at that point, and its length is proportional to the flux density.

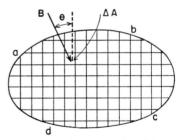

Fig. 7.12. The summation of $B \cos \theta\, \Delta A$ over the surface is equal to the total flux penetrating the surface.

Now suppose the surface to be divided into small areas ΔA, so small that the flux density may be considered as being uniform over ΔA. Then suppose we form products such as $B \cos \theta\, \Delta A$ by multiplying the area by the component of flux density perpendicular to the area, and finally that we sum up all the products over the specified surface and equate this to the flux ϕ which penetrates the surface.

$$\sum_{0}^{A} B \cos \theta \, \Delta A = \phi. \tag{7.47}$$

As ΔA is allowed to approach zero, the summation in Equation (7.47) becomes the definite integral

$$\int_{0}^{A} B \cos \theta \, dA = \phi. \tag{7.48}$$

This equation will serve as the defining equation of **magnetic flux.** *If the products of magnetic flux density with elements of area are taken as described above and summed up over any specified surface, the summation is equal to the magnetic flux penetrating the surface.*

Since magnetic flux density is measured in webers per sq m., it follows that the mks unit of magnetic flux is the weber.

Example 1: Owing to the earth's magnetism, the flux density at a certain place on its surface is 6×10^{-5} weber per sq m, and the magnetic lines make an angle of 30° with the vertical. What magnetic flux will link a circular coil 50 cm in diameter placed horizontally in this locality?

SOLUTION: The flux density being constant over the area of the coil, Equation (7.48) reduces to

$$AB \cos \theta = \phi,$$

$$A = \frac{\pi (0.5)^2}{4} = 0.196 \text{ sq m},$$

$$\cos \theta = \cos 30° = 0.866,$$

$$\phi = (0.196)(6 \times 10^{-5})(0.866) = 1.02 \times 10^{-5} \text{ weber}.$$

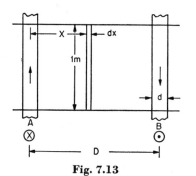

Fig. 7.13

Example 2: The parallel conductors of a two-wire transmission line are d m in diameter and are spaced D m apart (center to center). When the current in the line is I amperes, how much magnetic flux per meter of line passes between the conductors?

SOLUTION: Refer to Fig. 7.13 and let distances be measured to the right from the center of conductor A. At a distance x the magnetic field intensity due to conductor A is found, by use of Equation (7.9), to be

$$H_A = \frac{I}{2\pi x}. \tag{7.49}$$

The H_A vector is directed downward at a point on a line joining the two conductors. The H_B vector is also directed downward at this point and has a value

$$H_B = \frac{I}{2\pi(D - x)}.$$ (7.50)

Since H_A and H_B coincide, they may be added directly to get

$$H_R = \frac{I}{2\pi}\left[\frac{1}{x} + \frac{1}{(D - x)}\right].$$ (7.51)

Assuming the lines to be in free space or air, the flux density is given by Equation (7.8) as

$$B_R = \frac{\mu_0 I}{2\pi}\left[\frac{1}{x} + \frac{1}{(D - x)}\right].$$ (7.52)

B_R is directed downward as H_R.

The elemental flux passing downward through a rectangle 1 m long and Δx m wide in the plane of the two wires is

$$\Delta\phi = B_R\,\Delta x = \frac{\mu_0 I}{2\pi}\left[\frac{\Delta x}{x} + \frac{\Delta x}{(D - x)}\right].$$ (7.53)

The flux passing between the conductors can now be found by summing up $\Delta\phi$ from the surface of conductor A $(x = d/2)$ to the surface of conductor B $(x = D - d/2)$.

$$\phi = \frac{\mu_0 I}{2\pi}\sum_{d/2}^{D-d/2}\frac{\Delta x}{x} + \frac{\Delta x}{(D - x)}.$$ (7.54)

As Δx approaches zero, the summation becomes the definite integral

$$\phi = \frac{\mu_0 I}{2\pi}\int_{d/2}^{D-d/2}\frac{dx}{x} + \frac{dx}{(D - x)}.$$ (7.55)

The evaluation of the integral in Equation (7.55) gives

$$\phi = \frac{\mu_0 I}{2\pi}\left[\log_e x - \log_e (D - x)\right]_{d/2}^{D-d/2},$$ (7.56)

$$\phi = \frac{\mu_0 I}{2\pi}\left[\log_e\left(D - \frac{d}{2}\right) - \log_e\frac{d}{2} - \log_e\frac{d}{2} + \log_e\left(D - \frac{d}{2}\right)\right],$$ (7.57)

$$\phi = \frac{\mu_0 I}{\pi}\left[\log_e\frac{2D - d}{d}\right].$$ (7.58)

PROBLEMS

(13-VII) A rectangular exploring coil 1 in. by 2 in. is placed in a uniform magnetic field in which the flux density is 0.01 weber per sq m. Calculate the magnetic flux linking the coil (a) when the magnetic field is perpendicular to the face of the coil; (b) when the magnetic field makes an angle of 15 degrees with the face of the coil.

Fig. 7.14

(14-VII) A uniformly wound toroid of circular cross section has an inside diameter of 50 cm and an outside diameter of 60 cm. There are 900 turns in the winding. Assume no ferromagnetic material is used and that the average flux density is equal to the flux density on the axis of the toroid. Calculate the magnetic flux linking the toroid when the winding carries a current of 5 amp.

(15-VII) A long straight wire 0.1 in. in diameter carries a current of 50 amp. Calculate the flux surrounding the wire per meter of length between its surface and the surface of an imaginary circular cylinder 10 in. in diameter and coaxial with the wire.

(16-VII) Four long parallel wires are arranged in vertical alignment as in Fig. 7.14. The two upper wires carry a steady current of 15 amp with current directions as shown. Calculate the magnetic flux passing between the two lower wires per meter of line.

11. Magnetic flux linking a toroidal coil. From the symmetry of the windings it is obvious that the magnetic field in a uniformly wound toroidal coil (Fig. 7.11) is directed along the axis and has the same intensity at every point on the axis. The magnetic field intensity on the axis can be calculated by use of the circuital law, as in Example 2 of Section 9, and is found to be

$$H = \frac{NI}{2\pi R}. \tag{7.59}$$

For points not on the axis of the toroid, the magnetic field intensity can also be calculated by the circuital law, but the value of R will be more or less than for points on the axis, depending upon whether the point is toward the outer circumference or toward the inner circumference from the axis. The magnetic field intensity will therefore vary from a minimum value just inside the winding at the outer circumference to a maximum value just inside the winding at the inner circumference. It can be seen that the average magnetic field intensity is approximately the same as the magnetic field intensity at the axis.

Knowing the magnetic field intensity at specified points within the winding, we can find the magnetic flux density at these points by Equation (7.8) to be

$$B = \mu H = \frac{\mu N I}{2\pi R}. \tag{7.60}$$

If the space within the winding contains no ferromagnetic material, the permeability may be taken as μ_0, which is independent of field intensity or flux density. Therefore the flux density over a cross section of the toroid varies in exactly the same manner as the field intensity, being less on one side of the axis and more on the other. Since the average magnetic field intensity is approximately equal to the field intensity on the axis, the average flux density will be approximately equal to the flux density on the axis.

The total flux through any cross section of the toroid can be found by Equation (7.48)

$$\int_0^A B \cos \theta \, dA = \phi.$$

Since the flux density vector is perpendicular to the area, and since the average flux density is known, the flux becomes simply

$$\phi = BA,$$

$$\phi = \frac{\mu_0 NIA}{2\pi R} = \frac{\mu_0 NIA}{l} \text{ webers.} \tag{7.61}$$

Example: A uniformly wound toroid of circular cross section has an inside diameter of 40 cm and an outside diameter of 50 cm. There are 1500 turns in the winding. No ferromagnetic material is used. Calculate the flux linking the winding when the current is 2 amp.

SOLUTION: The mean length of path (along the axis) is

$$\frac{\pi \times 45}{4 \times 100} = 0.353 \text{ m.}$$

The average magnetic field intensity is

$$H = \frac{NI}{l} = \frac{1500 \times 2}{0.353} = 8500 \text{ ampere-turns per m.}$$

The average flux density is

$$B = \mu_0 H = (4\pi \times 10^{-7}) \times 8500 = 0.01068 \text{ weber per sq m.}$$

The cross-sectional area of the toroid is

$$\frac{\pi(0.05)^2}{4} = 0.001965 \text{ sq m.}$$

The flux linking the winding is

$$\phi = BA = (0.01068)(0.001965) = 2.1 \times 10^{-5} \text{ weber.}$$

The toroid affords a means of establishing a magnetic flux the magnitude of which can be calculated with reasonable accuracy, and which may be used as a standard for the calibration of flux-measuring devices. A long solenoid (i.e., a long straight tube, uniformly wound) can be shown to be linked at its mid-section by a flux calculated by Equation (7.61). (In this case l is the length of the solenoid, not the length of the mean flux path as in the toroid.) Since a solenoid is much easier to construct than a toroid, it is more often used as a standard in flux measurements.

12. Measurement of magnetic flux. Faraday's discovery of electromagnetic induction led to the formulation of the law as follows: *Whenever the number of magnetic lines which link a coil undergoes a change, an electromotive force is induced in the coil proportional to the number of turns and to the time rate of change of lines.* Although the law was actually stated by Neumann several years after Faraday's discovery, it is usually referred to as **Faraday's law of electromagnetic induction.**

The law furnishes us with a convenient basis for measuring magnetic flux, or more precisely, for measuring changes in flux. If a coil of N turns is so arranged that it is linked by the unknown flux, which is then caused to change in some predetermined way, an emf will be induced in the coil. In equation form the law is

$$E = N \frac{\Delta\phi}{\Delta T}, \tag{7.62}$$

where E is average emf in volts;
    N is number of turns in the coil;
    $\Delta\phi$ is change in flux in webers;
    ΔT is time in seconds for the change in flux to take place.

An alternative definition of the unit of flux would be: *One weber is that flux which, if brought to zero in one second, will cause an average emf of one volt to be induced in a one-turn coil which is interlinked with the flux.*

It is not usually practicable to measure directly the emf induced in the coil nor the time required for the change in flux. Instead, use is made of a fluxmeter or a ballistic galvanometer which, connected to the terminals of the coil, gives a maximum indication proportional to the change of flux.

$$\Delta\phi = Kd, \tag{7.63}$$

where $\Delta\phi$ is change of flux in webers;
    d is maximum reading in scale divisions;
    K is a constant which depends upon the number of turns in the coil, upon resistance of the galvanometer circuit, and upon the design of the galvanometer itself.

The galvanometer constant is determined experimentally by observing the deflection which occurs when a known change takes place in the flux which links a secondary winding placed upon an accurately constructed toroidal coil or solenoid (Section 11). An arrangement for determining the

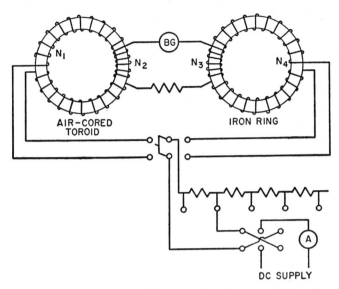

Fig. 7.15. Laboratory set-up for measuring the magnetic flux in an iron ring.

galvanometer constant and for measuring an unknown flux in an iron ring is shown in Fig. 7.15.

In order to determine the galvanometer constant, the dpdt switch is thrown to the left, and the current through N_1 is adjusted to any convenient value I_1. The flux established in the toroid and interlinked with N_2 can then be calculated by Equation (7.61),

$$\phi = \frac{\mu_0 N_1 I A}{l}.$$

The reversing switch is then operated, causing a change in flux from ϕ to $-\phi$; that is, a change $\Delta\phi = 2\phi$. This change in flux induces an emf in N_2, which sends current through the galvanometer circuit, resulting in a maximum deflection of d scale divisions. The constant of the galvanometer is then found by Equation (7.63),

$$K = \frac{\Delta\phi}{d}.$$

The dpdt switch is then thrown to the right, and the current through N_4 is adjusted to the desired value. The reversing switch is again operated, causing a change in flux, which induces an emf in N_3 and causes the galvanometer to be deflected. The observer reads the maximum swing, and having already determined the galvanometer constant, he is able to calculate the change in flux by Equation (7.63). If the flux in the iron ring has been put through several reversals before the reading is taken, it may usually be assumed to change from a certain value in one direction to an equal value in the opposite direction, and, on this assumption, may be taken as half the measured change.

The galvanometer constant is determined for a search coil of a certain number of turns (N_2), and for a certain circuit resistance R. A change in either of these quantities changes the constant. By connecting the secondary coils N_2 and N_3 permanently in series with the galvanometer, as in Fig. 7.15, constant circuit resistance is assured. Unless $N_3 = N_2$, however, the constant must be corrected for the difference in number of turns, using Equation 7.64.

Example 1: An air-cored toroid and an iron ring are connected as shown in Fig. 7.15. The toroid has a mean perimeter of 25 cm and a cross-sectional area of 5 sq cm. N_1 consists of 398 turns, N_2 and N_3 consist of 600 turns each. When a current of 5 amp is reversed in N_1, a deflection of 10 scale divisions is observed. When a current of 2 amp is reversed in N_4, a deflection of 140 scale divisions is observed. What is the galvanometer constant? What is the flux in the iron ring?

SOLUTION: From (7.61), the flux set up in the air-cored toroid is

$$\phi = \frac{\mu_0 N_1 I_1 A}{l} = \frac{(4\pi \times 10^{-7})(398)(5)(5 \times 10^{-4})}{(25 \times 10^{-2})} = 50 \times 10^{-7} \text{ weber.}$$

The change of flux, upon reversing the current, is

$$\Delta\phi = 2\phi = 100 \times 10^{-7} \text{ weber.}$$

The galvanometer constant is

$$K = \frac{\Delta\phi}{d} = \frac{100 \times 10^{-7}}{10} = 10 \times 10^{-7} \text{ weber per scale division.}$$

Since $N_3 = N_2$, the constant is the same when the change in flux occurs in the iron ring, and

$$\Delta\phi = Kd = (10 \times 10^{-7})(140) = 1400 \times 10^{-7} \text{ weber.}$$

Assuming that this change is from a certain value in one direction to an equal value in the other direction,

$$\phi = \frac{\Delta\phi}{2} = \frac{1400 \times 10^{-7}}{2} = 700 \times 10^{-7} \text{ weber.}$$

Had N_3 not been equal to N_2, the constant K would have to be corrected accordingly.

$$K \text{ corrected} = \frac{N_2}{N_3} K \text{ measured.} \tag{7.64}$$

That this is so can be seen from Faraday's law. Had N_2 been only 300 turns, the emf induced in it for $\Delta\phi = 100 \times 10^{-7}$ weber would have been half as much and the deflection half as much as observed above. Then K would have been found to be 20×10^{-7} weber per scale division. The correct value of K for $N_3 = 600$ turns would then be found by Equation (7.64).

A fluxmeter is essentially a ballistic galvanometer in which the restoring torque has been made as nearly zero as possible by suitably designing the leads by which connection to the moving coil is made. The moving coil will thus remain at rest in any position, and some means is usually provided for setting the indicator on zero before a reading is to be taken. The instrument is calibrated with a suitable search coil, and the scale is marked to read in webers or kilolines directly. The calibration is valid so long as the same search coil is used. Since there is no restoring torque it is not necessary to watch for a maximum deflection as with a ballistic galvanometer. The pointer comes to rest to indicate the change of flux linking the search coil. These features, and the portability of the fluxmeter, make it considerably more convenient to use than a ballistic galvanometer.

13. Magnetic units used in practice. The mks system of electrical and magnetic units has replaced the older cgs (centimeter-gram-second) system in most textbooks and electrical literature. However, in some calculations, particularly those for magnetic circuits (Section 15), the cgs electromagnetic unit of flux continues to be much used. This unit is the maxwell, or line, and for our purposes we can define it by the identity

$$1 \text{ maxwell} \equiv 1 \text{ line} \equiv 10^{-8} \text{ weber.} \qquad (7.65)$$

The kiloline (1000 lines) is also much used.

$$1 \text{ kiloline} \equiv 10^{-5} \text{ weber.} \qquad (7.66)$$

The cgs electromagnetic unit of flux density is the gauss (line per square centimeter), which is related to the mks unit by the identity.

$$1 \text{ gauss} \equiv 1 \text{ line per sq cm}$$
$$\equiv 10^{-4} \text{ weber per sq m.} \qquad (7.67)$$

In the United States, dimensions of apparatus are usually given in inches, and consequently flux density is often stated in lines per square inch or kilolines per square inch.

$$1 \text{ kiloline per sq in.} \equiv 0.0155 \text{ weber per sq m.} \qquad (7.68)$$

The cgs electromagnetic unit of magnetic field intensity is the oersted, or gilbert per centimeter.

$$1 \text{ oersted} \equiv 1 \text{ gilbert per cm}$$
$$\equiv 79.6 \text{ ampere-turns per m.} \qquad (7.69)$$

Since lengths are usually given in inches, magnetic field intensity can be more conveniently expressed in ampere-turns per inch than in ampere-turns per meter.

$$\text{1 ampere-turn per in.} \equiv 39.37 \text{ ampere-turns per m.} \qquad (7.70)$$

It is frequently necessary to find the magnetic field intensity in free space in ampere-turns per inch when the magnetic flux density in kilolines per square turns per inch is given. In mks units we have, by Equation (7.8),

$$B = \mu H.$$

From identities (7.68) and (7.70), the corresponding equations are

B (in webers per sq m) $= 0.0155\ B'$ (in kilolines per sq in.). $\qquad (7.71)$

H (in ampere-turns per m) $= 39.37\ H'$ (in ampere-turns per in.). $\qquad (7.72)$

Substituting (7.71) and (7.72) in (7.8) and putting $4\pi \times 10^{-7}$ for μ,

$$0.0155B' = (4\pi \times 10^{-7})\,39.37H',$$

$$B' = 0.00319H',$$

or $\qquad\qquad\qquad H' = 313B', \qquad\qquad\qquad\qquad (7.73)$

where H' is magnetic field intensity in ampere-turns per in.;
$\qquad B'$ is magnetic flux density in kilolines per sq in. (valid only in free space).

14. Energy of the magnetic field. The establishing of any magnetic field involves the storage of a definite amount of energy. This energy must necessarily come from the circuit containing the coil, or conductor, which establishes the field. If the field is in free space, all of the energy stored is recoverable, and is returned to the circuit when current ceases to flow and the field collapses. In general, however, some part of the energy is lost in

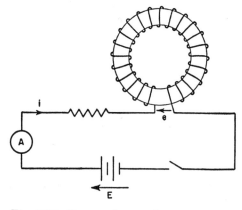

Fig. 7.16. Storage of energy in a magnetic field.

the medium, or substance, in which the field is established, and is not recoverable. The amount of energy stored in any magnetic field may be expressed in terms of the magnetic field intensity, the magnetic flux density, and the volume of the space occupied by the field. In working out this expression, we shall take advantage of the simplicity offered by the magnetic field of the toroid. If we close the switch in the circuit shown in Fig. 7.16, current will begin to flow, and the establishment of the magnetic field within the turns of the toroid will commence. As a result of the increasing number of magnetic lines, an emf,

$$E = N \frac{\Delta \phi}{\Delta T},$$
(7.62)

will be induced in the coil, according to Faraday's law. Now, it must be understood that this emf is induced only so long as the flux is increasing — which is to say, only so long as the current is increasing. It is a well-established fact that the current does not assume its steady-state value instantly upon closing the switch, but requires a definite length of time to increase from zero to the value finally indicated by the ammeter. How long a time is required depends upon the coil itself and upon the resistance included in the circuit; it may be only a few microseconds in the case of an air-cored coil with only a few turns, or several seconds for an iron-cored coil with many turns. But in any case, the emf persists as long as the current and the number of magnetic lines continue to increase. While this is going on, energy is being supplied to the coil at a rate

$$P = EI = N \frac{\Delta \phi}{\Delta T} I.$$
(7.74)*

But
$$\phi = BA$$
(7.48)

and
$$H = \frac{NI}{L},$$
(7.46)

from which
$$I = \frac{HL}{N}.$$

Substituting in (7.74),

$$P = N \frac{\Delta BA}{\Delta T} \left(\frac{HL}{N} \right)$$

$$= \frac{H \Delta B}{\Delta T} (AL).$$
(7.75)

The incremental amount of energy supplied during a time ΔT is

$$\Delta W = P \Delta T = H \Delta B (AL),$$
(7.76)

*It is assumed here that E and I are the average values of emf and current during the interval of time ΔT.

and the total energy that has to be supplied to establish a magnetic field of flux density B is the summation of all the incremental amounts of energy, beginning with B equal to zero, and continuing until B becomes equal to the desired value.

$$W = \Sigma H \, \Delta B (AL). \qquad (7.77)$$

But it can be seen that AL is simply the volume of the toroid; therefore, the energy per unit volume is

$$W = \Sigma H \, \Delta B. \qquad (7.78)*$$

The meaning of this expression can be made clear by referring to the graphical representation in Fig. 7.17. Here the flux density B is plotted against the magnetic field intensity H for a substance of constant permea-

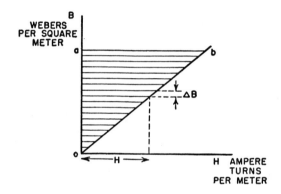

Fig. 7.17. Graphical representation of energy storage in a magnetic field.

bility, such as air. It can be seen that $H \, \Delta B$ is approximately the area of one of the strips of length H and width ΔB, and that the approximation becomes closer as ΔB is made smaller. $\Sigma H \, \Delta B$ is the total area of all such strips from $B = 0$ to $B = B$. Therefore, the stored energy can be found by determining the area oab in Fig. 7.17, taking into account the scale of H and the scale of B. Since this area is a triangle when the field is in air, its area is $\frac{1}{2} BH$, and the energy per unit volume is

$$W = \tfrac{1}{2} BH, \qquad (7.79)$$

or since

$$B = \mu_0 H, \qquad (7.80)$$

*As ΔB approaches zero the summation becomes the integral $\int H \, dB$. This expression is not particularly useful, because if permeability is constant, as in free space, the energy of the field can be calculated by (7.81) or (7.82). If permeability is not constant the integral is not readily evaluated, and it is simpler to use the summation for calculations.

$$W = \tfrac{1}{2} B^2/\mu_0 \qquad\qquad (7.81)$$

$$= \tfrac{1}{2} \mu_0 H^2, \qquad\qquad (7.82)$$

where B is the final value of the flux density in webers per square meter;

H is magnetic field intensity in ampere-turns per meter;

W is energy in joules per cubic meter.

It is important to recognize that Equation (7.78) is general and holds regardless of whether permeability is constant or not, whereas Equations (7.81) and (7.82) are useful only if the field was established in a medium of constant permeability.

PROBLEMS

(17-VII) Calculate the energy stored in the magnetic field of an air-cored toroid which has a mean diameter of 25 cm and a cross-sectional area of 5 sq cm when the winding of 800 turns carries a current of 2.5 amp. Assume that the field is confined to the space within the turns.

(18-VII) The air gaps of a six-pole dynamo are 0.275 in. long (in the direction of the magnetic lines) and the cross-sectional area under each pole is 100 sq in. Calculate the energy stored in the magnetic field in the air gaps when the flux density is 1.5 webers per sq m.

15. Reluctance and the magnetic circuit. When a magnetic field is practically confined to a definite region (as in the toroidal coil or in any instance where the path of the magnetic flux lines lies entirely in iron, or nearly so), we have what is called a **magnetic circuit.** This name was applied because of certain similarities between the establishment of magnetic flux lines in iron paths and the flow of current in electric circuits. These similarities are brought out in Fig. 7.18. In Fig. 7.18a, a battery having an

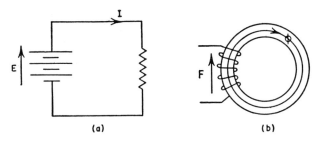

(a)   (b)

Fig. 7.18. Comparison of simple electric and magnetic circuits.

emf E causes a current I to flow around a circuit made up of conductors having a total resistance R. In Fig. 7.18b, a coil having an mmf F causes a magnetic flux ϕ to be established throughout a circuit consisting of an iron ring having a total **reluctance** $\mathcal{R}$. Reluctance is thus introduced as the magnetic equivalent of electrical resistance. No name has yet been assigned to the mks unit of reluctance, but the definition can be stated as follows: *A magnetic flux path has a reluctance of one mks unit if a magnetomotive force of one ampere-turn causes a flux of one weber.*

The defining equation is

$$\mathcal{R} = \frac{F}{\phi},\qquad(7.83)$$

where $\mathcal{R}$ is reluctance in mks units;
F is mmf in ampere-turns;
ϕ is magnetic flux in webers.

We may calculate the reluctance of a magnetic circuit from its dimensions and the permeability of the material, as will now be shown. From Equation (7.40).

$$F = HL,*$$

and from Equation (7.48),

$$\phi = BA.*$$

Substituting in (7.83),

$$\mathcal{R} = \frac{HL}{BA}.\qquad(7.84)$$

From Equation (7.8),

$$B = \mu H.$$

Substituting in (7.84),

$$\mathcal{R} = \frac{HL}{\mu HA} = \frac{L}{\mu A},\qquad(7.85)$$

where $\mathcal{R}$ is reluctance in mks units;
L is length of the magnetic circuit in meters;
μ is permeability of the material used, in mks units;

Equation (7.85) may be compared with Equation (6.7):

$$R = \frac{\rho L}{A},$$

which enables us to calculate the resistance of a conductor from its dimensions. Equation (7.83) is often called Ohm's law for magnetic circuits, from its similarity to the expression

$$R = \frac{V}{I}.\qquad(3.7)$$

*It is assumed here that the magnetic circuit is a uniformly wound iron ring.

This method of dealing with the magnetic field in certain instances as though it were a kind of circuit makes it possible for the student to understand and solve some of the most important magnetic problems. In general, the calculation of magnetic field intensities, even for simple conductor arrangements, is a formidable mathematical task, involving vectors in three-dimensional space. By making certain assumptions, which are not too far from true, we are often able to treat the field as though it were in one dimension only.

In some respects, however, the magnetic circuit is quite different from the electric circuit, and these differences should be understood. First, the magnetic circuit is not a circuit at all, in the sense that anything circulates around it. There is no magnetic particle comparable to the electron. The name magnetic flux implies *flow of something*, yet the magnetic lines, as has been pointed out, are purely imaginary.

The second difference to be pointed out lies in the available materials for constructing circuits. If it is desired to confine electric current to a certain path, it is readily done, because we have insulating materials that, as compared with the metals used for conductors, have practically zero conductivity. For low-voltage circuits, such as used in the laboratory, insulation presents so little difficulty that the student may well be unaware of the problem altogether. The task of confining magnetic lines to a certain path is not so easy. The permeability of most materials as compared with that of the best iron is by no means zero. As it is sometimes stated, there is no "magnetic insulator." Consequently, we must expect to find magnetic flux existing in paths other than the one which we wish it to take. It is this **leakage flux** about which assumptions must usually be made when setting up a magnetic-circuit problem.

A third difference is also attributable to the nature of magnetic materials as compared with those used for electric circuits. Metal wires, so long as their temperatures remain reasonably constant, have constant resistances. Since most circuits are constructed of metal wires, Ohm's law is applicable, and many calculations are made by use of it. Some circuits contain elements having variable resistances, and requiring special treatment, but these nonlinear circuits are the exception rather than the rule. Magnetic circuits, on the other hand, are built of iron or other ferromagnetic material of which the permeability is a function of flux density. The reluctance, in turn, depends upon permeability, and consequently can seldom be treated as a constant. The so-called "Ohm's law for the magnetic circuit," therefore, is by no means as useful as Ohm's law for the electric circuit. Magnetic circuits are nonlinear almost without exception, and require graphical or semigraphical treatment.

PROBLEMS

(19-VII) What is the reluctance of a magnetic circuit in which a mmf of 1525 ampere-turns establishes a flux of 0.083 weber?

(20-VII) What is the reluctance of an air gap in a magnetic circuit that is 0.1665 cm long and 5 sq cm in cross-sectional area?

(21-VII) An iron ring of rectangular cross section has an inside diameter of 6 in., an outside diameter of 8 in., and a thickness of 0.75 in. It is uniformly wound with a coil of 750 turns. When a current of 1.5 amp flows in the coil, a flux of 0.0002 weber is established. Calculate the mmf, the magnetic field intensity, the magnetic flux density, the reluctance, the permeability, and the relative permeability.

(22-VII) A toroidal coil of circular cross section is wound on a paper form and has an inside diameter of 12 in., an outside diameter of 15 in., and is wound with 1050 turns of wire. What flux will be set up in this coil by a current of 2 amp?

(23-VII) A 50-turn secondary coil is wound over the toroidal coil described in Problem 22-VII and connected in series with a 20,000-ohm resistance to a ballistic galvanometer. It is then found that reversing a current of 2 amp in the primary coil gives a deflection of 42 scale divisions. What is the galvanometer constant in webers per scale division? What precautions must be taken in using the galvanometer constant found by this procedure?

(24-VII) An air-cored toroid and an iron ring are connected as in Fig. 7.15 for taking magnetic data on the iron ring. The air-cored toroid has a mean diameter of 10 in. and a diameter of cross section of 1 in. The iron ring is rectangular in cross section, has an inside diameter of 6 in., an outside diameter of 8 in., and a thickness of $\frac{3}{4}$ in. The number of turns N_1 is 850, N_2 is 550, N_3 is 50, and N_4 is 1500. The resistance R is 20,000 ohms. Data are taken by the method of reversing the current and reading the deflection of the galvanometer, as described in Section 12. When a current of 4.5 amp is reversed in coil N_1, a deflection of 30 scale divisions is observed. When a current of 1.25 amp is reversed in coil N_4, a deflection of 210 scale divisions is observed. Calculate the magnetic field intensity in the ring in ampere-turns per in. Calculate the magnetic flux density in the ring in kilolines per sq in. By what number must the galvanometer deflection be multiplied to obtain flux density directly? Could this number be treated as a constant?

STUDY QUESTIONS

1. How would you obtain data for plotting a temperature field? Why is this a scalar and not a vector field?

2. How would you obtain data for plotting a gravitational field? Is it a scalar field or a vector field? Why?

3. Instead of the right-hand rule as stated in Section 2, many books state a "right-hand screw" relationship between current direction and direction of the magnetic field. What would the relationship be?

4. A toroidal coil is to be built for demonstrating the simplicity of the field as described in Section 11. A small magnetic needle is to be used to indicate field

direction and strength. What suggestions can you offer on how to design the coil (number of turns, spacing of turns, etc.)?

5. At Station A in an electrical laboratory a magnetic needle behaves in the normal manner, its north-seeking end pointing to the magnetic north. As the needle is moved toward station B, it begins to point east of the magnetic north and at Station B is violently deflected to point east. Make a sketch of the floor plan of the lab, showing the stations A and B and a hypothetical current-carrying conductor that would cause the needle to behave as outlined above.

6. Under what circumstances would magnetomotive force be numerically equal to the current producing it?

7. In a plane perpendicular to a long straight vertical wire carrying a current of $+I$ amp upward, a circle of radius R meters is drawn with the wire as the center. Sketch this arrangement as seen from above, and place a vector to indicate the magnetic field intensity at one point on the circle. Would you expect the magnetic field intensity at any other point on the circle to be the same in magnitude? In direction? If the summation of magnetic field intensity around the circle is taken according to Equation (7.36), what value must it have?

8. In a plane perpendicular to a long straight vertical wire carrying a current of $+I$ amp upward, a circle of radius R meters is drawn with its center $2R$ meters from the point where the wire intersects the plane. Sketch this arrangement as seen from above, and place a vector to indicate the magnetic field intensity at one point on the circle. Would you expect the magnetic field intensity at any other point on the circle to be the same in magnitude? In direction? If the summation of magnetic field intensity around the circle is taken according to Equation (7.36), what value must it have? How is this possible?

9. The magnetic field intensity at a point opposite the middle of a long straight current-carrying conductor is to be found by Ampere's law. Which segment of wire contributes the most? If the contribution of this segment is taken as 1.0, what would be the contribution of a segment 1 m further along the wire? Assume the point is 10 cm distant from the wire.

10. Could a ballistic galvanometer or a fluxmeter be correctly called a "volt-second meter"? What basis exists for this usage?

11. Interference with telephone and telegraph lines often results from alternating-current power lines running parallel to them and close by. Explain. Would there be interference from direct-current power lines carrying steady currents? Why?

12. Make sketches showing the flux lines in the vicinity of a long straight current-carrying conductor, both end-view and side-view. Indicate relative flux density by spacing of the flux lines. Indicate positive directions of flux lines and current. How far from the conductor do the flux lines extend?

13. Is it possible to have a flux density of 1 weber per sq m without having a total flux of 1 weber? Explain.

14. Permeability was introduced as that property of a substance which influences the force acting between current-carrying conductors placed in it. Later we find that permeability may also be regarded as that property of a substance. . . . Complete the statement.

15. Is any energy required to *maintain* a steady magnetic field after it is established? Explain.

16. A paramount principle in designing electrical machinery is to produce a given magnetic flux with as few ampere-turns as possible. What does this imply as to reluctance? How can this be brought about?

Chapter VIII

CHARACTERISTICS OF
FERROMAGNETIC MATERIALS

---

1. Magnetic properties of matter. The magnetic properties of most substances differ so little from the magnetic properties of free space that they are of no practical use in the construction of magnetic circuits. Substances generally may be classified as **diamagnetic,** having permeabilities slightly less than the permeability of free space, and **paramagnetic,** having permeabilities slightly greater than that of free space. Bismuth, silver, copper, and hydrogen, for example, are diamagnetic, but platinum, aluminum, and oxygen are paramagnetic. A few substances have permeabilities so much greater than free space that they are treated as a separate class, called **ferromagnetic.** The principal ferromagnetic element is iron. Iron and the various steels are used almost altogether in electrical machinery, though cobalt and nickel are also ferromagnetic, and various alloys containing these elements are used for special purposes.

The magnetic properties of substances are explained by supposing that there exist within the atoms themselves the equivalent of minute circuits in which currents flow. This theory was suggested by Ampère, long before anything was known of atomic structure, and it was necessarily vague as to the details until recent years. The present-day theory of atomic structure lends support to Ampère's theory of a hundred years ago. In addition to the magnetic effects of the electrons moving in their orbits about the nucleus of the atom (which would obviously be the equivalent of currents), the electrons themselves are believed to spin about their own axes, and thereby also to produce magnetic effects. The magnetic behavior of an atom of any particular element is then determined by the combined effects of all the orbital motions and all the electron spins within the atom. Since there is the possibility of the orbital motions or the spins having such senses and such orientations as to partially or wholly neutralize one another's effects, it is not surprising that atoms of various elements possess widely different magnetic properties. An atom in which the neutralization of all magnetic effects is complete would possess no **magnetic moment** — that is, no torque would act on such an atom to orient it in any particular way in a magnetic field. Magnetic moment is thus a measure of the extent to which atoms of any particular substance are magnetic.

In a paramagnetic substance, the atoms or molecules have small magnetic moments. If a paramagnetic substance is placed in a magnetic field, the atoms (or molecules in the case of a gas) are oriented just as small current-carrying loops would be. They then contribute their bit to the

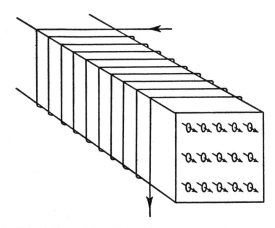

Fig. 8.1. Orientation of the atoms of a paramagnetic substance in a magnetic field.

effect of the current that sets up the field, and thus increase the flux density without any increase in magnetic field intensity. The permeability of the substance is, therefore, slightly greater than the permeability of space. It is not necessary that the entire atom change its angular position in the process of being oriented. Orientation can be accomplished by certain electron spins, or orbits, within the atom realigning themselves so that their magnetic effects coincide with the applied field.

If a diamagnetic substance is placed in a magnetic field, instead of the atoms being oriented so as to aid the field, the magnetic axis of each atom apparently takes up a precessional motion about the direction of the applied field, as the axis of a spinning top precesses about the vertical. Precession can be shown to have the same effect as would the realignment of the atoms in such a way as to oppose the applied field. There is, therefore, a decrease in flux density without any change in magnetic field intensity, and the permeability of the substance is slightly less than the permeability of space.

2. Theory of ferromagnetism. In ferromagnetic substances, the atoms, instead of acting independently, appear to be grouped magnetically into what are called **domains.** A domain may contain as many as 10^{15} atoms, and all of the atoms in a domain are believed to be so aligned that their magnetic effects are all in the same direction. The atoms are so inter- locked within the domain that the realignment of any must mean the realignment of all. A single, large magnetic moment is thus substituted for a larger number of small independent ones. At some temperature between 400° and 700° C, any specimen of iron or steel loses its ferromagnetic prop- erties. This is evidently due to the thermal agitation becoming so great that the regimentation of individual atomic magnetic moments into domains no longer exists. The temperature at which this occurs is called the **Curie point.**

Iron, like all metals, is crystalline in structure, the crystals being made up of atoms arranged geometrically in the space lattice. The arrangement in iron is cubic, with atoms at the corners of the cubes and at the centers, as shown in Fig. 8.2. This type of space lattice is known as **body-centered.** The normal direction of alignment of any particular domain is parallel to the edges of the cubes which make up the space lattice, in what is called, in

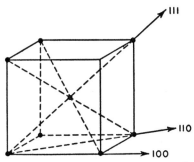

Fig. 8.2. Arrangement of the atoms in the space lattice of iron.

crystallography, a **100 direction.** Any diagonal of the faces of the cubes is a **110 direction,** and any diagonal of the cubes themselves is a **111 direc- tion.** The iron crystals are made up, in turn, of large numbers of domains. About one sixth of all the domains in a crystal have their magnetic axes aligned in each of the six possible 100 directions, so that the crystal as a whole has zero magnetic moment. Any ordinary specimen of iron consists of a large number of crystals, with no particular orientation of the space lattice of one relative to the space lattice of the next. It is possible, how- ever, to produce single crystals large enough to be tested magnetically, and much has been learned from the study of these crystals.

If a specimen of iron consisting of a single crystal is placed in a magnetic field so that the direction of the field coincides with one of the 100 directions of the crystal, part of the domains are already in alignment with the field, as shown in Fig. 8.3a. As the magnetic field intensity is increased, the remain-

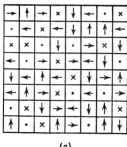

(a)

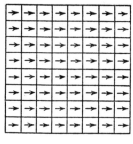

(b)

Fig. 8.3. Orientation of the domains in an iron cyrstal: (a) unmagnetized; (b) in a magnetic field.

der of the domains readily realign their magnetic axes to coincide with the particular 100 direction in which the field acts, as shown in Fig. 8.3b. The alignment of these domains gives rise to what is known as the **Barkhausen effect.** If a second coil is wound on the specimen of iron and connected to a suitable amplifier, which in turn operates a loud speaker, magnetization of the specimen is attended by a rapid succession of clicks, corresponding to the sudden orientation of domains from one of the 100 directions to another. It is believed, furthermore, that the domains which happen to be already in alignment gain slightly in size at the expense of neighboring domains when the field is applied. This is thought to be the explanation of the phenomenon known as **magnetostriction** — an actual change in the dimensions of a specimen of iron when it is magnetized.

Any 100 direction is referred to as an **easy axis** of magnetization. Domains will change readily from one 100 direction to another, but they are very reluctant to take up any in-between orientation. If magnetization of a single-crystal specimen is attempted in a 110 or a 111 direction, it is thus necessary for all the domains to realign themselves to directions that are not natural. They begin by changing to the 100 direction that is nearest to the direction of the field. Then gradually they allow themselves to be oriented closer and closer to the field direction. Complete alignment of all the domains necessitates the use of much greater magnetic field intensities than did the alignment in the easy direction. The 110 and 111 directions are, therefore, referred to as **difficult axes** of magnetization.

We are now in a better position to understand what happens when we undertake to magnetize an ordinary specimen of iron. The direction of magnetization makes little difference now because we are dealing with large aggregations of crystals the space lattices of which are oriented in every conceivable direction.* It is evident that, in any case, the flux density will be substantially increased by the contributions of the domains of the ferromagnetic material above what it would be in free space for the same field

*There is however, some difference in the magnetic properties of rolled steel, depending on whether magnetization is along the direction of rolling or across it. This is explained by differences in crystal orientation caused by the rolling.

intensity. The rate at which flux density increases with magnetic field intensity will vary widely with the material and with the field intensity itself, and we may now proceed to see how this relationship can best be expressed.

3. B-H curves. The relation of the magnetic flux density to the magnetic field intensity for any ferromagnetic material is nonlinear and is usually expressed graphically.* Such a graph, commonly called a *B-H* curve, is shown in Fig. 8.4. The curve rises rapidly at first owing to the

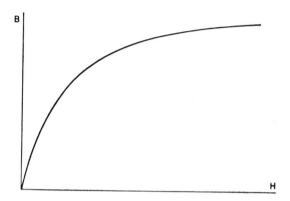

Fig. 8.4. *B-H* curve for a ferromagnetic substance.

alignment by relatively small magnetic field intensities of the domains in the more favorably oriented crystals. The gradual decrease in the slope of the curve is explained by the increasingly larger values of H required to orient the domains of crystals of which 110 or 111 axes lie in the direction of the field. The curve never becomes horizontal because B will always increase with increasing H, even in free space. When all the domains are oriented, the slope of the curve becomes constant at a value equal to μ_0, the permeability of free space. The condition known as **saturation** then prevails.

Flux density may thus be regarded in two different ways: (a) Consisting of two components, one due to the coil which sets up the magnetic field and equal to $\mu_0 H$; the other, called **intrinsic flux density,** owing to the domains of the magnetic material itself. (b) Equal simply to μH, where

*It is also possible to express the relation by an equation of the form

$$B = \frac{aH}{b + H},$$

where a and b are constants which have to be determined from data. This is known as Froelich's equation. Although it is of some interest to the student, it does not offer any saving in labor as compared with the graphical method when it comes to solving problems.

the permeability μ is a function of flux density. The second way is the simpler for engineering purposes and is more generally used. Unless stated to the contrary, the total flux density and not the intrinsic flux density is meant.

In using B-H curves for solving practical problems, the mks units for flux density and for field intensity are not particularly convenient. This is partly because, in the United States, we commonly express dimensions of apparatus in inches rather than meters. Accordingly, for the curves in this book, we shall take the units most commonly used in industry (H in ampere-turns per inch, B in kilolines per square inch). Curves for some commonly used materials appear on Appendix Fig. A.

4. Cyclic magnetization and hysteresis. If a specimen of any ferro-magnetic material be carried step by step through a complete cycle of magnetization and the flux density calculated for each step and plotted against the magnetic field intensity, a closed figure like that shown in Fig. 8.5 will result. The data for such a curve can readily be obtained by using an experimental set-up like that shown in Fig. 7.15. Beginning with the specimen carefully demagnetized, we start with the current at zero and

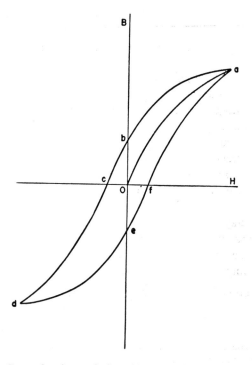

Fig. 8.5. Curve showing variation of B with H for cyclic magnetization.

increase it step by step, noting the deflection of the ballistic galvanometer caused by each increase, and calculating the corresponding change in flux density, which is plotted against magnetic field intensity. When maximum current is reached, the flux density and field intensity are those corresponding to point a, Fig. 8.5. The current is then reduced step by step and the resulting data plotted. It is seen that, instead of retracing the ascending curve, the points fall above it, and when H has been reduced to zero, B instead of being zero, as at the beginning, now has a value ob. This value is called the **residual flux density.**

The reversing switch is now thrown over, and the current again increased but in the opposite direction. The magnetic field intensity is, therefore, negative, and the value oc that will bring the flux density to zero is called **coercive force.** The increase of H in the negative direction is continued until a value equal to the previous maximum positive value is attained. This is point d. H is next reduced step by step to zero, corresponding to point e, at which point the reversing switch is again thrown to restore the current to its original direction. We are now beginning another cycle, but because the flux density starts from a negative value oe instead of zero as before, the original curve is not retraced, and the loop does not close at point a as shown. Upon each repetition of the cycle, the curve more nearly retraces the one before until a closed loop is obtained.

Cyclic magnetization occurs in electrical apparatus whenever a coil or conductor carries alternating current. The core of a transformer in service is being continually carried through the cycle of events just described, as is the iron adjacent to the windings of any a-c motor or generator. Cyclic magnetization also occurs in d-c motors and generators, owing to the rotation of the armature in the magnetic field set up by the stationary poles. A particle of iron in any given part of the armature is being magnetized, first in one direction, then in the opposite direction, as the armature rotates.

Residual flux density and coercive forces are peculiar to ferromagnetic materials. In all other substances, the descending B-H curve coincides with the ascending, zero flux density always corresponding to zero magnetic field intensity. The closed figure obtained when the magnetization of a ferromagnetic substance is carried through a complete cycle of magnetization is called a **hysteresis loop,** and the characteristic of a ferromagnetic material that gives rise to the loop is called **hysteresis.** Hysteresis is sometimes defined as the lag of flux density behind magnetic field intensity, but this definition must be qualified by stating that it is not a time lag. The residual flux density does not become zero after the passage of time, but only upon the application of a suitable coercive force.

5. Hysteresis loss. It was pointed out in Chapter VII that, in order to establish a magnetic field, a certain amount of energy has to be supplied.

If the field is in free space, this energy is stored, and it is returned to the circuit when the field collapses. If the field is wholly or partly in a ferromagnetic material, not all of the energy supplied can be returned, part of it having been converted into heat in the process of aligning the domains in the ferromagnetic substance. If the magnetization is carried through a complete cycle, the energy lost can be shown to be proportional to the area of the hysteresis loop. As the flux density is being changed from B_1, corresponding to the point e in Fig. 8.6, to B_2, corresponding to point a, the

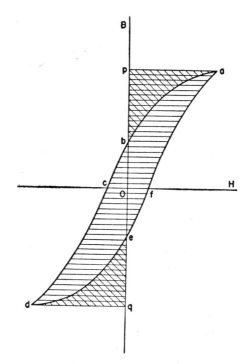

Fig. 8.6. Hysteresis loop.

amount of energy supplied, according to Equation (7.78), is

$$W_1 = \sum_{B_1}^{B_2} H \, \Delta B, \qquad (8.1)$$

which is represented (to scale) by the area $efapbo$ in Fig. 8.6. If H is ampere-turns per meter and B is webers per square meter, W will be in joules per cubic meter. As the flux density is changed from B_2, corresponding to point a, to B_3, corresponding to point b, the amount of energy returned to the circuit is

$$W_2 = \sum_{B_1}^{B_2} H \, \Delta B,$$ (8.2)

which is represented by the area apb. A net amount of energy $W_1 - W_2$, represented by the area $efabo$, has, therefore, been lost. In like manner, it can be shown that when the flux density is changed from B_3, corresponding to point b, to B_4, corresponding to point d, the energy supplied is

$$W_3 = \sum_{B_4}^{B_3} H \, \Delta B,$$ (8.3)

which is represented by the area $bcdqeo$, and that when the flux density is changed from B_4, corresponding to point d, to B_1, corresponding to point e, the energy returned is

$$W_4 = \sum_{B_4}^{B_1} H \, \Delta B,$$ (8.4)

which is represented by area dqe. A net amount of energy $W_3 - W_4$, represented by area $bcdeo$, has, therefore, been lost during this half cycle. Therefore, the energy lost per cycle is

$$W_T = (W_1 + W_2) + (W_3 - W_4) \text{ joules per cu m per cycle}, \quad (8.5)$$

which is represented to scale by the area $efabcd$, which is the area of the hysteresis loop. In determining the loss from area of the loop, the scales to which H and B are plotted must, of course, be taken into account.

Example: In order to determine the energy loss due to hysteresis in an iron ring, data are taken through a complete cycle of magnetization and plotted according to the following scales:

$H:$ 1 in. = 25 ampere-turns per in.

$B:$ 1 in. = 10 kilolines per sq in.

The area of the resulting loop is determined by means of a planimeter to be 5.6 sq in., and the volume of the ring is 50 cu in. What is the loss in joules per cycle?

SOLUTION: Changing to mks units, each inch represents

$H = 25 \times 39.37 = 985$ ampere-turns per m,

$B = 10 \times 10^{-5} \times (39.37)^2 = 0.155$ weber per sq m,

$$\text{Volume} = \frac{50}{(39.37)^3} = 0.00082 \text{ cu m},$$

$W = 5.6 \times 985 \times 0.155 \times 0.00082 = 0.7$ joule per cycle.

When placed in an alternating magnetic field, any specimen of iron or other ferromagnetic material will be carried repeatedly through the cycle of magnetization, and energy will be lost owing to hysteresis. Since the loss per cycle is a definite quantity at any particular maximum flux density, the power, which is the energy per unit time, will depend on the number of cycles per second through which the magnetization is carried. The power, or rate at which energy is lost, is called **hysteresis loss.**

The variation of hysteresis loss with flux density was studied by Steinmetz, who developed the empirical equation

$$P_h = K_h f B_m^x V, \tag{8.6}$$

where P_h is hysteresis loss in watts;

K_h is a constant which depends on the chemical analysis of the material and the heat treatment and mechanical treatment to which it has been subjected;

f is frequency in cycles per second;

B_m is maximum flux density in kilolines per square inch;

x is an exponent which depends on the material;

V is the volume of the material in cubic inches.

The constant K_h may be as low as 5×10^{-7} for permalloy and as large as 6×10^{-5} for cast iron. A typical value for electrical sheet steel is 4×10^{-6}.

The exponent x was determined by Steinmetz to be 1.6, and this value is found to hold fairly well for most materials at flux densities not exceeding 1 weber per sq m. For higher flux densities, however, the value of the exponent is not constant and may be as great at 2.5.

PROBLEMS

(**1-VIII**) A hysteresis loop is plotted according to the scales 1 cm = 5 ampere-turns per in. and 1 cm = 10 kilolines per sq in. The area of the resulting loop is found to be 25 sq cm, and the volume of the test specimen is 500 cu cm. Calculate the hysteresis loss for the specimen in joules per cycle.

(**2-VIII**) In order to determine the exponent in the empirical equation for hysteresis loss for a certain material, data for a loop are taken carrying the flux density to a maximum value of 50 kilolines per sq in. The resulting loop has an area of 3.21 sq in. Data for a second loop are then taken, carrying the flux density to a maximum value of 75 kilolines per sq in. The resulting loop has an area of 6.27 sq in. Calculate the exponent.

(**3-VIII**) The hysteresis loops in Problem 2-VIII were plotted to an H scale of 1 in. = 20 ampere-turns per in. and a B scale of 1 in. = 10 kilolines per sq in. Calculate K_h in the empirical equation for hysteresis loss.

(**4-VIII**) The hysteresis loss in the core of a certain transformer is known to be 37.5 w at a frequency of 60 cps and a flux density of 1 weber per sq m. If the frequency is decreased to 50 cps, and the flux density increased to 1.25 webers per sq m, find the new value of hysteresis loss. Assume a Steinmetz exponent of 1.9.

(5-VIII) The hysteresis loss in the core of a certain transformer is 7.17 w at a frequency of 400 cps and a flux density of 90 kilolines per sq in. To what value would the flux density have to be reduced to keep the loss the same when the frequency is increased to 500 cps? Assume the Steinmetz exponent to be 1.6.

6. Eddy currents and eddy-current loss. Whenever there is a change in the magnetic flux linking a coil, or a turn of wire, an emf is induced according to Faraday's law,

$$E = N \frac{\Delta \phi}{\Delta T}. \tag{7.62}$$

Electromotive forces are likewise induced in various paths in any piece of metal whenever there is a change in the flux that links them. As a consequence, currents known as **eddy currents** are caused to circulate in the metal. Eddy currents are not peculiar to ferromagnetic materials: they may occur in any conducting substance. Our present interest, however, is in the eddy currents that are set up in iron or other material used for magnetic circuits which are subjected to cyclic magnetization. In Fig. 8.7 is shown a cross section of a piece of iron so used.

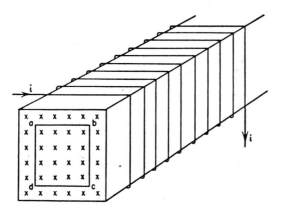

Fig. 8.7. Eddy-current path in a magnetic core.

The magnetization is caused by the alternating current i flowing in the coil. The magnetic flux is indicated by the small x marks, the positive direction selected for the flux being related to the positive direction of the current by Ampère's right-hand rule. The flux will increase and decrease with the current, being in the direction selected as positive when the current is positive, and reversing when the current reverses.

Now, consider a path *a-b-c-d* in the plane of the cross section shown in Fig. 8.7. When the flux is increasing in the positive direction, an emf will be induced in this path (and in any other path linked by the changing flux), in such a direction as to cause a counterclockwise current around the path. As a consequence of this current, energy will be converted into heat in the resistance of the path. There would be in the specimen a total loss that could be found by summing up the i^2R losses in all such elemental paths as *abcd*, beginning with a very small path near the center of the cross section and ending with a path lying just under the surface. This totalized i^2R loss is called **eddy-current loss.** In solid iron flux paths in which the flux varies with time, eddy-current losses may be so large as to create a serious problem as to how to dissipate the resulting heat.

It has been found that this loss may be materially reduced by building up the required cross section for the flux path by stacking thin pieces known as **laminations,** as shown in Fig. 8.8* Since the emf's set up in the mate-

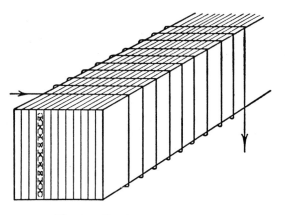

Fig. 8.8. Laminated magnetic core.

rial by the varying flux are usually of small magnitude, the natural oxide on the surface of the sheet iron or steel from which the laminations are punched will effectively insulate the laminations from one another, and thus limit each eddy-current path to a single lamination.

We shall now proceed to study mathematically the effect of the several variables, such as lamination thickness, frequency, and flux density, upon eddy-current loss. Figure 8.9 shows a magnified cross section of one of the laminations of the magnetic circuit shown in Fig. 8.8. The magnetic lines

---

*The loss may also be reduced by grinding the ferromagnetic material to a powder and mixing it with a binder that effectively insulates the particles one from another. This mixture is then formed under pressure into the desired shape and heat-treated. Magnetic cores for use in communication equipment are frequently made by this process.

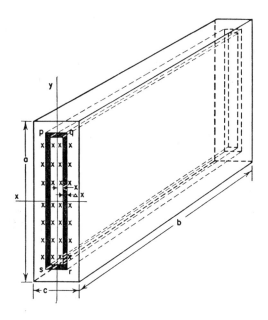

Fig. 8.9. Magnified view of a single lamination showing dimensions of eddy-current path.

are again represented by x marks, and we shall assume the eddy-current paths to be represented in the cross section by long, narrow rectangles, such as the one marked $pqrs$. All paths are assumed to extend in the y direction for the full distance a, but to vary from zero to c in the x direction.

Let us take the value of the flux density as B and assume it to vary sinusoidally according to the equation

$$B = B_{max} \sin \omega t \text{ webers per sq m.} \qquad (8.7)$$

The flux linking the eddy-current path $pqrs$ will then be

$$\phi = AB = 2xaB_{max} \sin \omega t \text{ webers.} \qquad (8.8)$$

The eddy-current path is equivalent to a single turn, and the emf induced in the path is, therefore,

$$e = \lim_{\Delta t \to 0} N \frac{\Delta \phi}{\Delta t} = N \frac{d\phi}{dt} = \frac{d[2xaB_{max} \sin \omega t]}{dt}$$

$$= 2\omega xaB_{max} \cos \omega t \text{ v.} \qquad (8.9)^*$$

*To find the instantaneous emf induced in the path, it is necessary to take the limit of $N(\Delta\phi/\Delta T)$ as ΔT approaches zero. This is known as the **derivative** and will be familiar to the student of calculus.

The resistance of the eddy-current path, ignoring the ends, is

$$R = \frac{\rho L}{A} = \frac{\rho(2a)}{b\,\Delta x} \text{ ohms.} \tag{8.10}$$

The current flowing in the path is then given by

$$i = \frac{e}{R} = \frac{\omega x B_{max} \cos \omega t\, b\,\Delta x}{\rho}, \tag{8.11}$$

and power loss can be calculated as

$$p = i^2 R = \frac{2\omega^2 B^2_{max} \cos^2 \omega t\, abx^2\,\Delta x}{\rho} \text{ w.} \tag{8.12}$$

To find the total eddy-current loss, it is now necessary to take the summation of the losses in all possible paths, from the one of zero thickness to the one of thickness c, just under the surface of the lamination.

$$\begin{aligned}
p_{total} &= \sum_0^{c/2} \frac{2\omega^2 B^2_{max} \cos^2 \omega t\, abx^2\,\Delta x}{\rho} \\
&= \left[\frac{2\omega^2 B^2_{max}\cos^2 \omega t\, abx^3}{3\rho} \right]_0^{c/2} \text{ w.}
\end{aligned} \tag{8.13}*$$

Substituting the limits and putting $\omega = 2\pi f$, we get

$$p_{total} = \frac{\pi^2 f^2 B^2_{max} \cos^2 \omega t\, abc^3}{3\rho} \text{ w,} \tag{8.14}$$

and since abc is the volume of the iron, we may write

$$p_{total} = \frac{\pi^2 f^2 c^2 B^2_{max} \cos^2 \omega t}{3\rho} \text{ w per cu m.} \tag{8.15}$$

The quantities B, e, and p are plotted against time in Fig. 8.10. It is seen that the power varies between zero and a maximum value

$$P_{max} = \frac{\pi^2 f^2 c^2 B^2_{max}}{3\rho}, \tag{8.16}$$

corresponding to a value of t that makes $\cos^2 \omega t = 1$. It can be shown by integrating (8.15) over a complete cycle and dividing by the corresponding time that

$$P_{average} = \frac{1}{2}P_{max} = \frac{\pi^2 f^2 c^2 B^2_{max}}{6\rho} \text{ w per cu m,} \tag{8.17}$$

where f is frequency in cycles per second;

*The actual evaluation of this summation must be carried out as a definite integral. The student of calculus will be able to check (8.13), but others will have to accept this equation on authority.

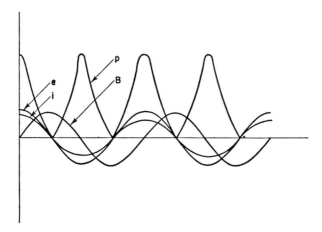

Fig. 8.10. Curves showing variation of flux density, induced emf, eddy current, and eddy-current loss in a magnetic core subjected to cyclic magnetization.

c is lamination thickness in meters;

B_{max} is maximum flux density in webers per square meter;

ρ is resistivity of material in ohm-meters.

Equation (8.17) may be used to calculate eddy-current loss in any magnetic circuit built of laminated material, or in general to calculate the eddy-current loss in thin metal strips, or sheets, placed in a magnetic field parallel to the direction of the lines of flux. It is not adapted to calculating the losses in very thick sheets, or in solid masses of metal of any kind.

It is interesting to note that the power loss decreases with increasing resistivity. Thus, everything else being equal, the loss in copper would be several times as much as in iron. It would not be practicable, however, to establish in copper the high flux densities that are commonly used in iron. Adding alloying materials, silicon in particular, to steel increases its resistivity, and thus decreases the eddy-current loss.

For practical calculations, Equation (8.17) may be rewritten

$$P_{average} = K_e f^2 c^2 B_{max}^2 \, V, \qquad (8.18)$$

where P is eddy-current loss in watts;

K_e is a constant which depends on the resistivity of the material;

f is frequency in cycles per second;

c is lamination thickness in inches;

B_{max} is maximum flux density in kilolines per square inch;

V is volume of the material in cubic inches.

The constant K_e varies from 1.5×10^{-5} to 6×10^{-5} for the steel sheets used in electrical apparatus, the smaller value corresponding to the greater resistivity.

PROBLEMS

(6-VIII) The eddy-current constant for a certain grade of 29-gage sheet steel (thickness 0.014 in.) is 2×10^{-5}. Calculate the eddy-current loss in a magnetic core made of this steel for a frequency of 500 cps and a flux density of 100 kilolines per sq in. The volume of the core is 107 cu in.

(7-VIII) The eddy-current loss in a sample of sheet steel is 12 w at a frequency of 100 cps and a flux density of 65 kilolines per sq in. What eddy-current loss might be expected in this sample at 120 cps and a flux density of 80 kilolines per sq in.?

(8-VIII) What would be the effect on eddy-current loss of redesigning a magnetic core to use laminations of 29-gage steel (thickness 0.014 in.) in place of 26-gage (thickness 0.0185 in.) steel of the same grade? Express your answer as a percentage.

(9-VIII) What would be the effect on eddy-current loss of doubling the cross-sectional area of a magnetic core, thus reducing the flux density to half and keeping the same total flux?

(10-VIII) The effective value of the emf induced in a winding on a core in which the magnetic flux varies sinusoidally is independent of changes in flux density, or in frequency, so long as the product of flux density and frequency remains constant. What would be the effect on the eddy-current loss in the core if the frequency were increased by 50 per cent, and the flux density reduced to keep the same induced emf in the winding?

7. Total core loss. In any ferromagnetic material that is subjected to cyclic magnetization there are losses due to (a) hysteresis and (b) eddy currents. These losses make themselves evident by converting energy to the heat form and raising the temperature of the material. The energy has to be supplied electrically, and the rate at which it is supplied can be measured by a wattmeter connected into the circuit, as shown in Fig. 8.11. The measure-

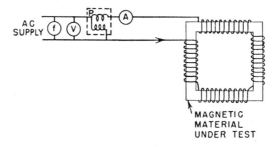

Fig. 8.11. Apparatus for measuring total core loss in a magnetic core.

ment may be made on a sample taken from a certain batch of steel especially for test purposes, or it may be made on a piece of apparatus already built, as a transformer. The wattmeter as here connected would read (a) the I^2R

loss in the wattmeter current coil, ammeter, connecting wire, and winding of the test specimen; and (b) the sum of the hysteresis and eddy-current losses in the test specimen. If the resistances of the various elements of the circuit are known and the current is measured, all of the items listed under (a) may be calculated. These items subtracted from the reading of the wattmeter give the combined hysteresis and eddy-current loss, or **core loss:**

$$P_c = K_h f B_{max}^x V + K_e f^2 B_{max}^2 c^2 V. \tag{8.19}$$

For some purposes, it is sufficient to know the combined loss, but it is occasionally desirable to be able to separate the losses and find what part of the total is due to hysteresis and what part to eddy currents. This may be done by measuring the total core loss at two different frequencies (or two different maximum flux densities, or both). We then have two equations which we may solve simultaneously to determine P_h and P_e.

Example: The core loss in a given specimen is found to be 65 w at a frequency of 30 cps and a flux density of 100 kilolines per sq in., and 190 w at 60 cps and the same flux density. What are the hysteresis loss and the eddy-current loss at each frequency?

Solution: Since the flux density, the volume of the specimen, and the thickness of the laminations remain constant in this problem, Equation (8.19) may be written as

$$P_c = K_h' f + K_e' f^2, \tag{8.20}$$

where $K_h' = K_h B_m^x V$ and $K_e' = K_e B_m^2 c^2 V$.

Substituting the data gives

$$65 = K_h'(30) + K_e'(30)^2,$$
$$190 = K_h'(60) + K_e'(60)^2.$$

Solving these equations gives

$$K_h' = 1.167, \quad K_e' = 0.0333.$$

At 30 cps, the losses would be

$$P_h = K_h'(30) = 35 \text{ w}, \quad P_e = K_e'(30)^2 = 30 \text{ w}.$$

At 60 cps,

$$P_h = K_h'(60) = 70 \text{ w}, \quad P_e = K_e'(60)^2 = 120 \text{ w}.$$

PROBLEMS

(11-VIII) The measured loss in a magnetic circuit built of sheet-steel laminations is 42 w at a frequency of 60 cps and a flux density of 1 weber per sq m. It is 28.5 w at the same frequency and a flux density of 0.8 weber per sq m. Determine the hysteresis loss and the eddy-current loss at each flux density.

(12-VIII) The measured loss in a magnetic circuit built of sheet-steel laminations is 80 w at a frequency of 600 cps and a flux density of 8000 gausses. It is 85 w at a frequency of 400 cps and a flux density of 12,000 gausses. Find the hysteresis loss and the eddy-current loss at each flux density.

(13-VIII) The measured loss in a magnetic circuit is 50 w at a frequency of 400 cps and flux density of 2000 gausses. Assuming that 75 per cent of this is hysteresis loss, what will be the measured total loss at 500 cps, 3000 gausses?

8. Application of ferromagnetic materials. In selecting a material for a particular magnetic circuit we must consider (a) permeability, (b) losses, and (c) mechanical properties. Permeability must be high enough so that the desired flux density can be secured with a reasonable magnetic field intensity. High magnetic field intensities can be attained only by using a large number of turns in the winding, or by using a large current in a normal number of turns. Either solution would result in abnormally large I^2R losses in the magnetizing winding, which implies reduced efficiency and excess heating. In case the material is subject to cyclic magnetization, the hysteresis and eddy-current losses must be kept low enough to avoid excess heating, and serious reduction in efficiency. In magnetic circuits, where the magnetization is always in one direction and essentially constant, losses, of course, do not have to be considered. The material must generally be workable — that is, it must be capable of being punched or machined to get it into the desired form. In the rotating parts of motors and generators, considerable mechanical strength is required. In a material for permanent magnets, high **retentivity,** or high ratio of residual flux density to maximum flux density is essential, as is high **coercivity,** or high ratio of coercive force to magnetic field intensity required for saturation.

These properties are all affected by (a) the chemical composition of the material and (b) the mechanical and heat treatment it received in production. The presence of carbon, oxygen, sulphur, and phosphorus in iron or steel tends to lower the permeability and increase the hysteresis loss; hence they are undesirable. The effect of silicon in reducing the hysteresis loss and increasing the electrical resistivity has already been mentioned, and since it does not affect permeability seriously, it is used in certain grades of sheet steel. The permeability of steel is increased, and its hysteresis loss decreased, by proper annealing. To secure the maximum advantage, annealing is done subsequently to punching and shearing operations, serving to relieve the abnormal stresses and the magnetic defects they cause. In general, soft materials have lower hysteresis losses and higher permeabilities than hard materials, but lower retentivity. Thus, suitable materials for permanent magnets are usually hard, and if subjected to varying flux, would have extremely high hysteresis losses.

Of the various forms in which iron and steel are used for magnetic circuits, rolled sheets are by far the most common. The thickness ordinarily ranges from gage No. 22 with a thickness of 0.031 in., to gage No. 29 with a thickness of 0.014 in. Heavier sheets or plates are used in fabricating parts not subject to cyclic magnetization, and sheets as thin as 0.005 in. are obtainable for use at higher frequencies. Several grades of steel are available in sheets, the best (lowest loss) grade containing about 4 per cent of silicon and costing the most per pound. The cheapest grade contains a fraction of 1 per cent of silicon and has the highest loss.

Rolled sections and castings of iron and steel are used in magnetic circuits where the flux is constant in magnitude and direction. In many instances, magnetic circuits are made up of several parts of different materials, often including one or more air gaps.

9. Magnetic materials for special purposes. For permanent magnets, the desired characteristics of high retentivity and high coercivity are obtained in steels containing carbon, tungsten, chromium, or cobalt. The carbon steels were the first used for this purpose, and they continue to be used in some apparatus because of their lower cost. They have, however, the disadvantage of losing their residual magnetism, particularly if subjected to vibration or high temperatures, and they cannot be depended on where constant strength is required, as in the magnets of D'Arsonval type meters. Tungsten and chromium steels have the same defect in lesser degree; cobalt steel is the most satisfactory of those mentioned. More recently, alloys of iron, nickel, cobalt, aluminum, and copper have been developed which are superior in retentivity and coercivity to any steel. These alloys, known as **alnico,** make it possible to produce permanent magnets of given strength which have only a fraction of the weight of steel magnets of like strength. Alnico has the disadvantage of being very difficult to machine, and has to be shaped mostly by grinding.

In the communications industries, currents of the order of a few milliamperes are commonly used. It is desirable, therefore, to build the magnetic circuits of the apparatus of some material which has very high permeability at very small values of the magnetic field intensity. A nickel-iron alloy known as permalloy was especially developed for this purpose, and permits flux densities as high as 0.5 weber per sq m to be established with small (5 ampere-turns per m) magnetic field intensities. The heat treatment of this alloy is as important as its chemical composition in securing the desired characteristics. One such product, known as supermalloy, has a maximum relative permeability of 10^6.

A recent development in nickel-iron alloys are the so-called "square-loop" materials, produced by maintaining the alloy for a time in a magnetic field at a temperature of 400° to 600° C. The result is to make the knee of the magnetization curve very sharp, the permeability high, and the

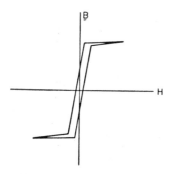

Fig. 8.12. Curve showing variation of B with H in a "square-loop" material.

coercive force small. The hysteresis loop for a specimen of such a material is shown in Fig. 8.12. These characteristics are especially useful in devices for the magnetic storage of information, as in computers.

Another development of especial importance in communications apparatus is the use of ferrites for magnetic cores. These cores are prepared by mixing the oxides of iron and other metals such as nickel or manganese in powdered form, pressing into the required shape, and firing at high temperature. The resulting material has reasonably good magnetic properties and the added advantage of extremely high resistivity, making the eddy-current loss low and its use possible in high frequency apparatus.

For certain devices, it is desirable to have a material the permeability of which changes with temperature. Iron has this property, but its Curie point is at a rather high temperature (400° C). Several alloys have been developed for which the Curie point is much lower and which show appreciable change in permeability for small changes in temperature.

For other purposes, a ferromagnetic material having constant permeability over a wide range of flux densities would be useful. A nickel-iron-cobalt-manganese alloy known as **perminvar** has been found which has this property.

Bismuth, although not a ferromagnetic material, has the unique property of changing its resistance when placed in a magnetic field. It is possible, therefore, to use a bismuth wire as the sensitive element of an instrument for measuring magnetic field intensity.

STUDY QUESTIONS

1. How is it possible for the atoms of a solid substance to be oriented by the action of a magnetic field?

2. Is a domain large enough to be seen with the aid of a microscope? (There are about 10^{23} atoms per cubic centimeter of iron.)

3. Is the Barkhausen effect evidence of the existence of domains? Would it occur if magnetization were the orientation of atoms individually?

4. Magnetization of a single-crystal specimen of iron is undertaken in one of its 100 directions. In what manner would the B-H curve differ from the one shown in Fig. 8.4?

5. After magnetic saturation is reached is it possible to increase further the flux density by increasing the magnetic field intensity? Why?

6. How can residual flux density be accounted for in terms of domain orientation?

7. In terms of domain orientation, how does the application of a coercive force bring the flux density to zero?

8. What would be the effect on the hysteresis loss in an iron core of each of the following changes: (a) doubling the frequency, (b) doubling the flux density, (c) doubling the cross section of the magnetic path, total flux and length of path to remain the same?

9. What would be the effect on the eddy-current loss in a laminated iron core of each of the following changes: (a) doubling the frequency, (b) rebuilding the core using laminations half as thick, (c) rebuilding the core using lamination material of twice the resistivity?

10. What reason, other than increased efficiency, makes it essential to reduce the hysteresis and eddy-current losses in the iron cores of electrical apparatus to the smallest practicable amount?

11. Why would a good permanent magnet material be a poor material for a transformer core which is subjected to cyclic magnetization?

12. What element is particularly useful in steel which is to be subjected to cyclic magnetization? Why?

13. For measurement of total core loss in sheet steel, the standard test specimen consists of four bundles of strips arranged to form a magnetic circuit in the form of a rectangle (Fig. 8.11). Depending upon how carefully the ends are abutted, the measured current and power are subject to considerable variation. Will this cause error in the core loss determination? Why?

14. Would the test specimen described above be suitable for determining points for a *B-H* curve? Why?

15. Is there any useful application of hysteresis and eddy-current loss? Explain.

Chapter **IX**

THE MAGNETIC CIRCUIT

---

1. Magnetic circuits in electrical apparatus. Magnetic flux paths constructed of ferromagnetic materials constitute important parts of many pieces of electrical apparatus. Every generator, every motor, and every transformer (except those which operate at high frequency) makes use of one or more such flux paths. The flux path of a D'Arsonval type meter, consisting of a U-shaped permanent magnet, pole pieces, air gaps, and central core, is shown in Fig. 5.2. Watt-hour meters, telephone receivers, loud speakers, relays for power, telephone, and telegraph circuits, and certain types of circuit breakers, all depend upon magnetic flux confined to paths of finite length and cross section. The variety of shapes and sizes which these magnetic circuits take is endless. Some are simple, as the iron ring considered in Chapter VII, which is used in practice in certain telephone apparatus. Some are rather complex, as the magnetic core of an ordinary watt-hour meter, shown in Fig. 9.1.

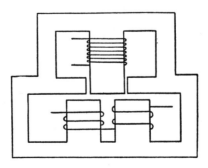

Fig. 9.1. Magnetic circuit of an a-c watt-hour meter.

A magnetic circuit is usually designed and built for the purpose of establishing, with as few ampere-turns as possible, a predetermined flux, in a certain definite space, as in the air gap between the armature and poles of a generator or motor. The utilization of the magnetic flux requires in most apparatus that one or more air gaps be included in the magnetic circuit. A notable exception is the transformer, in which the flux path may be in iron throughout its length, the operation of the transformer depending upon the variation of the flux with time.

The problems encountered in connection with magnetic circuits can usually be recognized as one of two types: (a) to find the magnetomotive force required to establish a given flux; or (b) to find the flux that will be established by a given magnetomotive force. The solution of these problems depends upon the application of the relationships developed in Chapter VII, and particularly upon Ampère's circuital law

$$\Sigma \, H \cos \theta \, \Delta l = NI. \tag{7.35}$$

In magnetic circuits the length of path is measured in the direction of the field, so that in most instances $\cos \theta$ is unity and Ampère's law becomes simply

$$\Sigma \, H \, \Delta l = NI. \tag{7.35a}$$

The relationship between flux density B and magnetic field intensity H can, for our present purposes, best be expressed graphically. The relationship

$$B = \mu H \tag{7.8}$$

is valid, but not particularly useful, since in ferromagnetic substances the permeability μ depends upon the flux density. For the same reason, the reluctance concept is useful for purposes of computation only if the reluctance is independent of flux density; that is, in air gaps, or parts of the magnetic circuit in which the flux path does not lie in iron.

For most purposes the relationship between magnetic flux density and magnetic field intensity is most conveniently found by referring to an experimentally determined B-H curve (Chapter VIII) for the particular ferromagnetic material concerned. Some B-H curves for commonly used materials are provided in Appendix Fig. A.

Let us now proceed to the consideration of some problems relating to simple magnetic circuits, and methods of solving them.

2. Magnetic circuits that are of same cross section and material throughout. This is the simplest problem of all. Suppose the magnetic circuit takes the form of an iron ring, such as the one illustrated in Fig. 9.2, and that we are required to calculate the number of ampere-turns necessary

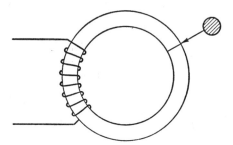

Fig. 9.2. Iron ring — the simplest possible magnetic circuit.

to establish a given flux. By measurements, we determine the cross-sectional area of the ring, and proceed to calculate the flux density. We then refer to the appropriate magnetization curve and find the magnetic field intensity that corresponds to this flux density. Then, knowing the magnetic field intensity and the mean length of the flux path, we calculate the mmf by Equation (7.35a).

> **Example:** Find the mmf necessary to establish a flux of 0.0006 weber in a cast-steel ring of circular cross section. The outside diameter of the ring is 8 in. and inside diameter 6 in.
>
> SOLUTION:
>
> $$\phi = 0.0006 \times 10^5 = 60 \text{ kilolines,}$$
>
> $$A = \text{(cross-sectional area)} = \pi(0.5)^2 = 0.785 \text{ sq in.,}$$
>
> $$B = \frac{\phi}{A} = \frac{60}{0.785} = 76.4 \text{ kilolines per sq in.,}$$
>
> $$H \text{ (from curve)} = 27.5 \text{ ampere-turns per in.,}$$
>
> $$l \text{ (mean length of path)} = \pi \times 7 = 22 \text{ in.,}$$
>
> $$F = \Sigma H \,\Delta l = Hl = 27.5 \times 22 = 605 \text{ ampere-turns.}$$

If we had been required to find the flux that would be established by a given mmf, our steps would have been (1) divide the given number of ampere-turns by the mean length of path to find H, (2) refer to curve to find B, and (3) multiply B by the cross-sectional area to find flux. For a magnetic circuit of this kind, it appears that one type of problem is no more difficult than the other.

PROBLEMS

(1-IX) What flux would be established in the cast-steel ring described in the foregoing example by a mmf of 850 ampere-turns?

(2-IX) What mmf will be required to establish a flux of 0.005 weber in the magnetic circuit shown in Fig. 9.3? The material is annealed sheet-steel laminations stacked to obtain the required thickness.

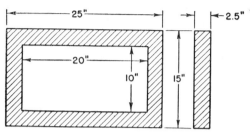

Fig. 9.3

(3-IX) What percentage of increase in mmf will result in a 25 per cent increase in flux in the magnetic circuit described in Problem 2-IX? What percentage of decrease in mmf will result in a 25 per cent decrease in flux?

(4-IX) What flux will be established in the magnetic circuit described in Problem 2-IX by a mmf of 1000 ampere-turns?

3. Magnetic circuits made up of two or more parts in series. Let us now consider a magnetic circuit that consists of two or more distinct parts so arranged that the flux path is through both. These parts are said to be in **series,** from the similarity of the arrangement to a series electric circuit. Since the parts do not, in general, have the same cross-sectional area, the flux density will be different in the different parts, and they must, therefore, be considered one at a time. If we are given the flux and required to find the mmf, we take one part at a time, finding the flux density, the magnetizing force (from a curve), and the product (Hl) for that part. The mmf will then be the sum of these products:

$$F = \Sigma H \, \Delta l = H_1 l_1 + H_2 l_2 + \ldots . \qquad (9.1)$$

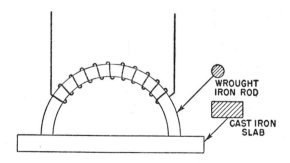

Fig. 9.4. Series magnetic circuit.

Example: A magnetic circuit consists of a wrought-iron rod, 1.5 in. in diam and 30 in. long bent into a semicircle, and a cast-iron slab, 2 in. thick and 4 in. wide, as in Fig. 9.4. A perfect contact between the slab and the ends of the rod is assumed. How many ampere-turns will be required to establish a flux of 0.002 weber?

SOLUTION: Here the magnetic flux path is partly through the wrought-iron rod and through the cast-iron slab for the remainder of its length. Since flux lines are continuous, the flux through the two parts of the circuit must be the same. Since the two parts have different cross-sectional areas, the flux densities must be different. The magnetic field intensities, which depend upon the flux densities and upon the materials in which the flux densities exist, may be expected to be different in the two parts. When the magnetic field intensities have been found (by reference to the magnetization curves) the application of the circuital law then gives the required number of ampere-turns.

$\phi = 0.002 \times 10^5 = 200$ kilolines (the same throughout both parts).

For the wrought-iron rod:

cross-sectional area $= \pi(0.75)^2 = 1.77$ sq in.,

$$B = \frac{\phi}{A} = \frac{200}{1.77} = 113 \text{ kilolines per sq in.,}$$

H (from curve) $= 80$ ampere-turns per in.,

$$Hl = 80 \times 30 = 2400 \text{ ampere-turns.}$$

For the cast-iron slab:

cross-sectional area $= 2 \times 4 = 8$ sq in.,*

$$B = \frac{\phi}{A} = \frac{200}{8} = 25 \text{ kilolines per sq in.,}$$

H (from curve) $= 16$ ampere-turns per in.

The length of the path in the slab is the diameter of the semi-circle formed by the rod and is given by

$$\pi l = 2 \times 30,$$

$$l = 19.1 \text{ in.,}$$

$$Hl = 16 \times 19.1 = 306 \text{ ampere-turns,}$$

$$F = \Sigma Hl = 2400 + 306 = 2706 \text{ ampere-turns.}$$

*This neglects the crowding together of the lines in the slab as they converge toward the ends of the rod. A correct average value to take for the cross-sectional area is hard to estimate without a knowledge of field mapping, but it is obviously less than 8 sq in.

PROBLEMS

(5-IX) How many ampere-turns are required to establish a flux of 180 kilolines in the magnetic circuit of the foregoing example?

(6-IX) Find the mmf required to establish a flux of 150 kilolines in the magnetic circuit in Fig. 9.5.

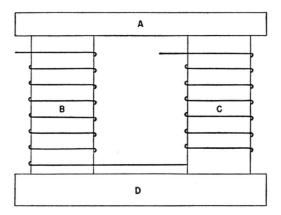

Fig. 9.5

Part	Material	Cross Section	Mean Length of Path
A	Cast steel	1.5 sq in.	5 in.
B, C	Wrought iron	1.4 sq in.	4 in.
D	Cast iron	3.0 sq in.	5 in.

(7-IX) How many ampere-turns are required to establish a flux of 120 kilolines in the magnetic circuit of Problem 6-IX?

4. Calculations involving air gaps. The magnetic circuits of generators and motors necessarily include one or more air gaps to permit the rotating parts to move. Air gaps are also included in the magnetic circuits of reactors and other apparatus to secure the desired characteristics. Since the permeability of air is constant, B-H curves are not necessary, calculations of flux or mmf being made from the defining equations. There are two convenient methods of calculating the number of ampere-turns required to establish a given flux across an air gap: (1) Calculate the reluctance of the air gap, and then find ampere-turns by taking the product of flux times reluctance; or (2) calculate the flux density in the air gap, find magnetic field intensity by use of Equation (7.73), then multiply by length of path to obtain ampere-turns. Since all quantities must be expressed in mks units if method 1 is used, method 2 will usually be shorter.

Example: A magnetic circuit contains an air gap 0.1 in. long and having a cross-sectional area which may be considered the same as the cross section of the steel faces between which it lies. These areas are each 4 sq in. How many ampere-turns are required to establish a flux of 400 kilolines across the gap?

SOLUTION 1:

$$\mathfrak{R} = \frac{l}{\mu_0 A} = \frac{(0.1/39.37)}{(4\pi \times 10^{-7})(4/39.37^2)} = 7.81 \times 10^5 \text{ mks units,}$$

$$\phi = 400 \times 10^{-5} \text{ weber,}$$

$$Hl = \phi\mathfrak{R} = (400 \times 10^{-5})(7.81 \times 10^5) = 3120 \text{ ampere-turns.}$$

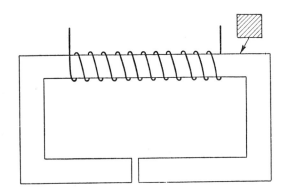

Fig. 9.6. Magnetic circuit with air gap.

SOLUTION 2:

$$B = \frac{400}{4} = 100 \text{ kilolines per sq in.,}$$

$$H = 313B = 31,300 \text{ ampere-turns per in.,}$$

$$Hl = 31,300 \times 0.1 = 3130 \text{ ampere-turns.}$$

The total number of ampere-turns required is then found by Ampère's circuital law

$$\Sigma Hl = NI.$$

That is, the ampere-turns required for the air gap must be added to the ampere-turns required for the other parts of the series circuit in order to find the total mmf.

There is always more or less "fringing" to be accounted for in problems involving air gaps. The flux lines, instead of being confined to the space defined by the metal faces of the air gap as in Fig. 9.7a, tend to bulge outward and increase the effective cross-sectional area of the gap, as in Fig. 9.7b. For short air gaps, this effect is sometimes taken into account in calculations by considering the cross section of the air gap to have been increased.

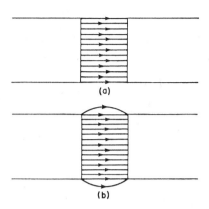

Fig. 9.7. "Fringing" of magnetic lines crossing an air gap.

When the air gap forms any considerable part of the total length of the magnetic circuit, the area of the path of the lines becomes so indefinite as to render a solution difficult or impossible by the methods here described.

PROBLEMS

(**8-IX**) An air gap 0.05 in. long is cut in the magnetic circuit described in Problem 2-IX. How many ampere-turns are now required to establish a flux of 500 kilolines?

(**9-IX**) The magnetic circuit shown in Fig. 9.4 consists of a wrought-iron rod 1.6 in. in diam and 32 in. long bent into a semicircle, and a cast-iron slab 1.75 in. thick and 3.5 in. wide. The ends of the rod are separated from the slab by air gaps 0.2 cm long. How many ampere-turns are required to establish a flux of 200 kilolines?

(**10-IX**) What should be the length of the air gaps in Problem 9-IX in order that a mmf of 4500 ampere-turns will establish a flux of 200 kilolines?

5. Composite magnetization curves. When our problem is to find the flux established by a specified number of ampere-turns in a magnetic circuit made up of two or more parts in series, our procedure must be modified. We cannot begin by dividing the number of ampere-turns by the length of path, as was done in Section 2. This can be done only if the magnetic circuit is of the same material and cross section throughout its length. Our best procedure is to plot a **composite,** or over-all, magnetization curve, showing the relationship of the flux to the magnetomotive force for various values of flux. Once such a curve is constructed for a particular magnetic circuit it can be used with equal facility to find (a) the magnetomotive force required to establish a given flux, or (b) the flux established by a given magnetomotive force.

In order to find a point on the composite magnetization curve we simply begin with a flux (any flux), and calculate, as outlined in Sections 3 and 4, the number of ampere-turns required to establish this flux in the magnetic circuit under consideration. It will usually be necessary to find at least three or four points; more if a wide range of fluxes and magnetomotive forces are encountered in the problem to be solved. The calculation of the points is not as laborious as it might appear, especially if the work is arranged in tabular form.

Example: Find points on the composite magnetization curve of the magnetic circuit described in the example in Section 3. From the curve, determine the flux established by a mmf of 2100 ampere-turns.

SOLUTION: In the foregoing example the dimensions were found as follows:

Wrought-iron rod: cross section 1.77 sq. in.
length of path 30 in.
Cast-iron slab: cross section 8 sq. in.
length of path 19.1 in.

ϕ (kilo-lines)	Rod			Slab			$\Sigma\, Hl$ (ampere-turns)
	B (kl per sq. in.)	H (a.t. per in.)	Hl (ampere-turns)	B (kl per sq. in.)	H (a.t. per in.)	Hl (ampere-turns)	
100	56.4	0.8	24	12.5	8	153	177
125	70.7	2.5	75	15.6	10	191	266
150	84.6	7	210	18.8	11.5	220	430
175	98.9	21.5	645	21.9	13.5	254	899
200	112.8	82	2460	25	16	306	2766
190	107.2	45	1350	23.8	14.5	276	1626
195	110	59	1770	24.3	15	286	2056

In making the tabulation, the first point was calculated for a flux of 100 kl and successive points at 125, 150, 175, and 200 kl. It was found that a flux of 200 kl requires a mmf of 2766 ampere-turns, which is greater than the specified mmf of 2100. Rather than calculate points for still larger values of flux, it was therefore expedient to go back and interpolate calculations between 175 kl and 200 kl. From these it is apparent that the flux established by 2100 ampere-turns will be slightly more than 195 kilolines.

PROBLEM

(11-IX) The magnetic circuit described in Problem 6-IX is changed by separating the parts B and C from the part D by air gaps each 0.075 in. long. Plot the composite magnetization curve, and from it determine what flux will be produced by a mmf of 3500 ampere-turns.

6. Magnetic circuits acted upon by two or more mmf's. The magnetic circuits of most electrical machines are acted upon simultaneously by two or more mmf's. These mmf's may aid or oppose one another, depending upon the relative directions of the currents in the several windings. The right-hand rule gives the direction of the mmf which corresponds to the direction of current in a given winding. The flux produced in a magnetic circuit by two or more mmf's acting simultaneously will not, in general, be the algebraic sum of the fluxes produced by the same mmf's acting separately. That is to say, if mmf F_1 produces a flux ϕ_1, and mmf F_2 produces a flux ϕ_2, both in the same direction around the circuit, then a mmf $F_1 + F_2$ will not produce a flux $\phi_1 + \phi_2$. This may be seen from the sketch of the composite magnetization curve shown in Fig. 9.8.

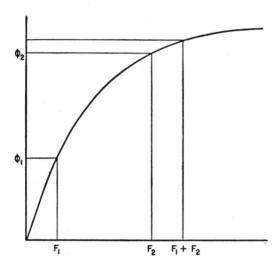

Fig. 9.8. Effect of two magnetomotive forces acting simultaneously.

PROBLEMS

(12-IX) The magnetic circuit shown in Fig. 9.9 is built of sheet-steel laminations. The cross-sectional area is the same throughout, and the air gap is 0.1 in. in length. The winding N_1 has 2000 turns of small-diameter wire, and N_2 has 40 turns of larger-diameter wire. Calculate and plot the composite magnetization curve and from it determine (a) flux established if $I_1 = 1.5$ amp and $I_2 = 0$, (b) flux established if $I_1 = 0$ and $I_2 = 25$ amp, (c) algebraic sum of the fluxes calculated in (a) and (b), and (d) flux established if $I_1 = 1.5$ amp and $I_2 = 25$ amp.

(13-IX) The magnetic circuit shown in Fig. 9.9 is built of sheet-steel laminations. The cross-sectional area is the same throughout, and the air gap is 0.05 in. long. The windings N_1 and N_2 each consist of 1000 turns. Calculate and plot the

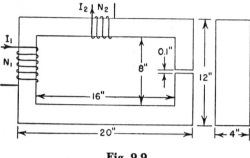

Fig. 9.9

composite magnetization curve and use it to determine the limits between which the flux will vary if I_1 is a direct current of 2 amp and I_2 is an alternating current that varies according to the equation $i_2 = 0.5 \sin 377t$.

7. Magnetic potential difference. Just as we speak of potential difference between two points on an electric circuit, we may speak of difference of magnetic potential between two points on a magnetic circuit. Difference of magnetic potential, like magnetomotive force, is measured in ampere-turns. The idea may be made clearer by reference to Fig. 9.10. In

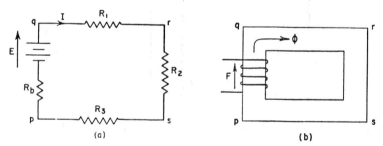

Fig. 9.10. Comparison of electric and magnetic potential differences.

the electric circuit, the potential difference between points r and s is commonly referred to as a *voltage drop*, or *IR drop*, and it is equal to the product of the current and the resistance R_2 of the part of the circuit lying between points r and s. In the magnetic circuit, the potential difference between points r and s could properly be referred to as an *ampere-turn drop*, or a $\phi \mathfrak{R}$ *drop*, since it is equal to the product of the flux and the reluctance of that part of the circuit. It is more usual, however, to think of the magnetic potential difference as being an *Hl drop*, a product of magnetic field intensity by length of path. This is because it is customary to work with *B-H* curves and read values of H rather than determine the new value of $\mathfrak{R}$ that corresponds to every change in flux.

Around the electric circuit, the emf of the battery equals the algebraic sum of IR drops in the various resistances according to Kirchhoff's voltage law

$$E = \Sigma \, IR.$$

Around the magnetic circuit the mmf of the coil equals the algebraic sum of the ϕR (or Hl) drops in the various sections of the core according to Ampere's circuital law

$$F = \Sigma \, Hl.$$

The electrical difference in potential between points p and q in Fig. 9.10a is equal to the emf of the battery less the IR drop in the internal resistance of the battery itself. The magnetic difference of potential between points p and q in Fig. 9.10b is equal to the mmf of the coil less the Hl for the section of the core lying within the coil itself. From this statement, it follows that if the winding be so distributed that the ampere-turns per unit length exactly equal the Hl per unit length for each and every part of a magnetic circuit, then no magnetic potential difference will exist between points along the magnetic path, no matter how widely they are separated. This would correspond to an electric circuit in which sources of emf were inserted at small intervals around the circuit so as to exactly supply the IR drops in every section of the circuit. In a magnetic circuit, the avoidance of large differences of magnetic potential is very desirable, as will be seen shortly. Unfortunately, it is seldom practicable to distribute the ampere-turns as described above, particularly in circuits containing air gaps. The air gap, where most ampere-turns per unit length are required, must be kept clear of any windings for mechanical reasons, and the ampere-turns demanded by the air gap must be made up by increasing the number on some other part of the circuit above the number required for that part.

8. Leakage flux. Magnetic flux lines will exist along all possible paths that connect any two points between which there is a magnetic potential difference. The principal path, in the case of a coil wound upon a closed iron core, is, of course, through the core, but this is not the only path. In Fig. 9.11, lines are drawn to indicate some of the other possible paths that may

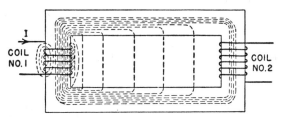

Fig. 9.11. Leakage flux paths in a magnetic circuit.

be taken by flux established by current in coil No. 1. If it is required that a certain definite amount of flux link coil No. 2 at the other end of the core, then any lines that fail to follow the core all the way around are useless, and are collectively called **leakage flux.** The calculation of the total amount of leakage flux is, in general, a formidable problem, and is often impossible. For magnetic circuits of simple geometry, however, we may make approximate calculations by determining the magnetic potential differences between certain points and estimating the reluctance of the paths that connect these points.

Example: The magnetic circuit in Fig. 9.12 is built of sheet-steel laminations. The over-all dimensions are 20 in. by 8 in., and the window is 16 in. by 4 in. The thickness of the core is 4 in. A flux of 720 kilolines is to link coil

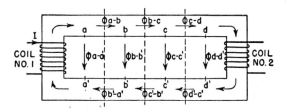

Fig. 9.12. Magnetic core for calculation of leakage flux.

No. 2. Determine the total flux that must be produced by coil No. 1, taking into account the leakage flux, and the ampere-turns required to establish this flux. Also find the ampere-turns that would have been required had there been no leakage flux.

SOLUTION: Let us begin by dividing the length of the window into four equal sections. The midpoints of these sections are designated aa', bb', cc', and dd', in Fig. 9.12. We shall assume that each of these sections forms a path for leakage flux to cross the window from top to bottom. The cross-sectional area of each path is 16 sq in. and the length is 4 in. The reluctance of each path will therefore be

$$\mathcal{R} = \frac{l}{\mu_0 A} = \frac{4/39.37}{(4\pi \times 10^{-7})16/(39.37)^2} = 7.83 \times 10^6 \text{ mks units.}$$

We shall now proceed to determine the magnetic potential difference that exists between the ends of each of these leakage paths, and the leakage flux which results. The flux density in the end section of the core at the extreme right is

$$B = \frac{\phi}{A} = \frac{720}{8} = 90 \text{ kilolines per sq in.,}$$

H (from curve) = 20.5 ampere-turns per in.

Assuming that the flux density is the same throughout the end section, the magnetic potential difference between points d-d' is

$$Hl_{d\text{-}d'} = 20.5 \times 12 = 246 \text{ ampere-turns.}$$

The flux over the leakage path d-d' is

$$\phi_{d\text{-}d'} = \frac{246}{7.83 \times 10^6} = 31.4 \times 10^{-6} \text{ weber} = 3.14 \text{ kilolines.}$$

The flux in the core in sections c-d and c'-d' will be greater than the flux in the end section by an amount equal to the leakage flux just calculated.

$$\phi_{c\text{-}d} = \phi_{c'\text{-}d'} = 720 + 3 = 723 \text{ kilolines,}$$

$$B_{c\text{-}d} = B_{c'\text{-}d'} = \frac{723}{8} = 90.4 \text{ kilolines per sq in.,}$$

$$H_{c\text{-}d} = H_{c'\text{-}d'} \text{ (from curve)} = 21 \text{ ampere-turns per inch.}$$

The magnetic potential difference between points c-c' can now be calculated:

$$Hl_{c\text{-}c'} = 246 + (21 \times 4) + (21 \times 4) = 414 \text{ ampere-turns.}$$

Repeating these calculations for each section in turn, we obtain

$$\phi_{c\text{-}c'} = \frac{414}{7.83 \times 10^6} = 52.9 \times 10^{-6} \text{ weber} = 5.29 \text{ kilolines,}$$

$$\phi_{b\text{-}c} = \phi_{b'\text{-}c'} = 723 + 5 = 728 \text{ kilolines,}$$

$$B_{b\text{-}c} = B_{b'\text{-}c'} = \frac{728}{8} = 91 \text{ kilolines per sq in.,}$$

$$H_{b\text{-}c} = H_{b'\text{-}c'} \text{ (from curve)} = 22.5 \text{ ampere-turns per in.,}$$

$$Hl_{b\text{-}b'} = 414 + (22.5 \times 4) + (22.5 \times 4) = 594 \text{ ampere-turns,}$$

$$\phi_{b\text{-}b'} = \frac{594}{7.83 \times 10^6} = 7.59 \text{ kilolines,}$$

$$\phi_{a\text{-}b} = \phi_{a'\text{-}b'} = 728 + 8 = 736 \text{ kilolines,}$$

$$B_{a\text{-}b} = B_{a'\text{-}b'} = \frac{736}{8} = 92 \text{ kilolines per sq in.,}$$

$$H_{a\text{-}b} = H_{a'\text{-}b'} \text{ (from curve)} = 25 \text{ ampere-turns per in.,}$$

$$Hl_{a\text{-}a'} = 594 + (25 \times 4) + (25 \times 4) = 794 \text{ ampere-turns,}$$

$$\phi_{a\text{-}a'} = \frac{794}{7.83 \times 10^6} = 10.1 \text{ kilolines,}$$

ϕ in extreme left-hand section of core is

$$736 + 10 = 746 \text{ kilolines.}$$

This is the total flux that must be produced by coil No. 1.

B in extreme left-hand section of core is

$$\frac{746}{8} = 93.3 \text{ kilolines per sq in.,}$$

H (from curve) $= 28$ ampere-turns per in.

Total ampere-turns required will be

$$F = \Sigma \, Hl = 794 + (12 \times 28) = 1130 \text{ ampere-turns.}$$

If there had been no leakage flux, the total ampere-turns required would have been

$$F = 20.5 \times 48 = 985 \text{ ampere-turns.}$$

Thus, we see that concentrating the winding on the left-hand end section of the core makes necessary the use of about 15 per cent more ampere-turns than would have been required had the winding been distributed around the core in such a manner as to avoid magnetic potential differences and leakage flux. In some instances, the additional ampere-turns necessary in a concentrated winding may even exceed 15 per cent of the requirements for a distributed winding, though practical designs require that the windings be so placed as to keep the excess as low as possible.

PROBLEM

(14-IX) A magnetic circuit is built of sheet-steel laminations in the form shown in Fig. 9.12. The over-all dimensions are 20 in. by 8 in. and the window is 18 in. by 6 in. The thickness of the core is 1.5 in. A flux of 140 kilolines is to link coil No. 2. Divide the length of the window into 3-in. sections, and determine (a) the magnetic potential difference between pairs of points located at the mid-sections, (b) the leakage flux over paths of cross-sectional area 3 in. by 1.5 in., corresponding to the sections for which potential differences are calculated, (c) total flux linking coil No. 1, (d) ampere-turns required to establish this flux, and (e) ampere-turns required to establish this flux, and (e) ampere-turns required to establish a flux of 150 kilolines had there been no leakage flux.

9. Magnetic circuits involving permanent magnets. Any magnetic circuit, when the mmf is removed, will retain a certain residual flux density, the value of which depends upon the material and the maximum flux density to which it has been subjected. It is thus a permanent magnet. In order to establish saturation flux density with as few ampere-turns as possible, any air gap in the circuit is bridged during the magnetizing process. To make the magnet useful, however, the bridge must be removed once the process is complete, and upon its removal the flux density decreases by a significant amount. The maintenance of flux across an air gap requires that there be a difference in magnetic potential between its faces, which must now be supplied by the domains remaining in alignment in the iron part of the circuit. The iron thus becomes the seat of a mmf equal to the drop in magnetic potential across the air gap. The supplying of this mmf by the iron has exactly the same effect as the application of a coercive force — that is, it results in a decrease in the residual flux density. If the magnet is of the bar or U type, so that the length of path in air is a considerable part of the total length of path, the calculation of the decrease is not readily made. In cases where the air gap is relatively short, however, the flux density in the air gap can be calculated with accuracy as high as that usually attained in magnetic-circuit calculations.

The basis of the calculation is Ampère's circuital law

$$\Sigma \, Hl = NI.$$

Suppose a magnetic circuit in the form of a ring, broken by a short air gap which has been temporarily bridged, is acted upon by a mmf F. After the mmf has been discontinued and the bridge removed, the equation around the ring is

$$0 = H_i l_i + H_a l_a, \tag{9.2}$$

where H_i is the magnetic field intensity in the iron;

l_i is the length of the magnetic path in the iron;

H_a is the magnetic field intensity in the air gap;

l_a is the length of the air gap.

It is obvious that unless H_i and H_a are both zero (in which case there could be no flux density in the air gap), then either H_i or H_a must be negative. If H_a were negative, the direction of the magnetic field in the air gap would reverse when the bridge was removed. H_i, then, must be negative, and thus is a coercive force so far as the iron is concerned, tending to reduce the residual flux density in the iron. The relation between residual flux density and coercive force for some materials commonly used for permanent magnets is given in Appendix Fig. B.

Since the air gap and iron part of the magnetic circuit are in series and equal in cross-sectional area (ignoring fringing), the flux density must be the same for each part:

$$B_i = B_a. \tag{9.3}$$

The determination of the flux density in the air gap, then, simply requires that we find a value which, for the particular material used, will satisfy Equation (9.2). This can readily be done by trial and error.

> **Example:** A ring of chrome steel, having a mean diameter of 7 in. and a cross-sectional area of ¾ sq in., contains an air gap ¼ in. long. It is magnetized to saturation with the air gap bridged. What flux density would exist in the air gap upon removal of the bridge?

SOLUTION: Let us assume a flux density of 20 kilolines per sq in. From the chrome-steel curve (Fig. 9.8) H is -112 ampere-turns per in.

$$l_i = 7\pi - \tfrac{1}{4} = 21.75 \text{ in.},$$

$$H_i l_i = (-112)(21.75) = -2440 \text{ ampere-turns.}$$

For the air gap the flux density will be

$$B_a = 20 \times 0.0155 = 0.31 \text{ weber per sq m,}$$

$$H_a = \frac{B_a}{\mu_0} = \frac{0.31}{4\pi \times 10^{-7}} = 2.47 \times 10^5 \text{ ampere-turns per m}$$

$$= 6270 \text{ ampere-turns per in.,}$$

$$H_a l_a = 6270 \times 0.25 = 1567 \text{ ampere-turns.}$$

These values obviously will not satisfy Equation (9.2), and it can be seen further that the assumed flux density must be increased. Let us try $B = 30$ kilolines per sq in. We then have

$$H_i \text{ (from curve)} = -105 \text{ ampere-turns per in.,}$$

$$H_i l_i = (-105)(21.75) = -2285 \text{ ampere-turns.}$$

The value of $H_a l_a$ will be increased in direct proportion to the flux density so that

$$H_a l_a = {}^{30}\!/_{20} \times 1567 = 2350 \text{ ampere-turns.}$$

These values satisfy Equation (9.2) within the allowable limits for magnetic calculations.

PROBLEMS

(15-IX) An air gap 0.2 in. long is cut in a ring of cobalt steel which has a mean diameter of 1.5 in. and a cross section of 0.25 sq in. The ring is magnetized to saturation with the air gap bridged. What will be the flux density in the air gap when the bridge is removed?

(16-IX) What would have been the flux density in the air gap of the ring described in Problem 15-IX if the material had been alnico?

(17-IX) The magnetic circuit of a D'Arsonval type meter consists of a permanent magnet of chrome steel, fitted with soft-iron pole pieces and core, as shown in Fig. 9.13. What flux density could be expected in the air gaps following magnetization to saturation with the air gaps bridged? *Suggestion:* Modify Equation (9.3) to take account of the difference in cross section of the air gap and magnet. Ignore the ampere-turns required by the soft iron.

10. Magnetic cores having parallel branches. Just as a single source of emf may cause current in a number of parallel circuits to which it is connected, a single coil carrying current may supply the mmf to establish

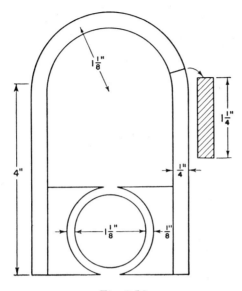

Fig. 9.13

flux in several parallel branches of a magnetic circuit. The core shown in Fig. 9.14 is typical of the kind used in shell-type transformers and reactors, the windings being placed on the middle leg, and the other two legs serving as return paths for the flux.

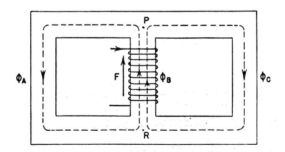

Fig. 9.14. Magnetic core with parallel branches.

Since magnetic lines are regarded as being always continuous, with no beginning and no end, it follows that in Fig. 9.14 the flux ϕ_B must be the sum of the fluxes ϕ_A and ϕ_C,

$$\phi_B = \phi_A + \phi_C. \tag{9.4}$$

In general, the flux entering any region in a magnetic field must equal the flux emerging from that region. This relationship is very similar to Kirchhoff's current law, which is applied at junction points in electrical networks.

In order to establish a given amount of flux in the center leg, enough ampere-turns must be provided to give the required magnetic field intensities in the center leg and in either outside leg according to the equations

$$F = H_B l_B + H_A l_A \qquad (9.5)$$

and
$$F = H_B l_B + H_C l_C. \qquad (9.6)$$

The relation between the fluxes expressed by Equation 9.4 must also be satisfied. The simplest case is the one in which the outside legs are exactly alike, so that it may be assumed that the flux ϕ_B divides equally between them, making

$$\phi_A = \phi_C = \tfrac{1}{2}\,\phi_B. \qquad (9.7)$$

Example 1: The dimensions of the magnetic core shown in Fig. 9.14 are as follows:

> Over-all: 28 in. by 16 in.
> Each window: 8 in. sq.
> Thickness of the core: 4 in.
> Material: sheet-steel laminations.

Required: number of ampere-turns on center leg to establish a flux $\phi_B = 1600$ kilolines.

SOLUTION: First we must determine the mean lengths and cross sections of the flux paths in the various legs. In doing this, we may consider each path to extend from point P to point R, midway of the core sections. On this basis we have

$$l_A = l_C = 36 \text{ in.},$$
$$l_B = 12 \text{ in.},$$
$$A_A = A_B = A_C = 16 \text{ sq in.}$$

Now, $\qquad B_B = \dfrac{\phi_B}{A_B} = \dfrac{1600}{16} = 100$ kilolines per sq in.,

H_B (from curve) $= 65$ ampere-turns per in.,

$$\phi_A = \phi_C = \frac{\phi_B}{2} = 800 \text{ kilolines},$$

$$B_A = B_C = \frac{800}{16} = 50 \text{ kilolines per sq in.},$$

$H_A = H_C$ (from curve) $= 2.5$ ampere-turns per in.

From Equation (9.5) or (9.6),

$$F = (65 \times 12) + (2.5 \times 36) = 870 \text{ ampere-turns}.$$

If legs A and C are not identical, we cannot assume the flux ϕ_B to divide equally, and the solution is more difficult.

Example 2: The magnetic core in Example 1 has an air gap 0.05 in. long cut in leg C. How many ampere-turns are now required to establish a flux of 1600 kilolines in leg B?

SOLUTION: Cutting the air gap in leg C makes it necessary to modify Equation (9.6), which now becomes

$$F = H_B l_B + H_C l_C + H_G l_G. \qquad (9.8)$$

The flux density in leg B is 100 kilolines per sq in. as before, and the magnetic field intensity H_B is 65 ampere-turns per in. It is obvious that the air gap in leg C will increase the reluctance of that leg and cause a decrease in the flux ϕ_C. We have no way of knowing in advance how much the decrease will be, so we are forced to assume a value. Let us assume $\phi_C = 400$ kilolines. Then,

$$B_C = \frac{400}{16} = 25 \text{ kilolines per sq in.,}$$

H_C (from curve) $= 1.6$ ampere-turns per in.,

$$H_C l_C = 1.6 \times 36 = 57.6 \text{ ampere-turns.}$$

The reluctance of the air gap is

$$\Re = \frac{l}{\mu_0 A} = \frac{0.05/39.37}{(4\pi \times 10^{-7})16/(39.37)^2} = 9.8 \times 10^4 \text{ mks units,}$$

$$H_G l_G = \phi_G \Re_G = (4 \times 10^{-3})(9.8 \times 10^4) = 392 \text{ ampere-turns.}$$

Equating the right-hand side of (9.5) to the right-hand side of (9.8),

$$H_A l_A = H_C l_C + H_G l_G \qquad (9.9)$$

$$= 57 + 392 = 449 \text{ ampere-turns,}$$

$$H_A = \frac{449}{36} = 12.5 \text{ ampere-turns per in.,}$$

B_A (from curve) $= 84.4$ kilolines per sq in.,

$$\phi_A = 84.4 \times 16 = 1350 \text{ kilolines.}$$

We can now check our assumption by substituting in Equation (9.4).

$$\phi_B = \phi_A + \phi_C = 1350 + 400 = 1750 \text{ kilolines.}$$

Since ϕ_B is to be only 1600 kilolines, we have evidently assumed too high a value for ϕ_C.

For our second trial let us assume $\phi_C = 320$ kilolines. We will then have

$$B_C = \frac{320}{16} = 20 \text{ kilolines per sq in.,}$$

H_C (from curve) $= 1.5$ ampere-turns per in.,

$$H_C l_C = 1.5 \times 36 = 54 \text{ ampere-turns,}$$

$$H_G l_G = \phi_G \Re_G = (3.2 \times 10^{-3})(9.8 \times 10^4) = 314 \text{ ampere-turns,}$$

$$H_A l_A = 54 + 314 = 368 \text{ ampere-turns,}$$

$$H_A = \frac{368}{36} = 10.2 \text{ ampere-turns per in.,}$$

B_A (from curve) = 82 kilolines per sq in.,

$$\phi_A = 82 \times 16 = 1310 \text{ kilolines,}$$

$$\phi_B = 1310 + 320 = 1630 \text{ kilolines.}$$

This is the required value of ϕ_B within the allowable limits of error. The ampere-turns required can now be found from either (9.5) or (9.8):

$$F = H_B l_B + H_A l_A \tag{9.5}$$

$$= (65 \times 12) + (10.2 \times 36) = 1147 \text{ ampere-turns.}$$

PROBLEMS

(18-IX) How many ampere-turns would have been required to establish a flux $\phi_C = 880$ kilolines in the magnetic core described in Example 1 if leg A had had a cross section of only 8 sq in.? What would have been the other fluxes?

(19-IX) How long an air gap should be cut in leg A of the magnetic circuit described in Example 1 in order that a mmf of 800 ampere-turns will establish a flux of 880 kilolines in leg C? What will be the other fluxes?

(20-IX) The following data are given on a magnetic core of the type shown in Fig. 9.14:

$l_A = l_C = 20$ in.   Material: annealed sheet-steel laminations.

$l_B = 8$ in.

$A_A = A_C = 4$ sq in.   Coil wound on leg A instead of leg B.

$A_B = 1.5$ sq in.

What mmf F_A will be required to establish a flux $\phi_C = 280$ kilolines? What values will the other fluxes have?

(21-IX) A magnetic core similar to that shown in Fig. 9.14 has the following dimensions:

$l_A = l_C = 16$ in.   Material: annealed sheet-steel laminations.

$l_B = 5$ in.

$A_A = A_B = A_C = 2.5$ sq in.

Windings are placed on leg A and also on leg B. The winding on leg B produces a mmf of 128 ampere-turns upward along the leg. What mmf on leg A will be required to establish a flux $\phi_B = 200$ kilolines? What will the other fluxes be?

(**22-IX**) Cores for small transformers and chokes are often built by stacking E-shaped laminations like those shown in Fig. 9.15. The completed coils are slipped on the center leg and the magnetic circuit closed by a stack of I-shaped laminations.

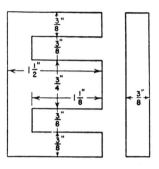

How many ampere-turns would be required to establish a flux of 50 kilolines in the center leg of a core 1 in. think? Assume a stacking factor of 0.9 (that is, in a stack 1 in. thick, there is a 0.1-in. space between laminations) and assume a 0.015-in. air gap at each joint.

Fig. 9.15

(**23-IX**) To what length would the air gaps of the core in Problem 22-IX have to be reduced in order that a flux of 50 kilolines in the center leg could be established by a current of 10 ma in a 4000-turn coil?

(**24-IX**) (a) The core described in Problem 22-IX is magnetized by a winding of 4000 turns carrying a direct current of 10 ma. What flux is established in the center leg? What is the permeability of the steel in mks units? (b) An alternating current ($i = 2 \sin 5000t$) is superimposed upon the direct current in the winding. What flux is established when the alternating current is maximum in the direction of the direct current? What is the incremental permeability (increase in B divided by increase in H) in mks units?

(**25-IX**) (a) The core described in Problem 22-IX is modified by reducing the air gaps at the joints to 0.0015 in. It is magnetized by a winding of 4000 turns carrying a direct current of 10 ma. What flux is established in the center leg? What is the permeability of the steel in mks units? (b) An alternating current ($i = 2 \sin 5000t$) is superimposed upon the direct current in the winding. What flux is established when the alternating current is maximum in the direction of the direct current? What is the incremental permeability (increase in B divided by increase in H) in mks units?

(**26-IX**) The magnetic circuit of a four-pole d-c dynamo is shown in Fig. 9.16. The poles, marked N,S, N,S, are bolted to the frame, and the armature is mounted upon a shaft so it may rotate in the space between the poles. Windings on each pole set up mmf's which establish flux, as shown by the dotted lines. Each flux path includes a section of the frame, two poles, two air gaps, and a section of the armature, and is acted upon by the mmf's of two windings. The dimensions shown below refer to one flux path.

Part	Material	Cross Section of Path	Length of Path
Frame	Cast steel	15 sq in.	17½ in.
1 pole	Cast steel	36 sq in.	4¾ in.
1 air gap		36 sq in.	⅛ in.
Armature	Sheet steel	16 sq in.	7 in.

How many ampere-turns per pole are required to set up a flux of 2500 kilolines per pole?

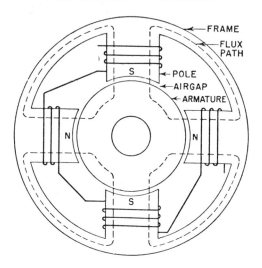

Fig. 9.16

(**27-IX**) What change in the magnetic circuit of the dynamo described in Problem 26-IX should be considered if it is required to radically reduce the ampere-turns per pole? Make calculations to justify your answer.

(**28-IX**) Calculate the composite magnetization curve for the magnetic circuit of the four-pole dynamo described in Problem 26-IX, and from it determine the flux per pole that would be established by a mmf of 2000 ampere-turns per pole.

(**29-IX**) The armature of the d-c dynamo described in Problem 26-IX carries windings that set up a mmf of 250 ampere-turns per pole when the dynamo is operating under rated load. This armature mmf, known as armature reaction, opposes that of the poles. Plot the composite magnetization curve of the dynamo and use it to calculate the percentage of change in flux per pole due to armature reaction when the number of ampere-turns per pole produced by the windings on the poles is (a) 2000, (b) 3500.

STUDY QUESTIONS

1. What magnetic flux density will be established in sheet steel by a magnetic field intensity of: (a) 1 ampere-turn per in., (b) 5 ampere-turns per in., (c) 20 ampere-turns per in., (d) 100 ampere-turns per in.? Use the curves in Appendix Fig. A.

2. For each of the four magnetic materials for which curves are shown in Appendix Fig. A, look up the magnetic flux density produced by a magnetic field intensity of 10 ampere-turns per in.

3. For each of the four magnetic materials for which curves are shown in Appendix Fig. A, look up the magnetic field intensity required to produce a magnetic flux density of 50 kilolines per sq in.

4. Why is it not possible to use a straight-forward procedure when it is desired to find the flux established by a certain magnetomotive force in a magnetic circuit made up of two or more parts in series?

5. Comment on the correctness of this statement: if a magnetic circuit has in it one or more very short air gaps these may be ignored without seriously affecting the results of a calculation of the number of ampere-turns required to establish a certain flux.

6. In general, what effect will the cutting of an air gap in a magnetic circuit have upon the shape of the composite magnetization curve?

7. It is known that a magnetomotive force F_1 will establish a flux ϕ_1 in a certain magnetic circuit, and that a magnetomotive force F_2 will establish a flux ϕ_2 in the same magnetic circuit. What is wrong with the assumption that the two magnetomotive forces acting in conjunction, will establish a flux $\phi_R = \phi_1 + \phi_2$?

8. The same magnetomotive force can be produced by a 1000-turn coil carrying 1 amp or by a 40-turn coil carrying 25 amp or by a 10-turn coil carrying 100 amp. What considerations will determine which coil is best suited in a particular case?

9. The number of ampere-turns needed to establish a certain flux in an iron ring is calculated in the usual way. What assumption is made here as to how the turns are to be distributed around the ring? What would happen if the turns were all concentrated in a small space? Explain.

10. Why does leakage flux in magnetic calculations often turn out to be an important factor, whereas in most electrical problems leakage current can be ignored?

11. Why is alnico a better permanent magnet material than chrome steel, which has greater retentivity? Explain.

12. In a magnetic circuit in the form of a ring of the same material and cross section throughout and magnetized by a uniformly distributed winding, a flux ϕ is established by a magnetomotive force F. How would the flux be affected by increasing the cross section of the ring from A to $2A$?

13. In the magnetic core shown in Fig. 9.14 the magnetomotive force set up by the winding on leg B establishes fluxes ϕ_A, ϕ_B and ϕ_C in legs A, B, and C, respectively. What would be the effect upon each of these fluxes of cutting an air gap in leg C?

Chapter **X**

ELECTROMAGNETIC FORCES

---

1. Forces between current-carrying conductors. The forces of attraction or repulsion between long parallel conductors which carry current furnished the basis for our definition of the mks unit of current in Chapter II. For conductors in free space the force is

$$F = \frac{(2 \times 10^{-7})LI_1I_2}{S}, \tag{2.1}$$

where F is force in newtons;

L is parallel length of the conductors in meters;

I_1 is current in amperes in the first conductor;

I_2 is current in amperes in the second conductor;

S is distance between the conductors in meters.

For the more general case where the conductors are in a medium of permeability μ, the equation becomes

$$F = \frac{\mu L I_1 I_2}{2\pi S}. \tag{7.3}$$

Thus, conductors embedded in iron, or other ferromagnetic substance having high relative permeability, experience forces many times greater than conductors in air or free space.

2. Force upon a current-carrying conductor in a magnetic field. The force acting upon a current-carrying conductor in a magnetic field served as the basis for defining magnetic flux density (Chapter VII). For

232

the case where the conductor is perpendicular to the magnetic lines, the force is

$$F = BLI,$$ (7.1)

where F is force in newtons;

B is magnetic flux density in webers per sq m;

L is length of conductor in meters;

I is current in amperes.

For the more general case where the conductor makes some angle θ with the magnetic lines, the equation becomes

$$F = BLI \sin \theta.$$ (10.1)

The magnetic field may be produced by a permanent magnet or by any arrangement of current-carrying conductors. The force is independent of the medium in which the field exists. The conductor upon which the force acts may be of any length, so long as there is a finite length, or component of length, perpendicular to the magnetic lines. Thus, in the still more general case where the flux density is not uniform in the region in which the conductor lies, or where the direction of the field relative to the conductor is not everywhere the same, we can express the force upon an elemental length of conductor as

$$\Delta F = B \, \Delta LI \sin \theta.$$ (10.2)

The force upon the conductor can then be found as

$$F = \sum_{0}^{L} B \, \Delta LI \sin \theta$$ (10.3)

or in the limit

$$F = \int_{0}^{L} BI \sin \theta \, dl.$$ (10.4)

It must be kept in mind that force is a vector quantity, and in adding forces their directions must always be considered.

A rule for finding the direction of the force may be obtained by a consideration of Fig. 10.1. These conductors carry current in the same direction, and hence the force is attraction, conductor No. 1 being pushed toward the right and conductor No. 2 toward the left. By the right-hand rule, the magnetic field produced by conductor No. 1 in the vicinity of conductor

Fig. 10.1. Strengthened and weakened field method of determining the direction of the force on a current-carrying conductor.

No. 2 is downward, as indicated by the arrows. By the same rule, the magnetic field produced by conductor No. 2 in its own vicinity is clockwise, as indicated by the arrows on the closed lines. Hence, the effect of conductor No. 2 is to modify the field produced by conductor No. 1, strengthening it on the right and weakening it on the left. The force on conductor No. 2, therefore, tends to move it from the strengthened toward the weakened part of the field. We may state the rule as follows: *A current-carrying conductor modifies a magnetic field in which it is placed, and is acted upon by a force which tends to move it from the strengthened toward the weakened part of the field.*

PROBLEMS

(1-X) Two parallel conductors lie in free space, one directly above the other. Each conductor weighs 0.1 lb per ft. The upper conductor floats freely between vertical guides, the separation depending upon the current flowing. For what current would the system be in equilibrium for a separation of 1 cm?

(2-X) Two conductors each 5 m long and each weighing 1 kg are suspended by means of threads 50 cm long so that they hang parallel in the same horizontal plane and 1 cm apart. Equal currents are now sent through the conductors and the separation increases to 2 cm. What are the magnitudes and directions of the currents?

(3-X) A straight conductor which carries a current of 50 amp lies perpendicular to the lines of a magnetic field in which the flux density is 0.8 weber per sq m. Calculate the force per meter of conductor.

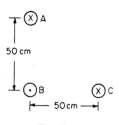

Fig. 10.2

(4-X) What would be the force on the conductor in Problem 3-X if it lay at an angle of 37 degrees with the lines of the field?

(5-X) Three long parallel conductors are arranged as shown in Fig. 10.2. The separations are as indicated. The currents are $I_A = 50$ amp, $I_B = 100$ amp, $I_C = 50$ amp. The conductors are in air. Calculate the magnetic flux density at conductor A due to the currents in B and C, and use it to find the force per meter on conductor A. Show the direction of the force.

(6-X) A one-turn rectangular coil 50 cm by 50 cm carries a current of 100 amp and lies in a uniform magnetic field in which the flux density is 1 weber per sq m. The field is perpendicular to the plane of the coil. Calculate the force on each coil side. Show the directions of current, force, and magnetic field on a diagram. Ignore the forces resulting from the interaction of the flux density due to one coil side with the current in another coil side.

(7-X) The coil in Problem 6-X is rotated so that the direction of the field is parallel to the plane of the coil, and perpendicular to two opposite coil sides. Calculate the force on each coil side. Show the directions of the current, force, and magnetic field on a diagram. Ignore the forces resulting from the interaction of the flux density due to one coil side with the current in another coil side.

(8-X) A one-turn rectangular coil 40 cm by 40 cm carries a current of 100 amp (Fig. 10.3). Consider the coil sides divided into 5-cm segments and measure distances from the middle of the segment. Assume that the flux density throughout the length of a segment is the same as at its midpoint. The coil is in free space. Calculate the approximate force on segment 1 due to (a) segment 10, (b) segment 20, (c) segment 25, (d) segment 3.

(9-X) Determine the direction of force on the conductors shown in Fig. 10.4.

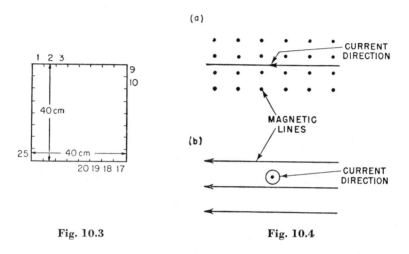

Fig. 10.3   Fig. 10.4

(10-X) Determine the direction of current in conductors shown in Fig. 10.5.

(11-X) Determine the direction of the field in which the conductors lie in Fig. 10.6.

3. Force upon a charged particle moving in a magnetic field.
Suppose a stream of small particles, such as electrons or charged atoms, consists of n particles per meter, each carrying a charge of e coulombs and moving with a velocity of v meters per second, at right angles to a magnetic field in which the flux density is B webers per square meter. The number of particles passing a reference point per second is

$$Z = nv, \tag{10.5}$$

and the quantity of electricity passing the reference point per second is

$$q = Ze = nve. \tag{10.6}$$

But quantity of electricity passing the reference point per second is current, so we may write

$$I = nve. \tag{10.7}$$

If we now substitute this expression for current into Equation (7.1) and put L equal to unity (because n is the number of particles *per meter*), we get

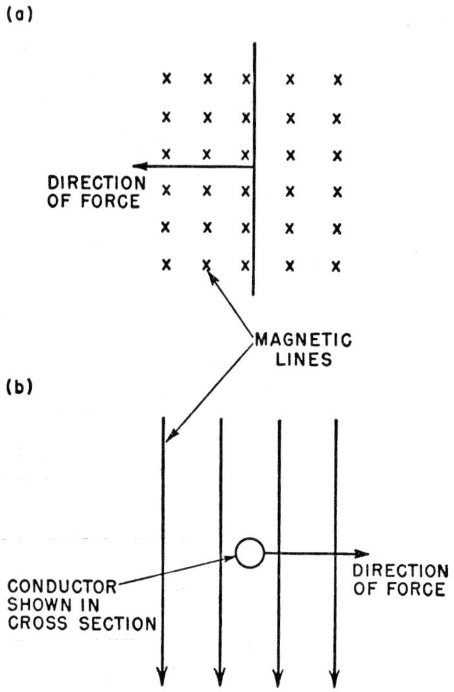

(a)

x x x x x

x x x x x

x x x x x

DIRECTION
OF FORCE   x x x x x

x x x x x

x x x x x

MAGNETIC
LINES

(b)

CONDUCTOR
SHOWN IN
CROSS SECTION

DIRECTION
OF FORCE

Fig. 10.5

$$f = BLI = Bnve, \tag{10.8}$$

where f is the force in newtons acting upon a stream consisting of n particles. By putting $n = 1$, Equation (10.8) becomes

$$f = Bve, \tag{10.9}$$

where f is the force acting upon a single particle.

The direction of the force on a particle depends on the sign of its charge. A positive particle in motion is the equivalent of current, and the local field about it may be determined by the right-hand rule. The direction of the force is, then, from the strengthened toward the weakened part of the field in which the particle moves. A negative particle in motion is the equivalent

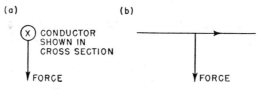

(a)

(x) CONDUCTOR
SHOWN IN
CROSS SECTION

FORCE

(b)

FORCE

Fig. 10.6

of current in the *opposite* direction and, consequently, in applying the right-hand rule, the thumb must be pointed in the direction opposite to the motion.

PROBLEMS

(12-X) Determine the force which acts upon an electron moving with a velocity of 30,000 m per sec perpendicular to a magnetic field in which the flux density is 1.5 webers per sq m.

(13-X) Determine the force which acts upon a positive particle having a charge equivalent in magnitude to one electron and moving with a velocity of 10^6 m per sec perpendicular to a magnetic field in which the flux density is 10,000 gausses.

4. Electromagnetic torque. We can now consider the effect of electromagnetic forces in causing rotation of a coil placed in a magnetic field. This is the underlying principle of the electric motor, and of D'Arsonval type electric meters, as was explained in Chapter V. In Fig. 10.7, a rectangular coil consisting of a single turn of wire lies in a magnetic field of uniform flux density of B webers per square meter. The coil has a length of L meters, a breadth of b meters, and it carries a current of I amperes. The coil is mounted so that it may rotate about its long axis, and its initial position is

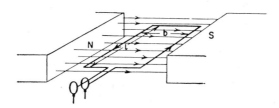

Fig. 10.7. Elementary a-c motor.

such that none of the magnetic lines link it. Figure 10.8a shows the sides of the coil in cross section as it lies in the initial position. Each of the long sides of the coil will experience a force, according to Equation (7.1), of

$$f = BLI \text{ newtons.}$$

These forces each act at right angles to a moment arm of $b/2$ m, and, as a consequence, the coil experiences a torque of

$$T = 2BLI\,\frac{b}{2} = BLbI \text{ newton-m,} \tag{10.10}$$

tending to rotate it clockwise about its axis. As it rotates from its initial position, the forces acting on the coil sides remain constant, but they are no longer at right angles to the moment arms, and, therefore, the torque

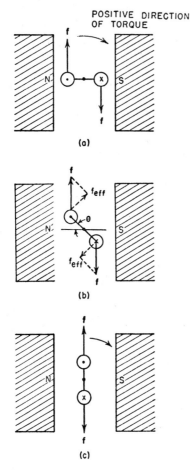

Fig. 10.8. Effect of coil position on torque.

decreases. After the coil has rotated through an angle θ, as shown in Fig. 10.8b, the component of force at right angles to the radius arm is

$$f_{\text{effective}} = f \cos \theta, \qquad (10.11)$$

and the torque is

$$T = BLbI \cos \theta. \qquad (10.12)$$

When the angle of rotation becomes 90°, as in Fig. 10.8c, the effective component of the force is zero and the coil, therefore, locks in this position. As may be seen, it is the position in which the coil is linked by the most magnetic lines.

If the coil is forced past the 90° position by an external torque, it will tend to return. The electromagnetic torque is negative (the clockwise direction being considered positive). We may plot the torque against angle of rotation from the initial position, obtaining a curve like that shown in Fig. 10.9. At the 270° position, there exists a condition of unstable equilibrium. As long as the angle is exactly 270°, there is no torque, and the coil remains at rest. But a small displacement either way gives rise to a positive or negative torque which, if unopposed, rotates the coil back to the 90° position.

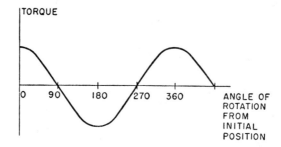

Fig. 10.9. Curve showing variation of torque with coil position.

PROBLEMS

(14-X) A one-turn coil, 20 by 30 cm, is mounted as in Fig. 10.7 so that it may rotate about its long axis in a uniform magnetic field of 0.2 weber per sq m. The coil carries a current of +100 amp. Calculate the torque at 30° intervals of displacement of the coil from the reference position from 0 to 360°. Use positive directions and reference position as in Fig. 10.8. Plot torque against displacement angle.

(15-X) Recalculate the torques and plot torque against displacement using the data in Problem 14-X and the positive directions and reference position shown in Fig. 10.10.

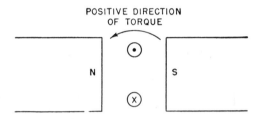

Fig. 10.10

5. Torque in D'Arsonval type meters.

As explained in Section 2 of Chapter V, the magnetic circuits of permanent-magnet moving-coil instruments are so designed that the magnetic lines are radially directed with respect to the axis of the coil. Thus, regardless of the position of the coil, the electromagnetic force will be perpendicular to the radius of the coil throughout the range of the meter (Fig. 5.2).

The force on each coil side is given by

$$f = NBLI, \qquad (10.13)$$

where f is the force in newtons;

  N is the number of turns on the coil;

  B is the flux density in webers per square meter (a constant which depends on the permanent magnet);

  L is the length of the coil side in meters;

  I is the current in amperes.

The deflecting torque for any coil position under the pole pieces is

$$T_d = 2Rf = 2NBLRI, \qquad (10.14)$$

where T_d is the deflecting torque in newton-meters;

  $2R$ is the breadth of the coil in meters.

The restoring torque is

$$T_r = K\theta, \qquad (10.15)$$

where T_r is the restoring torque in newton-meters;
    K is the spring constant in newton-meters per degree of turn;
    θ is the angle in degrees the coil has rotated from zero position.

For the moving system to be in equilibrium,

$$T_d = T_r, \tag{10.16}$$

$$2NBLRI = K\theta, \tag{10.17}$$

$$I = \frac{K\theta}{2NBLR}. \tag{10.18}$$

For any particular instrument, K, N, B, L, and R are constants and may all be combined into a single constant K'. Doing this, we have

$$I = K'\theta. \tag{10.19}$$

Thus, we have shown the deflection to be proportional to the current, and, consequently, that the scale of the meter will be uniform.

The constant K' can be calculated as indicated above, or it can be determined experimentally by observing the deflection that occurs when a known current is sent through the coil.

Example 1: A D'Arsonval instrument is designed to have a coil of 30 turns mounted in a magnetic field of 0.1 weber per sq m flux density. The coil is 3 cm long and 2 cm broad; the spring constant is to be 5×10^{-7} newton-meter per degree. The scale covers 60 degrees of arc, divided into 100 equal parts. What will be the current per degree? The current per scale division? The current required for full-scale deflection?

SOLUTION: The deflecting torque T_d by Equation (10.14) is

    $(30)(0.1)(3 \times 10^{-2})(2 \times 10^{-2})I$ newton-meters $= 18 \times 10^{-4}I$.

The restoring torque T_r by Equation (10.15) is

    $5 \times 10^{-7}\theta$ newton-meter.

For equilibrium at 1°,

$$18 \times 10^{-4}I = (5 \times 10^{-7})(1),$$
$$I = 2.78 \times 10^{-4} \text{ amp.}$$

For equilibrium at 1 scale division,

$$18 \times 10^{-4}I = (5 \times 10^{-7})^{60}\!/_{100},$$
$$I = 1.666 \times 10^{-4} \text{ amp.}$$

For equilibrium at full scale,

$$18 \times 10^{-4}I = (5 \times 10^{-7})60,$$
$$I = 1.666 \times 10^{-2}, \text{ or } 16.66 \text{ milliamperes (ma).}$$

Example 2: On test, the instrument described in Example 1 shows a deflection of 95 scale divisions for a current of 16.66 ma. What is the actual current for full-scale deflection? What could account for the difference between the calculated and the actual value?

SOLUTION: Current for full-scale deflection is

$$\frac{16.66}{95} \times 100 = 17.52 \text{ ma.}$$

The difference is due to the flux density of the permanent magnet or the constant of the spring differing somewhat from the design values.

PROBLEMS

(16-X) A D'Arsonval instrument has a 50-turn coil, 1.5 cm long by 1 cm broad, mounted in a magnetic field in which the flux density is 0.1 weber per sq m. The scale covers 65 degrees of arc divided into 50 equal parts. What should be the spring constant (newton-meters per degree) so that the current for full-scale deflection will be 10 ma?

(17-X) A D'Arsonval instrument has been designed to be deflected full scale by a current of 10 ma. What would be the effect on the current for full-scale deflection of: (a) Increasing the strength of the magnet by 10 per cent? (b) Increasing the number of turns on the coil by 10 per cent? (c) Increasing the strength of the spring by 10 per cent?

(18-X) What differences in design might be expected as between instrument A with a current of 1 ma for full-scale deflection, and instrument B with a current of 10 ma for full-scale deflection?

6. Electric motors. It is apparent that if continuous rotation of a coil like that in Fig. 10.8 is to be produced, there must be some means of reversing the current in the coil, and thereby maintaining the torque in the positive direction after the coil passes the 90° position. The simplest possible way of doing this is to use alternating current. This arrangement is not self-starting, because with the coil in the 90° position, there would be no torque, no matter what the magnitude and direction of the current. If, however, the coil be set in rotation by some means, without current flowing in it, at a speed equal to the frequency of the current to be used, and then the switch be closed at precisely the correct time (so that the current is positive maximum when the coil is in the initial position, as in Fig. 10.11a, torque will be developed always in the same direction, and the device will continue to run. It needs to be pointed out that the current directions marked in Fig. 10.11 are the directions selected as positive, not actual directions. The instantaneous values of current corresponding to coil positions a, b, and c are shown by the graph. Thus, in position b the current is zero, and in position c it is maximum negative. The torque fluctuates

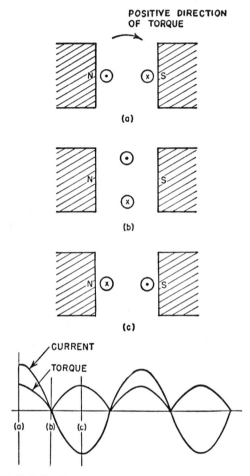

Fig. 10.11. Relation between current, coil position, and torque in an elementary a-c motor.

between zero and positive maximum but is never negative. This is an elementary synchronous motor. If it is to run at all, its time of rotation must be the same as the period of the alternating current which energizes it.

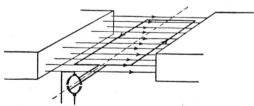

Fig. 10.12. Elementary d-c motor.

In order to obtain continuous rotation of the coil with direct current, it is necessary to provide a **commutator,** or switching device, to reverse the current in the coil at the proper time. The commutator is a metal ring, cut into two or more insulated segments, and mounted so that it rotates with the coil as in Fig. 10.12. The ends of the coil are connected to the commutator segments, and connection with the source of energy is through the **brushes** which maintain sliding contact with the commutator segments. In Fig. 10.13a, current flows through the coil in the direction marked as positive, which tends to rotate the coil clockwise in the direction selected as positive.

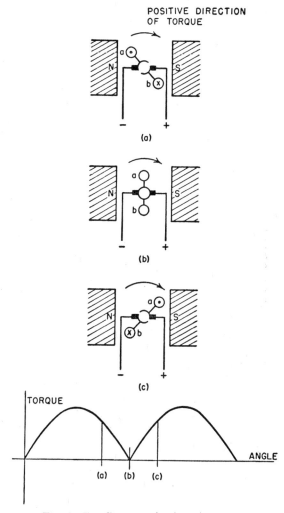

Fig. 10.13. Commutation in a d-c motor.

In Fig. 10.13*b*, both commutator segments are in contact with both brushes, and the coil is short-circuited. The current in the coil is effecting its change in direction during the time of short circuit, and is considered to be zero at the instant shown. In Fig. 10.13*c*, the short circuit no longer exists, and the current flows through the coil sides in the direction *opposite* to that selected as positive, thus maintaining torque in the clockwise direction. It is essential to understand that the current directions marked in Figs. 10.12 and 10.13 are the directions selected as positive, not actual directions.

Motors like those shown in Figs. 10.11 and 10.13 are not practical for several reasons. First, the torque of any single-coil motor is pulsating, and even though it is never in the negative direction, its magnitude falls to zero twice during a revolution. Such a motor cannot successfully deliver much mechanical power, and is able to run at all only because the inertia of the rotating parts carries it over the dead points, where no torque is developed. By using two coils having the same axis of rotation, but with their planes perpendicular to each other, as in Fig. 10.14, it is possible to eliminate the

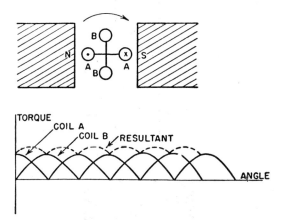

Fig. 10.14. Torque in a multicoil d-c motor.

dead points and make the torque much more uniform, for when one coil is in the 90° position, where it contributes nothing to the torque, the other is in the position to develop maximum torque. In practical motors, the number of coils is further increased, and the resultant torque made still more uniform. The problem of arranging the coils and connecting them to form a practical **winding** is treated in books on electrical machinery.

The production of any considerable torque also requires that the magnetic paths of the flux be mostly in iron, in order that large flux densities may be produced in the region occupied by the coils. This is accomplished by placing the coil sides in slots cut lengthwise in the surface of a cylindrical iron core, shaping the pole faces to conform to this cylinder, and completing the magnetic path through the frame of the machine. Magnetic problems involving such flux paths have already been considered in a previous chapter.

PROBLEM

(**19-X**) The armature of a d-c motor has 36 slots, in each of which there are two coil sides. There are 9 turns per coil, making a total of 18 conductors per slot, each of which carries a current of 50 amp. Of the 36 slots, 28 lie under the pole faces in a uniform flux density of 1.08 webers per sq m. The other 8 slots lie opposite the interpolar spaces, and the flux density will be considered to be zero. The flux entering the armature may be considered as perpendicular to the surface and to the conductors in the slots. The effective length of the armature conductors is 30 cm, and the effective radius of the armature is 25 cm. Calculate:
    (a) The force on each armature conductor.
    (b) The force on all the conductors in a slot.
    (c) The torque due to all the conductors in a single slot.
    (d) The total torque due to all the slots under the poles.

**7. Force acting to close the air gap in a magnetic circuit —
magnetic pull.** When an air gap exists in a magnetic circuit, forces act which tend to close the gap. The iron faces between which the air gap lies are magnetic poles, the north-seeking pole being the one at which the magnetic flux passes from iron to air, and the south-seeking pole the one at which it passes from air to iron. The force that tends to close the air gap may be regarded as being in part the attraction between the unlike magnetic poles, and it is sometimes referred to as **magnetic pull.**

In order to get a mathematical expression for calculating such a force, let us consider a magnetic circuit formed by cutting an iron ring into two halves and separating the halves to form two short air gaps of equal length, as shown in Fig. 10.15. Let the cross section of the ring be A square meters

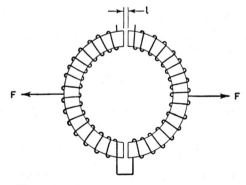

Fig. 10.15. Magnetic pull between halves of a magnetized iron ring.

and the length of each air gap l meters. The winding carries a current which establishes a flux density of B webers per square meter in each air gap and results in forces which tend to pull the two halves of the ring together. There will be energy stored in the air gaps in amount

$$W = \frac{1}{2}\frac{B^2}{\mu} \text{ joules per cu m.} \tag{7.81}$$

Since the volume of each air gap is lA cubic meters, the total energy stored in the air gaps is

$$W = \frac{B^2 lA}{\mu_0} \text{ joules.} \tag{10.20}$$

Now, suppose a force of F newtons is applied which overcomes the forces of attraction, and lengthens each air gap by an amount Δl. Meanwhile, the current in the windings is increased in order to maintain the flux density exactly constant. The work done by this force is

$$\Delta W = F \, \Delta l \text{ joules.} \tag{10.21}$$

This work will appear as additional energy stored in the lengthened air gaps:

$$\Delta W = \frac{B^2 \, \Delta lA}{\mu_0} \text{ joules.} \tag{10.22}$$

Equating the right-hand side of (10.21) to the right-hand side of (10.22) and solving for F we obtain

$$F = \frac{B^2 A}{\mu_0} \text{ newtons.} \tag{10.23}$$

This force is divided equally between the two air gaps. Consequently, the magnetic pull at each air gap is

$$\frac{1}{2} F = \frac{B^2 A}{2\mu_0} \text{ newtons.} \tag{10.24}$$

It can be seen from this equation that the magnetic pull might actually be increased in some instances by decreasing the cross section of the air gap. If the amount of magnetic flux remains constant, then since

$$B = \frac{\phi}{A},$$

a decrease in cross section would mean an increase in the flux density. Since flux density appears to the second power in Equation (10.24), and cross section to the first power only, a decrease in cross section means an increase in magnetic pull.

We now have an equation for calculating the pull exerted by all sorts of magnets, both permanent magnets and electromagnets, upon pieces of ferromagnetic material, provided there is a complete magnetic circuit and relatively short air gaps. The calculation of the pull of a lifting magnet, for instance, or of the magnets of an electric bell, can be made by use of this equation. Calculations for bar magnets and solenoids can seldom be made by Equation (10.24) because of the difficulty of determining flux density in cases where a larger part of the length of the magnetic path is in air.

Example: A wrought-iron ring having a mean diameter of 7 in. and a circular cross section of 1 sq in. is cut in half as in Fig. 10.15 and each half is uniformly wound with 760 turns of wire. With the halves separated 0.05 in., what will be the attractive force when the current in the windings is 2 amp?

SOLUTION: Solving for the flux density in the air gaps in the usual way, we find it to be 1.395 webers per sq m.

The area of the faces between which the pull is exerted is

$$\frac{1}{(39.37)^2} = 6.45 \times 10^{-4} \text{ sq m.}$$

The attractive force, by Equation (10.23), is

$$F = \frac{B^2A}{\mu_0} = \frac{(1.395)^2(6.45 \times 10^{-4})}{4\pi \times 10^{-7}} = 1000 \text{ newtons}$$

$$= 224 \text{ lb (total for both air gaps).}$$

PROBLEMS

(20-X) The magnetic circuit of a telegraph relay is constructed of wrought iron, with dimensions in inches as shown in Fig. 10.16. There are 1100 turns on each pole core. To attract the armature and close the relay against the pull of the spring requires a force of 5 g. What current in the winding will be necessary to close the relay? Ignore leakage flux.

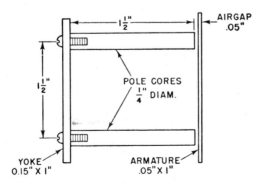

Fig. 10.16

(21-X) The magnetic circuit of a small lifting magnet is constructed of wrought iron with dimensions in centimeters as shown in Fig. 10.17. A 100-turn coil around the central core establishes flux over paths indicated by dotted lines. Assume that the surfaces of the magnet and armature are smooth enough to permit the armature and magnet to be fitted together with an effective air gap of 0.005 in. Determine the current in the coil to enable the magnet to exert a pull of 200 lb on the armature.

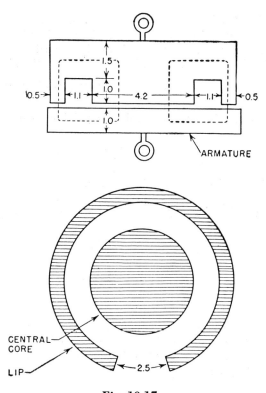

Fig. 10.17

STUDY QUESTIONS

1. What would be the effect on magnetic pull of chamfering the pole faces?

2. From Equation (10.23) it would seem that magnetic pull does not depend upon the distance between the pole faces. Explain.

3. In deriving the expression for magnetic pull it is assumed that all the additional energy stored in the air gaps when the pole faces are separated by an additional distance Δl comes from the agency that causes the separation. How can we be sure none of it comes from increasing the current in the winding?

4. How do we know that the magnetic field intensity is the same at all points which are equidistant from a very long straight wire which carries current? Why would it not be true for a short straight wire which carried current?

5. Would parallel streams of like-charged particles moving in free space be attracted as would current-carrying conductors? Explain.

6. Devise a simple statement of how a current-carrying loop will orient itself in a magnetic field.

7. The running of an elementary single-coil motor can sometimes be improved by adding a flywheel. Explain.

8. What is the function of the commutator in an elementary d-c motor? Why is it not required on an a-c motor?

9. In starting an elementary synchronous motor it is noticed that sometimes several trials are necessary. At other times the motor starts immediately. Explain.

Chapter XI

ELECTROMAGNETIC INDUCTION AND MOTIONAL ELECTROMOTIVE FORCE

---

1. Electromotive force caused by a changing magnetic field. Faraday's experiments in 1831 led him to the concept of lines of magnetic flux as a means of explaining how it was possible for a change in current in one circuit to cause a current in another circuit with which no electrical connections existed. This concept proved so useful that it has continued to occupy a principal place throughout the history of electrical science. Faraday's law of electromagnetic induction, which expresses the relationship between electromotive force and rate of change of magnetic flux,

$$E = N \frac{\Delta \phi}{\Delta T}, \tag{7.62}$$

served as an alternative definition of magnetic flux and its unit (Chapter VII). We shall now study this law more carefully, with the object of determining its usefulness and limitations, and also of trying to gain a better understanding of the magnetic flux concept itself.

In Faraday's original experiments, the changes in flux were basically changes in flux density, brought about by changing the current in some neighboring circuit. To illustrate this, let A and B in Fig. 11.1 represent circular turns of wire, fixed in position relative to one another and having a common axis. With the switch open in circuit A, no magnetic field exists

in the region of the coils because no
current is flowing. Upon closing the
switch, current begins to flow in circuit A,
establishing a magnetic field, some of the
lines of which link circuit B. As the current in circuit A increases, the magnetic
field intensity and magnetic flux density
in all the space surrounding circuit A will
increase, which will result in an increase
in the number of magnetic lines linking
circuit B, and, consequently, in an emf
induced in circuit B, which causes current
to flow, and the galvanometer to be deflected.

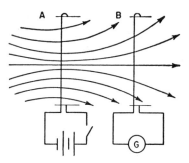

Fig. 11.1. Emf induced by a changing magnetic field.

That an emf will likewise be induced in circuit A is evident from the
same reasoning. Its effect is not so readily detected because there is another
source of emf (the battery) in that circuit. The effect of this emf will be
studied in more detail in Section 15. The emf in circuit B is called an **emf of
mutual induction,** that in circuit A is called an **emf of self-induction.**
These emf's, of course, will persist only as long as the current continues to
change in circuit A. When the current reaches its Ohm's law value (usually
in a very short time), the flux ceases to increase and the induced emf's
become zero.

If the switch is opened, or if any change is made in the current which
flows in circuit A, emf's appear in both circuits and persist as long as the
change continues. Thus, if a source of alternating current were substituted
for the battery in circuit A, the current in that circuit would be continually
changing, and both self and mutual emf's would always be present. Our two
circuits would then function as a **transformer.**

2. Lenz's law. We must now find some way to determine the **direction** of an induced emf. Let us first suppose that the emf in circuit B,
Fig. 11.1, acts to send current in the same direction as the current in circuit
A. Such a current would further strengthen the original magnetic field set
up by the increasing current in circuit A, and thus increase the induced emf,
which would increase the current, and so forth endlessly. This is obviously
impossible. Consequently, we must have been wrong when we supposed the
induced emf to be in the direction we did. It is in the contrary direction,
and acts to send current around circuit B in such a direction as to oppose the
increase in the original field, not aid it. This reasoning leads to **Lenz's law,**
which is a statement in electrical terms of the law of conservation of energy:
*The emf induced in a circuit by a change in flux will be in the direction current
would have to flow in order to oppose the change in flux.*

Lenz's law is readily applied to any complete circuit through which the flux is changing. It must be carefully noted that the law says "in order to oppose the **change** of flux," not "in order to oppose the flux." If the flux is decreasing, the emf is in the direction in which current must flow to aid the flux, and tends to prevent its decrease. Thus, referring again to Fig. 11.1, if the switch in circuit A is opened, the current and, therefore, the flux, must decrease to zero. The emf induced in circuit B will now actually be in such a direction as to send current in the same direction as the current in circuit A, thus aiding the flux and opposing its decrease.

The direction of the emf of self-induction set up in circuit A may likewise be determined by Lenz's law. It must always "be in the direction current would have to flow in order to oppose the **change** in flux." When the switch is closed and flux is increasing, the induced emf in circuit A opposes the battery emf, tending to prevent the increase in the current that is causing the flux. When the switch is opened and flux is decreasing, the induced emf in circuit A aids the battery emf, tending to maintain the current and prevent the decrease in flux.

PROBLEMS

(**1-XI**) Determine the actual direction of the induced emf in Fig. 11.2a and b.

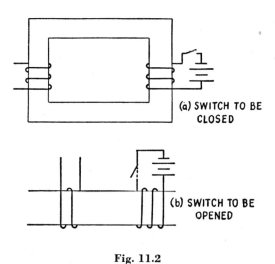

(a) SWITCH TO BE
CLOSED

(b) SWITCH TO BE
OPENED

Fig. 11.2

(**2-XI**) Determine the actual direction of the induced emf in Fig. 11.3a and b.
(**3-XI**) Determine the actual direction of the induced emf in Fig. 11.4a and b.

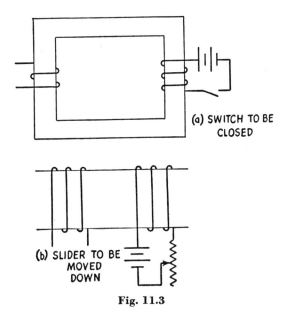

(a) SWITCH TO BE
CLOSED

(b) SLIDER TO BE
MOVED
DOWN

Fig. 11.3

3. Emf caused by a conductor moving in a magnetic field. It can be readily demonstrated that any change in the flux linking a circuit as a consequence of its motion in the magnetic field will also cause an emf. Such emf's are called **motional,** or **generated,** emf's as distinguished from induced emf's as discussed in the preceding section. Suppose, for example, that circuit B in Fig. 11.1 were pivoted so that it could be rotated about a diameter into the position shown in Fig. 11.5. With the current in circuit A, and, therefore, the magnetic field intensity and flux density at all points in the region remaining unchanged, the number of mag-

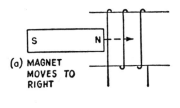

(a) MAGNET
MOVES TO
RIGHT

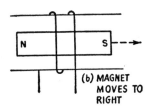

(b) MAGNET
MOVES TO
RIGHT

Fig. 11.4

netic lines linking circuit B will decrease from a maximum, when it is in the position shown in Fig. 11.1, to a minimum in the position shown in Fig. 11.5, and an emf will be set up in the coil while it is in motion, as will be demonstrated by the deflection of the galvanometer. Experiments show that Faraday's law is valid for motional emf's as it was for those induced by magnetic fields which varied in intensity.

It is not necessary that the entire circuit shift in position relative to the magnetic field. If any part of it moves in such a way as to increase or

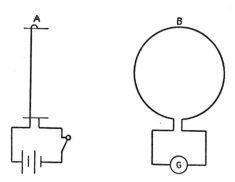

Fig. 11.5. Emf induced in a coil rotated in a fixed magnetic field.

decrease the total number of magnetic lines linked, the effect is the same.

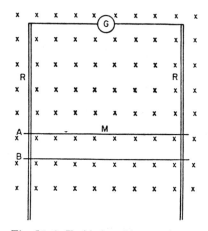

Fig. 11.6. Emf induced in a conductor which cuts magnetic lines.

Suppose a uniform magnetic field (that is, one having the same flux density at every point) is established perpendicular to the plane of the paper as indicated by the x arrows in Fig. 11.6. The circuit lies in the plane of the paper, and consists of two metal rails R, R, connected at the upper end by the galvanometer. A movable conductor M is arranged to slide along the rails, maintaining contact with them, and keeping always parallel to its initial position. As M moves from position A to position B, there is, obviously, an increase in the number of magnetic lines linking the loop, and, consequently, an emf (evidenced by the deflection of the galvanometer), and again found to be in accordance with Faraday's law.

Now the only way in which additional lines can be admitted to link the circuit is by the movement of the sliding conductor M. As it moves lines are cut by it — that is, they are transferred from one side of it to the other, and are admitted to link the circuit. Thus, in the particular case under consideration, the rate of increase of flux linking the loop,* and the electromotive force may be calculated on this basis.

4. The BlV rule. Since the rate at which the moving conductor is

*This is true provided the ends of the moving conductor do not project beyond the rails R, R, and provided, of course, there is no change in flux density.

cutting flux (for an arrangement such as that shown in Fig. 11.6) is equal to the rate of change of flux linking the circuit, we can obtain an expression for motional emf in terms of magnetic flux density, the length of the moving conductor, and its velocity relative to the field. Suppose the length of the moving conductor in Fig. 11.6 is l meters, and the distance traversed as it moves from position A to position B is ΔS meters. Then, if the magnetic flux density is B webers per square meter, the change in flux linking the loop is

$$\Delta \phi = Bl\Delta S. \tag{11.1}$$

If the average velocity at which the conductor moves is V meters per second, then the time required to move from position A to position B is

$$\Delta T = \frac{\Delta S}{V}. \tag{11.2}$$

Substituting (11.1) and (11.2) into the Faraday's law equation, we obtain

$$E = N\frac{\Delta \phi}{\Delta T} = \frac{Bl\,\Delta S}{\Delta S/V} = BlV. \tag{11.3}$$

To illustrate the equivalence of the two methods, we shall now consider a numerical example.

Example: A conductor 10 cm long moves as in Fig. 11.6, requiring 10^{-4} sec to move 2 cm from position A to position B. The flux density is 10^{-6} weber per sq m perpendicular to the paper. Determine the average emf generated in the conductor as it moves from position A to position B by (a) change-of-flux-linkage method and (b) flux-cut method.

SOLUTION: (a) The change in flux linking the loop is

$$\Delta \phi = Bl\,\Delta S$$

$$= (10^{-6})(0.1 \times 0.02) = 2 \times 10^{-9} \text{ weber,}$$

$$E = N\frac{\Delta \phi}{\Delta T}$$

$$= 1\frac{2 \times 10^{-9}}{10^{-4}} = 2 \times 10^{-5} \text{ v.}$$

(b) The velocity at which the conductor moves is

$$V = \frac{\Delta S}{\Delta T} = \frac{0.02}{10^{-4}} = 200 \text{ m per sec,}$$

$$E = BlV$$

$$= (10^{-6})(0.1)(200) = 2 \times 10^{-5} \text{ v.}$$

Equation (11.3) is based on a straight conductor that moves in a direction at right angles to the magnetic lines. If this condition is not met in a particular problem, it is necessary to find a component of flux density, or a component of the velocity, such that they are at right angles. Suppose the magnetic lines in Fig. 11.6 were not perpendicular, but inclined to the left, making an angle of θ degrees with the surface of the paper. The component of flux density perpendicular to the paper would be, then,

$$B_P = B \sin \theta, \tag{11.4}$$

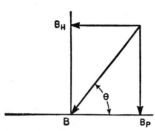

Fig. 11.7. Components of magnetic flux density.

as can be seen from a study of Fig. 11.7. In like manner, it can be seen that if the flux lines are perpendicular to the paper but both rails are tilted so that the plane in which the conductor moves makes an angle of α degrees with the paper, then a component of velocity

$$V_P = V \cos \alpha \tag{11.5}$$

would have to be used.

In the form in which it was stated in Section 2, Lenz's law cannot be applied to conductors that are not part of a complete circuit. Therefore, various rules of thumb have been devised which do apply to such conductors, and three such rules are given below.

1. *The emf in the moving conductor will be in such direction as to cause a current which would strengthen the field on the leading side of the conductor.*

2. *The emf will be in the direction pointed by the thumb if the conductor is allowed to strike the palm of the open right hand held with the fingers in the direction of the magnetic lines.*

3. *The emf will be in the direction pointed by the middle finger of the right hand held with the thumb, forefinger, and middle finger mutually perpendicular, the thumb pointing in the direction of motion and the forefinger pointing in the direction of the magnetic lines.*

There is no derivation for these rules: they simply are used because they happen to give the correct results. The student should verify all of them by applying them to Fig. 11.6.

PROBLEMS

(4-XI) In an apparatus like that in Fig. 11.6, the slide rails are 10 in. apart. The distance from the cross connection to the moving conductor in position A is 20 in.; to position B, 22 in. The lines of a uniform magnetic field in which the flux density is 5×10^{-7} weber per sq m are perpendicular to the plane of the apparatus. Calculate by Faraday's law the emf generated in the circuit if the conductor moves from A to B in 10^{-3} sec.

(5-XI) Recalculate the emf in Problem 4-XI, using the *BlV* rule.

(6-XI) What would have been the emf in Problem 5-XI if the lines had inclined to the right, making an angle of 50° with the paper? Use the *BlV* rule.

(7-XI) What would have been the emf in Problem 5-XI if the conductor were moved in a direction which makes an angle of 30° with the perpendicular to its length? Use the *BlV* rule.

(8-XI) The magnetic lines of the earth's field in a certain locality make an angle of 65° with the surface of the earth, entering the earth from the south. The flux density is 0.6 gauss. What emf would be generated in an axle of a railway train moving north at a speed of 75 mph? Take the length of the axle as 4 ft, 8½ in.

(9-XI) What emf would be generated in a vertical antenna 2 m long on an automobile going north at a speed of 75 mph in the locality of Problem 8-XI? What emf would be generated if the automobile were going east?

(10-XI) What is the direction of the emf induced in a loop of wire that is raised from a position flat on the floor to a position in an E-W vertical plane?

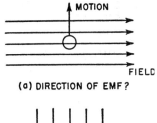

(a) DIRECTION OF EMF ?

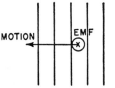

(b) DIRECTION OF FIELD ?

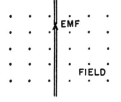

(c) DIRECTION OF MOTION ?

Fig. 11.8

(11-XI) Work out the thing called for in each of the cases of a conductor moving in magnetic field as shown in Fig. 11.8.

5. Limitations of the *BlV* rule. The questions may be asked, "Is an emf developed in a moving conductor that is not part of a loop? When is Equation (11.3) applicable?" It would seem that the answer to the first question could readily be found by experiment. However, when we connect a galvanometer or other measuring instrument to the ends of the moving conductor, we complete a circuit, and any emf that is measured could be attributed to a change of flux linking this circuit, unless it could be shown there were no such change. In certain arrangements of moving conductors, as in a Faraday disk generator (Section 10), it is possible to produce and measure an electromotive force in a loop when no change in the flux linking the loop is taking place. In such a case, Faraday's law would not give the right result: since there is no change in the flux linking the circuit, Faraday's law would give zero for the emf when actually an emf is being measured. We may conclude, therefore, that a change in flux linkages is not essential, and an emf will be generated when flux is cut by a conductor that is not part of a complete circuit. To calculate the magnitude of such an emf, the BlV rule must be used.

It is easy to see that Equation (11.3) would not be applicable to the calculation of an emf caused by a change in flux density. In Fig. 11.6, if there is no motion of the conductor M, Equation (11.3) would give zero for the emf when actually an emf would exist if the flux density were increasing or decreasing. To calculate the magnitude of such an emf, Faraday's law must be used.

Suppose now that in the arrangement shown in Fig. 11.6, the flux density were made to increase and the conductor M were moved downward at the same time. We would thus have the amount of flux linking the loop increasing for two reasons. Nevertheless, Faraday's law holds, and if we divide the change in flux by the time it took to bring it about, we find the average emf generated in the loop due to both motion and change in flux density. But using Equation (11.3) (after having determined the average flux density for the period of time the conductor M was in motion) will give the average emf due to motion only.

Thus we see that Equation (11.3) is applicable to the calculation of a motional emf when the conductor moves at right angles to a uniform magnetic field and to its own length.

Numerous paradoxical circuits and arrangements can be devised in which an emf might be predicted by one of the rules and experiment prove the emf non-existent, or on the other hand no emf might be predicted and experiment prove one to exist. In problems where both Faraday's law and the BlV rule give the same result, there is little question about its validity. If they do not give the same result the problem needs to be studied further to see whether in fact it involves a change of flux density, a conductor cutting flux, or a combination of the two.

6. Physical interpretation of emf's. We have seen that an emf may be produced by: (1) a change in the amount of magnetic flux linking a circuit, brought about by either: (a) a change in the magnetic flux density or (b) a change in position of the circuit or some part of it relative to the magnetic field; or by (2) cutting of magnetic flux by a moving conductor. Actually (1b) and (2) may be regarded as two ways of dealing with the same phenomenon. Let us now see whether we can find reasons why an emf should appear as a consequence of either a variation of magnetic flux density or a cutting of magnetic lines.

Let us begin with the flux-cut idea. In Fig. 11.9, a conductor M is represented as moving downward in a magnetic field perpendicular to the page, keeping always parallel to its initial position, exactly as described in Section 3. In the space lattice of the conductor are free electrons, which of necessity move downward as parts of the conductor itself. Now, any

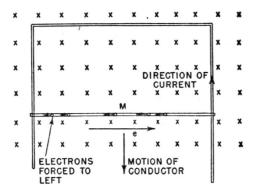

Fig. 11.9. Forces exerted on the free electrons of a moving conductor in a magnetic field.

moving charge is the equivalent of a current, and in a magnetic field will experience a force at right angles to its direction of motion and to the lines of the field. An electron moving downward is the equivalent of current upward, and will create a local field about itself which will strengthen the main field in Fig. 11.9 on the right and weaken it on the left, resulting in a force acting to move the electron to the left along the conductor. If the conductor is part of a complete circuit, as it is here, electrons are put in motion all the way around the circuit, and current will flow as long as the motion continues. The direction of the emf and the current will be contrary to the electron flow as shown, and will be found to agree with the direction as found by Lenz's law or by any of the various hand rules. The energy expended in maintaining the current through the resistance of the circuit can be shown to be equal to the energy required to move the conductor against the emf owing to its carrying current in a magnetic field, and, therefore, comes from the source that moves the conductor, not from the field.

If the conductor is insulated from the rails on which it slides, the free electrons will experience forces as before, and will move to the left until there is established throughout the length of the conductor an electric field of intensity $\mathcal{E}$* just sufficient to prevent any further motion of electrons. There would then exist between the ends of the conductor an emf,

$$E = BlV. \tag{11.6}$$

We have thus explained motional emf as being the direct consequence of the forces that act upon moving charges in a magnetic field and, therefore, of the forces that act between charges moving relative to one another. The concept of change of flux linkages, although valid in cases where the moving conductor is part of a complete circuit, is seen to be a somewhat indirect way

*Section 3, Chapter XII.

of explaining the phenomenon, though the laws of Faraday and of Lenz are nearly always the best and most convenient means of actually calculating the emf.

We now have to consider the origin of emf's that appear as a consequence of a change in the flux density of a magnetic field. Suppose the conductor M in Fig. 11.9 and all parts of the circuit remain at rest with respect to the field, but that the flux density increases owing to an increase in current in the circuit that establishes the flux. Since there is now no relative motion between the field and the circuit, our explanation of the emf as being due to magnetic forces acting upon moving electrons is no longer valid. We know, however, that electrons will experience forces in an *electric* field, regardless of whether they are in motion or at rest with respect to the field. We may, therefore, resolve our difficulty by supposing that a magnetic field in which the flux density varies with time gives rise to an electric field. The free electrons of the circuit would then experience electric forces, which, if the circuit were so placed that it coincided with the electric field throughout its length, would result in an emf which would act to cause a flow of current. In fact, it is not necessary that the circuit *coincide* with the field at every point, but simply that if we divide the circuit into segments, take the product of every segment's length by the component of the electric field intensity in the direction of the segment, and then sum up all these products, the summation should not be zero.

We need to emphasize at this point that we do not induce current: we induce emf, and the current that flows then depends upon the resistance of the circuit provided. Suppose we made up a circuit of glass tubing instead of wire. The emf induced in it (that is, the summation of the products of electric field intensity by length) would be precisely the same as for a copper conductor. Of course no current could be made to flow in such a circuit because of its enormous resistance.

When it comes to the matter of placing the circuit in the electric field to the best advantage (that is, so that it shall coincide as nearly as possible with the field) we usually find it expedient to make use again of the concept of lines of magnetic flux, and simply place the circuit so that the variation in the number of magnetic lines linking it will be a maximum. One thing is equivalent to the other, and the geometry of the varying magnetic field is usually more apparent than that of the associated electric field.

7. Representation of emf's. As we have already learned, the direction of a current is conveyed to a reader by telling him if it is positive or negative, and drawing an arrow to indicate which direction we are calling positive. Both these things are necessary: a statement that a certain current is positive is meaningless unless there is an indication of *which* direction is positive. These same statements may be made regarding emf's set up in coils and conductors. We select a direction in which the emf will be designated as positive, and plainly indicate this **positive direction** by placing an arrow beside the coil or conductor. We then proceed to apply Lenz's law to determine the actual direction of the emf. If the actual direction of the emf turns out to be in the arrow direction, it is accordingly written as positive; if opposite to the arrow, it is designated as negative. To illustrate this procedure, let us consider a coil like that shown in Fig. 11.10 which is linked by magnetic flux as shown, owing to current either in

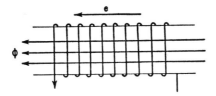

Fig. 11.10. Positive direction for induced electromotive force.

the coil itself, or in a neighboring circuit. The direction chosen as positive for the emf is indicated by the arrow marked e and placed alongside the coil. This arrow denotes that a rise of potential in the direction it points (from the right-hand terminal toward the left-hand terminal of the coil) will be considered positive. Now, let us suppose that the flux linking the coil is increasing. Lenz's law tells us that the induced emf is actually in the direction selected as positive, tending to cause current to flow out at the lefthand terminal, thereby opposing the increase in the flux. The emf is, therefore, positive, and we write

$$E = +N \frac{\Delta \phi}{\Delta T}. \tag{11.7}$$

If by chance we had selected the other direction as positive, it should be clear that since the actual direction of the emf is *not* the direction selected as positive, we would have had to write

$$E = -N \frac{\Delta \phi}{\Delta T}. \tag{11.8}$$

Let us now suppose that the flux linking the coil is decreasing. By applying Lenz's law, we find that the induced emf is actually in the direction opposite to that selected as positive, since it must tend to cause current to flow out at the right-hand terminal of the coil, thereby opposing the decrease in flux that is taking place. It is plain, then, that the emf is negative, but before writing it down, we must remember that in this case (flux decreasing) $\Delta \phi / \Delta T$ is itself a negative quantity, and the use of the minus sign is not only unnecessary, but wrong. Accordingly, we write

$$E = +N\frac{\Delta\phi}{\Delta T}. \tag{11.9}$$

It appears then, since (11.9) is identical with (11.7), that whether the flux is increasing or decreasing makes no difference in the expression to be used. The emf is actually in one direction for increasing flux and in the opposite direction for decreasing flux. The expression to be used is the same because $\Delta\phi/\Delta T$ itself is positive or negative according to whether the flux is increasing or decreasing.

To make the illustration complete, let us suppose we had taken the positive direction opposite to that in Fig. 11.10. With the flux decreasing, the emf would then actually be in the direction selected as positive and must, therefore, be represented as positive. But $\Delta\phi/\Delta T$ is itself negative. The correct expression is, therefore,

$$E = -N\frac{\Delta\phi}{\Delta T}. \tag{11.10}$$

The student may ask why we select a positive direction in advance at all. Why not apply Lenz's law at once and determine the actual direction in each case, then let this be the direction selected as positive? The answer to this is rather obvious. In a-c circuits, the flux linking the circuit first increases, then decreases, then increases in the opposite direction, then decreases, and so forth, repeating this cycle of variation over and over. The actual direction of the emf is not the same at every instant, and we have nothing to recommend the choice of one direction any more than the other as being the direction to consider positive. But a choice must be made if we are to speak intelligibly of positive or negative values of an emf. Even in problems where the flux change is limited to an increase or a decrease, the choice of a positive direction is arbitrary. In many textbooks the law is consistently written

$$E = -N\frac{\Delta\phi}{\Delta T},$$

which implies that the positive direction of the induced electromotive force was selected to agree with the direction of a current which is related to the changing flux by the right-hand rule.* Unfortunately, the positive direc-

---

*This is particularly true of books on electromagnetic theory. In electrical engineering books the positive directions of emf's are often chosen as best suits the immediate purpose of the writer, with the result that Faraday's law may sometimes have a negative, sometimes a positive sign. A further result is that on vector diagrams for alternating-current circuits and machines, an emf may either lead or lag by 90° the sinusoidal flux which produced it. If the positive directions for emf's were always chosen so that $E = -N\frac{\Delta\phi}{\Delta T}$, then the emf would in every case lag the sinusoidal flux by 90°.

tion is not always marked, and the student is sometimes given rather vague reasons why the law should be written with the minus sign. There is, of course, no objection to this particular choice; it is as logical as any other, but no more so, and it is essential for the student to know that the minus sign results from a choice of positive direction and to know which direction was chosen. The student will do well never to write the expression at all without first marking a positive direction and then using Lenz's law to determine the actual direction of the emf. If this is done there will never be any doubt as to the sign of the expression.

PROBLEMS

(12-XI) Write Faraday's law with the proper sign for the positive direction indicated in Fig. 11.11a and b.

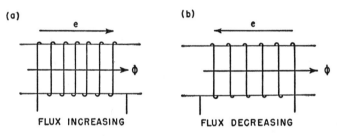

Fig. 11.11

(13-XI) What positive directions must have been assumed in Fig. 11.12a and b in order for the sign used in Faraday's law to be correct?

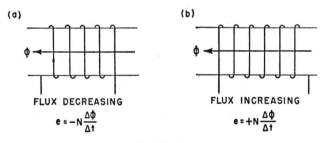

Fig. 11.12

(14-XI) Determine whether or not the emf is actually in the direction selected as positive in Fig. 11.13a and b.

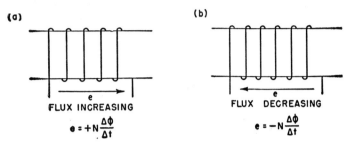

Fig. 11.13

8. Average, instantaneous, maximum, and effective values of emf. The emf's calculated in the present chapter thus far have been **average** for finite periods of time. If we use

$$E = N\frac{\Delta\phi}{\Delta T},$$ (7.62)

we obtain the average value for E over the period of time ΔT*. Now, the rate of change of flux (and consequently the emf) seldom remains the same for any time ΔT, and it is often necessary to determine **instantaneous** rates of change of flux and instantaneous emf's. If we take the limit of (7.62) as ΔT approaches zero, we obtain the instantaneous emf, designated usually by a small letter.

$$e = \lim_{\Delta T \to 0} N\frac{\Delta\phi}{\Delta T} = N\frac{d\phi}{dt}.$$ (11.11)

This is seen to be simply the derivative of the flux with respect to time. To actually calculate instantaneous values of e from this equation, it is, of course, necessary that we know the manner in which flux varies with time and that we be able to express the variation mathematically and perform the differentiation indicated in (11.11).

The **maximum,** or **peak,** value of an emf is the maximum instantaneous value which it has during a given period of time — usually one cycle.

The **effective,** or **root mean square,** value of an emf is the square root of the average squared value of the emf during a given period of time, usually one cycle. This is the value read by an a-c voltmeter. Any statement as to an a-c potential difference, unless it expressly says average, instantaneous, or maximum, is understood to mean effective value.

9. An elementary a-c generator. Suppose a conductor bent to form a one-turn rectangular coil is rotated in a uniform magnetic field, as shown in Fig. 11.14. In its initial position (shown in cross section in Fig. 11.15),

---

*In finding the average value of an alternating emf, ΔT is arbitrarily taken to correspond to a half cycle. The average value for one cycle is obviously zero.

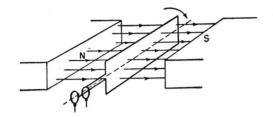

Fig. 11.14. Elementary a-c generator.

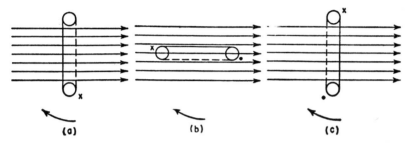

(a)   (b)   (c)

Fig. 11.15. Rotating coil of elementary alternator.

the plane of the coil is perpendicular to the magnetic field, and it is linked by the maximum flux, ϕ_M. The directions assumed as positive for the generated emf's are marked beside the conductors which form the coil sides. As the coil rotates, it is linked by less and less flux, until the angle θ, through which it has rotated, becomes 90°. The flux linking the coil for any position from $\theta = 0°$ to $\theta = 90°$ is obviously given by the equation

$$\phi = \phi_M \cos \theta. \tag{11.12}$$

For angles from 90° to 270°, the cosine is negative, and Equation (11.12) gives negative values for the flux through the coil. This can be interpreted to mean that flux that passes through the coil in the reference position from the face indicated by solid line to the face indicated by dotted line is positive, and that flux that passes through the coil in the opposite direction is negative. For angles from 270° to 360°, the cosine of θ is again positive, and the flux linking the coil is also positive.

Application of Lenz's law or any of the rules given in Section 4 shows that the actual emf is in the direction selected as positive as the coil moves from the position $\theta = 0°$ to the position $\theta = 90°$. Since $\Delta\phi/\Delta T$ is negative for flux decreasing, we must write the equation for the average emf as

$$E = -N\frac{\Delta\phi}{\Delta T}. \tag{11.13}$$

By considering various cases, the student may readily convince himself that (11.13) holds for any change in the position of the coil.

In order to find instantaneous emf's corresponding to various positions of the coil, we must take the limit of (11.13) as ΔT approaches zero, which is

$$e = -N \frac{d\phi}{dt}. \tag{11.14}$$

By substituting (11.12) in (11.14), we obtain

$$e = -N \frac{d(\phi_M \cos \theta)}{dt}. \tag{11.15}$$

If the coil is rotating at a uniform angular velocity of ω radians per second, where

$$\omega = 2\pi \times \frac{\text{revolutions per minute}}{60}, \tag{11.16}$$

the angle through which the coil has rotated from the reference position is given by

$$\theta = \omega t, \tag{11.17}$$

where t is the time in seconds elapsed since the coil passed through the reference position.

Substituting (11.17) in (11.15) gives

$$e = -N \frac{d(\phi_M \cos \omega t)}{dt},$$

and carrying out the differentiation, we obtain

$$e = N\omega\phi_M \sin \omega t. \tag{11.18}$$

If we plot the instantaneous emf against time (or against the angle wt), we obtain a wave like that shown in Fig. 11.16.

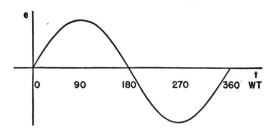

Fig. 11.16. Sine wave of emf produced by elementary alternator.

The greatest value the sine of an angle can have is 1; consequently, the maximum value of the emf is

$$E_M = N\omega\phi_M, \tag{11.19}$$

and we may write the equation for emf simply

$$e = E_M \sin \omega t. \tag{11.20}$$

Such an emf is called a sinusoidal emf, and would give rise to sinusoidal currents in any linear network. The effective value of a sinusoidal emf can be shown to be $1/\sqrt{2}$ times its maximum value.

Example: An elementary a-c generator like that shown in Fig. 11.14 has a single-turn coil 40 by 50 cm which rotates at a uniform angular speed of 1200 rpm in a uniform magnetic field in which the flux density is 15×10^{-5} weber per sq m. (a) What is the average emf as the coil rotates from the position $\theta = 0°$ to the position $\theta = 90°$? (b) What is the average emf as the coil rotates from $\theta = 45°$ to $\theta = 135°$? (c) What is the maximum emf? (d) What is the instantaneous emf at each of the following positions: $0°, 45°, 90°, 135°$? (e) What is the effective value of the emf?

SOLUTION: (a) When $\theta = 0°$,

$$\phi_1 = \phi_M = {}^{40}\!/_{100} \times {}^{50}\!/_{100} \times 15 \times 10^{-5} = 3 \times 10^{-5} \text{ weber.}$$

When $\theta = 90°$,

$$\phi_2 = \phi_M \cos 90° = 0,$$

$$\Delta\phi = 0 - (3 \times 10^{-5}) = -3 \times 10^{-5} \text{ weber,}$$

$$\Delta T = {}^{60}\!/_{1200} \times {}^{90}\!/_{360} = 0.0125 \text{ sec,}$$

$$E_{\text{average}} = -1 \frac{(-3 \times 10^{-5})}{0.0125} = 2.4 \times 10^{-3} \text{ v.}$$

(b) When $\theta = 45°$,

$$\phi_1 = \phi_M \cos 45° = 2.121 \times 10^{-5} \text{ weber.}$$

When $\theta = 135°$,

$$\phi_2 = \phi_M \cos 135 = -2.121 \times 10^{-5} \text{ weber,}$$

$$\Delta\phi = (-2.121 \times 10^{-5}) - (2.121 \times 10^{-5}) = -4.242 \times 10^{-5} \text{ weber,}$$

$$\Delta T = 0.0125 \text{ sec [same as in part (a)],}$$

$$E_{\text{average}} = -1 \frac{(-4.242 \times 10^{-5})}{0.0125} = 3.39 \times 10^{-3} \text{ v.}$$

(c) $E_{\text{max}} = N\omega\phi_M \tag{11.19}$

$$= (1) \left(\frac{2\pi \times 1200}{60} \right) (3 \times 10^{-5}) = 3.77 \times 10^{-3} \text{ v.}$$

(d) When $\theta = 0$ $e = 3.77 \times 10^{-3} \sin 0° = 0.$

When $\theta = 45°$ $e = 3.77 \times 10^{-3} \sin 45° = 2.67 \times 10^{-3}$ v.

When $\theta = 90°$ $e = 3.77 \times 10^{-3} \sin 90° = 3.77 \times 10^{-3}$ v.

When $\theta = 135°$ $e = 3.77 \times 10^{-3} \sin 135° = 2.67 \times 10^{-3}$ v.

(e) $E_{\text{effective}} = 1/\sqrt{2} E_{\text{max}} = 1/\sqrt{2} \times 3.77 \times 10^{-3} = 2.67 \times 10^{-3}$ v.

PROBLEMS

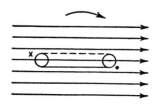

Fig. 11.17

(15-XI) An elementary alternator has one-turn coil 40 by 50 cm which rotates at a uniform speed of 1200 rpm in a uniform magnetic field in which the flux density is 15×10^{-5} weber per sq m. The reference position of the coil and the directions selected as positive for the emf are as shown in Fig. 11.17. (a) What is the average emf as the coil rotates from the reference position ($\theta = 0°$) to the position $\theta = 30°$? (b) What is the average emf as the coil rotates from $\theta = 30°$ to $\theta = 60°$? (c) What is the average emf as the coil rotates from $\theta = 60°$ to $\theta = 90°$? (d) What is the average emf as the coil rotates from 90° to 180°?

(16-XI) Find the equation for the instantaneous emf of the generator in Problem 15-XI. Plot the emf against angle and compare with Fig. 11.16.

(17-XI) An elementary alternator has a 50-turn coil 10 by 20 cm which rotates at a uniform speed of 900 rpm in a uniform magnetic field in which the flux density is 30 gausses. The reference position of the coil and the directions selected as positive for the emf are as shown in Fig. 11.18. Find the equation for the instantaneous emf, and plot emf against angle.

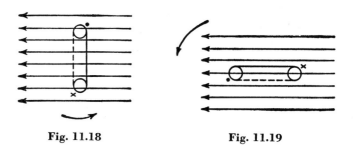

Fig. 11.18   **Fig. 11.19**

(18-XI) An elementary alternator has a one-turn circular coil 25 cm in diameter which rotates at a uniform speed of 1500 rpm in a uniform magnetic field in which the flux density is 30 gausses. The reference position of the coil and the directions selected as positive for the emf are as shown in Fig. 11.19. Find the equation for the instantaneous emf, and plot emf against angle.

10. Elementary d-c generators. If a metal disk is mounted on a shaft and rotated between the poles of a magnet, as shown in Fig. 11.20, an emf, constant in magnitude and direction, is developed between the shaft and the rim of the disk. This apparatus, first devised by Faraday, is a true d-c generator. The emf must be regarded as due to the cutting of flux by radial filaments of the disk: there is here no change in the flux linking the circuit.

An emf, always in the same direction though not constant in magnitude, can be readily obtained by adding a commutator to an elementary a-c generator like that described in Section 9. The emf's developed in the coil sides are alternating, the commutator serving as a switching device to keep the coil connected to the external circuit in such a way as to maintain current always in the same direction. Figure 11.21 shows three positions of the coil as it rotates in the field. The rotation of the commutator serves to keep the right-hand brush positive regardless of the position of the coil. The emf of such a generator pulsates, as shown graphically in Fig. 11.22.

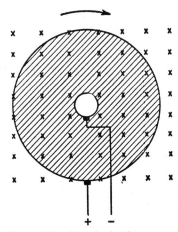

Fig. 11.20. Faraday's disk generator.

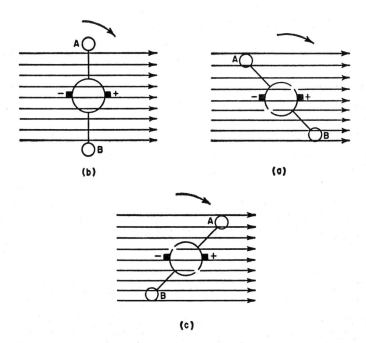

(b)

(a)

(c)

Fig. 11.21. Rotating coil and commutator of elementary d-c generator.

11. Inductance — the henry. When the flux linking a circuit is changing as a consequence of a changing current, either in some neighboring circuit or in the circuit itself, the induced emf may be expressed as a func-

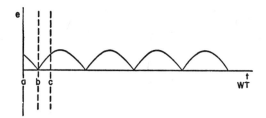

Fig. 11.22. Wave of emf produced by elementary d-c generator. *a, b,* and *c* correspond to coil positions *a, b,* and *c* in Fig. 11.21.

tion of the rate of change of current. If the changing current is in a neighboring circuit, the relation is written

$$e_1 = \pm M \frac{di_2}{dt},$$ (11.21)

where the subscripts refer to circuits 1 and 2, respectively, and M is called the **mutual inductance** of the two circuits. If the changing current is in the circuit itself, the relation is written

$$e = \pm L \frac{di}{dt},$$ (11.22)

and L is called the **self-inductance** of the circuit. The proper sign has to be determined in either case by first selecting a positive direction and then applying Lenz's law.

Both mutual inductance and self-inductance are measured in the same unit, the **henry,** defined as follows: *The inductance is one henry if current changing at the rate of 1 amp per sec induces an emf of 1 v.*

The inductance concept is extremely useful because it enables us to express an induced emf directly in terms of changing current, rather than having to go through the intermediate step of calculating the flux caused by the current, and then applying Faraday's law.

12. Factors affecting mutual inductance. Let us again consider two coils arranged as in Fig. 11.23, so that when coil No. 1 carries current, some of the magnetic flux established by this current will link coil No. 2. Any change in the current in No. 1 will result in a change in the flux linking No. 2 and, therefore, an emf will be set up in No. 2 according to Faraday's law:

$$e_2 = +N_2 \frac{d\phi_{12}}{dt}.$$ (11.23)

The subscript after ϕ denotes it as the flux produced by coil No. 1 which

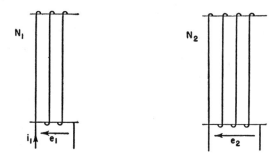

Fig. 11.23. Coils having mutual inductance.

links coil No. 2. The emf can also be found directly from the rate of change of current:

$$e_2 = +M \frac{di_1}{dt}. \tag{11.24}$$

Equating (11.23) and (11.24),

$$N_2 \frac{d\phi_{12}}{dt} = M \frac{di_1}{dt}, \tag{11.25}$$

from which

$$M = N_2 \frac{d\phi_{12}}{di_1}. \tag{11.26}$$

If the flux path is in air, then ϕ_{12} will be zero when i_1 is zero, and will be always in direct proportion to i_1, and we may write

$$M = \frac{N_2 \phi_{12}}{i_1}. \tag{11.27}$$

This equation tells us the mutual inductance is the flux-turns formed with coil No. 2, per ampere in coil No. 1. Obviously, then, if we want two circuits to have relatively great mutual inductance, we must place them so

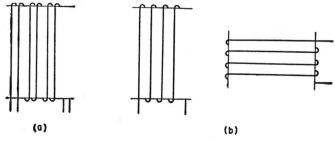

(a)   (b)

Fig. 11.24. Effect of coil arrangement on mutual inductance: (a) maximum mutual inductance; (b) minimum mutual inductance.

that one circuit is linked by a large percentage of the flux lines produced by the other circuit. This can be accomplished by making the two windings occupy the same space as nearly as possible, as in Fig. 11.24a. Conversely, if we want to avoid mutual inductance, we place the circuits so that few or no flux lines from one circuit can link the other, as in Fig. 11.24b.

Now, the flux is determined by the mmf $N_1 i_1$ of coil No. 1 and by the reluctance $\mathfrak{R}$ of the path taken by the flux:

$$\phi_{12} = \frac{N_1 i_1}{\mathfrak{R}}. \tag{11.28}$$

Substituting in (11.26), we obtain

$$M = N_2 \frac{d(N_1 i_1/\mathfrak{R})}{d i_1}. \tag{11.29}$$

If the flux path is in air, the reluctance is not a function of the current, and we may carry out the differentiation to obtain

$$M = \frac{N_1 N_2}{\mathfrak{R}}. \tag{11.30}$$

This equation tells us that mutual inductance varies as the product of the number of turns in each circuit and inversely as the reluctance. This assumes, however, that the percentage of the flux due to current in circuit No. 1 and linking circuit No. 2 is independent of the number of turns in both circuits. It is not always possible to change the number of turns and maintain this percentage constant; hence, in practice Equation (11.30) is an approximation only.

Finally, we see that by substituting a ferromagnetic material for air as the flux path through which the circuits are linked, we may very greatly decrease the reluctance and increase the mutual inductance. Since the reluctance of an iron flux path is a function of flux, however, and therefore of current, we see that mutual inductance is a function of current. A numerical value for the mutual inductance of two coils on an iron core is meaningless unless corresponding values of current are also given.

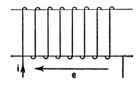

Fig. 11.25. Coil having self-inductance.

13. Factors affecting self-inductance. Any coil or circuit which is linked by flux due to current in its own turns will have an emf induced in it whenever the current is changing. Thus, in the coil in Fig. 11.25, a change in current will cause a change in flux, and an emf will be induced in the coil itself. According to Faraday's law, this emf is

$$e = +N \frac{d\phi}{dt}. \tag{11.31}$$

The emf can also be found directly from the rate of change of current:

$$e = +L\frac{di}{dt}.$$ (11.32)

Equating (11.31) and (11.32),

$$N\frac{d\phi}{dt} = L\frac{di}{dt},$$ (11.33)

from which

$$L = N\frac{d\phi}{di}.$$ (11.34)

If the flux path is in air, ϕ will be directly proportional to i at all times, and we may write

$$L = \frac{N\phi}{i}.$$ (11.35)

According to this equation, self-inductance is flux-turns per ampere. For a given number of turns, then, the self-inductance would be greatest when the turns were so arranged that all the flux linked all the turns. This condition can be most nearly realized by making a concentrated coil like that in Fig. 11.26a. Such a coil would have more self-inductance than a distributed coil of the same number of turns, as shown in Fig. 11.26b.

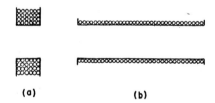

(a)   (b)

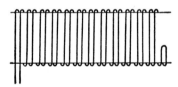

Fig. 11.26. Effect of distribution of turns on self-inductance: (a) maximum self-inductance; (b) minimum self-inductance.

Fig. 11.27. Coil wound to have zero self-inductance.

Equation (11.35) also indicates how we can wind a coil which has no self-inductance. If, after winding any number of turns, we double back and wind an equal number in the opposite direction, as in Fig. 11.27, the net mmf caused by a current in the winding will be zero. Consequently, no flux will link the turns, and the coil will have no self-inductance.

The flux linking the coil in Equation (11.35) may be expressed in terms of mmf and reluctance of the flux path as

$$\phi = \frac{Ni}{\mathcal{R}}.$$ (11.36)

Substituting in (11.35), we obtain

$$L = \frac{N\left(\dfrac{Ni}{\mathfrak{R}}\right)}{i} = \frac{N^2}{\mathfrak{R}}. \tag{11.37}$$

Thus, we see that the self-inductance varies as the square of the number of turns and inversely as the reluctance of the flux path. As in the case of Equation (11.30), the relation between self-inductance and turns is strictly true only when all the turns are linked by all the flux, though it is a useful approximation in the case of concentrated coils generally. The possibility of greatly increasing self-inductance by providing a flux path through iron is also obvious from (11.37). The inductance of any iron-cored coil, however, is a function of current, for the reason that the reluctance of the flux path varies with flux, which in turn depends upon current.

Equations (11.30) and (11.37) are of little use for actually calculating the self-inductance of a given coil. For such calculations, various empirical formulas have been devised.*

PROBLEMS

(19-XI) Current changing at the rate of 1000 amp per sec in circuit No. 1 induces an emf of 1.5 v in circuit No. 2. What is the mutual inductance of the circuits? What rate of change of current in circuit No. 1 would induce an emf of 0.3 v in circuit No. 2?

(20-XI) The self-inductance of a circuit is 0.15 h. What emf would be induced in the circuit by current changing at the rate of 400 amp per sec?

(21-XI) Two coils are wound side by side on a paper-tube form. An emf of 0.25 v is induced in coil A when the flux linking it changes at the rate of 10^{-3} weber per sec. A current of 2 amp in circuit B causes a flux of 10^{-5} weber to link coil A. What is the mutual inductance of the coils?

(22-XI) A coil of 250 turns has a self-inductance of 0.0145. Assuming that all the turns are linked by all the flux, what flux would be established by a current of 5 amp in this coil?

(23-XI) A concentrated coil of 250 turns has a self-inductance of 19 mh. How many turns should be added to increase the self-inductance to 25 mh? Assume that all the turns are linked by all the flux.

(24-XI) An air-cored toroid having a mean diameter of 20 cm and a diameter of cross section of 2.5 cm is provided with two uniform windings. Winding A consists of 1125 turns, and winding B consists of 775 turns. Calculate (a) self-inductance of coil A, (b) self-inductance of coil B, (c) mutual inductance of the coils, and (d) total inductance with coils connected in series.

*Terman, F. E., *Radio Engineer's Handbook*, Section 2. New York: McGraw-Hill Book Co., Inc., 1943.

(25-XI) A choke coil consists of 4000 turns of wire wound on the center leg of a magnetic core, such as that shown in Fig. 9.15. The thickness of core, stacking factor, and air gaps are as given in Problem 20-IX. Determine the self-inductance of the choke for (a) current of 10 ma and (b) current of 20 ma.

14. The effect of self-inductance in a circuit. Though self-inductance is a property of a circuit, just as resistance is, its effect is felt only when the current in the circuit is changing. For steady currents, the behavior of a circuit having self-inductance is no different from that of a circuit which is noninductive. Any change in current, however, will cause an emf to be set up in an inductive circuit, in such a direction as to oppose the change in current, and thus tend to prolong the time required for a given change to take place.

Let us consider the circuit shown in Fig. 11.28, which consists of a coil of wire having a self-inductance of L henrys and a resistance of R ohms connected to a battery of E volts. The resistance is indicated as apart from the coil itself, even though it is, in fact, distributed throughout the turns themselves, the connecting wires, and the battery. The procedure of representing all the resistance of a circuit as lumped together in a certain part and all the inductance as lumped together at another point is a convenient one, and much used in circuit analysis.

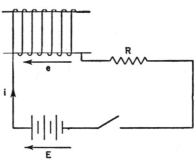

Fig. 11.28. Circuit consisting of resistance and self-inductance in series.

When the switch is closed, a current i begins to flow, and increases toward its limiting value

$$i = \frac{E}{R}. \tag{11.38}$$

The increasing current gives rise to an emf,

$$e = +L\frac{di}{dt}, \tag{11.39}$$

due to the self-inductance of the coil. Applying Kirchhoff's second law to the circuit gives

$$E - L\frac{di}{dt} = Ri. \tag{11.40}$$

This is a differential equation which may be readily solved to obtain an

expression for the current at any instant following the closing of the switch.*
The current is found to be

$$i = \frac{E}{R}[1 - \epsilon^{-Rt/L}]. \tag{11.45}$$

Study of this equation shows that the current does not increase instantaneously from zero to its final value, but increases according to an exponential law as shown graphically in Fig. 11.29. Greatest at the instant of

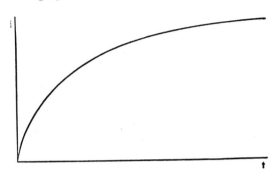

Fig. 11.29. Graph showing exponential increase of current in an inductive circuit.

*The solution of (11.40) can be carried out by various methods, one of which is
that of separating the variables. By this method, (11.40) is first manipulated to get it
into the form

$$-\frac{di}{\frac{E}{R} - i} = -\frac{R\,dt}{L}. \tag{11.41}$$

Both sides of (11.41) are then integrated to obtain

$$\log_\epsilon\left(\frac{E}{R} - i\right) = -\frac{Rt}{L} + K, \tag{11.42}$$

or

$$\frac{E}{R} - i = \epsilon^{(-Rt/L+K)} = \epsilon^{-Rt/L}\epsilon^k. \tag{11.43}$$

To evaluate ϵ^k, we take advantage of the known fact that at the instant of closing
the switch ($t = 0$), the current is zero. This gives

$$\epsilon^k = \frac{E}{R}, \tag{11.44}$$

which, substituted in (11.43), gives

$$\frac{E}{R} - i = \frac{E}{R}\epsilon^{-Rt/L},$$

$$i = \frac{E}{R}(1 - \epsilon^{-Rt/L}). \tag{11.45}$$

closing the switch, the rate of increase diminishes as time goes on, eventually becoming so small the current may be regarded as steady.

The time required for the current to reach any given percentage of its final value can be seen from Equation (11.45) to depend upon the self-inductance of the circuit. The larger the value of L, the greater is the value of t required for the exponential term to become negligible. A value of t equal to L/R is defined as the **time constant** of the circuit. It is the time required for the current to reach 63.2 per cent of its final value following the closing of the switch, as may be readily seen by putting L/R for t in Equation (11.45). The exponent becomes -1, and the current is

$$i = \frac{E}{R}[1 - \epsilon^{-1}] = \frac{E}{R}\left(1 - \frac{1}{\epsilon}\right) = 0.632\frac{E}{R}. \tag{11.46}$$

15. Energy storage in the magnetic field of an inductive circuit.
It was shown in Chapter VII that energy was stored in any magnetic field. When the field is due to a current of I amperes flowing in a circuit of self-inductance L henrys, the amount of energy stored can be shown to be*

$$W = \frac{LI^2}{2}. \tag{11.50}$$

This way of expressing the energy stored is extremely convenient. Since magnetic fields are generally indefinite in extent and vary in intensity from point to point, any attempt to calculate the total energy by using the

*This energy is furnished by the battery or other source that maintains the current I, and its storage is a direct consequence of establishing the current I in the circuit against the opposition of the self-induced emf. At any instant while the current is being established (Fig. 11.30), the emf is

$$e = +L\frac{di}{dt}. \tag{11.47}$$

The rate at which energy is being supplied is

$$p = ei = L\frac{di}{dt}i. \tag{11.48}$$

The energy supplied during an infinitesimal time dt is

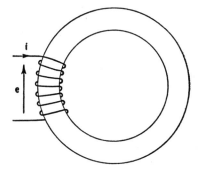

Fig. 11.30. Storage of energy in the magnetic field of an inductive circuit.

$$dw = p\,dt = Li\,di. \tag{11.49}$$

The total energy supplied while the current is being increased from zero to I is then found by summing up all the dw's as i varies from 0 to I. This is the definite integral,

$$W = \int_0^I Li\,di = \frac{LI^2}{2}. \tag{11.50}$$

expression for energy stored per unit volume would be hopeless. Equation (11.50) expresses it in terms of readily measurable quantities and avoids the difficulty entirely.

The energy represented by Equation (11.50) is partly recoverable. The arc which occurs upon opening an inductive circuit is made possible by the self-induced emf set up by the decreasing current, and the energy dissipated in the heat of the arc is in part the stored energy of the magnetic field.

PROBLEMS

(26-XI) A series circuit contains a coil having a self-inductance of 0.2 henry and negligible resistance, and a noninductive resistance of 50 ohms. This circuit is connected to a 10-v battery. (a) Determine the value of the current 0.004 sec later. (b) Repeat for time intervals of 0.008, 0.012, 0.016, 0.02, and 0.04 sec. (c) Plot the current against time.

(27-XI) (a) In Problem 26-XI, what is the initial rate of increase of current? (b) What is the initial induced emf? (c) What is the initial rate of energy storage? (d) What is the rate of increase of current 0.004 sec after connecting the circuit to the battery? (e) What is the induced emf after 0.004 sec? (f) What is the rate of energy storage after 0.004 sec?

(28-XI) A series circuit consists of a coil having a self-inductance of 1 h and a resistance of 5 ohms, and a 50-v battery. (a) Determine the value of the current 0.01 sec after closing the circuit. (b) Repeat for time intervals 0.03, 0.05, 0.1, 0.2, 0.3, 0.4, 0.5, and 1 sec. (c) Plot the curve of current against time.

(29-XI) (a) How long does it take the current in the above circuit to drop to 5 amp, after the battery is short-circuited? (b) Repeat for 1 amp, 0.1 amp, 0.01 amp.

(30-XI) How much energy is stored in the magnetic field of the coil in Problem 28-XI, when the current is 10 amp?

16. Self-inductance in a-c circuits — reactance. Since self-inductance manifests itself by opposing and slowing up any change in current, its effect will be most striking in a-c circuits. Suppose an a-c generator is connected to a coil having a self-inductance L and negligible resistance, as in Fig. 11.31. The emf of the alternator is adjusted to a value e_G, which causes a current

$$i = I_{max} \sin \omega t \qquad (11.51)$$

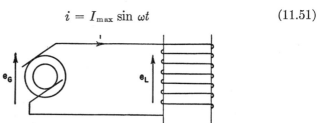

Fig. 11.31. Alternating emf applied to an inductive circuit.

to flow in the circuit. This varying current gives rise to a self-induced emf

$$e_L = +L\frac{di}{dt} = L\frac{d[I_{max}\sin \omega t]}{dt} \tag{11.52}$$

$$= \omega L I_{max}\cos \omega t. \tag{11.53}$$

Since the largest possible value of cos ωt is unity for values of ωt equal to $0°$, $180°$, $360°$, and so forth, the largest possible value of e_L is, obviously,

$$E_{Lmax} = \omega L I_{max}, \tag{11.54}$$

or
$$\frac{E_{Lmax}}{I_{max}} = \frac{E_{Leffective}}{I_{effective}} = \omega L. \tag{11.55}$$

The quantity ωL is called *inductive reactance*. Since it is the ratio of potential difference to current, it is dimensionally the same as resistance, and is expressed in ohms. It is commonly represented by the symbol X_L.

$$X_L = \omega L = 2\pi f L, \tag{11.56}$$

where X_L is inductive reactance in ohms;
　　　f is frequency in cycles per second;
　　　L is self-inductance in henrys.

It is seen that, whereas self-inductance (when no iron is in the vicinity of the circuit) is a constant independent of frequency* and current, reactance depends upon frequency directly. Thus, with direct current (frequency zero), a circuit with negligible resistance would permit the flow of an extremely large current when even a small voltage was applied. With alternating current (frequency $= f$), the current would be limited by reactance to a value inversely proportional to the frequency. A device known as a **choke coil,** consisting of a number of turns of copper wire (sometimes on an iron core) is often used in a branch of a network to impede the flow of alternating current while permitting direct current to flow unhindered.

Equation (11.55) gives a clue as to how self-inductance may be measured provided resistance is negligible. We may obtain readings of voltage and current when the coil or circuit carries alternating current of known frequency. We then divide voltage by current to obtain reactance, according to Equation (11.55). Maximum values of voltage and current are not readily measured directly, but the corresponding effective values can be read with ordinary iron-vane type voltmeters and ammeters, and are in the same ratio one to the other as are the maximum values. If the resistance of the circuit is not negligible, then Equation (11.55) gives **impedance,** not reactance, and the procedure outlined above is no longer valid.

*Not strictly true at high frequencies.

Example: When an alternating emf of 50 v is impressed across a coil of negligible resistance, a current of 2.5 amp flows. The frequency of emf is 60 cps. What is the self-inductance of the coil? What current would have flowed if the frequency of the impressed emf had been 400 cps?

SOLUTION:

$$X_L = \frac{E}{I} = \frac{50}{2.5} = 20 \text{ ohms at 60 cps,}$$

$$L = \frac{X_L}{2\pi f} = \frac{20}{2\pi \times 60} = 0.0531 \text{ h,}$$

$$X_L = 2\pi f L$$

$$= 2\pi \times 400 \times 0.0531 = 133.5 \text{ ohms at 400 cps,}$$

$$I = \frac{E}{X_L} = \frac{50}{133.5} = 0.375 \text{ amp.}$$

PROBLEMS

(31-XI) Calculate the reactance of a 1 microhenry (μh) inductance at frequencies of 0, 10, 10^2, and so forth, up to 10^9 cps.

(32-XI) The voltage drop across a coil of negligible resistance is found to be 105 v when the current is 2.1 amp. These measurements were made with a-c instruments at a frequency of 60 cps. What is the self-inductance of the coil?

STUDY QUESTIONS

1. In what two ways may we bring about a change in the magnetic flux linking a circuit?

2. A student offers the following as a statement of Lenz's law: The electromotive force induced in a circuit by a change in flux will be in the direction current would have to flow in order to oppose the flux. What is wrong? For what per cent of all flux changes would the statement be correct?

3. It is stated at the end of Section 1 that if alternating current flows in circuit A then both self and mutual electromotive forces would always be present. Is this literally true? Why?

4. Why is it not possible to measure directly the electromotive force generated in a straight piece of wire moving across a magnetic field?

5. Is it possible to have a conductor in motion in a steady magnetic field and yet have no electromotive force generated in it? Explain.

6. What is the physical explanation of the generation of an electromotive force in a conductor in motion in a magnetic field?

7. What is the physical explanation of the induction of an electromotive force in a loop of wire placed in a magnetic field in which the flux density is increasing or decreasing?

8. The terms "generator emf" and "transformer emf" are often used in analyzing the operation of electrical machinery. What distinction do you think is intended?

9. A spring clip like a bicyclist's trouser-guard is slipped over one pole of a U-shaped permanent magnet (Fig. 11.32a). The clip is then pulled to the right so that its ends spring apart (Fig. 11.32b) and it is removed from the magnet (Fig. 11.32c). A closed circuit is maintained at all times. Is an electromotive force induced in the clip? Why?

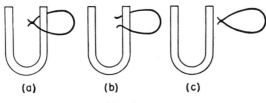

(a)   (b)   (c)

Fig. 11.32

10. The spring clip in Question 9 is slipped off over the end of the magnet instead of springing the ends apart. Will an electromotive force be induced in the clip? Why?

11. What is the significance of the positive direction arrow for an electromotive force? Without a positive direction arrow, what would be the significance of a plus or a minus sign before the expression $N\dfrac{\Delta\phi}{\Delta T}$?

12. Is it possible that $-N\dfrac{\Delta\phi}{\Delta T}$ could be a positive quantity? Explain.

13. The BlV rule as explained in Section 4 gives average electromotive force. How could it be modified to find instantaneous electromotive force? Under what circumstances will they be the same?

14. In an elementary alternating-current generator like the one described in Section 9, the electromotive force is zero at the instant the flux linking the coil is maximum and maximum at the instant the flux linking the coil is zero. Explain.

15. Equations (11.30) and (11.37) are useful in that they show approximately how inductance depends upon turns. They are not of much practical value for calculating inductance. Why?

16. Given a 100-foot length of copper wire, how would you arrange it to have maximum self-inductance? Minimum self-inductance?

17. Two direct-current circuits have equal resistances, and equal voltages are applied to their terminals. One circuit is known to be noninductive, the other highly inductive. The circuits themselves are concealed and cannot be examined, but they may be opened and closed at will, and electrical instruments may be connected at the terminals. Could the inductive circuit be distinguished? How?

18. A coil that is designed to be connected across a 115-volt a-c circuit is accidentally connected across a 115-volt d-c circuit and immediately smoke begins to appear. Explain.

Chapter XII

ELECTRIC FIELD CONCEPTS — CAPACITANCE

1. Charged bodies. A body that has either a deficiency or an excess of electrons is said to be **charged.** The charging of amber by friction is the earliest electrical phenomenon of which we have any record, and experiments with charged bodies were well advanced before anything was known of electric current. The outstanding property of charged bodies is, of course, that of attracting and repelling other charged bodies. A body that has an excess of electrons is arbitrarily designated as negatively charged and is repelled by any other body having a negative charge. A body that has a deficiency of electrons is designated as positively charged and is repelled by any other body having a positive charge. But a body that has a negative charge is attracted by any other body that has a positive charge.

Forces are continually at work in nature which tend to cause the molecules of all gases to lose electrons and, therefore, to become positively charged particles. The electrons thus lost attach themselves to other molecules which become negatively charged particles. Other forces in nature result in the separation of positive and negative electricity between the upper and lower strata of clouds, thus giving rise to the charges that produce lightning.

The charged bodies with which we work in electrical engineering usually become charged as a result of being connected to some source of emf, such as a battery or generator. Suppose, for example, the terminals of a battery to be connected to two well-insulated, parallel metal plates as in Fig. 12.1. The emf of the battery will cause electrons to move off plate *A* through the

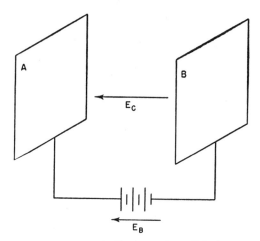

Fig. 12.1. Electrically charged parallel plates.

connecting wire and the battery onto plate B, leaving plate A with a deficiency of electrons and, therefore, positively charged, whereas plate B, with an excess of electrons, will be negatively charged.

This transfer of electrons constitutes a current in the connecting wires of momentary duration only, because every electron that moves toward plate B does so against the repelling force of all those which preceded it, and an equilibrium condition is soon reached where the battery is unable to move any more electrons against this opposing force. The potential difference between the plates is now equal to the emf of the battery. They may be disconnected from the battery, and if they are perfectly insulated, as we assumed them to be, they will maintain their charges and their potential difference indefinitely.

We have here a means of actually storing energy in electrical form. Energy had to be supplied by the battery to effect the removal of electrons from one plate to the other, and this energy is stored, just as energy is stored when a mass is raised to an elevation above the earth. In that case, mass is raised through a gravitational potential difference; in the electrical case, charge is raised through an electrical potential difference.*

The energy stored can be recovered by connecting a wire from one plate to the other. The displaced electrons then move back to their normal positions, constituting a current in the wire and dissipating the stored energy as I^2R loss. The plates are then said to be **discharged.**

2. The electric field. Suppose a very small, light ball be suspended by a thread and given a positive charge, either by friction or by allowing it to

---

*To be consistent with conventional rise in potential we will have to think of a positive charge as having been moved from plate B to plate A.

touch a larger object that is positively charged. If this charged ball is brought into the region between the charged plates shown in Fig. 12.1, it will be repelled by the positive plate and attracted by the negative plate, and will tend to move accordingly. Provided the battery used to charge the plates has sufficient emf and the ball is not too heavy, the motion can be readily observed, and the positively charged ball thus becomes a means of exploring the space between the plates, just as the compass needle was a device for exploring the space around a wire carrying current. The region between the plates is said to be an **electric field.** *Any region in which charged bodies are acted upon by forces is an electric field, and the direction in which a positive test charge is urged is the direction of the field.*

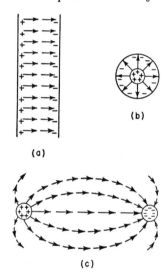

(a)

(b)

(c)

Fig. 12.2. Typical electric fields: (*a*) between oppositely charged parallel plates; (*b*) between oppositely charged coaxial cylinders; (*c*) between oppositely charged parallel wires.

If the force acting upon the test charge is observed in successive positions, taking care to move the charge always in the direction of the indicated force, we may map an electric field in much the same way that we mapped magnetic fields with an exploring coil or compass needle. The field between oppositely charged parallel plates that are separated by a distance that is small compared with the dimensions of the plates themselves is found to be directed at every point perpendicularly away from the positive and toward the negative plate, as indicated in Fig. 12.2*a*. The field between oppositely charged coaxial cylinders is found to be *radial*, as shown in Fig. 12.2*b*. This is typical of the field in coaxial cables used in high-frequency transmission. The field in the vicinity of two oppositely charged, parallel wires is shown in Fig. 12.2*c*. Here the description of the field is not so easy, since its direction changes from point to point, and it is not limited strictly to the space between the conductors.

We sometimes have occasion to speak of an "isolated charge." Since we charge a body by taking away electrons or by adding electrons, the very existence of a charge body implies the existence of a second charged body, which received the electrons taken away from the first body, or which supplied the electrons to it. The second body (and all other charged bodies) could, however, be carried so far away that its effect upon a test charge placed in the vicinity of the first body would be negligible. We would then have an isolated charge. It is easy to see that the electric field in the vicinity of our isolated charge would be radially directed, outward if the charge is positive, inward if the charge is negative.

The idea of a charge concentrated at a point will also arise. This, of course, is a concept that can be approached, but never realized. Point charges played an important part in the development of electrical science, and still serve as a useful concept.

One other matter to be considered here is the effect of the introduction of a test charge into a field. It can be seen that the field would be modified by the presence of a test charge just as an electric circuit is modified by connecting meters into it. For this reason we must stipulate that the test charge and the body which carries it be small.

3. Electric field intensity. To describe an electric field completely, we may specify its intensity at every point. The intensity may be defined in terms of the magnitude and direction of the force which acts upon a unit test charge placed at the point as follows: *The electric field intensity at a point has a value of 1 mks unit if a 1-coulomb test charge placed at the point is acted upon by a force of 1 newton. The direction of the electric field intensity is the direction of the force on a positive test charge.*

A descriptive name for the unit would therefore be the newton per coulomb. This name, although perfectly correct, is little used because, as we shall see, the unit may be described by another name to better advantage. The symbol most commonly used is $\mathcal{E}$ and the defining equation is

$$F = \mathcal{E}Q, \tag{12.1}$$

where F is force in newtons;

$\mathcal{E}$ is electric field intensity in newtons per coulomb;

Q is charge in coulombs.

In general, electric field intensity is a vector quantity which varies from point to point in magnitude and in direction. Consider a test charge of $+Q$ coulombs to be moved along a path a-b-c-d-e (Fig. 12.3) arbitrarily drawn between the faces of two oppositely charged parallel plates.

At every point on the path there will be an electric field intensity which can be represented by a vector $\mathcal{E}$ in the figure. Now suppose the path to be

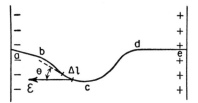

Fig. 12.3. The summation of $\mathcal{E}$ cos $\theta \, \Delta l$ along the path a–b–c–d–e is equal to the potential difference between the charged plates.

divided up into short segments Δl, so short that for the accuracy required, $\mathcal{E}$ may be considered the same in magnitude and direction all along a segment. Let us then form products by multiplying the length of each segment by the component of $\mathcal{E}$ that lies along the segment, and by Q, the magnitude of the test charge. Each of these products will be an amount of work done in moving the test charge through a length Δl, and if we take the summation of all such amounts of work, we will find the total work done in moving the test charge from one plate to the other:

$$\sum_a^e \mathcal{E} \cos \theta Q \, \Delta l = W. \tag{12.2}$$

In the limit, as Δl approaches zero,

$$\int_a^e \mathcal{E} \cos \theta Q \, dl = W. \tag{12.3}$$

But the work done in moving the test charge from one plate to the other is also given by

$$W = VQ, \tag{2.8}$$

where V is the potential difference between the plates. If we equate these two expressions and solve for V we obtain

$$\int_a^e \mathcal{E} \cos \theta \, dl = V. \tag{12.4}$$

For the special case of oppositely charged parallel plates which are separated by a distance which is small compared with the dimensions of the plates, the electric field intensity is the same at every point along a perpendicular path from one plate to the other. Equation (12.4) then becomes simply

$$\mathcal{E}S = V \tag{12.5}$$

or

$$\mathcal{E} = \frac{V}{S}, \tag{12.6}$$

where S is the distance between the plates.

Electric field intensity can, therefore, be expressed also in **volts per meter,** and this is the name most often used. For the simple field used in this instance, it is equal to the potential difference between the plates divided by the distance by which the plates are separated. In general, the electric field intensity varies from point to point, as we go from one extremity of the field to the other, and Equation (12.6) would yield **average** field intensity.

Example: Parallel plates 10 cm apart are maintained at a potential difference of 5000 v. What is the electric field intensity? What force would act upon a 10^{-2}-microcoulomb charge placed in the field?

Solution: By Equation (12.6), electric field intensity is

$$\mathcal{E} = \frac{V}{S} = \frac{5000}{0.1} = 50{,}000 \text{ v per m.}$$

By Equation (12.1), the force on the charge is

$$F = \mathcal{E}Q = 50{,}000 \times 10^{-8} = 0.0005 \text{ newton.}$$

PROBLEMS

(1-XII) What is the electric field intensity between parallel plates 1 cm apart and maintained at a potential difference of 250 v? What force would act upon an electron placed in this field?

(2-XII) A test charge of 10^{-10} coulomb in a uniform field is acted upon by a force of 10^{-7} newton. What is the potential difference between points 7.5 cm apart measured in the direction of the field?

4. Equipotential surfaces. The potential difference between two points is measured by the work done in moving a unit charge from one point to the other. If a unit positive charge is moved from the surface of the negative plate in Fig. 12.3 to a point x meters to the right, the work done and, therefore, the potential difference moved through, is

$$V_x = W_x = \mathcal{E}x. \tag{12.7}$$

The path taken in moving the charge would be immaterial, since work is only being done when the charge is being moved against the force of the electric field. Moving the charge at right angles to the field requires no work. Therefore, we may move the charge to *any* point x meters to the right of the negative plate with the same amount of work. Consequently, we see that all points in a parallel plane x meters to the right of the negative plate have the same potential difference with respect to it, and no potential

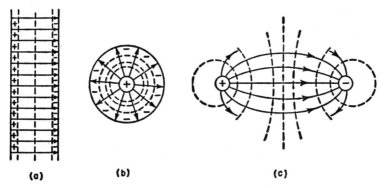

(a)   (b)   (c)

Fig. 12.4. Equipotential surfaces: (a) between oppositely charged parallel plates; (b) between oppositely charged coaxial cylinders; (c) between oppositely charged parallel wires.

difference with respect to one another. Such a plane is called an **equipo-tential surface.** Any number of equipotential surfaces may be drawn in a field, each containing those points which are at a certain potential difference with respect to another plane or with respect to one of the terminal elec-trodes of the field. A number of such surfaces for the field between parallel plates are indicated by the dotted lines in Fig. 12.4a.

Equipotential surfaces are not always planes. For the radial field between oppositely charged coaxial cylinders, the equipotential surfaces would also be cylinders, as represented by the dotted lines in Fig. 12.4b. For oppositely charged parallel wires, the equipotential surfaces are also circles, the centers of which are displaced from the centers of the wires, as in Fig. 12.4c. It will be noticed that in every instance the equipotential surfaces are perpendicular to the direction of the field.

By drawing the equipotential surfaces so that the potential difference between successive surfaces is the same, we obtain a sort of contour map of the electric field. Where the equipotential surfaces are close together, potential is changing rapidly, and there is considerable electric field inten-sity. Where the surfaces are far apart, the potential is changing slowly, and the electric field intensity is small. This is exactly like a topographical contour map where closely spaced contours indicate rapid change in eleva-tion (that is, steep grades).

5. Metal conductors in electric fields. Any metal is characterized by the presence in its atomic structure of free electrons which are capable, when acted upon by certain forces, of drifting through the space lattice of the substance. When a conductor, not part of a circuit, is placed in an electric field, all of its free electrons will be urged in the direction opposite to the direction of the field, thereby causing a momentary current in the conductor.

In Fig. 12.5, a straight conductor has been placed in the field between a pair of charged plates. The free electrons have moved to the left end of the

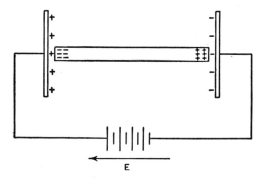

Fig. 12.5. Insulated metal rod in an electric field.

conductor, nearest the positive plate, making that end negatively charged with respect to the right end, which is positively charged. The charges are referred to as **induced charges,** since they were caused without any contact with the conductor itself. The effect of the charges at the ends of the conductor is to establish within the conductor an electric field equal and opposite to the field due to the charged plates, thus bringing to zero the net field that exists within the conductor itself. That this must be so is evident from the consideration that as long as any electric field exists within the conductor, the free electrons will experience forces which cause them to move in such a direction as to neutralize the field. We are thus led to the conclusion that *no steady electric field can be maintained within an isolated conductor.*

Any change in the electric field between the plates will result in a momentary current while the free electrons rearrange themselves. If the electric field between the plates were continually varying, as would be the case if the battery were replaced by an a-c generator, a varying field would exist in the conductor, under the influence of which the free electrons would be moving, first to the left, then to the right, and so forth, consituting an alternating current in the conductor. This is exactly what happens in radio reception. The transmitting antenna maintains a varying electric field in the vicinity of the receiving antenna. The free electrons in the receiving antenna, under the influence of this field, move back and forth, and thus establish in it an alternating current of the frequency of the transmitter.

A steady electric field may, and in fact always does, exist in a conductor which carries direct current. The free electrons of the conductor are continually acted upon by this field, giving rise to the forces that urge them along. The field required to do this is never of very great intensity, since it is only necessary for it to overcome the IR drop along the conductor. For example, the resistance of No. 10 copper wire is about 1 ohm per 1000 ft, or about 0.00328 ohm per m. To maintain a current of 25 amp in this wire thus requires an electric field intensity of $25 \times 0.00328 = 0.082$ v per m in the direction in which current flows along the wire.

In studying the function of the battery in an electric circuit in Chapter II, we spoke of it as supplying energy to the electrons as they passed through it. We may now take the optional viewpoint that the function of the battery is to maintain an electric field intensity along the circuit sufficient to maintain the desired current. The energy to maintain the current must, of course, come from the battery in the final analysis.

6. Insulators in electric fields. Substances act as insulators primarily because there are few, if any, free electrons in their structure. Such substances, collectively called **dielectrics,** include solids, liquids, and gases. When subjected to electric fields of less than a certain intensity, dielectrics permit only negligible current to flow. The molecules of the material, however, appear to be distorted by the field so that, in effect, the center of positive charge of a molecule no longer coincides with the center of negative charge. The dielectric and the molecules themselves are then said to be **polarized.** Figure 12.6*a* represents schematically a section of a dielectric in

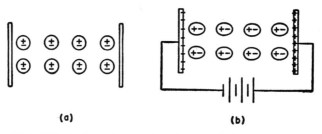

(a)   **(b)**

Fig. 12.6. Polarization of molecules of an insulating substance in an electric field; (*a*) molecules in normal state; (*b*) polarized molecules.

its normal state, and Fig. 12.6*b* shows the same section under the influence of an electric field. The degree of polarization depends upon the intensity of the field, the polarization increasing with electric field intensity up to the critical value.

A gaseous dielectric, once the field is removed, immediately returns to its normal state. In liquid and solid dielectrics, particularly in the latter, the state of polarization may continue for an appreciable time after the field is removed, the molecules returning gradually to their normal state. We have here, temporarily at least, a sort of electrical counterpart of residual magnetism.

A dielectric that is subjected to an alternating electric field would be polarized first in one direction, then in the other, at the frequency of the field. In the case of liquid and solid dielectrics, in which the polarized molecules do not relax instantaneously, there occurs a certain **dielectric loss,** not unlike hysteresis loss in magnetic materials. This loss is so large in some otherwise good insulating materials as to preclude their use in high-frequency apparatus. For very-high-frequency apparatus, it has been necessary to develop new synthetic insulations, such as polystyrene, in which the dielectric loss is low.

7. Dielectric strength. If the critical electric field intensity of a dielectric substance be exceeded, the molecules distorted by polarization are no longer able to hold together, and their breakdown into charged particles changes the nature of the substance from insulator to conductor. The electric field intensity at which breakdown occurs is known as the **dielectric strength** of the substance.

The dielectric strength of any particular insulating material depends upon attendant conditions, such as temperature, thickness of specimen, and length of time the specimen is subjected to the electric field. A surge voltage applied to a specimen of insulating material for a few microseconds might leave it unharmed, whereas a lesser voltage applied for several seconds might cause breakdown. In using published figures of dielectric strength, it is, therefore, necessary to know the conditions that prevailed when the tests were made. The values given in Table VI are for steady voltages applied to specimens not exceeding 1 mm in thickness.

The breakdown of a solid insulating material usually renders it unfit for further use by puncturing, burning, cracking, or otherwise damaging it. Gaseous and liquid dielectrics are self-healing and may be used repeatedly following breakdown.

PROBLEMS

(3-XII) What thickness of rubber insulation, allowing a safety factor of 2, is required between metal surfaces for a potential of 4000 v?

(4-XII) The windings of a certain transformer are insulated from the core by a layer of varnished cambric 0.036 in. thick. What voltage could be safely applied between windings and core?

(5-XII) What should be the minimum thickness of oiled-paper insulation to withstand a potential difference of 600 v?

Table VI. Dielectric Strength of Materials

Material	Dielectric Strength (kv per mm)	Dielectric Constant
Air..................................	3	1
Glass...............................	80–150	5–9
Vulcanized rubber....................	15–30	2–3
Mica................................	50–200	5–7
Paper, paraffined....................	40–60	2–3
Varnished cambric....................	50–70	2–3
Transformer oil.....................	12–20	2–3
Pure water..........................	......	81

8. Coulomb's law — permittivity. The first quantitative work in electricity (about 1785) was that of Charles Augustus Coulomb. Working with a torsion balance, Coulomb investigated the forces between two small charged bodies, which approximated point charges. He was able to show that the force was directly proportional to the product of the charges and inversely proportional to the distance between them.

$$F \propto \frac{Q_1 Q_2}{S^2}. \tag{12.8}$$

In Coulomb's experiments the charged bodies were in air. Later experiments and analysis showed that the force also depends upon some property of the medium by which they are surrounded. Thus, in oil the force is only about half as much as in air, and in pure water about $\frac{1}{81}$ times as great. This property of a substance is called **permittivity,** and the greater the permittivity of the surrounding medium, the less will be the force between charged bodies immersed in it. It is represented by the symbol ϵ. Taking the medium into account, then, the force can be written as

$$F \propto \frac{Q_1 Q_2}{\epsilon S} \tag{12.9}$$

or
$$F = \frac{K Q_1 Q_2}{\epsilon S}. \tag{12.10}$$

The value assigned to K in the mks system is $1/4\pi$, making

$$F = \frac{Q_1 Q_2}{4\pi \epsilon S^2}, \tag{12.11}$$

where F is force in newtons;
    Q_1 is charge on first body in coulombs;
    Q_2 is charge on second body in coulombs;
    ϵ is permittivity in mks units;
    S is distance in meters.

Permittivity in the mks system is measured in farads per meter, which will have more significance to the student further along in this chapter. The permittivity of free space (ϵ_0) is $1/36\pi \times 10^{-9}$ farads per meter. The permittivities of gases differ so slightly from this figure that extreme care is required in making the measurements if the difference is to be detected. Solid and liquid dielectrics have permittivities ranging from 2 to 80 times the permittivity of free space.

The ratio of the permittivity of any substance to the permittivity of free space is called **relative permittivity,** or more commonly, **dielectric constant,** and may be designated as ϵ_R. The actual permittivity of a substance in mks units would then be

$$\epsilon = \epsilon_0 \epsilon_R. \tag{12.12}$$

The dielectric constants of several materials commonly used for insulation are given in Table VI.

PROBLEM

(6-XII) What force would act between equal point charges of $+10^{-6}$ coulomb placed 20 cm apart in free space? What would be the force if the charges were immersed in alcohol (dielectric constant 23)?

9. Electric field intensity due to point charges. The force which acts upon a test charge Q_t concentrated at a point in space at a distance of S meters from a second point charge Q may be determined directly by Coulomb's law.

$$F = \frac{QQ_t}{4\pi\epsilon_0 S^2} \tag{12.13}$$

It may also be determined by considering that the second charge establishes at the point occupied by the test charge an electric field of intensity $\mathcal{E}$ volts per meter, and that the force on the test charge is then

$$F = \mathcal{E}Q_t. \tag{12.14}$$

Equating the two expressions for force and solving for $\mathcal{E}$,

$$\mathcal{E}Q_t = \frac{QQ_t}{4\pi\epsilon_0 S^2}, \tag{12.15}$$

$$\mathcal{E} = \frac{Q}{4\pi\epsilon_0 S^2} \text{ v per m}, \tag{12.16}$$

where ϵ_0 is the permittivity of free space. Equation (12.16) enables us to calculate the electric field intensity at any distance S from a point charge in free space. It must be remembered that $\mathcal{E}$ is a vector quantity and, therefore, its direction as well as its magnitude must be stated. The direction of the field due to a positive charge at a point is away from the point; that due to a negative charge at a point is toward the point.

If two or more point charges are present in a certain region, the electric field intensity at any specified point can be found by taking the resultant of the electric field intensities at this point due to the individual charges. That this is so will be clear when we remember that electric field intensity is measured by the force acting upon a unit positive charge placed at the point in question. When we add electric field intensities, we are, in effect, adding forces on a charge, and the resultant force will be the resultant electric field intensity.

Example: In a system of plane rectangular coordinates, charge A is $+2 \times 10^{-6}$ coulomb and is located at the point (0, 2), as shown in Fig. 12.7. Charge B is $+5 \times 10^{-6}$ coulomb and is located at the point (3, 0). The coordinates are expressed in meters. Determine the electric field intensity at the origin due to each charge and the resultant electric field intensity.

SOLUTION: Electric field intensity at the origin due to charge A is

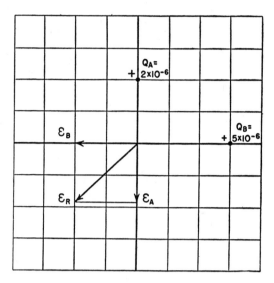

Fig. 12.7. Graphical determination of the electric field intensity due to two point charges.

$$\mathcal{E}_A = \frac{2 \times 10^{-6}}{4\pi\left(\frac{1}{36\pi} \times 10^{-9}\right)(2)^2} = 4500 \text{ v per m}$$

directed along the negative y axis as shown.

Electric field intensity at the origin due to charge B is

$$\mathcal{E}_B = \frac{5 \times 10^{-6}}{4\pi\left(\frac{1}{36\pi} \times 10^{-9}\right)(3)^2} = 5000 \text{ v per m}$$

directed along the negative x axis as shown.

	x Component	y Component
$\mathcal{E}_A$	0	-4500
$\mathcal{E}_B$	-5000	0
$\mathcal{E}_R$	-5000	-4500

$$\mathcal{E}_R = \sqrt{(5000)^2 + (4500)^2} = 6740 \text{ v per m.}$$

There is no limit to the number of point charges that may be taken into account by this method, nor is it necessary that all the charges lie in the same plane. If we are given the sign; magnitude; and x, y, and z coordinates of n point charges, we can find the electric field intensity at the origin, or at any specified point in space. Practically, the procedure is too laborious to apply to any but the simplest cases.

Point charges are, of course, fictitious, because any charge is distributed more or less uniformly over the surface of the body with which it is associated. Distributed charges may sometimes be replaced for purposes of calculation, however, by point charges properly placed. For instance, a charge uniformly distributed over the surface of a sphere can be replaced by an equal point charge placed at the center. A charged surface of any kind may be broken down into elements of area, and the charge on each element regarded as a point charge for the purpose of calculating electric field intensity by the method outlined above. The resultant field intensity would then be found as the vector summation of all the field intensities due to the elemental areas with their associated charges. However, this procedure, as indicated above, is too laborious to be very useful.

PROBLEMS

(7-XII) What is the electric field intensity in space 25 cm from a point charge of $+10^{-6}$ coulomb?

(8-XII) What is the electric field intensity at the origin if a point charge of $+2 \times 10^{-7}$ coulomb is located at the coordinate (30, 40) and a charge of -3×10^{-7} coulomb is located at the coordinate (-60, 80)? Coordinates are expressed in centimeters.

(9-XII) Calculate the electric field intensity at the point (20, -20) due to the arrangement of point charges described in Problem 8-XII.

10. Electric flux lines and electric flux density. In mapping an electric field by means of a positive test charge (Section 2), the direction of the field is found to be away from the positively charged body which is one boundary of the field, and toward the negatively charged body which is the other boundary. Suppose now continuous lines are drawn from the one boundary to the other so that at every point the direction of the line coincides with the direction of the field. These lines represent graphically the electric flux. As with magnetic flux lines, lines of electric flux have no real existence, they are simply a useful concept in representing and describing the fields. Unlike the lines of magnetic flux which are closed lines, with no terminations, the electric flux lines are conceived to have their beginnings on positive charges and to terminate upon negative charges. Figure 12.8 shows lines of electric flux in the field between oppositely charged parallel plates.

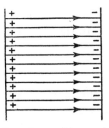

Fig. 12.8. Lines of electric flux between oppositely charged parallel plates.

We now proceed to define a concept called electric flux density by the equation

$$D = \epsilon \mathcal{E}, \qquad (12.17)$$

where D is the electric flux density in mks units;

     ϵ is permittivity of the medium;

     $\mathcal{E}$ is electric field intensity in volts per meter.

Electric flux density is thus seen to be directly related to electric field intensity, permittivity being the factor by which one quantity differs from the other. The mks unit of electric flux density has no special name.

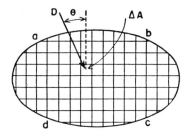

Fig. 12.9. The summation of $D \cos \theta \, \Delta A$ over the surface is equal to the total electric flux penetrating the surface.

11. Electric flux. Just as a magnetic field might be described by specifying for each point either the magnetic field intensity or the magnetic flux density, so an electric field may be described by specifying for each point either the electric field intensity or the electric flux density. Electric flux density is a vector quantity which may vary from point to point both in direction and in magnitude. Let us consider a surface a-b-c-d (Fig. 12.9), which is in an electric field and which is penetrated by the lines of electric flux. At every point there will be an electric flux density which can be represented by a vector such as D directed into the paper. The direction of the vector is the direction of the field at the point and its length is proportional to the flux density. Now suppose the surface to be divided into small areas ΔA, so small that the flux density may be considered as uniform over ΔA. Then suppose we form products such as $D \cos \theta \, \Delta A$ by multiplying the area by the component of the flux density perpendicular to the area, and finally that we sum up all such products over a specified surface and equate this to the electric flux ψ which penetrates the surface

$$\sum^{A} D \cos \theta \, \Delta A = \psi. \qquad (12.18)$$

In the limit, as ΔA approaches zero, the summation becomes the definite integral

$$\int^{A} D \cos \theta \, dA = \psi. \qquad (12.19)$$

This equation will serve as the defining equation of electric flux. If the products of the electric flux density with elements of area are taken as described above and summed up over any specified surface, the summation is equal to the electric flux penetrating the surface.

In the simple case of the field between oppositely charged parallel plates, the summation would become simply

$$DA = \psi \qquad (12.20)$$

or
$$D = \frac{\psi}{A}. \qquad (12.21)$$

Electric flux density is in this case seen to be electric flux per unit area, and so far as dimensions are concerned this is true in general. It must be remembered, however, that it is not usually possible to find the electric flux density at a point by simply dividing an electric flux by an area. This is valid only if the flux density is uniform over the area, or if average flux density is wanted.

The mks unit of electric flux has no special name.

PROBLEMS

(10-XII) Two parallel flat plates, each 10 by 5 cm and separated by 1 cm, are charged by transferring 0.1 microcoulomb from one plate to the other. What electric flux is established between the plates? What is the electric flux density?

(11-XII) What charge would be required to establish an electric flux density of 2×10^{-5} mks unit per sq m between parallel flat plates 20 cm in diameter?

12. Gauss's law. Consider a spherical surface of radius S meters, at the center of which is a positive point charge of Q coulombs (Fig. 12.10a). The

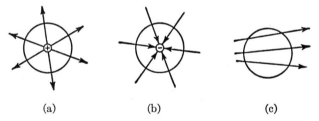

(a)   (b)   (c)

Fig. 12.10. Lines of electric flux penetrating a closed surface within which is: (a) a positive charge; (b) a negative charge; (c) no charge.

electric field intensity at a point on this surface is given by Equation (12.16) as

$$\mathcal{E} = \frac{Q}{4\pi\epsilon S^2} \text{ v per m.}$$

The electric flux density at the point can then be found by Equation (12.17) as

$$D = \epsilon\mathcal{E} = \frac{\epsilon Q}{4\pi\epsilon S^2} = \frac{Q}{4\pi S^2} \text{ mks units.}$$

Since the point charge is at the center of the sphere, the electric flux density is uniform over all the surface and perpendicular to the surface at every point. The electric flux passing outward through the surface is therefore

$$\psi = DA = \frac{Q}{4\pi S} \times 4\pi S = Q \text{ mks units.} \qquad (12.22)$$

The electric flux is thus shown to be numerically equal to the charge within the sphere. An alternative definition of the unit of electric flux would be: *One mks unit of electric flux is the amount which is associated with a charge of one coulomb.*

If the surface were drawn to enclose a net charge of $-Q$ coulombs as in Fig. 12.10b, an electric flux

$$\psi = Q \text{ mks units} \qquad (12.23)$$

would pass inward through the surface and terminate upon the charge. If the surface were so drawn that the net charge enclosed was equal to zero, the net flux passing in or out through the surface would be zero. Even if there were other charges in the vicinity, lines entering the specified surface due to these could not terminate within it (since it contains no net charge), but must again pass through the surface outward as in Fig. 12.10c.

It is not essential that the enclosing surface be spherical or that the charges be point charges. The above statements are summed up in Gauss's law as follows: *The net amount of electric flux passing through any closed surface is numerically equal to the net charge enclosed by the surface.*

PROBLEMS

(12-XII) What is the electric flux entering (leaving) a surface which encloses (a) the positive plate in Problem 11-XII, (b) the negative plate in Problem 11-XII, and (c) both plates in Problem 11-XII?

(13-XII) A spherical surface 50 cm in diameter is penetrated by an inward electric flux uniformly distributed over the surface, the electric flux density being 2.5×10^{-7} mks unit per sq m. What is the sign and magnitude of the charge enclosed by this surface?

13. Two experiments. The relationships among the various electric field quantities may be made clearer by consideration of two experiments. First suppose two flat plates maintained parallel at a fixed distance apart are connected to a battery and then immersed in an oil bath, as shown in Fig. 12.11a. The electric field intensity remains unchanged, since the potential difference between the plates is fixed by the battery. The molecules of oil, however, become polarized under the influence of the field, and, in effect, neutralize part of the charge, enabling the battery to crowd more charge onto the plates as can be demonstrated by connecting a galvanometer in series with the battery. More charge means more electric flux and greater electric flux density, as required by Equation (12.17).

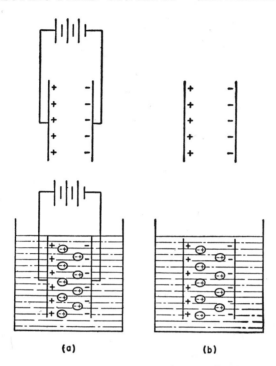

Fig. 12.11. Effect of immersing a pair of oppositely charged parallel plates in a liquid dielectric: (a) plates maintained at constant potential difference; (b) plates maintained at constant charge.

Now, suppose that after charging the plates (which are assumed to be perfectly insulated), the battery is disconnected and the plates are immersed in the oil as in Fig. 12.11b. The charge on the plates is now fixed, as are the electric flux and electric flux density. There is nothing to maintain the plates at a fixed potential difference, however, and the polarized molecules of oil set up an electric field in opposition to the field of the plates, and thus reduce the electric field intensity and the potential difference. An electrostatic voltmeter connected to the plates would thus indicate a decrease in potential difference as the plates are lowered into the oil.

PROBLEMS

(14-XII) What is the permittivity of a substance in which (a) an electric flux density of 1.018×10^{-7} mks unit per sq m is established by an electric field intensity of 500 v per m, (b) an electric flux density of 1.145×10^{-6} mks unit per sq m is established by an electric field intensity of 3.5×10^4 v per m, and (c) an electric flux density of 2.71×10^{-5} mks unit per sq m is established by an electric field intensity of 6×10^5 v per m? What is the dielectric constant of each of these substances?

(15-XII) A potential difference of 7500 v is established between parallel plates 30 by 40 cm which are separated by a sheet of glass (dielectric constant 8.35) 0.062 in. thick. Determine the charge on the plates.

(16-XII) What potential difference would be required to transfer a charge of 1 microcoulomb between parallel plates 25 cm in diameter which are spaced 1.5 cm apart and immersed in glycerin (dielectric constant 25)?

(17-XII) What is the maximum charge that can be transferred without causing breakdown of the air between parallel plates 5 cm in diameter and spaced 1 cm apart?

(18-XII) What is the maximum charge which may be placed upon a sphere 1 cm in diameter, located in air, before breakdown occurs?

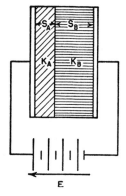

Fig. 12.12. Parallel plates insulated by slabs of two different dielectric substances.

14. Electric fields in nonhomogeneous dielectrics. Suppose an electric field is established between two plates which are separated by a layer of dielectric A, having a thickness S_A and a permittivity ϵ_A, and a layer of dielectric B, having a thickness S_B and permittivity ϵ_B, as shown in Fig. 12.12. Since there are no free charges within either layer of dielectric, nor at the boundary, lines of electric flux which originate on charges on the positive plate must be continuous through both layers and terminate on the negative plate. Since the cross section of the field is uniform, the electric density D must be the same in both layers:

$$D_A = D_B. \tag{12.24}$$

But since the permittivities are not the same, the electric field intensities must be different and must satisfy the equation

$$\epsilon_A \mathcal{E}_A = \epsilon_B \mathcal{E}_B \tag{12.25}$$

or, since $\epsilon_A = \epsilon_0 \epsilon_{RA}$ and $\epsilon_B = \epsilon_0 \epsilon_{RB}$,

$$\epsilon_{RA} \mathcal{E}_A = \epsilon_{RB} \mathcal{E}_B. \tag{12.26}$$

Also, the summation of the products of electric field intensity by thickness of the dielectric must equal the potential difference between the plates at the extremities of the field:

$$\mathcal{E}_A S_A + \mathcal{E}_B S_B = E. \tag{12.27}$$

If the dielectric constants, thicknesses, and potential difference are known, we may solve (12.26) and (12.27) to obtain the electric field intensity in each dielectric.

It is obvious from Equation (12.26) that the highest electric field intensity must exist in the medium of smallest dielectric constant. This is often of practical importance in the design of insulation, particularly if one of the layers is air. Air not only has a smaller dielectric constant, but also a smaller dielectric strength than most insulating materials and, consequently, an air film trapped between layers of other insulation is likely to break down, even when the stress in the other insulation is nominal. The heat resulting from breakdown of the air film may cause eventual deterioration and failure of the other insulation.

PROBLEMS

(19-XII) Two parallel plates are separated by a sheet of plate glass (dielectric constant 7.57) $\frac{3}{16}$ in. thick and a sheet of rubber (dielectric constant 2.3) $\frac{1}{4}$ in. thick. A potential difference of 50,000 v is established between the plates. Determine the electric field intensity in each substance.

(20-XII) The potential difference between the plates in Problem 19-XII is gradually raised until failure of one of the dielectrics occurs. Which dielectric fails first, and what will be the potential difference between the plates when failure occurs? Assume the dielectric strength of each substance to be the lower figure given in Table VI.

(21-XII) A sheet of fiber (dielectric constant 5) 0.23 cm thick is inserted between parallel plates 0.25 cm apart. A potential difference of 2500 v is applied between the plates. Determine the electric field intensity in the fiber and in the air film between the fiber and the plate. Will the air break down?

15. Capacitance. In order to charge one conductor with respect to another, it is necessary to establish between the conductors a certain potential difference. Conversely, if a potential difference be established between two conductors, a certain quantity of electricity is transferred from one to the other. The one thing implies the other. We never have potential difference without charge, nor charge without potential difference. The charge divided by the corresponding potential difference is defined as the **capacitance** of the two conductors.

The unit of capacitance is the **farad,** defined as follows: *The capacitance of two conductors is 1 farad if a potential difference of 1 volt corresponds to a charge of 1 coulomb.*

The definition in equation form is

$$C = \frac{Q}{V}, \tag{12.28}$$

where C is the capacitance in farads;

Q is the charge in coulombs;

V is the potential difference in volts.

The farad is too large a unit to be convenient for practical measurements. The charge corresponding to 1 v potential difference will never exceed more than a very small fraction of a coulomb, even for the largest conductors. Consequently, capacitance is usually expressed in microfarads (μf) or micromicrofarads ($\mu\mu$f). In making calculations in mks units, of course, farads must always be used.

Capacitance depends upon (a) the sizes and shapes of the two conductors, (b) their distance apart, and (c) the medium in which the conductors are located. In general, the larger the conductors and the closer together they are, the greater will be their capacitance. The capacitance will be several times as great if the conductors are separated by a solid or liquid dielectric as it will if the medium is air or free space.

Capacitance is frequently introduced deliberately into an electric circuit to secure certain desired behavior. On the other hand, it frequently occurs in circuits and apparatus as a consequence of other design considerations, without being particularly sought after. For example, the capacitance between the conductors of a transmission line, or a telephone cable, is an important factor in determining their performance characteristics, as is the capacitance between the various electrodes of any electronic tube. Often, the incidental capacitance is so high as to prevent the operation of the device as desired. For example, ordinary electronic tubes cannot be used at very high frequencies because of their too large interelectrode capacitances, and telephone conversations over most ocean cables are not practicable because of the large capacitances between the conductors.

PROBLEMS

(22-XII) What is the capacitance of a parallel-plate arrangement if a potential difference of 2500 v corresponds to a charge of 10^{-4} coulomb? What would be the charge if the potential difference were 7500 v? What potential difference would correspond to a charge of 10^{-3} coulomb?

(23-XII) The capacitance of a line consisting of two No. 10 gage wires spaced 18 in. apart is given in tables as 0.00762 μf per mile of line. What charge per mile would appear on each wire if the potential difference between the wires were 2300 v?

(24-XII) The plate-cathode capacitance of a 2A3 vacuum tube is 5.5 $\mu\mu$f. The normal potential difference between plate and cathode is 250 v. What is the charge on these electrodes at normal voltage?

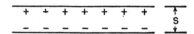

Fig. 12.13. Oppositely charged parallel plates.

16. Calculation of capacitance of parallel plates. The relationships between the various electric field concepts and capacitance will be further illustrated by the calculation of the capacitance of two parallel, flat plates. Suppose a quantity of electricity equivalent to Q coulombs be moved from one plate to the other as in Fig. 12.13. If we assume the plates to be separated by a distance which is small compared to their other dimensions, we may ignore any edge effects and assume the charge to be distributed uniformly over the inner surface of each plate.

The electric flux emerging from the positive plate and terminating on the negative plate is

$$\psi = Q \text{ mks units.} \tag{12.22}$$

Since the charge was assumed to be uniformly distributed, we may assume the electric flux to be uniformly distributed also. The electric flux density in any plane between the plates and parallel to them will, therefore, be

$$D = \frac{\psi}{A} = \frac{Q}{A} \text{ mks units per sq m,} \tag{12.29}$$

where A is the area in square meters of one side of one plate. If the plates are separated by a dielectric substance of permittivity ϵ, the electric field intensity will be

$$\mathcal{E} = \frac{D}{\epsilon} = \frac{Q}{\epsilon A} \text{ v per m.} \tag{12.30}$$

The electric field intensity will be constant from the surface of the positive plate to the surface of the negative plate. The potential difference between the plates is, therefore,

$$V = \mathcal{E}S = \frac{QS}{\epsilon A} \text{ v,} \tag{12.31}$$

where S is the plate separation in meters.

From the defining equation of capacitance, we then have

$$C = \frac{Q}{V} = \frac{Q}{QS/\epsilon A} = \frac{\epsilon A}{S} \text{ farads.} \tag{12.32}$$

Equation (12.32) not only enables us to calculate the capacitance of parallel plates when the permittivity of the dielectric is known, but also makes it possible to determine permittivity. If we *measure* the capacitance of a parallel-plate arrangement the dimensions of which are accurately known, we may use (12.32) to determine the permittivity of the substance used as the dielectric.

PROBLEMS

(25-XII) What is the capacitance of 2 parallel plates 20 by 25 cm, separated by 0.5 cm of air?

(26-XII) What should be the area of a pair of plates separated by mica (dielectric constant 6.5) 0.005 in. thick in order that their capacitance shall be 0.001 μf?

(27-XII) Two parallel metal plates each having a surface area of 100 sq cm (one side) and separated by 1 mm are immersed in oil. The capacitance is measured and found to be 0.00213 μf. What is the permittivity of the oil? What is its dielectric constant?

17. Energy stored in an electric field. It was pointed out in Section 1 that the charging of conductors by removing electrons from one to the other requires the expenditure of energy. This energy is not lost, but is stored in the electric field established between the conductors, and is recoverable in the form of heat when the conductors are discharged. We shall now look for a way to express the stored energy in terms of the electric field concepts.

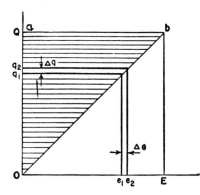

Fig. 12.14. Graphical determination of the energy stored in an electric field.

As the potential difference between the conductors is increased, the charge increases in direct proportion, as shown by the graph in Fig. 12.14. Corresponding to a potential difference e_1, there exists on each conductor a charge q_1. If the potential difference is increased by an amount Δe to a value e_2, the charge on each conductor increases by an amount Δq to a value q_2. The work done in moving this additional quantity of electricity Δq from one conductor to the other is, by the defining equation of potential difference, equal to the charge moved times the average potential difference that existed while it was being moved:

$$\Delta w = \frac{e_1 + e_2}{2} \Delta q. \tag{12.33}$$

If Δe is made very small, we can consider $e_1 = e_2$ and

$$\Delta w = e_1 \Delta q. \tag{12.34}$$

Graphically, Δw is represented in Fig. 12.14 by the area of the strip of width Δq and length e_1. To find the total energy required to move a quantity of electricity Q from one plate to the other and thus establish a potential difference E between the plates, we have to sum up the area represented by all such strips from $e = 0$ to $e = E$:

$$W = \sum_{e=0}^{e=E} e \, \Delta q. \tag{12.35}$$

Graphically, this energy is represented in Fig. 12.14 by the area of the triangle oab, which is

$$W = \frac{EQ}{2}. \qquad (12.36)$$

If the conductors are parallel plates, as used in defining the various electric field concepts, the field will be uniform, and we may write

$$E = (-)\mathcal{E}S, \qquad (12.37)$$

$$Q = \psi = DA. \qquad (12.38)$$

Upon substituting (12.37) and (12.38) in (12.36), we obtain

$$W = \frac{(\mathcal{E}S)(DA)}{2}. \qquad (12.39)$$

The product SA is the volume of the space between the plates. Consequently, the energy stored per unit volume is

$$W = \frac{\mathcal{E}D}{2} \text{ joules per cu m.} \qquad (12.40)$$

If the space between the plates is filled with a dielectric of permittivity ϵ, the energy storage per unit volume can also be expressed as

$$W = \frac{\mathcal{E}D}{2} = \frac{\mathcal{E}(\mathcal{E}\epsilon)}{2} = \frac{\mathcal{E}^2\epsilon}{2} \text{ joules per cu m,} \qquad (12.41)$$

or

$$W = \frac{\mathcal{E}D}{2} = \left(\frac{D}{\epsilon}\right)\frac{D}{2} = \frac{D^2}{2\epsilon} \text{ joules per cu m.} \qquad (12.42)$$

We may also obtain from (12.36) an expression for total stored energy in terms of capacitance and potential difference, because since

$$Q = CE,$$

substitution into (12.36) gives

$$W = \frac{E(CE)}{2} = \frac{CE^2}{2}. \qquad (12.43)$$

The student will note the similarity between the expressions obtained in this article and the corresponding expressions for the energy stored in the magnetic field. Equations (12.41) and (12.42) should be compared with Equations (7.81) and (7.82) in Chapter VII. Equation (12.43) should be compared with Equation (11.50) in Chapter XI.

18. Force between charged plates. We can make use of the expression just derived for the energy stored in an electric field to calculate the force with which oppositely charged plates attract each other. Suppose the plates are arranged so that they may be separated a further distance ΔS by exerting a force F newtons to overcome the force of attraction between them, as shown in Fig. 12.15.

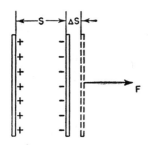

Fig. 12.15. Separation of oppositely charged parallel plates by an external force.

Before the separation of the plates is increased, the energy stored in the field, according to Equation (12.39), is

$$W = \frac{\mathcal{E}SDA}{2} \text{ joules.}$$

Increasing the separation by an amount ΔS involves the storage of an additional amount of energy

$$\Delta W = \frac{\mathcal{E}\,\Delta SDA}{2} \text{ joules.} \qquad (12.44)$$

Since the charge on the plates is fixed, the electric flux, electric flux density, and electric field intensity remain constant.

All of the increase represented by Equation (12.44) must have come from the mechanical force that pulled the plates apart. The energy supplied from this source is

$$\Delta W = F\,\Delta S \text{ joules.} \qquad (12.45)$$

Equating (12.44) and (12.45) and solving for F, we obtain

$$F = \frac{\mathcal{E}DA}{2} \text{ newtons,} \qquad (12.46)$$

or
$$F = \frac{D^2A}{2\epsilon} \text{ newtons.} \qquad (12.47)$$

Equation (12.47) may be compared with Equation (10.24), which gives the comparable magnetic force.

The force of attraction between charged plates may be utilized as a means of measuring potential difference. An instrument of this kind is known as an **electrostatic voltmeter.**

PROBLEMS

(28-XII) What is the energy storage per unit volume in an electric field in space where the intensity is 10^{-3} v per m? 10 v per m? 10^6 v per m?

(29-XII) How much energy is stored when a potential difference of 10,000 v is established between the plates of a parallel-plate arrangement which has a capacitance of 10^{-3} μf?

(30-XII) The capacitance of No. 10 wires spaced 18 in. apart in air is 0.00762 μf per mile. How much energy is stored in the electric field between the wires when the potential difference is 2300 v?

(31-XII) Parallel plates 10 cm in diameter are spaced 1 cm apart in air. With what force do the plates attract each other if the potential difference between them is 1500 v? What would the force become if the plates were immersed in oil (dielectric constant 2.5)?

(32-XII) What is the maximum attractive force that could be attained without breakdown of the air dielectric in the parallel-plate arrangement described in Problem 31-XII? Would this maximum force be more or less if the plates were immersed in oil (dielectric strength 100 kv per cm)?

19. Capacitors. An arrangement of insulated plates for obtaining a required capacitance in a limited space is known as a **capacitor** or **condenser.** The earliest capacitors were glass jars provided with inner and outer coatings of tin foil, and were called Leyden jars. They were used in connection with early-day electrostatic machines to accumulate electric charge as it was separated by the machine, and thus make possible the production of more spectacular discharges than could be obtained from the machine alone. No other form of capacitor was devised until about 1900 when the need for such a device in wireless telegraphy brought about the development of the parallel-plate type.

In present-day electrical engineering, immense numbers of capacitors of all types are used. The multiple-plate type consists of a stack of alternate plates and pieces of a dielectric material, such as mica, the odd-numbered plates being connected together to one terminal of the capacitor, and the even-numbered to the other. In other multiple-plate capacitors, the plates are held apart by spacers, and are so mounted that one group of plates may be moved relative to the other, and the groups interleaved to any desired extent. This is the familiar tuning condenser in any radio receiver.

Probably the most-used capacitor is of the type in which long, alternate strips of paper and metal foil are rolled together to form a compact unit of considerable capacitance. Paper capacitors are sometimes sealed into containers containing a liquid dielectric, which greatly improves the insulating qualities of the paper and makes the unit more reliable.

For applications in which a very large value of capacitance is required in small space, the electrolytic type of capacitor has been developed. The dielectric in this type is an extremely thin film deposited on an aluminum plate by the action of an electrolyte. The use of electrolytic capacitors is limited to d-c circuits and caution must be used to maintain the proper polarity.

A satisfactory explanation of the various uses to which capacitors are put is not easily made at this time. Most of the applications are in a-c circuits, and although one or two explanations will be attempted in the following sections, a full appreciation of the usefulness of capacitors is not possible until the student has more knowledge of alternating currents.

20. Rating of capacitors. Any capacitor is designed with two objectives in mind: the capacitance required and the potential difference to which the insulation will be subjected. The insulation aspect of the problem is usually the first one to be considered. The dielectric must be of such material and such thickness that its dielectric strength will not be exceeded when the capacitor is put into service. Since the properties of insulating materials vary somewhat, and since a capacitor may be momentarily subjected to overvoltage, it should be designed for a maximum safe voltage greater than the working voltage for which it is intended.

After having selected the dielectric material and calculated the proper thickness, there remains the calculation of the plate area to give the required capacitance, and the determination of the number of plates and their size to give the required area. In multiple-plate capacitors, the total plate area is given by

$$A = a(N - 1), \tag{12.48}$$

where A is total required plate area;

a is the area of one side of one plate;

N is the number of plates used.

Example: Design a capacitor that will have a capacitance of 0.01 μf and will work at a voltage of 2000.

SOLUTION: Let us consider mica as the dielectric. Table VI shows the dielectric strength of mica to be 50–200 kv per mm. Taking the minimum figure of 50 kv per mm and assuming that our capacitor may be subjected to as much as $1.5 \times 2000 = 3000$ v, we find the necessary thickness of the mica to be

$$\frac{3000}{50,000} \times 1 = 0.06 \text{ mm}$$

$$= 6 \times 10^{-5} \text{ m.}$$

The required plate area is given by Equation (12.32) for the capacitance of parallel flat plates:

$$C = \frac{\epsilon A}{S}.$$

From Table VI, we find the dielectric constant of mica to be 5–7. Again taking the minimum value, we find the permittivity of mica to be

$$\epsilon = \epsilon_0 \epsilon_R = 5 \times 8.85 \times 10^{-12} \text{ mks unit.}$$

Substituting in Equation (12.32) and solving for A, we obtain

$$0.01 \times 10^{-6} = \frac{(5 \times 8.85 \times 10^{-12})A}{6 \times 10^{-5}}$$

$$A = 136 \text{ sq cm.}$$

If we use 11 plates, then each plate must have an area of 13.6 sq cm.

PROBLEMS

(33-XII) What should be the effective surface area of each plate of a 1-μf paper-insulated capacitor using paper 2 mils thick? What would be the maximum voltage rating of such a capacitor?

(34-XII) A mica-insulated capacitor is to have a rating of 0.001 μf, 1000 v. What should be the effective area of the plates if a safety factor of 2 is allowed? If the capacitor is to be built up of alternate mica and metal disks, determine a suitable diameter and number of plates to give the proper area.

21. Capacitors in parallel and in series. Consider three capacitors having values of C_1, C_2, and C_3 farads, respectively, connected in parallel as shown in Fig. 12.16, and charged by a battery of constant voltage E. The final charges on the various capacitors will be

$$Q_1 = C_1E \text{ coulombs.} \tag{12.49}$$

$$Q_2 = C_2E \text{ coulombs.} \tag{12.50}$$

$$Q_3 = C_3E \text{ coulombs.} \tag{12.51}$$

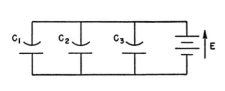 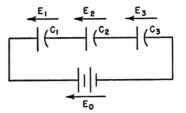

Fig. 12.16. Capacitors in parallel.   **Fig. 12.17.** Capacitors in series.

The total charge Q_0, transferred through the battery from the positive to the negative plates of the capacitors, will be the sum of the charges on the individual capacitors:

$$Q_0 = Q_1 + Q_2 + Q_3. \tag{12.52}$$

$$Q_0 = C_1E + C_2E + C_3E. \tag{12.53}$$

$$Q_0 = [C_1 + C_2 + C_3]E. \tag{12.54}$$

The total capacitance of the group is, therefore,

$$C_0 = \frac{Q_0}{E} = C_1 + C_2 + C_3. \tag{12.55}$$

Now, suppose three capacitors having capacitances C_1, C_2, and C_3 farads, respectively, are connected in series, as shown in Fig. 12.17, and charged from a battery of constant emf E_0. The charge on each capacitor in this case will be the same. The negative charge forced on to the right-hand plate of

C_3 will result in the displacement of an equal negative charge on to the right-hand plate of C_2, and finally of C_1, leaving the left-hand plate of each capacitor positively charged. In general, the emf's of the various capacitors will not be the same, since in each case the emf is determined by the charge and the capacitance. They are:

$$E_1 = \frac{Q}{C_1} \text{ v.} \tag{12.56}$$

$$E_2 = \frac{Q}{C_2} \text{ v.} \tag{12.57}$$

$$E_3 = \frac{Q}{C_3} \text{ v, respectively.} \tag{12.58}$$

By Kirchhoff's voltage law, the total voltage is

$$E_0 = E_1 + E_2 + E_3. \tag{12.59}$$

$$E_0 = \frac{Q}{C_1} + \frac{Q}{C_2} + \frac{Q}{C_3} = \left[\frac{1}{C_1} + \frac{1}{C_2} + \frac{1}{C_3}\right] Q. \tag{12.60}$$

Then the total capacitance is

$$C_0 = \frac{Q}{E_0} = \frac{Q}{\left[\dfrac{1}{C_1} + \dfrac{1}{C_2} + \dfrac{1}{C_3}\right] Q} = \frac{1}{\dfrac{1}{C_1} + \dfrac{1}{C_2} + \dfrac{1}{C_3}}, \tag{12.61}$$

or

$$\frac{1}{C_0} = \frac{1}{C_1} + \frac{1}{C_2} + \frac{1}{C_3}. \tag{12.62}$$

We may, therefore, state the rules for capacitors in parallel and series as follows:

The capacitance of a number of capacitors in parallel is the sum of the individual capacitances.

The capacitance of a number of capacitors in series is the reciprocal of the sum of the reciprocals of the individual capacitances.

Capacitors may be connected in parallel to obtain larger values of capacitance than are available from individual units. They are sometimes connected in series when the circuit voltage exceeds the working voltage of the individual units. In using the series connection, it is important to keep in mind that the voltages across capacitors in series are not the same unless the capacitances are equal. The greater voltage will be across the smaller capacitance, which may result in its failure if the capacitances differ very much.

One method of obtaining very high voltages in so-called "lightning generators" involves the charging of a number of capacitors in parallel, then reconnecting them in series for discharge. The reconnection is accomplished automatically by properly placed insulating gaps which break down when a predetermined voltage is reached.

PROBLEMS

(35-XII) Three capacitors of 2 μf, 3 μf, and 5 μf, respectively, are connected in parallel and charged from a 200-v battery. What is the group capacitance? What is the charge on each capacitor? What is the total charge?

(36-XII) Three capacitors of 2 μf, 3 μf, and 5 μf, respectively, are connected in series and charged from a 200-v battery. What is the group capacitance? What is the voltage across each capacitor? What is the charge on each capacitor? What is the total charge?

(37-XII) Three capacitors rated 1 μf, 300 v; 2 μf, 200 v; and 1.5 μf, 450 v are connected in series across a variable voltage, which is increased until one capacitor fails. Assume any capacitor will break down at 2 times its rated voltage. Which capacitor fails first, and what is the voltage across the group when failure occurs?

(38-XII) What will be the total capacitance of a parallel group made up of three capacitors having ratings of 20 μf, 30 μf, and 5 μf, respectively? What would be the total capacitance of a series group made up of these capacitors?

(39-XII) A laboratory capacitor is made up of four units arranged in a box, as in Fig. 12.18, so that various capacitances may be obtained by inserting plugs in positions A, B, C, . . . J. What capacitances are obtainable? Capacitances are expressed in μf.

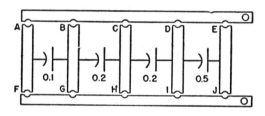

Fig. 12.18

(40-XII) A 2-μf capacitor is charged from a 100-v source. It is then connected, without loss of charge, to an uncharged 5-μf capacitor. What will be the final charge on each capacitor and the potential difference between their terminals?

(41-XII) Calculate the energy stored in the 2-μf capacitor in Problem 40-XII before it is connected to the other capacitor. Calculate the total energy stored in both capacitors after they are connected. Account for any discrepancy.

(42-XII) A 2-μf capacitor and a 5-μf capacitor are connected in series and charged from a 500-v battery. They are then disconnected from the battery and connected together, positive to positive and negative to negative. What will be the final charge on each capacitor and the potential difference at their terminals?

(43-XII) A 2-μf capacitor and a 5-μf capacitor are connected in series and charged from a 500-v battery. They are then disconnected from the battery and connected together, positive to negative and negative to positive. What will be the final charge on each capacitor and the potential difference at their terminals?

(44-XII) A surge generator consists of fifty 0.5-μf capacitors which are charged in parallel to 50,000 v. They are then reconnected in series and discharged. What is the charge on each capacitor and the total charge? What is the potential difference between terminals when the capacitors are reconnected in series? What quantity of electricity is available on discharge?

(45-XII) Calculate the total energy stored in the capacitors in Problem 44-XII during the charging period. Calculate the energy available on discharge. Account for any discrepancy.

22. Charging a capacitor. When a potential difference is applied to the terminals of a capacitor or to any conductors between which capacitance exists, electrons move as explained in Section 1 to charge the capacitor and establish at its terminals a potential difference equal to that applied. If the charging circuit contained no resistance, the charge would be completed instantaneously, and motion of electrons would cease. If, however, the charging circuit contains resistance, the rate at which charge can be transferred is limited, and electrons continue to move for an appreciable time before equilibrium is established. The movement of electrons in the charging circuit constitutes a measurable current which flows while the charging continues.

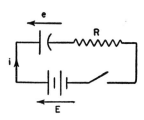

Fig. 12.19. Capacitor charged through a resistance by a source of constant emf.

Suppose a capacitor of C farads capacitance is being charged from a battery of E volts as indicated in Fig. 12.19. The circuit also contains a resistance of R ohms, as shown. At the instant of closing the switch, there is no charge on the plates of the capacitor, and the current is limited only by the resistance of the circuit:

$$i = \frac{E}{R}. \tag{12.63}$$

Electrons are thus transferred from the left-hand plate through the battery and resistance to the right-hand plate, charging it negatively and leaving the left-hand plate positive. The accumulation of charge on the plates establishes between them a potential difference

$$e = \frac{q}{C} \tag{12.64}$$

which opposes the emf of the battery and thus decreases the current.

If we apply Kirchhoff's voltage law to the circuit,

$$E - e = Ri. \tag{12.65}$$

Current is the time rate of transfer of charge and can be expressed as

$$I = \frac{\Delta Q}{\Delta T} \qquad (12.66)$$

if average current for a period of time ΔT is wanted, or

$$i = \frac{dq}{dt} \qquad (12.67)$$

if instantaneous current is wanted, as in this instance. Substituting in (12.65) the values of e and i from Equations (12.64) and (12.67), we have

$$E - \frac{q}{C} = R \frac{dq}{dt}. \qquad (12.68)$$

This is a differential equation which may be solved* to obtain an expression for the charge on the plates of the capacitor at any time following the closing of the switch. The solution is

$$q = CE(1 - \epsilon^{-t/RC}). \qquad (12.74)$$

Study of this equation shows that the charge does not increase instantaneously to its final value CE, but increases exponentially, as shown in Fig. 12.20, at a rate depending upon the capacitance and resistance of the circuit. In a time t equal to RC seconds, called the **time constant** of the circuit, the charge will have reached 63.2 per cent of its final value. That this is so can be readily seen by putting $t = RC$ in Equation (12.74), which then becomes

$$q = CE(1 - \epsilon^{-1}) = 0.632CE. \qquad (12.75)$$

Multiples of the time constant are always convenient instants at which to

---

*The solution of (12.68) may be carried out by various methods, one of which is that of separating the variables. By this method, (12.68) is first manipulated to get it into the form

$$-\frac{dq}{CE - q} = -\frac{dt}{RC}. \qquad (12.69)$$

Both sides of (12.69) are then integrated to obtain

$$\log_\epsilon(CE - q) = -\frac{t}{RC} + K, \qquad (12.70)$$

or

$$CE - q = \epsilon^{(-t/RC+K)} = \epsilon^{-t/RC}\epsilon^{K}. \qquad (12.71)$$

To evaluate ϵ^{K}, we take advantage of the known fact that at the instant of closing the switch ($t = 0$), the charge on the plates is zero. This gives

$$\epsilon^{K} = CE, \qquad (12.72)$$

which, substituted in (12.71), gives

$$CE - q = CE\epsilon^{-t/RC}, \qquad (12.73)$$

or

$$q = CE[1 - \epsilon^{-t/RC}]. \qquad (12.74)$$

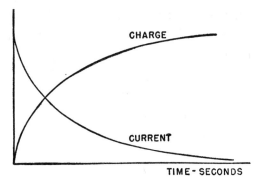

Fig. 12.20. Graphs showing charge and current as functions of time; capacitor being charged through a resistance.

calculate the charge because they result in integers (1, 2, 3, 4, and so forth) for the exponent in Equation (12.74).

We can readily find the current, which is the rate at which charge is being transferred from one plate to the other, by going back to Equation (12.67). Since

$$i = \frac{dq}{dt},$$

we may substitute for q the expression obtained above to obtain

$$i = \frac{d[CE(1 - \epsilon^{-t/RC})]}{dt}. \qquad (12.76)$$

Upon carrying out the differentiation, we obtain

$$i = \frac{E}{R}\epsilon^{-t/RC}. \qquad (12.77)$$

Study of this equation shows the current to be limited only by resistance at the instant the circuit is closed, and to decrease exponentially, as shown in Fig. 12.20, becoming less as the charge on the plates increases. The time constant $T = RC$ is a convenient value to use here also, since it gives integer values of the exponent.

> **Example:** A capacitor rated 0.1 μf is charged from a 100-v battery through a series resistance of 1000 ohms. Find (a) the time for the condenser to receive 63.2 per cent of its final charge, (b) the charge received in this time, (c) the initial rate of charging, and (d) the rate of charging when the charge is 63.2 per cent completed.
>
> SOLUTION: (a) The time to receive 63.2 per cent of the final charge is the time constant

$$T = RC$$

$$= (1000)10^{-7} = 10^{-4} \text{ sec.}$$

(b) The charge is found from Equation (12.74):

$$q = EC[1 - \epsilon^{-t/RC}]$$

$$= (100)(10^{-7})[1 - \epsilon^{-1}] = 0.632 \times 10^{-5} \text{ coulomb.}$$

(c) The initial rate of charging is found from Equation (12.77):

$$i = \frac{E}{R} \epsilon^{-t/RC}.$$

When $t = 0$, $\epsilon^{-t/RC} = 1$ and

$$i = \frac{E}{R} = \frac{100}{1000} = 0.1 \text{ amp.}$$

(d) The rate of charging when the charge is 63.2 per cent is

$$i = \frac{E}{R} \epsilon^{-1} = \frac{100}{1000} 0.368 = 0.0368 \text{ amp.}$$

PROBLEMS

(46-XII) A 1-μf capacitor is connected in series with a 1-megohm resistor and charged from a 100-v battery. (a) Find the time constant of the circuit. (b) Find the charge on the capacitor at times equal to 1, 2, 3, 4, and 5 times the time constant, and plot charge against time. (c) Find the initial rate of charging and rate of charging for times equal to 1, 2, 3, 4, and 5 times the time constant, and plot rate of charge against time.

(47-XII) A 0.002-μf capacitor is connected in series with a 50-ohm resistor and charged from a 100-v battery. Calculate (a) initial rate of charging, (b) time constant, (c) charging rate at a time equal to the time constant, and (d) charge at a time equal to the time constant.

23. Capacitance in alternating-current circuits — reactance. If a capacitor is connected to a source of alternating potential difference, as shown in Fig. 12.21, the charge on its plates must be continually changing in order that it may be proportional at every instant to the potential difference. The relation

$$q = Ce \qquad (12.28)$$

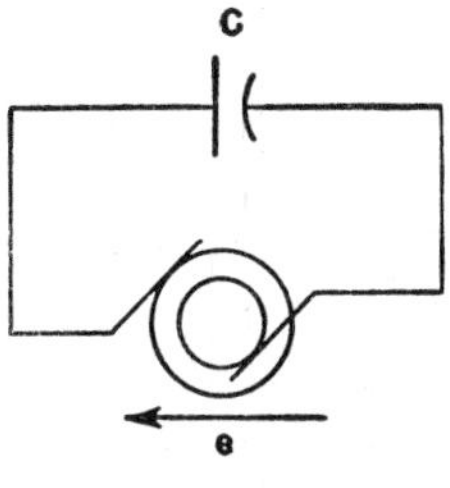

Fig. 12.21. Capacitor connected to a source of alternating emf.

must be satisfied at all times. This requires that current flow through the connecting wires in order that electrons may be shifted from one plate to the other as required by the changing potential difference. Then, since

$$i = \frac{dq}{dt}, \tag{12.67}$$

substituting gives

$$i = C\frac{de}{dt}. \tag{12.78}$$

The current at any instant is proportional to the rate of change of voltage at that instant.

Now, if e varies sinusoidally according to the equation

$$e = E_{\max} \sin \omega t, \tag{12.79}$$

the equation of the current can be found by substituting (12.79) in (12.78) and performing the differentiation as indicated:

$$i = C\frac{d[E_{\max} \sin \omega t]}{dt}. \tag{12.80}$$

$$i = \omega C E_{\max} \cos \omega t. \tag{12.81}$$

The maximum value of current will occur when $\cos \omega t = 1$, and its value will be

$$I_{\max} = \omega C E_{\max}. \tag{12.82}$$

From this expression, it can be seen that

$$\frac{E_{\text{effective}}}{I_{\text{effective}}} = \frac{E_{\max}}{I_{\max}} = \frac{1}{\omega C}. \tag{12.83}$$

The quantity $1/\omega C$ is thus seen to be dimensionally the same as resistance, since it is the ratio of voltage to current. It is called **capacitive reactance.**

The symbol for capacitive reactance is X_c, and it is defined by the equation

$$X_c = \frac{1}{\omega C} = \frac{1}{2\pi f C}, \tag{12.84}$$

where X_c is capacitive reactance in ohms;

f is frequency in cycles per second;

C is capacitance in farads.

The student should carefully compare Equation (12.84) with Equation (11.56) in Chapter XI. He will see at once that whereas inductive reactance increases with frequency, capacitive reactance becomes *less* as frequency is increased. The reactance of a capacitor is infinity for direct current and decreases with increasing frequency to very small values at high frequency. This suggests one purpose for which a capacitor can be used: if it is desired to prevent the flow of direct current in a certain branch of a network, and at the same time allow alternating current to flow, a capacitor should be inserted in the branch. A capacitor so used is called a **blocking capacitor.**

The fact that capacitive reactance and inductive reactance behave in inverse manner with change of frequency is the basis of the phenomena of resonance and tuned circuits, upon which depend the arts of radio and communication engineering generally. These phenomena form an important part of any course in alternating current circuits.

Example: What is the reactance of a 1-µf capacitor at a frequency of 60 cps?

SOLUTION:

$$X_c = \frac{1}{2\pi f C} = \frac{1}{2\pi \times 60 \times 10^{-6}} = 2660 \text{ ohms.}$$

24. Displacement current. The idea introduced in this chapter of current flowing in a circuit that is apparently incomplete will seem at first to be contradictory to what was said in the beginning chapters of this book. We have learned to think of current as flowing only in complete circuits, and as being the same in all parts of a series circuit. This is fundamentally correct, and instead of having to change our ideas about the continuity of current, what we need to do is to form a somewhat broader conception of what current is. Thus far, we have thought of current strictly in terms of moving electrons. From this limited viewpoint, we would be forced to say that, in the circuit in Fig. 12.1, current flows only as far as plate A; then there is a space between plate A and plate B where no current flows; and then from plate B the flow of current commences again. This is correct if we restrict ourselves to conduction current — the current accounted for by the motion of electrons. But if we define current as that which produces a magnetic field, then we may say that current flows in every part of the circuit in Fig. 12.1, because experiment shows that the part between plate A and plate B is as effective in producing a magnetic field as any other.

Although we have no free charges moving between the plates, we have or may have a changing electric field that is magnetically the equivalent of current. It is termed **displacement current** and may readily be expressed by Equation (12.67):

$$i = \frac{dq}{dt} = \frac{d\psi}{dt},$$

or by Equation (12.78)

$$i = C \frac{de}{dt},$$

or in the alternating-current case, by Equation (12.82)

$$I_{max} = \omega C E_{max}$$

or

$$I_{effective} = \omega C E_{effective}.$$

Example 1: What is the displacement current in a 1-μf capacitor when the voltage is changing at the rate of 10,000 v per sec?

SOLUTION: From Equation (12.78),

$$I = (10^{-6})(10,000) = 10^{-2} \text{ amp.}$$

Example 2: What is the effective value of the displacement current when an alternating voltage of 100 v at a frequency of 60 cps is applied to a 1-μf capacitor?

SOLUTION: From Equation (12.82),

$$I_{\text{effective}} = (2\pi \times 60)(10^{-6})(100) = 0.0377 \text{ amp.}$$

PROBLEMS

(48-XII) What is the reactance of a 0.001-μf capacitor at a frequency of (a) 0 cps (direct current)? (b) 1000 cps? (c) 10^6 cps? (d) 10^9 cps?

(49-XII) What is the effective value of the displacement current from one wire to the other when the two wires of the line described in Problem 23-XII are operated at an alternating voltage of 2300 v and a frequency of 60 cps?

STUDY QUESTIONS

1. What limits the quantity of electricity that can be transferred from one body to another?

2. Sketch the electric field in the vicinity of two parallel wires both positively charged.

3. It is a well-established fact that there is no electric field inside a charged hollow conductor, such as a sphere. Explain.

4. The definition of unit electric field intensity mentions a "1-coulomb test charge." Is such a charge practical? Why?

5. In Fig. 12.3, the work done in moving a test charge from the negative plate to the positive plate is independent of the path taken. Why is this so?

6. In Fig. 12.3, how much work would be done in moving a test charge of 10^{-8} coulomb once around a 5 cm by 5 cm square which lies entirely within the field and in a plane perpendicular to the plates, and which has two of its sides parallel to the plates? Take the electric field intensity as 10^{-4} newton per coulomb.

7. In Fig. 12.3, how much work would be done in moving a test charge of 10^{-8} coulomb once around a 5 cm by 5 cm square which lies entirely within the field and in a plane parallel to the plates? Take the electric field intensity as 10^{-4} newton per coulomb.

8. Are the algebraic signs in Equations (12.6) and (12.37) consistent with our definitions of E and V? Would it be correct to write $\mathcal{E} = E/S$?

9. In an arrangement like that shown in Fig. 12.5, what would happen if the metal rod were removed (still insulated) from between the plates? What would happen if the metal rod were allowed to touch the positive plate momentarily and then were removed (still insulated) from between the plates?

10. The lines of the electric field in the vicinity of a two-wire line carrying current are ordinarily thought of as originating on the positive wire, terminating on the negative wire, and lying in planes perpendicular to the line. Is this strictly correct? Why?

11. A capacitor with solid dielectric is charged to rated voltage and then discharged by short-circuiting its terminal momentarily. After a few seconds, the terminals are again short-circuited and a second discharge occurs. Explain.

12. Oil-insulated power cables, utilizing oil under pressure, are being specified for some purposes in preference to cables using solid insulation. What advantages can be claimed for the oil-insulated cable?

13. In what ways do lines of electric flux differ from lines of magnetic flux?

14. In Section 13, certain experiments designed to bring out the distinction between electric flux density and electric field intensity are described. Can you suggest parallel experiments to bring out the distinction between magnetic flux density and magnetic field intensity?

15. By means of dimensional analysis show that

$$D = M^{1/2}L^{-3/2}\mu^{-1/2}.$$

16. By means of dimensional analysis show that

$$\mathcal{E} = M^{1/2}L^{1/2}\mu^{1/2}T^{-2}.$$

17. By means of dimensional analysis show that

$$\frac{1}{\sqrt{\mu\epsilon}} = \text{velocity.}$$

18. An electrical worker, thinking to insulate better a part of an electrical machine, adds a layer of a different insulating material to that called for in the specifications. Is there any possibility that by doing this he may make breakdown of the insulation more likely? Explain.

19. An average electric field intensity of about 100 v per m is found to exist at the earth's surface, presumably because the earth itself carries a negative charge. What charge uniformly distributed over the earth's surface would give rise to this value of electric field intensity?

20. In the telephone industry, many long-distance circuits which were originally open-wire lines have been replaced by cables. What effect has this had upon the capacitance of such circuits?

21. Derive the expression for the capacitance per unit length of a coaxial conductor, the inner conductor of which has a diameter of d m, and the outer conductor an inside diameter of D m.

22. Discuss the practicability of storing in capacitors sufficient amounts of electrical energy to operate a lamp or lamps during an emergency. Make calculations to show the proposition is or is not feasible.

23. In one particular catalog, a capacitor rated 100 μf, 25 v direct current is listed for $0.74. However, a capacitor rated 1 μf, 2500 v direct current is listed for $7.06. Explain this apparent discrepancy in prices.

24. In designing a certain control circuit it is desired to have a certain 0.01-μf capacitor take 95 per cent of its final charge in $\frac{1}{500}$ sec, following the application of a direct-current voltage to its terminals. How can this be accomplished?

25. For what frequency is the reactance of a 1-μf capacitor numerically equal to the reactance of a coil having a self-inductance of 1 henry?

Chapter XIII

CONDUCTION IN LIQUIDS AND GASES. SEMICONDUCTORS. CHEMICAL, THERMAL, AND PIEZOELECTROMOTIVE FORCES

---

1. Conduction of electricity in liquids. Pure liquids, as a rule, are not conductors of electricity. Some liquids, such as mineral oils, are excellent nonconductors, or **insulators,** having resistivities as high as 10^{11} ohm-meters. Pure water is an extremely poor conductor, the conductivity of tap water being due to impurities which are always present. Mercury is, of course, a good conductor, as are all metals, even when melted. The most important liquid conductors, however, are solutions of substances known as **electrolytes.** If a salt, such as copper sulphate, be dissolved in water, it becomes possible to pass a current through the solution from one metal plate to another, as shown in Fig. 13.1. The plates are known as **electrodes;** the one by which the current enters the solution being called the **anode** and the one by which the current leaves the solution, the **cathode.** If these plates are copper and the electrolyte is copper sulphate, it is found that as conduction proceeds, the cathode gains weight but that the anode loses weight in equal amount. The gain in weight at the cathode is found to be due to the deposition on it of pure copper, and to be proportional to the quantity of electricity that has been passed through the solution. From these facts, it appears that particles of copper are, in effect, traveling

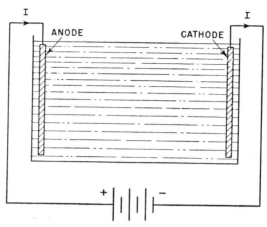

Fig. 13.1. Conduction of electricity through a liquid.

through the solution, and that these same particles are the carriers of the electric current. Conduction of electricity in an electrolyte, with the attendant results, is called **electrolysis.**

If we use silver nitrate in the solution and silver plates as the electrodes, we again find a transfer of metal from one plate to the other that is proportional to the quantity of electricity. We also find (1) in both instances the plate that gains is the cathode, or the one by which the current leaves the solution, and (2) if equal quantities of electricity are passed through the two cells, the mass of the metal deposited is directly proportional to its atomic weight and inversely proportional to its valence.

If we use a dilute solution of sulphuric acid and platinum electrodes, we find that at the cathode, hydrogen gas is liberated but that at the electrode by which the current enters, oxygen is set free. In this case, there is no gain or loss of mass of the electrodes, and we are apparently decomposing the water into its constituents. The same quantitative relations observed above, however, are found to hold in this case also. They are **Faraday's laws of electrolysis** and are here restated for reference:

1. *The mass of a substance liberated or deposited varies directly as the quantity of electricity.*

2. *The mass of substance liberated or deposited varies directly as its atomic weight and inversely as its valence.*

2. Dissociation and conduction. To account for the conductivity of solutions, the following theory was devised by Svante August Arrhenius in 1887. If a salt be dissolved in water, the molecules do not go into solution as such, but break up, or **dissociate,** into particles called **ions** which differ from atoms in that they are electrically charged.

It will be remembered from chemistry that a stable chemical compound is formed when an element such as sodium, which has one or more readily detached orbital electrons, or **valence** electrons, is combined with an element such as chlorine that needs one or more electrons to fill its orbits. When such a compound is put into solution, the electric forces which hold its parts together are weakened owing to the high permittivity of the water, and it breaks up. The chlorine takes with it the electron which normally belonged to the univalent sodium atom:

$$NaCl \rightarrow Na^+ + Cl^-. \tag{13.1}$$

Atomic groups or radicals, such as SO_4 and NO_3, dissociate as negatively charged ions, as

$$CuSO_4 \rightarrow Cu^{++} + SO_4^{--}. \tag{13.2}$$

In general any acid, base, or salt is an electrolyte. The metals and hydrogen dissociate as positive ions, and the nonmetals and radicals, as negative ions.

$$H_2SO_4 \rightarrow H^+ + H^+ + SO_4^{--}. \tag{13.3}$$

$$NaOH \rightarrow Na^+ + OH^-. \tag{13.4}$$

There is considerable difference in the extent to which dissociation takes place in different compounds. In some, such as HCl, KOH and KCl, ionization in 0.1 normal solutions is practically 100 per cent. In others, such as acetic acid and boric acid, ionization at this concentration is a fraction of 1 per cent. Dissociation is always greatest at small concentrations, the percentage of molecules which are dissociated becoming less as concentration is increased. Even pure water ionizes very slightly,

$$H_2O \rightarrow H^+ + OH^-, \tag{13.5}$$

and thus becomes a conductor to a small extent.

The phenomenon of dissociation is also encountered in melted salts. Thus, melted NaCl is a conductor, as is melted Al_2O_3, and several important electrochemical processes depend upon sending current through salts or ores in the molten state.

When an electric field of intensity ε volts per meter is established between two electrodes in a solution of an electrolyte or in an electrolyte in the molten state, the ions of both signs are acted upon by electric forces, according to the equation

$$F = \varepsilon Q, \tag{12.1}$$

where F is the force in newtons;

Q is the charge on an ion in coulombs.

The ions are caused to drift through the liquid — the positive ions toward the cathode and the negative ions toward the anode as shown in Fig. 13.2.

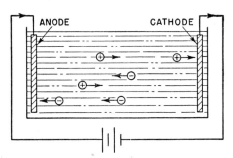

Fig. 13.2. Moving ions in a solution conducting electricity.

The positive ions, upon arrival at the cathode, take up sufficient electrons from the cathode to become neutral atoms which may stick to the cathode, pass off as a gas, fall to the bottom of the container as sludge, or enter into secondary chemical reactions, depending upon the particular conditions that exist in the cell. The negative ions, upon arrival at the anode, give up their excess electrons, becoming neutral atoms or atom groups. The electrons given up at the anode move through the external circuit to the cathode where they are available to neutralize the positive ions arriving there.

The current is thus seen to be carried within the electrolyte by ions, and in the external circuit, by electrons. The rate of transfer of charge across any boundary in the circuit must be the same; the net charge carried by positive ions and negative ions across a boundary surface set up midway between the electrodes must equal the net charge carried by electrons past a point on the external circuit in the same time.

3. Deduction of Faraday's laws. The theory of dissociation and conduction stated above leads logically to **Faraday's laws.** This may be shown as follows:

Let n = number of ions arriving at an electrode per second;

w = atomic weight of the substance liberated or deposited;

a = mass in grams of an atom having unit atomic weight;

m = mass of substance liberated or deposited (grams per sec).

Then

$$m = awn. \tag{13.6}$$

Let q = quantity of electricity in coulombs that passes through the cell per sec;

v = valence = number of electrons each ion has in excess or deficiency of normal atom;

e = charge in coulombs of an electron.

Then

$$q = nve. \tag{13.7}$$

Solving (13.7) for n and substituting in (13.6),

$$m = \frac{awq}{ve}. \tag{13.8}$$

From (13.8), it is obvious that m is proportional to q (**Faraday's first law**) and that m is proportional to w/v (**Faraday's second law**). The quantity a/e is a constant, which repeated experiments have shown to be equal to 1/96,485. Thus, we may write

$$m = \frac{1}{96,485} \frac{wq}{v}. \tag{13.9}$$

From this it can be seen that a quantity of electricity equal to 96,485 coulombs would liberate or deposit a number of grams of a substance equal to its atomic weight divided by its valence. This quantity of electricity is called **1 faraday.** For practical calculations, Equation (13.9) is a most useful relationship. It enables us to determine the mass of a certain substance that will be liberated, deposited, or consumed in a given electrochemical process by the passage of a given quantity of electricity.

Example: Copper is being deposited upon the cathode of a Cu-CuSO$_4$-Cu cell by a current of 1000 amp. How much copper is deposited in 24 hr?

Solution: The ion in which we are interested here is Cu^{++}, with an atomic weight of 63.57 and a valence of 2. Hence,

$$m = \frac{1}{96,485} \frac{63.57}{2} (1000 \times 24 \times 3600)$$

$$= 28,450 \text{ g.}$$

PROBLEMS

(1-XIII) If the potential difference at the terminals of the cell in the foregoing example is 0.25 v, and electrical energy costs 1 cent per kwhr, what is the cost per pound of depositing copper?

(2-XIII) How much silver would be deposited in 24 hr by a current of 1000 amp from an AgNO$_3$ solution? (Atomic weight of silver is 107.88, valence 1.)

(3-XIII) If the potential difference at the terminals of the cell in Problem 2-XIII is 3 v and the cost of electrical energy is 1 cent per kwhr, what is the cost per pound of depositing silver?

4. Digression upon the ratio a/e. Not only is Equation (13.9) useful for practical electrochemical calculations, but the fact that a/e is found to be a constant equal to 1/96,485 suggests an interesting possibility. If we know e, the charge on an electron in coulombs, we may find a, the mass in grams of an atom having unit atomic weight. Millikan's experiments showed e to be 1.60×10^{-19}; consequently,

$$a = \frac{1.60 \times 10^{-19}}{96,485} = 1.66 \times 10^{-24} \text{ g.} \qquad (13.10)$$

Since the atomic weight of hydrogen is 1.008, the above calculation gives approximately the mass in grams of the hydrogen atom. The mass in grams of any atom could be found by multiplying its atomic weight by 1.66×10^{-24}. Furthermore, $1/a$ gives the number of atoms in 1 gram of a substance having unit atomic weight, or the number of atoms in 1 g-atom of a substance of any atomic weight, or the number of molecules in 1 g-molecule of a compound of any molecular weight. This number, which comes out 6.02×10^{23}, is **Avogadro's number.** If, instead of taking the electronic charge as known, we had begun with Avogadro's number, we could have used our experimentally determined value of a/e to find the charge on an electron.

Example: What is the mass of an atom of chlorine? Of a molecule of KCl? How many molecules of KCl in 74.55 g?

SOLUTION: The mass of an atom of Cl is its atomic weight multiplied by a, the mass of an atom of unit atomic weight:

$$m = 35.46 \times 1.66 \times 10^{-24} = 58.8 \times 10^{-24} \text{ g.}$$

The mass of a molecule of KCl is its molecular weight multiplied by a:

$$m = (39.09 + 35.46)1.66 \times 10^{-24} = 124 \times 10^{-24} \text{ g.}$$

Since 74.55 is the molecular weight of KCl, this number of grams will contain 6.02×10^{23} molecules (Avogadro's number).

PROBLEMS

(4-XIII) What is the mass in grams of a copper atom? How many atoms are there in a cubic centimeter of copper? Atomic weight of copper is 63.57, valence 2, and density 8.89 g per cu cm.

(5-XIII) Using the results of Problem 4-XIII, determine the number of atoms per centimeter in No. 10 copper wire. On the assumption that there is 1 free electron per atom, determine the electron velocity in No. 10 copper wire carrying a current of 25 amp.

5. Gaseous ions and conduction in gases. In any volume of gas, there are always present at least a few positive and negative ions. In gases, ionization is not spontaneous, as in solutions, but is produced by the action of one or more of the following agencies: (1) ultraviolet light in the sun's rays, (2) radioactive substances that are present in minute quantities in the earth's crust and in water, and (3) cosmic radiation which reaches the earth from distant space. The ions share in the thermal agitation of the gas molecules, positive ions having approximately the same average velocity and mean free path as molecules. The negative ions begin their existence as electrons, and being smaller and lighter, their average velocities are greater and their mean free paths longer than those of positive ions. After a short interval of time, an electron may attach itself to a molecule, thus forming a negative ion that behaves more nearly like those of opposite sign. It might be expected that since the ionizing agencies are continually at work, eventually all molecules would be ionized. This would be true if it were not for the fact that positive ions and negative ions are continually recombining to form neutral molecules. The chance of a positive ion and a negative ion coming together in collision obviously depends on how many ions of each sign are present. The number of ions in any volume of gas will, therefore, increase until the rate of recombination equals the rate of ionization. In air, this ordinarily occurs when there are only a few hundred positive ions and an equal number of negative ions per cubic centimeter.

Suppose, now, a uniform electric field is established between parallel-plate electrodes a short distance apart in air at atmospheric pressure. To begin with, let the electric field intensity be 100 v per m. The positive ions will be urged in the direction of the field and the negative ions in the opposite direction. Instead of experiencing uniform acceleration, however, as do electrons in a vacuum, the positive and negative ions are found to acquire steady average velocities of 1.3 and 1.8 cm per sec, respectively. These drift velocities are governed by the collisions which the ions experience, and are superimposed upon the much higher velocities of thermal agitation. The drift velocities for an electric field intensity of 100 v per m, or 1 v per cm, are the mobilities of the ions. The drift velocities vary directly as the electric field intensity according to the equation

$$v = \mathcal{E}m \text{ cm per sec,} \tag{13.11}$$

where $\mathcal{E}$ is electric field intensity in volts per meter;
  m is mobility in centimeters per second in an electric field of 100 v per m.

It is to be observed that the mobilities of gaseous ions, even at atmospheric pressure, are very much greater than those of ions in solution. As the pressure is lowered, the mobilities of gaseous ions increase, as would be expected.

The electrons delivered to the anode by the negative ions move on around the external circuit and constitute a current. In the gas itself, the current consists of the oppositely directed streams of ions. With an electric field intensity of 100 v per m and air at normal pressure, the current would be too small to be measurable, but by the use of artificial ionizing agents, the number of ions present can be increased to where measurements of current are possible, if a very sensitive electrometer is used. If measurements of current are made for various values of potential difference between the plates, it is found that the current increases at first with potential difference, then becomes constant (as shown by the graph in Fig. 13.3) at

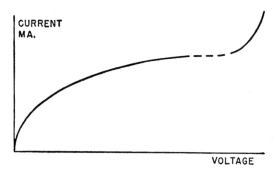

Fig. 13.3. Volt-ampere characteristic of low-voltage discharge, showing saturation effect.

what is called the **saturation value.** This must mean that the drift velocities of the ions have become high enough at some certain electric field intensity that the ions are carried to the electrodes (and lost by recombination) as fast as they are being formed. Beyond this point no increase in the current occurs until the electric field intensity has been increased to a very high value compared with those considered thus far. Before discussing this matter, however, it will be of interest to consider the effect of reducing the gas pressure.

6. Ionization by collision. Suppose we seal the electrodes into the ends of a glass tube, as in Fig. 13.4, from which we have pumped the air until the pressure is, say, $\frac{1}{1000}$ of atmospheric pressure. The saturation value of the current is now found to be less than before. There are fewer molecules and, consequently, fewer ions available to serve as carriers. But now we find that if we raise the electric field intensity to a moderately high value, say a few hundred volts per meter, the current begins again to in-

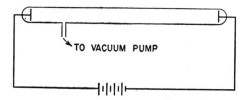

Fig. 13.4. Tube for study of conduction of electricity in gases.

crease. This must mean that some new source of ions has become available, since the current had previously ceased to increase with increased electric field intensity. The new source referred to is **ionization by collision.**

An ion, under the influence of the electric field between the electrodes, is accelerated and gains kinetic energy until it collides with a molecule and is stopped. At atmospheric pressure, the mean free path is so short that the ions seldom have the opportunity to gain much kinetic energy between collisions.

When the pressure is reduced, however, there are fewer molecules present in the space between the electrodes and, on the average, an ion travels further between collisions and possesses more kinetic energy at the time of collision. If its kinetic energy is sufficient, it may remove an orbital electron from the molecule with which it collides, thus producing a new pair of ions. These ions are then accelerated, gain kinetic energy, and experience collisions, which may result in further ionization. If new ions are produced by this means faster than they are being taken by the electrodes and lost by recombination, the current between the electrodes will increase, its limiting value being determined by the external resistance in the circuit.

Experiments show that the mobility of the negative ion increases tremendously with decreasing pressure. It is believed that this is due to the fact that at atmospheric pressure, the electron produced by ionizing a molecule attaches itself almost at once to another molecule, whereas at a lower pressure, it retains longer its original status as a free electron. Electrons, having only $\frac{1}{1837}$ of the mass of even the lightest atom, will be accelerated so much more rapidly than the heavier positive ions that they are almost wholly responsible for ionization by collision.

The energy that an electron must possess in order to ionize a molecule of any particular gas is a perfectly definite quantity. Although it might be expressed in ergs or joules, it is common practice to express it in terms of the number of volts potential difference through which the electron would have to move unhindered in order to acquire enough kinetic energy to ionize the given molecule. This potential difference is called the **ionization potential,** and the energy possessed by the electron is expressed in **electron volts** (ev).

The required ionization potential in any instance may be reached by (a) raising the potential difference between the electrodes or moving the electrodes closer together, thus enabling an electron to accelerate more rapidly and attain the required velocity and kinetic energy in a given distance, or (b) lowering the gas pressure and allowing the electron to move further before collision, thereby acquiring the necessary velocity and kinetic energy at a given acceleration. It must be made clear that the total amount of ionization by collision may be very small or very large. Even at fairly low potential differences between the electrodes, there must be an occasional electron that escapes collision long enough to acquire the ionization potential. Not every collision produces ionization, even when the electron possesses sufficient energy, and at low electric field intensities, the number of such electrons is itself so small that their total effect is negligible. At some rather well-defined value of electric field intensity, there will be enough electrons having free paths of sufficient length to enable them to attain the ionization potential so that the rate of ionization will exceed the rate of loss of ions, and the current will increase, limited only by the resistance of the external circuit. This is known as **breakdown,** and the potential difference between the electrodes when it occurs is called the **breakdown voltage** of the tube.

PROBLEMS

(6-XIII) What velocity would a positive ion acquire in an electric field intensity of 100,000 v per m in air at normal pressure (760 mm of mercury)?

(7-XIII) Taking the mass of an electron as 9.1×10^{-28} g, what must be its velocity when it has an energy of 1 ev? What force would have to act on the electron for it to acquire this velocity in a free path 0.05 cm long?

(8-XIII) The mean free path of electrons in a gas-filled tube is 0.05 cm and the electric field intensity is 100 v per cm. What energy would be acquired by an electron which had a free path equal to the mean free path?

7. Potential difference between an electrode immersed in a solution and the solution. Whenever a metal electrode is immersed in a solution of an electrolyte, a potential difference is established between the electrode and the solution. This potential difference is explainable in terms of certain forces, or pressures, that are not electrical in nature. The molecules of any metal tend to go into solution as positive ions, this tendency being known as **solution pressure.** On the other hand, the positive ions in the solution tend to be forced into the metal by **osmotic pressure.** The relative values of solution and osmotic pressure vary from one metal to another. In the case of zinc, for example, the solution pressure is the greater, and positive ions are forced into the solution. As positive ions leave the zinc, it acquires a negative charge, but the layer of solution immediately surrounding the zinc is positively charged. Thus, there is a difference of potential existing between the two surfaces, which may be regarded as separated by a distance of the order of one molecular diameter. Ions continue to be forced into the solution until the potential difference reaches such a value that equilibrium is brought about between the solution pressure, on the one hand, and the osmotic pressure plus the forces of electrical attraction, on the other hand.

If the immersed substance be a metal such as copper, the osmotic pressure exceeds the solution pressure, and positive ions are forced from the solution into the electrode, charging it positive and leaving the solution immediately around the electrode with a negative charge. Equilibrium is established when enough ions have been forced in to make the sum of the solution pressure and the electrical forces of attraction equal to osmotic pressure.

In order to measure the potential difference between the solution and an electrode, it is necessary to make contact with the solution with some sort of auxiliary electrode. But there must necessarily be a potential difference developed between the solution and the auxiliary electrode, and what is measured is, therefore, the algebraic sum of the two individual potential differences. For purposes of standardization, an electrode of hydrogen (formed by occluded hydrogen in a layer of platinum black deposited on platinum) shown in Fig. 13.5 is often used as the auxiliary electrode. By

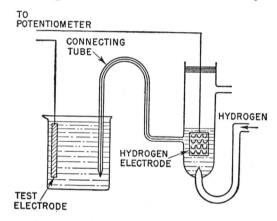

Fig. 13.5. Standard hydrogen electrode.

measuring the potential differences between a hydrogen electrode and electrodes of various metals, it is possible to make up a useful table from which the potential difference for any given combination may be found. The potential difference between the hydrogen electrode and the solution is arbitrarily taken as zero, and the table is based on each electrode being immersed in a normal solution of one of its own salts in which the valence of

Table VII. ELECTRODE POTENTIAL DIFFERENCES

Sodium	−2.70	Lead (2)	−0.13
Magnesium	−1.86	Hydrogen	0.00
Aluminum	−1.34	Bismuth	+0.20
Zinc	−0.76	Copper (2)	+0.34
Iron (2)	−0.43	Mercury (1)	+0.80
Nickel (2)	−0.23	Silver	+0.80
Tin (2)	−0.14	Gold (1)	+1.5

the elements is as shown in the table. For instance, if we make up a cell in which a zinc electrode is immersed in $ZnSO_4$ solution and a copper electrode is immersed in $CuSO_4$ solution, the two solutions being separated and prevented from mixing by a porous wall, the emf of such a cell would be $0.34 - (-0.76) = 1.1$ v.

A study of Table VII will show that the elements are arranged in the same order as in a chemical-displacement series, or activity series, with the most active element first. Much valuable information is contained in the series. If any element which precedes hydrogen in the series is immersed in an acid electrolyte, ions of the metal will replace hydrogen ions in the solution. Thus, zinc immersed in H_2SO_4 will replace H^+ ions in the solution with the formation of $ZnSO_4$. Furthermore, if any element in the series is immersed in a solution of a salt of a metal which follows it, its ions will replace those of the metal in solution. Iron immersed in $CuSO_4$ will be instantly covered with a layer of displaced copper ions.

If it were desired to deposit iron upon copper, however, it would be necessary to establish a potential difference of $0.34 - (-0.43) = 0.77$ v between the copper surface and the Fe^{++} ions in the solution in order that they might move against the solution pressure. If there were also present in the solution ions of another metal such as nickel, they would be deposited when a potential difference of only $0.34 - (-0.23) = 0.57$ v existed between the copper surface and the solution. The Ni^{++} ions are, therefore, deposited more easily than the Fe^{++} ions, and it would not be possible to deposit iron without depositing nickel also. On the other hand, if it were desired to deposit nickel, not iron, from a solution containing both ions, this could be done by properly adjusting the applied potential difference. Since hydrogen ions are always present in an acid solution, it will be impossible to deposit a metal standing before hydrogen in the series, without depositing hydrogen also.

PROBLEMS

(**9-XIII**) What metals from Table VII should be used as the electrodes of a primary cell to obtain the greatest possible emf? Would such a cell be practicable? Why?

(**10-XIII**) Electrochemical cells are set up using (a) zinc and lead electrodes, (b) copper and silver electrodes, and (c) tin and bismuth electrodes. Each electrode is immersed in a solution of one of its own salts. The solutions are separated by porous cups. What is the emf of each cell? Which is the positive electrode?

(**11-XIII**) The electrodes of a certain cell are copper and iron, respectively, and the electrolyte contains both Cu^{++} and Fe^{++} ions. What action would take place with (a) no connections to the electrodes, (b) the electrodes connected externally by a short piece of wire, (c) a battery with an emf of 0.77 v connected to the electrodes, positive to copper, and (d) a battery with an emf of 0.77 v connected to the electrodes, positive to iron?

8. Theory of a simple cell. Let us consider the Zn-HCl-Cu cell shown in Fig. 13.6. As explained in the preceding section, solution pressure forces Zn^{++} ions out of the zinc electrode into the surrounding solution until equilibrium is attained between solution pressure on the one hand and osmotic pressure plus electric forces of attraction on the other hand.* At the copper electrode, osmotic pressure forces H^+ ions onto the surface until equilibrium is reached between osmotic pressure on the one hand and solution pressure plus electric forces of

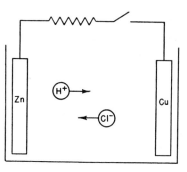

Fig. 13.6. Simple Zn-HCl-Cu primary cell.

attraction on the other hand. The equilibrium difference of potential between the electrodes will be approximately 1.1 v, as determined from Table VII.

Now, suppose the switch is closed to complete the external circuit between the electrodes. Electrons move through this circuit from the zinc electrode to the copper, seeking to equalize the potential difference. But this loss of negative charge by the zinc electrode upsets the equilibrium which existed there, and permits the solution pressure to force more Zn^{++} ions into solution. Likewise, the equilibrium at the copper electrode is upset by the arrival of electrons through the external circuit, and the osmotic pressure is able to force more H^+ ions onto the electrode. Within the cell, there are thus two streams of ions: Z^{++} and H^+ ions toward the cathode (copper), and Cl^- ions toward the anode (zinc). These streams of ions must transfer charge from one electrode to the other within the cell at exactly the same rate as it is transferred through the external circuit by free electrons.

Obviously, the flow of current through the resistance of the external circuit involves the expenditure of energy at a rate equal to I^2R joules per second. This energy must come from the chemical reaction within the cell—the reaction whereby zinc is converted into zinc chloride. If this reaction took place in a test tube, all of the energy involved would appear as heat. By having it take place in an electrochemical cell, a substantial part of it becomes available as electrical energy.

Faraday's laws of electrolysis apply to cells of this kind and Equation (13.9) may be used to determine the quantity of electricity available from the conversion of a given quantity of zinc. The product of this quantity of

---

*This equilibrium is not readily attained in practice because of local action due to impure zinc and agitation of the solution by displaced hydrogen ions.

electricity by the terminal voltage of the cell can then be taken to find the energy available from the given quantity of zinc.

Example: The terminal voltage of a Zn-HCl-Cu cell when delivering a current of 0.1 amp is found to be 0.7 v. How much electrical energy is available from such a cell per gram of zinc consumed?

SOLUTION: By Equation (13.9), the quantity of electricity per gram of zinc is

$$q = \frac{(1)(96500)(2)}{65.38} = 2950 \text{ coulombs.}$$

The energy is, therefore,

$$W = 2950 \times 0.7 = 2060 \text{ joules per g of zinc.}$$

PROBLEMS

(12-XIII) The zinc can of a certain dry cell weighs 4 oz. How long will this cell deliver a current of 1 amp before the zinc is 75 per cent consumed?

(13-XIII) If zinc costs 20 cents per lb, what is the cost per kwhr of supplying electrical energy from dry cells? Assume the zinc is the only cost and that a cell may be used until the zinc is 75 per cent consumed.

9. Thermoelectric effects. If two dissimilar metals are in contact, electrons from one diffuse into the other, as though the electron gas pressures in the two metals were different. This continues until the difference in potential across the boundary surface becomes high enough to establish equilibrium. Thus, there is established an emf known as the **Peltier electromotive force.** The direction and magnitude of the Peltier emf depend upon what metals are used and on the temperature of the junction. In the case of iron and copper at room temperature, electrons will move from the iron into the copper, and thus cause an emf to act in the direction shown in Fig. 13.7.

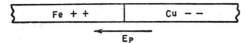

Fig. 13.7. Peltier electromotive force.

If a current is now sent through the junction in the direction indicated (using an external battery), heat energy is converted to electrical energy at a rate equal to $E_P \times I$ watts, and the junction will be cooled accordingly. Current in the other direction would heat the junction. This is known as the **Peltier effect.** At 0° C, the Peltier electromotive force for an iron-copper junction is 0.00432 v, with iron positive. It decreases to zero at

274.5° C, then increases to 0.0163 v at 600° C, with copper positive. It is evident that the amount of heating or cooling due to the Peltier effect is small, and it is masked by the much larger heating due to I^2R loss of the metals.

If one section of a wire is maintained at a higher temperature than another, the difference in electron gas pressures in the hot and cold parts causes a migration of free electrons from one part to the other until the potential difference, due to transfer of electrons, brings about equilibrium. The emf thus established is known is the **Thomson electromotive force.** The direction of the Thomson electromotive force depends upon the metal. In copper, the electrons are urged from hot to cold; in iron, the reverse is true. The magnitude of the Thomson electromotive force depends upon the temperatures of the sections. For copper with one section at 0° C and another section at 600° C, it is 0.00323 v with the hot parts positive. For iron with the same temperatures it is 0.0165 v with the cold part positive. If, by means of an external battery, current is sent through a wire in which Thomson electromotive forces are present, as in Fig. 13.8a, heat energy will

Fig. 13.8. Thomson electromotive forces: (a) in copper; (b) in iron.

be converted into electrical energy in the left end (thereby lowering its temperature), while electrical energy will be converted into heat energy in the right end (thereby raising its temperature). This is called the **Thomson effect.**

If two pieces of wire of dissimilar metals are joined at both ends to form a closed circuit, as shown in Fig. 13.9, and one junction is maintained at a higher temperature than the other, both Peltier and Thomson electromotive

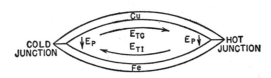

Fig. 13.9. Thermocouple circuit showing Peltier and Thomson electromotive forces.

forces will be present. For copper and iron with one junction, say, at 0° C and the other at 100° C, the directions of the electromotive forces would be as shown. If the hot junction temperature exceeded 274.5° C, the direction of E_P at that junction would be reversed. The resultant of the Peltier and Thomson electromotive forces in a closed circuit is known as the **Seebeck electromotive force,** and the flow of current in the circuit is called the **Seebeck effect.**

The three thermoelectric effects are of great significance in forming a theory of the conduction of electricity in metals. Any complete theory must explain them, and the data that can be obtained experimentally furnish a valuable check on the validity of any theory.

Apart from the theoretical significance, the Seebeck effect has a practical application in the **thermocouple.** We may cut into one of the wires which make up a circuit like that shown in Fig. 13.9 and insert a galvanometer to measure the current or a potentiometer to measure the Seebeck electromotive force, and as long as all parts inserted in the circuit remain at uniform temperature, the Seebeck electromotive force is unchanged. If we maintain one junction at a fixed temperature (usually done by inserting it in melting ice) and calibrate the other junction by observing electromotive forces for various temperatures, we have an excellent temperature-measuring device. Thermocouples may be inserted and read in inaccessible places or at temperatures that are too high for thermometers. They are very widely used in industry.

PROBLEM

(14-XIII) What is the Seebeck electromotive force in a copper-iron circuit if one junction is maintained at 0° C and the other at 600° C? What is the direction of this emf?

10. Piezoelectric effect. Certain crystalline solids, particularly quartz and Rochelle salt, have the unique property of becoming electrically charged between opposite faces when subjected to mechanical forces. This is known as the **piezoelectric effect.** Thus, if a piece of quartz is subjected to pressure, as in Fig. 13.10a, the surface becomes charged as indicated. If the same specimen is subjected to tension, as in Fig. 13.10b, the sign of the charge is reversed. The charge per unit area is small (about 2×10^{-12} coulomb per sq m per newton) and is proportional to the force.

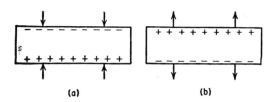

(a)   (b)

Fig. 13.10. Piezoelectric effects in crystal subjected to: (a) compression; (b) tension.

If a quartz crystal is placed in an electric field, the inverse effect is observed: the crystal expands or contacts, depending upon the direction of the field. Thus, in an alternating electric field, the crystal would expand and contract cyclically, and if the frequency of the field were made equal to a natural frequency of vibration of the crystal, the amplitude of motion might become considerable. Circuits have been devised whereby the vibrations of the crystal can in turn be made to control the frequency of the applied field, and the vibrations thus made continue at the natural frequency of the crystal. Such devices, known as **crystal oscillators,** provide the most reliable sources of constant-frequency alternating current available, and are widely used in controlling the frequency of radio transmitters. Since the natural frequency of a particular crystal depends upon its thickness and upon the orientation of the applied field relative to the axes of the crystal, it is possible to cut and finish a crystal so that it will have the desired natural frequency.

The amplitude of the piezoelectric effect in Rochelle salt is many times as great as in quartz, but its mechanical properties make it less satisfactory as a material for oscillator crystals.

11. Semiconductors. Certain elements, particularly silicon and germanium, have greater conductivities at room temperature than do the materials known as insulators, yet far less than the metals. These elements are called **semiconductors.** In the space lattice of metal crystals, as we have seen, at least one valence electron per atom is normally free from the nucleus, and these electrons move about within the space lattice in a random manner owing to thermal agitation. Conduction results when a drift motion in a definite direction is superimposed upon the random motion by the action of an electric field. In semiconductors, the valence electrons are normally required in the bonds which maintain the structure of the space lattice, and hence are not free to move about. That some small part of the total number of valence electrons are free, however, is evident from the fact that these substances have appreciable conductivities. The conductivity becomes greater with increased temperature (contrary to the behavior of metals), which must mean that more electrons are freed from their bonds by increased thermal agitation. The space lattice of germanium is represented in Fig. 13.11a. The atoms have four valence electrons, which are shown in their normal positions within the bonds.

When a valence electron is freed, its vacant position is known as a **hole.** A hole is not likely to remain for long. The motion of thermal agitation brings a free electron to fill the position, but this means that a hole must have appeared elsewhere in the structure. A hole may be thought of as moving about within the space lattice in a random manner, as are the free electrons. Now, if a drift motion of the free electrons is established in a

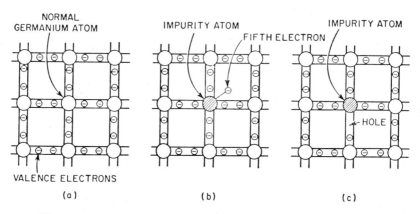

Fig. 13.11. Space lattice and bonding of the atoms in germanium.

certain direction (toward the positive terminal), this implies a drift motion of the holes in the opposite direction. The holes are regarded as being the equivalent of positive charges moving in the direction opposite to the electrons.

As mentioned above, the supply of free electrons (and of holes as well) is increased by raising the temperature. It may also be increased by introducing a trace of another element such as antimony, which has five valence electrons, into the semiconductor element in the process of manufacture. The atoms of the trace element find places in the space lattice, surrounded by atoms of the semiconductor, as shown in Fig. 13.11b. The fifth valence electron of the trace atom remains outside the bonds between the trace atom and the surrounding atoms and is free to drift through the space lattice. By rigorously controlling the percentage of the trace element present, the conductivity of the material can be significantly increased. Semiconductors of this kind and the conduction associated with them are designated as **N-type**.

On the other hand, the introduction of a trace of an element such as boron, which has only three valence electrons, leaves bonds unfilled, where an atom of the trace element is surrounded by four atoms of the semiconductor and a hole results (Fig. 13.11c). The hole may be filled by an electron, leaving a hole elsewhere, and so forth, and a drift of holes results. Semiconductors of this kind and the conduction associated with them are designated as **P-type**.

12. P-N junctions. If a junction is formed between N-type germanium and P-type germanium, as in Fig. 13.12, we have on one side of the junction a supply of free electrons and on the other side a supply of holes. This does not mean that the sides are oppositely charged: for each free elec-

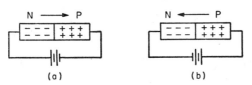

Fig. 13.12. P-N junction.

tron in the N-type material there is an equivalent positive charge. However, when the junction is formed, free electrons do migrate across it and fill holes on the other side. This results in a potential difference being established at the junction, and a state of equilibrum is brought about when the potential difference is just large enough to stop the migration.

Suppose now the P-N junction is made part of a circuit containing a battery. If the polarity of the battery is such that it establishes an electric field across the junction from N to P (Fig. 13.12a) little or no current can flow because there is no supply of holes — which could move with the field — in the N material, nor of electrons — which could move against the field — in the P material. If the polarity of the battery is such that it establishes an electric field across the junction from P to N (Fig. 13.12b), both the electrons on the left and holes on the right are acted upon by forces which cause them to drift across the barrier, and a current is established. This P-N junction thus becomes a unidirectional conductor, acting as though it had very high resistance to currents in the N-P direction and relatively low resistance to currents in the contrary direction. Such junctions are known as germanium (or silicon) diodes and are used as rectifier elements in many applications.

STUDY QUESTIONS

1. Criticize the statement "The cathode is the negative electrode." Under what conditions will the statement not be true?

2. What is the essential difference between the conduction of electricity in solutions and in metals?

3. Does ionization depend upon the passage of a current through the solution, or vice versa?

4. May a substance go into solution without forming ions? Explain.

5. Why is a smaller quantity of electricity required to deposit 100 g of lead (valence 2, atomic weight 207.2) than is required to deposit 100 g of copper (valence 2, atomic weight 63.57)?

6. Why is a smaller quantity of electricity required to deposit 100 g of silver (valence 1, atomic weight 107.88) than is required to deposit 100 g of cadmium (valence 2, atomic weight 112.41)?

7. How could electrochemical data be useful in determining the electronic charge? What other data would be necessary?

8. Is it possible to measure the potential difference established when a metal electrode is immersed in a solution? Why? How are the potential differences shown in Table VII obtained?

9. Theoretically a primary cell might be constructed with any two metals that stand far enough apart in Table VII to yield a substantial potential difference. Most such cells would be impractical. What characteristics, besides potential differences, should a cell for general use possess?

10. When a measuring instrument is inserted into a thermocouple circuit, at least two additional thermal junctions are introduced. Why is the Seebeck electromotive force not modified by the electromotive forces at these junctions?

Chapter **XIV**

TRANSIENT RESPONSE OF
SIMPLE CIRCUITS

---

1. Excitation functions. Most of the discussion of electric circuits in the preceding chapters has been limited to what is called the steady state. That is, the circuit in every case was assumed to have been closed, and its parameters unchanged for a sufficiently long time for the currents and voltages to have reached the values which they may be expected to have indefinitely. Exceptions to this have been (a) the circuit in Chapter XI, in which a coil having resistance and self-inductance was connected to a battery of constant voltage, and (b) the circuit in Chapter XII, containing a resistance and a capacitor in series, to which an emf source was connected. In the circuit in Chapter XI it was shown that the self-inductance had the effect of slowing up the rise of current and prolonging the time required for the current to reach a given percentage of its Ohm's law value. In the circuit in Chapter XII we saw how the resistance had the effect of slowing up the process of charging the capacitor and prolonging the time necessary for the charge to reach a given percentage of its final value.

We learned further that coils and capacitors are both capable of storing energy: a coil stores energy in the magnetic field interlinked with its turns whenever it carries current, and a capacitor stores energy in the electric field between its plates whenever a difference of potential exists between them. We shall now consider further the behavior of circuits containing one or both of these energy-storing elements, particularly during the time interval immediately following the closing of a switch to energize the circuit, or immediately following some change in the circuit itself. It should be specified further that all of the resistances, inductances, and capacitances (called the **parameters** of the circuit) shall be linear; that is, their values shall be independent of the current through them, or voltage across them.

When we close the switch to energize a circuit, we say that we are applying **excitation** to it. The source from which the circuit is energized may be either a voltage source or a current source (Chapter IV), and the manner in which the voltage or current varies with time describes what we call the **source function** or **excitation function.** The excitation function with which we dealt in the foregoing examples was a **step function of voltage.** It was applied by simply closing a switch. Before the switch was closed the voltage applied to the circuit was zero. At the instant the switch was closed it became (and remained) E. The graph of this function (from

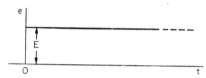

Fig. 14.1. Step function of voltage.

which its name is derived) is shown in Fig. 14.1. Time is usually (but not necessarily) measured from the instant the switch is closed, or in other words, the excitation function is ordinarily considered to be applied to the circuit at $t = 0$.

Other excitation functions that will be met with are **sinusoidal functions,** in which the voltage or current varies with the sine of an angle which increases with time at a constant rate (Section 15 of Chapter II), and **singularity functions,** in which the voltage or current varies with time in an arbitrary manner, often exhibiting discontinuities. The step function is actually a kind of singularity function.

2. Steady-state and transient response. The current, or charge, or voltage which results from the application of the excitation is the **response** of the circuit to that particular source function. Thus, the current

$$i = \frac{E}{R}(1 - \epsilon^{-Rt/L}) \tag{11.45}$$

was the response of the inductive circuit shown in Fig. 11.28 to the application of a step voltage E. The charge

$$q = CE(1 - \epsilon^{-t/RC}) \tag{12.74}$$

was the response of the capacitive circuit shown in Fig. 12.19 to the application of a step voltage E. These equations tell us the current, or charge, at any time following the closing of the switch.

If we study Equation (11.45) we see that the response of the inductive circuit is made up of two parts,

$$\frac{E}{R} \quad \text{and} \quad \frac{E}{R}\epsilon^{-Rt/L}.$$

The first of these we recognize as the steady-state or Ohm's law value of the current; the second is a term the value of which is E/R at $t = 0$, and which decreases in a short time to a value so small as to be insignificant. It thus represents a sort of transition current, or **transient** current, which at any instant represents the difference between the initial value of the current (zero) and its steady-state value E/R. This is made clear in Fig. 14.2, in

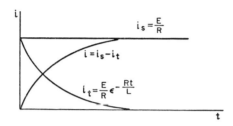

Fig. 14.2. Transient and steady-state components of current in R-L series circuit.

which the two terms are plotted separately. The circuit may be thought of as being forced by the source voltage E to change its current from zero to a value E/R, which is a function exactly like the applied voltage in form. Because the circuit has inductance, the change cannot take place instantly.

The expression for the charge on the capacitor [Equation (12.74)] is seen to be very similar to the one just considered. It consists of a steady-state term CE, which is the final charge the capacitor must have. The other term, $CE\epsilon^{-t/RC}$, is the transient term, and represents the difference at any instant between the initial charge (zero) and the final charge CE.

3. Solution of the equilibrium equation. The equations obtained by applying Kirchhoff's laws to circuits such as those in Figs. 11.28 and 12.19 are called **equilibrium equations.** Such an equation must be satisfied at any instant from the closing of the switch. The equilibrium equation for the inductive circuit in Fig. 11.28 was

$$E - L\frac{di}{dt} = Ri, \qquad (11.40)$$

and that for the capacitive circuit in Fig. 12.19 was

$$E - \frac{q}{c} = R\frac{dq}{dt}. \qquad (12.68)$$

Both of these equations were readily solved by the method of separating the variables and integrating each side. This method, however, is limited to equations in which there are no derivatives of higher order than the first. A method which is more generally applicable is suggested by the discussion in Section 2 concerning the steady-state and transient components of the circuit response. If we can find means of obtaining these partial solutions one at a time, we can then combine them to get the complete expression for circuit response.

For the circuits under consideration, the steady-state solutions seem extremely simple. When the current (or charge) has ceased to increase, the derivatives are zero. Thus, Equation (11.40) becomes

$$E = Ri,$$

from which
$$i = \frac{E}{R}. \tag{14.1}$$

That (14.1) is a solution of Equation (11.40) can be readily shown by substituting it back into the equation. Equation (12.68) becomes

$$E - \frac{q}{c} = 0,$$

from which
$$q = EC, \tag{14.2}$$

which obviously satisfies Equation (12.68). In mathematics the part of the solution corresponding to the steady-state term is called the **particular integral** because its form is determined by the form of the excitation function, and thus, for a specified excitation function, there is a particular form of steady-state solution.

The other part of the solution, the transient term, is called in mathematics the **complementary function.** While its magnitude depends upon the source function, its form does not. This part of the solution represents the free, or natural, behavior of the circuit, as opposed to the forced behavior represented by the particular integral. It therefore seems reasonable to attempt to find it by solving a **force-free equation,** which is the equilibrium equation with the excitation function left out. The force-free equation corresponding to Equation (11.40) is

$$-L\frac{di}{dt} = Ri. \tag{14.3}$$

It can be shown that the solution of this force-free equation added to the steady-state solution of Equation (11.40) is also a solution of Equation (11.40).

Having previously solved Equations (11.40) and (12.68) by the method of separating the variables, we know the transient term takes the form of an exponential function of time. Let us therefore assume that the solution of Equation (14.3) is

$$i = A\epsilon^{pt}, \tag{14.4}$$

where A and p are to be determined. Substituting the assumed solution into (14.3), we have

$$-LpA\epsilon^{pt} = RA\epsilon^{pt}. \tag{14.5}$$

$$p = -\frac{R}{L}. \tag{14.6}$$

The assumed solution thus satisfies Equation (14.3) if p is equal to $-R/L$. Therefore

$$i = A\epsilon^{-Rt/L}. \tag{14.7}$$

The complete solution of Equation (11.40) is then the sum of the steady-state part, or particular integral found in (14.1), and the transient part, or complementary function found in (14.7):

$$i = \frac{E}{R} + A\epsilon^{-Rt/L}. \tag{14.8}$$

It is obvious that A is the same quantity we called ϵ^k in Equation (11.43). Its evaluation requires that we have some information about the circuit in addition to that contained in the equilibrium equation. We need to know what the value of the current was at some specified time, say at $t = 0$. This is called an initial condition, or **boundary condition.** Taking the current as having been zero at $t = 0$, and putting these values in (14.8) we have

$$0 = \frac{E}{R} + A,$$

$$A = -\frac{E}{R}. \tag{14.9}$$

Putting the value of A thus found into Equation (14.8) we find the final solution of Equation (11.40) to be

$$i = \frac{E}{R} - \frac{E}{R}\epsilon^{-Rt/L}. \tag{14.10}$$

This can be verified by substituting the solution into the equation itself to obtain an identity.

The solution of Equation (12.68) can be carried out and verified by the same procedure.

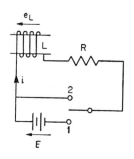

Fig. 14.3. *R-L* series circuit.

4. Response of the *R-L* series circuit to the removal of the excitation voltage. If the switch in Fig. 14.3 were moved from position 1 to position 2 (it being assumed that contact is made on position 2 before it is broken on position 1), the excitation voltage is instantaneously reduced from E to zero. If this switching operation is done a reasonably long time after closing the switch on position 1, the initial value of the current will be the steady-state value attained with the switch closed on position 1; that is, $i = E/R$. If the switch is moved to position 2 before the steady-state condition is reached on position 1, the initial current will be the instantaneous current at the time of moving the switch.

With the switch on position 2 the equilibrium equation is

$$-L\frac{di}{dt} = Ri. \tag{14.11}$$

This is identical with Equation (14.3) obtained above, and its solution is

$$i_t = A\epsilon^{-Rt/L}. \tag{14.12}$$

This is the complementary function, and the current found is the transient part of the complete solution. In this circuit, however, there is no energy source, and the steady-state term is obviously zero. Therefore,

$$i = 0 + A\epsilon^{-Rt/L} = A\epsilon^{-Rt/L}. \tag{14.13}$$

It remains to evaluate the constant A. If the current had a value I_0 at the instant of moving the switch ($t = 0$), substituting these values into (14.13) gives

$$I_0 = A. \tag{14.14}$$

Then
$$i = I_0\epsilon^{-Rt/L}. \tag{14.15}$$

Equation (14.15) gives the current in the circuit at any time t, measured from the time the switch was thrown to position 2. It represents the current decreasing exponentially toward zero, the rate of decrease becoming less as the limiting value is approached. This response can be thought of as due to the removal of the excitation voltage. It may also be thought of as due to the application of a second step voltage $-E$ which cancels the previous applied step voltage E.

The concept of time constant mentioned in Section 14 of Chapter XI provides a convenient means of studying a circuit such as this. For a time $t = L/R$, defined as the time constant, the exponent in Equation (14.15) is -1 and the value of i is

$$i = I_0\epsilon^{-1} = I_0\frac{1}{\epsilon} = 0.368I_0. \tag{14.16}$$

In this time the current has decreased to 36.8 per cent of its initial value, or has made 63.2 per cent of the total change from initial value to final value. For time $t = 2L/R$ (twice the time constant) the exponent is -2 and the value of i is

$$i = I_0\epsilon^{-2} = I_0\frac{1}{\epsilon^2} = 0.135I_0. \tag{14.17}$$

Thus, in a time 5 times the time constant, the current would decrease to $0.0067I_0$, or less than 1 per cent of its initial value, and in many problems could be regarded as insignificant.

PROBLEMS

(1-XIV) Solve Equation (12.68) by the method explained in Section 3.

(2-XIV) The rate of change of current in a series R-L circuit at the instant of applying a step voltage is 100 amp per sec and the steady-state value of the current is 5 amp. What is the time constant of the circuit?

(3-XIV) A step function of 100 v is applied at time $t = 0$ to a series circuit having a self-inductance L and resistance R. The response is

$$i = 2(1 - \epsilon^{-10t}).$$

Find (a) self-inductance, (b) resistance, (c) current at $t = 0.05$ sec, (d) time for current to reach 95 per cent of its steady-state value, (e) rate of change of current at $t = 0.2$ sec.

(4-XIV) A step function of $+500$ v is applied at $t = 0$ to a series circuit consisting of a 2-μf capacitor and a 1-megohm resistance. The capacitor has an initial charge of 0.005 coulomb, the positive terminal of the capacitor being connected to the positive terminal of the source. Find current and charge at 2-second intervals for the first 10 sec.

(5-XIV) The polarity of the capacitor in Problem 4-XIV is reversed, so that the negative terminal of the capacitor is connected to the positive terminal of the source. Find current and charge at 2-second intervals for the first 10 sec.

(6-XIV) In the circuit shown in Fig. 14.3, the source emf is 25 v, the inductance is 0.2 h, and the resistance 5 ohms. The switch has been on position 1 for several seconds. At $t = 0$ it is moved to position 2. (a) Calculate the points on the curve of current against time, beginning at $t = 0$. (b) Calculate points on the curve of stored energy against time, beginning at $t = 0$.

(7-XIV) A 5-μf capacitor is substituted for the inductance in the circuit shown in Fig. 14.3. The source emf is 50 v and the resistance is 1000 ohms. The switch has been on position 1 for several seconds. At $t = 0$ it is thrown to position 2. Calculate points on the curves of (a) current, (b) charge, and (c) stored energy against time beginning at $t = 0$.

(8-XIV) A 2-μf capacitor is given a charge of 200 μc and immediately connected to an uncharged 1-μf capacitor in series with a resistance of 1000 ohms. Obtain expressions for (a) current, (b) charge on the 2-μf capacitor, and (c) charge on the 1-μf capacitor as functions of time.

5. Superposition of response to step-voltage functions. Step functions of voltage (or current) may be of either sign, representing either increases or decreases of excitation, and they may be of any magnitude. By applying two or more step functions to a circuit in succession, by switching operations or otherwise, a variety of excitation functions can be simulated. For example, if after a short interval of time the switch in Fig. 14.3 is thrown back to position 1, the current again commences to increase according to Equation (14.10), its initial value being the value reached while the switch was in position 2. In this manner the response of the circuit to a

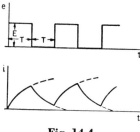

Fig. 14.4

succession of excitation functions may be studied. Successive operations of the switch may be regarded as the successive application at predetermined times of step-voltage functions +E, −E, +E, etc., as shown in Fig. 14.4. We can calculate points on the response curve by using Equations (14.10) and (14.15) as explained above, taking care to use as the initial value of current in each calculation the value reached in the preceding time interval.

We can also calculate points on the response curve by using the superposition theorem. To do this, we find the response of the circuit, at the specified time, to each step voltage which has been applied up to that time. The total response is then found by adding algebraically, or superimposing, the individual responses.

Example: Let the parameters in the circuit in Fig. 14.3 be $R = 10$ ohms, $L = 1$ h. The battery emf is 10 v. The switch is initially on position 2. At $t = 0$ it is moved to position 1. At the end of a time t equal to the time constant of the circuit, it is moved back to position 2; at the end of another T seconds, back to position 1, etc. Find the current at a time $t = 4T$.

SOLUTION: The steady-state current I (for the switch in position 1) is

$$\frac{E}{R} = \frac{10}{10} = 1 \text{ amp.}$$

The time constant T is

$$\frac{L}{R} = \frac{1}{10} = 0.1 \text{ sec.}$$

Calculating the current at the end of each period of T seconds we have:
1. At the end of T seconds:

$$i = \frac{E}{R}(1 - \epsilon^{-Rt/L})$$

$$= 1(1 - \epsilon^{-1}) = 0.632 \text{ amp.}$$

2. At the end of $2T$ seconds:

$$i = I_0\epsilon^{-Rt/L}$$

$$= 0.632\epsilon^{-1} = 0.232 \text{ amp.}$$

3. At the end of $3T$ seconds:

$$i = [(1 - 0.232)(1 - \epsilon^{-1})] + 0.232 = 0.717 \text{ amp.}$$

(The current starts at 0.232 amp, increases, completes 63.2 per cent of the change from 0.232 amp to its steady-state value in a time equal to the time constant.)

4. At the end of $4T$ seconds:

$$i = 0.717\epsilon^{-1} = 0.264 \text{ amp.}$$

Calculating the current by the superposition theorem:

1. A step voltage of $+10$ v is applied at $t = 0$;
at the end of $4T$ seconds $i = 1(1 - \epsilon^{-4}) = 0.9818$ amp.

2. A step voltage of -10 v is applied at $t = T$;
at end of $3T$ seconds $i = -1(1 - \epsilon^{-3}) = -0.9504$ amp.

3. A step voltage of $+10$ v is applied at $t = 2T$;
at end of $2T$ seconds $i = 1(1 - \epsilon^{-2}) = 0.8650$ amp.

4. A step voltage of -10 v is applied at $t = 3T$;
at end of T seconds $i = 1(1 - \epsilon^{-1}) = -0.6320$ amp.

Adding the responses of the circuit to the four step voltages individually we find

$$i = 0.2644 \text{ amp.}$$

PROBLEMS

(9-XIV) A step function of $+30$ v is applied at time $t = 0$ to a series circuit having 50 ohms resistance and 0.5 h self-inductance. At time 0.01 sec another step function of $+40$ v is applied. Find the response of the circuit at intervals of 2 milliseconds for the first 0.02 sec.

(10-XIV) A voltage which varies with time as indicated in Fig. 14.4 is applied to a series circuit made up of a 0.1-h inductance and a 50-ohm resistance. The voltage steps have a uniform height of 1 v and are spaced 0.002 sec apart, with the first step at $t = 0$. Calculate the response of the circuit at 0.002-second intervals for the first 0.01 sec.

(**11-XIV**) A voltage which varies with time as indicated in Fig. 14.4 is applied to a series circuit consisting of a 1-μf capacitor and a resistance of 10^4 ohms. The voltage steps have a uniform height of 1 v and are spaced 0.01 sec apart, with the first step at $t = 0$. Calculate current and charge at 0.01-second intervals for the first 0.05 sec.

(**12-XIV**) A voltage which varies with time as indicated in Fig. 14.5 is impressed upon a series circuit consisting of a 0.1-h inductance and a resistance of 50 ohms. The voltage steps have a uniform height of 1 v (zero to maximum) and are spaced 0.002 sec apart, with the first step at $t = 0$. Calculate the current at 0.002-second intervals for the first 0.01 sec.

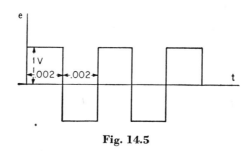

Fig. 14.5

(**13-XIV**) A voltage which varies with time as indicated in Fig. 14.6 is impressed upon a series circuit consisting of a 1-μf capacitor and a resistance of 10^4 ohms. The voltage steps have a uniform height of 1 v and are spaced at 0.01-second intervals, with the first step at $t = 0$. Find the current at 0.01-second intervals for the first 0.05 sec.

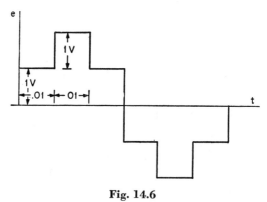

Fig. 14.6

6. Step-current source applied to the *R-L* parallel circuit. It will be remembered from Chapter IV that an ideal current source is capable of maintaining a current I in any circuit connected to its terminals, being able to accommodate its terminal voltage to suit the circuit resistance. We will suppose that the source in Fig. 14.7 is normally short-circuited, and that

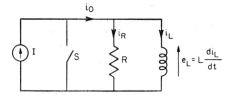

Fig. 14.7. *R-L* parallel circuit with current source.

excitation is applied to the circuit by opening the switch *S*. A step-current function is thereby impressed upon the circuit, and the current i_0 must instantaneously become *I* amperes. We will assume the initial condition of $i_L = 0$. There are, in this case, two conditions of equilibrium, expressed in equation form as follows:

$$I = i_R + i_L. \tag{14.18}$$

$$L\frac{di_L}{dt} = Ri_R. \tag{14.19}$$

We must therefore solve these equations to obtain expressions for i_R and i_L at any specified time. By solving (14.18) for i_R and substituting this value into (14.19), we obtain

$$L\frac{di_L}{dt} = RI - Ri_L \tag{14.20}$$

or

$$RI - L\frac{di_L}{dt} = Ri_L. \tag{14.21}$$

Equation (14.21) is seen to be identical in form with Equation (11.40), the solution of which we have already obtained. The solution of (14.21) can therefore be written as

$$i_L = I(1 - \epsilon^{-Rt/L}). \tag{14.22}$$

Substituting (14.22) into (14.18), we obtain

$$i_R = I\epsilon^{-Rt/L}. \tag{14.23}$$

It can be seen from these equations that, upon closing the switch, the current in the resistance branch instantly becomes equal to *I* and then decreases exponentially to zero. The current in the inductance branch cannot change instantaneously, and beginning at zero it increases exponentially to become equal to *I*. The current thus shifts from the resistance branch to the inductance branch of the circuit, the time required depending upon the time constant L/R. In this interval of time, the shift would be 63.2 per cent completed. Had the current source had associated with it a parallel resistance of its own, this resistance would, upon opening the switch, be in parallel with R, and the combined resistance R' would be used in the equation above. At any instant, the current i_R given by (14.23) would be divided between the two parallel resistances, the currents being inversely proportional to the resistances.

7. Step-current source applied to the R-C parallel circuit. We may now consider the response to a step-current source function of a parallel circuit with branches having resistance and capacitance, respectively, as in Fig. 14.8. As in the preceding section, we shall apply the source

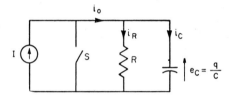

Fig. 14.8. R-C parallel circuit with current source.

function by opening the switch S, thereby causing the current i_0 to instantly assume the value I. We will take the initial condition to be $q = 0$ (capacitor uncharged). The equilibrium equations are then

$$I = i_R + i_c. \tag{14.24}$$

$$\frac{q}{C} = Ri_R. \tag{14.25}$$

Solving (14.24) for i_R and substituting in (14.18), we have

$$\frac{q}{C} = RI - Ri_c. \tag{14.26}$$

In order to solve this equation we need either to express q in terms of i_e and t, or to express i_c in terms of q and t. To do the former we may differentiate both sides of (14.26) with respect to time, obtaining

$$\frac{1}{C}\frac{dq}{dt} = -R\frac{di_c}{dt}. \tag{14.27}$$

But dq/dt is i_c, and therefore we have

$$i_c = -RC\frac{di_c}{dt}. \tag{14.28}$$

We then assume the solution to take the exponential form

$$i_c = A\epsilon^{pt}, \tag{14.29}$$

Then $$\frac{di_c}{dt} = pA\epsilon^{pt} \tag{14.30}$$

and
$$A \epsilon^{pt} = -RCpA \epsilon^{pt}, \tag{14.31}$$

from which
$$p = -\frac{1}{RC}, \tag{14.32}$$

$$i_c = A \epsilon^{-t/RC}. \tag{14.33}$$

It is obvious from (14.28) that the steady-state value of i_c is zero, therefore (14.33) is the complete solution of (14.28). Having assumed the initial condition $q = 0$, we can see from Equation (14.25) that i_R is zero at the instant of opening the switch. Since $i_0 = I$, Equation (14.24) tells us that i_c must instantly become equal to I. Therefore, at $t = 0$, Equation (14.33) gives

$$I = A \tag{14.34}$$

and
$$i_c = I\epsilon^{-t/RC}. \tag{14.35}$$

Then, by substituting in (14.24), we find

$$i_R = I - I\epsilon^{-t/RC}. \tag{14.36}$$

Had we chosen the second method of handling Equation (14.26), our procedure would have been to replace q by the time integral of current

$$q = \int i_c \, dt. \tag{14.37}$$

Equation (14.26) would thus become

$$\frac{1}{C}\int i_c \, dt = RI - Ri_c. \tag{14.38}$$

The corresponding force-free equation is

$$\frac{1}{C}\int i_c \, dt = -Ri_c. \tag{14.39}$$

Assuming
$$i_c = A \epsilon^{pt} \text{ as before,}$$

$$\int i_c = \frac{I}{p} A \epsilon^{pt} + K, \tag{14.40}$$

and Equation (14.39) becomes

$$\frac{1}{Cp} A \epsilon^{pt} + K = -RA \epsilon^{pt}. \tag{14.41}$$

There is no constant that we may add to an exponential function to obtain another exponential function. Therefore, K is zero and

$$\frac{1}{Cp} = -R, \tag{14.42}$$

$$p = -\frac{1}{RC},$$

as found above. Equations (14.35) and (14.36) show the current i_c to instantly assume the value I and then decrease exponentially to zero. The current i_R is zero at $t = 0$ and then increases exponentially to the value I.

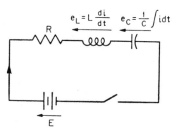

Fig. 14.9. RLC series circuit.

8. The RLC series circuit with step-voltage excitation. Let us now set up the equilibrium equation for a series circuit containing resistance, self-inductance, and capacitance, and attempt to solve it by the procedure explained in Section 3. We will take as initial conditions that there is no current in the circuit and no charge on the capacitance. Upon closing the switch, the source function E causes the growth of the current i. As a consequence of the increasing current an emf equal to $L\,di/dt$ volts appears at the terminals of the inductance, its actual direction positive. As a consequence also of the current and its time integral $q = \int i\,dt$, an emf equal to $1/C\int i\,dt$ volts appears at the terminals of the capacitance, its actual direction positive. By Kirchhoff's voltage law, the equilibrium equation is

$$E - L\frac{di}{dt} - \frac{1}{C}\int i\,dt = Ri. \qquad (14.43)$$

From our previous experience with circuits containing capacitance we can predict that, regardless of what takes place in the time interval immediately following the closing of the switch, eventually di/dt will become zero, i will become zero, and the circuit will be in equilibrium with e_c equal and opposite to E. This prediction is correct, but it should be mentioned that if R is very small, the time required to reach the steady-state condition will be prolonged, and if R could be made zero, the steady-state condition would never be attained. This will become clear as we go along. For the present it need not concern us, and we may write for the steady-state solution

$$i = 0. \qquad (14.44)$$

To find the transient solution, or complementary function, we write the force-free equation

$$0 = L\frac{di}{dt} + \frac{1}{C}\int i\,dt + Ri. \qquad (14.45)$$

The solution of this equation we assume to be an exponential function of time as

$$i = A\,\epsilon^{p\,t}. \qquad (14.46)$$

We now try to find the value (or values) of p such that the assumed solution will satisfy the equation

$$\frac{di}{dt} = pA\,\epsilon^{pt} \tag{14.47}$$

and

$$\int i\,dt = \frac{1}{p}A\,\epsilon^{pt} + K. \tag{14.48}$$

Substituting into the force-free equation,

$$0 = LpA\,\epsilon^{pt} + \frac{1}{Cp}A\,\epsilon^{pt} + RA\,\epsilon^{pt} + K. \tag{14.49}$$

There is no constant other than zero that can be added to an exponential function, or to the sum of several exponential functions, to obtain zero. Therefore K is zero in Equation (14.49), leaving

$$0 = LpA\,\epsilon^{pt} + \frac{1}{Cp}A\,\epsilon^{pt} + RA\,\epsilon^{pt}, \tag{14.50}$$

$$0 = Lp + \frac{1}{Cp} + R, \tag{14.51}$$

or

$$0 = p^2 + \frac{R}{L}p + \frac{1}{LC}. \tag{14.52}$$

Solution of Equation (14.52) yields the two roots

$$p_1 = -\frac{R}{2L} + \sqrt{\left(\frac{R}{2L}\right)^2 - \frac{1}{LC}}, \tag{14.53}$$

$$p_2 = -\frac{R}{2L} - \sqrt{\left(\frac{R}{2L}\right)^2 - \frac{1}{LC}}. \tag{14.54}$$

Examination of these roots reveals three possibilities:

(1) If $\left(\dfrac{R}{2L}\right)^2 > \dfrac{1}{LC}$ the roots are real numbers and they are unequal (the overdamped case).

(2) If $\left(\dfrac{R}{2L}\right)^2 = \dfrac{1}{LC}$ the roots are real numbers and equal (the critically damped case).

(3) If $\left(\dfrac{R}{2L}\right)^2 < \dfrac{1}{LC}$ the roots are complex conjugate numbers (the underdamped case).

Considering first the case of the roots real and unequal, let us rewrite (14.53) and (14.54) as

$$p_1 = -\alpha + \beta, \tag{14.55}$$

$$p_2 = -\alpha - \beta, \tag{14.56}$$

where $\alpha = R/2L$;

$$\beta = \sqrt{(R/2L)^2 - 1/LC}.$$

The solution which we are looking for is then

$$i = A_1\epsilon^{(-\alpha+\beta)t} + A_2\epsilon^{(-\alpha-\beta)t}. \tag{14.57}$$

Since Equation (14.52) has two roots, it is necessary to determine two constants of integration A_1 and A_2. This is where we need the information as to what the initial conditions of the circuit were. One condition was that $i = 0$ when $t = 0$, and putting these values into (14.57) yields

$$0 = A_1 + A_2. \tag{14.58}$$

The other condition was that q (the charge on the capacitor) was zero when $t = 0$. Going back to the equilibrium equation

$$E - L\frac{di}{dt} - \frac{1}{C}\int i\,dt = Ri \tag{14.43}$$

it is obvious that at $t = 0$, for the initial conditions specified,

$$E - L\frac{di}{dt} = 0, \tag{14.59}$$

$$\frac{di}{dt} = \frac{E}{L}. \tag{14.60}$$

Let us therefore take the derivative of Equation (14.57):

$$\frac{di}{dt} = (-\alpha+\beta)A_1\epsilon^{(-\alpha+\beta)t} + (-\alpha-\beta)A_2\epsilon^{(-\alpha-\beta)t}. \tag{14.61}$$

This equation gives the rate of change of current at any time t. Equation (14.60) gives the rate of change of current for $t = 0$. At $t = 0$, then, Equation (14.61) becomes

$$\frac{E}{L} = (-\alpha+\beta)A_1 + (-\alpha-\beta)A_2. \tag{14.62}$$

But since

$$A_2 = -A_1, \tag{14.58}$$

$$\frac{E}{L} = (-\alpha+\beta)A_1 - (-\alpha-\beta)A_1 = 2\beta A_1, \tag{14.63}$$

and

$$A_1 = \frac{E}{2\beta L}, \qquad A_2 = -\frac{E}{2\beta L}.$$

Putting these values back into Equation (14.57),

$$i = \frac{E}{2\beta L}\epsilon^{(-\alpha+\beta)t} - \frac{E}{2\beta L}\epsilon^{(-\alpha-\beta)t}. \tag{14.64}$$

$$i = \frac{E}{2\beta L}\left[\epsilon^{(-\alpha+\beta)t} - \epsilon^{(-\alpha-\beta)t}\right]. \tag{14.65}$$

$$i = \frac{E}{\beta L}\epsilon^{-\alpha t}\left(\frac{\epsilon^{\beta t} - \epsilon^{-\beta t}}{2}\right). \tag{14.66}$$

Now $(\epsilon^{\beta t} - \epsilon^{-\beta t}/2)$ can be shown to be the hyperbolic sine of βt. Therefore Equation (14.66) may be written as

$$i = \frac{E}{\beta L}\epsilon^{-\alpha t}\sinh \beta t. \qquad (14.67)$$

Since the steady-state current is zero, the transient current found in Equation (14.64) or (14.67) is the solution of Equation (14.43) for the case of $(R/2L)^2 > 1/LC$ and for the initial conditions specified.

It is seen that each term in (14.64) represents an exponential function of time. At $t = 0$ the terms are each equal to $E/2\beta L$, and the current, which is their difference, is zero. For increasing values of t, both terms decrease, but the second term, having a larger negative exponent, will decrease more rapidly. The current will therefore increase until such time as the second term has become so small that its more rapid decrease can no longer offset the decrease in the first term. This time can be found by setting the rate of change of current equal to zero and solving for t to obtain

$$t = \frac{1}{\beta}\tanh^{-1}\frac{\beta}{\alpha}. \qquad (14.68)$$

Shortly thereafter the value of the second term becomes insignificant, after which the current decreases according to the equation represented by the first term

$$i = \frac{E}{2\beta L}\epsilon^{(-\alpha+\beta)\,t}. \qquad (14.69)$$

The two exponentials and their difference for a typical case are shown in Fig. 14.10.

If we consider now the case in which the roots of Equation (14.52) are real and equal, we see that if

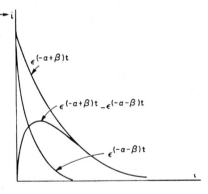

Fig. 14.10. Current response of series RLC circuit $(R/2L)^2 > 1/LC$.

$$\left(\frac{R}{2L}\right)^2 = \frac{1}{LC},$$

then β is zero and equation (14.66) reduces to

$$I = \frac{E}{L}\epsilon^{-\alpha t}\left(\frac{0}{0}\right). \qquad (14.70)$$

We may avoid this indeterminate expression by considering that β is small but not zero, and differentiating numerator and denominator of (14.66) with respect to β to obtain

$$i = \frac{E}{2L}\epsilon^{-\alpha t}\left(\frac{t\epsilon^{\beta t} + t\epsilon^{-\beta t}}{1}\right).$$ (14.71)

If now we let β approach zero, the limit of (14.71) is

$$i = \frac{E}{2L}\epsilon^{-\alpha t}(2t) = \frac{E}{L}t\epsilon^{-\alpha t}.$$ (14.72)

$$i = \frac{E}{L}t\epsilon^{-Rt/2L}.$$ (14.73)

This is called the critical case; any decrease in R would result in the roots of Equation (14.52) becoming complex conjugate quantities and in the behavior of the circuit becoming oscillatory, as discussed below.

Let us now consider the third possibility which may occur when we solve Equation (14.52) and find the roots

$$p_1 = -\frac{R}{2L} + \sqrt{\left(\frac{R}{2L}\right)^2 - \frac{1}{LC}},$$ (14.53)

$$p_2 = -\frac{R}{2L} - \sqrt{\left(\frac{R}{2L}\right)^2 - \frac{1}{LC}}.$$ (14.54)

This is the possibility that

$$\left(\frac{R}{2L}\right)^2 < \frac{1}{LC},$$

making the quantity under the radical negative in sign. We may rewrite the radical as

$$\sqrt{(-1)\left[\frac{1}{LC} - \left(\frac{R}{2L}\right)^2\right]}$$ (14.74)

or

$$\sqrt{-1}\sqrt{\frac{1}{LC} - \left(\frac{R}{2L}\right)^2}$$ (14.75)

or

$$j\sqrt{\frac{1}{LC} - \left(\frac{R}{2L}\right)^2}.*$$ (14.76)

Let us use the symbols

$$\omega_0^2 \quad \text{for} \quad \frac{1}{LC},$$ (14.77)

$$\alpha \quad \text{for} \quad \frac{R}{2L}.$$ (14.78)

*The symbol j used for $\sqrt{-1}$ is identical with i used in algebra for $\sqrt{-1}$. Its significance is to place the quantity before which it appears along the axis of imaginaries, 90° counterclockwise from the axis of reals. Thus, if the number 5 were laid off along the x axis in the usual way, the number $j5$ would be laid off along the y axis. The number $j^2 5$ would be -5, laid off along the negative x axis, and $j^3 5$ would be $-j5$ laid off along the negative y axis.

Then the radical becomes

$$j \sqrt{\omega_0^2 - \alpha^2}. \tag{14.79}$$

If we further use the symbol

$$\omega_d^2 = \omega_0^2 - \alpha^2, \tag{14.80}$$

the expressions for p_1 and p_2 become

$$p_1 = -\alpha + j\omega_d, \tag{14.81}$$

$$p_2 = -\alpha - j\omega_d. \tag{14.82}$$

The solution of Equation (14.52) can now be written as

$$i = A_1 \epsilon^{(-\alpha + j\omega_d)\,t} + A_2 \epsilon^{(-\alpha - j\omega_d)\,t}. \tag{14.83}$$

For the initial conditions specified (at $t = 0$, $i = 0$ and $q = 0$) it has been shown above that the initial rate of change of current is

$$\frac{di}{dt} = \frac{E}{L}. \tag{14.60}$$

Differentiation of (14.83) gives

$$\frac{di}{dt} = (-\alpha + j\omega_d)A_1 \epsilon^{(-\alpha + j\omega_d)\,t} + (-\alpha - j\omega_d)A_2 \epsilon^{(-\alpha - j\omega_d)}. \tag{14.84}$$

For $t = 0$, then, Equation (14.83) becomes

$$0 = A_1 + A_2, \tag{14.85}$$

and Equation (14.84) becomes

$$\frac{E}{L} = (-\alpha + j\omega_d)A_1 + (-\alpha - j\omega_d)A_2 \tag{14.86}$$

$$= 2j\omega_d A_1.$$

$$A_1 = \frac{E}{2j\omega_d L}, \qquad A_2 = -\frac{E}{2j\omega_d L}. \tag{14.87}$$

Substituting these values in Equation (14.83),

$$i = \frac{E}{2j\omega_d L}\epsilon^{(-\alpha + j\omega_d)\,t} - \frac{E}{2j\omega_d L}\epsilon^{(-\alpha - j\omega_d)\,t}. \tag{14.88}$$

$$i = \frac{E}{2j\omega_d L}(\epsilon^{-\alpha t}\epsilon^{j\omega_d t} - \epsilon^{-\alpha t}\epsilon^{-j\omega_d t}). \tag{14.89}$$

$$i = \frac{E\epsilon^{-\alpha t}}{\omega_d L}\left(\frac{\epsilon^{j\omega_d t} - \epsilon^{-j\omega_d t}}{2j}\right). \tag{14.90}$$

But $\dfrac{\epsilon^{j\omega_d t} \; - \; \epsilon^{-j\omega_d t}}{2j}$ can be shown to be equal to sin $\omega_d t$.*

Therefore

$$i = \frac{E}{\omega_d L}\epsilon^{-\alpha t} \sin \omega_d t. \tag{14.91}$$

In Equation (14.91) the factor $E/\omega_d L$ is independent of time. The factor $\epsilon^{-\alpha t}$ decreases with time and ultimately brings the current to zero. In the factor sin $\omega_d t$, $\omega_d t$ is an angle that is zero when t is zero and which increases uniformly with time. Thus, the current varies as the sine of an angle, at the same time decreasing exponentially. The response of the circuit is said to be oscillatory and damped. At some time $t = 2\pi/\omega_d$, the angle $\omega_d t$ would have reached 360°, and the current would have completed one cycle. This time is the period of the sine wave, and its reciprocal $\omega_d/2\pi$ is the frequency, or number of periods completed per second. A typical graph of the current in the circuit is shown in Fig. 14.11.

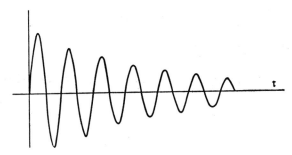

Fig. 14.11. Current response of series RLC circuit $(R/2L)^2 < 1/LC$.

If all resistance could be removed from the circuit, α, called the **damping factor**, would become zero.

$$\alpha = \frac{R}{2L} = 0, \tag{14.92}$$

and

$$\omega_d^2 = \omega_0^2 = \frac{1}{LC}. \tag{14.93}$$

Here ω_0 is the undamped angular frequency, or **natural frequency,** of the circuit. The term ω_d is the damped angular frequency, and its value depends upon the natural frequency of the circuit and also upon the circuit resistance, according to Equation (14.80).

*This can be done by expanding each of the functions $\epsilon^{j\omega_d t}$, $\epsilon^{-j\omega_d t}$, and sin $\omega_d t$ by Mc Laurin's series. It is then obvious that the difference of the first two series divided by $2j$ is identical with the third series.

If the circuit resistance could be reduced to zero, the equation for current would be

$$i = \frac{E}{\omega_0 L} \sin \omega_0 t, \tag{14.94}$$

and the circuit would continue to oscillate indefinitely at the undamped angular frequency ω_0.

It is of interest to consider from the physical standpoint how a response in the nature of a sinusoidally varying current can result from the application of a step-voltage source — a battery. Basically, the explanation lies in the energy-storing properties of inductance coils and capacitors and in the inertia-like behavior of inductances in opposing any change in the current.

Let us consider first the nature of the response of the circuit without resistance. During the first quarter cycle the current is increasing and the capacitor is being charged. The coil voltage e_L opposes the source voltage, as does the capacitor voltage e_c. At the instant the current reaches positive maximum, its rate of change, and therefore the coil voltage e_L, is zero. The energy stored in the magnetic field of the coil is maximum. The capacitor voltage e_c is equal and opposite to the source voltage E. Equilibrium does not exist because there is no voltage to maintain the current. The current now begins to decrease, and as it does so, e_L reverses and now aids the source voltage. The capacitor continues to charge, and e_c continues to increase. At the instant the current reaches zero, its rate of change is maximum, and therefore e_L is maximum. The capacitor voltage e_c and the energy stored in the electric field of the capacitor reach maximum values. Part of the energy added to the capacitor in the quarter cycle just ended has come from the magnetic field of the coil, in which the energy at this instant is zero. As the current passes through zero, its rate of change begins to decrease and e_L decreases. The capacitor voltage e_c is now predominant, and it causes the increase of current in the negative direction. The capacitor is thereby discharged, its voltage and stored energy decreasing as the current increases. Again at the instant the current is negative maximum, the stored energy in the field of the coil is maximum, this energy having come from the capacitor. During the remaining quarter cycle, the circuit returns to its original condition of $i = 0$, $q = 0$, and the same series of events is repeated.

It is assumed, in the above explanation, that the circuit has no resistance and that the source is capable of delivering and reabsorbing energy as required. Since there is no resistance, no energy is lost during the exchanges of energy between the source, coil, and capacitance. Any resistance in the circuit would result in energy loss during the flow of current which is associated with exchanges of energy. It might seem that energy loss would be of no consequence, since the source voltage remains in the circuit and can furnish energy as required. However the presence of resistance results in the capacitor retaining charge at the end of a cycle. Consequently the next cycle begins, not with $i = 0$ and $q = 0$ as in the resistanceless circuit, but with $i = 0$ and $q = Q_0$. This results in each successive current maximum being less than the preceding one (by how much depends, of course, upon how much resistance is present). Eventually a state of equilibrium is reached, wherein the current is zero and e_c is equal and opposite to the source voltage E.

PROBLEMS

(**14-XIV**) A series circuit consists of an inductance of 0.11 h, a capacitance of 19.9 µf, and a resistance of 300 ohms. A step voltage of $E = 32$ v is applied to the circuit at $t = 0$. Calculate the current response from $t = 0$ until the current falls to 1 per cent of its maximum value. Tabulate the values of each exponential term and their difference. Determine the maximum value of the current and the time at which it occurs.

(**15-XIV**) The resistance of the series circuit described in Problem 14-XIV is changed to 150 ohms. Calculate the current response, tabulating values and determining maximum current and time at which it occurs as called for above.

(**16-XIV**) What is the critical resistance of the series circuit described in Problem 16-XIV? What is the natural frequency of oscillation?

(**17-XIV**) The resistance of the series circuit described in Problem 14-XIV is changed to 50 ohms. What is the damped frequency of oscillation? Calculate and plot the current response of the circuit for the first two cycles.

(**18-XIV**) The resistance of the series circuit described in Problem 14-XIV is changed to 4.55 ohms. What is the damped frequency of oscillation? Calculate and plot the current response of the circuit for the first two cycles.

APPENDIX

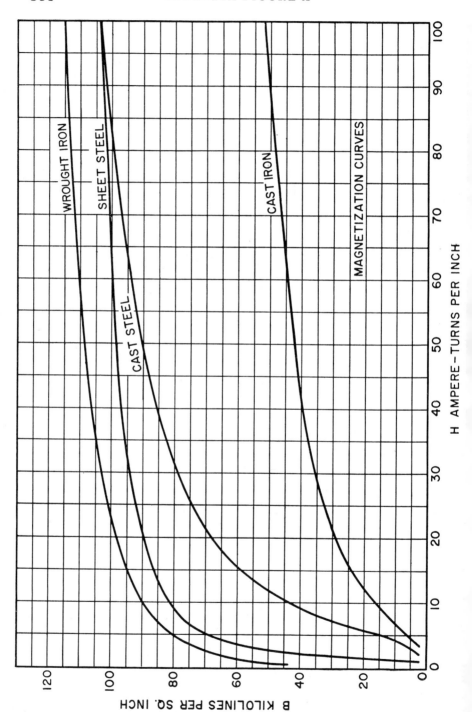

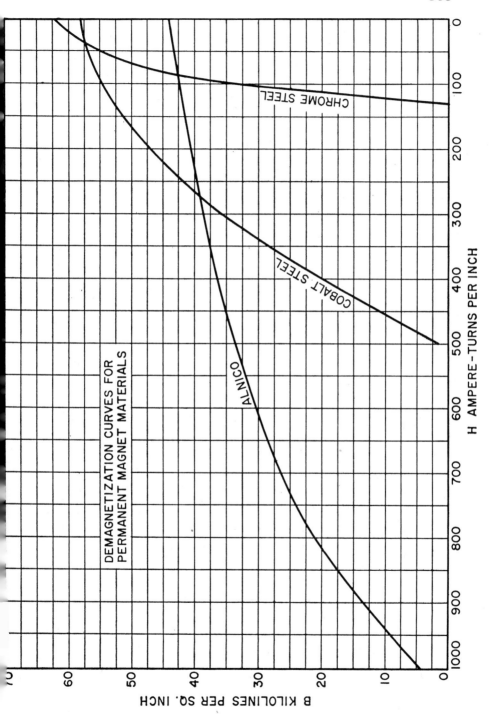

DEMAGNETIZATION CURVES FOR
PERMANENT MAGNET MATERIALS

CHROME STEEL

COBALT STEEL

ALNICO

H AMPERE-TURNS PER INCH

B KILOLINES PER SQ. INCH

INDEX

Energy *(cont.)*:
  radiant, 8
  stored in electric field, 304
  stored in magnetic field, 178
  supplied to electrons, 28
  thermal, 7
Energy transmission, 48
Equipotential surfaces in electric fields, 287
Equivalence of voltage and current
  sources, 86
Excitation functions, 342
Exploring coil, 153

F

Farad, 301
Faraday, Michael, 4, 155
Faraday's law of electromagnetic induction, 250
Faraday's laws of electrolysis, 322
  deduction of, 324
Faraday, unit of quantity of electricity
  defined, 325
Ferrites, 206
Ferromagnetic substances, 187
Ferromagnetism, theory of, 189
Fields:
  electric, 282
  magnetic, 152
Flux density:
  electric, 295
  intrinsic, 191
  magnetic, 156
  residual, 193
Forces:
  electric, 5, 292, 305
  electromagnetic, 19, 232
Franklin, Benjamin, 3
Frequency:
  classification of, 24
  alternating current, 24
Fringing of magnetic lines, 214
Froelich's equation, 191

G

Galvani, Luigi, 4
Galvanometer, D'Arsonval, 120
Gauss's law, 297
Gauss, unit of magnetic flux density, 177

Generator:
  elementary a-c, 264
  elementary d-c, 268
Gilbert, Sir William, 2
Graphs, network, 71
Gray, Stephan, 3

H

Henry, unit of inductance, 270
Hysteresis, 193
Hysteresis loss, 193

I

Induced charges, 289
Inductance, 270
Instruments, indicating, 109
Ionization by collision, 329
Ionization potential, 329
Ions:
  in gases, 326
  in liquids, 323

J

Joule, unit of energy defined, 11
Junction point, 71

K

Kelvin bridge, 124
Kirchhoff's laws:
  current, 53
  voltage, 45

L

Laminations, 198
Leakage flux, 219
Lenz's law, 251
Line, unit of magnetic flux, 177
Lorentz, H.A., 5

M

Magnetic circuit:
  parallel, 224
  series, 211
  simple, 209